FAULT-TOLERANT COMPUTING
Theory and Techniques

FAULT-TOLERANT COMPUTING
Theory and Techniques
Volume I

DHIRAJ K. PRADHAN, *Editor*

University of Massachusetts

PRENTICE-HALL
Englewood Cliffs, New Jersey 07632

Library of Congress Cataloging-in-Publication Data
Main entry under title:

Fault tolerant computing : theory and techniques.

Includes bibliographies and index.
1. Fault-tolerant computing.   I. Pradhan, D. K.
QA76.9.F38F38 1986   004.2   85-23238
ISBN 0-13-308230-X (v. 1)
ISBN 0-13-308222-9 (v. 2)

Editorial/production supervision: Nancy Milnamow and Diana Drew
Cover design: Edsal Enterprises
Manufacturing buyer: Gordon Osbourne

ISBN 0-13-308230-X 025

Prentice-Hall International (UK) Limited, *London*
Prentice-Hall of Australia Pty. Limited, *Sydney*
Prentice-Hall Canada Inc., *Toronto*
Prentice-Hall Hispanoamericana, S.A., *Mexico*
Prentice-Hall of India Private Limited, *New Delhi*
Prentice-Hall of Japan, Inc., *Tokyo*
Prentice-Hall of Southeast Asia Pte. Ltd., *Singapore*
Editora Prentice-Hall do Brasil, Ltda., *Rio de Janeiro*
Whitehall Books Limited, *Wellington, New Zealand*

CONTENTS

Chapter 2
DESIGN FOR TESTABILITY   **95**

E. J. McCluskey, *Stanford University*

Chapter 3
FAULT SIMULATION

184

Y. Levendel, *Bell Laboratories*

P. R. Menon, *Bell Laboratories*

Chapter 4
CODING THEORY FOR FAULT-TOLERANT SYSTEMS   **265**

B. Bose and J. Metzner, *Oregon State University and Oakland University*

Chapter 5
CODING TECHNIQUES IN FAULT-TOLERANT, SELF-CHECKING, AND FAIL-SAFE CIRCUITS   *336*

Yoshihiro Tohma, *Tokyo Institute of Technology*

Chapter 6
ARCHITECTURE OF FAULT-TOLERANT COMPUTERS   **417**

D. Siewiorek, *Carnegie-Mellon University*

PREFACE

Fault-tolerant computing has evolved into a broad discipline, one that encompasses all aspects of reliable computer design. Diverse areas of fault-tolerant study range from failure mechanisms in integrated circuits to the design of robust software.

High reliability in computer design was first achieved through so-called fault-avoidance techniques; these involved computer design which used high-quality, thoroughly tested components. Sometimes, simple redundancy techniques were employed to achieve limited fault tolerance. Automated recovery techniques were seldom used as there was little confidence in the hardware. The drastically increased reliability requirements as well as the increased computer speed quickly made manual recovery obsolete. One example of this is the 1964 *Saturn V* launch computer, which had a reliability requirement of only 0.99 for 250 hours; this compares to the late-1970s FTMP and SIFT computers, with reliability requirements of 10^{-9} failures per hour over the 10-hour mission time.

Besides ultrahigh-reliability needs, fault-tolerant computing is driven by other key factors, such as ultrahigh availability, reduced life-cycle costs, and long-life applications. A good illustration is the ESS system of Bell Telephone, which has an availability requirement of only 2 minutes downtime per year. Because reduction of the life-cycle costs of commercial computers has become a major objective of manufacturers, fault-tolerance techniques have become increasingly important, such as using low-cost error-correction/detection codes and maintenance processors like those utilized in systems such as the IBM 3081 and Sperry 1100/60 models. Still another major thrust behind strong development of fault-tolerant computing are the long-life applications. A prime example here is the very high survival probability warranted in spacecraft computers such as the one planned for the upcoming *Galileo* spacecraft.

Other major factors influencing growth and development of fault-tolerant computing include the intangible trade-offs between the lack of high reliability and the loss of computational power, including gaining consumer confidence. This is to say that a loss of availability of a supercomputer, even during a small amount of time each day, can actually result in a loss of computing energy equivalent to the entire throughput of a mainframe computer. Also, we cannot afford to overlook the critical point that the wide use of computers now makes it essential that they be not only highly available, but especially, reliable, so as to heighten their acceptance and use by the general public. A good example here is the ultimate goal of "paperless" offices and banks—impossible to achieve without the availability of low-cost, highly available, *and* highly reliable computers.

The design of reliable computers is actually much more complex than the design of other complex human-made objects (robots, airplanes, etc.). Perhaps this can better be grasped by looking at one statement in the *IEEE Spectrum* (Oct. 81, p. 41): "Information-processing errors can occur through a failure lasting a billionth of a second in one of the hundreds of thousands of digital components that switch billions of times a day." It is no exaggeration to say that fault-tolerant computer design requires a real understanding of a large and complex set of interrelated subjects. The goal of this book, then, is to provide a strong, broad base for general understanding. Particularly emphasized is the theory itself, as well as how the theory works to pave the way for the implementation of practical techniques.

Basic to the design of reliable computers is the availability of defect-free parts. Effective testing strategy becomes critically important to determine the presence or absence of defects and faults. This book's first three chapters are devoted to an in-depth focus on three major aspects of the testing of integrated circuits: test generation, fault simulation, and design for testability.

Test generation for digital circuits is one of the oldest areas of study in fault-tolerant computing. But this field has had to undergo rapid revamping to keep pace with the nearly revolutionary changes in circuit technology. The factors affecting the test generation problems are twofold, while the number of components that can be supported on a chip is increasing. The chip itself is becoming susceptible to a more diverse variety of failures, ranging from internal opens and shorts to encapsulation and bonding failures. Sounder understanding of these failures has yielded newer fault models, such as bridging faults, stuck-open faults, and crosspoint faults. Abraham and Agarwal's opening chapter gives us this necessary current perspective of the testing and test generation area. Not only is a good overview of the basic theoretical issues presented, but various practical state-of-the-art test generation algorithms such as PODEM, function testing, and random testing are also included.

With limited internal access to increasingly complex circuits, the test generation problem is a most untenable one. The use of testability as a *design criterion* is one particularly successful solution to this "testing problem." Dubbed "design for testability," this area has received much current attention, especially since the introduction by IBM in the late 1970s of the level-sensitive scan design (LSSD). Various techniques and issues involved in the design for testability area are given a very thorough treatment in the chapter by McCluskey.

The third chapter, written by Levendel and Menon, gives a highly useful and easy-to-understand treatment of the principles as well as the practices of the area known as fault simulation—a most practical technique for both test generation and test validation.

One interesting tool, used to depict the failure characteristic of components over time, is the "bath-tub" curve. What this implies is that a large initial failure rate is likely for components for a short duration, known as the "burn-in period." Following this, the components may experience a failure rate which is small, if steady, all through their operational life. Then the failure rate rapidly increases because of wear-out and the like. Therefore, a small probability of component failure exists during the useful life. The following two chapters go into detail as to the theory and techniques involved in the design of circuits which are fault tolerant. To begin with, error-correcting and error-detecting codes have been used quite successfully, providing low-cost error control. The chapter by Bose and Metzner provides a sharp, concise treatment of the theory and application of error-correcting codes at the subsystem level, such as RAMs and ALUs. Following this, Tohma's chapter yields a well-delineated view of the error-detection/correction techniques available at the gate level for the design of fault-tolerant and self-checking circuits.

The issues of organization and architecture of computers are key ones to the design of fault-tolerant computers. The next two chapters tackle these issues. The chapter by Siewiorek gives an in-depth survey of various existing fault-tolerant architectures. Included here is a discussion of a broad range of fault-tolerant architectures, incorporating those that are available commercially. It should be noted that the recent computer architecture thrust has been concerned with the area of multiprocessors and distributed processors. One can say nothing less than that it is expected that the next generation of computers will consist of innovative interconnections of multiple computing elements. Fault-tolerance issues in interconnecting multiple computing elements therefore will inevitably receive increasing attention. The chapter by Pradhan provides an overview of various architectures which are suitable for yielding robust interconnections between computing elements. Also discussed are some of the recent research results in the area of fault-tolerant VLSI (very large scale integration) and WSI (wafer-scale integration) interconnections.

With this feasibility of interconnecting a large number of computing elements to build an integrated system, the issue of *self*-diagnosis becomes a critical one. Self-diagnosis techniques have already become commercially feasible with the use of maintenance processors with computers such as the IBM 3081, Honeywell DPS 88, and Sperry 1100/60. These maintenance processors, although logically built and electronically separate, are located with the mainframe; they are capable of performing both diagnosis and recovery. Other commercial systems, such as those DEC has employed, take the form of remote computers that perform automated diagnosis.

An elegant theory, known as system diagnosis, provides an understanding of various fundamental relationships in the framework itself when computing elements that can test other computing elements. Kime's chapter gives a very comprehensive overview of the various models developed and their results.

Determining the reliability of ultrareliable systems through life testing is an awesome task. For example, in order to test that the failure probability of an FTMP system does not exceed 10^{-9} for a 10-hour mission, 10 million computer-years would be required. In other words, this translates to running 1000 FTMP computers for 10,000 years. Consequently, analytical and simulation techniques provide our only other practical alternatives. Stiffler's chapter examines this analytical approach and provides a detailed overview of the CARE III technique.

Although a major body of theory of software fault tolerance is not yet in place, the problem of software fault tolerance is one not to be taken lightly. That is, one significant cause of system failure can be attributed to software failure. As an illustration, both the *Apollo* and the Space Shuttle missions were aborted at least once because of software failures. Reliability in software has been achieved primarily through fault-avoidance techniques, principally because software faults are design errors (as opposed to wear-out faults experienced by hardware). Although software reliability increases with its heightened use, the possibility exists of an unforeseen combination of environmental factors causing catastrophic failure. Redundancy techniques, analogous in principle to those found in the design of fault-tolerant hardware, have been formulated to avoid such catastrophes. Although deceptively simple, these techniques can be very difficult to implement because of the intrinsic complexities of the software itself. Because these inherent problems make software reliability a new, important, and distinct area of research, it is well surveyed by Hecht and Hecht in the book's final chapter.

This book is intended to be both introductory and suitable for advanced-level graduates. It is suggested that the chapters be selected in different combinations to provide courses with different orientations.

Course Topic	Chapter Combinations
Introduction to fault-tolerant computing	7, 1, 3, 5, and 10
Testing and diagnosis	1, 2, 3, 5, and 8
Fault-tolerant hardware design	7, 1.1, 1.2, 2, 4.1–4.3, 4.6–4.9, 5, 6.1–6.4
Fault-tolerant system design	7, 4, 5, 6, 8, 9, and 10
Theoretical issues in fault-tolerant computing	1, 2.1, 2.5, 2.6, 4, 5, 6.1, 6.6–6.9, 8, 9, and 10.1–10.4

Chapter 1

TEST GENERATION
FOR DIGITAL SYSTEMS

Jacob A. Abraham
Vinod K. Agarwal

1.1. INTRODUCTION

Rapid advances in integrated circuit (IC) technology have made possible the fabrication of digital circuits with a very large number of devices on a single chip. This complexity is coupled with an increase in the ratio of logic to pins which drastically reduces the controllability and observability of the logic on the chip. In addition, there are new and subtle failures being observed with very large scale integrated (VLSI) circuits. These problems are already causing difficulties with the testing of the existing complex chips, and testing is expected to be even more difficult with the higher-complexity chips that are being proposed. When one considers that a complete system consists of many boards, each consisting of many chips, the magnitude of the task is overwhelming.

1.1.1. Levels of Testing

Testing is done in order to discover defects in a digital system which could be caused either during manufacture or because of wear-out in the field. Testing is done at various stages in the production of a system [MANN80, MYER83]: the dies are tested during fabrication, the packaged chips before insertion in the boards, the boards after assembly, and the entire system is tested when complete. The choice of test patterns for each of these tests is determined by factors such as the time available for test, the degree of access to internal circuitry, and the percentage of failures which are required to be detected. A simplified discussion of the type of hardware needed and the methods used to apply a test pattern to a unit under test (UUT) which could be a chip or board, for example, is given below. [BENN82], [HEAL81], and papers in [CHER00] provide a detailed treatment of various problems and approaches to solutions in this area.

Table 1.1.1 indicates some of the tests performed at various steps during the manufacturing process of a system. (All of these tests, of course, would not necessarily be applied to any single product.) Many identical integrated circuits, called dies, are fabricated on a single silicon wafer. The first major test performed checks the process. This test uses sophisticated probes on special transistor structures in order to screen out problem wafers during the manufacturing process. The test structures could be on special dies on the wafer, part of a die could be dedicated to this test structure, or the test structures could be placed in between dies and be destroyed when the dies are cut up for packaging. A typical test structure, for example, would be a ring oscillator, the frequency of oscillation of which would check the parameters of the process.

TABLE 1.1.1   TYPES OF TESTS PERFORMED

Unit under test			
Wafer	Chip	Board	System
Parametric	Chip test	Incoming inspection	System test
Die probe	Burn-in test	Bare board	Field diagnosis
	QA sample	Board in-circuit	
		Board functional	
		Burn-in test	

The next step tests the individual dies using probes. Both digital and analog tests are performed on the circuits to determine the ones that have not been manufactured properly. The dies failing the test are marked. The wafer is then sliced into individual dies and the ones that have passed the test are mounted in packages with wire bonds providing the electrical connection between the pads on the die and the leads of the package. The use of a scanning electron microscope has been suggested as a way of testing the dies before encapsulation [FAZE81]. This technique is based on the fact that electrons are scattered differently by areas on the powered-up chip which have a high voltage and those which have a low voltage. This technique provides a high degree of observability and can also be used to detect potential failure points such as thin wires.

The packaged chip is then tested using a chip tester. These testers are very expensive, very complicated systems which can drive signals on pins at very high speeds and compare the actual values on the pins with stored correct values [MARU79, SWAN83, DOWN80]. There is usually a minicomputer connected to the tester interface hardware which serves the function of generating patterns and analyzing the responses. Thus the tester interface to the chip consists of very fast circuitry and the responses obtained in real time are analyzed at much slower speeds. To obtain chips with even higher reliability, they may be burned in at high temperatures to accelerate failures, at the end of which process there is a testing step to screen out the failed devices. Some of the chips may even be sampled and tested more thoroughly to ensure the quality of the shipped chips.

Recent advances in packaging technology have resulted in packages incorporating over 100 chips [BLOD82]; each package can have hundreds of pins. The very large amount of logic in a package is practically impossible to test thoroughly if techniques for testability are not incorporated in the design. Test techniques for such packages are discussed in [CURT83] and the tester itself is described in [PIER83].

The packaged chips are then mounted on modules such as printed circuit boards. The manufacturer of the boards may obtain the chips from various sources, so there may be a test of the incoming chips to ensure that they are working properly. The printed circuit board is tested first as a bare board and again after mounting the tested packages on it. In the early generation of board testers, the board was tested by applying test signals at the board edge connectors and by monitoring the output signals, again at the edge connectors [STON79, HEAL81, BENN82]. The tester system usually includes a minicomputer with fault simulation capability. Test patterns produced using the software on the computer are applied to the board which is connected to the tester interface. To increase the accessibility and improve the probability of locating faulty chips, a *guided probe* technique is sometimes used where the test system asks the operator to probe certain points on the board and reads those probed values and thus guides the operator, step by step, to the fault. Another technique in board testing which is now popular is called *in-circuit testing,* where each individual component is tested separately by applying test patterns directly to the inputs of the chip and measuring the response directly at the output of the chip [BATE83, MASC83, SNOO83]. This, of course, requires much more sophisticated electronics to overdrive certain pins and check the values without destroying the components.

The fabricated boards are finally put together into a system and the system is then tested before shipping it to a customer. The system test is usually a high-speed test which executes the programs normally run on the system. For example, a computer would be tested by actually running its operating system and application programs on it. When the system is in the field, it is periodically tested to ensure that it has no latent failures. When a system fails in the field, a test is run to determine the failed part. This type of testing is usually called *diagnosis.* Field diagnosis involves a series of tests which are stored either in backup storage in the system itself, or loaded by phone lines from a remote site [SWAR78]. The diagnostics may also be stored in microcode, in which case they are called microdiagnostics [RAMA72]. The objective of field diagnosis is to locate a failure down to a field-replaceable unit (FRU). Fault diagnosis is usually aided greatly by on-line error detection mechanisms (described in Chapter 5). The FRU, for example a printed circuit board, is usually exchanged in the field and the potentially faulty board is sent back to the factory for repairs.

When testing a complex circuit such as a microprocessor, there are two different ways of sequencing the tests. In one case, called *open-loop testing,* the inputs come from the tester in a sequence completely under tester control. The tester software can interpret the outputs of the circuit under test and send the appropriate next input vector. A good example is a test of the "jump" instructions in a microprocessor. The tester can send an instruction for the microprocessor to branch to a specified address (say A_1). The microprocessor should emit address A_1 during the next fetch cycle. The tester can issue the next instruction at this point. In the second case, the UUT itself determines the sequencing. This case is called *closed-loop testing*. Using the same microprocessor example, there would be no tester between the microprocessor and the memory. If the test involves a jump instruction, say to address A_1, the next instruction in the test must be stored at that address. This clearly is more restrictive for test sequence design but can be used to make the circuit test itself. Open-loop testing is usually used during manufacturing test, and closed-loop testing is used for field testing.

1.1.2. Test Economics

As digital systems become more complex, it is feared that the cost of testing will become a major part of the cost of the system. Thus there is much activity in trying to reduce the cost of testing by improved testing techniques and test generation techniques, such as described in this chapter, and by design for testability, as described in Chapter 2. [SIEW81], [DAVI82], and various papers in [CHER00] discuss aspects of the economics of testing in greater detail. An interesting figure that has been cited is that the cost to find a defective unit goes up by a factor of 10 for each level of assembly; that is, if it costs 30 cents to find a defective component, it will cost $3 to find and replace it on a board, $30 at the system level (in the factory), and $300 in the field [OBER78, STEW78]. Thus it is imperative that failures be detected as early as possible in the manufacturing process in order to minimize the cost of testing. This also points out a need for designing the circuits to be easily testable so that failures can be detected with a very high degree of probability. Examples of the dramatic savings that result from designing for testability are also described in [STEW78].

1.1.3. Measures of Test Quality

When considering which test patterns to generate for testing a complex circuit, one should first consider how good the patterns are for detecting the possible physical failures in the circuit. As we will see in the next section, it may be impossible to consider all possible physical failures; test patterns are generated to detect some set of modeled faults in the circuit, for example, any line in the gate-level representation of the circuit permanently "stuck" at logic 0 or 1. The measure of test quality in this case could be the percentage of these "stuck-at" faults detected by the patterns, and is called the *fault coverage* for the fault class. A typical goal might be to achieve a fault coverage for single stuck faults of 98% for all boards in the system, and a goal for system diagnosis might be to have a probability of 95% of isolating a fault to one board.

Fault coverage is determined by a fault simulation program (Chapter 3). Simulation of all faults in a large circuit with many tens of thousands of gates may take a prohibitive amount of computer time. Statistical sampling procedures for simulating a fraction of the total faults and the relationship between sample size and confidence are discussed in [AGRA81b]. It was found that for large circuits, reasonably good results can be obtained by simulating only 1000 to 2000 faults.

Another measure of test quality is the amount of product that is defective after completion of testing [CLEV83], termed the *product quality level*. This can only be estimated, of course, and a good measure of the quality level of a product is the *field reject rate* of the units that have been tested as good by the test patterns (assuming that a field failure has not occurred). Since stuck-at faults are only a representative model for possible physical failures, the measure of fault coverage for these faults can only be regarded as a figure of merit for the overall quality of the test patterns. Thus units that pass the stuck-type tests will fail in the field when the physical failures become exposed. The relationship between fault coverage and field reject rate or defect level is statistically developed in [AGRA81c, WILL81]. These papers give analyses for determining the value of fault coverage required for a given field reject rate of the tested chips. Methods of monitoring and testing to improve product quality are described in [CLEV83].

In many cases it may be desirable to have a measure of how easy a module is to test before the actual patterns are derived. A measure of testability enables poor designs to be identified early in the design cycle, so that these may be redesigned for improved testability at a stage where the redesign will not incur a high cost. A requirement is that the measure of testability be evaluated without a high cost in computation, and approximate measures based on the circuit topology have been proposed [DEJK77, KEIN77, DUSS78, GOLD79, GRAS79, BENN81, KOVI81, RATI82]. Methods for interpreting the testability measures are discussed in [AGRA82].

1.1.4. Scope of This Chapter

Even though there is a wide variety of testing techniques used at various phases during the manufacture and life of a system, the fundamental problems in generating tests are common to all these situations and are explored in this chapter. [CHAN70], [FRIE71], [BREU76b] and papers in [FTCS00 and CHER00] provide further detail in this area.

This chapter does not consider the problem of testing in order to verify the correctness of a design, which is a subject in itself. The test generation procedures will assume that the designs are logically correct. (Some of the testing techniques described in the chapter can, in fact, be used to find design "bugs," but this is not pursued here.)

Other chapters in the book are related to this. Chapter 2 discusses methods of designing complex systems so as to ease the testing problem. Chapter 3 treats automated techniques for grading the quality of a test set. Finally, Chapters 4 and 5 describe ways of detecting errors caused by faulty circuits and correcting them during normal operation.

1.2. PHYSICAL FAILURES AND FAULT MODELS

1.2.1. Introduction

We wish to derive test patterns to identify circuits which have become faulty because of physical failures. It would, therefore, be instructive to look at the types of failures that can occur in integrated circuits. Unfortunately, one cannot find an all-encompassing set of failures. Failures differ according to the technology (bipolar, MOS, etc.), the density of integration, and other factors, such as the operating temperature and operating voltage. A detailed study of physical failure mechanisms is thus beyond the scope of this book. We will briefly describe below some of the failures that can be expected in present-day ICs.

1.2.2. Physical Failures in ICs

Wire bond failures were the most common type of failure in early small-scale ICs. Since the ratio of pins to logic was relatively high, early test techniques concentrated on detecting failures on the input and output leads of gates. VLSI systems, because of their increased complexity and reduced geometries, exhibit more complex failure modes. These failures can be broadly divided into two classes: those induced primarily during manufacture (defects in the fabricated chip), and those which are more long term and which tend to occur in the field (because of wear-out). These classes are not exclusive since anomalies during fabrication can result in failure in the field. Information on failure modes of various IC technologies is available in [PEAT74], [COLB74], [SCHN78], and [ROSE79], and extensive failure rate data can be found in [RADC81].

Manufacturers are very concerned about reducing the incidence of fabrication-related failures in order to increase the yield and thus lower the cost of ICs. Recent high-density memory chips, for example, are being fabricated with redundant elements that can be switched into operation to take over the function of faulty elements by the use of a laser beam or current pulses [SUD81, ABBO81]. There is less information available on long-term failures since many of the new devices have not been out in the field for very long. Test generation techniques, however, should be applicable to both kinds of failures since circuits have to be tested soon after manufacture to weed out faulty units and also in the field to detect occurrences of wear-out failures.

Failures that occur during fabrication include faulty devices, breaks in lines at some level (polysilicon, diffusion, metal, etc.), and shorts between levels and among levels. Defects in the crystalline structure of silicon cause devices in the region of the defect to be faulty. Because of extremely small geometries and resulting close toler-ances, alignment errors, mask failures, and problems with photolithographic tech-niques can result in pinholes in oxide, faulty contacts, defective devices (missing or extra devices), and shorts. Improper doping profiles can result in devices with un-wanted characteristics, which in turn can result in intermittent or permanent faulty behavior. Improper handling can result in input gate breakdown due to static electricity, especially for MOS circuits. Poor encapsulation can result in the penetration of moisture into the package (which in turn leads to long-term corrosion-related failures) and in thermal coefficient mismatches which can lead to breakage of the substrate or interconnect. Finally, impurities in the packaging can lead to low-level radiation which can cause charge stored in a memory cell to be lost.

Long-term failure mechanisms in ICs include breaks in lines, shorts between lines, and degradation and breakdown of active devices. Aluminum metal can be subject to corrosion. High current densities in thin wires can result in metal migration, eventually leading to a break in the wire. Formation of spurious "whiskers" can lead to resistive shorts. Migration of alkali ions can cause a shift in the thresholds of transistors. High field intensities can impart energy to electrons, causing these "hot" electrons to move into and be trapped in the gate oxide in MOS transistors. This will also cause shifts in threshold voltages which will initially manifest themselves as intermittent failures which will eventually become permanent.

The types of failures that are seen also vary with the technology. For example, bipolar circuits usually have a higher device power dissipation and are more likely to exhibit hot spots and temperature-related problems. They are also prone to metal migration problems because of high current densities. Metal migration and hot spots are expected to be a problem in MOS circuits as they are scaled down, increasing their current and device densities. Defects in the epitaxial layer and clamping diode failures are other problems seen in bipolar circuits. An increase in the leakage current in bipolar circuits affects their fan-in and fan-out capabilities. On the other hand, CMOS circuits are affected by latch-up problems due to the formation of spurious lateral bipolar transistors.

It is important to note that as a technology matures and existing problems are corrected, the failure modes (both manufacturing and long term) will change. This makes it almost impossible to have a list of failures that can be used to derive tests for faulty circuits.

1.2.3. Fault Models

The large number and complex nature of physical failures dictates that a practical approach to testing should avoid working directly with the physical failures. In most cases, in fact, one is not usually concerned with discovering the exact physical failure; what is desired is merely to determine the existence of (or absence of) any physical failure. A physical failure that changes the function (in some sense) of a circuit can be detected by applying an appropriate sequence of input vectors (tests) to the circuit and monitoring its outputs for errors. Many different physical failures may very well cause the same error under that test.

One approach for solving this problem is to describe the effects of physical failures at some higher level (logic, register transfer, functional block, etc.). This description is called a *fault model*. If the fault model accurately describes all the physical failures of interest, then one only needs to derive tests to detect all the faults in the fault model. This offers several possible advantages. A higher-level fault can include many physical failures, thus reducing the number of primitive entities to be considered in deriving a test. Even if the details of the physical failure mechanisms are not known, a fault model can be hypothesized to cover most of the possible failures; this is especially useful in deriving tests for circuits that may later be fabricated with a reduced geometry or in a different technology. Finally, the existence of fault models at the various levels of a hierarchical design will be useful for finding the effects of faults and deriving tests in a hierarchical fashion, treating the testing problem in much the same way as the original design problem.

Gate-level fault models.   Note that since a fault model can be formulated at any level, at the lowest level the description of the physical failure is the same as the fault model. This is usually at the layout (mask) or transistor level. At the next level, the fault model is usually formulated in terms of logic gates. Classically, this has been the most popular level for the treatment of faults, and the preponderance of publications deal with faults described at the gate level.

The classical gate-level fault model has been the *stuck-at* fault model, where the effects of physical failures are supposed to be described by the inputs and outputs of logic gates permanently "stuck" at logic 0 or 1. Since much of the work in the testing field has been in terms of this model, a major portion of this chapter is devoted to studying test generation techniques under this fault model. This fault model is quite accurate for small- and medium-scale ICs where bonding failures will look like permanently stuck lines at the logic level. A related fault model is the *bridging* fault model, which describes shorts between lines at the logic level in a circuit.

We will go through an example below to describe the development of a fault model at various levels. We will start at the transistor level and go through the gate level to a functional block. The example uses CMOS transistors; this was chosen partly because of the widespread use of MOS technology, and partly because CMOS transistors have some interesting failure modes. The ideas presented here can readily be extended to other technologies. No detailed knowledge of transistor electronics is required in the following; a simplified analysis will be performed, treating the transistor as a simple switch.

Figure 1.2.1 shows the two types of MOS transistors which we will consider, a p-channel transistor in part (a) and an n-channel transistor in part (b). In both types, a voltage (logic value) applied to the gate controls conduction between the source and the drain. Thus, for the n-channel transistor, a gate voltage close to the supply voltage of V_{DD} (this can be considered to be logic 1) will cause the switch to close, and source and drain are essentially connected together; a voltage close to ground (considered to be logic 0) will cause the switch to be open. The p-channel transistor works in a complementary fashion, as can be seen from the figure. In practice, the transistors are fabricated symmetrically, and the source and drain are interchangeable, so that MOS circuits have a very close analogy to classical relays. One point to note is that charges stored in the lines of the integrated circuit can activate switches, even though an explicit voltage is not applied to them.

Figure 1.2.2 shows the basic CMOS inverter. A logic 1 applied to the input x

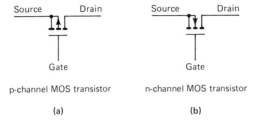

p-channel MOS transistor   n-channel MOS transistor

(a)   (b)

Type	Gate voltage	Source-drain conduction
p-channel	$\approx V_{DD}$	No
	≈ 0	Yes
n-channel	$\approx V_{DD}$	Yes
	≈ 0	No

V_{DD} typically around 5 volts   **Figure 1.2.1** MOS transistors.

will cause the lower n-channel transistor to conduct, bringing the output z close to ground, or logic 0; the upper p-channel transistor will be open (nonconducting) at this point. A logic 0 at the input will cause the p-channel transistor to close (turn on), and the n-channel transistor to open, causing the output z to be close to V_{DD}, or logic 1.

Now let us consider what happens to this inverter under some physical failures, such as open lines, shorts between lines, and failed transistors. (This discussion is not meant to be comprehensive but is merely intended to provide the reader with an idea about physical failures and fault models.) If the input is shorted to ground, the output will be permanently at logic 1. The same happens if there is a break in the input line at A, since after any residual charge at the gate of the p-channel transistor has leaked off, the output will remain at logic 1, because the input cannot affect the inverter. Now consider a break in the line at B, just before the gate of the n-channel transistor. If the input is a 0, the output will clearly be at logic 1. However, if an input of logic 1 is

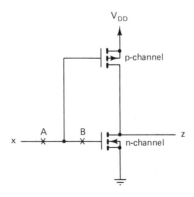

Figure 1.2.2 CMOS inverter.

now applied at x, the p-channel transistor will turn off, but the n-channel transistor will remain off because of the break. The output will now retain its previous value of logic 1 for a period of time which is dependent on the leakage currents, usually on the order of milliseconds. Therefore, if 0s and 1s are applied regularly to the inverter during normal operation, the output will, for all practical purposes, look like a stuck-at-1. The same effect happens if there is a failure of the n-channel transistor so that it is permanently off. Thus many physical failures will cause the inverter to behave as if its input (or output) is permanently stuck at logic 0 or 1. However, other failures will have more complex effects. An example will be the failure where the n-channel transistor fails permanently in the on state. If an input of 1 is applied, no error will be produced by the inverter. On the other hand, if an input of 0 is applied, both the transistors will be conducting (the n-channel because of failure), and the output will be at some intermediate voltage between 0 and V_{DD} whose value depends on the ratio of the resistances of the two transistors. Such "indeterminate" voltages cause problems in testing, especially since they may be interpreted differently by different parts of the circuit.

Figure 1.2.3 shows CMOS NOR and NAND gates and their truth tables. Failures in these gates can be analyzed in a similar manner as above, and many of them cause the gates to behave as if their inputs or outputs are stuck at 0 or 1. There is one class of failures, however, which makes the gate behave in a much more complex fashion, and we analyze this here. Consider the NOR gate in Fig. 1.2.3a and suppose that a break occurs at point A, just before the gate of the n-channel transistor. When $x = 1$ and $y = 0$, the output should normally be 0; however, because of the failure, there will be no path from the output z to either ground or V_{DD}, so that the output is floating and retains its previous value. The output can be forced to 0 by setting $y = 1$, and to logic 1 by setting both x and y to 0. Thus, under this failure, the circuit sometimes retains memory of its previous state and has, therefore, become sequential. A fault model for this type of failure, called a *stuck-open fault,* was first described in [WADS78]. Detection of such a fault involves the application of a specific sequence of test patterns. The particular failure described here can be detected, for example, by forcing the output to a $1(x = y = 0)$, and then changing x to a 1; the output will not change if there is a break at A.

A detailed analysis can similarly be carried out for other failures in the NOR and NAND gates in Fig. 1.2.3. It will be seen that many of the physical failures can be described by single stuck-at faults at the inputs or the outputs of the gates. Other failures, however, will result in indeterminate logic outputs or will cause the gates to have memory [WADS78, BANE82, TIMO83a]. Failures can also result in timing errors [BANE82, CLEV83]; there has not been much research into this problem and we can merely suggest this as an area for future work. A fault model that incorporates memory in gates will, of course, make the test generation process much more difficult. More complex logic functions can be formed by the series and parallel interconnections of MOS transistors. Galiay et al. [GALI80] describes short-circuit and open-circuit failures in complex nMOS circuits and points out some which cannot be described by a stuck-at fault model.

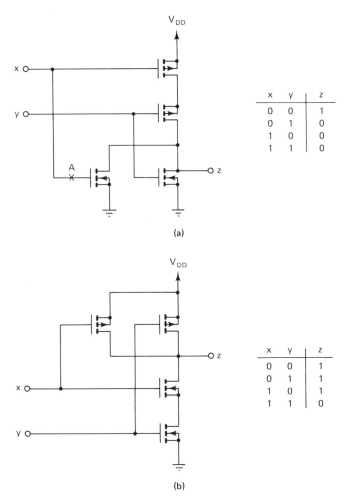

Figure 1.2.3   CMOS NOR (a) and NAND (b) gates.

Recent work has addressed the question of whether tests generated for single stuck faults at the gate level will detect physical failures. Analysis of a TTL NAND circuit [BEH82, CLEV83] showed that some failures can be modeled by single stuck faults on the lines of the gate; others can be detected by single stuck fault tests even though they cannot be modeled as stuck faults. There are a few failures that cannot be detected by a solely logic test, but can be detected by one which uses timing information (an *ac* test) since they would cause delay changes [CLEV83]. Tests generated on the basis of an equivalent gate model of a functional block, actually implemented as a complex interconnection of transistors, do not necessarily detect physical failures in the transistors [BEH82]. Another study showed that many physical failures can be modeled by multiple stuck-at faults [TIMO83a]. An analysis of MOS gates showed that tests for stuck-at faults would detect most physical failures [BANE83]; however, some failures can be detected only by ac tests since they cause delay changes. This work also showed that very short and thorough tests can be derived by considering the transistor level rather than the equivalent gate level in some cases. A hardware model of a commercially available CMOS microprocessor, into which faults can be injected, was used to study the effectiveness of pseudorandom patterns [TIMO83b]. It was found that 512,000 vectors detected 98% of stuck-at faults but only 85% of stuck-open faults.

Fault model for a functional block.   We will now discuss the formulation of a fault model for a functional block which includes many gates. We will use, for simplicity of analysis, the stuck-at fault model for the gates themselves but will also allow shorts between lines in the functional block. The example chosen is an 8-to-1 multiplexer shown in Fig. 1.2.4. The logic values for the select inputs p, q, and r determine which of the eight inputs is selected to the output. The result of a short is assumed to be a logically determinate value. The value depends on the "strengths" of the transistors which are driving the two shorted nodes; a treatment of this is beyond the scope of this book.

If any data input line is stuck at some logic value, we will not be able to select the opposite logic value at that input. If a select line is stuck (either the select inputs or the outputs of the inverters), the effect will be that some input cannot be selected or that an incorrect input will be selected in addition to the correct input with the output being the OR function of the two. Consider the topmost NAND gate; suppose that the input line marked A (corresponding to select input $\bar{p}$) is stuck at 1. When we attempt to select input x_1, the output will be equal to $x_0 + x_1$ (i.e., the wrong input x_0 has been additionally selected). If the outputs of gates are stuck, the effect will be the inability to select certain values on some of the data inputs. A short between two lines results in the two lines having the AND or OR function of their original values, depending on the technology. (In nMOS technology, for example, the AND function results.) In some cases, however, a short can result in an indeterminate logic value at the point of the short. Suppose that an OR type of fault occurs between lines B and C in Fig. 1.2.4. This will result in the inability to select a logic 1 on either x_3 or x_4. An AND-type short between lines D and E will leave the output permanently at 0. (Clearly, the complementary type of short in the two cases above will have no effect on the function of the circuit.) An OR type of short between input line x_0 and line A will result in the inability to select a 0 on input x_0, as well as in the selection of x_0 additionally when attempting to select x_1 (among others). It is left to the reader as an exercise to determine the effects of other faults for the example multiplexer.

We can now formulate a fault model for the multiplexer functional block. Under a fault, one or more of the following will happen.

1. We cannot select a 0 and a 1 on every input line, or
2. When selecting some input, another input will be selected instead of or in addition to the correct input (producing the AND or OR of the two values).

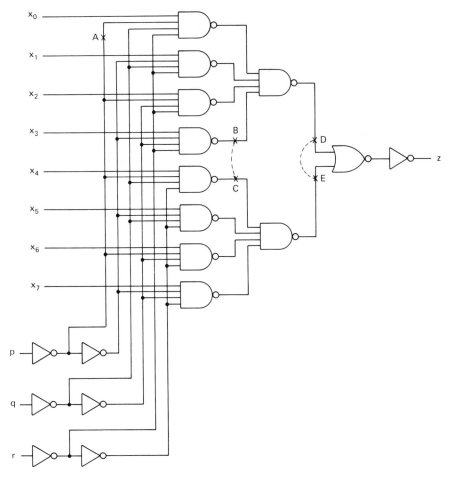

Figure 1.2.4 8-to-1 multiplexer.

If stuck-open faults can occur in the gates, we also have

3. Selection of a value on an input followed by its complement on the same input will result in error at the output, or
4. Selection of a value on an input followed by the selection of the opposite value on a line whose address differs in exactly one bit from the first address will result in error.

A test for this block will now consist of input patterns which will guarantee that the faults above are not present.

We will now consider a fault model for another realization of the multiplexer functional block. Figure 1.2.5 shows a CMOS transmission gate and its function. This primitive is used much like a classical relay to easily realize complex functions. In this circuit, if either transistor fails so that the drain is shorted to the source, the switch is stuck closed. If any transistor fails open, the switch will function essentially correctly because of its inherent redundancy. However, since the n-channel (p-channel) transistor passes a 0(1) well but not a 1(0), the output voltage would be degraded under this failure. A short between the x input and the $\bar{s}$ control line will cause the behavior shown in the figure. Note that the output is incorrect for two of the input combinations. Thus we cannot pass an input of 1 to the output, and the output is essentially stuck at 0. (It is left to the reader to determine the effect of a short between the x input and the s control line and between the output and the control lines.)

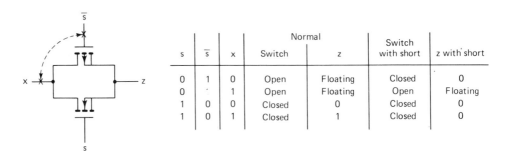

			Normal		Switch	
s	$\bar{s}$	x	Switch	z	Switch with short	z with short
0	1	0	Open	Floating	Closed	0
0		1	Open	Floating	Open	Floating
1	0	0	Closed	0	Closed	0
1	0	1	Closed	1	Closed	0

Figure 1.2.5   CMOS transmission gate and effect of short between x and $\bar{s}$.

Figure 1.2.6 gives a realization of the 8-to-1 multiplexer using transmission gates. (Note that the number of transistors has been drastically reduced in this realization compared with the previous gate-level design.) An analysis of the effects of various failures can be carried out in the same way as for the previous realization and is left to the reader. We will just consider an AND type of short between the inverted x_0 input and the point marked A as shown in the figure. When input p is 0, we will be unable to select a 0 on x_0 because of the fault. When p is 1 and x_0 is 1, the short will cause point A to become 0, which leads to the incorrect selection of $x_0, x_2, \ldots,$ in addition to the input desired.

Thus, interestingly, the higher-level fault model formulated above based on a gate-level realization of a multiplexer is still quite accurate for a transmission gate realization. The advantage of the higher-level fault model, in addition to its simplicity, is that it is not dependent on the details of the implementation. It is not always possible to develop useful functional fault models which are independent of the implementation. Also, different functional blocks will have different fault models, so this approach, if used indiscriminately, can lead to a proliferation of fault models. This type of approach to treating faults is still in its infancy, and much work needs to be done. Later in this chapter the ideas developed here will be used for deriving tests for memories, programmable logic arrays, microprocessors, and structured implementations of functions.

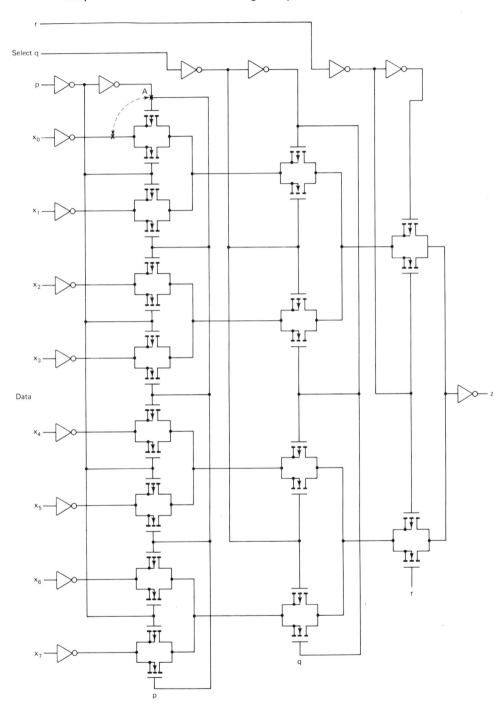

Figure 1.2.6   8-to-1 multiplexer using transmission gates.

1.3. ELEMENTARY TESTING CONCEPTS

1.3.1. Introduction

The basic testing problem is to determine an optimal testing procedure for a given circuit C and a set F of faults which models most of the failures likely to occur in C. The testing procedure consists of three steps: test generation, test application, and test verification. Testing procedure optimality is usually in terms of the time and effort required to carry out all three steps. Given C and F, the test generation step generates (randomly and/or algorithmically) a set $T(F)$ of input vectors called test patterns or test vectors. Each test pattern when applied to C will cause it to produce incorrect logic values (errors) at one or more output lines of C in the presence of certain specific faults belonging to F. For $T(F)$ to be a complete test set for F, it is essential that for every fault $f \in F$, there must exist at least one test vector in $T(F)$ which will detect f. It will be seen later that a complete test set is often not a practical possibility. Once a $T(F)$ is generated, it is then applied to the circuit C through test equipment [BENN82], which converts each test vector into the corresponding physical signals, and applies it to the appropriate pins of C with the necessary timing constraints. The same test equipment is also used to collect the response generated by test vector applications. In the final step, the test responses are analyzed (either by the same test equipment or by another machine) to determine whether circuit C is faulty, and if it is, what the fault is. The first part of this final step is called *fault detection,* and the second part is called *fault location* or *fault diagnosis.* The detection step is simpler and easier to implement, but does not inform one of the source of the error, if any. It is, however, useful in such applications as wafer testing, where the faulty dies are simply discarded before encapsulating them into expensive packages. Fault location, on the other hand, is useful in prototyping a new device, or in field repair where a faulty chip on a board can be replaced. Since the process of location is much more demanding, one has to develop a trade-off between the cost of locating the faulty chip and the cost of discarding the faulty board and replacing it with a new board. In this chapter the main emphasis is on test generation for fault detection. The test application and verification steps require a detailed understanding of the device under test and of the test equipment, and they are, therefore, beyond the scope of this chapter.

Given a combinational circuit C and a fault f in it, the set of all the input vectors which can detect f will be denoted by $T(f)$. If C is a single output circuit with n primary inputs, $x_1, x_2, \ldots, x_n$, the symbol $Z[X]$ will be used to denote the Boolean function realized by C, wherein $X = \{x_1, x_2, \ldots, x_n\}$. Moreover, let $Z_f[X]$ represent the Boolean function realized by C in the presence of f. It is then clear that any input vector X_t which produces different binary values on $Z[X_t]$ and $Z_f[X_t]$ is a test vector for f. More particularly,

$$T(f) = \{X_t \mid Z[X_t] \neq Z_f[X_t]\}$$

Consider now a set $F = \{f_1, f_2, \ldots, f_r\}$ of faults that are likely to occur in C. Each fault $f_j \in F$ can be detected by any test vector from $T(f_j)$. However, if any input vector $X_t \in T(f_j)$ is applied to C and the resulting output is not the same as $Z[X_t]$, then although one would know that C is faulty, there would be no guarantee that the fault present is f_j. This can happen if X_t belonged to more than one $T(f)$, $f \in F$. For instance, if X_t belongs only to $T(f_j)$ and $T(f_k)$, then X_t can be used to detect whether C contains f_j or f_k, but it cannot be used to determine whether the fault present if any is f_j or f_k. Similar concepts also apply to digital devices which are not just combinational circuits, and will be discussed later in this chapter.

The possibility that a test vector may belong to more than one $T(f)$ suggests that if one is simply interested in detecting that no fault from F is present in C, the set $T(F)$ could be any set of representatives of $\{T(f_1), T(f_2), \ldots, T(f_r)\}$. The problem of determining a minimal size or near-minimal size $T(F)$ in the smallest time possible is probably the most researched problem in the testing area. Over the last 15 years, various books [CHAN70, FRIE71, BREU76b, ROTH80], *Digest of Papers of the Fault-Tolerant Computing Symposia* [FTCS00], *Proceedings of the International Test Conference* [CHER00], *IEEE Transactions on Computers,* and numerous other references have presented very large numbers of algorithms and procedures for generating a complete test set $T(F)$ for various classes of digital circuits and fault sets. Some basic results from these research efforts will form the core of this chapter. By necessity, the descriptions here will be concise and will illustrate only the fundamental and/or most commonly used approaches. The richness of the testing problem demands that one must study the references cited in this chapter to fully appreciate and to gain a complete understanding of this exciting area. In the following pages, three fundamental concepts which are central to most of the research in this area are explained: those of *sensitization, consistency,* and *undetectability.*

1.3.2. Sensitization

In order to explain the basic concepts of testing, we consider the very specific situation of testing combinational circuits under the well-known model of stuck-at faults. In this model, a fault is said to be a single stuck-at fault if any one line of a circuit permanently assumes a specific logic value of 0 or 1 (or a multiple stuck-at fault if there are stuck faults on more than one line). In this chapter a single stuck-at fault on a line l stuck-at-α, $\alpha \in \{0, 1\}$, will often be denoted by l/α, and a multiple stuck-at fault involving line l_1 stuck-at-α_1, line l_2 stuck-at-α_2, $\ldots$, line l_k stuck-at-α_k will be denoted by $(l_1/\alpha_1, l_2/\alpha_2, \ldots, l_k/\alpha_k)$. Consider now the circuit of Fig. 1.3.1 and the

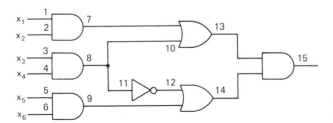

Figure 1.3.1   Example circuit to describe sensitization.

fault f, which is 7/0. In order to detect this fault by a procedure that allows access only to the primary input lines (1, 2, 3, 4, 5, and 6) and the primary output line (15), it is essential that a test vector must somehow create a change on line 7 and ensure that the change can be seen on line 15. That is, the test vector must produce a 1 on line 7, and line 15 should be sensitized to line 7 in the sense that the output created on line 15 clearly shows whether the signal on line 7 is 0 or 1. If the path from line 7 to line 15 is traced in Fig. 1.3.1, the first condition for sensitization is that line 10 be a 0. Indeed, if line 10 is a 1, then line 13 would be a 1 irrespective of the value on line 7. In other words, a 1 on line 10 would desensitize line 7 to line 13. Moreover, since there is no other path to transmit the value on line 7 to line 15, line 10 being a 1 will also desensitize line 7 to line 15. Thus, assuming that line 10 is a 0, the next condition for the sensitization is that line 14 be a 1. If both of these conditions exist in the circuit, then when a 0(1) is applied to line 7, the circuit output is going to be a 0 (respectively, a 1). In other words, any input vector that can create a 1 on line 7, a 0 on line 10, and a 1 on line 14 will in the fault-free circuit produce a 1 on the output line, and in the faulty circuit a 0 on the output line, and will, therefore, be a test vector for 7/0. In general, any vector is a test vector for a fault l/α if the vector produces the complement of α on l, and sensitizes l to a primary output line.

The concept of sensitization needs to be explained further in the situations involving more than one path from the faulty line to a primary output line, and in the case of multiple stuck-at faults. To consider the former, let the fault under consideration be 8/0 in Fig. 1.3.1. Since there are two distinct paths, one along lines 8, 10, 13, and 15, and the other along 8, 11, 12, 14, and 15, the sensitization can take place along either path or both the paths simultaneously. Notice that when a line is sensitized to a primary output line, this means that a change of binary signal on that line will result in a change on the primary output line as well. This change, however, can be propagated to the output line along many paths at the same time, and leads to what is referred to above as simultaneous multiple-path sensitization. It is important to point out here that attempts to create a simultaneous sensitization along many paths by considering one path at a time may not be successful. For instance, coming back to the example, one sees that by setting line 7 to 0, line 8 can be sensitized along the path 8, 10, 13. Similarly, by setting line 9 to 0, line 8 is sensitized along the path 8, 11, 12, 14. However, the two changes propagated along each path are such that they cancel each other out at the final AND gate, and, therefore, the two paths are not simultaneously sensitized by setting lines 7 and 9 to 0 at the same time. Equally important to notice is the complementary situation in which if some two paths are simultaneously sensitized, the constituent paths may not be. For instance in Fig. 1.3.2, the paths 1, 2, 4, 5 and 1, 3, 4, 5 are simultaneously sensitized, but none of the single paths are sensitized.

Finally, the sensitization problem becomes even worse in the case of multiple faults. For example, an input vector may detect the multiple fault (7/0, 12/1) in the circuit of Fig. 1.3.1 by one of the following five different sensitization possibilities:

1. Changes on both lines 7 and 12 are created, but only the change from line 7 is propagated. That is, path 7, 13, 15 is sensitized.

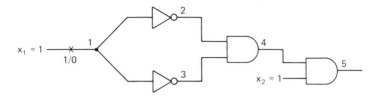

Figure 1.3.2   Sensitization through multiple paths.

2. Changes on both lines 7 and 12 are created, but only the change from line 12 is propagated. That is, path 12, 14, 15 is sensitized.
3. Changes on both lines 7 and 12 are created, and both the changes are simultaneously propagated without canceling out each other. That is, both the paths, 7, 13, 15 and 12, 14, 15 are sensitized simultaneously.
4. Change is created only on line 7 and is propagated to 15. That is, path 7, 13, 15 is sensitized.
5. Change is created only on line 12 and is propagated to 15. That is, path 12, 14, 15 is sensitized.

Unfortunately, no vector satisfies cases 1 and 3 due to contradictory requirements in this example situation. However, the sets of test vectors that satisfy cases 2, 4, and 5, respectively, in the cubic notation are $\{11110x, 1111x0\}$, $\{110xxx, 11x0xx\}$, and $\{0x110x, 0x11x0, x0110x, x011x0\}$ (where x represents a don't-care value on an input line).

   The multiple-fault situation is further complicated when one of the possible sensitizing paths has a faulty line on the path. Consider again the circuit of Fig. 1.3.1 and the multiple fault $(7/0, 8/\alpha, 12/1)$. Among the various ways of detecting this fault is the sensitization of line 8 to line 15 along the path 8, 11, 12, 14, 15. It is, however, clear that due to line 12 being stuck-at 1, the change coming from line 8 may or may not be propagated even if line 9 was set to 0. In particular, if line 8 is stuck-at-1, the faulty value propagated along line 11 will be 1, and will be passed to line 12 as 0. However, since line 12 is stuck-at-1, this faulty value coming from line 8 cannot be propagated any farther along this path. In general, only that faulty value will be propagated which is the same as the fault lying on the path.

   In summary, the concept of sensitization is fundamental to understanding how a fault is detected from the input and output lines only. However, the process of determining a sensitized path (or paths) in a general situation is not a simple procedure, except in certain specific types of circuits, as will be seen in Section 1.4.

1.3.3. Consistency

Consider again the fault 7/0 in Fig. 1.3.1. It was discussed earlier that any input vector which can set line 7 to 1 (i.e., create a change on line 1), and set line 10 to 0 and line 14 to 1 (i.e., sensitize line 7 to line 15) should be able to detect 7/0. However, as was seen above in some other situations, just formulating such conditions does not always mean that an input vector satisfying such conditions also exists. Thus, formulating conditions to create a change and to propagate the change along a sensitized path is just one step. The second, equally important, step is to determine which if any vector(s) satisfies such conditions. When this process is carried out by exploring the circuit structure, it is often referred to as the line justification or consistency process. In the example under discussion, line 7 needs to be set to a 1. Looking back from line 7 immediately shows that the only way to satisfy this condition is to set both lines 1 and 2 to 1. Similarly, line 10 can be set to 0 by any of the following three options: line 3 is 0 and line 4 is 0; line 3 is 0 and line 4 is 1; or line 3 is 1 and line 4 is 0. Finally, line 14 can be made 1 by three similar options on lines 12 and 9. However, line 10 being a 0 implies that line 12 is a 1. Therefore, line 14 is also a 1. All the vectors that satisfy all these requirements simultaneously are $\{110xxx, 11x0xx\}$. In other words, these vectors form $T(7/0)$.

In general, consistency or line justification is not a simple process since different conditions may result in contradictory requirements. To illustrate, consider the fault $(7/0, 12/1)$ such that it is tested by creating changes on both the faulty lines, and the change is propagated only from line 7. This will require that the following conditions be satisfied: line 7 is 1, line 12 is 0, line 10 is 0, and line 9 is 1. However, since lines 10 and 12 require the same binary signal, but can have only complementary values, it is clear that no vector will satisfy this particular set of conditions. In Section 1.4 various ways of implementing this line justification step will be described. An ideal line justification algorithm will at each step make a decision that will not have to be changed. In general, however, this is not possible since making an irreversible decision requires knowledge which is not available at the time of decision, and can be obtained only by reversing the decision and starting again. The most one can do in this situation is to use some insights or heuristics so that as few decisions as possible are changed. This decision process is clearly not unique to test generation as evidenced in many well-known problems [KNUT75]. In Section 1.4.2 on the complexity of test generation, it will be shown that, due to this decision process, the test generation problem is NP-complete [FUJI82].

1.3.4. Redundancy and Undetectability

Given a fault f on line l in a circuit C, if it so happens that there is no vector to detect f, that is, $T(f)$ is empty, then f is termed an *undetectable fault*, and the line l is called a *redundant line* with respect to f. For instance, in the trivial circuit of Fig. 1.3.3, the fault 5/1 is undetectable, since sensitizing it would require that each of lines 3, 4, and 6 be a 1, implying in turn that $x_1 = 1$, $x_2 = 1$, and $x_1x_2 = 0$. These being contradictory requirements, one can conclude that if 5/1 existed in the circuit, then as far as the input/output behavior is concerned, the circuit is going to behave as if there is no fault in it. Such undetectable faults seem to be harmless when not probed further. However, as a fair amount of research in this area has demonstrated, one must know

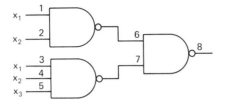

Figure 1.3.3 Example of redundancy.

where the redundant lines in the circuit are to be able to carry out an effective detection of the detectable faults. For instance, notice that in the circuit above, the input vector $(1, 1, 0)$ is a test vector for $1/0$. However, in the presence of the undetectable fault $5/1$, $(1, 1, 0)$ cannot test $1/0$. Thus, if one applied $(1, 1, 0)$ to C and determined that there is no fault, the conclusion would be wrong if the fault present were $(1/0, 5/1)$. In other words, the undetectable faults can invalidate the testing of some detectable faults if both are present simultaneously.

Another effect of an undetectable fault is its impact on the test generation efforts for a given C and a fault set F. If, in fact, a fault is undetectable, any resources spent in trying to obtain a test vector are wasted. It is thus useful to remove all the undetectable faults from the set F before the test generation step. As it turns out, even the process of determining whether a fault is detectable or not is as complex (i.e., NP-complete) as the test generation process. The best hope, therefore, is to avoid the appearance of redundant lines during the design phase of the circuit under consideration. In most of the discussions in this chapter, faults under treatment will be assumed to be detectable faults.

1.3.5. Summary

Three concepts, sensitization, consistency, and undetectability, were described in this section. Although most of the discussions were limited to combinational circuits and stuck-at faults, these basic concepts can be extended for any digital circuit and any fault model, as will be seen in the later parts of the chapter.

The test generation for a given device is affected by many factors, such as the complexity of the device, the description level (transistor, gate, register-transfer, or functional level), and fault model. A convenient classification of the various known test generation procedures for various types of devices is in terms of structural-level or functional-level generation. The implication in the term "structural level" is that the test generation step will usually require a detailed transistor or gate-level structure of the device under test. Such a description is, however, not always available (e.g., of a microprocessor chip in the market) or is not best suited due to the complexity of the device. Functional-level test generation, on the other hand, exploits only the minimal amount of structural information, but is almost exclusively based on input/output information only. The following section discusses structural-level testing and Section 1.5 considers functional-level test generation.

1.4. STRUCTURAL-LEVEL TEST GENERATION

1.4.1. Introduction

Structural-level testing is usually based on the concept that if the structure of the device under test conforms to that of the fault-free device, the device has gone through an acceptable fabrication process. As a result, the most commonly used fault model at this level of testing is to test for the presence of every line in the device, and its capability to carry both a 0 and a 1 signal. This fault model is also referred to as the single stuck-at fault model, as alluded to earlier in Sections 1.2 and 1.3. A single stuck-at fault in a circuit is a good model of various physical failures, such as a break in a diffusion line caused by an unintentional scratch on an IC chip. However, due to the shrinking line widths on such chips, a scratch may affect not one but many lines. The fault model to cover such cases is the multiple stuck-at model. In newer technologies, such as CMOS and nMOS, a break in a diffusion line cannot always be modeled (see Section 1.2) as a single or multiple stuck-at fault. A model that has recently been investigated to cover such situations is the shorts/opens model. In this section, single and multiple stuck-at test generation is covered first, followed by test generation for some short/open-type faults. The device under consideration will be primarily a combinational circuit, except for an introductory discussion on sequential circuit testing. Despite a large amount of research in sequential testing in the past, the best approach to testing a sequential circuit seems first to be to convert it into a combinational circuit at the time of testing (see more in Chapter 2) and, hence, the preoccupation with combinational testing in this chapter. Throughout this section, only single-output circuits will be considered in order to avoid notational inconvenience.

1.4.2. Stuck-at Fault Testing

The general problem of stuck-at fault testing is extremely complex, as pointed out in the preceding section. A valid approach, therefore, is to develop a good insight into this problem by considering special classes of the circuits, and then employing these insights for the general problem. Consequently, this section is divided into two major parts: combinational circuits and sequential circuits. The treatment of combinational circuits is further subdivided into three parts. First, test generation algorithms for those special combinational circuits which are simple and straighforward (i.e., NP-completeness does not exist) will be developed. The results and understanding developed there will then be used to describe the test generation process for general combinational circuits. Finally, the complexity of the test generation process will be considered in the last part on sequential circuits.

Combinational circuits. The main interest in this section is to develop a $T(F)$ for a combinational circuit, where F is either the set F_s of all the single stuck-at circuits in C or the set F_m of all the single and multiple stuck-at faults in C. It has been noted in Section 1.3 that a $T(F)$ is basically a set of representatives of $\{T(f_1), T(f_2),$ $. . . , T(f_r)\}$ if $F = \{f_1, f_2, . . . , f_r\}$. However, for most circuits of interest, $T(F)$ is built up incrementally by using the following procedure (assuming only detectable faults):

Begin
    $T(F) = \emptyset;$
    While F is not empty do
    Begin
        Choose X_t (randomly or algorithmically) such that
        $X_t \in T(f)$ for some $f \in F$;
        $T(F) \leftarrow T(F) \cup \{X_t\};$
        $F \leftarrow F - F'$, where F' is the largest set such that for each
        $f \in F'$, $T(f)$ contains X_t;
    End;
End.

It may be obvious that such a procedure will usually not lead to a minimal $T(F)$; nonetheless, the convenience of generating a $T(F)$ without calculating all $T(f)$s explicitly is normally worth the extra vectors in a nonminimal $T(F)$. In fact, further savings can be accrued by realizing that many faults have some similarity which can be exploited to generate a $T(F)$ by considering a reduced set $F'' \subset F$. More specifically, the following two relations are very useful [MCCL71b]:

Relation 1:   A fault f_i covers a fault f_j if $T(f_i) \subseteq T(f_j)$.
Relation 2:   A fault f_i is functionally equivalent to a fault f_j if $T(f_i) = T(f_j)$.

Thus if all those faults which are functionally equivalent and/or are covered by some other detectable faults are removed from F to form F'', it would immediately follow that $T(F) = T(F'')$. In most situations of interest, phenomenal savings can be accrued by considering only the set F''. For instance, it is easily seen that on an AND gate with k input lines, all the single and multiple faults involving at least one line being stuck-at-0 are functionally equivalent. Similarly, any input line stuck-at-1 can be seen to cover the output line stuck-at-1.

    Various results in this area can be classified under two very distinct categories: one category consists of determining the smallest set of single (multiple) stuck-at faults in a circuit that will cover all the single (multiple) stuck-at faults; the other category consists of results that attempt to determine and characterize those multiple stuck-at faults in combinational circuits which are/cannot be covered by single stuck-at fault test sets. A major result in the first category is that the set of check-point faults, which are the stuck-at faults on primary input lines that do not fan out as well as on all the fan-out branches in a circuit, to cover all the single and multiple stuck-at faults in the circuit [BOSS71]. In the second category, the characterization of multiple faults not detected by a $T(F_s)$ has been a difficult problem. The best effort in this direction seems to be the calculation of a greatest lower bound on the number of multiple faults detected by a $T(F_s)$ [AGAR81, AGAR80a].

Based on these general discussions, test generation algorithms for special and general circuits are now presented in the following sections.

Special circuits

Elementary Gates. Consider the testing of a simple AND gate G with k input lines. At any given time, each line of G can be normal (i.e., fault-free), stuck-at-0, or stuck-at-1. Since there are $k + 1$ lines in G, the total number of different single stuck-at faults which could possibly occur in G is $2(k + 1)$, and the total number of different single and multiple faults is $3^{(k + 1)} - 1$. However, all these faults can be partitioned into 2^k functionally equivalent classes, as shown in Fig. 1.4.1, for $k = 2$. Moreover, the following set of $k + 1$ faults can be shown [HAYE71a] to cover all $3^{(k + 1)} - 1$ faults. In other words, a complete $T(F)$ for G is:

Vector number	Vector X_t	Single stuck-at fault f such that $T(f) = \{X_t\}$
1	$(0, 1, 1, \ldots, 1, 1)$	$1/1$
2	$(1, 0, 1, \ldots, 1, 1)$	$2/1$
.	.	.
.	.	.
.	.	.
k	$(1, 1, 1, \ldots, 1, 0)$	$k/1$
$k + 1$	$(1, 1, 1, \ldots, 1, 1)$	$i/0$, for any i

The discussions above are equally valid for all other basic gates, OR, NAND, NOR, and NOT, as a little reflection will convince the reader. The most obvious extension of elementary gates is the next class of special circuits.

$S_0 = \{(3/0), (3/0, 1/0), (3/0, 2/0),$
$\quad (3/0, 1/1), (3/0, 2/1), (3/0, 1/0, 2/0),$
$\quad (3/0, 1/0, 2/1), (3/0, 1/1, 2/0),$
$\quad (3/0, 1/1, 2/1), (1/0), (2/0), (1/0, 2/0),$
$\quad (1/0, 2/1), (1/1, 2/0)\}$

$S_1 = \{(3/1), (3/1, 1/0), (3/1, 2/0),$
$\quad (3/1, 1/1), (3/1, 2/1), (3/1, 1/0, 2/0),$
$\quad (3/1, 1/0, 2/1), (3/1, 1/1, 2/0),$
$\quad (3/1, 1/1, 2/1), (1/1, 2/1)\}$

$S_2 = \{(1/1)\}$

$S_3 = \{(2/1)\}$

Figure 1.4.1 Sets of equivalent faults for an AND gate.

Completely Fan-out-free Circuits.   A CFOF circuit has the unique property that from each primary input line there is only one path to the primary output line [HAYE71b, AGAR78]. Thus it is possible to write the Boolean expression realized by such a circuit in a form wherein each input variable appears exactly once, either complemented or uncomplemented. Such a form is referred to as the *fan-out-free form,* and any function that can be written in this form is referred to as a *fan-out-free function.* Each CFOF circuit thus realizes a fan-out-free function and, conversely, each fan-out-free function can be realized by a CFOF circuit. Due to the simplicity of CFOF circuits, many useful results on test generation, on their implementation, and on their various properties have been reported.

The simplest property to notice is that if a test vector is generated for a primary input line, say $i/0$, then since there is exactly one path from i to the primary output, the sensitization can easily be carried out, as shown in the circuit in Fig. 1.4.2. Equally important to notice is that, due to the lack of fan out in the circuit, the line justification operation is also straightforward, since any decision at each step will not have to be retracted. Thus the test vectors for all single stuck-at faults on primary input lines can easily be obtained. It can be shown that any such set of vectors is a $T(F_s)$; that is, it will also detect all other single stuck-at faults in the circuit. This is possible since when a vector detects a fault $i/0$ on a primary input line, it also detects one stuck-at fault on each line on the path from line i to the primary output. Again refer to Fig. 1.4.2 for an illustration.

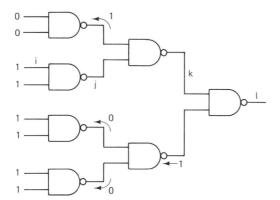

Figure 1.4.2 $(0, 0, 1, 1, 1, 1, 1, 1)$ detects $(i/0)$, $(j/1)$, $(k/0)$, and $(l/1)$ along the sensitized path.

What is most interesting about CFOF circuits is that if a $T(F_s)$ is obtained with a little extra care, the $T(F_s)$ will also be a $T(F_m)$. In other words, a procedure can be developed [HAYE71b, KOHA75] such that a $T(F_m)$ for a CFOF circuit can be generated simply by generating test vectors for single stuck-at faults at the primary inputs only.

Two-level Circuits.   A two-level circuit usually has all the gates at each level of the same type. A common practice is to use AND gates at the first level and OR gates at the second level. Such a circuit is also referred to as a two-level AND–OR circuit. Another practice is to use two-level NAND–NAND circuits. It is well known that each two-level AND–OR circuit has a one-to-one correspondence with a two-level NAND–NAND circuit, and vice versa. To avoid duplication and difficult notation, a test generation procedure for two-level circuits will be developed in the following pages for AND–OR-type circuits only. This test procedure will generate a $T(F_m)$ to test all single and multiple stuck-at faults. In newer technologies such as nMOS and CMOS, a two-level circuit is often implemented as a programmable logic array (PLA). The test generation problem for PLAs is discussed elsewhere in the chapter.

A two-level AND–OR circuit in which every fault is detectable has the property that each product term realized by an AND gate is a prime implicant of $Z[X]$. Since each prime implication can be represented by a cube, a convenient way to represent $Z[X]$ is by the set of all prime implicant cubes [BREU72]. For example, in circuit C of Fig. 1.4.3,

$$Z[X] = \bar{x}_1\bar{x}_3 + \bar{x}_3x_4 + x_1x_2x_4 + x_2x_3\bar{x}_4$$

The cube associated with $\bar{x}_1\bar{x}_3$ is $(0x0x)$, with $\bar{x}_3x_4$ is $(xx01)$, with $(x_1x_2x_4)$ is $(11x1)$, and with $x_2x_3\bar{x}_4$ is $(x110)$. Thus the function realized by C in Fig. 1.4.3 can also be represented by the set $S(Z) = \{0x0x, xx01, 11x1, x110\}$.

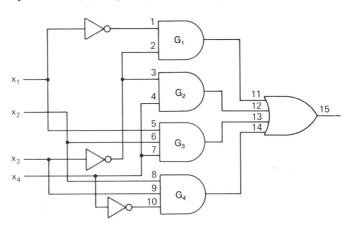

Figure 1.4.3 Two-level AND-OR circuit.

Consider now the set of faults $\{(1/1), (2/1), (11/0)\}$ which will cover all the other faults in G_1. If the fault $11/0$ occurs in C, it would completely remove the prime implicant $\bar{x}_1\bar{x}_3$ from $Z[X]$. Thus the faulty function realized by C in the presence of $11/0$ would be $S(Z_f) = \{xx01, 11x1, x110\}$. Recall that a test vector for f is any input vector which belongs to either $S(Z)$ or $S(Z_f)$ but not to both. Since the 0-cubes (that is, the true minterms) in $S(Z_f)$ form a subset of 0-cubes in $S(Z)$, the set $T(11/0)$ of all the test vectors for $11/0$ is simply

$$T(11/0) = \text{set of 0-cubes in } (S(Z) - S(Z_f))$$

$$= \{(0000), (0100)\}$$

In general, for any AND gate's output stuck-at-0 fault in a two-level AND–OR circuit,

$T(f)$ is the set of all those 0-cubes which belong to the cube realized by that gate and do not belong to any other cube in $S(Z)$. Thus

$$T(12/0) = \{(1001)\}$$

$$T(13/0) = \{(1111)\}$$

$$T(14/0) = \{(0110), (1110)\}$$

The manner in which these test sets are obtained implies that they all are pairwise mutually exclusive. Hence a minimal set of tests representative for all AND gates stuck-at-0 can be found by arbitrarily choosing an element of each test set.

Refer next to the fault $1/1$. In the presence of this fault, the faulty function is such that the prime implicant $0x0x$ realized by $G1$ is modified to $xx0x$. In other words, the faulty function $S(Z_f) = \{xx0x, xx01, 11x1, x110\}$. As above, the set $T(1/1)$ is the set of all those 0-cubes which belong to $(S(Z_f) - S(Z))$. One can be even more specific. Notice that the only cube which is in $S(Z_f)$ and not in $S(Z)$ is $C_1 = xx0x$, and the only cube which is in $S(Z)$ and not in $S(Z_f)$ is $C_2 = 0x0x$. Moreover, C_1 is obtained from C_2 by replacing the first (corresponding to line 1) 0 by x. Therefore, $T(1/1)$ is the set of those 0-cubes which belong to $xx0x$ but not to $S(Z)$. $T(2/1)$ similarly is the set of 0-cubes which belong to $0xxx$ but not to $S(Z)$. In general, for any AND gate G with k input variables, $xl_1, xl_2, \ldots xl_k$, and realizing the prime implicant C_i, the set $T(xl_j/1), 1 \leq j \leq k$, is the set of all the 0-cubes in a cube C_1 but not in $S(Z)$, wherein C_1 is obtained by replacing the 0 or 1 entry for the xl_j variable in C_i by x. All the k test sets $T(xl_j/1)$, $1 \leq j \leq k$, are pairwise mutually exclusive, and, therefore, a set of test representatives for stuck-at 1 on G can be determined by input lines arbitrarily choosing any vector from each test set.

Once the test vectors for all the covering faults on each gate are obtained, it is easily shown that the set of such vectors will not only be a $T(F_s)$ but also a $T(F_m)$ [KOHA71]. In other words, every $T(F_s)$ for a two-level circuit is also a $T(F_m)$. The most general class of circuits for which $T(F_s) = T(F_m)$ is the cascaded two-level circuit discussed in [SCHE71, AGAR81].

Circuits Realizing Unate Functions.   A Boolean function $Z[X]$ is said to be positive (negative) in a variable x_j if for any two input vectors

$$X_{t_1} = (a_1, a_2, \ldots, a_{j-1}, a_j, a_{j+1}, \ldots, a_n)$$

$$X_{t_2} = (a_1, a_2, \ldots, a_{j-1}, b_j, a_{j+1}, \ldots, a_n), a_j \geq b_j \ (a_j \leq b_j)$$

implies that $Z[X_{t_1}] \geq Z[X_{t_2}]$ (correspondingly, $Z[X_{t_1}] \leq Z[X_{t_2}]$). If $Z[X]$ is either positive or negative in x_j, it is said to *be unate in x_j*. A function $Z[X]$ is *unate* if it is unate in all its variables. A function is *positive unate (negative unate)* if it is positive (negative) in all its variables. (We also write $X_{t_1} \geq X_{t_2}$ if $a_j \geq b_j$ for all j.)

A unate function when realized by an irredundant circuit C has the property that the parity of all the paths connecting any given primary input to the primary output is the same. Using this property, C can be transformed [REDD73] into another circuit C' such that C' has the general form shown in Fig. 1.4.4, and a set $T(F'_m)$ for C' is

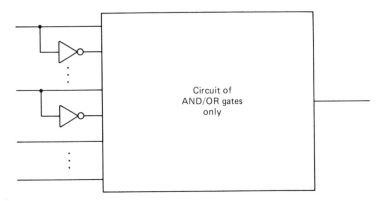

Figure 1.4.4 Irredundant circuit realizing transformed structure of unate function.

also $T(F_m)$ for C. The transformation procedure is best described by an example. Consider the unate function $Z[X] = x_1x_2 + x_1x_3 + x_1x_4 + x_2x_3 + x_2x_4 + x_3x_4$. An irredundant realization of $Z[X]$ is shown in Fig. 1.4.5. To transform this circuit into the form of Fig. 1.4.6 requires that all the inversions on internal lines be pushed back to the primary input lines. Starting from line 20, the NAND gate can be replaced by an OR gate with inversions on lines 17, 18, and 19. This new inversion on line 19, together with the NAND gate therein, can be replaced by an AND gate. Similarly, the NAND gate on line 17 can be replaced by an AND gate. Finally, the inversion on line 18 can be pushed to lines 12 and 13 by replacing the OR gate by an AND gate. Since there are two consecutive inversions on each of lines 12 and 13, they can be canceled to result eventually in circuit C' shown in Fig. 1.4.6. Notice that because of the property mentioned earlier, the foregoing procedure to convert C into C' would never result in the unamanageable situation wherein one fan-out branch of a stem line has one inversion to be pushed back to the primary input line, and the other branch has

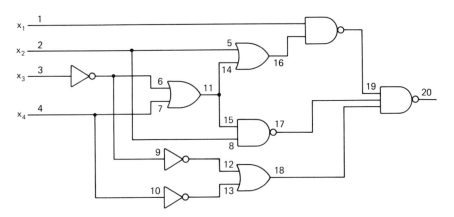

Figure 1.4.5 Irredundant realization of unate function.

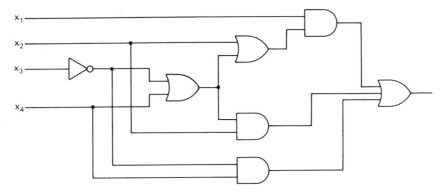

Figure 1.4.6   Transformed circuit of Fig. 1.4.5.

no inversion at all. Thus all the branches will have either exactly one inversion each or no inversion at all.

Given a unate function $Z[X]$ which is realized by a circuit C in the form of Fig. 1.4.4, a $T(F)$ for C can be obtained just by knowing $Z[X]$. (In fact, for any $Z[X]$ which is realized by a circuit in this form, irrespective of its redundancy and unateness properties, a $T(F)$ for the circuit can be obtained by knowing $Z[X]$ [REDD73].) For notational convenience, the following results are described for positive unate functions only. Their extension to general unate functions simply requires the complementation of those variables that are nonpositive unate in $Z[X]$.

Definition: *A minimal true minterm* of a function $Z[X]$ is an input vector X_t such that $Z[X_t] = 1$ and for any input vector $X_s < X_t$, $Z[X_s] = 0$. Similarly, a maximal false minterm of $Z[X]$ is an input vector X_t such that $Z[X_t] = 0$ and for any input vector $X_s > X_t$, $Z[X_s] = 1$.

Let S_0 be the set of all the maximal false minterms and S_1 the set of all the minimal true minterms of a positive unate function $Z[X]$. It has been shown [REDD73] that the set $S_0 \cup S_1$ is a complete $T(F)$ for any irredundant circuit C that realizes $Z[X]$ in the form shown in Fig. 1.4.6. There are many approaches available to calculate S_0 and S_1 for a given function [BETA70]. Since their description is not within the scope of this chapter, the only points important to note here are that (1) none of the available approaches is practical for large functions and (2) the set $T(F) = S_0 \cup S_1$ is not a minimal test set unless the circuit belongs to a special class of two-level circuits [BETA70, DAND73].

In each of the special cases discussed above, the processes of sensitization and line justification are easily implementable. A major reason is that every single stuck-at-fault f on any primary input line has the property that for each $X_t \in T(f)$ the fault-free output is, say, α, and the faulty output is $\bar{\alpha}$, $\alpha \in \{0, 1\}$. This property ensures that either there is only one sensitization path or, if there are many sensitization paths, they do not cancel out each other's propagation of changes. Another reason for the simplicity is that by constraining the structure and/or functions realized by a circuit, the line justification can be performed without changing any decisions made previously.

A general combinational circuit does not have the foregoing conveniences and, therefore, needs the general test generation algorithms of the next section. However, it is possible to exploit the results of this section in testing general circuits that have the special type of subcircuits. In particular, the FAN algorithm described in the next section identifies all the CFOF subcircuits in the circuit under test, and does not treat their test generation as a part of the general problem, thereby reducing the total computational effort.

General circuits. The class of test generation algorithms which is useful for any combinational circuit can be partitioned into two groups. One group consists of the *algebraic algorithms* because the test generation for a given stuck-at fault is done by exploiting some algebraic representations of the fault-free and faulty circuits. The other group of algorithms, called *structural algorithms*, generate the test vector by exploiting the transistor or gate-level representation. The first group of algorithms is not very practical since the heuristics required to tolerate the NP-completeness of the test generation problem are not available. Yet this group of algorithms serves the very important purpose of enlightening the fundamental nature of testing problems [AGAR81]. The structural algorithms, on the other hand, have been extensively used in the semiconductor industry and will continue to play an important practical role in the near future. In this section, the group of algebraic algorithms will be represented by the Boolean difference method, although many other schemes have also been reported in the literature. The group of structural algorithms, on the other hand, will be described by considering three examples: D-algorithm [ROTH66], PODEM [GOEL81], and FAN [FUJI83]. Many other structural algorithms are available in the literature. All the discussions in the following relate to single stuck-at faults only.

Boolean Difference Method. To describe this well-known method, consider the circuit in Fig. 1.4.7 and the fault 6/0. The first step in this method is to express the Boolean equation of the circuit in terms of not only the primary input variables, but also the Boolean variable of the faulty line. Letting Y_6 represent the Boolean function realized by line 6 in terms of the primary input variables, suppose that $Z[X, Y_6]$ represents the required circuit equation:

$$Z[X, Y_6] = (x_2 + \bar{x}_1\bar{x}_3)(x_3 + \bar{x}_2\bar{x}_4)(x_1 + Y_6)(x_4 + Y_6)$$

If the fault 6/0 were present in the circuit, the output function of the faulty circuit would simply be

$$Z[X, 0] = (x_2 + \bar{x}_1\bar{x}_3)(x_3 + \bar{x}_2\bar{x}_4)x_1x_4$$

Thus any vector X_t which is such that $Z[X_t, Y_6] \neq Z[X_t, 0]$ should be a test vector for 6/0. More specifically,

$$T(6/0) = \{X_t \mid Z[X_t, Y_6] \neq Z[X_t, 0]\}$$

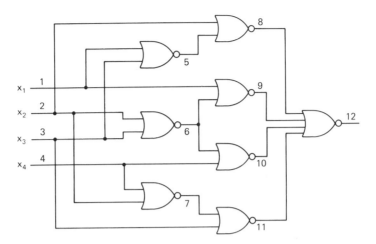

Figure 1.4.7   Example circuit for Boolean difference method.

By using Shannon's expansion theorem, it is possible to rewrite the above as

$$T(6/0) = \{X_t \mid Y_6 * (Z[X_t, 0] \oplus Z[X_t, 1]) = 1\}$$

This equation clearly shows that every test vector for $T(6/0)$ should set Y_6 equal to a 1, and be able to create a different primary output depending on whether line 6 carries a 0 or a 1.

The expression $Z[X, 0] \oplus Z[X, 1]$ is referred to as the Boolean difference of $Z[X, Y_6]$ with respect to Y_6. Various properties of this difference operator and its extension to multiple stuck-at faults are available [KU75]. The elegant representation of $T(l/\alpha)$ in the Boolean difference method has made it very useful in developing certain other results in the testing area [AGAR81].

D-Algorithm. As discussed earlier, two problems have to be solved by every test generation procedure:

1. Creation of a change at the faulty line
2. Propagation of the change to the primary output line.

In the D-algorithm and the following two algorithms, a symbol D and its complement $\overline{D}$ are used to refer to the change. If a line has a value 1 in the presence of no fault, and 0 otherwise, this change is denoted by D. The complementary situation is, of course, denoted by $\overline{D}$. The D-algorithm [ROTH66] is probably the best known test generation algorithm. It develops a five-valued $\{0, 1, x, D, \overline{D}\}$ calculus to be able to carry out the sensitization and line justification procedures in a very formal manner. In this calculus, each line can be either 0, 1, x (unknown), D, or $\overline{D}$. The faulty line is first assigned a D or $\overline{D}$ depending on the fault on the line. The next step then is to use the calculus and the circuit structure information to determine values on the other lines so that the D or $\bar{D}$ can be sensitized to the primary output line. A line justification step is then carried out to justify the values assigned in the preceding step. Notice, however, that both the sensitization and line justification steps may have to be carried out many times before a test vector is obtained.

The following three terms must first be defined before proceeding further:

1. A propagation D-cube of a gate G specifies signals on all the input lines except one (or more) under which a change of signal in this input (inputs) induces a change on the output of the gate.

   Example: The propagation D-cubes of an AND gate with two input lines are shown below:

1	2	3
D	1	D
1	D	D
D	D	D
$\bar{D}$	1	$\bar{D}$
1	$\bar{D}$	$\bar{D}$
$\bar{D}$	$\bar{D}$	$\bar{D}$

   Each row represents a D-cube and the conditions under which change on one or more lines can be propagated to the output of the gate.

2. The primitive D-cube of a failure is a D-cube associated with a fault l/α on the output line l of a gate G such that a D or $\bar{D}$ is assigned to line l and other values to the input lines of G so that $\bar{\alpha}$ is produced on l.

   Example: For the fault $3/0$ on the AND gate, the primitive D-cube of failure is

1	2	3
1	1	D

3. The singular cover of a gate is a compact truth-table representation in terms of the $\{0, 1, x\}$ variables.

   Example: The singular cover of the two-input AND gate is

1	2	3
0	x	0
x	0	0
1	1	1

The three concepts above are used as follows. First, the propagation D-cubes of all the gates in the circuit under test are listed in one table in which the rows correspond to the cubes and the columns to the lines in the circuit. Figure 1.4.8 shows an example circuit and Table 1.4.1 the propagation D-cubes for the circuit. Notice that this table also contains the circuit structure information in an indirect manner. The table contains blanks for all the entries that should have been xs. Moreover, the D-cubes corresponding to $\bar{D}$ propagation are not listed for convenience, but are assumed to be available.

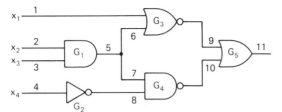

Figure 1.4.8 Example circuit illustrating D-algorithm.

TABLE 1.4.1 PROPAGATION D-CUBE TABLE FOR CIRCUIT IN FIG. 1.4.8

Cube label	1	2	3	4	5	6	7	8	9	10	11	
a		1	D		D							} G1
b		D	1		D							
c				D			$\overline{D}$					} G2
d	0					D			$\overline{D}$			} G3
e	D					0			$\overline{D}$			
f							1	D		$\overline{D}$		} G4
g							D	1		$\overline{D}$		
h									0	D	D	} G5
i									D	0	D	
j					D	D	D					} Fan-out

A second table is similarly created which contains all the singular covers of all the gates. The singular covers for the circuit of Fig. 1.4.8 are shown in Table 1.4.2.

Given this information, the test generation procedure starts with a cube containing xs on all the lines except the ones involved in the primitive D-cube of the failure under consideration. The aim then is to change these xs into Ds and/or 1s and 0s such

TABLE 1.4.2 SINGULAR COVER TABLE FOR CIRCUIT OF FIG. 1.4.8

1	2	3	4	5	6	7	8	9	10	11	
	0	x		0							} G1
	x	0		0							
	1	1		1							
			0				1				} G2
			1				0				
1					x			0			} G3
x					1			0			
0					0			1			
						0	x		1		} G4
						x	0		1		
						1	1		0		
								1	x	1	} G5
								x	1	1	
								0	0	0	

that the resulting cube has a D or $\bar{D}$ assigned to the primary output line and binary values to the primary input lines. Moreover, the final cube must correspond to the creation of a change and its sensitization to the primary output line. Both the tables are used in determining such a final cube. The values on the primary input lines of the cube form the required test vector. Various heuristics are used to speed up the test generation process. A very detailed example illustrating all the aspects of the D-algorithm is provided in [CHAN70]. In the following, a simple example illustrates some of the salient features. Consider the process of generating a test for line 5/0 in Fig. 1.4.8. We start with the following cube, which includes the primitive D-cube of failure for this fault:

	1	2	3	4	5	6	7	8	9	10	11
cube k:	x	1	1	x	D	x	x	x	x	x	x

The next step is to propagate this D farther toward line 11. Referring to propagation D-cubes in Table 1.4.1, cube j shows that the D in cube k is automatically propagated to lines 6 and 7. Consider now the propagation along the path 6, 9, 11. Table 1.4.1 again shows that the D on line 6 can be moved to line 9 by using cube d. In other words, a new cube can be obtained by combining cubes d and k. This process of combination is referred to as D-cube intersection, and is defined in Table 1.4.3.

	1	2	3	4	5	6	7	8	9	10	11
cube k:	x	1	1	x	D	D	D	x	x	x	x
cube d:	0	x	x	x	x	D	x	x	$\bar{D}$	x	x
cube l:	0	1	1	x	D	D	D	x	$\bar{D}$	x	x

TABLE 1.4.3 INTERSECTION TABLE FOR D-CUBES

$\cap$	0	1	x	D	$\bar{D}$	
0	0	ϕ	0	ψ	ψ	ϕ, ψ: inconsistency, empty
1	ϕ	1	1	ψ	ψ	μ, λ: can be made consistent if
x	0	1	x	D	$\bar{D}$	only λ or μ but not both
D	ψ	ψ	D	μ	λ	occur
$\bar{D}$	ψ	ψ	$\bar{D}$	λ	μ	λ: made consistent by changing

to a cube where $D \to \bar{D}$
or $\bar{D} \to 1$

μ: made consistent by placing
D or $\bar{D}$ where
appropriate

Lines 7 and 9 now contain the "change" which can be propagated further. The set of such lines is referred to as the D-frontier. By referring to Table 1.4.1, it is noticed that if cube i is used with $\overline{D}$ instead of D, then the $\overline{D}$ on line 9 can be propagated to the primary output line.

	1	2	3	4	5	6	7	8	9	10	11
cube l:	0	1	1	x	D	D	D	x	$\overline{D}$	x	x
cube i:	x	x	x	x	x	x	x	x	$\overline{D}$	0	$\overline{D}$
cube m:	0	1	1	x	D	D	D	x	$\overline{D}$	0	$\overline{D}$

The next aim is to determine a value for the primary input line 4 since that is the only line that has not been assigned a value. This is where the line justification starts. By referring to Table 1.4.2, notice that to create a 0 on line 10, both lines 7 and 8 must be a 1. However, in cube m, line 7 is a D, indicating that cube m cannot result in a test vector if the fault is propagated along path 5, 6, 9, and 11. One thus starts again from cube k and starts propagating along the path 5, 7, 10, 11. A similar process leads to the following cube:

	1	2	3	4	5	6	7	8	9	10	11
cube n:	x	1	1	x	D	D	D	1	0	$\overline{D}$	$\overline{D}$

Here, the values on lines 1 and 4 are required. Table 1.4.2 shows that the 1 on line 8 is the same as 0 on line 4. Moreover, the 0 on line 9 can be obtained by applying a 1 on line 1 irrespective of the value on line 6. These considerations result in the final cube $1\ 1\ 1\ 0\ D\ D\ D\ 1\ 0\ \overline{D}\ \overline{D}$, with the conclusion that a test vector for 5/0 is (1, 1, 1, 0) with the fault-free value of the circuit as 0 and the faulty value as 1.

The D-algorithm has over the years been enhanced to generate test vectors for shorts/opens, perform design verification, and for other such related problems [ROTH80].

PODEM Algorithm.   Both PODEM [GOEL81] and FAN [FUJI83] algorithms are outcomes of the desire to improve the performance of the structural algorithms by employing better heuristics. The PODEM algorithm was introduced in particular to perform better than the D-algorithm for circuits containing mostly Exclusive-OR gates. It was, however, demonstrated to have a better performance than the D-algorithm for various other types of circuits as well. The approach taken by the PODEM appears to be the first to treat the test generation problem as a classic branch-and-bound problem. Most fundamentally, the algorithm starts by assigning a value of 0 or 1 to a selected primary input (pi) line, and then determines its implication on the propagation of the D or $\overline{D}$ to a primary output line. If no inconsistency is found, it again somehow selects another pi line and assigns a 0 or 1 and repeats the process, which is referred to as *branching*. If, however, at any time in this branching, an inconsistency is determined, the branching stops and the bounding starts. The pi line which was most recently assigned a binary value is assigned the complementary value, and the branching is started again. If, however, both the values on the most recent line result in the bounding step, then the pi line next to the most recent is treated in a similar manner. The complete process stops when either a test vector is found or when the fault is determined to be undetectable.

The implementation of PODEM is best described by considering two different graphs. One is a binary tree, Fig. 1.4.9, wherein a node corresponds to a pi line and its two branches to the assignment of a 0 or a 1 to that pi line. The two sons of a node recursively correspond to the next pi lines, each for one of the two possible values on the farther node. The process of finding a test vector can be seen as that of finding a path from the root node to a leaf node in this binary tree. The branching step is simply to go as deeply into the tree as possible. The bounding step is going to the brother of the last node, provided that the brother node has not already been tried. Or else one goes to the first ancestor node of the last node that has an untried brother node and starts branching from that new node. It is a classic branch-and-bound algorithm employed in various artificial intelligence and operation research problems [KNUT75].

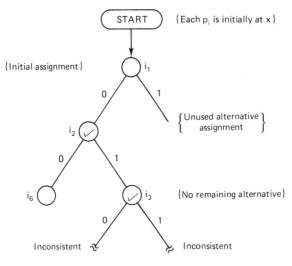

Figure 1.4.9 Binary search tree in PODEM.

Nodes i_2 and i_3 are flagged

The other graph employed in PODEM is the graph of the circuit itself. Each node in the graph corresponds to a gate of the circuit, and those nodes are connected by directed edges whose corresponding gates are connected. One of the edges in this graph has a D or $\overline{D}$ corresponding to the fault under consideration. Recall now that the aim is to propagate this D or $\overline{D}$ to one of the edges corresponding to a primary output line.

Every branch step (i.e., the selection of a new node in the binary tree) results in having specific binary values on certain pi lines. These values are then applied to the circuit graph to determine their implication in propagating the D or $\overline{D}$. If it is determined, by using the rules to be described later, that it cannot be propagated any further, the bounding step starts, or else the branching continues. To continue the branching, one needs to select the next pi line and the binary value to be assigned to it. Here again, some heuristics are used on the circuit graph to determine which is the next pi line and what the value on it should be. In other words, the branch-and-bound steps are constrained by the circuit graph. It is, therefore, important to keep in mind that one travels the tree graph and the circuit graph in both the forward direction and the backward direction, but the two travels should not be intermixed.

Implementation of Bound Step.   Consider that the binary tree is implemented as a last-in, first-out stack (LIFO). An initial pi-line assignment results in pushing the associated node into the stack. It is called an *unflagged node,* implying that the brother of this node is still untried. If by using the following two rules it is ever determined that the bounding process is required, it can easily be implemented by popping the LIFO stack until an unflagged node is on the top of the stack. As mentioned previously, this process is repeated iteratively until a test is found, or it is determined that new untried nodes are available, or the stack becomes empty. The rules for bounding are:

> *Rule 1:* The line value for the faulty line has the same value as that of the stuck-at fault.
>
> *Rule 2:* There is no path from an internal line to a primary output line such that the internal line is at the D or $\overline{D}$ value, and all other lines on the path have yet-unassigned values.

Indeed, in both cases, the fault cannot be detected by the node selections mode thus far in the binary tree. Therefore, instead of going further, it is essential to bound, change the current assignments, and try again.

Implementation of Branch Step.   The branch step basically consists of making an intelligent choice on the next pi line to be selected and the binary value to be assigned to it. In PODEM, this choice is made by first defining an objective for the choice which is to bring the test generation process closer to its goal of propagating a D or $\overline{D}$ to a primary output. The chosen pi line and the value on that line are those which help toward meeting this objective, which is defined as follows: If the output line of the faulty gate does not have a D or $\overline{D}$, the objective is directed toward promoting setup for that gate. Once this setup exists, the objective is aimed at propagating a D or $\overline{D}$ one level closer to a primary output line. This is implemented by simply selecting that gate from the D-frontier which is closest to a primary output line.

Once the objective is determined in terms of which line inside the circuit should be assigned a specific value, the next step is to trace backward in the circuit graph to determine a pi line and the value on it which will help meet the objective. This backtrace operation is very similar to, although not as complex as, the consistency operation described earlier for the *D*-algorithm.

Consider that the objective is to set a 0(1) on the output line of an AND gate (correspondingly, an OR gate). In the backtrace operation, any input of the gate under consideration can be set to 0(1) to achieve the objective. However, an intelligent choice can be made here by choosing that input which is most controllable among all the inputs to that gate. Similarly, if the objective was to set a 1(0) on the output line of an AND gate (an OR gate), all the input lines to that gate must be set 1(0). The backtrace operation requires that only one of these input lines be selected. Here again, the intelligent choice is to choose that input line which is the least controllable, since an early determination of the inability to set the chosen input will avoid time wasted attempting to set the remaining inputs of the gate. Similar observations can be made about NAND and NOR gates. This process repeated iteratively will eventually lead to a pi line and a value for it. That is where the branching process picks up a new node to be pushed into the LIFO stack.

Various formal details on PODEM and its performance comparison (see Table 1.4.4) with the *D*-algorithm are available in [GOEL81], and the reader is encouraged to refer to these references for a further understanding of the algorithm.

TABLE 1.4.4 COMPARISON OF PODEM AND DALG

Test case	Type	Number of blocks	Normalized run time		Test coverage (%)	
			PODEM	DALG	PODEM	DALG
1	ECAT	828	1	34.5	100.0	99.7
2	ECAT	935	1	12.8	100.0	93.1
3	ECAT	2002	1	[a]	100.0	31.2
4	ECAT	948	1	5.7	100.0	95.7
5	—	951	1	2.2	99.5	99.5
6	—	1249	1	3.5	98.2	98.2
7	—	1172	1	2.6	98.5	98.5
8	ALU	1095	1	15.3	96.5	96.2
9	MUX	1082	1	3.2	96.6	96.6
10	—	915	1	3.9	96.3	96.3
11	ALU	919	1	1.7	99.7	99.8
12	DECODER	1018	1	3.8	99.1	99.1
13	PLA	538	1	2.5	94.5	94.5
14	PLA	682	2.6	1	89.4	89.4
15	PLA	1566	1	3.1	97.4	97.4

[a] Test coverage from DALG was much lower, making a run-time comparison lose its significance.

FAN Algorithm.   The FAN algorithm started with the basic conjecture that the PODEM does not fully exploit the excellent framework in which it works. More specifically, it was felt that the heuristics employed in bounding-and-branching steps could be made stronger. The following definitions will be useful in describing the basic implementation of FAN.

A line is said to be a *bound line* if it can be reached from a fan-out point in the circuit. All the other lines are called *free lines*. A free line adjacent to a bound line is called a *head line*. For example, if a fan-out stem line is a free line, it is also a head line. See Fig. 1.4.10 for more examples of these definitions. It is interesting to note here that since a head line is the output line of a completely fan-out-free subcircuit, any assignment of a 0 or a 1 on a head line can always be achieved without affecting the assignment of other lines (except, of course, those feeding the head line) in the circuit. In other words, in a consistency like backtrace operation, one does not have to go all the way back to the primary input lines. The backtrace operation can be stopped at a head line, since the value of the head line can always be realized without any inconsistencies. Given a circuit, a linear algorithm can be used to determine which lines are free, bound, and head lines.

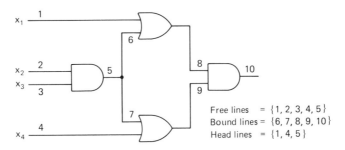

Free lines   = {1, 2, 3, 4, 5}
Bound lines = {6, 7, 8, 9, 10}
Head lines   = {1, 4, 5}

Figure 1.4.10   Free, bound, and head lines.

Another definition used later on is that of unique sensitization. If the D-frontier in the circuit at any time consists of a single gate, it is obvious that there is no choice in deciding how the D or $\bar{D}$ can be propagated further to a primary output line. If the resulting new D-frontier also consists of a single gate, the choice is again obvious. The concept of unique sensitization is based on determining the largest such path wherein the D-frontier on each line of the path always consists of a single gate. Given a circuit and a fault under consideration, it is possible to determine unique sensitization path(s) from the faulty line to all the primary output lines. During the actual execution of the FAN algorithm, this information is very useful in avoiding unnecessary branch-and-bound steps.

Finally, one needs to define the concept of multiple backtrace. Recall that in PODEM, the step of branching requires the selection of a new pi line and a value on it. This is achieved by defining an initial objective, and performing a backtrace operation to determine which pi line will best satisfy the initial objective. The backtrace selects one line at each step. In FAN, the backtrace operation does not choose just one line at each step. In fact, the FAN tries to backtrace along as many paths as possible, and stops the backtrace at an appropriate time by using certain criteria which are detailed in [FUJI83]. The stopping usually occurs either at a fanout point or a head line, and is used to determine what is called a *final objective*.

With these definitions, one can compare PODEM and FAN in their major distinguishing factors as follows:

PODEM	FAN
1. Backtracing goes all the way to primary input lines.	Backtracing goes only up to the head lines.
2. The initial objective in the branching step is based on moving a D closer to a primary output line.	The branching process is made more intelligent by utilizing the concepts of unique sensitization and multiple backtrace.
3. The backtracing goes along one path only.	The backtracing goes along multiple paths.

The details of how these differences result in FAN being better than PODEM are available in [FUJI83]. Notice here that the bound step in the branch-and-bound procedure is referred to as the backtracking operation in [GOEL81] and [FUJI83]. However, to avoid the confusion between backtrace and backtracking, we have used a different terminology here.

Complexity considerations.   The area of digital system testing, despite its steady growth in the last two decades, has yet to witness the development of a consistent framework which can provide efficient testing algorithms for large and complex systems. Most of the work in this area is useful under very specific circumstances. It is, therefore, reasonable to expect that in practice many testing schemes used are based on experience, and not on some unified theory. As the system complexity and inaccessibility to system components grows due to VLSI technology, mere experience may not suffice. There is clearly a need for developing broad concepts for large systems and various fault models. Unfortunately, however, this task is complicated by the fact that the test generation problem for combinational circuits is NP-complete [IBAR75]. In other words, it is in the same class of problems as the traveling salesman problem, Boolean satisfiability problem, knapsack problem, and so on. As there are no known efficient solutions to such problems, one should not expect efficient solutions to the test generation problem either. Maybe the solution to this dilemma lies in designing circuits for easy testability (see Chapter 2).

The aim of this section is to present various bounds on the complexity of the test generation problem under some general and specific situations. The concept of NP-completeness will first be introduced, followed by discussions that unless a circuit is CFOF or two-level, the problem of determining whether there exists a test vector for a given single stuck-at fault is NP-complete. Various ramifications of this result will then be described. Specific situations will be considered next, and bounds on the size of minimal test sets for CFOF and two-level circuits will be provided. Finally, the problem of covering multiple stuck-at faults by single fault test sets will be considered and some bounds regarding this coverage capability will be established.

NP-complete problems.   The concept of NP-completeness is used to prove that the amount of time, that is, the number of steps, required to solve some specific problems is beyond a certain practical limit [AHO74]. In particular, a problem that can be solved in polynomial time on a nondeterministic machine is referred to as an *NP-problem*. Many such NP-problems can be solved in polynomial time on a deterministic machine as well. Of those NP-problems that are not known to have any deterministic polynomial solution, a special subclass exists which is referred to as the *NP-complete class*. All the problems in the NP-complete class are equivalent in the sense that if a deterministic polynomial algorithm can be found for any one such problem, a similar algorithm can also be found for all the problems in the class. In some sense, these are the hardest NP-problems.

One way to show that a problem P is NP-complete is to prove that P is in NP (i.e., it can be solved in polynomial time by a nondeterministic machine) and a previously known NP-complete problem P' is polynomially transformable to P. A problem P' is said to be polynomially transformable to P if the existence of a polynomial algorithm for P implies the existence of a polynomial algorithm for P'. For our purpose in this section, we will take P' to be a modification of a well-known NP-complete problem, called the *Boolean satisfiability problem,* which is to determine if a given Boolean expression of n variables in the conjunctive normal form (the product-of-sums form) is true for any of the 2^n possible vectors. The satisfiability problem remains NP-complete even when each clause in the product-of-sums form has at most three literals [AHO74]. We will refer to this problem as the 3-CNF satisfiability problem. Another modification that keeps the NP-completeness intact for the satisfiability problem is when the product of sums form is *clause monotone,* wherein each clause contains either only negated variables or unnegated variables [FUJI82].

NP-completeness of test generation.   Consider the following problem, P: Does there exist a test vector for a given single stuck-at fault in a combinational circuit C?

If C is completely fan-out-free, then every single stuck-at fault is known to be detectable and, therefore, the answer to P is yes. If, however, C is a general circuit, then P is not known to be solvable in polynomial time unless C is a two-level circuit. In fact, one can consider three-level monotone circuits to be the simplest class of circuits that are neither CFOF nor two-level and show that problem P for such circuits is NP-complete [FUJI82].

The NP-completeness property of the test generation necessitates that various heuristics be developed to create practical solutions to the problem. The PODEM and FAN algorithms are elegant examples in this regard. Many other fault analysis problems, such as a priori determination of size of minimal test sets, coverage of multiple faults by single-fault test sets, coverage of faults by randomly generated test sets, and so on, are similarly besieged by their inherent complexity, and their solutions require thoughtful insights. In the remainder of this section, some known results pertaining to some of these problems will be described.

Bounds on minimal test sets.   It was shown in Section 1.4.2. that the minimal test set for an elementary gate with n inputs consists of $n + 1$ test vectors. For the class of completely fan-out-free circuits, it has been proven [HAYE71b] that the minimal test set, T_m, for any n-input circuit must satisfy the following equation:

$$2\sqrt{n} \leq |T_m| \leq n + 1$$

The linear complexity of $|T_m|$ and the ease with which T_m can be generated (see Section 1.4.2) make CFOF circuits most attractive from the testability point of view. Unfortunately, however, the ratio of the total number of completely fan-out-free functions of n variables to the total number of all functions of n variables tends to zero even for moderate values of n. Consequently, very few functions of interest can be realized as CFOF circuits.

Every function can nonetheless be realized by a two-level network in which primary input lines may fan out. In such networks, every single-fault detection test set is also a multiple-fault detection test. Moreover, as seen from Section 1.4.2, the single-fault detection test set for a two-level network is easily generated. The size of the minimal test set for a two-level network, however, is not always of practical magnitude. It has been shown [HAYE71b] that for most functions, the size is of the order of 2^{n-1}.

More reasonable bounds on general circuits are known for the class of tree circuits, which can be used to realize many functions of interest [ABRA81a]. For a tree of depth d with each module containing m inputs, it is clear that there are m^d primary inputs. By a simple recursion on the procedure (see Section 1.5.4) to generate a test set for a tree circuit, it can be shown that the size of the test set is of the order of $2^m m^d$. This almost linear bound is obtained due to the fan-out-free interconnection of the modules in the tree circuit. For the special class of linear circuits in which each module is a two-input Exclusive-OR gate, the size of the test is $2^2 = 4$, independent of the depth of the tree [HAYE71b].

Except for the special classes of circuits discussed above, no useful general bounds on minimality of test sets are known. It should be pointed out here that the minimality of test sets is not an absolute requirement, and thus near-minimal test sets are often generated to save the effort required in minimizing a test set. However, minimal bounds discussed earlier provide some framework for the size of near-minimal test sets.

Multiple fault coverage by single-fault test sets.   Intuitively, one is liable to conclude that if a test set T can detect every single stuck-at fault in a circuit, it should surely be able to detect the simultaneous presence of two or more single stuck-at faults. However, unlike what happens in most physical observations, and as pointed out earlier in this chapter, logical circuits have the capability of masking [DIAS75] the effect of one fault f_1 by the presence of another fault f_2. Two different possibilities exist:

Case 1: f_2 may mask f_1 in such a manner that the combined effect of (f_1, f_2) makes the circuit behave as if there were no faults in the circuit at all.

Case 2: f_2 may mask f_1 in such a manner that a particular test vector or set of test vectors expected to detect f_1 does not detect f_1 in the combined presence of (f_1, f_2).

Case 3: f_1, f_2, f_3, f_4 or any combination of up to three of these faults may be detectable, but (f_1, f_2, f_3, f_4) is undetectable [DAND74, SMIT78].

The straightforward approach to this problem is to determine by simulation whether or not a given single-fault test set T covers (to a reasonable degree) all multiple faults of interest. This approach is quite impractical, however, as the total number of multiple faults of interest [GOLD77], say up to size 6, in a circuit with 1000 lines is close to 10^{17}.

A more formal and systematic approach to this problem was developed in [AGAR80a, AGAR81], wherein some sort of generic properties of a circuit structure are exploited to determine, in an a priori manner, the greatest lower bound on the capability of any single-fault test set to cover multiple faults up to a given size. A concept of G-expressions is employed to list all possible generic circuit structures feasible for a given number of lines in any circuit belonging to a specific class. The greatest lower bound is then determined simply by manipulating G-expressions, a process that does not require any further information about the circuit or the test set under consideration. Averaging over all such G-expressions, the following results have been reported:

Each single-fault detection test set in any internal fan-out-free circuit covers all faults of sizes 2 and 3 and at least 98% of all multiple faults of size 6 and less.

The inclusion of a single internal fan-out point in an otherwise internal fan-out-free circuit reduces the average coverage by single-fault test sets of multiple faults on gates involving the fan-out gate by approximately 5%.

In the case of circuits with more than one fan-out point, the use of the formalism becomes quite complex. However, an example is presented in [AGAR81] in which a circuit with three internal fan-out points and a single-fault detection test set covers only 76.5% of multiple faults of size 4 on gates with fan-out points. This drop of almost 22% is a cause for concern if one intuitively believes that every single-fault detection set covers almost all multiple faults.

Test generation for sequential circuits.   A fault in a sequential circuit requires, in general, a *sequence* of vectors in order to detect it. This makes sequential circuit testing a much more difficult problem than testing combinational circuits. The need to generate sequences is not the only problem associated with sequential circuit testing. Some memory elements within the circuit may require a sequence of input vectors to initialize them to a known value; until this is done, the propagation of faults may be difficult. A more severe problem is that faults may cause memory elements to become uninitializable and it may not be possible to find a test for such faults. Faults may cause oscillations (and unwanted state changes) within the circuit. The fault-free

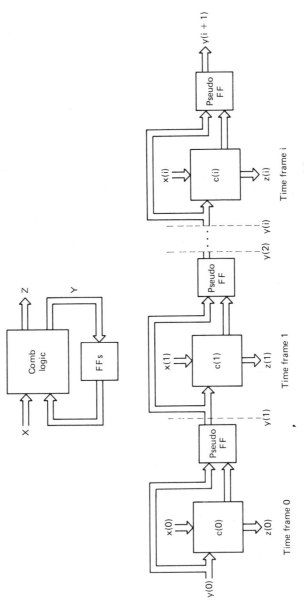

Figure 1.4.11 Sequential circuit and its iterative array model.

44

circuit may be designed to be free of races and hazards, but these could occur as a result of faults. The circuit may be designed so that only one state variable changes during a state transition, but it cannot be guaranteed that this condition will hold under failure and a critical race may result. A fault could cause the number of states in a circuit to increase (this is quite possible since a stuck-open fault could cause a combinational circuit to become sequential). Failures can also transform a synchronous circuit into an asynchronous one. Many of these problems have to be also addressed during fault simulation, and are discussed in Chapter 3.

The extension of the test generation techniques discussed previously to sequential circuits is, therefore, a very difficult problem and it has been the subject of much research. The extension of the D-algorithm to the sequential case is studied in [KUBO68], [BOUR71], and two heuristic methods of generating tests are introduced. One transforms the sequential circuit into an iterative combinational circuit, and the other uses complex primitives such as latches to represent the circuit to be tested. [BREU71] describes an algorithmic path-sensitizing procedure and an adaptive random procedure for sequential circuit testing. A heuristic algorithm (based on the D-algorithm) for asynchronous sequential circuits is described in [PUTZ71]. The procedure involves cutting the feedback loops, generating a potential test with the D-algorithm, and simulating the circuit to determine whether the sequence will in fact detect the fault. Heuristic tree search procedures for sequential circuit test generation are discussed in [HILL77]. The Boolean difference technique has been extended to sequential circuits in [HSIA71] and [CHIA72a]. Other work in the area of sequential circuit test generation includes [FUJI72], [AZEM72], [PAYA76], and [BHAT79].

The iterative array model for sequential circuits is illustrated in Fig. 1.4.11. The original circuit is replicated, each copy corresponding to a time frame. The flip-flops are modeled as combinational pseudo-flip-flops. Then a test for a single fault in the original sequential circuit can be obtained by finding a test for the corresponding multiple fault in the combinational array model (since each copy of the circuit will have the fault in it). Unfortunately, the model may not always represent the original circuit faithfully since, for example, delays in the feedback path may not be represented correctly in the combinational model. Thus simulation is usually used to verify the validity of the tests generated from such models.

The idea of viewing sequential circuits as a series of time frames can be used to generate tests for them even when there are faults in the flip-flops. This is shown by means of an example. Figure 1.4.12 shows a sequential circuit with one of the lines stuck at 0. The circuit is assumed to be initially in the state $Q = 0$. A test for this fault will consist of a sequence of input values applied to I and W, with the output at Z being observed. This sequence of inputs is illustrated in Fig. 1.4.13 as a series of time frames. Thus, initially in time frame 0, we have $Q = 0$ and $\overline{Q} = 1$. To activate the fault, we want to set $Q = 1$ (by $I = W = 1$); this is analogous to the primitive D-cube of failure. This D value at the point of failure can be propagated to Q by setting $W = 0$ (the propagation cube for the gate being $D0$), which will also propagate a D to the output.

In contrast to combinational circuits, algorithms have not been found which will

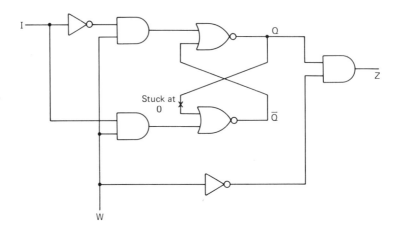

Figure 1.4.12   Sequential circuit with stuck-at fault.

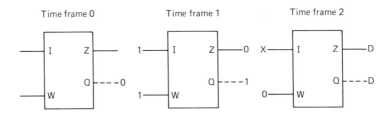

Figure 1.4.13   Derivation of test for fault circuit of Fig. 1.4.12.

be guaranteed to produce a test sequence, if one exists, for a fault in an arbitrary sequential circuit. Fault simulation is used in practice to determine the validity of proposed test sequences for detecting faults [PUTZ71, CHAP74]. In light of the difficulty of testing sequential circuits, the trend at this time is to redesign circuits (in particular the memory elements) so that the sequential testing problem is essentially reduced to a combinational testing problem; this is discussed in Chapter 2.

1.4.3. Testing Shorts and Opens

Introduction. Various physical failures result in creating a short between two lines, or an open path on a conducting line. As was pointed out earlier in this chapter, most of these shorts/opens can be accounted for by the stuck-at fault model. On the other hand, many shorts/opens do not have any representation as a stuck-at fault. The test generation problem for such faults is the subject of this section. Many researchers [MEI74, ELZI81, JAIN83, CHAN83] in this area have made significant contributions, yet many problems remain unsolved.

The usual approach in this area is to demonstrate that a certain single stuck-at fault test set T, can also detect shorts/opens which cannot be modeled as stuck-at faults. In other words, if T_s were generated with some constraints, the same test set would also be able to test for shorts/opens. This approach is particularly useful since most of the testing environment in the electronics industry is geared to perform stuck-at testing only. In the next section, various shorts/opens failures and their effects will be described. Some of the test generation procedures for such faults will then be considered, followed by some concluding remarks.

Shorts and open failures.   Any short or open in a circuit results in behavior which is heavily dependent on the technology of the circuit. Thus one single-fault model cannot possibly account for all different types of effects observed in different technologies. The following four examples from nMOS, CMOS, ECL, and TTL technologies are used to provide the flavor of the problem.

Consider the nMOS circuit shown in Fig. 1.4.14, wherein the output of the fault-free circuit is $(\overline{x_1 x_2 + x_3 x_4})$. Suppose next that there is a failure in this circuit which results in a short between points a and b. The output of the faulty circuit would then be $(\overline{x_1 + x_3)(x_2 + x_4})$, which cannot be accounted for by any stuck-at fault in the circuit. On the other hand, a short between points b and d, a and d, or c and d will correspond to a stuck-at-1 fault.

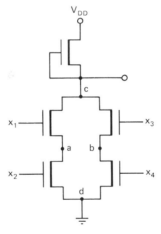

Figure 1.4.14   Complex nMOS gate.

As the next example, consider the CMOS NAND gate of Fig. 1.4.15. As mentioned in Section 1.2, any of the opens on the marked positions in the circuit will make it behave like a sequential circuit. Table 1.4.5 shows the complete truth table for all the opens. Such failures have been called stuck-open faults [WADS78].

Another class of shorts, called *bridging faults,* occurs when two lines in a circuit are shorted and wired logic is performed at the interconnection. Consider, for instance, the circuit in Fig. 1.4.16 in ECL (emitter-coupled logic) and a short between lines 2 and 3 which results in a wired OR. The fault-free and the faulty functions realized by this circuit are $x_1 x_2 + x_3 x_4$ and $x_1(x_2 + x_3) + (x_2 + x_3)x_4 = x_1 x_2 + x_2 x_3 + x_3 x_4$, respectively. Here again, the bridge fault cannot be modeled by a stuck-at fault.

Finally, there are shorts and opens which result in an indeterminate behavior.

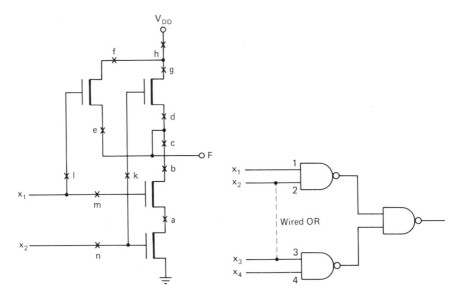

Figure 1.4.15 CMOS NAND gate.   **Figure 1.4.16** Short in ECL technology.

TABLE 1.4.5 TRUTH TABLE FOR NORMAL AND FAULTY NAND GATE OF FIG. 1.4.15[a]

								Faulty values						
x_1	x_2	f	a	b	c	d	e	f	g	h	k	l	m	n
0	0	1	1	1	θ^n	1	1	1	1	θ^n	1	1	1	1
0	1	1	1	1	θ^n	θ^n	1	1	θ^n	θ^n	θ^n	1	1	1
1	0	1	1	1	θ^n	1	θ^n	θ^n	1	θ^n	1	θ^n	1	1
1	1	0	θ^n	θ^n	0	0	0	0	0	0	0	0	θ^n	θ^n

[a]θ^n corresponds to the previous output value.

For instance, two lines shorted in a TTL circuit could both acquire an intermediate value between 0 and 1, and thus cannot be treated by "logical" fault models.

Test generation algorithms

Bridging faults.   One of the first attempts in this area was made on detecting bridging faults. In [ROTH80], the D-algorithm is used to generate a test for a bridging fault by defining a primitive D-cube of the fault under consideration. More systematic work is reported in [MEI74], wherein it is shown that any single stuck-at fault test set T_s for a circuit will always be able to detect any bridging fault between any two or more input leads of an elementary gate, and any bridging fault which results in a feedback such that the total number of inversions in the loop is odd. All bridging faults are assumed to exclude fan outs. Interesting results on undetectable bridging faults are provided in [FRIE74, KODA80].

Stuck-open Faults.   The stuck-open faults in CMOS have attracted wide attention [WADS78, ELZI81, JAIN83, CHAN83]. In [WADS78], a simulation strategy for dealing with stuck-open faults is described. A test generation algorithm for stuck-open faults which considers stuck-at fault test vectors is available in [ELZI81]. Various insights into stuck-open testing by stuck-at tests are provided in [CHAN83]. In particular, it is shown that if a single stuck-at test set for a circuit, with fan out on primary input lines only, is rearranged in a specific manner, the new test set will be able to detect all stuck-open faults in the circuit. Similar results are also obtained for general combinational circuits in [CHAN83]. Finally, Jain and Agarwal [JAIN83] provide a method to represent stuck-open faults in a manner that will allow the use of the D-algorithm to generate test vectors for any stuck-open fault. Recently, it was shown that tests to detect stuck-open faults in CMOS circuits can be invalidated due to delays in the circuit under test. This problem is still under investigation; however, some very interesting results on tests that will remain valid in the presence of arbitrary circuit delays are obtained in [REDD83] and [REDD84].

Non-stuck-at Faults.   The shorts/opens in nMOS which do not correspond to any stuck-type faults have been referred to as *non-stuck-at* (NSA) *faults* in [LAMO83] and have been treated in [GALI80], [CHIA82], and [LAMO83]. An NSA fault usually drastically changes the function realized by the fault-free circuit. Galiay et al. [GALI80] provide reasons for the need to concentrate on NSA faults by practical investigation of failure modes of various chips. Some exhaustive test generation algorithms for such faults are also given in [GALI80] and in [CHIA82], wherein a graph-theoretic model for such faults is introduced. Various heuristics provided in [LAMO83] help simplify the test generation task for NSA faults. Banerjee and Abraham [BANE83] showed that, in some cases, deriving tests for open and shorts at the transistor level produced very short test sets compared with sets derived at the equivalent gate level.

Summary.   The newer technologies of the future may involve failure modes which are completely unrelated to stuck-at and/or shorts/opens models. Moreover, the increasing complexity of future systems may make it extremely impractical to test at such a low level in terms of every single line. Until then, however, the need to understand test generation problems, and attempts to discover better and more practical solutions, remains necessary.

1.5. FUNCTIONAL-LEVEL TEST GENERATION

1.5.1. Introduction

As the systems to be tested became larger, one approach taken to reduce the complexity of test generation was to test a system by applying inputs which would verify that its designed functions were indeed performed correctly. This is frequently called *functional testing* and is often the only method by which some circuits are tested.

However, it is very difficult to grade the quality or the fault coverage of these tests, and it has been observed that in many cases these tests do not detect existing failures.

The example of a higher-level fault model derived earlier in this chapter showed that faults could cause the system to apparently perform its function correctly, while also performing other spurious tasks. The multiplexer in the example could select an incorrect data line in addition to the correct one, and the fault would be detected only if the intended data line was 0 and the incorrect one was 1. Clearly, it is not sufficient merely to check out all the functions of a system.

The two rules given below should be followed when using a higher-level approach to testing so that test patterns of reasonable length which will detect the most likely physical failures can be derived.

> *Rule 1:* It is not sufficient for a functional test to determine whether the intended function has been performed correctly; a test must also verify that no unintended function was performed in addition to the intended function.
>
> *Rule 2:* In order to generate tests of reasonable length for a complex system, information about the structure or the faulty behavior of the system should also be available (in addition to the functional information).

The necessity for rule 1 was discussed above. Unfortunately, for a complex system, the number of possible erroneous functions to be checked is extremely large, and the test length would be prohibitive. If no information is available about the structure or the faulty behavior, one is left with this impractical test or is forced to reduce it in some arbitrary fashion to a reasonable length, but with questionable fault coverage.

We, therefore, use the term *functional-level test generation* to mean an approach whereby a higher-level fault model is first derived for the system under test to include the most likely physical failures; test sequences are then derived to detect faults in this fault model. In some cases, structural information about the system is utilized to reduce the length of the test set.

1.5.2. Extension of Classical Testing to Functional Modules

The test generation problem can be simplified for large circuits if primitives more complex than gates are used, thus reducing the number of primitive elements. The techniques of propagating D values through functional modules, generating tests for simple modules, and partitioning to reduce the test complexity are considered here.

Extension of the D-algorithm to circuits with functional primitives and circuits described using a computer hardware description language have been studied [HUEY75, BREU80, ABRA82, LEVE82]. Table 1.5.1 shows the propagation of D values through a *JK* flip-flop; this can be derived from the algebraic expression describing the flip-flop [LEVE82]. Other examples from the same paper include the D-propagation table for an adder shown in Table 1.5.2 (the sum and carry functions

TABLE 1.5.1 PROPAGATION OF D VALUES THROUGH A JK FLIP-FLOP

J	K	q	Q
0	0	D	D
D	0	D	D
—	$\overline{D}$	1	D
0	$\overline{D}$	D	D
D	$\overline{D}$	$\overline{D}$	D
1	1	$\overline{D}$	D
D	1	$\overline{D}$	D
D	—	0	D
1	$\overline{D}$	D	D
D	$\overline{D}$	D	D

are shown), and that for a counter in Table 1.5.3. For the counter, $k, m \geq 0$, Φ represents a don't-care value not affected by counting, and a^n denotes n repetitions of a, while a,b^n denotes a sequence of length n of members of the set $\{a, b\}$. Examples of D-propagation through a decoder and a multiplexer are shown in Figs. 1.5.1 and 1.5.2, respectively. Note how D values on the control inputs of the multiplexer can be propagated to the output by the appropriate choice of input values. The use of this type of functional-level propagation information could drastically reduce the amount of computation needed in fault simulation and test generation.

Higher-level fault models were developed in Section 1.2 with a multiplexer as an example. Table 1.5.4 shows the test patterns for detecting stuck-at and short faults in the multiplexer of Fig. 1.2.4. It is left to the reader to extend this test to include stuck-open faults.

These ideas can be applied to complex circuits by partitioning the circuit into functional modules, applying functional patterns to the modules and propagating the errors to the output, and backtracking to find a consistent set of values on the input lines.

1.5.3. Functional-Level Test Generation for Complex Modules

The preceding section described methods of extending classical test generation techniques to functional modules when fault models were available for these modules and

TABLE 1.5.2 D-PROPAGATION FOR AN ADDER

Sum	0	1	D	$\overline{D}$	x	Carry	0	1	D	$\overline{D}$	x
0	0	1	D	$\overline{D}$	x	0	0	0	0	0	0
1	1	0	$\overline{D}$	D	x	1	0	1	D	$\overline{D}$	x
D	D	$\overline{D}$	0	1	x	D	0	D	D	0	x
$\overline{D}$	$\overline{D}$	D	1	0	x	$\overline{D}$	0	$\overline{D}$	0	$\overline{D}$	x
x	x	x	x	x	x	x	0	x	x	x	x

TABLE 1.5.3 *D*-PROPAGATION FOR A COUNTER

	Counter pattern	Next state
1	$\Phi 0\{\overline{D}, 1\}^{K}\overline{D}1^{m}$	$\Phi\overline{D}\{0, \underline{D}\}^{K}\underline{D}0^{m}$
2	$\Phi 0\{\underline{D}, 1\}^{K}D 1^{m}$	$\Phi D\{0, \overline{D}\}^{K}\overline{D}0^{m}$
3	$\Phi\underline{D}\{\overline{D}, 1\}^{K}\overline{D}1^{m}$	$\Phi 1\{0, \underline{D}\}^{K}D0^{m}$
4	$\Phi\overline{D}\{D, 1\}^{K}D 1^{m}$	$\Phi 1\{0, \overline{D}\}^{K}\overline{D}0^{m}$
5	$\Phi 01^{m}$	$\Phi 10^{m}$
6	$\Phi 0$	$\Phi 1$

	Counter pattern	Next pattern
1	$\Phi 0\{\overline{D}, 1, x\}^{K}x\{\overline{D}, 1\}^{m}$	$\Phi xx^{K}xA\,(m)$
2	$\Phi D\overline{D}\{\overline{D}, 1, x\}^{K}x\{\overline{D}, 1\}^{m}$	$\Phi xxx^{K}xA\,(m)$
3	$\Phi 0\{D, 1, x\}^{K}x\{D, 1\}^{m}$	$\Phi xx^{K}xB\,(m)$
4	$\Phi\overline{D}D\{D, 1, x\}^{K}x\{D, 1\}^{m}$	$\Phi xxx^{K}xB\,(m)$

	Counter state	Next state
1	$0111\overline{D}xx1$	$xxxxxxx0$
2	$011D\overline{D}\,\overline{D}xx11$	$011xxxxx00$
3	$0\overline{D}\,\overline{D}xx11$	$xxxxx00$
4	$0xxDD$	$xxx0\overline{D}$

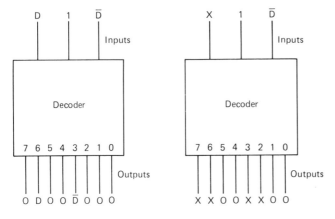

(a)   (b)

Figure 1.5.1 Example of *D*-propagation through a decoder.

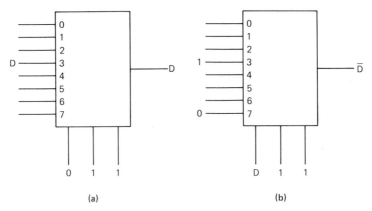

Figure 1.5.2   Example of D-propagation through a multiplexer.

TABLE 1.5.4   TESTS FOR STUCK FAULTS AND SHORTS IN MULTIPLEXER OF FIG. 1.2.4

x_0	x_1	x_2	x_3	x_4	x_5	x_6	x_7	p	q	r
0	1	1	1	1	1	1	1	0	0	0
1	0	1	1	1	1	1	1	0	0	1
1	1	0	1	1	1	1	1	0	1	0
.	.	.	.	.	.	.	.	.	.	.
1	1	1	1	1	1	1	0	1	1	1
1	0	0	0	0	0	0	0	0	0	0
0	1	0	0	0	0	0	0	0	0	1
0	0	1	0	0	0	0	0	0	1	0
.	.	.	.	.	.	.	.	.	.	.
0	0	0	0	0	0	0	1	1	1	1

their interconnection structure was known. This section will consider some complex functional elements for which we derive tests based on more general fault models.

Memory testing.   A good example of the application of the functional-level test generation approach is the derivation of tests for a large semiconductor memory. There is no meaningful gate-level description for memories, and a large memory chip consists of many hundreds of thousands of transistors. In addition, the detailed transistor-level description of a memory is usually unavailable to the user. Thus test procedures for memories are usually produced at a higher level. We first mention some of the popular test procedures in use for memory testing, then develop a functional-level fault model and, finally, provide an example of an algorithm that will detect the faults in the fault model.

A semiconductor random access memory (RAM) stores information in a memory cell array, each bit of information being typically stored in a single transistor cell. The address of the cell to be accessed is provided to decoders which activate the appropriate select lines. Amplifiers and drivers provide the necessary translation of voltages to levels which can be interpreted as logic values.

Test procedures for a semiconductor RAM can be divided into two broad areas, parametric testing and functional testing [MUEH81]. *Parametric testing* involves measuring the dc parameters such as output levels, power consumption, fan-out capability, leakage current, noise margins, and so on. It also involves ac parameters such as the dynamic behavior, setup and hold times, access time, recovery times, and so on. Testing for these parameters requires detailed knowledge of the memory chip as well as the availability of test equipment which has the ability to apply patterns and to capture the responses at the required speeds and with the necessary resolution. Therefore, we will not consider parametric testing in this chapter. *Functional testing* involves the detection of physical failures which cause the RAM to function incorrectly. These include faults in memory cells, address logic, drivers or amplifiers, noise coupling between cells, and so on.

In a general sense, a memory is said to be *functional* if it is possible to change every cell from a 0 to a 1 as well as from a 1 to a 0 and to read every cell correctly when it stores a 0 as well as when it stores a 1, independent of the state of the remaining cells. Unfortunately, checking every cell for all possible states of the other cells requires an exhaustive test which is on the order of 2^n in length, where n is the number of cells in the memory [HAYE75]. Therefore, a useful test would be to check for a subset of faults which would include all the physical failures of practical interest.

Various functional tests have been proposed for RAMs [SOHL77, KNAI77]. They range in complexity from test lengths which grow linearly with n to those which grow as the square of n. The fault coverage of the tests also varies considerably. Some representative tests are described briefly below. The notation used to describe the memory tests is given in Table 1.5.5.

TABLE 1.5.5 NOTATION USED IN
DESCRIBING MEMORY TESTS

0:	Write a 0 in cell
1:	Write a 1 in cell
R:	Read cell and verify
$\updownarrow$:	Complement the contents of the cell

March test.   A set of 1s or 0s is made to "march" down the memory addresses. A background pattern of all 0s is written in the memory. For each address in some sequence, the bit is read (should be a 0) and a 1 is written into the location. Now, for each address in the reverse order, the bit is read (should be a 1) and a 0 is written into the location. The entire test is repeated with complementary data.

This test takes a time proportional to n, but is not very comprehensive. An improved "march test" will be described later in this section.

GALPAT test.   This is a widely used test which has a length proportional to the square of n but which is considered to be very comprehensive. This test is described in Table 1.5.6. It consists of first writing a background pattern of all 0s or

TABLE 1.5.6 GALPAT TEST

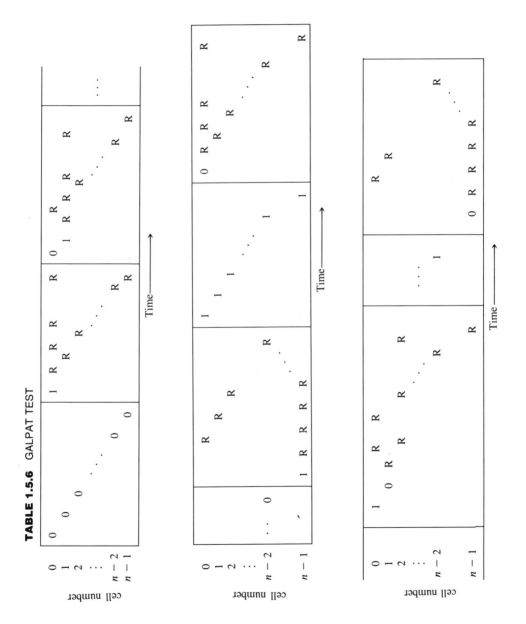

all 1s. A test cell is then complemented; a sequence of reads is performed of the test cell, followed by every other cell in turn. This is repeated for every cell. This test was designed to detect interactions between any pair of cells, as well as to detect problems in transitioning between any pair of addresses. Unfortunately, this test takes too long to be practical for large RAM chips. Modified versions of this test have been proposed to reduce the test time [SOHL77]. One such test is GALTCOL, which, rather than make transitions between all pairs of cells, makes transitions only between a cell and other cells in the same row (of the actual implementation). This test takes a time proportional to $n^{3/2}$ but requires detailed knowledge of the internal memory structure. This might vary among manufacturers (even of the same part number); and as redundant cells are incorporated into chips to increase the yield (see Section 1.2), the structure of a memory might vary even among chips from the same lot.

Functional fault model for memories.   A set of functional faults was proposed for memories by [THAT77] and [NAIR78] and augmented by [SUK81]. This fault model is as follows.

1. One or more cells are stuck-at 0 or stuck-at 1.
2. One or more cells fail to undergo a 0-to-1 or a 1-to-0 transition.
3. There exist one or more cells which are *coupled*. By this is meant that a 0-to-1 (or a 1-to-0) transition in a cell (due to a write into that cell) changes the contents of another cell from 0 to 1 or from 1 to 0. This does not imply that if a transition in cell i changes the state of cell j, a transition in cell j will change the state of cell i.
4. More than one memory cell is accessed during a Read or a Write operation.

A comprehensive march test.   Although the fault model allows interaction between any pair of cells, tests of length proportional to n (rather than n^2) can be devised to detect all these faults. A test requiring $30n$ operations was given in [NAIR78] to detect faults in this fault model. An improved test, requiring $14n$ operations, was derived in [SUK81] to detect the occurrence of the functional faults given above as long as only one type of fault is present. This test is given in Table 1.5.7 using the notation in Table 1.5.5. Intuitively, in order to detect a coupling fault, one must force a transition in a cell and read the coupled cell before the faulty value in it is changed. Since a cell could be coupled to one with a higher addresses or to one with a lower address, one must exercise the memory by going from lower addresses to higher addresses as well as from higher addresses to lower addresses in order to detect both types of couplings. Various complex coupling faults were analyzed in [SUK81] and it was shown that a read followed by two writes, each complementing the cell, as well as a read followed by three complementing writes, was necessary to detect all the coupling faults. For a detailed explanation of the algorithms and the proofs that the tests indeed detect any of the faults in the fault model, the reader is referred to the papers cited above.

TABLE 1.5.7 COMPREHENSIVE MARCH TEST FOR RAMS

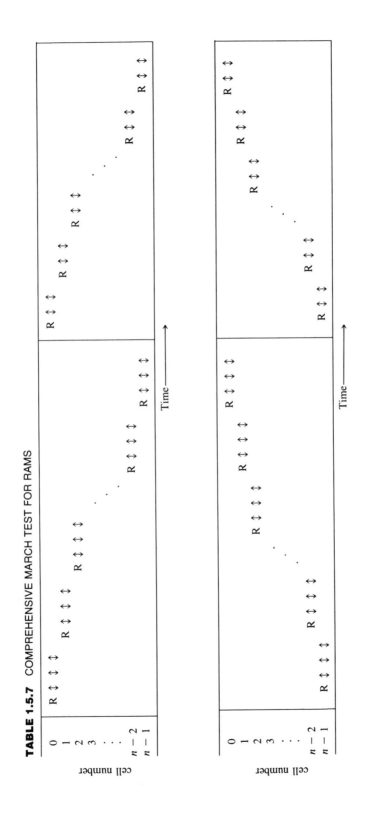

A comparison of the functional fault and tests presented here with the GALPAT test procedure shows that both procedures detect interactions between any pair of cells in the memory, and both are independent of the actual implementation of the memory cell array. The GALPAT test, however, detects address sequence problems, where a specific pair of addresses presented in sequence to the memory cause problems; this type of fault is not detected by the shorter tests presented here. Clearly, any algorithm which detects such a fault and which does not have any information of the internal design of the memory will be fairly complex.

Testing of programmable logic arrays. Programmable logic arrays (PLAs) are becoming very popular primitive blocks in the design of complex systems. They have a very regular structure and can be "programmed" easily to be functional blocks for random logic. With the addition of registers and feedback, they can be made into finite-state machines. Thus it is no wonder that many of the complex micro-processors today have PLAs implementing part of their control logic.

A schematic representation of a PLA is shown in Fig. 1.5.3a. This particular PLA has four inputs, two outputs, and can be programmed with up to four product terms. The programming is indicated by the presence or absence of "contacts" be-tween the horizontal and vertical lines. The logic function implemented by the PLA is given in Fig. 1.5.3b.

A PLA is another good target for the development of a higher-level fault model. We will briefly describe the fault model here and will indicate how tests may be generated. The details of the tests can be found in the references. Recent work on the testing of PLAs includes [OSTA79], [SMIT79], and [BOSE82]. A structural-level fault model for the PLA includes faults such as stuck faults on lines and bridging faults between lines. In addition, a class of faults peculiar to PLAs, known as *contact faults* or *crosspoint faults,* has to be considered. A contact fault is caused by the spurious presence or absence of a contact in a PLA. It has been shown in the references given here that a complete contact fault detection test set inherently covers most of the other types of faults.

In [SMIT79] and [BOSE82] a fault model was derived for contact faults in terms of the product terms of the PLA (which is how a PLA is specified). The fault model is that, under contact faults, the following can happen:

1. A product term can grow (i.e., cover more minterms)
2. A product term can shrink (cover fewer minterms)
3. A product term can disappear from a function
4. A product term from one function can spuriously appear in another function.

Figure 1.5.4 gives examples of these faults for the PLA in Fig. 1.5.3. The growth is caused by the loss of the original contact at q_1; a spurious contact at q_2 causes a product term to shrink. A wrong contact at q_3 can cause a new product term to appear for f_1, while the loss of the contact at q_4 can result in the disappearance of a product term.

From the fault model above it can be seen that tests can be derived by consid-

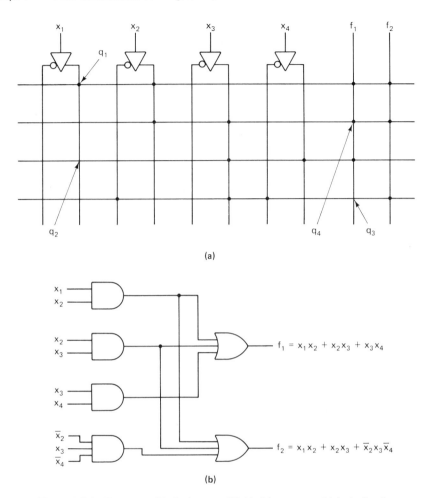

Figure 1.5.3   Programmable logic array (PLA): (a) structure; (b) logic function.

ering only the original product terms (describing the PLA) and their mutations. To check whether a product term has grown, for example, minterms which would be covered by the growth of the term and which are not covered by any other product term are chosen as test vectors. The reader is referred to the literature cited in [AGAR80b] for details which are beyond the scope of this chapter. Chapter 2 also discusses the design of PLAs which are slightly modified so that they can be tested with a universal set of tests, thus obviating any test generation.

Test generation for microprocessors.   Our final example in the derivation of tests at the functional level without any knowledge of the internal structure will consider microprocessors. This is a difficult problem compared to those considered earlier since the microprocessor is a much more complex device. Thus there is the

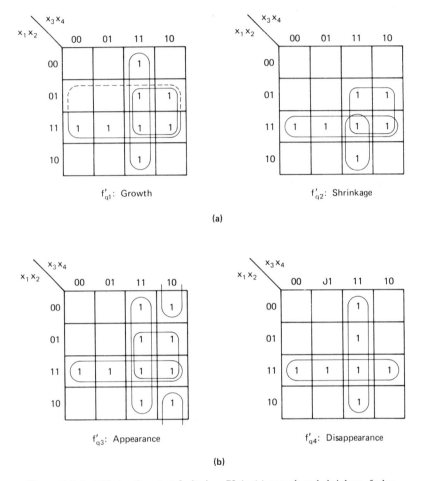

Figure 1.5.4   Effects of contact faults in a PLA: (a) growth and shrinkage faults;
(b) appearance and disappearance faults.

added difficulty that even the description of the fault-free microprocessor is not very simple.

A gate-level approach to testing a microprocessor is admittedly inappropriate because of its complexity. The approach taken in many cases is to check out each instruction or to run application programs. General fault models have been proposed for microprocessors [THAT80, ROBA75, ROBA78, BRAH84]; techniques have also been given to derive tests for general microprocessors to detect faults in the fault model. The particular case of testing bit-sliced microprocessors was considered in [SRID81]. In the following, we will outline briefly the approach taken in [BRAH84]. The reader is referred to the papers cited for more details.

As will be seen below, the fault model is developed at the instruction and register transfer level for a microprocessor. It follows the principles outlined earlier, including, for example, the execution of additional spurious instructions in addition to the desired instruction. The problem is in deriving tests for the faults. This is because in order to check for an instruction or internal state of the microprocessor, other (possibly faulty) instructions have to be executed, and faults in these instructions might mask the faults they are attempting to detect.

The approach is to model the microprocessor and its various functions, and to define the faulty behavior for the functions at the control sequencing level [THAT80, ABRA81b, BRAH84]. The detailed model at the control sequencing level is used to obtain general results about the type of test patterns necessary. The actual test patterns can be produced without this detailed knowledge. A microprocessor is modeled as a graph where each node represents a register or set of registers $R_i \in \mathbf{R}$. An edge represents data or information transfer. Instructions are modeled as consisting of sequences of microinstructions, with each microinstruction consisting of a set of micro-orders. Note that this is only conceptual, and will also apply to non-microprogrammed processors. Figure 1.5.5 gives the graph of the Motorola MC68000 and Table 1.5.8 the set of micro-orders. The eight data registers D0–D7 of the

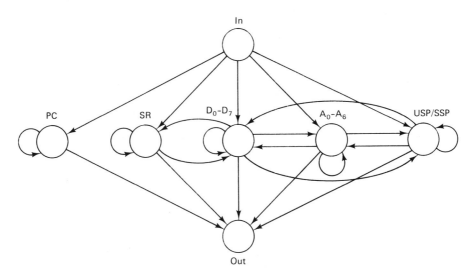

Figure 1.5.5   Data transfer graph representing the Motorola MC68000.

TABLE 1.5.8   SET OF MICRO-ORDERS FOR THE MC68000

Type 0	SWAP,CLR,NOT,NEG BTST,BSET,BCLR BCHG,SHIFTLEFT,SHIFTRIGHT
Type 1	MOV,AND,OR,EOR,EXG
Type 2	ADD,MUL,SUB,DIV

MC68000 form a set of equivalent registers, as do the seven address registers A0–A6. However, address register A7 does not belong to the same equivalence class, because A7 is used as an implicit stack pointer in addition to being accessed explicitly like registers A0–A6. Thus there are instructions, such as MOVE USP, which refer to A7 implicitly but which cannot reference A0–A6 and, hence, A7 cannot belong to the same equivalence class as A6. The external environment is represented by two nodes, IN and OUT. All data input and output (information) is done through the IN and OUT nodes, respectively. The micro-orders are divided into three types depending on their function. A micro-order is of type 0 if it operates on one register, it is of type 1 if it involves a transfer of data from one register to another or if it is a logical operation (e.g., AND), and it is of type 2 if it is an arithmetic operation (e.g., ADD).

Fault models are then defined for various functions of the microprocessor. A microprocessor is decomposed into the following functional units: (1) register decoding function, (2) arithmetic and logic unit, (3) data transfer paths, and (4) the instruction sequencing and control function.

Fault model for the register decoding function. Let $f_D(R_i)$ denote the register decoding function. Then under a fault $f_D(R_i) = R_j$ or

$$f_D(R_i) = \emptyset \text{ or } f_D(R_i) = \{R_i, R_j\}.$$

Fault model for the data transfer function. Under a fault (1) any number of lines can be stuck at 0 or 1, and (2) any pair of lines i, j can be coupled. Two lines i and j are coupled if the value of j depends on the value of i.

Fault model for the data manipulation function. No specific fault model is presented for the data manipulation function. It is assumed that the complete test set for any given ALU can be determined. Thus the test set for the data manipulation function consists of instructions to transfer the operands from memory to the source registers, instructions to perform the operation under test, and instructions to read the result from the destination register into memory.

Fault model for the instruction sequencing function. Under a fault we could have one or all of the following events:

1. One or more micro-orders are inactive; therefore, the instruction is not executed completely.
2. Micro-orders which are normally inactive become active.
3. A set of microinstructions is active in addition to or/instead of the normal microinstructions. (The following assumptions are made. The number of memory write operations does not increase under fault. Under fault the maximum number of microinstructions in an instruction does not exceed K, and the maximum number of micro-orders in a microinstruction does not exceed M.)

It can be seen that the model is quite comprehensive. The bounds on the number of microinstructions and micro-orders are just to bound the test length; the values for these can easily be estimated for any microprocessor.

A faulty microinstruction is detected by storing appropriate data in the registers of the microprocessor so that the fault will destroy some of the data. A suggested set of code words for the MC68000 is given in Table 1.5.9. This is based on a $\binom{d}{p}$ code. It has the property that any fault resulting in one additional micro-order with two code words as the source will produce a noncode word in the destination.

TABLE 1.5.9 CODE WORD ASSIGNMENT TO THE REGISTERS OF THE MC68000

Register	Code pattern
D0	11111101111111111111111111111111
D1	11111110111111111111111111111111
D2	11111111011111111111111111111111
D3	11111111101111111111111111111111
D4	11111111110111111111111111111111
D5	11111111111011111111111111111111
D6	11111111111101111111111111111111
D7	11111111111110111111111111111111
A0	11111111111111011111111111111111
A1	11111111111111101111111111111111
A2	11111111111111110111111111111111
A3	11111111111111111011111111111111
A4	11111111111111111101111111111111
A5	11111111111111111110111111111111
A6	11111111111111111111011111111111
USP	11111111111111111111101111111111
SSP	11111111111111111111110111111111

The most difficult part of test generation for microprocessors is in finding tests for instruction decoding and control. Test generation algorithms for detecting faults in the instruction execution process are based on testing the Read(R_i) instruction for all R_i for the presence of faults by executing the Read(R_i) instructions in a particular order. It should be noted that the Read(R_i) instructions themselves could be faulty. Table 1.5.10 gives the high-level description of the algorithm to detect faults in instruction sequencing and control. A core set of instructions (needed for the micro-

TABLE 1.5.10 TEST ALGORITHM TO DETECT FAULTS IN INSTRUCTION DECODING AND CONTROL

1. Check that a core set of instructions (LOAD, COMPARE, BRANCH) is executed completely.
2. Check that every register can be correctly read out without disturbing other registers.
3. Check that every register can be loaded (the LOAD REGISTER instruction is tested for all addressing modes).
4. Check the correct operation of all the remaining instructions.

Read (R_i) is a sequence of instructions which transfers data in register i to a location in memory and leaves the internal state of the microprocessor as it was before executing the instructions.

In the self-test mode, this sequence should include a comparison with the stored data value for the register followed by a branch to "error" if the comparison failed.

processor to test itself) is first checked, followed by instructions to read and load registers; the remaining instructions can then be easily tested. Table 1.5.11 gives the details of the test for core instructions. The compare and branch instructions are tested for all conditions. The compare instruction is executed $M * K + 1$ times to guarantee that faults will not mask each other; it can be proved that any existing fault will be detected in the worst case after this repeated loop.

TABLE 1.5.11 PROCEDURE TO TEST CORE INSTRUCTIONS

	MOV $\#d_1, R_1$	;Move d_1 to R_1
	MOV $\#d_1, R_2$	;Move d_1 to R_2
	CMP R_1, R_2	
	BEQ a	
	BRA error	
	.	
	.	
a:	MOV $\#d_2, R_1$	;$d_1 \neq d_2$
	MOV $\#d_3, R_2$	;$d_2 \neq d_3$
	CMP R_1, R_2	;$d_1 \neq d_3$
	BEQ error	
b:	MOV $\#d_1, R_1$	
	MOV $\#d_1, R_2$	
	do $M * K + 1$ times BEQ error	
	CMP R_1, R_2	
	BEQ C	
	BRA error	
	.	
	.	
c:	MOV $\#d_2, R_1$	
	MOV $\#d_3, R_2$	
	BEQ error	
	.	
	.	
d:	CMP R_1, R_2	
	BEQ error	
	BRA success	
error:	write error!	
success:	NOP	

The next step is to test that all the registers can be read correctly. This is done in three subtasks based on the type of operation. Three sets are defined, and the procedures operate on these sets. S_0 is the set of registers i for which there is an operation using i as both source and destination. S_1 consists of pairs of distinct registers i and j for which there is an operation using i as source and j as destination. S_2 consists of triples of registers i, j, and k (i and j distinct) for which an operation exists which uses i and j as source and k as destination. One of the procedures is given in Table 1.5.12; as before, the multiple execution of an instruction is to guarantee that faulty microinstructions do not mask each other. The other procedures are similar and can be found in the references cited.

TABLE 1.5.12 PROCEDURE TO
DETECT FAULTS OF TYPE 2 IN READ
REGISTER INSTRUCTIONS

	for all $i \in \mathbf{R}$ and for all $(j, k, l) \in S_2$ do {
1.	Read (i)
2.	Read (j)
3.	{Read (k) $M * K + 1$ times}
4.	{Read (l) $M * K + 1$ times}
5.	{Read (k); Read (l) $M * K + 1$ times}
6.	Read (i)
7.	Read (j)

The load register instruction is then checked by moving data into each register and reading it out. (We know that the read instructions are working correctly at this point.) This instruction is checked for all addressing modes, while the remaining instructions are checked for only one addressing mode. This is primarily to reduce the number of instructions that must be executed for the test, since checking all instructions for all addressing modes would require a very large number of instructions. This simplification is quite reasonable if the microprocessor is designed so that faults in the instruction sequencing are independent of faults in the addressing modes. Most modern microprocessors are, in fact, designed in this way. Table 1.5.13 gives the test procedure.

Finally, the remaining instructions can be checked out using the procedure given in Table 1.5.14; reading the internal registers after each instruction ensures that no information has been destroyed when executing the instruction.

Table 1.5.15 gives the test procedures for the data storage and data transfer functions. A more comprehensive RAM test can be used if desired for internal register files or on-chip RAMs.

The internal data manipulation units should now be tested since it is known that

TABLE 1.5.13 TEST
PROCEDURE TO
DETECT FAULTS IN
LOAD REGISTER
INSTRUCTIONS[a]

	for all $i \in \mathbf{R}$ do { for all $j \in \mathbf{R}$ do {
1.	Read (j)
2.	MOV d_i, R_i
3.	Read (j) enddo}}

[a] This test is done for all addressing modes.

TABLE 1.5.14 PROCEDURE TO CHECK
OUT ALL INSTRUCTIONS

	for all $I_i \in \mathbf{I}$ do {
1.	Load the registers with the code words.
2.	Execute I_i.
3.	Read all the internal registers. enddo}

TABLE 1.5.15 TEST PROCEDURE FOR DATA STORAGE AND DATA TRANSFER

Use the data patterns below to check all logical transfer paths and all registers (patterns are shown for a 32-bit transfer path)

0	1	2	3	4	5	6	7	8	9	10	11	12	13	14	15	16	17	18	19	20	21	22	⋯	30	31
0	0	0	0	0	0	0	0	0	0	0	0	0	0	0	0	0	0	0	0	0	0	0		0	0
1	1	1	1	1	1	1	1	1	1	1	1	1	1	1	1	1	1	1	1	1	1	1		1	1
0	0	0	0	0	0	0	0	0	0	0	0	0	0	0	0	1	1	1	1	1	1	1		1	1
1	1	1	1	1	1	1	1	1	1	1	1	1	1	1	1	0	0	0	0	0	0	0		0	0
0	0	0	0	0	0	0	0	1	1	1	1	1	1	1	1	0	0	0	0	0	0	0		1	1
1	1	1	1	1	1	1	1	0	0	0	0	0	0	0	0	1	1	1	1	1	1	1		0	0
0	0	0	0	1	1	1	1	0	0	0	0	1	1	1	1	0	0	0	0	1	1	1		1	1
1	1	1	1	0	0	0	0	1	1	1	1	0	0	0	0	1	1	1	1	0	0	0		0	0
0	0	1	1	0	0	1	1	0	0	1	1	0	0	1	1	0	0	1	1	0	0	1		1	1
1	1	0	0	1	1	0	0	1	1	0	0	1	1	0	0	1	1	0	0	1	1	0		0	0
0	1	0	1	0	1	0	1	0	1	0	1	0	1	0	1	0	1	0	1	0	1	0		0	1
1	0	1	0	1	0	1	0	1	0	1	0	1	0	1	0	1	0	1	0	1	0	1		1	0

test data can be applied to these units and the results read out correctly. It is, unfortunately, not a simple matter to derive test patterns for a function unit without knowing anything about its structure. If the adder is known to be a ripple carry adder, or if it has a tree structure for carry lookahead, exhaustive tests can be generated [DIAS76, ABRA81a, MONT83]. Another alternative is to apply pseudorandom patterns supplemented with deterministic tests for exception conditions such as divide-by-zero.

The length of the test sequence to detect faults in the Read register instruction is proportional to n_R^4, where n_R is the number of internal registers in the microprocessors. The length of the procedure for detecting the faults in the remaining instructions of the instruction set is $(n_1 * n_R)$, where n_1 is the number of instructions in the instruction set. Thus the test length is quite reasonable even for complex microprocessors.

It is difficult to determine the quality of the functional test patterns. One way would be to correlate with failures in the field or to check the test against units which were suspected to have failed in the field. The fault coverage for a given fault set (single stuck faults, for example) is another good measure. This requires the knowledge of the details of the microprocessor and a fault simulator. Another study using a simple 8-bit microprocessor showed that patterns similar to those described here would give excellent stuck-at fault coverage [ABRA79]. A detailed fault simulation was done on 2200 faults. The interesting result here was that 90% of the stuck faults were detected by exercising each instruction, while about 6% of the stuck faults were detected only by the instruction sequencing tests and they caused incorrect functions in addition to the desired function. (The remaining 4% were found to be redundant or undetectable.)

These tests can be stored in a ROM or loaded from disk into RAM to make the microprocessor test itself. During the test procedure, checksums can be updated in memory after each subtest to ensure that the faulty microprocessor does not branch to the end of the test and indicate that it is good.

1.5.4. Exhaustive Testing

The functional-level test generation examples discussed so far used a higher-level fault model but did not use any knowledge of the internal structure of the system. There are cases, however, where it is not clear how a higher-level fault model should be derived. However, in many cases, the structure of the circuit is known, even though the details of the modules are unknown. In VLSI circuits, the modules are usually inter-connected, if possible, in a regular structure. The regularity of the structure can be exploited to derive simple tests. [MCCL81] describes methods of partitioning a circuit so that the modules comprising the circuit can be tested exhaustively, and [SAVI80b] discusses methods of designing a circuit so that the output values from an exhaustive test can be compressed into a single syndrome.

   Testing of iterative arrays.   Consider a 32-bit adder; if one counts the carry in, this is a 65-input circuit. How does one describe a functional-level fault model for this adder? Of course, in the absence of a functional fault model and any structural information, a test for the adder would consist of applying 2^{65} inputs. (At the rate of one input every nanosecond, this would take over 1000 years!) Such a test would still not allow faults which caused the adder to become sequential.

   An idea of a possible solution to this dilemma comes from the fact that the adder is known to be implemented as a ripple carry adder, as shown in Fig. 1.5.6. It can be

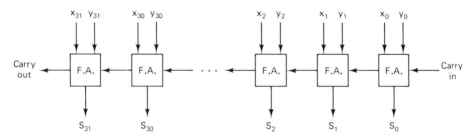

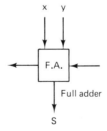

Figure 1.5.6 Ripple carry adder.

exhaustively tested for failure of a single cell with eight tests, as given in Table 1.5.16. Note that we are applying all eight combinations to each of the three-input combinational cells, thus testing them exhaustively. This is obvious for the S output of a cell. Examination of Table 1.5.16 reveals that if a cell produces an incorrect C_{out} as a result of a fault, the next cell (to the left) will produce an incorrect S output as a result of its incorrect C input. Therefore, we do not care about the actual realization of the full-adder cells. The only faults that are not allowed are those which cause a cell to become sequential. Thus implementation of function with regular structures can drastically reduce the length of the test sets. This has important implications in VLSI design, where layouts are typically done by replication of a subcell.

TABLE 1.5.16 EXHAUSTIVE TEST FOR RIPPLE CARRY ADDER

	BIT								
Test	31	30	·	·	·	2	1	0	
1	0	0	·	·	·	0	0	0	x
	0	0	·	·	·	0	0	0	y
								0	carry in
2	1	0	·	·	·	0	1	0	x
	1	0	·	·	·	0	1	0	y
								1	carry in
3	0	0	·	·	·	0	0	0	x
	1	1	·	·	·	1	1	1	y
								0	carry in
4	0	0	·	·	·	0	0	0	x
	1	1	·	·	·	1	1	1	y
								1	carry in
5	1	1	·	·	·	1	1	1	x
	0	0	·	·	·	0	0	0	y
								0	carry in
6	1	1	·	·	·	1	1	1	x
	0	0	·	·	·	0	0	0	y
								1	carry in
7	0	1	·	·	·	1	0	1	x
	0	1	·	·	·	1	0	1	y
								0	carry in
8	1	1	·	·	·	1	1	1	x
	1	1	·	·	·	1	1	1	y
								1	carry in

Any iterative array can be tested with a test that is linear in the size of the array. Iterative arrays that could be tested with a constant number of tests, independent of the size of the array, were studied and characterized by [KAUT67, FRIE73b, DIAS76, and PART81]. Dias [DIAS76] presents a procedure to derive such a test for an iterative logic array whose basic cell is reduced and has strongly connected components. Any fault that changes the truth table of the combinational array cell is allowed, and any number of cells are allowed to be faulty at any time. The approach is to verify each transition in the flow table of the iterative array by applying inputs to force the transition while applying inputs to $k - 1$ other cells so that the transition can be checked and the last cell is in the same state as the first cell. This pattern can be applied at the same time to blocks of k cells over the array. If $k - 1$ shifts of the basic pattern are applied to the blocks in the same fashion, it can be shown that this will check the transition in every cell. Repeating this for every transition will check the truth table of every cell in the array.

Testing of tree structures.   Iterative realizations of functions such as described above are slow because of the propagation delay from one end of the array to the other. For high-speed realizations of functions, a tree-type realization is usually used. The technique for testing arbitrary tree structures was described in [ABRA81a] where a recursive procedure is given to generate a test for an arbitrary tree network. The fault model used is that any node (cell) of the tree can fail in an arbitrary fashion as long as the failure does not cause the cell to become sequential. Any number of cells is allowed to be faulty.

We now show that a test $T(F)$ for a uniform tree can easily be determined by a recursive procedure. With appropriate notational changes, the procedure can also be applied to any general tree circuit. Let $T(F)$ for a tree of depth d, TREE (d), be denoted by $T_d(F)$. Assume that $T_1(F)$ consists of all the 2^m input vectors to M. Moreover, let S_i for a module M be a vector to M which will make the output of M dependent on the ith input line of M. Finally, for any TREE(d), let X_d^0 and X_d^1 be any input vectors which produce, respectively, a 0 and 1 on the output of the tree.

Procedure to calculate $T_d(F)$.   Consider the module at the root of the tree and the m subtrees of depth $d - 1$.

Step 1: Using only the vectors X_{d-1}^0 and X_{d-1}^1 for each of the m subtrees, apply $T_1(F)$ to the module at the root.

Step 2:

If $d > 2$ then
    begin
        for $i = 1$ to m do
            begin
                keeping S_i constant at the input to the root module
                (using X_{d-1}^0 and X_{d-1}^1 for the $m - 1$ subtrees), apply
                test $T_{d-1}(F)$ to the ith subtree TREE $(d - 1)$
            end
    end
  else return.

Thus if a function is realized in a cellular fashion as a linear array or as a tree, there are very efficient ways of deriving tests for it, with each cell being tested exhaustively. Chapter 2 also describes techniques whereby arbitrary circuits can be partitioned with additional logic so that the subcircuits can be tested exhaustively.

Checking experiments for sequential circuits. The final case of testing under general fault models is that of sequential circuits. This type of test, known as a *checking experiment,* can be used to test circuits exhaustively with a small number of states [HENN68, BOUT74]. The only assumption usually made is that the number of states does not increase under failure (or that there is a bound on the number of states).

The test involves various input sequences which are derived from knowledge of the function of the circuit under test. A *distinguishing sequence* is one that produces a unique output sequence when the sequence is applied to the circuit starting in each state; it serves to distinguish state from another. All sequential machines do not have distinguishing sequences; tests may still be derived for such machines but the test procedure will be complex and the tests will be very long.

A *homing sequence* is one which when applied to the circuit in an unknown starting state leaves the circuit in a known final state. (A special case of this is a synchronizing sequence which leaves the circuit in a specific state; "reset" control inputs usually synchronize the circuit to a particular state.)

A checking experiment then consists of the following steps:

Step 1: Apply a homing sequence to bring machine to a known state, followed by an input sequence to maneuver the machine into some fixed state.

Step 2: Apply an input sequence that causes the correctly operating machine to display the response of each of its states to the distinguishing sequence. This may also verify some of the machine's transitions.

Step 3: Apply an input sequence that verifies those transitions not checked in Step 2.

As an example, Fig. 1.5.7 shows the state table of the sequential circuit in Fig. 1.4.11. Table 1.5.17 describes the development of the test with the comments indicating the reason for each of the input vectors. It is clear that such an exhaustive test is practical only for very small circuits. On the other hand, since the circuit described in Fig. 1.5.7 is a 1-bit register, a register with many bits can be tested exhaustively by testing each bit exhaustively, as long as a failure in a bit will not affect other bits.

State	w = 0		w = 1	
	I = 0	I = 1	I = 0	I = 1
0 = A	A, 0	A, 0	A, 0	B, 0
1 = B	B, 1	B, 1	A, 0	B, 0

Next state, output

Figure 1.5.7 State diagram of a sequential circuit.

TABLE 1.5.17   CHECKING EXPERIMENT FOR SEQUENTIAL CIRCUIT OF FIG. 1.5.7

Input		Output	
W	I	Z	Comment
1	0	0	Put circuit in state A (synchronizing sequence)
0	0	0	Read (distinguishing sequence for state)
0	0	0	Read to check $W = 0, I = 0$ transition from state A
1	1	0	Move to state B
0	0	1	Read (distinguishing sequence)
0	0	1	Read to check $W = 0, I = 0$ transition from state B
0	1	1	Check various transitions from B each followed by
0	0	1	distinguishing sequence to verify final state
1	1	0	
0	0	1	
1	0	0	
0	0	0	Check various transitions from A followed
0	1	0	by distinguishing sequence
0	0	0	
1	0	0	
0	0	0	

1.6. RANDOM TESTING

1.6.1. Introduction

The concept of generating test vectors for a digital circuit by some random process provides probably the simplest approach to the test generation problem. A large interest [RAUL71, HUAN73, AGRA75, SCHN75, PARK75, SHED76, SHED77, PARK78, THEV78, THEV81, DAVI81, THEV83] in this area, however, deals with some of the problems faced in applying this simple concept. In this section the concept of random testing and various associated problems are described. Application of this concept to combinational circuits, sequential circuits, and microprocessors is dealt with, and concluding remarks indicating the future of random testing are presented. Throughout this section the random process that generates the input vectors is considered to be a stationary multinomial process, implying that successive input vectors are chosen independently according to some fixed probability distribution.

1.6.2. Concept and Problems

As amply noticed in Section 1.4, each input vector is, in general, known to be able to detect a large number of distinct faults. Deterministic approaches such as the D-algorithm generate a test vector X_t for a specific fault, but then simulate the vector to determine what other faults can be detected by it. If one moves a step further and generates X_t, not based on a fault in mind, but randomly, then S_t may still be perceived to be capable of detecting many faults. A large number L of test vectors generated randomly can then be applied to the circuit under test and the output compared with a fault-free reference unit or a simulator to determine whether or not the circuit is faulty.

Three difficult problems must, however, be solved before applying random testing. What is the value of L? What is the fault coverage provided by applying L random vectors? What is the confidence in the fault coverage results? All the three problems are clearly interrelated. To determine the value of L in general, the simplest approach would be to consider some specific type (Δ) of faults for which L can easily be obtained, and then extrapolate it to general situations. This approach, however, leads to the next two problems. If the extrapolation procedure is approximate, the fault coverage may not be guaranteed. In fact, a general procedure to determine the effectiveness of a random testing procedure with a high degree of confidence will necessarily entail an analysis which can be more complicated than the deterministic test generation procedure being replaced [SHED77]. Thus the choice to use random testing should be based on a clear analysis of the situation under consideration.

1.6.3. Combinational Circuits

A simple example will first be used to demonstrate the problems raised earlier. Consider an AND gate with k input lines. If the probability of producing a 0(1) on each input line is $\frac{1}{2}$, the probability of generating any specific input vector is 2^{-k}. From the discussions in Section 1.4 on special circuits, it follows that since there is exactly one test vector for each of the $k + 1$ faults, $1/1$, $2/1$, . . . , $k/1$, or $(k + 1)/0$, the probability of detecting each of these faults is only 2^{-k}. For $k = 32$, this probability is almost 0. Thus even if a million random vectors were applied to the AND gate with $k = 32$, there is a good probability that none of these single stuck-at faults would have been accounted for. Recall here that a complete deterministic test set for such a gate consists of 33 vectors only!

Various papers [SCHN75, PARK75, RAUL71, HUAN73, DAVI81, AGRA75] have considered the general problem of combinational circuit testing by random vectors. In [AGRA75], an analytical value of L is first determined for completely fan-out-free NAND networks, and then the results are extrapolated for general networks. A practical confirmation of such extrapolation has been determined to be very satisfactory [AGRA75]. A completely different approach is taken in [DAVI81], wherein L is determined for a so-called "most-difficult-to-detect fault," with a certain specified confidence $1 - \theta_D$. In particular,

$$L \approx \frac{2^n \log (1 - \theta_D)}{\sigma}$$

where n is the number of primary input lines and σ is the number of input vectors allowing the detection of the most-difficult-to-detect fault. If for instance, $1 - \theta_D = 0.999$ and $\sigma = 1$, then $L = 3 \times 2^n$, which is worse than the exhaustive testing. However, the equation above provides a quick solution to the value of L and the required confidence level.

1.6.4. Sequential Circuits

The problem of random testing a sequential circuit is worsened by the "memory" property of such circuits. A concept of error latency has been defined [SHED76] to analyze this situation:

> The error latency EL_k of a fault f_k is the number of input vectors applied to a digital circuit while f_k is active, until the first incorrect output vector due to f_k is observed.

The number of inputs until a given fault is detected during a random test is clearly the error latency of the fault. The confidence in the random test procedure for a fault f_k is the probability that the test detects f_k. That is, the confidence in an L-length random test is equal to $\Pr[EL_k \leq L]$. If the fault f_k is the worst-case fault, then the value of L to a specified confidence can be obtained by considering $\Pr[EL_k \leq L]$. Shedletsky and McCluskey [SHED76] provide results on how to obtain $\Pr[EL_k \leq L]$ and how to use these results very effectively to determine L for a given confidence level. Various other researchers [PARK78, THEV78, RAUL71] have also dealt with the sequential testing problem.

1.6.5. Microprocessors

Due to the inherent complexity of a microprocessor or any other LSI/VLSI chip, the random testing results above cannot be applied to such chips in an efficient manner. Instead, a random testing approach that can exploit the architectural information of complex systems under test can be much more effective. In [THEV81] and [THEV83], very useful results on microprocessor random testing are provided. The problem is treated in two parts: the random testing of the data section [THEV81] and the random testing of the control section [THEV83]. In both cases, the fault model is developed at the register-transfer level, resulting in the consideration of such faults as stuck-at faults in registers, faults in operators, faults in register decoding, faults in instruction decoding, and faults in control functions. A graph-theoretic model of microprocessors [THAT79], which was described in Section 1.5, is used to determine the bounds on the probability of each of the foregoing types of faults in terms of the instruction set and the register-transfer-level architecture of a microprocessor.

Based on this analysis, the most-difficult-to-detect faults are determined and the value of L is obtained for such faults. For a microprocessor such as the Motorola 6800, L is shown to be of the order of 6 million vectors. This test may correspond to just a few seconds of testing and will provide a confidence level of 0.999. L might be much greater for a more complex microprocessor such as the Motorola 68000.

1.6.6. Summary

Random testing is becoming a reasonable alternative to deterministic testing in various situations, most specifically in the case of microprocessors. Its full potential can, however, be realized only after it is adopted as a practical choice by manufacturers of digital systems. Various researchers have done considerable analytical work to demonstrate the viability of the random testing concept.

Due to the advancement of built-in testing (see Chapter 2), the random testing concept has taken another turn. In all the discussions in this section, the response generated by random testing was assumed to be verified at each step with the expected response. In built-in testing, however, the response to an L-length random test is first compressed into a small signature, and then only this signature is compared with the expected signature. A different set of analysis problems is created due to the compression step. Nonetheless, it is probably safe to assume that in the near future random testing will continue to become increasingly more important and more widely used.

REFERENCES

[ABBO81] Abbott, R., et al., "Equipping a Line of Memories with Spare Cells," *Electronics,* pp. 127–130, July 28, 1981.

[ABRA79] Abraham, J. A., and S. M. Thatte, "Fault Coverage of Test Programs for a Microprocessor," *Dig. 1979 IEEE Test Conf.,* pp. 18–22, Oct. 23–25, 1979.

[ABRA80] Abramovici, M., and M. A. Breuer, "Multiple Fault Diagnosis in Combinational Circuits Based on Effect–Cause Analysis," *IEEE Trans. Comput.,* vol. C-29, no. 6, pp. 451–460, June 1980.

[ABRA81a] Abraham, J. A., and D. D. Gajski, "Design of Testable Structures Defined by Simple Loops," *IEEE Trans. Comput.,* vol. C-30, pp. 875–884, Nov. 1981.

[ABRA81b] Abraham, J. A., and K. P. Parker, "Practical Microprocessor Testing: Open and Closed Loop Approaches," *COMPCON Spring 81,* pp. 308–311, Feb. 23–26, 1981.

[ABRA82] Abramovici, M., "A Hierarchical, Path-Oriented Approach to Fault Diagnosis in Modular Combinational Circuits," *IEEE Trans. Comput.,* vol. C-31, pp. 671–677, July 1982.

[AGAR78] Agarwal, V. K., "Fanout-Free Circuits and L-Expressions," *Proc. Conf. Inf. Sci. Sys.,* Johns Hopkins University, Baltimore, Md., pp. 227–233, Mar. 29–31, 1978.

[AGAR80a] Agarwal, V. K., and G. M. Masson, "Generic Fault Characterization for Table-Look-Up Coverage Bounding," *IEEE Trans. Comput.,* vol. C-29, no. 4, pp. 288–300, Apr. 1980.

[AGAR80b] Agarwal, V. K., "Multiple Fault Detection of Programmable Logic Arrays," *IEEE Trans. Comput.,* vol. C-29, pp. 518–523, June 1980.

[AGAR81] Agarwal, V. K., and A. S. F. Fung, "Multiple Fault Testing of Large Circuits by Single Fault Test Sets," *IEEE Trans. Comput.,* vol. C-30, no. 11, pp. 855–865, Nov. 1981.

[AGRA72] Agrawal, V. D., and P. Agrawal, "An Automatic Test Generation System for Illiac IV Logic Boards," *IEEE Trans. Comput.*, vol. C-21, no. 9, pp. 1015–1017, Sept. 1972.

[AGRA75] Agrawal, P., and V. D. Agrawal, "Probabilistic Analysis of Random Test Generation Method for Irredundant Combinational Logic Network," *IEEE Trans. Comput.*, vol. C-24, no. 7, pp. 691–695, July 1975.

[AGRA78] Agrawal, V. D., "When to Use Random Testing," *IEEE Trans. Comput.*, vol. C-27, no. 11, pp. 1054–1055, Nov. 1978.

[AGRA81a] Agrawal, V. D., "An Information Theoretic Approach to Digital Fault Testing," *IEEE Trans. Comput.*, vol. C-30, no. 8, pp. 582–587, Aug. 1981.

[AGRA81b] Agrawal, V. D., "Sampling Techniques for Determining Fault Coverage in LSI Circuits," *J. Digit. Syst.*, vol. 5, no. 3, pp. 189–202, 1981.

[AGRA81c] Agrawal, V. D., S. Seth, and P. Agrawal, "LSI Product Quality and Fault Coverage," *Proc. 18th Des. Autom. Conf.*, Nashville, Tenn., p. 196, June 29–July 1, 1981.

[AGRA82] Agrawal, V. D., and M. R. Mercer, "Testability Measures—What Do They Tell Us?" *Proc. IEEE Semiconduct. Test Conf.*, Philadelphia, pp. 391–396, Nov. 15–18, 1982.

[AHO74] Aho, A. V., J. E. Hopcroft, and J. D. Ullman, *The Design and Analysis of Computer Algorithms*, Addison-Wesley, Reading, Mass., 1974.

[AKER73] Akers, S. B., "Universal Test Sets for Logic Networks," *IEEE Trans. Comput.*, vol. C-22, no. 9, pp. 835–839, Sept. 1973.

[AKER76a] Akers, S. B., "Binary Decision Diagrams," *IEEE Trans. Comput.*, vol. C-27, no. 6, pp. 509–516, June 1976.

[AKER76b] Akers, S. B., Jr., "A Logic System for Fault Test Generation," *IEEE Trans. Comput.*, vol. C-25, no. 6, pp. 620–629, June 1976.

[AKER78] Akers, S. B., "Functional Testing with Binary Decision Diagrams," *Dig., 8th Annu. Int. Symp. Fault-Tolerant Comput.*, Toulouse, France, June 21–23, 1978.

[AKER79] Akers, S. B., "Probabilistic Techniques for Test Generation from Functional Descriptions," *Dig., 9th Annu. Int. Symp. Fault-Tolerant Comput.*, Madison, Wis., June 20–22, 1979.

[AKER74] Akers, S. J., Jr., "Fault Diagnosis as a Graph Coloring Problem," *IEEE Trans. Comput.*, vol. C-23, no. 7, pp. 706–713, July 1974.

[AMAR67] Amar, V., and N. Condulmari, "Diagnosis of Large Combinational Networks," *IEEE Trans. Electron. Comput.*, vol. EC-16, no. 5, pp. 675–680, Oct. 1967.

[APTE73] Apte, R. M., "Derivation of Near Minimal Test Sets and Fault Partitioning Techniques," Ph.D. thesis, Southern Methodist University, Dallas, Aug. 1973.

[ARMS66] Armstrong, D. B., "On Finding a Nearly Minimal Set of Fault Detection Tests for Combinational Logic Nets," *IEEE Trans. Electron. Comput.*, vol. EC-15, no. 1, pp. 66–73, Feb. 1966.

[AZEM72] Azema, P., M. Courvoisier, and J. P. Richard, "Fault Detection Method in Sequential Systems," *Abstr. IFAC 5th World Congr.*, Paris, p. 167, June 12–17, 1972.

[BALL69] Ball, M., and F. Hardie, "Effect on Detection of Intermittent Failure in Digital Systems," *AFIPS Conf. Proc.*, vol. 35, pp. 329–335, 1969 FJCC.

[BANE82] Banerjee, P., "A Model for Simulating Physical Failures in MOS VLSI Circuits," Tech. Rep. CSG-13, Coordinated Science Laboratory, University of Illinois, 1982.

[BANE83] Banerjee, P., and J. A. Abraham, "Generating Tests for Physical Failures in MOS Logic Circuits," *Proc. IEEE Semiconduct. Test Conf.*, Philadelphia, pp. 554–559, Oct. 18–20, 1983.

[BATE83] Bates, S. L., "High Speed In-Circuit Testing," *1983 IEEE Int. Test Conf.*, Philadelphia, pp. 57–63, Oct. 18–20, 1983.

[BEAR71] Bearnson, L. W., and C. C. Carroll, "On the Design of Minimum Length Fault Tests for Combinational Circuits," *IEEE Trans. Comput.*, vol. C-20, no. 11, pp. 1353–1356, Nov. 1971.

[BEH82] Beh, C. C., K. H. Arya, C. E. Radke, and K. E. Torku, "Do Stuck Faults Models Reflect Manufacturing Defects?" *Proc. IEEE Semiconduct. Test Conf.*, Philadelphia, pp. 35–42, Nov. 15–18, 1982.

[BENN72] Bennetts, R. G., "A Realistic Approach to Detection Test Set Generation for Combinational Logic Circuits," *Comput. J.*, vol. 15, no. 3, pp. 238–246, Oct. 1972.

[BENN81] Bennetts, R. G., C. M. Maunder, and G. D. Robinson, "CAMELOT: A Computer-Aided Measure for Logic Testability," *Proc. IEEE*, vol. 128, pp. 177–189, Sept. 1981.

[BENN82] Bennetts, R. G., *Introduction to Digital Board Testing*, Crane Russak, New York, 1982.

[BERG73] Berger, I., and Z. Kohavi, "Fault Detection in Fanout-Free Combinational Networks," *IEEE Trans. Comput.*, vol. C-22, no. 10, pp. 908–914, Oct. 1973.

[BETA70] Betancourt, R., "Derivation of Minimum Test Sets for Unate Logical Circuits," AD-720 330, Aug. 1970.

[BHAT79] Bhattacharya, A., "Fault Detection in Moore-Model Sequential Machine Using Counter-Cycle," *Electron. Lett.*, vol. 15, pp. 402–403, June 21, 1979.

[BLOD82] Blodgett, A. J., and D. R. Barbour, "Thermal Conduction Module: A High-Performance Multilayer Ceramic Package," *IBM J. Res. Dev.*, vol. 26, pp. 30–36, 1982.

[BOGO66] Bogomolov, A. M., et al., "The Theory of Binary Relations Applied to Detecting and Locating Faults in Complex Systems," *Vychisl. Metody Program. Vychisl. Mash.*, pp. 103–125 (IZD-Vo Saratovskovo Universiteta, 1966).

[BOGO68] Bogomolov, A. M., and V. A. Tverdokhlovov, "The Conditions for the Existence of Diagnostics Tests," *Kibernetika*, no. 3, pp. 9–19, 1968.

[BOSE82] Bose, P., and J. A. Abraham, "Test Generation for Programmable Logic Arrays," *Proc. 19th Des. Autom. Conf.*, pp. 574–580, June 14–16, 1982.

[BOSS71] Bossen, D. C., and S. J. Hong, "Cause Effect Analysis for Multiple Fault Detection in Combinational Networks," *IEEE Trans. Comput.*, vol. C-20, no. 11, pp. 1252–1257, Nov. 1971.

[BOUR71] Bouricius, W. G., E. P. Hsieh, G. R. Putzolu, J. P. Roth, R. R. Schneider, and C. J. Tan, "Algorithms for Detection of Faults in Logic Circuits," *IEEE Trans. Comput.*, vol. C-20, no. 11, pp. 1258–1264, Nov. 1971.

[BOUT74] Boute, R. T., "Optimal and Near-Optimal Checking Experiments for Output Faults in Sequential Machines," *IEEE Trans. Comput.*, vol. C-23, pp. 1207–1213, Nov. 1974.

[BRAH84] Brahme, D., and J. A. Abraham, "Functional Testing of Microprocessors," *IEEE Trans. Comput.*, vol. C-33, July 1984.

[BREU71] Breuer, M. A., "A Random and an Algorithmic Technique for Fault Detection Test Generation for Sequential Circuits," *IEEE Trans. Comput.*, vol. C-20, pp. 1364–1370, Nov. 1971.

[BREU72] Breuer, M. A., "Generation of Fault Tests for Linear Logic Networks, *IEEE Trans. Comput.*, vol. C-21, no. 1, pp. 79–83, Jan. 1972.

[BREU73] Breuer, M. A., "Testing for Intermittent Faults in Digital Circuits," *IEEE Trans. Comput.*, vol. C-22, pp. 241–246, Mar. 1973.

[BREU74] Breuer, M. A., "The Effects of Races, Delays, and Delay Faults on Test Generation," *IEEE Trans. Comput.*, vol. C-23, no. 10, p. 1078–1092, Oct. 1974.

[BREU76a] Breuer, M. A., et al., "Identification of Multiple Stuck-Type Faults in Combinational Networks," *IEEE Trans. Comput.*, vol. C-25, no. 1, pp. 44–59, Jan. 1976.

[BREU76b] Breuer, M. A., and A. D. Friedman, *Diagnosis and Reliable Design of Digital Systems*, Computer Science Press, Woodland Hills, Calif., 1976.

[BREU80] Breuer, M. A., and A. D. Friedman, "Functional Level Primitives in Test Generation," *IEEE Trans. Comput.*, vol. C-20, pp. 223–234, Mar. 1980.

[CARR74] Carrol, B. D., et al., "An Examination of Algebraic Test Generation Methods for Multiple Faults," *IEEE Trans. Comput.*, vol. C-23, no. 7, pp. 743–746, July 1974.

[CERN78] Cerny, E., "Controllability and Fault Observability in Modular Combinational Circuits," *IEEE Trans. Comput.*, vol. C-27, no. 10, pp. 896–904, Oct. 1978.

[CERN79] Cerny, E., D. Mange, and E. Sanchez, "Synthesis of Minimal Binary Decision Trees," *IEEE Trans. Comput.*, vol. C-28, no. 7, pp. 472–483, July 1979.

[CHA78] Cha, C. W., et al., "9-V Algorithm for Test Pattern Generation of Combinational Digital Circuits," *IEEE Trans. Comput.*, vol. C-27, no. 3, pp. 193–200, Mar. 1978.

[CHAL79] Chalkey, M. J., "Trends in VLSI Testing," *Dig., 1979 IEEE Test Conf.*, Cherry Hill, N.J., p. 3, Oct. 1979.

[CHAN65] Chang, H. Y., "An Algorithm for Selecting an Optimum Set of Diagnostic Tests," *IEEE Trans. Electron. Comput.*, vol. EC-14, no. 5, pp. 706–711, Oct. 1965.

[CHAN70] Chang, H. Y., E.G. Manning, and G. Metze, *Fault Diagnosis of Digital Systems*, Wiley-Interscience, New York, 1970.

[CHAN83] Chandramouli, R., "On Testing Stuck-Open Faults," *Dig., 13th Annu. Int. Symp. Fault-Tolerant Comput.*, Milan, Italy, pp. 258–264, June 1983.

[CHAP74] Chappell, S. G., "LAMP: Automatic Test Generation for Asynchronous Digital Circuits," *Bell Syst. Tech. J.*, vol. 53, pp. 1477–1503, Oct. 1974.

[CHER00] Various papers in the *IEEE Int. Test. Conf.*, Cherry Hill, N.J., and Philadelphia, 1970–1982.

[CHIA72a] Chia, D. K., and M. Y. Hsiao, "A Homing Sequence Generation Algorithm for Fault Detection in Asynchronous Sequential Circuits," *Dig., 2nd Annu. Int. Symp. Fault-Tolerant Comput.*, Newton, Mass., pp. 137–142, June 19–21, 1972.

[CHIA72b] Chiang, A. C. L., I. S. Reed, and A. V. Banes, "Path Sensitization, Partial Boolean Difference, and Automated Fault Diagnosis," *IEEE Trans. Comput.*, vol. C-21, no. 2, pp. 189–195, Feb. 1972.

[CHIA73] Chia, D. K., J. W. A. Y. Cho, M. Y. Hsiao, and A. M. Patel, "Algorithm for Generating a Complete Minimum Set of Test Patterns for Combinational Circuits," *IBM Tech. Disclosure Bull.*, vol. 14, pp. 3060–3063, Mar. 1973.

[CHIA82] Chiang, K. W., and Z. G. Vranesic, "Test Generation for MOS Complex Gate Networks," *Dig., 12th Annu. Int. Symp. Fault-Tolerant Comput.*, Santa Monica, Calif., pp. 149–157, June 22–24, 1982.

[CHIP70] Chipulis, V. P., "On the Construction of Tests for Checking Combinational Circuits," *Autom. Remote Control,* Oct. 1970.

[CHUA71] Chuang, Y. H., and S. R. Vishnubhotla, "A Path Analysis Approach to the Diagnosis of Combinational Circuits," 8th Des. Autom. Workshop, 28–30 June 1971.

[CLEG71] Clegg, F. W., "The Algebraic Approach to Faulty Logic Networks," Proc. Int. Symp. Fault-Tolerant Comput., Pasadena, Calif., pp. 44–45, 1–3 Mar. 1971.

[CLEG73] Clegg, F. W., "Use of Spoofs in the Analysis of Faulty Logic Networks," *IEEE Trans. Comput.,* vol. C-22, no. 3, pp. 229–234, Mar. 1973.

[CLEV83] Cleverly, D. S., "The Role of Testing in Achieving Zero Defects," *Proc. IEEE Semiconduct. Test Conf.,* Philadelphia, Oct. 18–20, pp. 248–253, 1983.

[COHN71] Cohn, M., and G. Ott, "The Design of Adaptive Procedures for Fault Detection and Isolation," *IEEE Trans. Reliab.,* vol. R-20, no. 1, pp. 7–10, Feb. 1971.

[COLB74] Colbourne, E. D., G. P. Coverly, and S. K. Behera, "Reliability of MOS LSI Circuits," *Proc. IEEE,* vol. 62, pp. 244–259, Feb. 1974.

[COUR81] Courtois, B., "Failure Mechanism, Fault Hypothesis and Analytical Testing of LSI-NMOS (HMOS) Circuits," *VLSI Conf.,* Edinburgh, Aug. 1981.

[COY80] Coy, W., "A Remark on the Nonminimality of Certain Multiple Fault Detection Algorithms," *IEEE Trans. Comput.,* vol. C-29, no. 8, pp. 757–759, Aug. 1980.

[CURT83] Curtin, J. J., and J. A. Waicukausi, "Multi-chip Module Test and Diagnostic Methodology," *IBM J. Res. Dev.,* vol. 27, pp. 27–34, Jan. 1983.

[DAND73] Dandapani, R., "Derivation of Minimal Test Sets for Monotonic Logic Circuits," *IEEE Trans. Comput.,* vol. C-22, no. 7, pp. 657–661, July 1973.

[DAND74] Dandapani, R., and S. M. Reddy, "On the Design of Logic Networks with Redundancy and Testability Considerations," *IEEE Trans. Comput.* vol. C-23, no. 11, pp. 1139–1148, Nov. 1974.

[DASG80] DasGupta, S., C. R. P. Hartmann, and L. D. Rudolph, "Dual-Mode Logic for Function-Independent Fault Testing," *IEEE Trans. Comput.,* vol. C-29, pp. 1025–1029, Nov. 1980.

[DAVI81] David, R. and P. Thevenod-Fosse, "Random Testing of Integrated Circuits," *IEEE Trans. Instrum. Meas.,* vol. IM-30, pp. 20–25, Mar. 1981.

[DAVI82] Davis, P., *The Economics of Automatic Testing,* McGraw-Hill, New York, 1982.

[DEJK77] Dejka, W. J., "Measures of Testability in Device and System Design," *Proc. 20th Midwest Symp. Circuits Syst.,* pp. 39–52, Aug. 1977.

[DIAS75] Dias, F. J. O., "Fault Masking in Combinational Logic Circuits," *IEEE Trans. Comput.,* vol. C-24, no. 5, pp. 476–482, 1975.

[DIAS76] Dias, F. J. O., "Truth Table Verification of an Iterative Logic Array," *IEEE Trans. Comput.,* vol. C-25, pp. 605–613, June 1976.

[DIEP69] Diephuis, R. J., "Fault Analysis for Combinational Logic Networks," Ph.D. dissertation, MIT, Department of Electrical Engineering, Sept. 1969.

[DOWN80] Downey, A. L., "Test Program Optimization Techniques for a High-Speed Performance VLSI Tester," *1980 IEEE Int. Test Conf.,* Philadelphia, pp. 33–38, Nov. 11–13, 1980.

[DU73] DU, M. W., and C. D. Weiss, "Multiple Fault Detection in Combinational Circuits: Algorithms and Computational Results," *IEEE Trans. Comput.*, vol. C-22, no. 3, pp. 235–240, Mar. 1973.

[DUSS78] Dussault, J., "A Testability Measure," *Proc. IEEE Semiconduct. Test Conf.*, Cherry Hill, N.J., pp. 113–116, Oct. 1978.

[DWYE69] Dwyer, T. F., "Comments on Faulty Testing and Diagnosis in Combinational Digital Circuits," *IEEE Trans. Comput.*, vol. C-18, no. 8, p. 760, Aug. 1969.

[EICH65] Eichelberger, E. B., "Hazard Detection in Combinational and Sequential Switching Circuits," *IBM J. Res. Dev.*, Mar. 1965.

[ELZI81] El-Ziq, Y. M., "Automatic Test Generation for Stuck-Open Faults in CMOS VLSI," *ACM 18th Des. Autom. Conf.*, pp. 347–352, June 1981.

[ELZI82] El-Ziq, Y. M., and S. Y. H. Su, "Fault Diagnosis of MOS Combinational Networks," *IEEE Trans. Comput.*, vol. C-31, no. 2, pp. 129–139, Feb. 1982.

[FANT74] Fantanzzi, G., and A. Marsella, "Multiple Fault Detection and Location in Fan-Out-Free Combinational Circuits," *IEEE Trans. Comput.*, vol. C-23, no. 1, pp. 48–55, Jan. 1974.

[FAZE81] Fazekas, P., et al., "Scanning Electron Beam Probes VLSI Chips," *Electronics*, vol. 54, no. 14, p. 105, July 14, 1981.

[FEE78] Fee, W. G., *Tutorial: LSI Testing*, 2nd ed., IEEE Computer Society Publ. EHP 122-2, 1978.

[FLOM73] Flomenhoft, S. S., and A. K. Susskind, "Algebraic Techniques for Finding Tests for Several Fault Types," *Dig., 3rd Annu. Int. Symp. Fault-Tolerant Comput.*, Palo Alto, Calif., pp. 85–90, June 20–22, 1973.

[FRID74] Fridrich, M., and W. A. Davis, "Minimal Fault Test Sets for Combinational Networks," *IEEE Trans. Comput.*, vol. C-23, no. 8, pp. 850–860, Aug. 1974.

[FRID77] Fridrich, M., and W. A. Davis, "Minimal Fault Tests for Redundant Combinational Networks," *IEEE Trans. Comput.*, vol. C-26, no. 10, pp. 1057–1060, Oct. 1977.

[FRIE71] Friedman, A. D., and P. R. Menon, *Fault Detection in Digital Circuits*, Prentice-Hall, Englewood Cliffs, N.J., 1971.

[FRIE73a] Friedman, A. D., "Diagnosis of Short Faults in Combinational Circuits," *Dig., 3rd Annu. Symp. Fault-Tolerant Comput.*, Palo Alto, Calif., pp. 95–99, June 20–22, 1973.

[FRIE73b] Friedman, A. D., "Easily Testable Iterative Systems," *IEEE Trans. Comput.*, vol. C-22, pp. 1061–1064, Dec. 1973.

[FRIE74] Friedman, A. D., "Diagnosis of Short-Circuit Faults in Combinational Circuits," *IEEE Trans. Comput.*, vol. C-23, no. 7, pp. 746–752, July 1974.

[FTCS00] Various papers in *Dig., Annu. Int. Symp. Fault-Tolerant Comput.*, 1970–1985.

[FUJI72] Fujiwara, H., and K. Kinoshita, "A Method of Constructing Fault Detecting Sequences of Sequential Circuits with Shift Registers," *J. Electron. Commun. Jap.*, vol. 54, pp. 113–120, Feb. 1972.

[FUJI81] Fujiwara, H., "On Closedness and Test Complexity of Logic Circuits," *IEEE Trans. Comput.*, vol. C-30, no. 8, pp. 556–562, Aug. 1981.

[FUJI82] Fujiwara, H., and S. Toida, "The Complexity of Fault Detection Problems for Combinational Logic Circuits," *IEEE Trans. Comput.*, vol. C-31, no. 6, pp. 555–560, June 1982.

[FUJI83] Fujiwara, H., and T. Shimono, "On the Acceleration of Test Generation Algorithms," *Dig., 13th Annu. Int. Symp. Fault-Tolerant Comput.*, Milan, Italy, pp. 98–105, June 1983.

[GALI80] Galiay, J., et al., "Physical versus Logical Fault Models in MOS LSI Circuits, Impact on Their Testability," *IEEE Trans. Comput.*, vol. C-29, pp. 527–531, June 1980.

[GAUL72] Gault, J. W., J. P. Robinson, and S. M. Reddy, "Multiple Fault Detection in Combinational Networks," *IEEE Trans. Comput.*, vol. C-21, no. 1, pp. 31–36, Jan. 1972.

[GOEL81] Goel, P., "An Implicit Enumeration Algorithm to Generate Tests for Combinational Logic Circuits," *IEEE Trans. Comput.*, vol. C-30, no. 3, pp. 215–222, Mar. 1981.

[GOLD77] Goldstein, L. H., "A Probabilistic Analysis of Multiple Faults in LSI Circuits," IEEE Comput. Rep. R77-304, 1977.

[GOLD79] Goldstein, L. H., "Controllability/Observability Analysis of Digital Circuits," *IEEE Trans. Circuits Syst.*, vol. CAS-26, pp. 685–693, Sept. 1979.

[GORO68] Gorovoi, V. R., "On the Diagnosis of Combinational Switching Devices," *Autom. Remote Control,* Nov. 1968.

[GOUN80] Goundan, A., and J. P. Hayes, "Identification of Equivalent Faults in Logic Networks," *IEEE Trans. Comput.*, vol. C-29, no. 11, pp. 978–986, Nov. 1980.

[GRAS79] Grason, J., "TMEAS, A Testability Measurement Program," *Proc. 16th Des. Autom. Conf.,* San Diego, Calif., pp. 156–161, June 25–27,

[GRAY71] Gray, F. G., and J. F. Meyer, "Locatability of Faults in Combinational Networks," *IEEE Trans. Comput.*, vol. C-20, no. 11, pp. 1407–1412, Nov. 1971.

[GRAY79] Gray, F. G., L. C. C. Shih, and R. A. Thompson, "Diagnosis of Faults in Modular Trees," *IEEE Trans. Comput.*, vol. C-28, no. 5, pp. 342–353, May 1979.

[HADJ73] Hadjilogiou, J., and B. Patel, "Design of Minimum Number of Fault Tests for Combinational Switching Circuits," *Proc. IEEE Region III Conv.*, 1973.

[HADL67] Hadlock, F., "On Finding a Minimal Set of Diagnostic Tests," *IEEE Trans. Electron. Comput.*, vol. C-16, no. 5, pp. 674–675, Oct. 1967.

[HAYE71a] Hayes, J. P., "NAND Model for Fault Diagnosis in Combinational Logic Networks," *IEEE Trans. Comput.*, vol. C-20, no. 12, pp. 1496–1506, Dec. 1971.

[HAYE71b] Hayes, J. P., "On Realizations of Boolean Functions Requiring a Minimal or Near Minimal Number of Tests," *IEEE Trans. Comput.*, vol. C-20, no. 12, pp. 1506–1513, Dec. 1971.

[HAYE75] Hayes, J. P., "Detection of Pattern-Sensitive Faults in Random Access Memories," *IEEE Trans. Comput.*, vol. C-24, pp. 150–157, Feb. 1975.

[HAYE76] Hayes, J. P., "On the Properties of Irredundant Logic Network," *IEEE Trans. Comput.*, vol. C-25, no. 9, pp. 884–892, Sept. 1976.

[HEAL81] Healy, J. T., *Automatic Testing and Evaluation of Digital Integrated Circuits,* Reston, Reston, Va., 1981.

[HENN68] Hennie, F. C., *Finite State Models for Logical Machines,* Wiley, New York, 1968.

[HILL77] Hill, F. J., and B. Huey, "SCIRTSS: A Search System for Sequential Circuit Test Sequences," *IEEE Trans. Comput.*, vol. C-26, pp. 490–502, Mar. 1977.

[HONG81] Hong, S. J., and D. L. Ostapko, "A Simple Procedure to Generate Optimum Test Patterns for Parity Logic Networks," *IEEE Trans. Comput.*, vol. C-30, no. 5, pp. 356–359, May 1981.

[HORN69] Hornbuckle, G. D., and R. N. Spann, "Diagnosis of Single-Gate Failures in Combinational Circuits," *IEEE Trans. Comput.*, vol. C-18, no. 3, pp. 216–220, Mar. 1969.

[HSIA70] Hsiao, M. Y., and D. K. Chia, "Boolean Difference for Automatic Test Pattern Generation," Open workshop on Fault Detection and Diagnosis in Digital Circuits and Systems, Lehigh University, Pa., pp. 43–44, Dec. 1970.

[HSIA71] Hsiao, M. Y., and D. K. Chia, "Boolean Difference for Fault Detection in Asynchronous Sequential Machines," *IEEE Trans. Comput.*, vol. C-20, pp. 1356–1361, Nov. 1971.

[HUAN71] Huang, H. H. C., "Analysis of Random Test Pattern Generation for Combinational Circuits," Ph.D. dissertation, University of Southern California, Los Angeles, Jan. 1971. Computer Science Press, Woodland Hills, Calif., 1976.

[HUAN73] Huang, H., and M. A. Breuer, "Analysis of the Detectability of Faults by Random Test Patterns in a Special Class of NAND Networks," *Comput. Electron. Eng.*, vol. 1, pp. 171–186, 1973.

[HUEY75] Huey, B. M., and F. J. Hill, "Test Generation Using a Design Language," *Proc. Symp. Hardware Descr. Languages,* pp. 91–95, 1975.

[IBAR75] Ibarra, O. H., and S. K. Sahni, "Polynomially Complete Fault Detection Problems," *IEEE Trans. Comput.*, vol. C-24, no. 3, pp. 242–249, 1975.

[IBAR81] Ibaraki, T., T. Kameda, and S. Toida, "On Minimal Test Sets for Locating Single Link Failures in Networks," *IEEE Trans. Comput.*, vol. C-30, no. 3, pp. 182–190, Mar. 1981.

[IOSU78] Iosupovicz, A., "Optimal Detection of Bridge Faults and Stuck-At Faults in Two-Level Logic," *IEEE Trans. Comput.*, vol. C-27, no. 5, pp. 452–455, May 1978.

[JAIN83] Jain, S. K., and V. D. Agarwal, "Test Generation for MOS Circuits Using *D*-Algorithm," *ACM 20th Des. Autom. Conf.*, pp. 64–70, June 1983.

[JOHN60] Johnson, R. A., "An Information Theory Approach to Diagnosis," *IRE Trans. Reliab. Quality Control,* p. 35, Apr. 1960.

[JONE67] Jones, E. R., and C. H. Mays, "Automatic Test Generation Methods for Large Scale Integrated Logic," *IEEE J. Solid State Circuits*, vol. SC-2, no. 4, pp. 221–226, Dec. 1967.

[KAJI69] Kajitani, K., Y. Tezuka, and Y. Kasahara, "Diagnosis of Multiple Faults in Combinational Circuits," *Electron. Commun. Jap.*, vol. 52-C, pp. 123–131, Apr. 1969.

[KAMA75] Kamal, S., "An Approach to the Diagnosis of Intermittent Faults," *IEEE Trans. Comput.*, vol. C-24, no. 5, pp. 461–467, 1975.

[KARA73] Karavai, M. K., "Construction of Tests for Finding Multiple Faults in Combinational Devices in Arbitrary Basis," *Autom. Remote Control*, vol. 34, no. 4, pp. 656–657, Apr. 1973.

[KARP80] Karpovsky, M., and S. Y. H. Su, "Detection and Location of Input and Feedback Bridging Faults among Input and Output Lines," *IEEE Trans. Comput.*, vol. C-29, pp. 523–527, June 1980.

[KAUT61] Kautz, W. H., "Automatic Fault Detection in Combinational Switching Networks," *Proc. Symp. Switching Theory Logic Des.*, pp. 195–214, and AD-267 005, Apr. 1961.

[KAUT67] Kautz, W. H., "Testing for Faults in Cellular Logic Arrays," *Proc. Switching Automata Theory Symp.*, pp. 161–174, 1967.

[KAUT68] Kautz, W. H., "Fault Testing and Diagnosis in Combinational Digital Circuits," *IEEE Trans. Comput.*, vol. C-17, no. 4, pp. 352–366, Apr. 1968.

[KEIN77] Keiner, W., and R. West, "Testability Measures," *Proc. AUTOTESTCON 1977*, pp. 49–55.

[KINS65] Kinsht, N. V., "Criteria for the Optimization of the Fault Detection Process," Izvestiya Sibirskovo Otdeleniya A.N. SSSR, *Ser. Tekh. Nauk*, vol. 3, no. 10, 1965.

[KLAY71] Klayton, A. R., and A. K. Susskind, "Multiple Fault-Detection Tests for Loop-Free Logic Networks," *1971 Int. IEEE Comput. Conf.*, pp. 77–78.

[KNAI77] Knaizuk, J., and C. R. P. Hartmann, "An Optimal Algorithm for Testing Stuck-At Faults in Random-Access Memories," *IEEE Trans. Comput.*, vol. C-25, pp. 1141–1144, Nov. 1977.

[KNUT75] Knuth, D. E., "Estimating the Efficiency of Backtrack Programs," *Math. Comput.*, vol. 29, no. 129, pp. 121–136, Jan. 1975.

[KODA80] Kodandapani, K. L., and D. K. Pradhan, "Undetectability of Bridging Faults and Validity of Stuck-At Fault Test Sets," *IEEE Trans. Comput.*, vol. C-29, no. 1, pp. 55–59, Jan. 1980.

[KOGA70] Koga, Y., T. C. Chen, and K. Naumura, "A Method of Test Generation for Fault Location in Combinational Logic," *FJCC*, pp. 69–73, 1970.

[KOGA72] Koga, Y., and F. Hirata, "Fault-Locating Test Generation for Combinational Logic Networks," *Dig., 2nd Annu. Int. Symp. Fault-Tolerant Comput.*, Newton, Mass., pp. 131–136, June 19–21, 1972.

[KOHA68] Kohavi, I., and Z. Kohavi, "Variable Length Distinguishing Sequences and Their Application to the Design of Fault Detection Experiments," *IEEE Trans. Comput.*, vol. C-17, no. 40, pp. 792–795, Aug. 1968.

[KOHA71] Kohavi, Z., and D. A. Spires, "Designing Sets of Fault-Detection Tests for Combinational Logic Circuits," *IEEE Trans. Comput.*, vol. C-20, no. 12, pp. 1463–1479, Dec. 1971.

[KOHA72] Kohavi, I., and Z. Kohavi, "Detection of Multiple Faults in Combinational Logic Networks," *IEEE Trans. Comput.*, vol. C-21, no. 6, pp. 556–568, June 1972.

[KOHA75] Kohavi, Z., and I. Berger, "Fault Diagnosis in Combinational Tree Networks," *IEEE Trans. Comput.*, vol. C-24, no. 12, pp. 1161–1167, Dec. 1975.

[KORE79] Koren, I., and Z. Kohavi, "On the Properties of Sensitized Paths," *IEEE Trans. Comput.*, vol. C-28, no. 3, pp. 268–269, Mar. 1979.

[KOVI77] Kovijanic, P. G., "A New Look at Test Generation and Verification," *Proc. 14th Des. Autom. Conf.*, 77CH1216-IC, pp. 58–63, June 1977.

[KOVI81] Kovijanic, P., "Single Testability Figure of Merit," *Proc. IEEE Semiconduct. Test Conf.*, Philadelphia, pp. 521–529, Oct. 27–29, 1981.

[KRIZ69] Kriz, T. A., "Machine Identification Concepts of Path Sensitizing Fault Diagnosis," *10th Annu. Symp. Switching Automata Theory*, pp. 174–181, Oct. 1969.

[KU75] Ku, C.-T., and G. M. Masson, "The Boolean Difference and Multiple Fault Analysis," *IEEE Trans. Comput.*, vol. C-24, no. 1, pp. 62–71, Jan. 1975.

[KUBO68] H. Kubo, "A Procedure for Generating Test Sequences to Detect Sequential Circuit Failures," NEC Research Development, No. 12, pp. 69–78.

[LAMO83] Lamoureax, P., and V. K. Agarwal, "Non-Stuck-At Fault Detection in nMOS Circuits by Region Analysis," *IEEE 1983 Int. Test Conf.*, Philadelphia, pp. 129–137, Oct. 1983.

[LEE74] Lee, H.-P. S., and E. S. Davidson, "Redundancy Testing in Combinational Networks," *IEEE Trans. Comput.*, vol. C-23, no. 10, pp. 1029–1047, Oct. 1974.

[LESS80] Lesser, J. D., and J. J. Shedletsky, "An Experimental Delay Test Generator for LSI Logic," *IEEE Trans. Comput.*, vol. C-29, no. 3, pp. 235–248, Mar. 1980.

[LEVE82] Levendel, Y. H., and P. R. Menon, "Test Generation Languages for Hardware Description Languages," *IEEE Trans. Comput.*, vol. C-31, pp. 577–588, July 1982.

[LIN78] Lin, C. H., and S. Y. J. Su, "Feedback Bridging Faults in General Combinational Circuits," *Dig., 8th Annu. Int. Symp. Fault-Tolerant Comput.*, Toulouse, France, June 21–23, 1978.

[LYUB68] Lyubatov, Y. V., and M. H. Gaimalov, "A Bound on the Diagnostic Efficiency of Tests," *Eng. Cybern.*, no. 5, pp. 102–106, 1968.

[MANN80] Mann, W. R., "Microelectronic Device Test Strategies—A Manufacturer's Approach," *1980 IEEE Int. Test Conf.*, Philadelphia, pp. 195–202, Nov. 11–13, 1980.

[MARI70] Marinos, P. N., "Partial Boolean Differences and Their Application to Fault Detection," *4th Asilomar Conf. Circ. Syst.*, Pacific Grove, Calif., Nov. 1970.

[MARI71] Marinos, P. N., "Derivation of Minimal Complete Sets of Test-Input Sequences Using Boolean Differences," *IEEE Trans. Comput.*, vol. C-20, no. 1, pp. 25–32, Jan. 1971.

[MARK79] Markowsky, G., "Diagnosing Single Faults in Fanout-Free Combinational Circuits," *IEEE Trans. Comput.*, vol. C-28, no. 11, pp. 863–874, Nov. 1979.

[MARU79] Maruyama, H., et al., "A Hundred MHz Test Station for High Speed LSI Testing," *1979 IEEE Test Conf.*, Cherry Hill, N.J., pp. 369–376, Oct. 23–25, 1979.

[MASC83] Masciola, J., and G. Roberts, "Testing Microprocessor Boards and Systems—A New Approach," *1983 IEEE Int. Test Conf.*, Philadelphia, pp. 46–50, Oct. 18–20, 1983.

[MCCL62] McCluskey, E. J., "Transients in Combinational Logic Circuits," in *Redundancy Techniques for Computing Systems*, Spartan Books, Bensalem, Pa., 1962, pp. 9–46.

[MCCL71a] McCluskey, E. J., "Test and Diagnosis Procedures for Digital Networks," *Computer*, pp. 17–20, Jan.–Feb. 1971.

[MCCL71b] McCluskey, E. J., and F. W. Clegg, "Fault Equivalence in Combinational Networks," *IEEE Trans. Comput.*, vol. C-20, no. 11, pp. 1286–1293, Nov. 1971.

[MCCL81] McCluskey, E. J., and S. Bozorgui-Nesbat, "Design for Autonomous Test," *IEEE Trans. Comput.*, vol. C-31, pp. 866–875, Nov. 1981.

[MEI74] Mei, K. C. Y., "Bridging and Stuck-At-Faults," *IEEE Trans. Comput.*, vol. C-23, no. 7, p. 720, July 1974.

[MEYE75] Meyer, J. F., and R. J. Sundstrom, "On-Line Diagnosis of Unrestricted Faults," *IEEE Trans. Comput.*, vol. C-24, no. 5, pp. 468–476, 1975.

[MIOT72] Miotke, T. F., "Systematic Testing of Boolean Functions," *Comput. Des.*, pp. 99–101, Mar. 1972.

[MONT83] Montoye, R. K., and J. A. Abraham, "Built-In Tests for Arbitrarily Structured Carry-Lookahead VLSI Adders," *Proc. VLSI 83, Int. Conf. Very Large Scale Integration*, Trondheim, Norway, pp. 361–371, Aug. 16–19, 1983.

[MUEH77] Muehldorf, E. I., and T. W. Williams, "Optimized Stuck Fault Test Patterns for

PLA Macros," *Digit. 1977 Semiconduct. Test Symp.*, 77CH1216-7C, pp. 89–101, Oct. 1977.

[MUEH81] Muehldorf, E. I., and A. D. Savkar, "LSI Logic Testing—An Overview," *IEEE Trans. Comput.*, vol. C-30, pp. 1–17, Jan. 1981.

[MULL54] Muller, D. E., "Application of Boolean Algebra to Switching Circuit Design and to Error Detection," *IRE Trans. Electron. Comput.*, vol. EC-13, no. 3, pp. 6–11, Sept. 1954.

[MUTH76] Muth, P., "A Nine-Valued Circuit Model for Test Generation," *IEEE Trans. Comput.*, vol. C-25, no. 6, pp. 630–636, June 1976.

[MYER83] Myers, M. A., "An Analysis of the Cost and Quality Impact of LSI-VLSI Technology on PCB Test Strategies," *1983 IEEE Int. Test Conf.*, Philadelphia, Oct. 18–20, pp. 382–395, 1983.

[NAIR78] Nair, R., S. M. Thatte, and J. A. Abraham, "Efficient Algorithms for Testing Semiconductor Random-Access Memories," *IEEE Trans. Comput.*, vol. C-27, pp. 572–576, June 1978.

[OBER78] Oberly, R. B., and J. E. Strenk, "Prediction of Printed Circuit Board Fallout," *Dig. 1978 IEEE Semiconduct. Test Conf.*, Cherry Hill, N.J., pp. 293–295, 1978.

[OGUS75] Ogus, R. C., "The Probability of a Correct Output from a Combinational Circuit," *IEEE Trans. Comput.*, vol. C-24, no. 5, pp. 534–544, May 1975.

[OSTA79] Ostapko, D. L., and S. J. Hong, "Fault Analysis and Test Generation for Programmable Logic Arrays," *IEEE Trans. Comput.*, vol. C-28, pp. 617–626, Sept. 1979.

[PAPA77] Papaioannou, S. G., "Optimal Test Generation in Combinational Networks by Pseudo-Boolean Programming," *IEEE Trans. Comput.*, vol. C-26, no. 6, pp. 553–559, June 1977.

[PARK73] Parker, K., "Probabilistic Test Generation," *Dig., 3rd Annu. Int. Symp. Fault-Tolerant Comput.*, Palo Alto, Calif., June 20–22, 1973.

[PARK75] Parker, K. P., and E. J. McCluskey, "Analysis of Logic Circuits with Faults Using Input Signal Probabilities," *IEEE Trans. Comput.*, vol. C-24, no. 5, pp. 573–578, May 1975.

[PARK78] Parker, K. P., and E. J. McCluskey, "Sequential Circuit Output Probabilities from Regular Expressions," *IEEE Trans. Comput.*, vol. C-27, no. 3, pp. 222–231, Mar. 1978.

[PART81] Parthasarathy, R., and S. M. Reddy, "A Testable Design of Iterative Logic Arrays," *IEEE Trans. Comput.*, vol. C-30, pp. 833–841, Nov. 1981.

[PAYA76] Payan, C., and J. Sifakis, "Universal Preset Tests of Sequential Circuits," *Dig., 6th Annu. Int. Symp. Fault-Tolerant Comput.*, Pittsburgh, Pa., pp. 75–79, June 21–23, 1976.

[PEAT74] Peattie, C. G., et al., "Elements of Semiconductor Device Reliability," *Proc. IEEE*, vol. 62, 149–168, Feb. 1974.

[PIER83] Pierson, R. L., and T. B. Williams, "The LT1280 for Through-the-Pins Testing of the Thermal Conduction Module, *IBM J.Res. Dev.*, vol. 27, pp. 35–40, Jan. 1983.

[POAG63] Poage, J. F., "Derivation of Optimum Tests to Detect Faults in Combinational Circuits," *Proc. Symp. Math. Theory Automata*, Polytechnic Press, pp. 483–528, Apr. 1963.

[POWE69] Powell, T. J., "A Procedure for Selecting Diagnostic Test," *IEEE Trans. Comput.*, vol. C-18, no. 2, pp. 168–175, Feb. 1969.

[PRAD78] Pradhan, D. K., "Universal Test Sets for Multiple Fault Detection in AND-EXOR Arrays," *IEEE Trans. Comput.*, vol. C-27, no. 2, pp. 181–186, Feb. 1978.

[PREI72] Preiss, R. J., "Fault Test Generation," Chapter 7 in *Design Automation of Digital Systems*, M. A. Breuer, ed., Prentice-Hall, Englewood Cliffs, N.J., 1972.

[PUTZ71] Putzulo, G. R., and J. P. Roth, "A Heuristic Algorithm for the Testing of Asynchronous Circuits," *IEEE Trans. Comput.*, vol. C-20, pp. 639–647, June 1971.

[RADC81] *Digital Failure Rate Data Book, 1981*, Rome Air Development Center, MDR-17.

[RAMA71] Ramamoorthy, C. V., and W. Mayeda, "Computer Diagnosis Using the Blocking Gate Approach," *IEEE Trans. Comput.*, vol. C-20, no.11, pp. 1294–1300, Nov. 1971.

[RAMA72] Ramamoorthy, C. V., and L. C. Chiang, "System Modeling and Testing Procedures for Microdiagnostics," *IEEE Trans. Comput.*, vol. C-21, pp. 1169–1183, Nov. 1972.

[RATI82] Ratiu, I. M., A. Sangiovanni-Vincentilli, and D. O. Pederson, "VICTOR: A Fast VLSI Testability Analysis Program," *Proc. IEEE Semiconduct. Test Conf.*, Philadelphia, pp. 397–401, Nov. 15–18, 1982.

[RAUL71] Rault, J. C., "A Graph Theoretical and Probabilistic Approach to the Fault Detection of Digital Circuits," *Proc. Int. Symp. Fault-Tolerant Comput.*, Pasadena, Calif., pp. 26–29, Mar. 1971.

[REDD73] Reddy, S. M., "Complete Test Sets for Logic Functions," *IEEE Trans. Comput.*, vol. C-22, no. 11, pp. 1016–1020, Nov. 1973.

[REDD83] Reddy, S. M., M. K. Reddy, and J. G. Kuhl," On Testable Design for CMOS Logic Circuits," *Proceedings of the 1983 International Est Conference*, Philadelphia, Oct. 1983, pp. 435–445.

[REDD84] Reddy, S. M. and M. K. Reddy, "Testable Realizations for FET Stuck-Open Faults in CMOS Combinational Logic Circuits," Submitted to *IEEE Trans. On Computers*, November, 1984.

[REYN78] Reynolds, D. A., and G. Metze, "Fault Detection Capabilities of Alternating Logic," *IEEE Trans. Comput.*, vol. C-27, no. 12, pp. 1093–1098, Dec. 1978.

[RICH72] Richard, J. P., M. Courvosier, M. Diaz, and P. Azema, "Detection of Multiple Faults in Combinational Circuits," *Dig., 2nd Annu. Symp. Fault-Tolerant Comput.*, Newton, Mass., pp. 36–41, June 19–21, 1972.

[RICH73a] Richard, J. P., and P. Azema, "Detection of Multiple Faults in Monotomic Networks and the Synthesis of Easily Testable Circuits," *Dig., 3rd Annu. Int. Symp. Fault-Tolerant Comput.*, Palo Alto, Calif., June 20–22, 1973.

[RICH73b] Richards, D. L., "Efficient Exercising of Switching Elements in Combinational Nets," *J. ACM*, vol. 20, no. 2, pp. 320–322, April 1973.

[ROBA75] Robach, C., and G. Saucier, "Diversified Test Methods for Local Control Units," *IEEE Trans. Comput.*, vol. C-24, pp. 562–567, May 1975.

[ROBA78] Robach, C., and G. Saucier, "Dynamic Testing of Control Units," *IEEE Trans. Comput.*, vol. C-27, pp. 617–623, July 1978.

[ROSE79] Rosenberg, S. J., et al., "H-MOS Reliability," *IEEE Trans. Electron Devices*, vol. ED-26, no. 1, p. 48, Jan. 1979.

[ROTH60a] Roth, J. P., "Diagnosis of Automata Failures," Research Memo SR-114, IBM Corp., July 1960.

[ROTH60b] Roth, J. P., "On Computing Diagnostic Tests for Circuits with Feedback," IBM Research Memo SR-140, IBM Corp., Nov. 1960.

[ROTH65] Roth, J. P., "Algorithms for Diagnosis for Automata Failures," *IBM J. Res. Dev.*, Apr. 1965.

[ROTH66] Roth, J. P., "Diagnosis of Automata Failures: A Calculus and a Method," *IBM J. Res. Dev.*, vol. 10, pp. 278–291, July 1966.

[ROTH67] Roth, J. P., W. G. Bouricius, and P. R. Schneider, "Programmed Algorithms to Compute Tests to Detect and Distinguish between Failures in Logic Circuits," *IEEE Trans. Electron. Comput.*, vol. EC-16, no. 5, pp. 567–580, Oct. 1967.

[ROTH80] Roth, J. P., *Computer Logic, Testing and Verification*, Computer Science Press, Woodland Hills, Calif., 1980.

[ROY74] Roy, B. K., "Diagnosis and Fault Equivalence in Combinational Circuits," *IEEE Trans. Comput.*, vol. C-23, no. 9, pp. 955–963, Sept. 1974.

[RUSS71] Russell, J. D., and C. R. Kime, "Structural Factors in the Fault Diagnosis of Combinational Networks," *1971 Int. Symp. Fault-Tolerant Comput.*, and *IEEE Trans. Comput.*, vol. C-20, no. 11, pp. 1276–1285, Nov. 1971.

[SALU72] Saluja, K. K., and S. M. Reddy, "Multiple Faults in Reed-Muller Canonic Networks," *Proc. 1972 Switching Automata Theory*, pp. 185–191, 1972.

[SALU74] Saluja, K. K., and S. M. Reddy, "On Minimally Testable Logic Networks," *IEEE Trans. Comput.*, vol. C-23, no. 5, pp. 552–554, May 1974.

[SANG78] Sangani, S. H., and B. Valitski, "In-Situ Testing of Combinational and Memory Circuits Using a Compact Tester," *Dig., 8th Annu. Int. Symp. Fault-Tolerant Comput.*, Toulouse, France, p. 214, June 21–23, 1978.

[SAVC66] Savchenko, Yu. G., "Some Problems of Fault Detection in Redundant Automata," *SB. Avtomatizatsiya Proektirovanie, Tekhnologiya i Programmirovannoe Upravlenie*, pp. 149–156, Izdat Tekhnika, Kiev, 1966.

[SAVI79] Savir, J., "Testing for Single Faults in Modular Combinational Networks," *J. Des. Autom. Fault-Tolerant Comput.*, vol. 3, no. 2, pp. 69–82, Apr. 1979.

[SAVI80a] Savir, J., "Testing for Single Intermittent Failures in Combinational Circuits by Maximizing the Probability of Fault Detection," *IEEE Trans. Comput.*, vol. C-29, no. 5, pp. 410–416, May 1980.

[SAVI80b] Savir, J., "Syndrome-Testable Design of Combinational Circuits," *IEEE Trans. Comput.*, vol. C-29, pp. 442–451, June 1980.

[SCHE68] Schertz, D. R., and G. A. Metze, "On the Indistinguishability of Faults in Digital Systems," *Proc. 6th Annu. Allerton Conf. Circuits Syst. Theory*, pp. 752–760, 1968.

[SCHE71] Schertz, D. R., and G. A. Metze, "On the Design of Multiple Fault Diagnosable Networks," *IEEE Trans. Comput.*, vol. C-20, no. 11, pp. 1361–1364, Nov. 1971.

[SCHE72] Schertz, D. R., and G. A. Metze, "New Representation for Faults in Combinational Digital Circuits," *IEEE Trans. Comput.*, vol. C-21, no. 8, pp. 858–866, Aug. 1972.

[SCHE73] Schertz, D. R., "Applications of a Fault Class Representation to Diagnosis," *Dig., 3rd Annu. Int. Symp. Fault-Tolerant Comput.*, Palo Alto, Calif., June 20–22, 1973.

[SCHN67] Schneider, P. R., "On the Necessity to Examine D-Chains in Diagnostic Test Generation—An Example," *IBM J. Res. Dev.*, vol. 11, no. 1, p. 114, Jan. 1967.

[SCHN75] Schnurmann, H. D., E. Lindbloom, and R. G. Carpenter, "The Weighted Random

Test-Pattern Generator," *IEEE Trans. Comput.*, vol. C-24, no. 7, pp. 695–700, July 1975.

[SCHN78] Schnable, G. L., L. G. Gallace, and H. J. Pujol, "Reliability of CMOS Integrated Circuits," *Computer,* vol. 11, pp. 6–17, Oct. 1978.

[SELL68] Sellers, F. F., L. W. Bearnson, and M. Y. Hsiao, "Analyzing Errors with the Boolean Difference," *IEEE Trans. Electron. Comput.*, vol. EC-17, pp. 676–683, July 1968; Errata in *IEEE Trans. Electron. Comput.*, vol. C-18, no. 2, p. 381, Apr. 1969.

[SELL69] Sellers, F. F., M. Y. Hsiao, and L. W. Bearnson, *Error Detecting Logic for Digital Computers,* McGraw-Hill, New York, 1969.

[SESH62] Seshu, S., and D. N. Freeman, "The Diagnosis of Asynchronous Sequential Switching Systems," *IRE Trans. Electron. Comput.*, vol. EC-11, pp. 459–465, Aug. 1962.

[SETH73] Seth, S. C., "Distance Measures on Detection Test Sets and Their Application," *Dig., 3rd Annu. Int. Symp. Fault-Tolerant Comput.*, Palo Alto, Calif., June 20–22, 1973.

[SETH77] Seth, S. C., and K. L. Kodandapani, "Diagnosis of Faults in Linear Tree Networks," *IEEE Trans. Comput.*, vol. C-26, no. 1, pp. 29–33, Jan. 1977.

[SETH81] Seth, S. C., and V. D. Agrawal, "Forecasting Reject Rate of Tested LSI Chips," *IEEE Electron Device Lett.*, vol. EDL-2, no. 11, p. 286, Nov. 1981.

[SHED76] Shedletsky, J. J., and E. J. McCluskey, "The Error Latency of a Fault in a Sequential Digital Circuit," *IEEE Trans. Comput.*, vol. C-25, pp. 655–659, June 1976.

[SHED77] Shedletsky, J. J., "Random Testing: Practicality vs. Verified Effectiveness," *Dig., 7th Annu. Int. Symp. Fault-Tolerant Comput.*, Los Angeles, pp. 175–179, June 28–30, 1977.

[SHOR71] Short, R. A., and J. Golberg, "Soviet Progress in the Design of Fault-Tolerant Digital Machines," *IEEE Trans. Comput.*, vol. C-20, no. 11, pp. 1337–1352, Nov. 1971.

[SHUK71] Shukla, V. M., "Functional Testing of Complex Logic Circuits," *Symp. Hybrid Microelectron.*, pp. 9-5-1 to 9-5-9, 1971.

[SIEW81] Siewiorek, D. P., and L. K. Lai, "Testing of Digital Systems," *Proc. IEEE,* vol. 69, pp. 1321–1333, Oct. 1981.

[SKLY70] Sklyarevich, A. N., "Function for Testing the Working Order of a Logic Element in a Combinational Automat," *Vychisl. Tekh.*, no. 3, pp. 55–61, 1970.

[SMIT78] Smith, J. E., "On the Existence of Combinational Logic Circuits Exhibiting Multiple Redundancy," *IEEE Trans. Comput.*, vol. C-27, no. 12, pp. 1221–1226, Dec. 1978.

[SMIT79] Smith, J. E., "Detection of Faults in Programmable Logic Arrays," *IEEE Trans. Comput.*, vol. C-28, pp. 845–853, Nov. 1979.

[SNOO83] Snook, M., and B. Illick, "A New Hardware Architecture for Digital In-Circuit Testing," *1983 IEEE Int. Test Conf.*, Philadelphia, pp. 64–71, Oct. 18–20, 1983.

[SOHL77] Sohl, W. E., "Selecting Test Patterns for 4K RAMs," *IEEE Trans. Manuf. Technol.*, vol. MFT-6, pp. 51–60, Sept. 1977.

[SPIL77] Spillman, R. J., and S. Y. H. Su, "Detection of Single, Stuck-Type Failures in Multivalued Combinational Networks," *IEEE Trans. Comput.*, vol. C-26, no. 12, pp. 1242–1250, Dec. 1977.

[SRID81] Sridhar, T., and J. P. Hayes, "Design of Easily Testable Bit-Sliced Systems," *IEEE Trans. Comput.*, vol. C-30, pp. 842–854, Nov. 1981.

[STEW78] Stewart, J. H., "Application of Scan/Set for Error Detection and Diagnosis," *Dig. 1978 IEEE Semiconduct. Test Conf.,* Cherry Hill, N.J., pp. 152–158.

[STOF80] Stoffers, K. E., "Test Sets for Combinational Logic—The Edge-Tracing Approach," *IEEE Trans. Comput.,* vol. C-29, no. 8, pp. 741–746, Aug. 1980.

[STON79] Stone, P. S., and J. F. McDermid, "Circuit Board Testing: Cost Effective Production Test and Trouble-Shooting," *Hewlett-Packard J.,* pp. 2–8, Mar. 1979.

[SU72] Su, S. Y. H., and Y. C. Cho, "A New Approach to the Fault Location of Combinational Circuits," *IEEE Trans. Comput.,* vol. C-20, no. 1, pp. 21–30, Jan. 1972.

[SUD81] Sud, R., and K. C. Hardee, "Designing Static RAMs for Yield As Well As Speed," *Electronics,* pp. 121–126, July 28, 1981.

[SUK81] Suk, D. S., and S. M. Reddy, "A March Test for Functional Faults in Semiconductor Random Access Memories," *IEEE Trans. Comput.,* vol. C-30, pp. 982–984, Dec. 1981.

[SUSS72] Susskind, A. K., "Additional Applications of the Boolean Difference to Fault Detection and Diagnosis," *Dig., 2nd Annu. Int. Symp. Fault-Tolerant Comput.,* Newton, Mass., pp. 58–61, June 19–21, 1972.

[SWAN83] Swan, R., and C. McMinn, "General Purpose Tester Puts a Separate Set of Resources behind Each VLSI-Device Pin," *Electronics,* vol. 56, pp. 101–106, Sept. 8, 1983.

[SWAR78] Swarz, R. S., "Reliability and Maintainability Enhancements for the VAX-11/780," *Dig., 8th Annu. Int. Symp. Fault-Tolerant Comput.,* Toulouse, France, pp. 24–28, June 21–23, 1978.

[SZYG71] Szygenda, S. A., "Problems Associated with the Implementation and Utilization of Digital Simulators and Diagnostic Test Generation Systems," *Proc. Int. Symp. Fault-Tolerant Comput.,* pp. 51–53, Mar. 1971.

[TAKE72] Takesue, M., "Relations between Diagnostic Resolution and Structure of Logical Circuits," *Electron. Comm. Lab. Tech. J.,* vol. 21, no. 2, pp. 291–301, 1972.

[TAMM67] Tammaru, E., and J. B. Angell, "Redundancy for LSI Yields Enhancement," *IEEE J. Solid State Circuits,* vol. SC-2, no. 4, pp. 172–182, Dec. 1967.

[TASA77] Tasar, D., and V. Tasar, "A Study of Intermittent Faults in Digital Computers," *AFIPS Conf. Proc.,* pp. 807–811, 1977 NCC.

[THAT77] Thatte, S. M., and J. A. Abraham, "Testing of Semiconductor Random Access Memories," *Dig., 7th Annu. Int. Symp. Fault Tolerant Comput.,* Los Angeles, pp. 81–87, June 28–30, 1977.

[THAT79] Thatte, S. M., "Test Generation for Microprocessors," Rep. R-842, Coordinated Science Laboratory, University of Illinois, May 1979.

[THAT80] Thatte, S. M., and J. A. Abraham, "Test Generation for Microprocessors," *IEEE Trans. Comput.,* vol. C-29, pp. 429–441, June 1980.

[THAY72] Thayse, A., "Multiple-Fault Detection in Large Logical Networks," *Philips Res. Rep.,* vol. 27, pp. 583–602, 1972.

[THEV78] Thevenod-Fosse, P., and R. David, "A Method to Analyze Random Testing of Sequential Circuits," *Digit. Process.,* vol. 4, pp. 313–332, 1978.

[THEV81] Thevenod-Fosse, P., and R. David, "Random Testing of the Data Processing Section of a Microprocessor," *Dig., 11th Annu. Int. Symp. Fault-Tolerant Comput.,* Portland, Me., pp. 275–280, June 24–26, 1981.

[THEV83] Thevenod-Fosse, P., and R. David, "Random Testing of the Control Section of a Microprocessor," *Dig., 13th Annu. Int. Symp. Fault-Tolerant Comput.*, Milan, Italy, pp. 366–373, June 1983.

[TIMO83a] Timoc, C., et al., "Logical Models of Physical Failures," *Proc. IEEE Semiconduct. Test Conf.*, Philadelphia, pp. 546–553, Oct. 18–20, 1983.

[TIMO83b] Timoc, C., F. Stott, K. Wickham, and L. Hess, "Adaptive Self-Test for a Microprocessor," *Proc. IEEE Semiconduct. Test Conf.*, Philadelphia, pp. 701–703, Oct. 18–20, 1983.

[TO71] To, K., "Fault Folding, A Unified Approach to Fault Analysis in Combinational Logic Networks," *1971 IEEE Comput. Soc. Conf.*, pp. 81–82, 1971.

[TO73] To, K., "Fault Folding for Irredundant and Redundant Combinational Circuits," *IEEE Trans. Comput.*, vol. C-22, no. 11, pp. 1008–1015, Nov. 1973.

[TURC79] Turcat, C., and A. Verdillon, "Symmetry, Automorphism, and Test," *IEEE Trans. Comput.*, vol. C-28, no. 4, pp. 319–325, Apr. 1979.

[TZID78] Tzidon, T., et al., "A Practical Approach to Fault Detection in Combinational Networks," *IEEE Trans. Comput.*, vol. C-27, no. 10, p. 968–971, Oct. 1978.

[UNGE72] Unger, S. H., "Fault Checking of Combinational Circuits with Input Reconvergent Fan-Out," *Colloque Int. Conception Maintenance Automatismes Logiques*, Toulouse, France, Sept. 27–28, 1972; also N73-12257.

[VANE72] Vane, K. L., "Construction of a Diagnostic Test Sequence for a Combined Automaton," in *Problems of Synthesis of Finite Automata*, V. I. Levin, Ed., Izdatel'stvo Izinatne', Riga, USSR, 1972.

[VARS79] Varshney, P. K., "On Analytical Modeling of Intermittent Faults in Digital Systems," *IEEE Trans. Comput.*, vol. C-28, no. 10, pp. 786–791, Oct. 1979.

[VEDE68] Vedeshenkov, V. A., "Construction of Test Tables for Detecting Logical Errors of Electronic Combinational Devices," *Autom. Remote Control*, vol. 23, no. 3, pp. 491–500, Mar. 1968.

[VERD73] Verdillon, A., "Failures in Acyclic Networks," *Dig., 3rd Annu. Int. Symp. Fault-Tolerant Comput.*, Palo Alto, Calif., June 19–22, 1973.

[VIRU83] Virupakshia, A. R., and V. C. V. P. Reddy, "A Simple Random Test Procedure for Detection of Single Intermittent Faults in Combinational Circuits," *IEEE Trans. Comput.*, vol. C-32, pp. 594–597, June 1983.

[VISH71] Vishnubhotla, S. R., and Y. H. Chuang, "A Path Analysis Approach to the Diagnosis of Combinational Circuits," *8th Des. Autom. Workshop*, 1971.

[WADS78] Wadsak, R. L., "Fault Modeling and Logic Simulation of CMOS and MOS Integrated Circuits," *Bell Syst. Tech. J.*, vol. 57, pp. 1449–1474, May–June 1978.

[WANG75] Wang, D. T., "An Algorithm for the Generation of Test Sets for Combinational Logic Networks," *IEEE Trans. Comput.*, vol. C-24, no. 7, pp. 742–746, July 1975.

[WEIS72] Weiss, C. D., "Bounds on the Length of Terminal Stuck-Fault Tests," *IEEE Trans. Comput.*, vol. C-21, no. 3, pp. 305–309, Mar. 1972.

[WHIT71] Whitney, G. E., "Algebraic Fault Analysis for Constrained Combinational Networks," *IEEE Trans. Comput.*, vol. C-20, no. 2, pp. 141–148, Feb. 1971.

[WILL73] Williams, M. J. Y., and J. B. Angell, "Enhancing Testability of Large-Scale Integrated Circuits via Test Points and Additional Logic." *IEEE Trans. Comput.*, vol. C-22, no. 1, pp. 46–60, Jan. 1973.

[WILL81] Williams, T. W., and N. C. Brown, "Defect Level as a Function of Fault Coverage," *IEEE Trans. Comput.*, vol. C-30, pp. 987–988, Dec. 1981.

[WILL82] Williams, T. W., and K. P. Parker, "Design for Testability—A Survey," *IEEE Trans. Comput.*, vol. C-31, no. 1, pp. 2–16, Jan. 1982.

[YAU71] Yau, S. S., and Y. H. Tang, "An Efficient Algorithm for Generating Complete Test Sets for Combinational Logic Circuits," *IEEE Trans. Comput.*, vol. C-20, no. 11, pp. 1245–1251, Nov. 1971.

[YAU75] Yau, S. S., and S.-C. Yang, "Multiple Fault Detection for Combinational Logic Circuits," *IEEE Trans. Comput.*, vol. C-24, no. 3, pp. 233–241, Mar. 1975.

[YETT71] Yetter, I. H., "Fault Isolation Dictionary for the Univac 9200/9300," *Comput. Designer's Conf.*, Anaheim, Calif., pp. 433–443, Jan. 1971.

[YOSH69] Yoshikazu, K. K., and Y. Kasahara, "Diagnosis of Multiple Faults in Combinational Circuits," *Electron. Commun. Jap.*, vol. 52-C, no. 4, pp. 123–131, 1969.

REFERENCES BY MAJOR AREAS

Books [AHO74], [BENN82], [CHAN70], [DAVI82], [FRIE71], [HEAL81], [HENN68], [PREI72], [RADC81], [ROTH80], [SELL69].

Failure Modes and Fault Models [ABBO81], [BANE82], [BANE83], [BEH82], [CLEV83], [COLB74], [COUR81], [GALI80], [PEAT74], [RADC81], [ROSE79], [SCHN78], [SUD81], [TIMO83a], [TIMO83b], [WADS78].

Fault Interrelationship [DIAS75], [GOUN80], [MCCL71b], [MEI74], [ROY74], [SCHE68], [SCHE72], [TAKE72], [TO71], [TO73].

Sensitization/Structural Approach [APTE73], [ARMS66], [BEAR71], [BOSS71], [BOUR71], [CHA78], [CHIA72b], [CHIA73], [CHIP70], [CHUA71], [DIEP69], [DWYE69], [FUJI83], [GAUL72], [GOEL81], [GOLD77], [KOHA71], [KOHA72], [KOHA79], [KRIZ69], [MUEH77], [POAG63], [ROTH65], [ROTH66], [SAVI79], [SCHN67], [STOF80], [UNGE72], [VISH71], [WANG75].

Boolean Difference/Algebraic Approach [AKER74], [AKER78], [AMAR67], [CHIA72b], [CLEG71], [CLEG73], [HORN69], [HSIA70], [KAUT61], [KAUT68], [KU75], [MARI70], [MARI71], [MIOT72], [MULL54], [REDD73], [SELL68], [SUSS72], [VEDE68], [WHIT71], [YAU71].

Redundancy [DAND74], [FRID77], [KODA80], [LEE74], [SAVC66], [SMIT78], [TAMM67].

Multiple Faults [ABRA80], [AGAR81], [AGAR81a], [BREU76a], [CARR74], [DU73], [KAJI69], [KARA73], [KLAY71], [KU75], [RICH72], [RICH73a], [SALU72], [THAY72], [YAU75].

Unate/Special/CFOF [AGAR78], [BERG73], [BETA70], [FANT74], [HONG81], [KOHA75], [SALU74], [SETH77], [TZID78].

Fault Location [CHAN65], [COHN71], [GORO68], [GRAY71], [GRAY79], [HADL67], [KARI65], [KOGA70], [KOGA72], [MARK79], [MEYE75], [POWE69], [RAMA71], [ROTH60a], [ROTH60b], [ROTH67], [RUSS71], [SCHE71], [SCHE73], [SU72], [VANE72], [YETT71], [YOSH69].

Shorts/Opens [CHAN83], [CHIA82], [ELZI81], [ELZI82], [FLOM73], [FRIE73a], [FRIE74], [GALI80], [IOSU78], [JAIN83], [KARP80], [LAMO83], [LIN78], [MEI74], [ROTH66], [WADS78].

Transients/Intermittents/Timing/Delay [BALL69], [BREU73], [BREU74], [KAMA75], [LESS80], [MCCL62], [SAVI80a], [TASA77], [VARS79], [VIRU83].

Bounds/Complexity [AGAR80a], [AGAR81], [AGRA81a], [COY80], [DAND73], [FUJI81], [FUJI82], [HAYE71a], [HAYE71b], [IBAR75], [IBAR81], [KINS65], [LYUB68], [SETH73], [WEIS72].

Testability Measures and Fault Coverage [AGRA81b], [AGRA81c], [AGRA82], [BENN81], [DEJK77], [DUSS78], [GOLD79], [GRAS79], [KEIN77], [KOVI77], [KOVI81], [RATI82], [SETH81], [WILL81], [WILL82].

Functional Testing [ABRA79], [ABRA81a], [ABRA81b], [ABRA82], [BOSE82], [BRAH84], [BREU80], [DIAS76], [HAYE75], [HUEY75], [KNAI77], [LEVE82], [MASC83], [MONT83], [MUEH81], [NAIR78], [OSTA79], [ROBA75], [ROBA78], [SMIT79], [SOHL77], [SRID81], [SUK81], [THAT77], [THAT79], [THAT80].

Exhaustive Testing [ABRA81a], [DIAS76], [FRIE73b], [KAUT67], [MCCL81], [PART81], [SAVI80b].

Sequential Circuit Testing [AZEM72], [BHAT79], [BOUR71], [BOUT74], [BREU71], [CHIA72a], [EICH65], [FUJI72], [HENN68], [HILL77], [HSIA71], [KOHA68], [PAYA76], [PUTZ71], [SESH62].

Random Testing [AGRA72], [AGRA75], [AGRA78], [AGRA81a], [AKER79], [DAVI81], [HUAN71], [HUAN73], [OGUS75], [PARK73], [PARK75], [PARK78], [RAUL71], [SCHN75], [SHED76], [SHED77], [THEV78], [THEV81], [THEV83].

Miscellaneous/General [AGRA72], [AKER73], [AKER76a], [AKER76b], [AKER78], [BENN72], [BLOD82], [BOGO66], [BOGO68], [BREU72], [BREU76b], [CERN78], [CERN79], [CHAL79], [CHAN70], [CHER00], [CURT83], [DASG80], [DOWN80], [FAZE81], [FEE78], [FRID74], [FRIE71], [FTCS00], [HADJ73], [HAYE71a], [HAYE71b], [HAYE76], [JOHN60], [JONE67], [KNUT75], [KORE79], [KOVI65], [MANN80], [MARU79], [MCCL71a], [MUEH81], [MUTH76], [MYER83], [OBER78], [PAPA77], [PIER83], [PRAD78], [PREI72], [RAMA72], [REYN78], [RICH73b], [ROTH80], [SANG78], [SELL69], [SHOR71], [SHUK71], [SIEW81], [SKYL70], [SNOO83], [SPILL77], [STEW78], [STON79], [SWAN78], [SWAR78], [SZYG71], [TURC79], [VANE72], [VERD73], [WILL73].

PROBLEMS

1.1. The front ends of chip testers have sophisticated circuitry which can apply patterns to the UUT and capture the responses at very high speeds. Comment on the problem of testing the chips which go into the front end of a state-of-the-art tester.

1.2. Incorporating a built-in test into a chip reduces the need for an expensive tester. Discuss the trade-offs between the extra cost for each chip for the built-in test and the one-time cost for a chip tester.

1.3. Catalog the effects of all opens and shorts between all pairs of lines for the CMOS inverter and NOR and NAND gates; attempt to formulate a fault model for the gates that includes these failures.

1.4. Analyze the effects of various opens and shorts for the CMOS transmission gate and formulate a fault model.

1.5. Research the effects of physical failures on nMOS and bipolar (I^2L, STL, for example) technologies.

1.6. Attempt a general fault model for a multiplexer for the failures found above.

1.7. Investigate functional fault models for other functional blocks (e.g., comparators, parity trees, flip-flops, registers, counters).

1.8. (a) Consider the sensitization of fault $l/0$ in the circuit shown in Fig. P1.8. List all possible ways in which this fault can be sensitized to the primary output line.
  (b) Perform a backtrace for creating a change on line l and for each of the sensitization possibilities. Determine a complete $T(l/0)$.

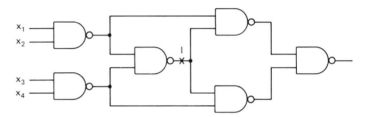

Figure P1.8

1.9. Are there any undetectable stuck-at faults in the circuit of Fig. 1.3.1? If yes, locate them all.

1.10. For each vector X_t in $T(l/0)$ of Problem 1.8, determine the set of all the faults in addition to $l/0$ which can be detected by X_t. [*Hint:* Consider the corresponding sensitization path(s) and notice how a change on that path is propagated to the primary output.]

1.11. For the circuit shown in Fig. P1.11, prepare a truth table with 64 rows, one for each input vector, and seven columns, one for each of the input variables and one for the fault-free output. Append to this table 22 more columns corresponding to the faulty output for each of the following 22 faults: l/α, $l \epsilon \{1, 2, ..., 11\}$, and $\alpha \epsilon \{0, 1\}$. Determine $T(l/\alpha)$ for each of the 22 faults, and a $T(F)$ where F is the set of 22 faults. How many different $T(F)$ are possible? Can this method easily be extended to any size of circuit? Discuss its advantages and disadvantages.

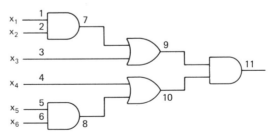

Figure P1.11

1.12. Design a circuit which has an undetectable fault of size 4 but no undetectable fault of any smaller size.

1.13. A fault f is said to be detected by the single-path-sensitization (SPS) scheme if there exists a test vector which can test f by sensitizing only one path. What is the largest class of circuits in which every fault is detected by the SPS scheme and only by the SPS scheme? Can any given Boolean function be realized by a circuit of such a class?

1.14. Consider the class of circuits consisting of Exclusive-OR gates only. Is the backtracking a serious problem in such circuits? Determine an algorithm for generating a test vector for any given single stuck-at fault for such a class of circuits. What is the minimum size of $T(F)$ for any such circuit?

1.15. Determine a fault location test set for an AND gate with k inputs.

1.16. What is the number of functionally equivalent fault classes for a completely fan-out-free circuit (CFOF) with n inputs?

1.17. (a) Show that the number of true minterms for any completely fan-out-free function is always odd.
  (b) Given a CFOF circuit, show that the number of true minterms of the faulty CFOF under any single or multiple stuck-at fault is always even.
  (c) Determine an exhaustive testing scheme for CFOF circuits in which the output response verification consists of only one bit comparison.

1.18. Determine an algorithm for generating a minimal complete $T(F_m)$ for CFOF circuits.

1.19. For the circuit shown in Fig. P1.19, obtain a $T(F_s)$ which detects every single stuck-at fault but not all the multiple stuck-at faults.

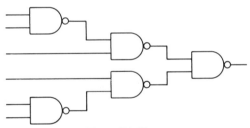

Figure P1.19

1.20. Can a two-level circuit with no fan-out contain a redundancy? Can a unate circuit with no fan-out contain a redundancy? If not, why?

1.21. Prove that a $T(f_s)$ for a two-level circuit is always a $T(f_m)$ as well.

1.22. Suppose that a test vector X_t is obtained for a single stuck-at fault f in a circuit by using the D-algorithm. What is the easiest way to determine the set of all the other single stuck-at faults which also are detected by X_t?

1.23. Show how the D-algorithm can be extended to circuits in which gates may be replaced by multi-input, multi-output modules with no information about their internal structure.

1.24. Can the D-algorithm be applied to generate test vectors for faults that result in a short between two lines? If yes, sketch the general outline.

1.25. Derive a functional test for an 8-to-1 CMOS multiplexer which will detect all stuck values, shorts, and opens in the circuit. Prove that the test set will indeed detect these faults.

1.26. Derive a memory test for the fault where a particular pair of addresses in sequence causes the second cell addressed to be disturbed:
(a) With no knowledge of the assignment of cells to rows or columns.
(b) Given the exact assignment of cells in every row and column.

1.27. Derive an appropriate fault model and tests for an n-bit by m-word memory chip.

1.28. Write an efficient memory test for a large (several-megabyte) memory with 32 bits per word, which uses 64K by 1-bit RAM chips. Note that your test should detect external decoder failures and board failures in addition to chip failures.

1.29. For a microprocessor of your choice, write an assembly language program which will guarantee that every internal storage element can be written and read without disturbing any other storage element.

1.30. Extend the technique of microprocessor testing to a peripheral control chip of your choice.

1.31. Indicate how you would test a microprocessor board (with memory and I/O chips on the board):
(a) Using an external tester.
(b) Using the microprocessor itself.
Comment on the fault coverage in both cases.

1.32. Give a high-level language test program to test exhaustively any one-dimensional array with a test which grows linearly with the size of the array. Now derive a test program which generates a test that is independent of the size of an array, for a strongly connected array with cells having a reduced flow table.

1.33. A high-speed ALU can be built out of TTL using 74181 and 74182 chips. (This set is used in many computers.) Although the interconnection is not quite a tree, derive a test for a 32-bit ALU using the principles developed for testing pure tree networks.

Chapter 2

DESIGN FOR TESTABILITY

E. J. McCluskey

2.1. INTRODUCTION

In spite of the great effort that has been devoted to developing testing techniques, a number of serious problems exist. The following list of difficulties with through-the-pins testing is taken from a presentation by Paul H. Bardell of IBM at the *Eleventh Annual International Symposium on Fault-Tolerant Computing* [BARD81].

Test Generation
  Single stuck-fault model
  CPU run times
  CPU memory-size limitations
  Test coverage not high enough
Test Application
  Immense test data volumes
  High capital/operating costs of testers
  Long socket times
  Diagnostic resolution

The list of difficulties would be even longer except for the fact that Bardell assumed that LSSD design rules (to be explained below) were used so that problems such as sequential circuit testing and hazard detection could be ignored.

Research on better testing methods continues. However, it seems unlikely that techniques for economical testing of arbitrary designs will result. More probably, economical testing will be possible only for designs that include explicit features to facilitate testing.

There are actually two types of testing which are important for computer systems:

> *Implicit or concurrent testing:* This is sometimes called *checking*. It refers to on-line testing to detect errors that occur during normal system operation. Parity codes or duplication techniques are used. The relevant theoretical techniques deal with self-checking circuits [WAKE78].
>
> *Explicit testing:* This is the testing that is carried out while the tested circuit is not in use. It includes the tests done on chips while still on a wafer, production tests on packaged chips and on boards, acceptance tests, maintenance tests, and repair tests.

The present discussion will be restricted to explicit testing and the terms *testing* and *test* will be used to refer only to explicit testing and tests.

The term *design for testability* (DFT) describes design techniques that are used to make testing of the resulting product economical. This chapter presents current DFT practice as well as proposed improvements.

Testability tends to be used somewhat imprecisely since there are various factors that contribute to test or maintenance cost. Testing cost is determined mainly by the cost of test pattern generation and by the cost of test application. Test pattern generation cost depends on either the computer time required to run the test pattern generation program plus the (pro-rated) capital cost of developing the program or on the number of man-hours required to write the test patterns plus the increase in system development time caused by the time taken to develop tests. Test application cost is determined by the cost of the test equipment plus the tester time required to apply the test (sometimes called *socket time*). There is a trade-off between test cost and repair cost. The cost of testing can be reduced by using tests which either fail to detect many faults or cannot locate many of the detected faults. This can cause a substantial increase in system production or maintenance costs. It is much more expensive to repair a faulty printed circuit (PC) board than to discard a faulty chip, and it is much more expensive to repair a faulty system than to repair a faulty PC board.

No attempt will be made to give a precise definition of testability. Instead, it will be assumed that testability is increased whenever the costs of test generation or of test application are decreased, or the fault coverage or fault diagnosability is increased. Of course, testability will be decreased by any increase in test cost or by any decrease in fault coverage or diagnosability.

Most DFT techniques increase testability by both decreasing test cost and increasing coverage and diagnosability. The exceptions to this will be pointed out when the corresponding techniques are presented.

Attempts to understand circuit attributes that influence testability have produced the two concepts of observability (visibility) and controllability (control). *Observability* refers to the ease with which the state of internal signals can be determined at the circuit output leads. *Controllability* refers to the ease of producing a specific internal signal value by applying signals to the circuit input leads. Attempts to assign specific values to these attributes will be described in a later section. Many of the DFT techniques to be described are attempts to increase the observability or controllability of a circuit design. The most direct way to do this is to introduce *test points,* that is, additional circuit inputs and outputs to be used during testing. There is always a cost associated with adding test points. For circuit boards the cost of test points is often well justified. On the other hand, for ICs the cost of test points can be prohibitive because of IC pin limitations. Some of the techniques to be described are aimed at obtaining the benefits of test points without incurring the full cost of additional board connectors or IC pins.

The new DFT techniques are general: they involve the overall circuit structure, or they are implemented by general design rules. Older techniques are more ad hoc and typically consist of a set of guidelines listing features that enhance or detract from "ease of testing" or testability. They are aimed at the circuit designer and depend on his insight and willingness to worry about testability. Ad hoc techniques will be presented first, followed by presentations of more systematic DFT methods.

In addition to the references cited in the text, a bibliography of relevant items for further reading is included for each section topic.

2.2. AD HOC TECHNIQUES

This approach to testability enhancement is aimed at the designer. It typically consists of a list of design features that create testing problems together with suggestions of preferred implementations. Table 2.2.1 lists ad hoc techniques for testability enhancement.

TABLE 2.2.1   AD HOC LOGIC TECHNIQUES FOR TESTABILITY ENHANCEMENT

Feature	Ad hoc technique
Unknown initial state	Initialization circuitry
Internal clock	Circuitry to disconnect internal clock and substitute tester clock
Feedback loops	Circuitry to permit tester to break feedback loop
Deep sequential circuits (counters and divider chains)	Circuitry to segment circuits into more easily controlled portions
Wired logic	Avoid
Fan-in and fan-out points	Add test access to these points

Initialization refers to the ability to control the initial state of registers and sequential circuits. The *initial state* of a circuit describes the contents of the memory elements right after power is first applied. Many designs do not require a specified initial state for correct functioning: they will work properly for any arbitrary initial state. There is no need to include circuitry to control the state in order to obtain correct functionality.

To test the circuitry it is necessary to place it in a known state.* This can be done by applying an initialization sequence as the first portion of the test input. However, such an initialization sequence can be very lengthy (particularly if long counter chains are contained in the circuit). It can also require a large amount of computation time in order to discover such a sequence. These expenses of initialization can be drastically reduced by incorporating initialization circuitry in the design. The initialization circuitry can take two forms: the circuit can be designed to be self-initializing as in Fig. 2.2.1a, or additional control inputs can be provided, as in Fig. 2.2.1b, to allow the tester to set the circuit state. By connecting circuits such as those of Fig. 2.2.1 to all the flip-flop clear inputs, the initial state is fixed with all the flip-flops cleared. If it is desired to have some of the flip-flops initially set, it is only necessary to connect the initialization circuits to the flip-flop preset inputs (asynchronous set)—rather than to the clear inputs.

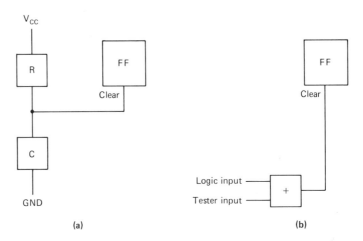

Figure 2.2.1   Initialization techniques: (a) power-up reset; (b) tester reset.

Circuits for the other techniques listed in Table 2.2.1 are straightforward and will not be shown here. Detailed diagrams can be found in the items cited in the References and Bibliography. Table 2.2.1 deals with the logic aspects of a product to be tested. The electrical and mechanical characteristics of the product are also important to its testability. These are not discussed here because they are outside the

*It may seem paradoxical that the state must be controlled for testing when it need not be controlled for correct operation. A simple resolution of the paradox can be seen by remembering that standard commercial testers do not alter the input sequence on the basis of the outputs received, while the system in which a circuit is embedded does typically determine the inputs sent to the circuit on the basis of the outputs received from the circuit.

planned scope of this presentation, not because they are felt to be unimportant. DFT techniques relating to electrical and mechanical properties are discussed in [WRIT75].

2.3. TESTABILITY MEASURES

The techniques listed in Table 2.2.1 require the addition of extra logic or extra connections. These additions add to the cost of the design. Thus it is desirable to limit the additions to those necessary to assure adequate testability of the design. To do this, a method of estimating the design's testability is required.

A straightforward method for determining the testability of a circuit is to use an *automatic test pattern generation* (ATPG) program to generate the tests and the fault coverage. The running time of the program, the number of test patterns generated, and the fault coverage then provide a measure of the testability of the circuit. The difficulty with this approach is mainly the large expense involved in running the ATPG program. Also, the ATPG program may not provide sufficient information about how to improve the testability of a circuit with poor testability. To overcome these difficulties, a number of programs have been written to calculate estimates of the testability of a design without actually running an ATPG program: TMEAS (Testability Measure Program) [STEP76, GRAS79]; SCOAP (Sandia Controllability/Observability Analysis Program) [GOLD78, GOLD79a, GOLD79b, GOLD80]; TESTSCREEN [KOVI79a, KOVI79b]; CAMELOT (Computer-Aided Measure for Logic Testability) [BENN80, BENN81]; VICTOR (Vlsi Identifier of Controllability, Testability, Observability, and Redundancy) [RATI82].

These *testability measure* (TM) *programs* implement algorithms that attempt to predict, for a specific circuit, the cost (running time) of generating test patterns. In the process of calculating the testability measure, information is developed identifying those portions of the circuit which are difficult to test. This information can be used as a guide to circuit modifications that improve testability.

No accurate relationship between circuit characteristics and testability has yet been demonstrated. Thus the circuit parameters calculated by the TM programs are heuristic and have been chosen on the basis of experience and study of existing ATPG programs. It is not surprising that the various authors of TM programs have chosen different circuit characteristics for their estimates of testability. The technique used to demonstrate that a given TM program does indeed give an indication of circuit testability is to run both the TM program and also an ATPG program on a number of different circuits. A monotonic relation between the TM and the ATPG run time is offered as "proof" that the TM program produces a good estimate of circuit testability. The difficulty with this validation technique is the high cost of running enough examples to be meaningful. Some interesting results obtained by using statistical methods to evaluate the testability measure program approach are presented in [AGRA82].

All the TM programs base their estimates of testability on "controllability" and "observability" values for each circuit component. They differ in the precise definitions used for obtaining these estimates. The concepts of controllability and observability are derived from the techniques used for ATPG. They are defined in [STEP76] as:

> *Controllability:* "the ease of producing an arbitrary valid signal at the inputs of a component by exercising the primary inputs of the circuit."
>
> *Observability:* "the ease of determining at the primary outputs of the circuit what happened at the outputs of a component."

The *components* referred to in the definitions are standard ICs (SSI and MSI) for board-level circuits and are standard cell library modules for LSI or VLSI circuits. It is assumed that the components are interconnected by unidirectional links.

2.3.1. TEMAS

In TEMAS an observability value, OY, and a controllability value, CY, are assigned to each link. These values are normalized to be between 0 and 1, with 1 being the best possible value. For primary inputs, $CY = 1$ since they are assumed to have perfect controllability. Primary outputs have $OY = 1$ since perfect observability is assumed for them. Internal link values are calculated by associating with each component a *controllability transfer factor* (CTF) and an *observability transfer factor* (OTF). Two systems of N (N equals the number of components) simultaneous equations are used to determine the link CY and OY values.

Sequential components are handled by introducing implicit feedback links to represent the state transitions. No other modifications are required in TEMAS to handle sequential circuits.

The input controllability of a component is defined as the average of the input link controllabilities, and the same controllability value is assigned to all the component output links. The component output observability is the average of the output link observabilities, and the component input links are all assigned a common observability.

In defining the controllability transfer factor it is assumed that all valid input signal values can be achieved with equal ease and that all valid output signal values are equally important. Based on these assumptions the CTF is defined as a measure of the uniformity of the input output mapping produced by the component. For a single-output component with output = 0 for half of the possible input patterns, the value of CTF would be 1. (Thus CTF for an XOR gate is 1.) For an n-input, single-output component (such as an OR gate or a NAND gate) that has output = 0 for only one input pattern, the value of CTF is 2^{n-1}. This is also the CTF for a gate whose output is 1 for only one input pattern (AND, NOR gates). The CTF measures only the uniformity of the component input output mapping. (Thus CTF is $\frac{1}{2}$ for a two-input OR gate and CTF is $\frac{1}{4}$ for a three-input NOR gate.) The controllability of the output links of a component is calculated by multiplying the component input controllability by the CTF.

The observability transfer factor is specified to approximate the probability that observation of the component outputs will permit the determination of whether an input fault has occurred. The observability of the input links of a component is calculated by multiplying the output observability by the OTF.

The overall observability of the circuit is defined as the average of the component output observabilities, and the overall controllability is the average of the component input controllabilities. The overall circuit testability is defined as the geometric mean of the overall observability and overall controllability.

In TEMAS and CAMELOT two values (one for controllability and one for observability) are determined for each node. SCOAP and TESTSCREEN each calculate a vector of six values for each node. TESTSCREEN and SCOAP differ in the methods used to calculate the values.

2.3.2. SCOAP

In SCOAP the circuit nodes are characterized as sequential or combinational according to the following definitions:

> A *combinational node* is a primary circuit input or a combinational standard cell output node.
>
> A *sequential node* is an output node of a sequential standard cell.

The controllability/observability properties of each node are represented by a vector with six elements representing the following measures:

> *CC0(N), combinational 0-controllability:* the minimum number of combinational node assignments required to set the node N value to 0
>
> *CC1(N), combinational 1-controllability:* the minimum number of combinational node assignments required to set the node N value to 1
>
> *SC0(N), sequential 0-controllability:* the minimum number of sequential nodes that must be set to specified values in order to justify a 0 on node N
>
> *SC1(N), sequential 1-controllability:* the minimum number of sequential nodes that must be set to specified values in order to justify a 1 on node N
>
> *C0(N), combinational observability:* both the number of combinational standard cells between node N and a primary output terminal and the minimum number of combinational node assignments required to propagate the value of node N to a primary circuit output
>
> *S0(N), sequential observability:* both the number of sequential standard cells between node N and a primary output terminal and the minimum number of sequential standard cells that must be controlled in order to propagate the value of node N to a primary circuit output

The controllability/observability measures of SCOAP are not normalized like those in TMEAS. In SCOAP higher values for the measures correspond to nodes that are more difficult to test. The sequential controllabilities and observability are related to the number of time frames necessary to observe or control the value of an internal node.

In calculating the parameter values for SCOAP, all the internal node parameters are initially set to infinity. The initial settings for primary input and output nodes are given in Table 2.3.1.

TABLE 2.3.1 SCOAP INITIAL PARAMETER VALUES FOR PRIMARY INPUTS AND OUTPUTS

	CC0(X)	CC1(X)	SC0(X)	SC1(X)	C0(X)	S0(X)
Input	1	1	0	0	∞	∞
Output	∞	∞	∞	0	0	0

Each standard cell must have a set of rules determined for obtaining its output controllability parameters from the input controllability parameter values, and for obtaining the input observability parameter values from the output observability parameter values. The rules for some combinational cells are given in Table 2.3.2. Table 2.3.3 gives the rules for the D flip-flop shown in Fig. 2.3.1 (negative edge-triggered

TABLE 2.3.2 PARAMETER TRANSFORMATION RULES FOR SOME TYPICAL CELLS

	Buffer Y = X	Inverter Y = X′	AND GATE Y = X1*X2
CC0(Y)	CC0(X) + 1	CC1(X) + 1	min[CC0(X1), CC0(X2)] + 1
CC1(Y)	CC1(X) + 1	CC0(X) + 1	CC1(X1) + CC1(X2) + 1
SC0(Y)	SC0(X)	SC1(X)	min[SC0(X1), SC0(X2)]
SC1(Y)	SC1(X)	SC0(X)	SC1(X1) + SC1(X2)
C0(X)	C0(Y) + 1	C0(Y) + 1	See below
S0(X)	S0(Y)	S0(Y)	See below
CO(X1)	See above	See above	CO(Y) + CC1(X2) + 1
S0(X1)	See above	See above	S0(Y) + SC1(X2)

TABLE 2.3.3 TRANSFORMATION RULES FOR D FLIP-FLOP OF FIG. 2.3.1

CC0(Q):	min[CC1(R) + CC0(C), CC0(D) + CC1(C) + CC0(C) + CC0(R)]
CC1(Q):	CC1(D) + CC1(C) + CC0(C) + CC0(R)
SC0(Q):	min[SC1(R) + SC0(C), SC0(D) + SC1(C) + SC0(G) + SC0(R)] + 1
SC1(Q):	SC1(D) + SC1(C) + SC0(C) + SC0(R) + 1
C0(D):	C0(Q) + CC1(C) + CC0(C) + CC0(R)
S0(D):	S0(Q) + SC1(C) + SC0(C) + SC0(R) + 1

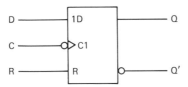

Figure 2.3.1 D flip-flop corresponding to Table 2.3.3.

with asychronous reset). A detailed discussion of the formation of these rules is given in [GOLD78] and [GOLD79b].

The controllability parameters are calculated by starting at the primary inputs and using the transformation rules to determine the internal and primary output controllabilities. Several iterations can be required if there are feedback loops present. The observability parameter calculations start with the primary output node values. The internal and primary input observability parameters are determined by means of the cell transformation rules. The observability of a fan-out node is defined to be the minimum of the observabilities of the nodes to which it fans out. There can be some parameter values which remain equal to infinity. This is an indication that the corresponding nodes are uncontrollable or unobservable, demonstrating a redundancy in the circuit. This is not a complete test for redundancy since it is possible to have a redundant node that does not lead to an infinite parameter value. This phenomenon is discussed in [GOLD79b].

No single measure of the circuit testability is defined in SCOAP. Instead, controllability and observability profiles (density plots) are used in which the number of nodes having a given controllability or observability value are plotted against the corresponding values. There are, in general, six such profiles for each circuit analyzed. Figure 2.3.2 shows the sequential controllability profiles generated by SCOAP for the circuit of Fig. 2.3.3. The data for these profiles, shown in Table 2.3.4, are taken from [GOLD80]. The highest value occurs for the 1-controllability of node FB, reflecting the difficulty of placing a 1 on this node. This is an indication that some modification, such as adding an asynchronous reset to flip-flop FF3, should be considered.

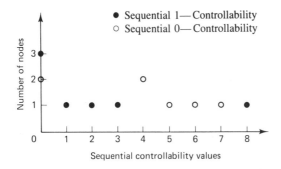

Figure 2.3.2 Profiles for the circuit of Fig. 2.3.3.

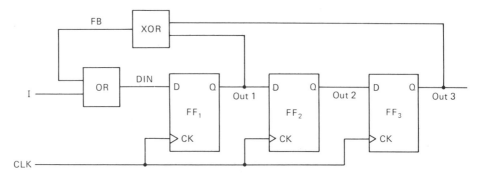

Figure 2.3.3   Circuit to illustrate SCOAP.

TABLE 2.3.4   SEQUENTIAL CONTROLLABILITY PARAMETER VALUES FOR FIG. 2.3.3

Sequential	CLK	I	DIN	FB	OUT1	OUT2	OUT3
0-controllability	0	0	4	4	5	6	7
1-controllability	0	0	0	8	1	2	3

2.3.3. TESTSCREEN, CAMELOT, and VICTOR

TESTSCREEN is similar to SCOAP in that a six-element vector is associated with each node. The same six parameters are represented, but a different technique is used to compute their values. In TESTSCREEN the number of primary inputs that must be fixed in order to control a node value is used as the value of the node combinational controllability. Combinational observability is based on the number of primary inputs that must be fixed in order to sensitize a fault from the node to a primary output. Thus the major change from the SCOAP program is the use of primary inputs rather than the total number of nodes which need to be controlled. The use of primary inputs is justified as a measure of the logic conflicts that occur in trying to control or observe a node value. The sequential measures in TESTSCREEN are defined as the number of clock changes needed to control or observe the node's logic signal.

CAMELOT, like TMEAS, derives a controllability value and an observability value for each node. Unlike TMEAS, CAMELOT makes use of controllability values in determining the node observabilities. This is done to account for the necessity of placing values on internal nodes to sensitize a path to the output. There are other differences in the details of how the controllability and observability calculations are specified.

VICTOR is restricted to combinational circuits. It differs from the other programs in its emphasis on detecting redundant faults. It is typical in VICTOR to identify many nodes as "potentially redundant" even if few or no redundant faults are present. The potentially redundant nodes may represent nodes that are difficult to test rather than nodes that can be removed without altering the circuit function. As discussed above, SCOAP identifies some but not all redundant faults. In a sense, all the TM programs give some indication of potentially redundant faults. However, some redundant faults may be missed. It is possible for a node to be easy to control and easy to observe, but impossible to both control and observe simultaneously. Such nodes correspond to redundant faults that could be missed by the TM programs. For a discussion of redundancy, see [FLOU79].

2.4. SCAN TECHNIQUES

A major difficulty with the ad hoc techniques of Section 2.2 is the requirement of adding extra control inputs or observation outputs. Testability measures help by allowing the use of only those additional external connections that are important for satisfying the testability requirements. The techniques to be described in this section permit access to the internal nodes of a circuit without requiring a separate external connection for each node accessed. Very few (from one to four) additional external connections are used to access many internal nodes. This is made possible at the cost of additional internal logic circuitry used primarily for testing.

Besides increased accessibility the scan-path techniques have another very important benefit. It is possible to test the entire circuit outside of the scan path by generating test patterns only for its combinational portions.

The first description of the use of scan techniques for testing appears to have been in [CART64]. This paper describes a technique of storing test patterns on a serial storage device (disk or tape) and then reading them into a computer main memory for periodic testing of the computer. Special circuitry is included to allow the CPU flip-flops to be initialized from the memory. After a fixed number of machine cycles the flip-flop contents are compared with a precomputed result. The scan-path techniques to be described here differ in that they are not limited to self-test of a stored program system, but are applicable on a circuit level and can be used for production testing as well as system maintenance.

2.4.1. Scan Path

In the scan-path technique [WILL73], the circuit is designed so that it has two modes of operation: one that is the normal functional mode, and another that is a test mode in which the circuit flip-flops are interconnected into a shift register. With the circuit in the test mode it is possible to shift an arbitrary test pattern into the flip-flops. By returning the circuit to the normal mode for one clock period the combinational circuitry acts on the flip-flop contents and primary input signals and stores the results in the flip flops. If the circuit is then placed in the test mode, it is possible to shift out the contents of the flip-flops and compare these contents with the correct response.

In the following discussion of scan-path techniques it is assumed that the circuit is constructed of flip-flops interconnected by combinational networks. It will also be assumed initially that all the flip-flops are clocked by a single common clock signal. These assumptions mean that the circuit can be considered to have the general structure shown in Fig. 2.4.1. Drawing the circuit in this form is done to simplify the following discussion, but is not meant to imply any restrictions on the designer other than those stated above.

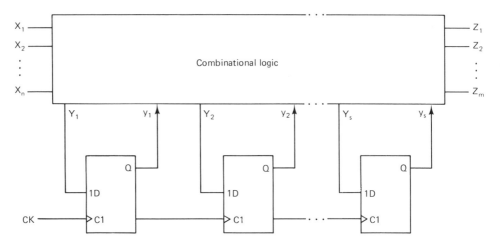

Figure 2.4.1   General structure of circuit for scan-path discussion.

While the application of these techniques to other circuit types was discussed in [WILL73], the structure considered here is the most common type of digital circuit and is the easiest to modify with the scan-path technique. D flip-flops are shown in Fig. 2.4.1 and will be used in the following discussion. The same general results hold true if other types of flip-flops (SR, JK, T, . . .) are used. Since the extension to other flip-flops is straightforward, the details will not be presented here.

In the following discussion of various scan-path techniques it is important to distinguish between latches and flip-flops. This distinction is illustrated in Fig. 2.4.2. A latch has the transparency property: if the data input changes while the clock is active, the latch output will follow the data input change. This is illustrated in Fig. 2.4.2 by the changes in the Q-latch waveforms at times 31, 38, and 40. A flip-flop changes only when the clock input makes a specific transition—the active transition. For the flip-flop in Fig. 2.4.2, the active transition of the clock input occurs when the clock changes from 0 to 1. The flip-flop output takes on the value present at the data input when this active transition occurs. Subsequent changes of the data input have no effect until the next active transition of the clock. An important characteristic of flip-flops is that a shift register can be constructed by connecting the output of one flip-flop directly to the data input of the next flip-flop; the conversion of a latch register to a shift register requires an extra latch between each register stage.

The symbols used in this chapter for bistable logic elements follow the revision of the IEEE Standard for Graphic Symbols for Logic Functions (ANSI/IEEE std. 91–1984) as described in [MANN81].

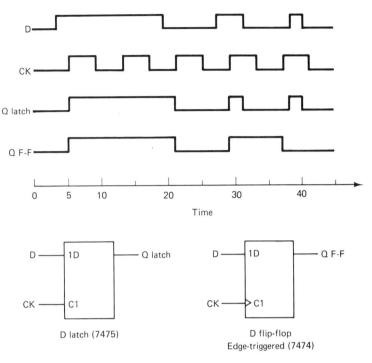

Figure 2.4.2   Latches and flip-flops: symbols and waveforms.

2.4.2. Stanford Scan-Path Design

The first published description of a scan-path design-for-testability structure was [WILL73], a paper based on the Stanford Ph.D. research of Michael Williams. In this technique each of the circuit flip-flops is replaced by the flip-flop structure shown in Fig. 2.4.3. A multiplexer is placed at the data input to permit a selection of two different data inputs: d_0 (normal system operation) and d_1 (test mode). The choice of data input is based on the value of the control input, T. When $T = 0$, data are gated from the d_0 input on an active clock transition. Data are taken from d_1 if T is equal to 1. A D flip-flop with multiplexed data inputs as in Fig. 2.4.3 will be called a *multiplexed data* (MD) *flip-flop*.

It should be noted that the design of Fig. 2.4.3 has the undesirable feature of increasing the propagation delay of the flip-flop. This is not inherent in a multiplexed data flip-flop. The additional delay can be eliminated (except possibly for the effect of additional gate fan-in) by redesigning the flip-flop to incorporate the multiplexer into the flip-flop circuitry.

The modification of the basic circuit structure of Fig. 2.4.1 to obtain a scan-path architecture using MD flip-flops is shown in Fig. 2.4.4. One additional input, the T input, has been added. For normal operation, T is equal to 0 and the circuit is

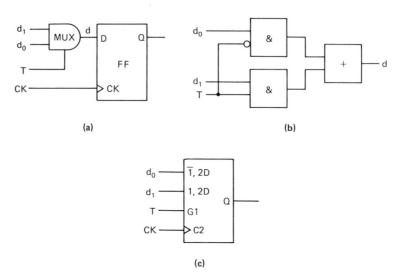

(a)   (b)

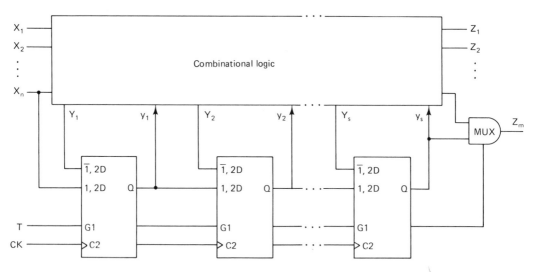

(c)

Figure 2.4.3   Multiplexed data flip-flop: (a) flip-flop with multiplexer (MUX); (b) multiplexer circuit diagram; (c) symbol for multiplexed data flip-flop.

Figure 2.4.4   Stanford scan-path architecture; MD flip-flops used to provide scan path.

connected as in Fig. 2.4.1. The upper data inputs ($y_1, \ldots, y_s$) act as the flip-flop D inputs. To test the circuit, T is set equal to 1. The lower data inputs become the flip-flop D inputs. Thus $D_i = Q_i - 1$ for i from 2 to s, and a shift register is formed. The primary input X_n is connected to D_1, becoming the shift register input, and Q_s, the shift register output, appears at the primary output Z_m.

Testing of the combinational logic is accomplished by:

1. Setting $T = 1$ (scan mode).
2. Shifting the test pattern y_j values into the flip-flops.
3. Setting the corresponding test values on the X_i inputs.
4. Setting $T = 0$ and, after a sufficient time for the combinational logic to settle, checking the output Z_k values.
5. Applying a clock signal to CK.
6. Setting $T = 1$ and shifting out the flip-flop contents via Z_m. The next y_j test pattern can be shifted in at the same time. The y_j values shifted out are compared with the good response values for y_j.

The flip-flops must also be tested. This is accomplished by shifting a string of 1s and then a string of 0s through the shift register to verify the possibility of shifting both a 1 and a 0 into each flip-flop.

A number of manufacturers have adopted design-for-testability methods which are very similar to the Stanford scan-path scheme. The different variations will be described next. They fall into two general categories: the basic scan-path flip-flop design and the way in which the scan path is interfaced with the functional circuitry.

2.4.3. Scan-Path Flip-Flop Designs

A basic requirement of the scan-path technique is that it be possible to gate data into the system flip-flops from two different sources. One method of doing this is to add multiplexers to the system flip-flops as shown in Fig. 2.4.3. In this method, data are entered into the scan-path input by first placing a 0 on the T input to the multiplexer and then pulsing the flip-flop clock input. Another possibility is to replace each system flip-flop by a *two-port flip-flop*, a flip-flop having two clock inputs with the data source determined by which of the clocks is pulsed.

A circuit for a two-port flip-flop is shown in Fig. 2.4.5. When a pulse is applied to $C1$, data are entered from $D1$; and when a pulse occurs at $C2$, data are entered from $D2$. This circuit is shown in [FUNA78] in connection with a discussion of the design-for-testability methods used at NEC (Nippon Electric Co.). In this paper a comparison is made between the use of two-port flip-flops and MD flip-flops. The two-port flip-flops were preferred. It was found easier to implement the control for a structure using such devices than for an MD flip-flop structure. An earlier paper [FUNA75] shows a detailed logic diagram for a two-port flip-flop.

Figure 2.4.6 shows the structure of a network with two-port flip-flops used to provide the scan path. The testing procedure must be modified slightly and becomes:

1. Scan in the test vector y_j values via X_n using the test clock TCK.
2. Set the corresponding test values on the X_i inputs.
3. After sufficient time for the signals to propagate through the combinational network, check the output Z_k values.

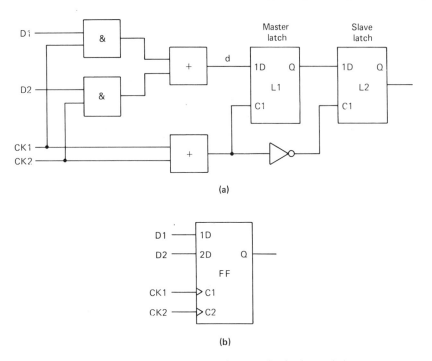

(a)

(b)

Figure 2.4.5 Two-port D flip-flop: (a) circuit; (b) symbol.

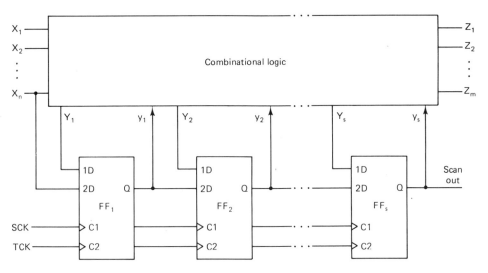

Figure 2.4.6 General structure of circuit using two-port flip-flops to provide scan path.

4. Apply one clock pulse to the system clock SCK to enter the new values of Y_j into the corresponding flip-flops.

5. Scan out and check the Y_j values by pulsing the test clock TCK.

2.4.4. Latch-Based Structures

Some systems are designed using latches rather than flip-flops as the bistable elements. The scan-path techniques presented in the previous sections cannot be applied directly to such systems; these techniques depend on the direct conversion of flip-flop registers into shift registers. For latch-based systems it is not possible to reconfigure the system bistable elements directly into a shift register for test purposes. Several different approaches have been developed which permit control and/or observation of the system latches through a small number of I/O pins.

The most popular technique for introducing scan-path testability into latch-based systems is IBM's LSSD (level-sensitive scan design). This requires the use of extra latches to allow the system latches to be connected into a shift register. The Univac scan-set technique avoids the necessity of configuring the system latches into a shift register by using a separate test data shift register. This register can load test data in parallel to or from the system latches. Univac has also proposed the use of multiplexers to scan out latch contents. Fujitsu and Amdahl avoid the use of test shift registers entirely. They use a combination of demultiplexing and multiplexing to set and scan out the system latches. More details on these techniques will be presented next.

Level-sensitive scan design: LSSD.   A scan-path design method, called *level-sensitive scan design* (LSSD), for latch-based systems was presented in [EICH77]. It is the standard design technique in current use at IBM. In this method each system latch is replaced by a two-port latch ($L1$ latch),* and a second (single-port) latch ($L2$ latch) is added to permit reconfiguration of the system latches into a shift register for test purposes.

The reason that this method is called "level sensitive" has to do with the design of the latches (which will be discussed below) and on the fact that if the design rules are followed, correct operation is not dependent on signal rise and fall times or on internal delays.

A general structure for a system designed using the LSSD technique is shown in Fig. 2.4.7. This particular structure is called a *double-latch design*. Examples of some specific designs using this structure are presented in [DASG78]. During normal operation the system is clocked with two interleaved nonoverlapping pulse trains applied to the CK1 and CK2 inputs. Other possible structures are discussed in

---

*A two-port latch is directly analogous to a two-port flip-flop. It is a latch with two data inputs, each of which is controlled by a separate clock.

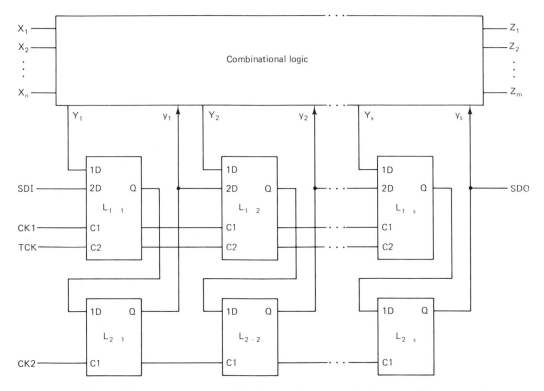

Figure 2.4.7 General structure of a circuit using two-port latches to provide a scan path—LSSD double-latch design. SDI represents scanned-in test data, SCO scanned-out test data. TCK is the test clock.

[EICH77]. The way a system designed using this technique is tested is very similar to testing a system using two-port flip-flops:

1. Scan in the test vector y_j values via SDI by applying pulses alternately to the test clock input TCK (called the A clock in some LSSD papers) and the system clock input CK2 (also called the B clock).

2. Set the corresponding test values on the X_i inputs.

3. After sufficient time for the signals to propagate through the combinational network, check the output Z_k values.

4. Apply one clock pulse to the system clock CK1 to enter the new values of y_j into the corresponding $L1$ latches.

5. Scan out and check the y_j values by applying clock pulses alternately to CK2 and TCK.

Scan-set structures.   All of the previous methods use the functional system flip-flops or latches to scan test data into and out of the circuit. It is also possible to add to the functional circuitry a shift register whose sole purpose is the shifting in and out of test data. A design technique based on the introduction of such a shift register is proposed in [STEW77] and [STEW78]. (*Caution:* Stewart uses the term "flip-flop" to mean either a latch or a flip-flop. When it is necessary to distinguish, he calls a latch a "latch flip-flop" and a flip-flop as defined in Section 2.4.1 an "edge-triggered flip-flop.") The resulting structure is shown in Fig. 2.4.8.

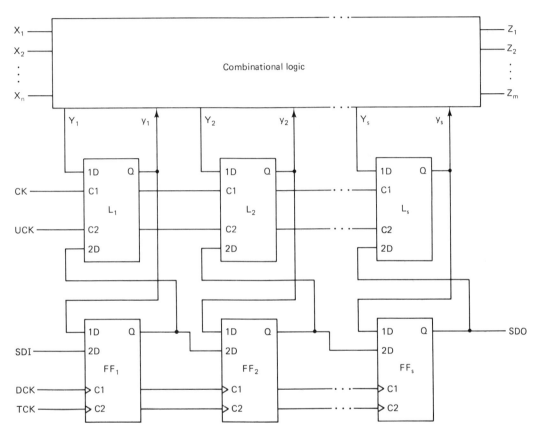

Figure 2.4.8   General structure of a circuit using the scan-set technique. FF1-FFs make up a shift register added for test purposes. L1-LNs are system latches converted to two-port latches.

Test data are shifted into the flip-flop register (FF1–FFs) from the SDI (scan data in) connection by clocking TCK. The test data are transferred to the system latches in parallel through their 2D inputs by applying a pulse to UCK. Scanning out the latch data is the reverse process: the latch contents are loaded in parallel into the shift register by pulsing DCK. Shifting out the register contents is accomplished by clocking TCK. The data are shifted to the SDO (shift data out) terminal.

To implement the structure of Fig. 2.4.8, the system latches must be converted into two-port latches. There is more hardware overhead in this technique than for LSSD: two latches per system latch for scan-set versus one latch per system latch for

LSSD. (Both techniques require the conversion of the system latches into two-port latches. Scan-set requires one shift register stage per system latch and each such stage requires the equivalent of two latches.)

Scan-set does have an important advantage compared to the techniques described above: with scan-set it is possible to gate the latch contents into the test shift register during normal system operation. This provides a means for getting a "snapshot" of system status. A technique for augmenting the LSSD structure to obtain a similar facility is discussed in [DASG81].

Another important feature of scan-set is the ability to scan circuit nodes other than latch outputs into the test shift register. Thus it has the ability to introduce observation test points at nonlatch nodes.

Multiplexer scan structures.   All of the preceding scan-path techniques use a shift register to convert between serial and parallel data. Serialization of parallel data can also be done with a multiplexer. A circuit structure with a multiplexer used to scan out the system latches is shown in Fig. 2.4.9. This type of structure is discussed in [STEW78], in which the use of a 4-bit-wide multiplexer is suggested. Use of more than one scan-out point increases the speed of scanning but also increases the number of I/O connections required. One possibility for avoiding this increase is to place

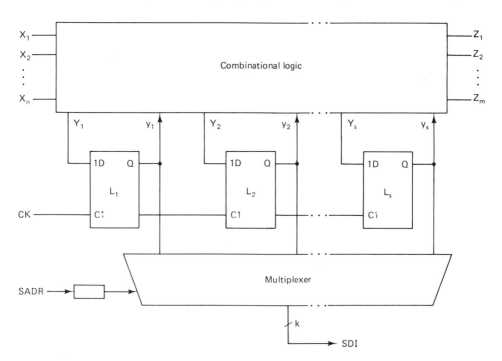

Figure 2.4.9   General structure of a circuit using multiplexer to scan latch contents out. SADR is the address of point(s) to be scanned out. SDI is a k-bit-wide bus with scanned-out latch values.

multiplexers on output pins to permit some of the output pins to be used both for system output and for scanning out test data [MCCL81].

With a multiplexer scan structure, nodes other than latch outputs can be accessed. The scanning operation can take place while the system is operating. Complete scan-out of all scan points is simplest if the scan data address register can be configured as a counter that steps through all addresses when clocked.

This multiplexer structure improves the observability of a design but does nothing for the controllability. Setting of the system latches can be accomplished with a demultiplexer. The use of a demultiplexer for setting the system latches and a multiplexer for scan-out forms the basis for the random access structure to be described next.

Random access scan design. Fujitsu and Amdahl use the principles of multiplexing and demultiplexing to implement a scan technique for latch-based systems [ANDO80, WAGN83]. A simplified version of the latch design used is shown in Fig. 2.4.10. This is called an *addressable latch*. Inputs 1D(Yi) and C1(CK) are used during normal system operation.

To access latch *i* for test purposes, the signal "Select *i*" must be set to 1. With Select *i* = 1, the latch content is placed on SDO(*i*), and SDI is clocked into the latch if TCK is pulsed. The structure of a system using these latches is shown in Fig. 2.4.11.

There is associated with the circuit an address register whose contents are decoded to produce the "Select *i*" signals. At most one of these signals is equal to 1 at a time. Data are scanned into the latches by placing the latch *i* data value on SDI, the *i* address in the address register, and then pulsing TCK. The address register is

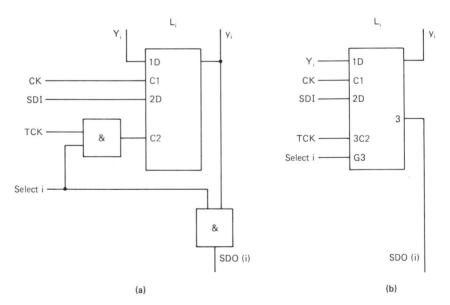

Figure 2.4.10   Addressable latch: (a) circuit diagram; (b) symbol.

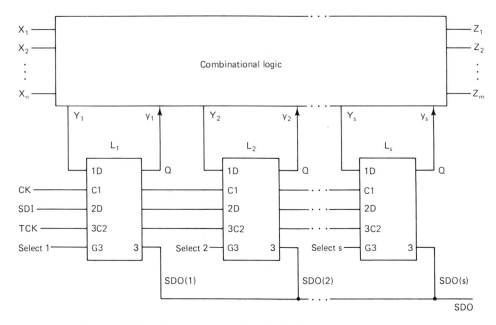

Figure 2.4.11   General structure of a circuit using random access scan.

implemented as a counter. Thus a sequence of data can be scanned into the latches by placing the sequence on SDI and pulsing the address register counter and TCK in the proper time relationship. The latch contents are scanned out via SDO by pulsing the address register to select the latches in turn.

An important feature of this structure is the ability to scan out the latches during normal system operation.

The actual implementations of this technique using addressable latches have two or three select signals per latch. These signals are decoded at each latch using the circuit shown in Fig. 2.4.12 for the case of two select signals. Somewhat more complex latches are used in the actual systems to take advantage of the technology (ECL) and minimize the penalties due to addressability. These are described in [ANDO80] and [WAGN83].

2.4.5. I/O Scan-Path Structures

The scan-path techniques described in Sections 2.4.1 through 2.4.4 improve testability by increasing controllability and observability (because of better internal access), and by eliminating the necessity of sequential circuit test pattern generation. The technique of this section improves testability by reducing the requirements placed on the physical test equipment.

The general I/O scan-path structure is shown in Fig. 2.4.13. The circuit latches are implemented in an LSSD-type design so that they form a scan path (called *internal scan path* or *ring*) for test purposes. A pair of scan-path latches are introduced for each

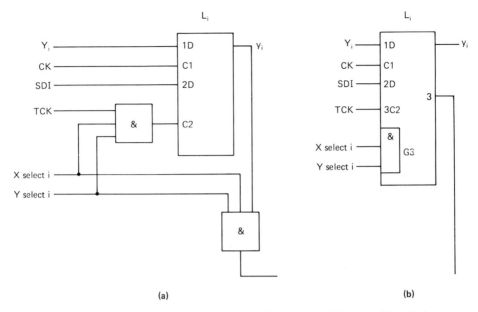

Figure 2.4.12   Addressable latch with coincident selection; (a) circuit; (b) symbol.

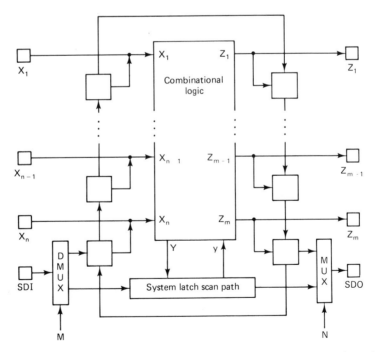

Figure 2.4.13   General structure of a circuit using scan latches on input pins and output pins.

I/O bonding pad. These I/O latches are configured as another LSSD-type scan path (called *external scan path* or *ring*). The details of the circuitry for input bonding pads are shown in Fig. 2.4.14. The output bonding pad latches are connected in an analogous fashion. More complete circuits are given in [ZASI83].

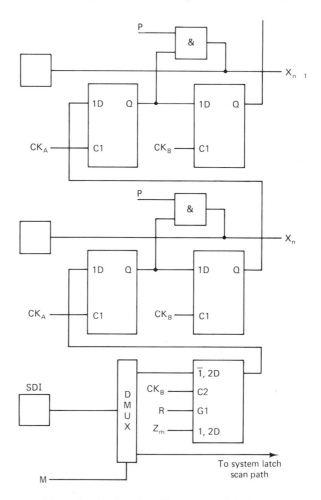

Figure 2.4.14 Details of input scanpath latches.

The test procedure is very similar to that described in Section 2.4.4 for LSSD structures. The necessary modifications are that the X_i values are scanned in via the SDI pin (the DMUX control must be set to direct its inputs to the external ring). The Z outputs from the combinational logic must be clocked into the external ring latches, which are then shifted out via the SDO pin.

The presence of the external scan path allows the chip to be tested through a small number of probe pins: seven control pins plus two pins for power and ground for the design described in [ZASI83]. This design demonstrates the testing of a 256-pin chip.

Another feature of this structure is the ability to qualify chips for speed at wafer probe by configuring the external ring as a ring oscillator. This is done by connecting the last latch in the external ring back as the input to the first latch in the ring.

Finally, this structure can easily be modified for use in a built-in self-test configuration. This application will be discussed in the section on self-test.

2.4.6. Scan-Path Bistable Element Design

The costs associated with the scan-path designs are:

1. Additional circuitry is added to each flip-flop or latch. Thus the flip-flops used for scan-path designs are more expensive than standard flip-flops.
2. One or more additional circuit pins are required. (If this is a critical design parameter, it is possible to use voltage multiplexing of the pins for test purposes.)
3. Testing time is increased by the need to shift the test patterns into the flip-flops serially. This may not be a net increase in test time; the modified circuit requires shorter test sets than the original circuit because only combinational logic test patterns are used.
4. There can be a performance penalty. The speed of normal operation may be decreased due to increased propagation delay in the scan-path latches or flip-flops.
5. Available functional area can be reduced due to the increased interconnect. This additional interconnect can also introduce a performance penalty.

Most of the overhead associated with the scan-path designs results from the modifications of the bistable elements: flip-flops or latches. Since the bistables make up only a small portion of an entire system, the scan-path system overhead is probably at least an order of magnitude less than the overhead associated with a single bistable. The overhead can be minimized by optimizing the design of the scan-path bistables. Efficient LSSD latch designs are discussed in [EICH83a].

The performance penalty can be minimized by designing the bistables so that no additional gate delays are introduced in series with the data inputs. A design for the LSSD latches is shown in Fig. 2.4.15. Since the two data inputs are effectively in parallel, no additional gate delay is introduced by the inclusion of a second data port. (There may be some decrease in speed due to increased loading.) Another feature of this design is that the latches are hazard-free: no spurious signals (glitches or spikes) are produced on the outputs when the state is changed. It is this feature that is important for level-sensitive operation. A detailed discussion of the hazard-free aspect of the design is given in [EICH77]. Elimination of hazards in a random-access scan design is discussed in [WAGN83].

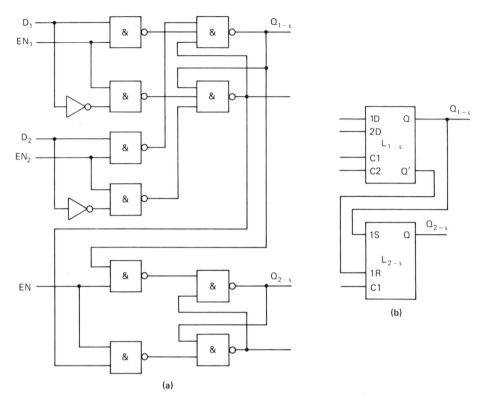

Figure 2.4.15 Design of LSSD latches to eliminate data delay and hazards: (a) NAND-gate circuit; (b) corresponding logic symbol.

The pairs ($L1$ and $L2$) of LSSD latches can be converted into master-slave flip-flops by the modification shown in Fig. 2.4.16. If the resulting two-port flip-flops are used in the structure of Fig. 2.4.6, a design is obtained in which there is no delay penalty due to the use of two-port flip-flops, and static hazards are avoided. However, the use of master-slave flip-flops does introduce an essential hazard which is inherent in all flip-flops. A different two-port flip-flop design which does not have a delay penalty but which does have static hazards is presented in [FUNA75] and [YAMA78].

2.4.7. Extensions

A number of testing problems can still arise in systems designed using scan-path techniques. Extensions to the basic scan-path technique have been proposed to overcome these problems.

Test pattern generation cost. The cost of automatic test pattern generation for the combinational portion of a large circuit can be excessive. The computation time for test generation increases rapidly with network size. (The growth in test generation

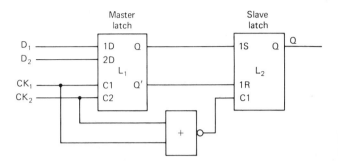

Figure 2.4.16 Master-slave flip-flop using LSSD latches.

time is demonstrated in [GOEL80] to be proportional to G^2, where G is the number of gates in the circuit. Although this result is not universally accepted, there is general agreement that the growth is faster than linear.) The test generation cost can be substantially reduced by generating tests for subcircuits and then combining the subcircuit tests to obtain the complete network test. In [BOTT77] an algorithm for preprocessing an LSSD circuit description to obtain subcircuit descriptions for an automatic test pattern program is described:

1. A backtrace is performed from each primary output and from each latch. The backtrace is stopped when a primary input or latch is reached. This identifies a "cone" of all logic elements and interconnections (nets) which control the value of the starting point of the backtrace.

2. The cones are combined into subcircuits for test generation. The size and number of the subcircuits is determined by the circuit structure and the characteristics of the test generation program to be used. An attempt is made to minimize the logic which appears in more than one subcircuit by choosing cones with common logic for combination.

Sometimes this procedure fails to obtain subcircuits which are small enough for efficient test pattern generation. For such cases it has been proposed in [HSU78] to incorporate selective control circuitry at the subassembly (module, dip) outputs. Division of a circuit into subcircuits for test generation is also discussed in [YAMA78]. Both of these papers call the subcircuits "partitions," although they are not partitions in a strict sense since the subcircuits will typically not be disjoint.

Embedded memory. It is becoming increasingly common to have memory (ROM or RAM) included as part of a circuit. Testing of such designs using scan-path techniques is not straightforward. Four specific problems arise:

1. Tests for some of the faults in the combinational logic may require that the memory outputs be set to specified values.

2. Tests for some of the faults in the combinational logic may require that the effect

of the fault be propagated through the memory in order for the effect to appear at a latch or primary output.

3. To test a RAM fully it is necessary to write and read both a 1 and a 0 for each cell. For a ROM test, each cell must be read.

4. The combinational logic in the part of the "cone" driving the RAM tends to be rather large.

A modification of the basic LSSD design method to permit efficient testing of circuits with embedded memory is presented in [EICH78c]. Different methods for testing such circuits are discussed in [FUNA78] and [ANDO80]. In these papers the embedded memories are called "arrays," although the techniques described are not intended to apply either to programmed logic arrays or to gate arrays.

Miscellaneous extensions.   The use of a random test pattern generator to obtain tests for an LSSD design is described in [WILL77]. Modifications to the basic LSSD latch design for a variety of applications, including those in which an LSSD design is interfaced with non-LSSD circuitry, are presented in [DASG81].

2.5. EASILY TESTABLE NETWORKS AND FUNCTION-INDEPENDENT TESTING

Most of the recent work on DFT has assumed that standard design techniques would be used to implement the functional logic. These techniques aim at producing circuits which represent some compromise between maximizing the performance and minimizing the cost. The DFT techniques are design modifications that attempt to limit their impact on cost and performance while improving testability. There is an older DFT approach called *easily testable network design* which is aimed at developing design techniques that start with a functional specification and result in networks which are easy to test. In this approach there are no constraints on the cost or performance of the resulting design. The easily testable network design techniques are described in this section. Desirable properties for *easily testable* (ET) *networks* were specified in [REDD72] as:

1. Small test sets.
2. No redundancy.
3. The test set can be found without much extra work.
4. The test set can be easily generated.
5. The test set outputs should be easily interpreted.
6. The faults should be locatable to the desired degree.

The requirement of no redundancy is present because it is not possible to test for a fault on a redundant lead, but the presense of such a fault can prevent a test set from detecting a fault on a nonredundant lead [FRIE67]. This requirement does not create any particular difficulties; any testing scheme will be more efficient if redundancy is not present.

Test application cost is made low both by keeping socket time short and by using a simple tester. The short socket time results from the small test set property (1). A simple tester can be used because of requirement 4—that the test set be easily generated (by a simple logic network) so that it is not necessary to have a large memory to store precalculated test patterns—and requirement 5—that outputs be easily interpreted, which avoids the necessity of storing output response patterns.

Low maintenance cost is the aim of requirement 6 on fault locatability. Test pattern generation cost is small because of requirement 3—that the test set be found without much extra work. Some of the techniques result in test sets that do not depend on the function realized by the network. They are said to allow *function-independent testing*.

2.5.1. RM Networks

The design procedure presented in [REDD72] responds to properties 1 and 3 by constraining the final form of the network. An example of a network designed using this procedure is shown in Fig. 2.5.1a. (The function is available at the output marked f. The e output is used only during testing.) Such networks will be called *RM networks*. Their design is based on the Reed-Muller canonical form for switching functions [MULL54], in which the switching function is expressed as the Exclusive-OR (sum modulo 2) of products of the independent variables.

The network form is such that it can be tested for all single stuck-at faults on the inputs or the AND gates as well as any combinational fault of the XOR gates with a set of $n + 4$ test inputs (n is the number of primary network inputs) that does not depend on the function realized by the network. For an arbitrary network structure the number of patterns required to test for all single stuck-at faults is proportional to the number of gates in the network [GOEL80]. There are usually many more gates than network inputs. Thus it seems reasonable to accept $n + 4$ as a small number of test inputs. Since the test set is independent of the function realized by the network, a tester circuit can be designed that will test any n-input design. The block diagram for such a test circuit is given in [REDD72]. The generalization to a test circuit that can test for any number of inputs up to some maximum seems straightforward. No extra work is required to get the test set for a specific function, so property 3 is surely satisfied. The test circuit is not costly to implement, hence property 4 is taken care of. Ease of interpretation of the test outputs (property 5) is also direct. A simple circuit is given in [REDD72] that produces the same output as the network being tested for each of the test inputs. Since this circuit need only have its outputs specified for the test pattern inputs, it is much simpler than the circuit under test. In fact, this test-output circuit can be realized in a general form which permits it to be "programmed" for a specific function.

A number of extensions to the original scheme of [REDD72] have been proposed

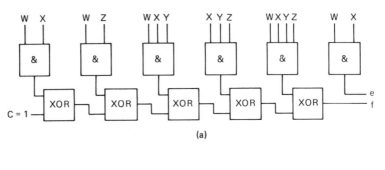

(a)

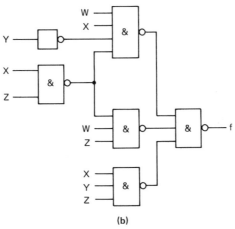

(b)

Figure 2.5.1 Networks for function $f = wxy'z' + wx'z + xyz$: (a) easily testable realization; (b) NAND realization.

[KODA74, KODA77, PRAD78, PAGE80, SALU75]. These all preserve the RM network structure and do not change the fundamental nature of the technique.

A RM network is made up of two parts: a cascade connection of XOR gates and a number of AND gates. The XOR cascade part can be tested for any faulty gate with just four tests [KAUT71]. This is the basic property that makes the RM network testable with a small test set. The AND-gate portion can be tested for any stuck fault with an additional n tests, provided that an extra output (e in Fig. 2.5.1a) is used. The extra output is derived from an AND gate that has as inputs all those primary inputs that are connected to an even number of AND gates in the circuit for f.* (In Fig. 2.5.1a, W is connected to four AND gates in the f network; thus W is connected to the e AND gate. Y is connected to three AND gates in the f network and is thus missing from the e gate.)

*The additional output can be avoided at the cost of adding $2E$ tests to the test set, where E equals the number of inputs connected to an even number of AND gates. In this case the test set depends on the function realized.

The RM network technique has three very serious flaws:

1. It can require many more gates than are necessary to implement the function. Figure 2.5.1b shows a NAND-gate realization for the same function as the RM network of Fig. 2.5.1a. The NAND network uses five NAND gates and one inverter. The RM network has six AND gates and five XOR gates. For this simple function of only four variables the RM network has about twice as many gates as does an efficient network. In many technologies the XOR gates are much more expensive than NAND gates.

2. There is a long delay in producing the output from the RM network because of the necessity to propagate signals through the XOR cascade (six-gate maximum delay for Fig. 2.5.1a versus three-gate delay for Fig. 2.5.1b). There is usually a longer propagation delay for an XOR gate than for a NAND gate.

3. The RM network must be designed from a Boolean specification. Thus efficient techniques of combining known modules such as adders, multiplexers, and so on, cannot be used.

Several other techniques have been proposed for designing ET networks. These techniques avoid the third flaw mentioned in connection with RM networks by starting with an efficient network design obtained by standard design techniques and then modifying the network to make it possible to use a small test set. In [HAYE74] the network is converted to a network of two-input NAND gates and inverters. The inverters are replaced by XOR gates and XOR gates are inserted into all gate inputs not driven by inverters. The second inputs to the XOR gates all become additional primary control inputs and all of the XOR gate outputs become additional primary test outputs. The modified network can be tested with five test inputs. The objective of having a small test set is clearly satisfied. The extra XOR gates can easily double the total number of gates in the network and also the delay in forming the output. A related technique is described in [SALU74], in which each original gate is replaced by a network of gates and the test set consists of three test inputs. It suffers from the same problems of many extra gates and long propagation delays.

Rather than modifying the functional network, the technique proposed in [DASG80] embeds it in a larger network in order to obtain the ET network properties. The assumption is made that it is only necessary to test for faults at input/output terminals. Four extra inputs are added for test purposes, and only two test input patterns are required. Although the number of added gates and delay is modest, the restriction to input/output faults is probably acceptable only in very special situations.

2.5.2. FITPLA

To my knowledge none of the techniques just described has ever been used in an actual system design. Methods that are more promising for practical application involve modifying the PLA structure to make it easily testable. Since the PLA structure is one that is frequently used in real systems, a modification of this structure which makes it easy to test has the possibility of wide usage.

A modified PLA structure has been proposed that can be tested with a fixed test set that depends only on the size of the PLA and not on the functions realized. Further, the output response can be checked by the structure itself, so that storage of test responses is not necessary. Thus this structure realizes a PLA for which function-independent testing is possible. The number of input vectors in the test set is of the order of $n + w$, where n is the number of input variables and w is the number of word lines (product terms). The following description of the FITPLA, a modified PLA that can be tested by a function-independent test set, is based on [HONG80] and [FUJI81].

The basic PLA structure is shown in Fig. 2.5.2a and an example of a specific implementation is given in Fig. 2.5.2b. In the following discussion it will be assumed that the signal on a word line is the logical product of the signals on the bit lines connected to the word line with crosspoints and that the signal on an output line is the logical sum of the signals on the word lines connected to the output line with crosspoints. Thus, in Fig. 2.5.2b, the signal on word line 4 is given by $X_2' X_3'$. For MOS PLAs some of the signal polarities should be modified to reflect the fact that NOR functions are realized by the arrays rather than AND and OR functions.

The strategy used in deriving the FITPLA is to provide mechanisms whereby the selection of either a single bit line or a single word line can be forced. Selection of a single bit line is made possible by replacing the input decoders (which provide X_i

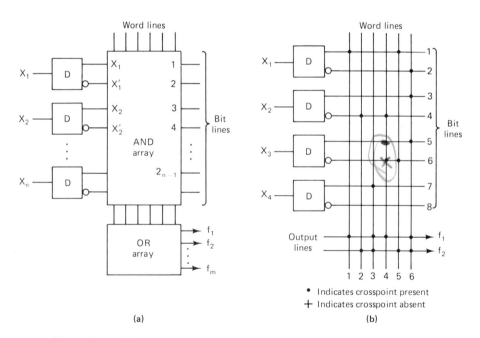

(a)   (b)

Figure 2.5.2 PLA networks: (a) general structure; (b) example of PLA realizing
$f_1 = x_1 + x_4 + x_2' x_3 + x_1' x_2 x_3, f_2 = x_2' + x_4 + x_1 x_3' + x_1' x_2 x_3.$

and X_i') with modified decoders (which provide $X_i + y_1$ and $X_i' + y_2$). Circuits for the decoders are shown in Fig. 2.5.3 and their operation is illustrated in Table 2.5.1. During normal operation of the PLA both y_1 and y_2 are set equal to 0. With $y_1 = 0$ and $y_2 = 1$, all of the bit lines driven by complemented variables are forced to 1. All those variables which are equal to 1 will have the corresponding bit lines equal to 1. Thus by setting only one of the input variables to 0 and $y_1 y_2 = 01$, a single bit line will be equal to 0. Similarly, setting only one of the input variables (X_i) equal to 1 and $y_1 y_2 = 10$ will cause only one of the bit lines corresponding to X_i' to equal 0.*

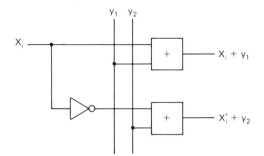

Figure 2.5.3 Design of modified input decoders.

TABLE 2.5.1 ILLUSTRATION OF OPERATION OF MODIFIED INPUT DECODERS FOR $n = 4$

						Bit Lines							
X_1	X_2	X_3	X_4	y_1	y_2	1	2	3	4	5	6	7	8
X_1	X_2	X_3	X_4	0	0	X_1	X_1'	X_2	X_2'	X_3	X_3'	X_4	X_4'
X_1	X_2	X_3	X_4	0	1	X_1	1	X_2	1	X_3	1	X_4	1
X_1	X_2	X_3	X_4	1	0	1	X_1'	1	X_2'	1	X_3'	1	X_4'
1	1	1	1	0	1	1	1	1	1	1	1	1	1
0	0	0	0	1	0	1	1	1	1	1	1	1	1
0	1	1	1	0	1	0	1	1	1	1	1	1	1
1	0	0	0	1	0	1	0	1	1	1	1	1	1

The next modification is the addition of one word line, the *parity word line*, to the AND ARRAY. The connections to the parity word line are made to ensure that there are an odd number of crosspoints on each bit line. A circuit that checks the parity of the signals on the word line is also added to the PLA. The PLA of Fig. 2.5.2b with these modifications is shown in Fig. 2.5.4.

By selecting each of the bit lines individually and observing the signal on E_1, it is possible to detect any single stuck-at-1 fault on a bit line and any single crosspoint fault (a crosspoint missing or an extra crosspoint) in the AND array. This requires $2n$

---

*If the input variables are decoded two at a time, a similar modification can be used to permit selection of a single bit line. In this situation, four y control variables are required rather than two.

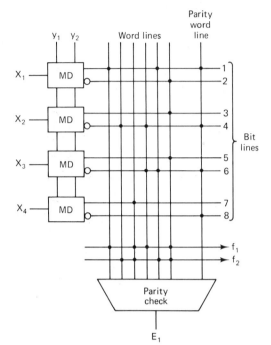

Figure 2.5.4 PLA of Figure 2.5.2b with AND array modifications.

test inputs since there are $2n$ bit lines. These $2n$ test inputs will be called the *A test set* (the AND array is being tested). The eight vectors of the A test set for the four-input example of Fig. 2.5.4 are shown in Table 2.5.2.

Testing of the OR array is done by selecting the word lines one at a time. This is made possible by an extra bit line, called the *word select line,* in the AND array. The word select line has crosspoints connected to each of the word lines. Together with the word select line, a shift register, SHR, is also added to the PLA. This shift register has one stage per word line and each stage output is connected to one of the word select line crosspoints. During normal operation an all-1 pattern is held in SHR. These modifications are shown in Fig. 2.5.5.

TABLE 2.5.2 TEST SET FOR THE PLA OF FIG. 2.5.4

Test set A						Bit lines							
X_1	X_2	X_3	X_4	y_1	y_2	1	2	3	4	5	6	7	8
0	1	1	1	0	1	0	1	1	1	1	1	1	1
1	0	0	0	1	0	1	0	1	1	1	1	1	1
1	0	1	1	0	1	1	1	0	1	1	1	1	1
1	1	0	0	1	0	1	1	1	0	1	1	1	1
1	1	0	1	0	1	1	1	1	1	0	1	1	1
1	0	1	0	1	0	1	1	1	1	1	0	1	1
1	1	1	0	0	1	1	1	1	1	1	1	0	1
0	0	0	1	1	0	1	1	1	1	1	1	1	0

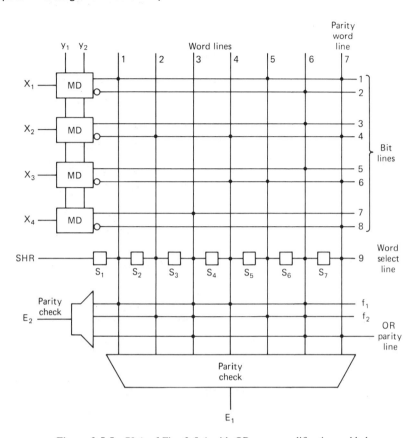

Figure 2.5.5 PLA of Fig. 2.5.4 with OR array modifications added.

Detection of faults in the OR array is based on the addition of an output line, the *OR parity line*, which has crosspoints to ensure that there is an odd total number of crosspoints on each word line in the OR array. Verification of this odd parity is done by means of a parity checker, the E_2 checker, which is connected to all the output lines.

Selection of a single word line is accomplished by shifting into SHR a pattern having 0s in all stages except that corresponding to the word selected, and setting 1s on all bit lines by placing appropriate signals on the X_i and y_j lines. These are shown in Table 2.5.3. Any single crosspoint fault in the OR array or stuck fault on a single (output) line in the OR array will be indicated by a change in the E_2 signal. Single stuck faults on the word lines are indicated by an incorrect E_1 signal. (A stuck-at-0 fault will be discovered when the faulty word line is selected. Single stuck-at-1 faults will be indicated by more than one word line having a 1 on it.) A single stuck-at-0 on a bit line will be detected at E_1 by the failure to select the word line having a crosspoint on the stuck bit line.

A summary of the fault detection in the FITPLA is given in Table 2.5.4. During the application of the A test set, an all-1 pattern should be present in SHR. In addition

TABLE 2.5.3 TEST SET B FOR THE PLA OF FIG. 2.5.4

X_1	X_2	X_3	X_4	y_1	y_2	S_1	S_2	S_3	S_4	S_5	S_6	S_7	Bit line 12345678	Word line 1234567	E_1	E_2
1	1	1	1	0	1	1	0	0	0	0	0	0	11111111	1000000	1	1
0	0	0	0	1	0	1	0	0	0	0	0	0	11111111	1000000	1	1
1	1	1	1	0	1	0	1	0	0	0	0	0	11111111	0100000	1	1
0	0	0	0	1	0	0	1	0	0	0	0	0	11111111	0100000	1	1
1	1	1	1	0	1	0	0	1	0	0	0	0	11111111	0010000	1	1
0	0	0	0	1	0	0	0	1	0	0	0	0	11111111	0010000	1	1
1	1	1	1	0	1	0	0	0	1	0	0	0	11111111	0001000	1	1
0	0	0	0	1	0	0	0	0	1	0	0	0	11111111	0001000	1	1
1	1	1	1	0	1	1	0	0	0	1	0	0	11111111	0000100	1	1
0	0	0	0	1	0	1	0	0	0	1	0	0	11111111	0000100	1	1
1	1	1	1	0	1	0	0	0	0	0	1	0	11111111	0000010	1	1
0	0	0	0	1	0	0	0	0	0	0	1	0	11111111	0000010	1	1
1	1	1	1	0	1	0	0	0	0	0	0	1	11111111	0000001	1	1
0	0	0	0	1	0	0	0	0	0	0	0	1	11111111	0000001	1	1

TABLE 2.5.4 FAULT DETECTION SUMMARY

Single stuck faults				Crosspoint faults		
Value	Location	Test set	Checker	Location	Test set	Checker
0	Bit line	B	E_1	AND array	A	E_1
1	Bit line	A	E_1	OR array	B	E_2
0, 1	Output line	B	E_2			
0, 1	Word line	B	E_1			
0	X_i, y_j input	B	E_1			
1	X_i, y_j input	A	E_1			
0	OR gate input	B	E_1			
1	OR gate input	A	E_1			

to testing for faults in the PLA proper, it is necessary to test the two parity-check circuits. This is discussed in [HONG80]. Subsequent research has resulted in techniques for designing the parity checkers so that they are self-checking [KHAK84, KHAK83a, KHAK82].

Extension of the FITPLA design so that multiple as well as single faults are detected is discussed in [SALU81].

A number of other techniques for designing PLAs have been presented. Some of them [KHAK83b, PRAD80, RAMA82], and [SON80] are aimed at designs that require test pattern generation but significantly reduce the amount of computation required. The Khakbaz technique requires the addition of a shift register and gets very high fault coverage. Very good fault coverage is also obtained by the Ramanatha technique by adding control inputs, observable outputs, and product lines. Self-testing

PLAs are the aim of the papers [DAEH81], [GRAS82], and [YAJI81]. The issues involved in self-testing designs are discussed in the next section.

2.6. BUILT-IN SELF-TEST (BIST)

Testing a circuit requires the application of an appropriate set of test vectors and the comparison of the actual circuit response with the correct response. The techniques presented in the preceding sections are aimed at facilitating the application of the test vectors (controllability) and the observation of the circuit response (observability). It is assumed that the test vectors will be applied to the circuit by a tester that is capable of storing the test patterns and the corresponding correct responses. Such testers are expensive.

Several techniques have been proposed for reducing the complexity of the external tester by moving some or all of the tester functions onto the chip itself. These techniques are presented in this section.

Tester cost is not the only difficulty encountered in using an external tester. As discussed in the introduction, there are also problems with

1. Generating the test patterns. The turnaround time to obtain the test patterns and the computation cost are becoming too large.
2. The number of test patterns becoming too large to be handled efficiently by the tester hardware.
3. The time taken to apply the test patterns.

The techniques of this section are intended to solve these problems as well as to reduce the tester cost.

The inclusion of on-chip circuitry to provide test vectors or to analyze output reponses is called *built-in self-test* (BIST), *built-in test (BIT), self-test, autonomous test,* or *self-verification*. There is some ambiguity in the use of these terms. In particular, *BIT* and *self-test* are sometimes used to mean implicit testing (concurrent checking) or system-level periodic testing [CLAR79]. The discussion in this chapter is restricted to explicit testing techniques.

Any test method must consist of (1) a strategy for generating the inputs to be applied, (2) a strategy for evaluating the output responses, and (3) the implementation mechanisms. Each of these topics will be considered in turn. The various options for strategies and implementations suitable for BIST will be presented.

2.6.1. Input Test Stimulus Generation

Test vectors can be generated (manually or by a test pattern generation program) and stored, called *off-line test pattern generation,* or they can be calculated while they are being applied, called *concurrent test pattern generation.* In theory it would be possible to generate test vectors off-line and store them in an on-chip ROM. This has not been an attractive scheme; it does nothing to reduce the cost of test pattern generation and it requires a very large ROM. All the BIST methods to be described here rely on concurrent test pattern generation.

A number of techniques have been proposed for concurrent test pattern generation. If the chip includes a processor and memory, it is possible to use a test program to generate appropriate signals to stimulate the circuitry.* It has been suggested that it is sufficient that this program be written to force state changes or "wiggle" the circuit nodes [GORD77]. More systematic approaches to writing test programs are described in [HAYE80]. The test programs usually rely on a *functional test approach:* they typically are written to exercise the functionality of the various system components. They can be based on the system diagnostic programs. Some reconfiguration of the circuit during test mode (to permit initialization and perhaps to break feedback loops) may be necessary to ensure good fault coverage [GORD77].

Two concurrent test pattern generation approaches which do not depend on the availability of an instruction processor have been proposed. Since these can be used with or without an instruction processor they are more general than the test program approach. One of these, *random testing,* uses a set of randomly generated patterns as test patterns. The other, *exhaustive testing,* uses all possible input combinations as test patterns. The random technique has the advantage of being applicable to sequential as well as combinational circuits; however, there are difficulties in determinimg the required test sequence length and fault coverage. Some circuits may require modification to obtain adequate coverage with reasonable test lengths, [EICH83b]. Exhaustive testing eliminates the need for a fault model and fault simulation. For large numbers of inputs this technique may require too much time. Some form of circuit partitioning is required to reduce the number of inputs in this case.

An important problem connected with concurrent random test pattern generation is the determination of the length of the random sequence that is required to obtain a satisfactory fault coverage. One straightforward technique uses fault simulation to determine fault coverage. The difficulty with simulation is its high cost. An analytical method of estimating fault coverage would be preferable. A number of approaches have been suggested [RAUL71, SHED77]. None of the techniques yet developed is capable of getting accurate fault coverage estimates without a great deal of computation.

Another approach is aimed at discovering those faults that are hard to detect with random patterns [SAVI83]. Two schemes for coping with these "random-pattern resistant" faults have been proposed. One would generate test patterns for these faults (using a deterministic technique such as the D-algorithm) and store these patterns in a ROM. Thus some few patterns would be obtained from the ROM and the remaining patterns would be randomly generated [SAVI83]. The other scheme modifies the network being tested so that none of its faults are random-pattern resistant [EICH83b, SAVI83].

---

*This test program may be stored in ROM. This should not be confused with the technique of storing the actual test patterns in ROM.

Random testing.   If an instruction processor is available, the random test patterns can be generated by a program. A thorough discussion of random number programs is given in [KNUT69]. For random test pattern generation it is not so important that the numbers used be strictly random since they are not being used for statistical purposes. A simple program for random test pattern generation is presented in [BRAC79].

Random test patterns can also be generated by means of a simple circuit called an *autonomous linear feedback shift register* (ALFSR). An autonomous linear feedback shift register is a series connection of delay elements (*D* flip-flops) with no external inputs and with all feedback provided by means of Exclusive-OR gates (XORs). A four-stage ALFSR is shown in Fig. 2.6.1a and the general standard form of ALFSR is shown in Fig. 2.6.1b. The symbol h_i in Fig. 2.6.1b indicates the possible presence of a feedback connection from the output of each stage. If $h_i = 1$, there is feedback from stage *i*; and if $h_i = 0$, the stage *i* output is not connected to the XOR

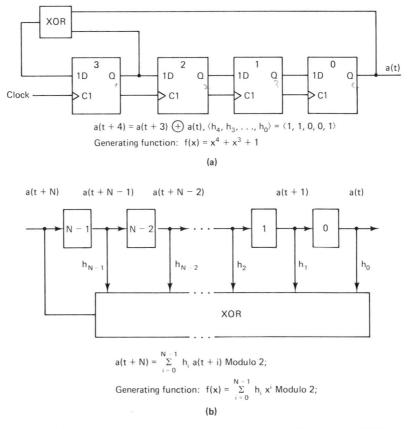

$a(t + 4) = a(t + 3) \oplus a(t), \langle h_4, h_3, \ldots, h_0\rangle = \langle 1, 1, 0, 0, 1\rangle$

Generating function: $f(x) = x^4 + x^3 + 1$

(a)

$$a(t + N) = \sum_{i=0}^{N-1} h_i \, a(t + i) \text{ Modulo 2};$$

Generating function: $f(x) = \sum_{i=0}^{N-1} h_i \, x^i \text{ Modulo 2};$

(b)

Figure 2.6.1   Standard form of autonomous linear feedback shift register, AFLSR: (a) four-stage circuit; (b) *N*-stage circuit.

feedback network. The ALFSR can be specified by just listing the values of the h_i or by specifying the generating function, as shown in Fig. 2.6.1.

Another possible realization of an ALFSR, called a *modular realization*, is shown in Fig. 2.6.2. There are as many XOR gates in the modular realization as there are feedback taps in the standard circuit. The gates are placed in the "reverse" positions from the locations of the feedback taps. If in the standard LFSR there are m "taps," inputs to the XOR network generating the feedback signal, $m - 1$ two-input XOR gates are required if an iterative structure is used to realize the XOR network. This is the minimum-gate realization. It is slower than a tree network which also requires $m - 1$ gates, but has a delay of log m gate propagations rather than $m - 1$ gate delays. The modular circuit also requires $m - 1$ XOR gates. It has a delay of only one gate propagation. For circuits with more than two feedback signals, faster operation always results with the modular rather than the standard LFSR.

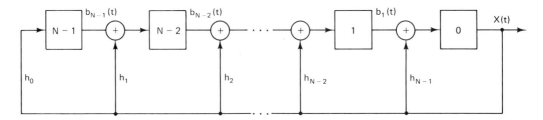

Figure 2.6.2   General modular realization of an ALFSR.

The sequence of states for the ALFSR of Fig. 2.6.1 is shown in Table 2.6.1. Note that the sequence repeats after 15 ($2^n - 1$) clocks. This is the maximum period for a four-stage ALFSR; The all-0 state of the register cannot occur in the maximum-length cycle since an all-0 state always has a next state that is also all 0s, due to the use of XORs to form the feedback signal. In general, the maximum period for an n-stage ALFSR is $2^n - 1$. There are maximum-length realizations for all values of n. The generating function corresponding to a maximum-length ALFSR is called a *primitive polynomial*. Tables of primitive polynomials can be found in [GOLU82], [PETE72], and many other publications.

TABLE 2.6.1   STATE SEQUENCE FOR FIG. 2.6.1A

State	Q_1	Q_2	Q_3	Q_4	State	Q_1	Q_2	Q_3	Q_4
0	1	0	0	0	8	1	1	0	1
1	1	1	0	0	9	0	1	1	0
2	1	1	1	0	10	0	0	1	1
3	1	1	1	1	11	1	0	0	1
4	0	1	1	1	12	0	1	0	0
5	1	0	1	1	13	0	0	1	0
6	0	1	0	1	14	0	0	0	1
7	1	0	1	0	15 = 0	1	0	0	0

Of course, the signals produced by an ALFSR are not really random since they are produced by a fixed circuit. Truly random signals are not required for test pattern generation. What is necessary is signals that produce the same types of test patterns as random signals. The output of an ALFSR can be shown to possess many of the properties of random signals. The sequences produced by maximum-length ALFSRs are called *pseudorandom* (pr) *sequences* or *pseudo-noise sequences* to distinguish them from truly random sequences. For test pattern generation pseudorandom sequences are better than random sequences since the pr-sequences can be reproduced for simulation. One period of the output sequence produced by the ALFSR of Fig. 2.6.1a is

$$(0\ 0\ 0\ 1\ 1\ 1\ 1\ 0\ 1\ 0\ 1\ 1\ 0\ 0\ 1)$$

The five-stage ALFSR with feedback connections given by $H = <5, 2, 0>$ has the following output sequence:

$$(111110001101110101000 0100101100)$$

There are three properties of pr-sequences that are used to demonstrate their randomness characteristics:

Property 1: A pr-sequence has 2^{n-1} 1s and $(2^{n-1} - 1)$ 0s.

Property 2: There is one run of n (consecutive) 1s and one run of $n - 1$ 0s. For $n - 1 > r > 0$, there are $2 \exp [n - (r + 2)]$ runs of length r for 1s and the same number of runs of 0s. Thus for the $<5, 2, 0>$ sequence given above there are one run of 5 1s, one run of 4 0s, one run each of 3 0s or 1s, two runs of 2 0s or 2 1s, and four single 1s or 0s.

Property 3: This is the autocorrelation property that measures the similarity between a pr-sequence and a shifted version of the same sequence. Any pair of such sequences will be identical in $2^{n-1} - 1$ positions and will differ in 2^{n-1} positions. For the Fig. 2.6.1a sequence there are seven matches and eight mismatches between pairs of shifted sequences:

$$(0\ 0\ 0\ 1\ 1\ 1\ 1\ 0\ 1\ 0\ 1\ 1\ 0\ 0\ 1)0$$

$$(0\ 0\ 0\ 1\ 1\ 1\ 1\ 0\ 1\ 0\ 1\ 1\ 0\ 0\ 1)$$

The randomness characteristics of pr-sequences are discussed and proved in [GOLO82].

For each $n > 4$ there are a number of different LFSRs that all produce maximal-length sequences. The maximal-length LFSR sequences occur in pairs. With each sequence is associated another sequence, called the *reverse sequence*, which consists of the symbols of the original sequence in reverse order. Thus the $<5, 2, 0>$ LFSR has the following sequence:

$$(111110001101110101000 0100101100)$$

and the reverse sequence

(00110100100001010111011100011111)

is produced by the $<5, 3, 0>$ LFSR. The specification for the LFSR corresponding to the reverse sequence is obtained by replacing each entry i in the original specification by $n - i$. There is only one pr-sequence that is self-reverse, the sequence for $n = 2$. Since the characteristics of the reverse sequence are easily determined from the original sequence, it is only necessary to study half of the total number of pr-sequences in detail. Two pr-sequences will be said to be distinct if neither is the reverse of the other. The number of distinct pr-sequences (LFSRs) for n from 2 to 32 is given in Table 2.6.2. It is clear that there are lots of choices of ALFSRs for n larger than 10. The best choice for any given application is not always clear and often the design requiring the simplest feedback circuitry is chosen. There is some evidence that when the number of circuit inputs is larger than the size of the ALFSR, better fault coverage is obtained by an ALFSR with more than the minimum number of feedback taps.

TABLE 2.6.2 $N(n)$ = NUMBER OF DISTINCT PR-SEQUENCES FOR n-STAGES LFSRs

n	$N(n)$	n	$N(n)$
2	1	18	3,888
3	1	19	13,797
4	1	20	12,000
5	3	21	42,336
6	3	22	60,016
7	9	23	178,480
8	8	24	138,240
9	24	25	648,000
10	30	26	859,950
11	88	27	2,101,248
12	72	28	2,370,816
13	315	29	9,203,904
14	378	30	8,910,000
15	900	31	34,636,833
16	1,024	32	33,554,432
17	3,855		

Exhaustive and pseudo-exhaustive testing. The application of all 2^n input combinations to the (combinational) circuit being tested will be called *exhaustive testing*. Any binary counter can be used to develop these signals. Since the order of generation of the combinations is not important, it may be more efficient to use an ALFSR modified so that it cycles through all states. To do this it is necessary to modify the ALFSR so that the all-0 state is included in the state sequence [DEVI71, MCCL81].

The result of modifying the four-stage ALFSR of Fig. 2.6.1a in this fashion is shown in Fig. 2.6.3a. A term equal to $Q_1' Q_2' Q_3'$ is added to the XOR gate inputs to inhibit the introduction of a 1 into the low-order stage for the state 0001. This causes the next state to become 0000 and the following state to be 1000. The general form

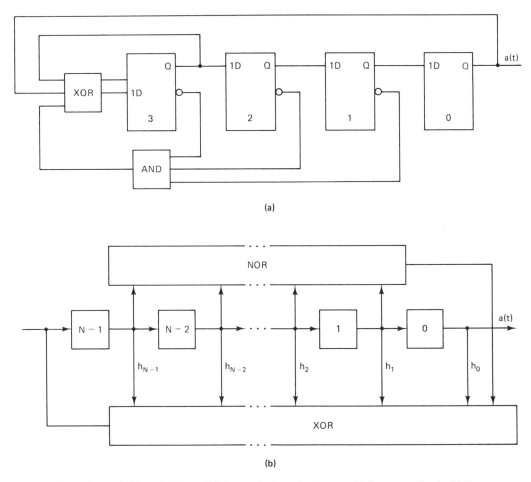

Figure 2.6.3 ALFSR modified to cycle through all states: (a) four-stage circuit; (b) *N*-stage circuit.

of full-cycle ALFSR is shown in Fig. 2.6.3b. By algebraic simplification it is possible to reduce the required circuitry. The simplified version of the circuit of Fig. 2.6.3a is shown in Fig. 2.6.4.

Exhaustive testing provides a thorough test but can require a prohibitively long test time for networks with many (20 or more) inputs. It is possible to reduce the test time to a practical value while retaining many of the advantages of exhaustive testing with the techniques to be described next. These *pseudo-exhaustive* techniques apply all possible inputs to portions of the circuit under test rather than to the entire circuit. The first technique is applicable to multioutput circuits in which none of the outputs depends on all the inputs. It is called *verification testing* [MCCL82a, MCCL82b].

Most combinational networks have more than one output. In many cases each of the outputs depends on only a subset of the inputs. For example, the parity generator

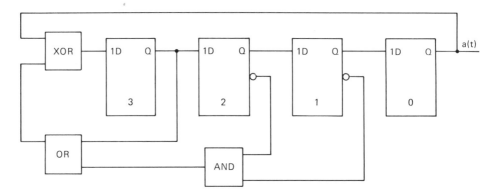

Figure 2.6.4   Simplified form of circuit in Fig. 2.6.3a.

network of the TI SN54/74LS630 (shown in Fig. 2.6.5) has 23 inputs and six output functions, but each output depends on only 10 of the inputs. It may not be practical to exhaustively test the outputs by applying all combinations of the network inputs (2^{23} for the example). However, it may be possible to exhaustively test each output by applying all combinations of only those inputs on which the output depends. For the SN74LS630, each output can be exhaustively tested with $2^{10} = 1024$ input patterns and all six outputs tested one after another with $(6)(1024) = 6144$ patterns. In fact, for this circuit it is possible by an appropriate choice of input patterns to apply all possible input combinations to each output concurrently rather than serially. Thus, with only 1024 rather than $(6)(1024)$ test patterns, each output can be tested exhaustively by using the verification testing techniques described in [MCCL82a] and [BARZ81].

The SN74LS630 is an example of a circuit for which it is possible to test all outputs concurrently by applying (to the entire circuit) only as many patterns as are necessary to exhaustively test one of the outputs. Two inputs that never appear in the same output function can have the same test signal applied to both. This fact can be used to reduce the number of required test signals. If the number of required test signals is equal to the maximum number of inputs upon which any output depends, the circuit is called a *maximal test concurrency* (MTC) *circuit*.

An example of a very simple MTC circuit with three inputs and two outputs is shown in Fig. 2.6.6. The f output depends only on inputs w and x, while the g output depends on x and y. It is possible to apply the same test signal to both w and y since no output depends on both of these inputs. The four input patterns shown in the figure are such that all possible combinations of values are applied to w and x, and also all combinations of x and y are present. Thus outputs f and g are both tested exhaustively by only four input patterns rather than the eight patterns required for a full exhaustive test.

Figure 2.6.7 shows a very simple example of a non-MTC circuit. There are three inputs and each possible pair occurs in some output function. Thus no two inputs can have the same test signal applied to both. Three test signals are required; however, it is possible to test each of the output functions exhaustively with only four test patterns.

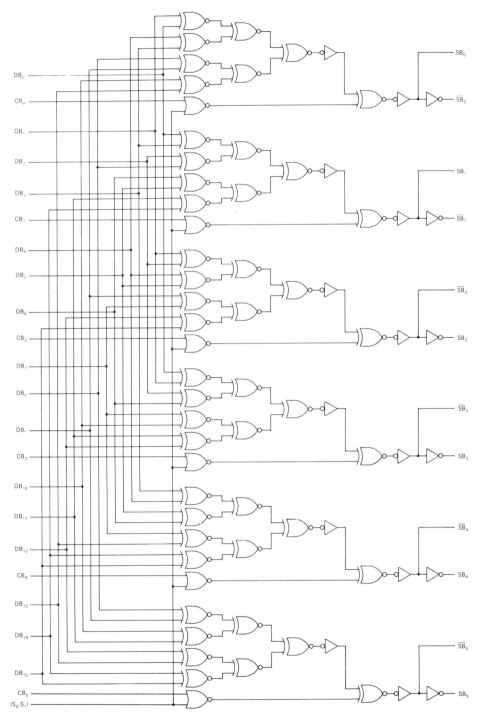

Figure 2.6.5 Parity generator network of the TI SN54/74LS630.

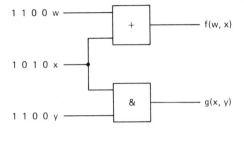

Figure 2.6.6 Simple example of an MTC circuit with verification test inputs.

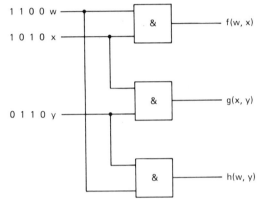

Figure 2.6.7 Simple example of a three-input, three-output non-MTC circuit with verification test inputs.

All outputs are tested concurrently with the same number of test patterns that are necessary to test one of the outputs. This is an example of the general situation of an n-input circuit in which each output depends on at most $n - 1$ inputs. Such circuits can always have all outputs tested concurrently with at most 2^{n-1} test patterns. The appropriate patterns are all n-bit vectors having the same parity (either all even parity as in Fig. 2.6.7, or all odd parity).

A simple example of a non-MTC circuit for which it is not possible to verify (test concurrently) all outputs with the same number of patterns required for testing a single output is shown in Fig. 2.6.8. In this circuit each of the six outputs depends on two of the four inputs. All six outputs are verified with the five input patterns shown on the figure. To test the circuit exhaustively would require 16 patterns. Testing exhaustively each of the output functions in succession takes $(4)(6) = 24$ patterns. It is possible to test pairs of outputs such as $f1$ and $f6$ at the same time since they depend on disjoint sets of inputs. This strategy requires three tests of four patterns each or 12 total patterns. The numbers of inputs and outputs used in this example are too small to be significant. However, it does serve to illustrate the percentage reduction in test length obtainable with verification test techniques.

It has been shown in [MCCL82b] that any network for which no output depends on all inputs can be tested pseudo-exhaustively with fewer than 2^n test patterns. This paper also derives a specification for test sets that consist of constant-weight vectors. These test sets are suitable for concurrent test pattern generation since they are simply

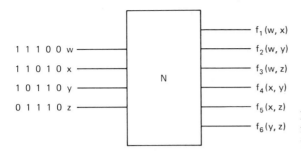

Figure 2.6.8 Simple example of a four-input, six-output non-MTC circuit with verification test inputs.

generated by constant-weight counters. The constant-weight test set is shown to be a minimum-length test set for many networks. Even for those networks for which the constant-weight type of test set is not minimum length, it may be advisable to use this test set because of its ease of generation.

It is still possible that a verification test set, even though smaller than 2^n, is too long. Also, there are many circuits with an output that depends on all inputs. Such circuits require 2^n inputs for an exhaustive test and this may be too large a set. In other words, there are circuits for which the verification test approach does not result in a satisfactory test procedure. A pseudo-exhaustive test is still possible for such circuits, but it is necessary to resort to a partitioning or segmentation technique. Such a procedure is described in [MCCL81]. The technique presented in this paper relies on exhaustive testing, but divides the circuit into segments or partitions to avoid excessively long input test sequences. It differs from previous attempts along these lines in that the partitions may divide the signal path through the circuit rather than just separating the signal paths from one another. Although it is possible to use multiplexers to enforce the segmentation, they are not necessary. A partitioning method that does not alter the functional circuitry is described in [MCCL81].

To exhaustively test each subcircuit, all subcircuit inputs must be controllable at the input of the circuit and all subcircuit outputs must be observable at the circuit outputs. This can be achieved in two ways: (1) hardware partitioning and (2) sensitized partitioning.

Access to the embedded inputs and outputs of the subcircuit under test can be achieved by inserting multiplexers and connecting the embedded inputs and outputs of each subcircuit to those primary inputs and outputs that are not used by the subcircuit under test [BOZO80]. By controlling the multiplexers, all the inputs and outputs of each subcircuit can be accessed using primary input and output lines.

Multiplexers can reduce the operating speed of the circuit and are costly to implement. However, it is possible to achieve the same testing discipline without actually inserting any multiplexers at all. Thus the previous discussion should be regarded as an introduction to the technique, to be described next, which is the actual suggested implementation.

Circuit partitioning and subcircuit isolation can be achieved by applying the appropriate input pattern to some of the input lines. The effect achieved is similar to that of hardware partitioning: paths from the primary inputs to the subcircuit inputs and paths from the subcircuit output to the primary output can be sensitized. Using these paths each subcircuit can be tested exhaustively.

2.6.2. Output Response Analysis

Storage of a fault dictionary (all test inputs with the correct output responses) [BREU76] on chip requires too much memory to be a practical technique. The simplest practical method for analyzing the output response is to match the outputs of two identical circuits. Identical circuits may be available either because the function being designed naturally leads to replicated subfunctions [SRID79] or because the functional circuitry is duplicated redundantly for concurrent checking [SEDM79]. If identical outputs are not available it is necessary to resort to some technique for compacting the response pattern. Techniques for reducing the volume of output data were originally developed in connection with portable testers. Their use is usually called *compact testing* [LOSQ78], but this technique is sometimes also called *response compression*. In compact testing, the output response pattern is passed through a circuit, called a *compacter*, that has fewer output bits than input bits. The output of the compacter is called the *signature* of the test response. The aim is to reduce the number of bits that must be examined to determine whether the circuit under test is faulty.

Many portable testers use transition counting as a compaction technique. This involves counting the number of transitions (0 following a 1 or 1 following a 0) in the response sequence [HAYE76]. Transition counting has not received serious consideration for BIST since recent research has developed better methods.

The choice of a compaction technique is influenced mainly by two factors: (1) the amount of circuitry required to implement the technique, and (2) the loss of "effective fault coverage." In general a fault will go undetected if none of the input test patterns produces an incorrect circuit output in the presence of the fault. With output response compaction it is also possible for a fault to fail to be detected even though the output response differs from the fault-free response. This will happen whenever the output response from a faulty circuit produces a signature that is identical to the signature of a fault-free circuit. This phenomenon is called *aliasing*.

Definition. A faulty circuit test output response signature that is identical to the fault-free signature is called an *alias*.

Many compaction schemes have been studied. A list of relevant papers is included in the Bibliography. These techniques can be grouped into three classes:

1. Parity techniques
2. Counting techniques
3. Linear feedback shift register (LFSR) techniques

A comparison of parity techniques, LFSR techniques, and combined parity and LFSR techniques is given in [BENO75] for pseudorandom test patterns. No advantages were discovered for the use of parity techniques. The use of parity techniques in connection with exhaustive testing is discussed in [CART82a] and [CART82b]. High values for stuck fault detection are demonstrated.

The only counting technique that has been seriously considered for BIST is called *syndrome analysis* [SAVI80]. This technique is applicable only to exhaustive testing and requires counting the number of 1s in the output response stream. It has been shown that it is possible to detect any single stuck fault in the circuit using this method, although some circuit modification may be required [SAVI81]. A generalization of syndrome testing that uses Walsh coefficients has been studied [SUSS81] but has yet to have its practicality demonstrated.

All the actual implementations of BIST using compaction rely on LFSR techniques; thus these will be described in more detail.

The compaction techniques all require that the fault-free signature for the circuit be known. This can be found by (fault-free) simulation of the design or by measurement on an actual circuit that has been verified to be fault-free by some other method.

Signature analysis.   The most popular BIST compaction circuit is an LFSR with its input equal to the output response of the circuit under test. This circuit was called a *cyclic code checker* when it was first proposed in [BENO75]. Figure 2.6.9 shows a cyclic code checker based on the circuit of Fig. 2.6.1a.

This method of output response compaction is most often called *signature analysis,* a term coined by Hewlett-Packard to describe its use in their product, the 5004A Signature Analyzer [CHAN77]. The term "signature" was coined by them to describe the LFSR contents after shifting in the response pattern of the circuit being tested.

The usefulness of signature analysis depends on the fact that the final values of the LFSR flip-flops, the signature, depends on the bit pattern that is applied at the input. If a fault causes the output bit sequence to change, this will usually result in a

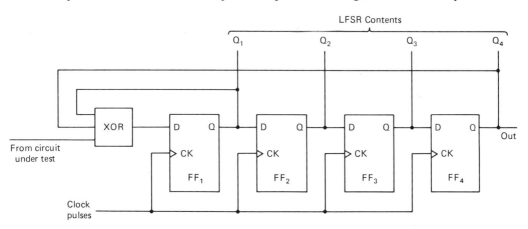

Figure 2.6.9   A four-stage linear feedback shift register used as a serial signature analyzer.

different signature in the LFSR. However, aliasing can occur. It is possible for a fault to cause an output bit sequence that produces the same final LFSR contents as the fault-free circuit. In this case the fault will be undetected. The output sequences that have this property depend on the structure of the LFSR used. They are characterized in [BENO75] in terms of division of the Galois field polynomial representation of the LFSR and the output response sequences.

Table 2.6.3 illustrates the alias phenomenon for the LFSR of Fig. 2.6.9. Both the faulty and the fault-free sequences shown in the table will leave the same signature—1001—in the LFSR. The error sequence is determined as the (bitwise) sum modulo 2 of the faulty and fault-free sequences. It can be shown that aliasing will occur whenever the error sequence is equal to the LFSR feedback vector $<H>$ or to the sum (bitwise modulo 2) of shifted versions of $<H>$.

TABLE 2.6.3 ALIASING WAVEFORMS FOR LFSR OF FIG. 2.6.9

Time:	0	1	2	3	4	5	6	7
Fault-free output sequence:	0	1	1	0	1	0	0	1
Faulty output sequence:	0	0	0	0	0	0	0	1
Error sequence:	0	1	1	0	1	0	0	0
$\langle H \rangle = \langle 1$		1	0	0	1$\rangle$			
Other alias error sequences								
		1	1	0	1	0	0	0	0
		1	1	0	1	1	1	0	1
		1	0	1	1	1	0	0	0
		1	0	0	0	0	0	0	1

Any compaction technique can cause some loss of effective fault coverage due to aliasing. Experience with the HP product and simulation studies of BIST designs [PERK80] have not discovered any signature analysis applications for which aliasing is a problem. However, it has not been possible to derive any general properties of the effective fault coverage obtained by signature analysis. As discussed in connection with Table 2.6.3, it is possible to characterize the alias error sequences; but no simple relationship between the circuit faults and the resulting errors has yet been found. The problem of determining effective coverage loss for LFSR compaction is discussed in [SMIT80].

Two methods are suggested in [BENO75] for signature analysis for a multi-output circuit under test. One of them, the *serial signature analyzer,* uses a multiplexer to direct each of the outputs to the LFSR in turn. A circuit for this is shown in Fig. 2.6.10a. With this scheme the input test patterns would have to be applied to the network *m* times for an *m*-network.

The other technique, the *parallel signature analyzer,* compacts *K* network outputs in parallel using a *K*-bit parallel code checker (Fig. 2.6.10b). The parallel technique requires each test pattern to be applied only *m/K* times. In the parallel technique, network outputs are connected to the LFSR through XOR gates added to

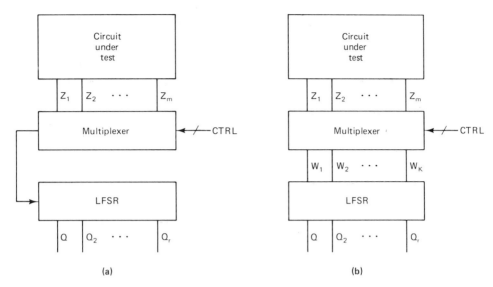

Figure 2.6.10 Connection of multioutputs to LFSR signature analyzer: (a) serial signature analysis using a multiplexer; (b) parallel signature analysis.

the shift lines between stages as well as connecting a network output to the first LFSR stage. The design of a four-stage parallel signature analyzer is detailed in Fig. 2.6.11.

In general, the parallel signature analyzer is faster but requires more added circuitry than the serial signature analyzer [BENO75]. A detailed comparison of these two techniques in a particular system is presented in [BENO76]. Fault coverage data, derived by hardware fault insertion, are also reported. Another study of fault coverage for a parallel signature analyzer is reported in [KONE80]. Physical fault insertion was carried out on an experimental microprocessor with an 8-bit parallel signature analyzer. In this paper, the term "multiple-input signature register" is used. The serial signature analyzer is not discussed.

Besides requiring more hardware than the serial analyzer, the parallel signature analyzer has an additional alias source. An error in output Z_j at time t_i followed by an error in output Z_{j+1} at time t_{i+1} will have no effect on the signature. More generally, an error in output Z_j at time t_i followed by an error in output Z_{j+h} at time t_{i+h} will have no effect on the signature [HASS82, SRID82, HASS83].

2.6.3. Circuit Structures for BIST

Several schemes for incorporating BIST techniques into a design have been proposed. They fall naturally into four classes: those that assume no special structure to the circuit under test, those that make use of scan paths in the circuit under test, those that reconfigure the scan paths for test application and analysis, and those that use the concurrent checking (implicit test) circuitry of the design.

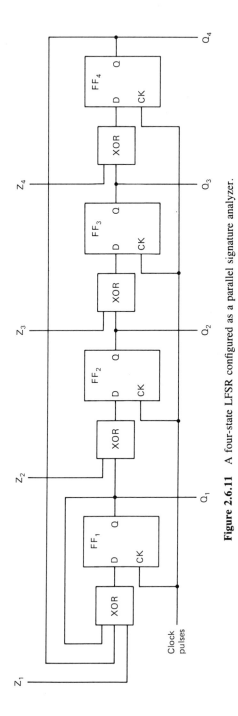

Figure 2.6.11 A four-state LFSR configured as a parallel signature analyzer.

BIST structure for circuits without scan paths.   Figure 2.6.12 shows the method described in [BENO75]. Two LFSRs and two multiplexers are added to the circuit. One multiplexer (MUX 1) selects the inputs to the circuit—normal inputs for regular operation and the LFSR pseudorandom pattern output for testing. The other multiplexer (MUX 2) routes the circuit outputs in turn to the serial signature analyzer during test. This serial signature analyzer has circuitry to match the final signature with the known correct signature. It provides a failure indication if a different pattern results after the test phase. The only assumptions made about the circuit under test are that it not contain memory. Sequential as well as combinational logic circuits can be present in the circuit under test.

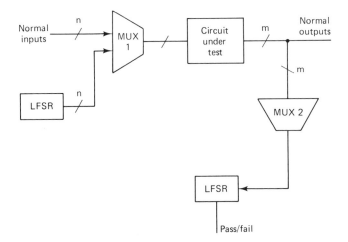

Figure 2.6.12   Circuit with LFSRs added to generate random test patterns and to compute output signature.

A similar structure is described in [PERK80]. This structure makes use of a tester circuit that is external to the chip but could be located on the same board. Pseudorandom patterns are applied in parallel to the chip inputs and a parallel signature analyzer receives both the chip outputs as well as the test inputs. A special feature of this design is its ability to be configured by means of a tester circuit register to apply input signals to the appropriate chip input pins. Testing of RAM and ROM chips is discussed. The most novel feature of the structure of [PERK80] is the inclusion of a source resistance detector at each logic input and an output current detector at each logic output. The main purpose of these detectors is to watch over the integrity of the interconnection system.

BIST structure for circuits with scan paths.   For designs that incorporate a scan path, it is possible to make use of this feature for the BIST circuitry. A structure that does this was proposed in [EICH83b] and is shown in Fig. 2.6.13. In addition to the internal LSSD scan latches, a scan path must be connected to the primary inputs and outputs (similar to that shown in Fig. 2.4.13). This is called the *boundary scan path*. Its scan input is connected to the scan-out point of the internal scan path.

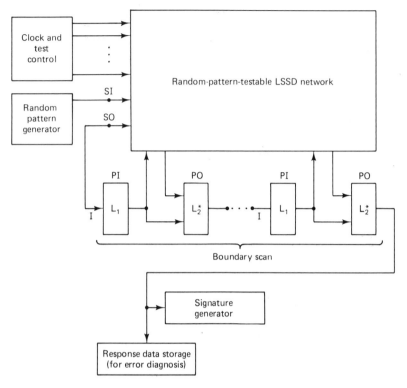

Figure 2.6.13 BIST structure using scan paths.

Pseudorandom test patterns are generated in a pattern generator circuit and are scanned into the combined scan path. The system clocks are pulsed and the scan-path latches are scanned out into the serial signature analyzer circuit. The resulting signature is then compared in the analyzer with a precalculated fault-free signature in order to generate a failure signal. The scan-out point is also connected to a pin so that, in case of a failure, intermediate signatures can be examined externally for diagnostic purposes.

A similar design for a multichip module is presented in [BARD82]. This design, shown in Fig. 2.6.14, uses a special test chip added to the module. The test chip contains a shift register pattern generator and a parallel signature analyzer. The scan paths on each chip are loaded in parallel from the pattern generator. The system clocks are then pulsed and the test results are scanned out to the parallel signature analyzer. New test patterns can be scanned in at the same time that the test results are being scanned out.

BIST structure using register or scan-path reconfiguration.   A concern with BIST designs is the amount of extra circuitry required. One technique for reducing the extra circuitry is to make use of the flip-flops or latches already in the design for test generation and analysis. The system registers are redesigned so that they can function as pattern generators or signature analyzers for test purposes.

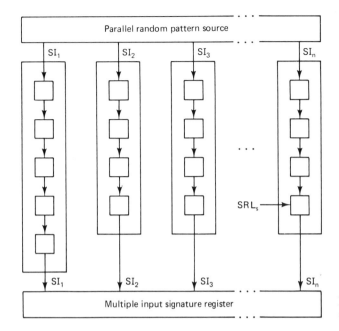

Parallel random pattern source

SI$_1$ SI$_2$ SI$_3$ SI$_n$

SRL$_s$

SI$_1$ SI$_2$ SI$_3$ SI$_n$

Multiple input signature register

Figure 2.6.14 Multichip module BIST structure using chip scan paths.

The structure described in [KONE79] and [KONE80] applies to circuits that can be partitioned into independent modules. Each module is assumed to have its own input and output registers, or such registers are added to the circuit where necessary. No precise definition of a module is given, nor is the problem of identifying modules discussed. It is assumed that the circuit modularity is evident. The registers are redesigned so that for testing purposes they can act as either shift registers or parallel signature analyzers. The redesigned register is called a BILBO (built-in logic block observer).

The details of the BILBO design for a four-stage register are shown in Fig. 2.6.15. When both control inputs B_1 and B_2 are equal to 1, the circuit functions as a parallel read-in register with the inputs Z_i gated directly into the flip-flops. When both control inputs are equal to 0, the register is reconfigured into a serial read-in shift register. Test data can be scanned-in via the serial input port or scanned-out via the serial output port. Setting $B_1 = 1$ and $B_2 = 0$ converts the register into a parallel signature analyzer. It can be used in this configuration as a test vector generator by holding the Z_i inputs fixed. The register is reset when $B_1 = 0$ and $B_2 = 1$.

It is possible to design reconfigurable registers using the multiport flip-flops discussed in Section 2.4.3. Designs using this technique are discussed in [MCCL81] in connection with pseudo-exhaustive testing. The circuit that results from using this approach to convert the LFSR of Fig. 2.6.3a to a reconfigurable circuit is shown in Fig. 2.6.16. In this design the circuit functions as a parallel read-in and read-out register under control of the system clock input, SCK. When a clock pulse is applied to SCK it is routed to the CK_1 terminals of the flip-flops, causing the Z_i data to be entered into the flip-flops via the D_1 inputs. For testing use, the test clock, TCK, is

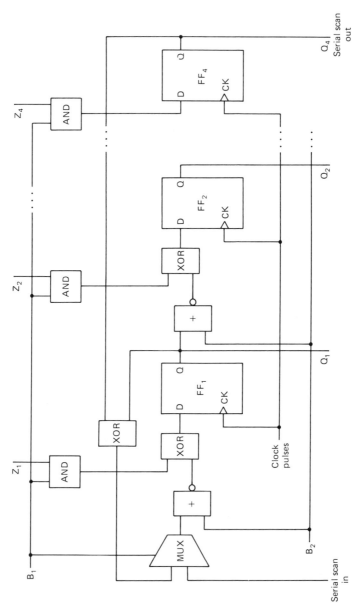

Figure 2.6.15 Four-stage BILBO. The details of stages 3 and 4 are omitted.

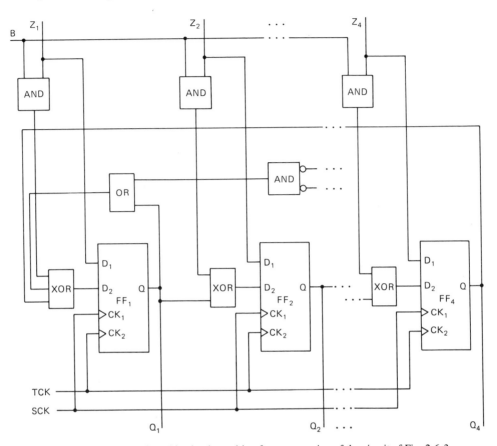

Figure 2.6.16 Reconfigurable circuit resulting from conversion of the circuit of Fig. 2.6.3a.

pulsed. If control input B is held at 1, the register functions as a parallel signature analyzer. If $B = 0$, the register functions as a counter to generate the input test vectors. The B control input has been added to avoid the necessity of holding the Z_i inputs fixed when using the register to generate test vectors (as is required in the BILBO design of Fig. 2.6.15). If this feature is not desired, the B input and all the AND gates to which it is connected can be removed and replaced with a straight-through connection of the Z_i. Serial shifting is not accommodated with this design, although the modification to add it is simple.

In [MCCL81], the use of this type of reconfigurable register is described in connection with exhaustive testing of subcircuits having few enough inputs to make the application of all input patterns economical. Circuit partitioning and subcircuit isolation can be achieved by applying the appropriate input pattern to some of the input lines. The effect achieved is similar to that of hardware partitioning using multi-plexers: paths from the primary inputs or register outputs to the subcircuit inputs and paths from the subcircuit output to the primary output or register inputs can be sensitized. This technique is called *sensitized partitioning*.

The two techniques just described are most suitable for circuits that can be partitioned so that the input and output registers of the resulting modules can be reconfigured separately. They can be used for scan-path designs, but the existence of scan paths is not a requirement. There are other reconfiguration techniques that are suitable for scan-path designs.

A very good technique is that used by Storage Technology Corporation (STC) as described in [KOMO82] and [KOMO83]. The basic design of the STC circuits incorporates both an internal LSSD scan path and an external scan path for the I/O pads as described in connection with Fig. 2.4.13. The BIST modification provides for the reconfiguration of the input scan path latches into an ALSFR for use as a pseudo-random pattern generator and the reconfiguration of the output scan path latches into a signature analyzer. A test pattern is generated in the ALFSR, scanned into the internal latches, the system clock is pulsed, and the resulting latch contents are scanned out to the signature analyzer. The details of the design are presented in the two references cited. Other BIST designs using LFSRs for test vector generation and signature analysis are described in [EIKI80], [HECK81], and [FASA80].

BIST structure using concurrent checking circuits.   For systems that include concurrent checking circuits, it is possible to use this circuitry to verify the

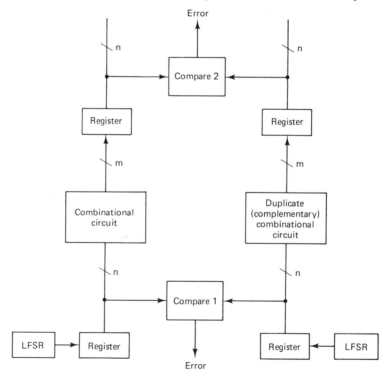

Figure 2.6.17   BIST using concurrent checking compare circuits for output response analysis.

response during explicit (off-line) testing. Thus the necessity of implementing a separate response analysis circuit such as a signature analyzer is avoided. This approach to BIST is described in [SEDM79] and [SEDM80]. Since the checking circuitry recommended in this paper involves duplication of the functional circuitry and comparison of the outputs of the two implementations, this technique avoids the alias problem and consequent loss of effective fault coverage of a signature analyzer. Figure 2.6.17 shows a suggested BIST implementation using this scheme. (The duplicate circuitry is actually realized in complementary form to reduce design and common mode faults.) The test patterns are shifted serially into the input registers from the ISG (input stimulus generator) circuits which are added for test pattern generation. The ISG cycles through all input patterns thus generating exhaustive test patterns. The contents of the two input registers are checked by the compare 1 circuit. The output response of the combinational circuitry is checked by the compare 2 circuit. Another design that uses the concurrent check circuits for BIST is described in [LU83].

REFERENCES

[AGRA82] Agrawal, V. D., and M. R. Mercer, "Testability Measures—What Do They Tell Us?" *Dig., 1982 IEEE Test Conf., Cherry Hill '82*, Philadelphia, Paper 13.3, pp. 391–396, 1982.

[ANDO80] Ando, H. "Testing VLSI with Random Access Scan," *Dig., COMPCON Spring 80*, San Francisco, pp. 50–52, Feb. 25–28, 1980.

[BARD81] Bardell, P. H., and W. H. McAnney, "A View from the Trenches: Production Testing of a Family of VLSI Multichip Modules," *Dig., 11th Annu. Int. Symp. Fault-Tolerant Comput.*, Portland, Me., pp. 281–283, June 24–26, 1981.

[BARD82] Bardell, P. H., and W. H. McAnney, "Self-Testing of Multichip Logic Modules," *Dig., 1982 IEEE Test Conf.*, Philadelphia, pp. 200–204, Nov. 15–18, 1982. (Reprinted in *Test Meas. World*, pp. 26–29, Mar. 1983.)

[BARZ81] Barzilai, Z., et al., "The Weighted Syndrome Sums Approach to VSLI Testing," *IEEE Trans. Comput.*, pp. 996–1000, Dec. 1981.

[BENN80] Bennetts, R. G., G. D. Robinson, and C. M. Maunder, "Computer-Aided Measure for Logic Testability: The CAMELOT Program," *Proc. IEEE Int. Conf. Circuits Comput.*, Port Chester, N.Y., pp. 1162–1165, Oct. 1980.

[BENN81] Bennetts, R. G., C. M. Maunder, and G. D. Robinson, "CAMELOT: A Computer-Aided Measure for Logic Testability," *IEE Proc. Comput.*, Sept. 1981.

[BENO75] Benowitz, N., D. F. Calhoun, G. E. Alderson, J. E. Bauer, and C. T. Joeckel, "An Advanced Fault Isolation System for Digital Logic," *IEEE Trans. Comput.*, vol. C-24, no. 5, pp. 489–497, May 1975.

[BENO76] Benowitz, N., D. F. Calhoun, and G. W. K. Lee, "Fault Detection/Isolation Results from AAFIS Hardware Built-In Test," *NAECON '76 Rec.*, pp. 215–222, 1976.

[BOTT77] Bottorf, P. S., R. E. France, N. H. Garges, and E. J. Orosz, "Test Generation for Large Logic Networks," *Dig., 14th Des. Autom. Conf.*, New Orleans, pp. 479–485, June 20–22, 1977.

[BOZO80] Bozorgui-Nesbat, S., and E. J. McCluskey, "Structured Design for Testability to Eliminate Test Pattern Generation," *Dig., 10th Annu. Int. Symp. Fault-Tolerant Comput.*, Kyoto, Japan, pp. 158–163, Oct. 1–3, 1980.

[BRAC79] Brack, J. W., "Random Numbers with Software," *Mach. Des.*, pp. 76–77, Feb. 8, 1979.

[BREU76] Breuer, M. A., and A. Friedman, "Design to Simplify Testing," in *Diagnosis and Reliability of Digital Systems,* Computer Science Press, Woodland Hills, Calif., pp. 291–303, 1976.

[CART64] Carter, W. C., H. C. Montgomery, R. J. Preiss, and H. J. Reinheimer, "Design of Serviceability Features for the IBM System/360," *IBM J.*, pp. 115–126, Apr. 1964.

[CART82a] Carter W. C., "The Ubiquitous Parity Bit," *Dig., 12th Annu. Int. Symp. Fault Tolerant Comput.*, Santa Monica, Calif., pp. 289–296, June 22–24, 1982.

[CART82b] Carter W. C., "Signature Testing with Guaranteed Bounds for Fault Coverage," *Dig., 1982 IEEE Test Conf., Cherry Hill '82,* Philadelphia, pp. 75–82, Nov. 11–13, 1982.

[CHAN77] Chan, A. Y., "Easy-to-Use Signature Analyzer Accurately Troubleshoots Complex Logic Circuits," *Hewlett-Packard J.*, pp. 9–14, May 1977.

[CLAR79] Clary, J. B., and R. A. Sacane, "Self-Testing Computers," *Computer,* vol. 12, no. 10, pp. 49–59, Oct. 1979.

[DAEH81] Daehn, W., and J. Mucha, "A Hardware Approach to Self-Testing of Large Programmable Logic Arrays," *IEEE Trans. Comput.*, vol. C-30, no. 11, pp. 829–833, Nov. 1981.

[DASG78] Das Gupta, S., E. B. Eichelberger, and T. W. Williams, "LSI Chip Design for Testability," *Dig., 1978 IEEE Int. Solid-State Circuits Conf.,* San Francisco, Sess. XVI, pp. 216–217, Feb. 15–17, 1978.

[DASG80] Das Gupta, S., C. R. P. Hartmann, and L. D. Rudolph, "Dual-Mode Logic for Function-Independent Fault Testing," *IEEE Trans. Comput.*, vol. C-29, no. 11, pp. 1025–1029, Nov., 1980.

[DASG81] Das Gupta, S., R. G. Walther, and T. W. Williams, "An Enhancement to LSSD and Some Applications of LSSD in Reliability, Availability, and Serviceability," *Dig., 11th Annu. Int. Symp. Fault-Tolerant Comput.*, Portland, Me., pp. 32–34, June 24–26, 1981.

[DEVI71] deVisme, G. H., *Binary Sequences,* English Universities Press, London, 1971.

[EICH77] Eichelberger, E. B., and T. W. Williams, "A Logic Design Structure for LSI Testability," *Proc. 14th Des. Autom. Conf.,* New Orleans, pp. 462–468, June 20–22, 1977.

[EICH78] Eichelberger, E. B., T. W. Williams, E. I. Muehldorf, and R. G. Walther, "A Logic Design Structure for Testing Internal Array," *Dig., 3rd USA–Japan Comput. Conf.,* San Francisco, Sess. 14–4, pp. 266–272, Oct. 10–12, 1978.

[EICH83a] Eichelberger, E. B., "Latch Design Using 'Level Sensitive Scan Design.'" *Dig., COMPCON Spring 83,* San Francisco, pp. 380–383, Feb. 28–Mar. 3, 1983.

[EICH83] Eichelberger, E. B., and E. Lindbloom, "Random-Pattern Coverage Enhancement and Diagnosis for LSSD Logic Self-Test," *IBM J. Res. Develop.*, vol. 27, no. 3, pp. 265–272, May 1983.

[EIKI80] Eiki, H., K. Inagaki, and S. Yajima, "Autonomous Testing and Its Application to

Testable Design of Logic Circuits," *Dig., 10th Annu. Int. Symp. Fault-Tolerant Comput.,* Kyoto, Japan, pp. 173–178, Oct. 1–3, 1980.

[FASA80] Fasang, P. P., "BIDCO, Built-In Digital Circuit Observer," *Dig., 1980 IEEE Test Conf.,* Philadelphia, pp. 261–266, Nov. 11–13, 1980.

[FLOU79] Floutier, D., "Some Basic Properties of Redundancy in Combinational Logic Networks," unpublished, 1979.

[FRIE67] Friedman, A. D., "Fault Detection in Redundant Circuits," *IEEE Trans. Electron. Comput.,* pp. 99–100, Feb. 1967.

[FUJI81] Fujiwara, H., and K. Kinoshita, "A Design of Programmable Logic Arrays with Universal Tests," *IEEE Trans. Comput.,* vol. C-30, no. 11, pp. 823–828, Nov. 1981.

[FUNA75] Funatsu, S., N. Wakatsuki, and T. Arima, "Test Generation Systems in Japan," *Dig., 12th Annu. Des. Autom. Conf.,* Boston, pp. 114–122, June 23–25, 1975.

[FUNA78] Funatsu, S., N. Wakatsuki, and A. Yamada, "Designing Digital Circuits with Easily Testable Consideration," *Dig., 1978 IEEE Semiconduct. Test Conf.,* Cherry Hill, N.J., pp. 98–102, Oct. 31–Nov. 2, 1978.

[GOEL80] Goel, P., "Test Generation Costs Analysis and Projections," *17th Annu. Des. Autom. Conf.,* Minneapolis, Minn., pp. 77–84, June 23–25, 1980.

[GOLD78] Goldstein, L. H., "Controllability/Observability Analysis of Digital Circuits," SAND78-1895, Sandia Laboratories, Albuquerque, N. Mex., Nov. 1978.

[GOLD79a] Goldstein, L. H., "Controllability/Observability Analysis of Digital Circuits," Design for Testability Workshop, Boulder, Colo., Apr. 1979.

[GOLD79b] Goldstein, L. H., "Controllability/Observability Analysis of Digital Circuits," *IEEE Trans. Circuits Syst.,* vol. CAS-26, no. 9, pp. 685–693, Sept. 1979.

[GOLD80] Goldstein, L. H., and E. L. Thigpen, "SCOAP: Sandia Controllability/Observability Analysis Program," *Dig., 17th Des. Autom. Conf.,* Minneapolis, Minn., pp. 190–196, June 23–25, 1980.

[GORD77] Gordon, G., and H. Nadig, "Hexadecimal Signatures Identify Troublespots in Microprocessor Systems," *Electronics,* pp. 89–96, Mar. 3, 1977.

[GRAS79] Grason, J., "TMEAS, A Testability Measure Program," Bell Laboratories, 1979.

[GRAS82] Grassl, G., and H.-J. Pfleiderer, "A Self-Testing PLA," *Dig., 1982 IEEE Int. Solid-State Circuits Conf.,* pp. 60–61, Feb. 10, 1982.

[HASS82] Hassan, S. Z., "Algebraic Analysis of Parallel Signature Analyzers," Center for Reliable Computing Tech. Rep. 82-5, Computer Systems Laboratory, Stanford University, Stanford, Calif., June 1982.

[HASS83] Hassan, S. Z., D. J. Lu, and E. J. McCluskey, "Parallel Signature Analyzers— Detection Capability and Extensions," *Dig., COMPCON Spring 83,* San Francisco, Feb. 28–Mar. 3, 1983.

[HAYE74] Hayes, J. P., "On Modifying Logic Networks to Improve Their Diagnosability," *IEEE Trans. Comput.,* vol. C-23, no. 1, pp. 56–62, Jan. 1974.

[HAYE76] Hayes, J. P., "Transition Count Testing of Combinational Logic Circuits," *IEEE Trans. Comput.,* vol. C-27, no. 6, pp. 613–620, June 1976.

[HAYE80] Hayes, J. P., and E. J. McCluskey, "Testability Considerations in Microprocessor-Based Design," *Computer,* pp. 17–26, Mar. 1980. Reprinted in *Tutorial: Microcomputer System Software and Languages,* B. E. Allen, ed., IEEE Cat. EHO 174-3, pp. 198–206.

An expanded version was issued as Stanford Computer Systems Laboratory Tech. Rep. 179, Nov. 1979.

[HECK81] Heckelman, R. W., and D. K. Bhavsar, "Self-Testing VLSI," *Dig., 1981 IEEE Solid State Circuits Conf.*, pp. 174–175, Feb. 19, 1981.

[HONG80] Hong, S. J., and D. L. Ostapko, "FITPLA: A Programmable Logic Array for Function Independent Testing," *Dig., 10th Annu. Int. Symp. Fault-Tolerant Comput.*, Kyoto, Japan, pp. 131–136, Oct. 1–3, 1980.

[HSU78] Hsu, F., P. Lolechy, and L. Zobniw, "Selective Controllability: A Proposal for Testing and Diagnosis," *Dig., 1978 IEEE Semiconduct. Test Conf.*, Cherry Hill, N.J., pp. 170–175, Oct. 31–Nov. 2, 1978.

[KAUT71] Kautz, W. H., "Testing Faults in Combinational Cellular Logic Arrays," *Proc. 8th. Annu. IEEE Symp. Switching Automata Theory*, pp. 161–174, Oct. 1971.

[KHAK82] Khakbaz, J., "Self-Testing Embedded Parity Trees," *Dig., 12th Annu. Int. Symp. Fault-Tolerant Comput.*, Santa Monica, Calif., pp. 109–116, June 22–24, 1982.

[KHAK83a] Khakbaz, J., and E. J. McCluskey, "Self-Testing Embedded Code Checkers," *Dig., COMPCON Spring 1983*, San Francisco, Feb. 28–Mar. 3, pp. 452–457, 1983.

[KHAK83b] Khakbaz, J., "A Testable PLA Design with Low Overhead and High Fault Coverage," *Dig., 13th Annu. Int. Symp. Fault-Tolerant Comput.*, Milan, Italy, June 1983. See also Stanford CRC Tech. Reps. 83-3 and 82-17.

[KHAK84] Khakbaz, J., and E. J. McCluskey, "Self-Testing Embedded Parity Checkers," *IEEE Trans. Comput.*, vol. C-33, no. 8, pp. 753–756, Aug. 1984.

[KNUT69] Knuth, D. E., *The Art of Computer Programming*, vol. 2: Seminumerical Algorithms, Addison-Wesley, Reading, Mass., 1969.

[KODA74] Kodandapani, K. L., "A Note on Easily Testable Realizations for Logic Functions," *IEEE Trans. Comput.*, vol. C-23, no. 3, pp. 332–333, Mar. 1974.

[KODA77] Kodandapani, K. L., and R. V. Setlur, "A Note on Minimal Reed-Muller Canonical Forms of Switching Functions," *IEEE Trans. Comput.*, vol. C-26, no. 3, pp. 310–313, Mar. 1977.

[KOMO82] Komonytsky, D., "LSI Self-Test Using Level Sensitive Scan Design and Signature Analysis," *Dig., 1982 IEEE Test Conf.*, Philadelphia, pp. 414–424, Nov. 15–18, 1982.

[KOMO83] Komonytsky, D., "Synthesis of Techniques Creates Complete System Self-Test," *Electronics*, pp. 110–115, Mar. 10, 1983.

[KONE79] Konemann, G., J. Mucha, and G. Zwiehoff, "Built-In Logic Block Observation Technique," *Dig., 1979 IEEE Test Conf.*, Cherry Hill, N.J. pp. 37–41, Oct. 23–25, 1979.

[KONE80] Konemann, B., J. Mucha, and G. Zwiehoff, "Built-In Test for Complex Digital Integrated Circuits," *IEEE J. Solid-State Circuits*, vol. SC-15, no. 3, pp. 315–318, June 1980.

[KOVI79a] Kovijanic, P. G., "Computer-Aided Testability Analysis," *AUTOTESTCON*, pp. 292–294, Sep. 1979.

[KOVI79b] Kovijanic, P. G., "Testability Analysis," *Dig., 1979 IEEE Test Conf.*, Cherry Hill, N.J., pp. 310–316, Oct. 23–25, 1979.

[LOSQ78] Losq, J., "Efficiency of Random Compact Testing," *IEEE Trans. Comput.*, vol. C-27, no. 6, pp. 516–525, June 1978.

[LU83] Lu, D. J. and E. J. McCluskey, "Recurrent Test Patterns," *Dig., 1983 IEEE Test Conf.*, Philadelphia, pp. 76–82, Nov. 1983.

[MANN81] Mann, F. A., "Explanation of New Logic Symbols," Chapter 5 in 1981 Supplement to the *TTL Data Book for Design Engineers*, 2nd ed., Texas Instruments, Inc., Dallas.

[MCCL81] McCluskey, E. J., and S. Bozorgui-Nesbat, "Design for Autonomous Test," *IEEE Trans. Comput.*, vol. C-30, no. 11, pp. 866–875, Nov. 1981.

[MCCL82a] McCluskey, E. J., "Verification Testing," *Dig., 19th Annual Design Automation Conf.*, Las Vegas, pp. 495–500, June 14–16, 1982.

[MCCL82b] McCluskey, E. J., "Built-In Verification Test," *Dig., 1982 IEEE Test Conf.*, Philadelphia, pp. 183–190, Nov. 11–13, 1982.

[MULL54] Muller, D. E., "Application of Boolean Algebra to Switching Circuit Design and Error Detection," *IRE Trans. Electron. Comput.*, pp. 132–140, Sept. 1954.

[PAGE80] Page, E. W., "Minimally Testable Reed-Muller Canonical Forms," *IEEE Trans. Comput.*, vol. C-29, no. 8, pp. 746–750, Aug. 1980.

[PERK80] Perkins, C. C., S. Sangani, H. Stopper, and W. Valitski, "Design for In-Situ Chip Testing with a Compact Tester," *IEEE Test Conf.*, Philadelphia, PA, pp. 29–41, Nov. 11–13, 1980.

[PETE72] Peterson, W. W., and E. J. Weldon, *Error-Correcting Codes*, 2nd ed., Colonial Press, 1972.

[PRAD78] Pradhan, D. K., "Universal Test Sets for Multiple Fault Detection in AND-EXOR Arrays," *IEEE Trans. Comput.*, vol. C-27, no. 2, pp. 181–187, Feb. 1978.

[PRAD80] Pradhan, D. K., and K. Son, "The Effect of Untestable Faults in PLAs and a Design for Testability," *Dig., 1980 IEEE Test Conf.*, Philadelphia, pp. 359–367, Nov. 11–13, 1980.

[RAMA82] Ramanatha, K. S., "A Design for Complete Testability of Programmable Logic Arrays," *Dig., 1982 IEEE Test Conf., Cherry Hill 82*, Philadelphia, pp. 67–74, Nov. 11–13, 1982.

[RATI82] Ratiu, I. M., A. Sangiovanni-Vincentelli, and D. O. Pederson, "VICTOR: A Fast VLSI Testability Analysis Program," *1982 IEEE Test Conf., Cherry Hill 82*, Philadelphia, pp. 397–401, Nov. 11–13, 1982.

[RAUL71] Rault, J.-C., "A Graph Theoretical and Probabilistic Approach to the Fault Detection of Digital Circuits," *Dig., 1971 Int. Symp. Fault-Tolerant Comput.*, Pasadena, Calif., pp. 26–29, Mar. 1971.

[REDD72] Reddy, S. M., "Easily Testable Realizations for Logic Functions," *IEEE Trans. Comput.*, vol. C-21, pp. 1183–1188, Nov. 1972.

[SALU74] Saluja, K. K., and S. M. Reddy, "On Minimally Testable Logic Networks," *IEEE Trans. Comput.*, vol. C-23, no. 5, pp. 552–554, May, 1974.

[SALU75] Saluja, K. K., and S. M. Reddy, "Fault Detecting Test Sets for Reed–Muller Canonic Networks," *IEEE Trans. Comput.*, vol. C-24, no. 10, pp. 995–998, Oct. 1975.

[SALU81] Saluja, K. K., K. Kinoshita, and H. Fujiwara, "A Multiple Fault Testable Design of Programmable Logic Arrays," *Dig., 11th Annu. Int. Symp. Fault-Tolerant Comput.*, Portland, Me., pp. 44–46, June 24–26, 1981.

[SAVI80] Savir, J., "Syndrome-Testable Design of Combinational Circuits," *IEEE Trans. Comput.*, pp. 442–451, June 1980.

[SAVI81] Savir, J., "Syndrome-Testing of 'Syndrome-Untestable' Combinational Circuits," *IEEE Trans. Comput.*, vol. C-30, no. 8, pp. 606–608, Aug. 1981.

[SAVI83] Savir, J., G. Ditlow, and P. H. Bardell, "Random Pattern Testability," *Dig., 13th Annu. Int. Symp. Fault-Tolerant Comput.*, Milan, Italy, pp. 80–89, June 28–30, 1983.

[SEDM79] Sedmak, R. M., "Design for Self-Verification: An Approach for Dealing with Testability Problems in VLSI-Based Designs," *Dig., 1979 IEEE Test Conf.*, Cherry Hill, N.J., pp. 112–124, Oct. 23–25, 1979.

[SEDM80] Sedmak, R. M., "Implementation Techniques for Self-Verification," *1980 IEEE Test Conf.*, pp. 267–278, 1980.

[SHED77] Shedletsky, J. J., "Random Testing: Practicality vs. Verified Effectiveness," Dig., *7th Annu. Int. Symp. Fault-Tolerant Comput.*, Los Angeles, pp. 175–179, June 28–30, 1977.

[SMIT80] Smith, J. E., "Measure of the Effectiveness of Fault Signature Analysis," *IEEE Trans. Comput.*, vol. C-29, no. 6, pp. 510–514, June 1980.

[SON80] Son, K., and D. K. Pradhan, "Design of Programmable Logic Arrays for Testability," *Dig., 1980 IEEE Test Conf.*, Philadelphia, Paper 7.2, pp. 163–166, Nov. 11–13, 1980.

[SRID79] Sridhar, T., and J. P. Hayes, "Testing Bit-Sliced Microprocessors," *Dig., 9th Annu. Int. Symp. Fault-Tolerant Comput.*, Madison, Wis., pp. 211–218, June 20–22, 1979.

[SRID82] Sridhar, R., D. S. Ho, T. J. Powell, and S. M. Thatte, "Analysis and Simulation of Parallel Signature Analyzers," *Dig., 1982 IEEE Test Conf., Cherry Hill '82*, Philadelphia, pp. 656–661, Nov. 11–13, 1982.

[STEP76] Stephenson, J. E., and J. Grason, "A Testability Measure for Register Transfer Level Digital Circuits," *Dig., 6th Annu. Int. Symp. Fault-Tolerant Comput.*, Pittsburgh, Pa., pp. 101–107, June 21–23, 1976.

[STEW77] Stewart, J. H., "Future Testing of Large LSI Circuit Cards," *Dig., 1977 Semiconduct. Test Symp.*, Cherry Hill, N.J., pp. 6–15, Oct. 25–27, 1977.

[STEW78] Stewart, J. H., "Application of Scan/Set for Error Detection and Diagnostics," *Dig., 1978 IEEE Semiconductor Test Conf.*, Cherry Hill, N.J., pp. 152–158, Oct. 31–Nov. 2, 1978.

[SUSS81] Susskind, A., "Testability and Reliability of LSI," RADC Rep. RADC-TR-80-384, Rome Air Development Center, Griffiss Air Force Base, N.Y., Jan. 1981.

[WAGN83] Wagner, K. D., "Design for Testability in the Amdahl 580," *Dig., COMPCON Spring 83*, San Francisco, pp. 384–388, Feb. 28–Mar. 3, 1983.

[WAKE78] Wakerly, J. F., *Error-Detecting Codes, Self-Checking Circuits, and Applications*, Elsevier North-Holland, New York, 1978.

[WILL73] Williams, M. J. Y., and J. B. Angel, "Enhancing Testability of Large Scale Integrated Circuits via Test Points and Additional Logic," *IEEE Trans. Comput.*, vol. C-22, no. 1, pp. 46–60, Jan. 1973.

[WILL77] Williams, T. W., and E. B. Eichelberger, "Random Patterns within a Structured Sequential Logic Design," *Dig., IEEE 1977 Semiconduct. Test Conf.*, Cherry Hill, N. J., pp. 19–27, Oct. 25–27, 1977.

[WRIT75] Writer, P. L., "Design for Testability," *'75 ASSC Conf. Rec. (Autom. Support Syst. Symp. Adv. Maintainability)*, pp. 84–87, Oct. 1975.

[YAJI81] Yajima, S., and T. Aramaki, "Autonomously Testable Programmable Logic Arrays," *Dig., 11th Annu. Int. Symp. Fault-Tolerant Comput.*, Portland, Me., pp. 41–43, June 24–26, 1981.

[YAMA78] Yamada, A., N. Wakatsuki, T. Fukui, and S. Funatsu, "Automatic System Level Test Generation and Fault Location for Large Digital Systems," *Dig., 15th Des. Autom. Conf.*, Las Vegas, Nev., pp. 347–352, June 19–21, 1978.

[ZASI83] Zasio, J. J., "Shifting Away from Probes for Wafer Test," *Dig., COMPCON Spring 83*, San Francisco, pp. 395–398, Feb. 28–Mar. 3, 1983.

BIBLIOGRAPHY

Section 2.1

[BARD81] Bardell, P. H., and W. H. McAnney, "A View from the Trenches: Production Testing of a Family of VLSI Multichip Modules," *Dig., 11th Annu. Int. Symp. Fault-Tolerant Comput.*, Portland, Me., p. 281–283, June 24–26, 1981.

[BREU76] Breuer, M. A., and A. Friedman, "Design to Simplify Testing," in *Diagnosis and Reliability of Digital Systems*, Computer Science Press, Woodland Hills, Calif., 1976, pp. 291–303.

[FOX75] Fox, J. L., "Availability Design of the System 370 Model 168 Multi Processor," *Dig., 2nd USA–JAPAN Comput. Conf.*, Tokyo, pp. 52–57, Aug. 26–28, 1975.

[GRAS80] Grason, J., and A. W. Nagle, "Digital Test Generation and Design for Testability," *Dig., 17th Des. Autom. Conf.*, Minneapolis, Minn., pp. 175–189, June 23–25, 1980.

[HAYE74] Hayes, J. P., "On Modifying Logic Networks to Improve Their Diagnosability," *IEEE Trans. Comput.*, vol. C-23, no. 1, pp. 56–62, Jan. 1974.

[HAYE80] Hayes, J. P., and E. J. McCluskey, "Testability Considerations in Microprocessor-Based Design," *Computer*, pp. 17–26, Mar. 1980.

[HSIA81] Hsiao, M. Y., W. C. Carter, J. W. Thomas, and W. R. Stringfellow, "Reliability, Availability, and Serviceability of IBM Computer Systems: A Quarter Century of Progress," *IBM J. Res. Dev.*, vol. 25, no. 5, pp. 453–465, Sept. 1981.

[MCCL78] McCluskey, E. J., "Design for Maintainability and Testability," *Dig., Govt. Microcircuit Appl. Conf.*, (GOMAC), Monterey, Calif., pp. 44–47, Nov. 14–16, 1978.

[MUEH81] Muehldorf, E. I., and A. D. Savkar, "LSI Logic Testing—An Overview," *IEEE Trans. Comput.*, vol. C-30, no. 1, pp. 1–17, Jan. 1981.

[OBER78] Oberly, R., "Testability and Test Methods," *Electron. Test*, pp. 71–73, Oct./Nov. 1978.

[OKLO82] Oklobdzija, V. G., "Design for Testability of VLSI Structures through the Use of Circuit Techniques," UCLA Computer Science Dept., Rep. CSD 820820, Aug. 1982.

[STEW77] Stewart, J. H., "Future Testing of Large LSI Circuit Cards," *Dig., 1977 IEEE Semiconduct. Test Symp.*, Cherry Hill, N.J., pp. 6–15, Oct. 25–27, 1977.

[STEW79] Stewart, J. H., "Testing Computers in the Year 1990," *Dig., 1979 IEEE Test Conf.*, Cherry Hill, N.J., pp. 125–126, Oct. 23–25, 1979.

[SUSS81] Susskind, A., "Testability and Reliability of LSI," RADC Rep., RADC-TR-80-384, Jan. 1981.

[SWAR78] Swarz, R. S., "Reliability and Maintainability Enhancements for the VAX-

11/780," *Dig., 8th Annu. Int. Symp. Fault-Tolerant Comput.*, Toulouse, France, pp. 24–28, June 21–23, 1978.

[WAKE78] Wakerly, J. F., *Error-Detecting Codes, Self-Checking Circuits, and Applications*, Elsevier North-Holland, New York, 1978.

[WILL79] Williams, T. W., and K. P. Parker, "Testing Logic Networks and Designing for Testability," *Computer*, vol. 12. no. 10, pp. 9–21, Oct. 1979.

[WILL82] Williams, T. W., and K. P. Parker , "Design for Testability—A Survey," *IEEE Trans. Comput.*, vol. C-31, no. 1, pp. 2–15, Jan. 1982.

[WILL83] Williams, T. W., "Design for Testability—A Survey," *IEEE Proc.*, vol. 71, no. 1, pp. 98–112, Jan. 1983.

Section 2.2

[CHAN74] Chang, H. Y., and G. W. Heimbigner, "LAMP: Controllability, Observability, and Maintenance Engineering Technique (COMET)," *Bell Syst. Tech. J.*, vol. 53, no. 8, pp. 1505–1534, Oct. 1974.

[GIBS78] Gibson, J. M., "Digital Logic Design for Testability," *Electron. Test*, pp. 10–11, July/Aug. 1978.

[HP] Hewlett-Packard, "Designing Digital Circuits for Testability," Appl. Note 210-4, (AN 210-4), DTS-70, Digital Test System.

[TORI79a] Torino, J., "Testability Guidelines," *Electron. Test*, pp. 18–20, Apr. 1979.

[TORI79b] Torino, J., "Design for Testability," Logical Solutions, Inc., Campbell, Calif., 1979.

[VOGE78] Vogel, A., and W. Coy, "Improving Testability by Simple Modifications of Combinational Nets," *Dig., 8th Annu. Int. Symp. Fault-Tolerant Comput.*, Toulouse, France, p. 216, June 21–23, 1978.

[WRIT75] Writer, P. L., "Design for Testability," *'75 ASSC Conf. Rec., (Autom. Support Systems Symp. Adv. Maintainability)*, pp. 84–87, Oct. 1975.

Section 2.3

[AGRA82] Agrawal, V. D., and M. R. Mercer, "Testability Measures—What Do They Tell Us?" *Dig., 1982 IEEE Test Conf., Cherry Hill '82*, Philadelphia, Paper 13.3 pp. 391–396, 1982.

[BENN80] Bennetts, R. G., G. D. Robinson, and C. M. Maunder, "Computer-Aided Measure for Logic Testability: The CAMELOT Program," *Proc. IEEE Int. Conf. Circuits Comput.*, Port Chester, N.Y., pp. 1162–1165, Oct. 1980.

[BENN81] Bennets, R. G., C. M. Maunder, and G. D. Robinson, "CAMELOT: A Computer-Aided Measure for Logic Testability," *IEE Proc. Comput.*, Sept. 1981.

[BERG82] Berg, W. C., and R. D. Hess, "COMET; A Testability Analysis and Design Modification Package," *Dig., 1982 IEEE Test Conf., Cherry Hill 82*, Philadelphia, pp. 364–378, Nov. 11–13, 1982.

[CONS80] Consolla, W. M., and F. G. Danner, "An Objective Printed Circuit Board Testability Design Guide and Rating System," Rep. RADC-TR-79-327, Rome Air Development Center (RBET), Griffiss AFB, N.Y., 11714, Jan. 1980.

[DANN79] Danner, F., and W. Consolla, "An Objective PCB Testability Rating System," *1979 IEEE Test Conf.*, Cherry Hill, N.J., pp. 23–28, Nov. 11–13, 1979.

[DEJK75] Dejka, W. J., "Measure of Testability in Device and System Design," *Dig., 20th Midwest Symp. Circuits Syst.,* Texas Tech. University, Lubbock, Tex., pp. 39–52, Aug. 15–17, 1977.

[DUNN81] Dunning, B., and P. Kovijanic, "Demonstration of a Figure of Merit for Inherent Testability," *Proc., IEEE AUTOTESTCON,* Orlando, Fla., pp. 515–520, Oct. 1981.

[DUSS78] Dussault, J. A., "A Testability Measure," *Dig., 1978 IEEE Semiconduct. Test Conf.,* Cherry Hill, N.J., pp. 113–116, Oct. 31–Nov. 2, 1978.

[FLOU79] Floutier, D., "Some Basic Properties of Redundancy in Combinational Logic Networks," unpublished, 1979.

[FONG82a] Fong, J. Y. O., "A Generalized Testability Analysis Algorithm for Digital Logic Circuits," *Proc., IEEE Int. Symp. Circuits Syst.,* Rome, pp. 1160–1163, May 1982.

[FONG82b] Fong, J. Y. O., "On Functional Controllability and Observability Analysis," *Dig., 1982 IEEE Test Conf., Cherry Hill 82,* Philadelphia, pp. 170–175, 1982.

[FUNG82] Fung, H. S., and J. Y. O. Fong, "An Information Flow Approach to Functional Testability Measures," *Proc., IEEE Int. Conf. Circuits Syst.,* New York, pp. 460–463, Sept. 1982.

[GOEL82] Goel, P., and McDermott, "An Interactive Testability Analysis Program—ITTAP," *Dig., 19th Annu. Des. Autom. Conf.,* Las Vegas, Nev., p. 581–586, June 14–16, 1982.

[GOLD78] Goldstein, L. H., "Controllability/Observability Analysis of Digital Circuits," SAND78-1895, Sandia Laboratories, Albuquerque, N.M., Nov. 1978.

[GOLD79a] Goldstein, L. H., "Controllability/Observability Analysis of Digital Circuits," Design for Testability Workshop, Boulder, Colo., Apr. 1979.

[GOLD79b] Goldstein, L. H., "Controllability/Observability Analysis of Digital Circuits," *IEEE Trans. Circuits Syst.,* vol. CAS-26, no. 9, pp. 685–693, Sept. 1979.

[GOLD80] Goldstein, L. H., and E. L. Thigpen, "SCOAP: Sandia Controllability/Observability Analysis Program," *Dig., 17th Des. Autom. Conf.,* Minneapolis, Minn., pp. 190–196, June 23–25, 1980.

[GRAS79] Grason, J., "TMEAS, A Testability Measure Program," Bell Laboratories, 1979.

[HESS82] Hess, R. D., "Testability Analysis: An Alternative to Structured Design for Testbility," *LSI Des.,* pp. 22–27, Mar./Apr. 1982.

[KEIN77] Keiner, W., and R. West, "Testability Mesaures," *Dig., Autotestcon '77,* Hyannis, Mass., pp. 49–55, Nov. 2–4, 1977.

[KEIN78] Keiner, W. L., "A Framework for Testable Digital Designs," *Dig., Govt. Microcircuit Appl. Conf. (GOMAC),* Monterey, Calif., pp. 456–459, Nov. 14–16, 1978.

[KIRK83] Kirkland, T., and V. Flores, "Software Checks Testability and Generates Tests of VLSI Design," *Electronics,* pp. 120–124, Mar. 10, 1983.

[KOVI79a] Kovijanic, P. G., "Computer-Aided Testability Analysis," *AUTOTESTCON,* pp. 292–294, Sep. 1979.

[KOVI79b] Kovijanic, P. G., "Testability Analysis," *Dig., 1979 IEEE Test Conf.,* Cherry Hill, N.J., pp. 310–316, Oct. 23–25, 1979.

[KOVI81] Kovijanic, P. G., "Single Testability Figure of Merit," *1981 IEEE Test Conf.,* pp. 521–529, 1981.

[RATI82] Ratiu, I. M., A. Sangiovanni-Vincentelli, and D. O. Pederson, "VICTOR: A Fast

VLSI Testability Analysis Program," *1982 IEEE Test Conf., Cherry Hill 82*, Philadelphia, pp. 397–401, Nov. 11–13, 1982.

[STEP76] Stephenson, J. E., and J. Grason, "A Testability Measure for Register Transfer Level Digital Circuits," *Dig., 6th Annu. Int. Symp. Fault-Tolerant Comput.*, Pittsburgh, Pa., pp. 101–107, June 21–23, 1976.

[TAKA81] Takasaki, S., M. Kawai, S. Funatsu, and A. Yamada, "A Calculus of Testability Measure at the Functional Level," *Dig., 1981 IEEE Int. Test Conf.*, Philadelphia, pp. 95–101, Oct. 1981.

Section 2.4, Part 1: SCAN

[ANDO80] Ando, H. "Testing VLSI with Random Access Scan," *COMPCON*, pp. 50–52, Feb. 1980.

[BOTT77] Bottorf, P. S., R. E. France, N. H. Garges, and E. J. Orosz, "Test Generation for Large Logic Networks," *Dig., 14th Des. Autom. Conf.*, New Orleans, pp. 479–485, June 20–22, 1977.

[CART64] Carter, W. C., H. C Montgomery, R. J. Preiss and H. J. Reinheimer, "Design of Serviceability Features for the IBM System/360," *IBM J.*, pp. 115–126, Apr. 1964.

[CORR82] Correale, A., "Physical Design of a Custom 16-Bit Microprocessor," *IBM J. Res. Dev.*, vol. 26, no. 4, pp. 446–453, July 1982.

[FASA80] Fasang, P. P., "BIDCO, Built-In Digital Circuit Observer," *Dig., 1980 IEEE Test Conf.*, Philadelphia, pp. 261–266, Nov. 11–13, 1980.

[FUNA75] Funatsu, S., N. Wakatsuki, and T. Arima, "Test Generation Systems in Japan," *Dig., 12th Annu. Des. Autom. Conf.*, Boston, pp. 114–122, June 23–25, 1975.

[FUNA78] Funatsu, S., N. Wakatsuki, and A. Yamada, "Designing Digital Circuits with Easily Testable Consideration," *Dig., 1978 IEEE Semiconduct. Test Conf.*, Cherry Hill, N.J., pp. 98–102, Oct. 31–Nov. 2, 1978.

[GOEL82] Goel, P., and M. T. McMahon, "Electronic Chip-In-Place Test," *Dig., 1982 IEEE Test Conf.*, Paper 3.6, pp. 83–90, 1982.

[HOLL82] Holland, E. R., and J. L. Robertson, "GUEST—A Signature Analysis Based Test System for ECL Logic," *Hewlett-Packard J.*, pp. 26–29, Mar. 1982.

[KAWA80] Kawai, M., S. Funatsu, and A. Yamada, "Application of Shift Register Approach and its Effective Implementation," *Dig., 1980 Test Conf.*, Philadelphia, pp. 22–25, Nov. 11–13, 1980.

[LAMP80] Lampson, B. W., and K. A. Pier, "A Processor for a High-Performance Personal Computer," Xerox Research Center, Palo Alto, Calif.

[LEE83] Lee, F., V. Coli, and W. Miller, "On-Chip Circuitry Reveals System's Logic States," *Electron. Des.*, pp. 119–124, Apr. 14, 1983.

[PORT] Porter, E. H., "Testability Considerations in a VLSI Design Automation System," STC-Microtechnology.

[STEW77] Stewart, J. H., "Future Testing of Large LSI Circuit Cards," *Dig., 1977 Semiconduct. Test Symp.*, Cherry Hill, N.J., pp. 6–15, Oct. 25–27, 1977.

[STEW78] Stewart, J. H., "Application of Scan/Set for Error Detection and Diagnostics," *Dig., 1978 IEEE Semiconduct. Test Conf.*, Cherry Hill, N.J., pp. 152–158, Oct. 31–Nov. 2, 1978.

[TOTH74] Toth, A., and C. Holt, "Automated Database-Driven Digital Testing," *Computer*, pp. 13–19, Jan. 1974.

[WAGN83] Wagner, K. D., "Design for Testability in the Amdahl 580," *Dig., COMPCON Spring 83*, San Francisco, pp. 384–388, Feb. 28–Mar. 3, 1983.

[WILL73] Williams, M. J. Y., and J. B. Angel, "Enhancing Testability of Large Scale Integrated Circuits via Test Points and Additional Logic," *IEEE Trans. Comput.*, vol. C-22, no. 1, pp. 46–60, Jan. 1973.

[YAMA78] Yamada, A., N. Wakatsuki, T. Fukui, and S. Funatsu, "Automatic System Level Test Generation and Fault Location for Large Digital Systems," *Dig., 15th Des. Autom. Conf.*, Las Vegas, Nev., pp. 347–352, June 19–21, 1978.

[ZASI83] Zasio, J. J., "Shifting Away from Probes for Wafer Test," *Dig., COMPCON Spring 83*, San Francisco, pp. 395–398, Feb. 28–Mar. 3, 1983.

Section 2.4, Part 2: LSSD

[BERG78] Berglund, N. C., "Processor Development in the LSI Environment," in *IBM System/38 Technical Developments*, pp. 7–10, 1978; reprinted in *Electronics*, Mar. 15, 1979.

[DASG78] Das Gupta, S., E. B. Eichelberger, and T. W. Williams, "LSI Chip Design for Testability," *Dig., 1978 IEEE Int. Solid-State Circuits Conf.*, San Francisco, Sess. XVI, pp. 216–217, Feb. 15–17, 1978.

[DASG81] Das Gupta, S., R. G. Walther, and T. W. Williams, "An Enhancement to LSSD and Some Applications of LSSD in Reliability, Availability, and Serviceability," *Dig., 11th Annu. Int. Symp. Fault-Tolerant Comput.*, Portland, Me., pp. 32–34, June 24–26, 1981.

[EICH74a] Eichelberger, E. B., "Level Sensitive Logic System," U.S. Patent 3,783,254, International Business Machines (Assignee), Jan. 1, 1974.

[EICH74b] Eichelberger, E. B., "Method of Propagation Delay Testing a Functional Logic System," U.S. Patent 3,784,907, International Business Machines (Assignee), Jan. 8, 1974.

[EICH77a] Eichelberger, E. B., and T. W. Williams, "A Logic Design Structure for LSI Testablity," *Proc. 14th Des. Autom. Conf.*, New Orleans, pp. 462–468, June 20–22, 1977.

[EICH77b] Eichelberger, E. B., E. I. Muehldorf, R. G. Walther, and T. W. Williams, "Level Sensitive Embedded Array Logic System," U.S. Patent 4,051,352, International Business Machines (Assignee), Sept. 27, 1977.

[EICH78a] Eichelberger, E. B., "A Logic Design Structure for LSI Testability," *Dig., COMPCON*, 1978.

[EICH78b] Eichelberger, E. B., and T. W. Williams, "A Logic Design Structure for LSI Testability," *J. Des. Autom. Fault-Tolerant Comput.*, vol. 2, no. 2, pp. 165–178, May 1978.

[EICH78c] Eichelberger, E. B., T. W. Williams, E. I. Muehldorf, and R. G. Walther, "A Logic Design Structure for Testing Internal Array," *Dig., 3rd USA–Japan Comput. Conf.*, San Francisco, Sess. 14-4, pp. 266–272, Oct. 10–12, 1978.

[EICH83a] Eichelberger, E. B., "Latch Design Using 'Level Sensitive Scan Design'," *Dig., COMPCON Spring 83*, San Francisco, pp. 380–383, Feb. 28–Mar. 3, 1983.

[FREC79] Frechette, T. J., and F. Tanner, "Support Processor Analyzes Errors Caught by Latches," *Electronics,* pp. 116–118, Nov. 8, 1979.

[GRAN83] Grant, B., "A 55K Transistor NMOS Microprogrammable Microprocessor," *Dig., IEEE Int. Solid-State Circuits Conf.,* Sess. II, pp. 30–31, Feb. 23, 1983.

[HSU78] Hsu, F., P. Lolechy, and L. Zobniw, "Selective Controllability: A Proposal for Testing and Diagnosis," *Dig., 1978 IEEE Semiconduct. Test Conf.,* Cherry Hill, N.J., pp. 170–175, Oct. 31–Nov. 2, 1978.

[MUEH76] Muehldorf, E. I., "Designing LSI Logic for Testability," *1976 IEEE Semiconduct. Test Symp.,* Cherry Hill, N.J., pp. 45–49, Oct. 19–21, 1976.

[STOL79] Stolte, L. A., and N. C. Berglund, "Design for Testability of the IBM System/38," *Dig., 1979 IEEE Test Conf.,* Cherry Hill, N.J., Oct. 23–25, 1979.

[WILL77] Williams, T. W., and E. B. Eichelberger, "Random Patterns within a Structured Sequential Logic Design," *Dig., IEEE 1977 Semiconduct. Test Conf.,* Cherry Hill, N.J., pp. 19–27, Oct. 25–27, 1977.

[WILL78] Williams, T. W., "Utilization of a Structured Design for Reliability and Serviceability," *Dig., Govt. Microcircuit Appl. Conf. (GOMAC),* Monterey, Calif., pp. 441–444, Nov. 14–16, 1978.

Section 2.5.1

[AKER73] Akers, S. B., "Universal Test Sets for Logic Networks," *IEEE Trans. Comput.,* vol. C-22, no. 9, pp. 835–839, Sept. 1973.

[BENN76] Bennets, R. G., and R. V. Scott, "Recent Developments in the Theory and Practice of Testable Logic Design," *Computer,* vol. 9, no. 6, pp. 47–63, June 1976.

[CHUA75] Chuang, C. S., and S. J. Oh, "Testability Enhancement in Digital System Design," *Dig., 1975 IEEE Intercon Conf. Rec.,* Sec. 11, Paper 3, 1975.

[DASG80] Das Gupta, S., C. R. P. Hartmann, and L. D. Rudolph, "Dual-Mode Logic for Function-Independent Fault Testing," *IEEE Trans. Comput.,* vol. C-29, no. 11, pp. 1025–1029, Nov., 1980.

[FRIE67] Friedman, A. D., "Fault Detection in Redundant Circuits," *IEEE Trans. Electron. Comput.,* pp. 99–100, Feb. 1967.

[FUJI74]P Fujiwara, J., and K. Kinoshita, "Design of Diagnosable Sequential Machines Utilizing Extra Outputs," *IEEE Trans. Comput.,* vol. C-23, no. 2, pp. 138–145, Feb. 1974.

[GOEL80] Goel, P., "Test Generation Costs Analysis and Projections," *17th Annu. Des. Autom. Conf.,* Minneapolis, Minn., pp. 77–84, June 23–25, 1980.

[GOUN80] Goundan, A., and J. P. Hayes, "Design of Totally Fault Locatable Combinational Networks," *IEEE Trans. Comput.,* vol. C-29, no. 1, pp. 33–44, Jan. 1980.

[HAYE71] Hayes, J. P., "On Realizations of Boolean Functions Requiring a Minimal or Near-Minimal Number of Tests," *IEEE Trans. Comput.,* vol. C-20, no. 12, pp. 1506–1513, Dec. 1971.

[HAYE74] Hayes, J. P., "On Modifying Logic Networks to Improve Their Diagnosability," *IEEE Trans. Comput.,* vol. C-23, no. 1, pp. 56–62, Jan. 1974.

[HLAV78] Hlavicka, J., and J. Klikar, "Easily Tested Tree Realization of Reed–Muller Expansion," *Dig., 8th Annu. Int. Symp. Fault-Tolerant Comput.,* Toulouse, France, p. 217, June 21–23, 1978.

[KAUT71] Kautz, W. H., "Testing Faults in Combinational Cellular Logic Arrays," *Proc. 8th. Annu. IEEE Symp. Switching Automata Theory*, pp. 161–174, Oct. 1971.

[KODA74] Kodandapani, K. L., "A Note on Easily Testable Realizations for Logic Functions," *IEEE Trans. Comput.*, vol. C-23, no. 3, pp. 332–333, Mar. 1974.

[KODA77] Kodandapani, K. L., and R. V. Setlur, "A Note on Minimal Reed–Muller Canonical Forms of Switching Functions," *IEEE Trans. Comput.*, vol. C-26, no. 3, pp. 310–313, Mar. 1977.

[MULL54] Muller, D. E., "Application of Boolean Algebra to Switching Circuit Design and Error Detection," *IRE Trans. Electron. Comput.*, pp. 132–140, Sept. 1954

[MURA70] Murakami, S.-I., and K. Kinoshita, "Sequential Machines Capable of Fault Diagnosis," *IEEE Trans. Comput.*, vol. C-19, no. 11, pp. 1079–1084, Nov. 1970.

[PAGE80] Page, E. W., "Minimally Testable Reed–Muller Canonical Forms," *IEEE Trans. Comput.*, vol. C-29, no. 8, pp. 746–750, Aug. 1980.

[PRAD78] Pradhan, D. K., "Universal Test Sets for Multiple Fault Detection in AND-EXOR Arrays, " *IEEE Trans. Comput.*, vol. C-27, no. 2, pp. 181–187, Feb. 1978.

[REDD72a] Reddy, S. M., "Easily Testable Realizations for Logic Functions," *IEEE Trans. Comput.*, vol. C-21, pp. 1183–1188, Nov. 1972.

[REDD72b] Reddy, S. M., "A Design Procedure for Fault-Locatable Switching Circuits," *IEEE Trans. Comput.*, vol. 21, no. 12, pp. 1421–1426, Dec. 1972.

[SALU74] Saluja, K. K., and S. M. Reddy, "On Minimally Testable Logic Networks," *IEEE Trans. Comput.*, vol. C-23, no. 5, pp. 552–554, May 1974.

[SALU75] Saluja, K. K., and S. M. Reddy, "Fault Detecting Test Sets for Reed–Muller Canonic Networks," *IEEE Trans. Comput.*, vol. C-24, no. 10, pp. 995–998, Oct. 1975.

[SALU78] Saluja, K. K., "A Testable Design of Sequential Machines," *Dig., 8th Annu. Int. Symp. Fault-Tolerant Comput.*, Toulouse, France, pp. 185–190, June 21–23, 1978.

[SALU80] Saluja, K. K., "Synchronous Sequential Machines: Modular and Testable Design," *IEEE Trans. Comput.*, vol. C-29, no. 11, pp. 1020–1025, Nov. 1980.

Section 2.5.2

[DAEH81] Daehn, W., and J. Mucha, "A Hardware Approach to Self-Testing of Large Programmable Logic Arrays," *IEEE Trans. Comput.*, vol. C-30, no. 11, pp. 829–833, Nov. 1981.

[FUJI80] Fujiwara, H., K. Kinoshita, and H. Ozaki, "Universal Test Sets for Programmable Logic Arrays," *Dig., 10th Annu. Symp. Fault-Tolerant Comput.*, Kyoto, Japan, pp. 137–142, Oct. 1–3, 1980.

[FUJI81] Fujiwara, H., and K. Kinoshita, "A Design of Programmable Logic Arrays with Universal Tests," *IEEE Trans. Comput.*, vol. C-30, no. 11, pp. 823–828, Nov. 1981.

[GRAS82] Grassl, G., and H.-J. Pfleiderer, "A Self-Testing PLA," *Dig., 1982 IEEE Int. Solid-State Circuits Conf.*, pp. 60–61, Feb. 10, 1982.

[HONG80] Hong, S. J., and D. L. Ostapko, "FITPLA: A Programmable Logic Array for Function Independent Testing," *Dig., 10th Annu. Int. Symp. Fault-Tolerant Comput.*, Kyoto, Japan, pp. 131–136, Oct. 1–3, 1980.

[KHAK82] Khakbaz, J., "Self-Testing Embedded Parity Trees," *Dig., 12th Annu. Int. Symp. Fault-Tolerant Comput.*, Santa Monica, Calif., pp. 109–116, June 22–24, 1982.

[KHAK83a] Khakbaz, J., and E. J. McCluskey, "Self-Testing Embedded Code Checkers, *Dig., COMPCON Spring 1983*, San Francisco, Feb. 28–Mar. 3, pp. 452–457, 1983.

[KHAK83b] Khakbaz, J., "A Testable PLA Design with Low Overhead and High Fault Coverage," *Dig., 13th Annu. Int. Symp. Fault-Tolerant Comput.*, Milan, Italy, pp. 426–429, June 1983. See also Stanford CRC Tech. Reps. 83-3 and 82-17.

[KHAK84] Khakbaz, J., and E. J. McCluskey, "Self-Testing Embedded Parity Checkers," *IEEE Trans. Comput.*, vol. C-33, no. 8, pp. 753–756, Aug. 1984.

[PRAD80] Pradhan, D. K., and K. Son, "The Effect of Untestable Faults in PLAs and a Design for Testability," *Dig., 1980 IEEE Test Conf.*, Philadelphia, pp. 359–367, Nov. 11–13, 1980.

[RAMA82] Ramanatha, K. S., "A Design for Complete Testability of Programmable Logic Arrays," *Dig., 1982 IEEE Test Conf., Cherry Hill 82*, Philadelphia, pp. 67–74, Nov. 11–13, 1982.

[SALU81] Saluja, K. K., K. Kinoshita, and H. Fujiwara, "A Multiple Fault Testable Design of Programmable Logic Arrays," *Dig., 11th Annu. Int. Symp. Fault-Tolerant Comput.*, Portland, Me., pp. 44–46, June 24–26, 1981.

[SON80] Son, K., and D. K. Pradhan, "Design of Programmable Logic Arrays for Testability," *Dig., 1980 IEEE Test Conf.*, Philadelphia, Paper 7.2, pp. 163–166, Nov. 11–13, 1980.

[YAJI81] Yajima, S., and T. Aramaki, "Autonomously Testable Programmable Logic Arrays," *Dig., 11th Annu. Int. Symp. Fault-Tolerant Comput.*, Portland, Me., pp. 41–43, June 24–26, 1981.

Section 2.6

[ALUN82] Alunkal, J., "Diagnostic Design Principles for Computer Systems: A Self-Testing Perspective," *Electron. Test,* pp. 69–82, Oct. 1982.

[BENO74] Benowitz, N., J. E. Bauer, and C. T. Joeckel, "Advanced Avionics Fault Isolation System for Digital Logic," *1974 ASSC Conf. Rec.*, San Diego, Calif., pp. 195–201, Oct. 30–Nov. 1, 1974.

[BENO75] Benowitz, N., D. F. Calhoun, G. E. Alderson, J. E. Bauer, and C. T. Joeckel, "An Advanced Fault Isolation System for Digital Logic," *IEEE Trans. Comput.*, vol. C-24, no. 5, pp. 489–497, May 1975.

[BENO76] Benowitz, N., D. F. Calhoun, and G. W. K. Lee, "Fault Detection/Isolation Results from AAFIS Hardware Built-In Test," *NAECON '76 Rec.*, pp. 215–222, 1976.

[BUEH82] Buehler, M. G., and M. W. Sievers, "Off-Line, Built-In Test Techniques for VLSI Circuits," *Computer,* pp. 69–82, June 1982.

[CART77] Carter, W., G. R. Putzolu, A. B. Wadia, W. G. Bouricius, D. C. Jesssep, E. P. Hsieh, and C. J. Tan, "Cost Effectiveness of Self Checking Computer Design," *Dig., 7th Annu. Int. Symp. Fault-Tolerant Comput.*, Los Angeles, pp. 117–123, June 28–30, 1977.

[CLAR79] Clary, J. B., and R. A. Sacane, "Self-Testing Computers," *Computer,* vol. 12, no. 10, pp. 49–59, Oct. 1979.

[COME82] Comerford, R. W., "Automation Promises to Lighten the Field-Service Load," *Electronics,* pp. 110–123, Apr. 7, 1982.

[COME83] Comerford, R. W., and J. Lyman, "Self-Test, Special Report," *Electronics,* pp. 109, Mar. 10, 1983.

[COUR83] Courtois, B., "Built-In Self Test during the Life Cycle of Integrated Circuits," RR 364, Laboratoire d'Informatique et de Mathématiques Appliquées de Grenoble, BP 68, 38402 Saint Martin d'Hères, Cedex, France, Apr. 1983.

[EICH83a] Eichelberger, E. B., "Latch Design Using 'Level Sensitive Scan Design,'" *Dig., COMPCON Spring 83,* San Francisco, pp. 380–383, Feb. 28–Mar. 3, 1983.

[EICH83b] Eichelberger, E. B., and E. Lindbloom, "Random-Pattern Coverage Enhancement and Diagnosis for LSSD Logic Self-Test," *IBM J. Res. Develop.,* vol. 27, no. 3, pp. 265–272, May 1983.

[GORD77] Gordon, G., and H. Nadig, "Hexadecimal Signatures Identify Troublespots in Microprocessor Systems," *Electronics,* pp. 89–95, Mar. 3, 1983.

[HANS81] Hansen, P., "Functional and In-Circuit Testing Team up to Tackle VLSI in the '80s," *Electronics,* pp. 189–195, Apr. 21, 1981.

[HAYE80] Hayes, J. P., and E. J. McCluskey, "Testability Considerations in Microprocessor-Based Design," *Computer,* pp. 17–26, Mar. 1980.

[JONE81] Jones, D., "Built-In Test Capabilities Could Cure μP-Based-System Ills," *EDN,* pp. 105–109, Apr. 15, 1981.

[KOPN74] Kopnin, Y. I., "Synthesis of Built-In Test Circuits for Combinational Networks," *Avtom. Telemekh.,* no. 3, pp. 132–139, Mar. 1974; translated by Consultants Bureau, a division of Plenum, New York, 1974.

[LINE81] Lineback, J. R., "Self-Testing Processors Cut Costs," *Electronics,* pp. 110–112, Dec. 15, 1981.

[LYMA80] Lyman, J., "VLSI Spurs Self-Testing," *Electronics,* pp. 76–78, Dec. 18, 1980.

[LYMA82] Lyman, J., and R. W. Comerford, "On-Chip and Functional Testing Spearhead Attack on VLSI Systems," *Electronics,* pp. 100–104, Nov. 3, 1982.

[RTI76] Research Triangle Institute, "A Study of a Standard BIT Circuit," Interim Report, for the Naval Avionics Facility, Indianapolis, Ind., Sept. 1976.

[SCHI81] Schindler, M., "Self-Testing of Full Wafer Cuts Production Costs," *Electron. Des.,* pp. 35–36, Aug. 1981.

[SMIT81] Smith, K., "Wafer Prepares to Turn Itself into a Computer," *Electronics,* pp. 73–74, Sept. 22, 1981.

[SOGO74] Sogomonyan, E. S., "Design of Built-In Self-Checking Monitoring Circuits for Combinational Devices," *Avtom. Telemekh.,* no. 2, pp. 121–133, Feb. 1974; translated by Consultants Bureau, a division of Plenum, New York, 1974.

[TOID82] Toida, S., "A Graph Model for Fault Diagnosis," *J. Digit. Syst.,* vol. VI, no. 4, pp. 345–365, 1982.

[WAKE74] Wakerly, J. F., and E. J. McCluskey, "Design of Low-Cost General-Purpose Self-Diagnosing Computers," *Inf. Process. Congr., 1974,* Stockholm, vol. 1. pp. 108–111, Aug. 5–10, 1974.

[WALZ82] Walz, G. A., "ATE Self-Testing—Concepts and Methods," *Test Meas. World,* pp. 14–19, Dec. 1982.

Section 2.6.1

[AGRA72] Agrawal, V. D., and P. Agrawal, "An Automatic Test Generation System for Illiac IV Logic Boards," *IEEE Trans. Comput.,* vol. C-21, no. 9, pp. 1015–1017, Sept. 1972.

[AGRA78] Agrawal, V. D., "When to Use Random Testing," *IEEE Trans. Comput.*, vol. C-27, no. 11, pp. 1054–1055, Nov. 1978.

[AGRA75a] Agrawal, P., and V. D. Agrawal, "On Improving the Efficiency of Monte Carlo Test Generation," *Dig., 5th Annu. Int. Symp. Fault-Tolerant Comput.*, Paris, pp. 205–209, June 18–20, 1975.

[AGRA75b] Agrawal, P., and V. D. Agrawal, "Probabilistic Analysis of Random Test Generation Method for Irredundant Combinational Logic Networks," *IEEE Trans. Comput.*, vol. C-24, no. 7, pp. 691–695, July 1975.

[AGRA76] Agrawal, P., and V. D. Agrawal, "On Monte Carlo Testing of Logic Tree Networks," *IEEE Trans. Comput.*, vol. C-25, no. 6, pp. 664–669, June 1976.

[BARZ83] Barzilai, Z., D. Coppersmith, and A. L. Rosenberg, "Exhaustive Generation of Bit Patterns with Applications to VLSI Self-Testing, *IEEE Trans. Comput.*, vol. C-32, no. 2, pp. 190–194, Feb. 1983.

[BOZO80] Bozorgui-Nesbat, S., and E. J. McCluskey, "Structured Design for Testability to Eliminate Test Pattern Generation," *Dig., 10th Annu. Int. Symp. Fault-Tolerant Comput.*, Kyoto, Japan, pp. 158–163, Oct. 1–3, 1980.

[DAVI76] David, R., and G. Blanchet, "About Random Fault Detection of Combinational Networks," *IEEE Trans. Comput.*, vol. C-25, no. 6, pp. 659–663, June 1976.

[DAVI79] David, R., and R. Tellez-Giron, "Comments on the Error Latency of a Fault in a Sequential Digital Circuit," *IEEE Trans. Comput.*, vol. C-27, no. 1, pp. 85–85, Jan. 1979.

[DAVI80] David, R., "Testing by Feedback Shift Register," *IEEE Trans. Comput.*, vol. C-29, no. 7, pp. 668–673, July 1980.

[DAVI81] David, R., and P. Thevenod-Fosse, "Random Testing of Integrated Circuits," *IEEE Trans. Instrum. Meas.*, vol. IM-30, no. 1, pp. 20–25, Mar. 1981.

[DAVI] David, R., X. Fedi, P. Thevenod-Fosse, "Test aléatoire de microprocesseurs: étude théorique et expérimentations," Laboratoire d'Automatique de Grenoble, Institut National Polytechnique de Grenoble, BP. 46, 38402, Saint-Martin D'Heres, France.

[ELEC82a] Electronics Test Staff Report, "Built-In Testing: The Future of ATE for VLSI Systems?" *Electron. Test,* pp. 38–40, July 1982.

[ELEC82b] Electronics Test Staff Report, "Designing VLSI Chips for Testability," *Electron. Test,* Nov. 1982.

[GIED71] Giedd, G. R., G. A. Maley, and M. H. Perkins, "Random Number Statistical Logic Test System," U.S. Patent No. 3,614,608, International Business Machines (Assignee), Oct. 19, 1971.

[HOLL82] Holland, E. R., and J. L. Robertson, "GUEST–A Signature Analysis Based Test System for ECL Logic," *Hewlett-Packard J.,* pp. 26–29, Mar. 1982.

[HUAN73] Huang, H., and M. A. Breuer, "Analysis of Detectability of Faults by Random Patterns in a Special Class of NAND Networks," *Comput. Electr. Eng.*, vol. 1, pp. 171–186, 1973.

[LOSQ76] Losq, J., "Referenceless Random Testing," *Dig., 6th Annu. Int. Symp. Fault-Tolerant Comput.*, Pittsburgh, Pa., pp. 108–113, June 21–23, 1976.

[LOSQ77] Losq, J., "Efficiency of Compact Testing for Sequential Circuits," *Dig., 7th Annu. Int. Conf. Fault-Tolerant Comput.*, Los Angeles, pp. 168–174, June 28–30, 1977.

[LOSQ78] Losq, J., "Efficiency of Random Compact Testing," *IEEE Trans. Comput.*, vol. C-27, no. 6, pp. 516–525, June 1978.

[MCCL81] McCluskey, E. J., and S. Bozorgui-Nesbat, "Design for Autonomous Test," *IEEE Trans. Comput.* vol. C-30, no. 11, pp. 866-875, Nov. 1981.

[MCCL82a] McCluskey, E. J., "Verification Testing," *Dig., 19th Annual Design Automation Conf.*, Las Vegas, pp. 495–500, June 14–16, 1982.

[MCCL82b] McCluskey, E. J., "Built-In Verification Test," *Dig., 1982 IEEE Test Conf.*, Philadelphia, pp. 183–190, Nov. 11–13, 1982.

[MUEH82] Muehldorf, E. I., and T. W. Williams, "Analysis of the Switching Behavior of Combinatorial Logic Networks," *Dig., 1982 IEEE Test Conf., Cherry Hill '82*, Philadelphia, pp. 379–390, Nov. 11–13, 1982.

[PAL79] Pal, A., "Pseudorandom Generator Has Programmable Sequence Length," *Electronics*, pp. 129, Oct. 11, 1979.

[RAUL71] Rault, J.-C., "A Graph Theoretical and Probabilistic Approach to the Fault Detection of Digital Circuits," *Dig., 1971 Int. Symp. Fault-Tolerant Comput.*, Pasadena, Calif., pp. 26–29, Mar. 1971.

[SAVI83] Savir, J., G. Ditlow, and P. H. Bardell, "Random Pattern Testability," *Dig., 13th Annu. Int. Symp. Fault-Tolerant Comput.*, Milan, Italy, pp. 80–89, June 1983.

[SCHN75] Schnurmann, H. D., E. Lindbloom, and R. G. Carpenter, "The Weighted Random Test Pattern Generator," *IEEE Trans. Comput.*, vol. C-24, no. 7, pp. 695–700, July 1975.

[SHED75] Shedletsky, J. J., "A Rationale for the Random Testing of Combinational Digital Circuits," *Dig., COMPCON Fall 75*, Washington, D. C., Sept. 9–11, 1975.

[SHED77] Shedletsky, J. J., "Random Testing: Practicality vs. Verified Effectiveness," *Dig., 7th Annu. Int. Symp. Fault-Tolerant Comput.*, Los Angeles, pp. 175–179, June 28–30, 1977.

[SRID82] Sridhar, T., D. S. Ho., T. J. Powell, and S. M. Thatte, "Analysis and Simulation of Parallel Signature Analyzers," *Dig., 1982 IEEE Test Conf., Cherry Hill '82*, Philadelphia, pp. 656–661, Nov. 11–13, 1982.

[THEV78a] Thevenod-Fosse, P., and R. David, "A Method to Analyse Random Testing of Sequential Circuits," *Digit. Process.*, vol. 4, pp. 313–332, 1978.

[THEV78b] Thevenod-Fosse, P., "Asynchronous Random Testing of Sequential Circuits," *Dig., 8th Annu. Int. Symp. Fault-Tolerant Comput.*, Toulouse, France, p. 213, June 21–23, 1978.

[THEV81] Thevenod-Fosse, P., and R. David, "Random Testing of the Data Processing Section of a Microprocessor," preprint of a paper presented at the *11th Annu. Int. Symp. Fault-Tolerant Comput.*, Portland, Me., June 24–26, 1981.

[WILL83] Williams, R. W., and K. P. Parker, "Design for Testability—A Survey," *Proc. IEEE*, vol. 71, no. 1, pp. 98–112, Jan. 1983.

Section 2.6.2

[BARZ81] Barzilai, Z., et al., "The Weighted Syndrome Sums Approach to VLSI Testing," *IEEE Trans. Comput.*, pp. 996–1000, Dec. 1981.

[BHAV81] Bhavsar, D. K., and R. W. Heckelman, "Self-Testing by Polynomial Division," *Dig., 1981 Int. Test Conf.*, Philadelphia, pp. 208–216, Oct. 27–29, 1981.

[BHAV82] Bhavsar, D. K., and R. W. Heckelman, "Self-Testing by Polynomial Division," *J. Digit. Syst.,* vol. VI, no. 2/3, pp. 139–160, Summer/Fall 1982.

[CART82a] Carter, W. C., "The Ubiquitous Parity Bit," *Dig., 12th Annu. Int. Symp. Fault-Tolerant Comput.,* Santa Monica, Calif., pp. 289–296, June 22–24, 1982.

[CART82b] Carter, W. C., "Signature Testing with Guaranteed Bounds for Fault Coverage," *Dig., 1982 IEEE Test Conf., Cherry Hill '82,* Philadelphia, pp. 75–82, Nov. 11–13, 1982.

[CHAN77] Chan, A. Y., "Easy-to-Use Signature Analyzer Accurately Troubleshoots Complex Logic Circuits," *Hewlett-Packard,* pp. 9–14, May 1977.

[DAVI80] David, R., "Testing by Feedback Shift Register," *IEEE Trans. Comput.,* vol. C-29, no. 7, pp. 668–673, July 1980.

[FROE79] Froehlke, T., "Signature Analysis in Practice," *Electron. Test,* pp. 29–31, Dec. 1979.

[FROH77] Frohwerk, R. A., "Signature Analysis: A New Digital Field Service Method," *Hewlett-Packard J.,* pp. 2–8, May 1977.

[FUJI80] Fujiwara, H., and K. Kinoshita, "Testing Logic Circuits with Compressed Data," *J. Des. Autom. Fault-Tolerant Comput.,* vol. 3, no. 3/4, pp. 211–225, 1980.

[GORD77] Gordon, G., and H. Nadig, "Hexadecimal Signatures Identify Troublespots in Microprocessor Systems," *Electronics,* pp. 89–96, Mar. 3, 1977.

[GRAS] Grason, J., and A. W. Nagle, "Digital Test Generation and Design for Testability," unpublished.

[HASS83a] Hassan, S. Z., D. J. Lu, and E. J. McCluskey, "Parallel Signature Analyzers—Detection Capability and Extensions," *Dig., COMPCON Spring 83,* San Francisco, Feb. 28–Mar. 3, 1983.

[HASS83b] Hassan, S. Z., and E. J. McCluskey, "Testing PLA's Using Multiple Parallel Signature Analyzers," *Dig., 13th Annu. Int. Symp. Fault-Tolerant Comput.,* Milan, Italy, pp. 422–425, June 28–30, 1983.

[HAYE76a] Hayes, J. P., "Transition Count Testing of Combinational Logic Circuits," *IEEE Trans. Comput.,* vol. C-27, no. 6, pp. 613–620, June 1976.

[HAYE76b] Hayes, J. P., "Check Sum Methods for Test Data Compression," *J. Des. Autom. Fault-Tolerant Comput.,* vol. 1, no. 1, pp. 3–17, 1976.

[HAYE78] Hayes, J. P., "Generation of Optimal Transition Count Tests," *IEEE Trans. Comput.,* vol. C-27, no. 1, pp. 36–41, Jan. 1978.

[HECK81a] Heckelman, R. W., and D. K. Bhavsar, "Problems and Approaches with Polynomial Division Testing," *Dig., IEEE 1981 Des. Testability Workshop,* Vail, Colo., 1981.

[HECK81b] Heckelman, R. W., and D. K. Bhavsar, "Self-Testing VLSI," *Dig., 1981 IEEE Solid State Circuits Conf.,* pp. 174–175, Feb. 19, 1981.

[HOLL82] Holland, E. R., and J. L. Robertson, "GUEST—A Signature Analysis Based Test System for ECL Logic," *Hewlett-Packard J.,* pp. 26–29, 1982.

[HP77a] Hewlett-Packard, "A Designer's Guide to Signature Analysis," Appl. Note 222, HP Publ. 02-5952-7465, Apr. 1977.

[HP77b] Hewlett-Packard, "5004A Signature Analyzer . . . a Microprocessor Service Solution," HP Publ. 02-5952-7464, Apr. 1977.

[HP77c] Hewlett-Packard, *Hewlett-Packard J.,* May 1977.

[HP78] Hewlett-Packard, "Signature Analysis Seminar," HP Publ. 02-5952-7503, 1978.

[HP80] Hewlett-Packard, "A Manager's Guide to Signature Analysis," Appl. Note 222-3, HP Publ. 02-5952-7592, Oct. 1980.

[HP81a] Hewlett-Packard, "Model 5005A Signature Multimeter, Model 5004A Signature Analyzer, Combined Data Sheets," HP Publ. 02-5952-7584, Mar. 1981.

[HP81b] Hewlett-Packard, "Remarkble Performance, Choice and Value in Electronic Counters," HP Publ. 02-5952-7606, Apr. 1981.

[HP81c] Hewlett-Packard, "An Index to Signature Analysis Publications," Appl. Note 222-0, HP Publ. 02-5952-7625, May 1981.

[HUMP81] Humphrey, J. R., and K. Firooz, "Signature Analysis for Board Testing," Radio Electron. Eng., vol. 51, no. 1, pp. 37–50, Jan. 1981.

[MEGG61] Meggitt, J. E., "Error Correcting Codes and Their Implementation," IRE Trans. Inf. Theory, pp. 234–244, Oct. 1961.

[NADI77] Nadig, H. J., "Signature Analysis—Concepts, Examples, and Guidelines," Hewlett-Packard J., pp. 15–21, May 1977.

[REDD77] Reddy, S. M., "A Note on Testing Logic Circuits by Transition Counting," IEEE Trans. Comput., vol. C-26, no. 3, pp. 313–314, Mar. 1977.

[RHOD81] Rhodes-Burke, R., "Applying Signature Analysis to Existing Processor-Based Products," Electronics, pp. 127–133, Feb. 24, 1981.

[ROBI79] Robinson, J. P., "Test Sequences for Fault Signature Analysis," Proposal to the National Science Foundation, Nov. 9, 1979.

[SALU81] Saluja, K. K., K. Kinoshita, and H. Fujiwara, "A Multiple Fault Testable Design of Programmable Logic Arrays," Dig., 11th Annu. Int. Symp. Fault-Tolerant Comput., Portland, Me., pp. 44–46, June 24–26, 1981.

[SAVI80] Savir, J., "Syndrome-Testable Design of Combinational Circuits," IEEE Trans. Comput., pp. 422–451, June 1980.

[SETH77] Seth, S. C., "Data Compression Techniques in Logic Testing: An Extension of Transition Counts," J. Des. Autom. Fault-Tolerant Comput., vol. 1, no. 2, pp. 99–114, Feb. 1977.

[SLOA81] Sloane, E. A., "Applying Walsh Functions to Converter Testing," Electron. Test, pp. 32–40, Apr. 1981.

[SMIT80] Smith, J. E., "Measures of the Effectiveness of Fault Signature Analysis," IEEE Trans. Comput., vol. C-29, no. 6, pp. 510–514, June 1980.

[YATE83] Yates, W., "Signature Analyzer Update," Electronics, pp. 51–54, Mar. 4, 1983.

[WEIS80a] Weisberg, M. J., "Study the Life Cycle to Uncover Complex Test Problems," Designer's Guide to: Testing and Troubleshooting μP-based Products—Part 1, reprinted from EDN, Mar. 20, 1980.

[WEIS80b] Weisberg, M. J., "Development-Phase Tools Unravel the Hard/Software Knot," Designer's Guide to: Testing and Troubleshooting μP-based Products—Part 2, reprinted from EDN, Mar. 20, 1980.

[WEIS80c] Weisberg, M. J., "Production-Phase Testing Increases Product Throughput," Designer's Guide to: Testing and Troubleshooting μP-based Products—Part 3, reprinted from EDN, Mar. 20, 1980.

[WEIS80d] Weisberg, M. J., "Clever Portable Test Tools Help Find System Field Failures," Designer's Guide to: Testing and Troubleshooting μP-based Products—Part 4, reprinted from EDN, Mar. 20, 1980.

[WONG79] Wong, J., W. Kolofa, and J. Krause, "Software Error Checking Procedures for Data Communication Protocols," *Comput. Des.*, pp. 122–126, Feb. 1979.

Section 2.6.3

[ALBE76] Alberts, R. D., et al., "A Study of A Standard BIT Circuit," Systems Instrumentation Department, Research Triangle Institute, Research Triangle Park, N.C., Sept. 1976.

[BARD83] Bardell, P. H., and W. H. McAnney, "Self-Testing of Multichip Logic Modules," *Test Meas. World*, pp. 26–29, Mar. 1983. (Also appears in *1982 IEEE Test Conf.*, pp. 200–204).

[BUEH82] Buehler, M. G., and M. W. Sievers, "Off-Line, Built-In Test Techniques for VLSI Circuits," *Computer*, pp. 69–82, June 1982.

[D'AMB78] d'Ambra, F. P., M. A. Menezes, H. H. Mueller, H. Stopper, and R. C. Yuen, "On-Chip Monitors for System Fault Isolation," *ISSCC Tech. Dig.*, pp. 218–219, Feb. 1978.

[EICH83] Eichelberger, E. B., and E. Lindbloom, "Random-Pattern Coverage Enhancement and Diagnosis for LSSD Logic Self-Test," *IBM J. Res. Dev.*, vol. 27, no. 3, pp. 265–272, May 1983.

[EIKI80] Eiki, H., K. Inagaki, and S. Yajima, "Autonomous Testing and Its Application to Testable Design of Logic Circuits," *Dig., 10th Annu. Int. Symp. Fault-Tolerant Comput.*, Kyoto, Japan, pp. 173–178, Oct. 1–3, 1980.

[FASA80] Fasang, P. P., "BIDCO, Built-In Digital Circuit Observer," *Dig., 1980 IEEE Test Conf.*, Philadelphia, pp. 261–266, Nov. 11–13, 1980.

[FASA82a] Fasang, P. P., "A Built-In Self Test Technique for Digital Circuits," *Siemens Forsch*, vol. 11, no. 2, pp. 65–68, 1982.

[FASA82b] Fasang, P. P., "Circuit Module Implements Practical Self-Testing," *Electronics*, pp. 164–167, May 19, 1982.

[FASA83a] Fasang, P. P., "MICROBIT, a Method of Built-In Test for Microcomputers," *Siemens Res. Dev. Rep.*, vol. 12 (1983), no. 1, pp. 47–54, 1983.

[FASA83b] Fasang, P. P., "Microbit Brings Self-Testing on Board Complex Microcomputers," *Electronics*, pp. 116–119, Mar. 10, 1983.

[GRAS82] Grassl, G., and H.-J. Pfleiderer, "A Self-Testing PLA," *Dig., 1982 IEEE Int. Solid-State Circuits Conf.*, pp. 60–61, Feb. 10, 1982

[KONE79] Konemann, B., J. Mucha, and G. Zwiehoff, "Built-In Logic Block Observation Technique," *Dig., 1979 IEEE Test Conf.*, Cherry Hill, N.J., pp. 37–41, Oct. 23–25, 1979.

[KONE80] Konemann, B., J. Mucha, and G. Zwiehoff, "Built-In Test for Complex Digital Integrated Circuits," *IEEE J. Solid-State Circuits*, vol. SC-15, no. 3, pp. 315–318, June 1980.

[PERK80] Perkins, C. C., S. Sangani, H. Stopper, and W. Valitski, "Design for In-Situ Chip Testing with a Compact Tester." *Dig., 1980 IEEE Test Conf.*, Philadelphia, Nov. 11–13, 1980.

[SANG76] Sangani, S. H., and R. Saeks, "A Spectral Theoretical Approach to Fault Analysis in Sequential Circuits," *J. Franklin Inst.*, vol. 302, no. 3, pp. 239–258, Sept. 1976.

[SANG78] Sangani, S. H., and B. Valitski, "In-Situ Testing of Combinational and Memory

Circuits Using a Compact Tester," *Dig., 8th Annu. Int. Symp. Fault-Tolerant Comput.,* Toulouse, France, p. 214, June 21–23, 1978.

[SEDM78] Sedmak, R. M., and H. L. Liebergot, "Fault-Tolerance of a General Purpose Computer Implemented by Very Large Scale Integration," *Dig., 8th Annu. Int. Symp. Fault-Tolerant Comput.,* Toulouse, France, pp. 137–143, June 21–23, 1978.

[SEDM79] Sedmak, R. M., "Design for Self-Verification: An Approach for Dealing with Testability Problems in VLSI-based Designs," *Dig., 1979 IEEE Test Conf.,* Cherry Hill, N.J., pp. 112–124, Oct. 23–25, 1979.

[SEDM80] Sedmak, R. M., "Implementation Techniques for Self-Verification," *1980 IEEE Test Conf.,* pp. 267–278, 1980.

[STOP77] Stopper, H., "Circuit Design for Fault Analysis," *Dig., 20th Midwest Symp. Circuits Syst.,* Lubbock, Tex., Aug. 1977.

[STOP80] Stopper, H., "The BCML Circuit and Packaging System," *IEEE Trans. Components, Hybrids, Manuf. Technol.,* vol. CHMT-3, no. 1, pp. 110–120, Mar. 1980.

[ZWIE79] Zwiehoff, G., B. Konemann, and J. Mucha, "Experimente mit einem Simulationsmodell für selbst-testende IC's," Apr. 1979.

PROBLEMS

2.1. Use SCOAP testability analysis rules for the following problem.

(a) Function $F(A, B, C, D) = ABCD$ can be realized in two forms using three AND gates. These are shown in Fig. P2.1(a). For each implementation determine the combinational observabilities and controllabilities of all the nets in the circuit. Which one of these two implementations, in your opinion, is a more testable circuit?

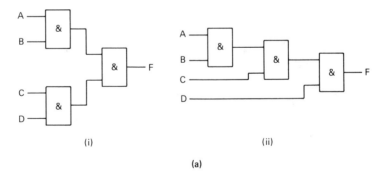

(a)

Figure P2.1(a)

(b) Function $F(A, B, C, D) = A + B + C + D$ can be realized in two forms, using three two-input OR gates. For each implementation shown in Fig. P2.1(b), determine the combinational observabilities and controllabilities of the nets in the circuit. Make comments similar to part (a) about the relative testability of the two implementations.

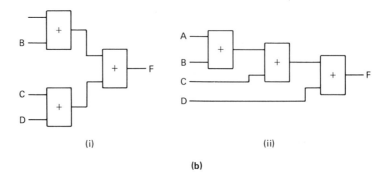

(i)   (ii)

(b)

Figure P2.1(b)

2.2. A measure of the testability of a fault, or how easy it is to test for a particular fault, can be defined as follows:

$$\text{testability of fault } F_i = \frac{\text{no. of input patterns that detect } F_i}{2^{\text{no. of inputs}}}$$

Using this definition and the combinational circuit shown in Fig. P2.2, calculate the testability of the following faults:

(a) $b/0$

(b) $h/1$

(c) $h/0$

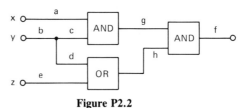

Figure P2.2

2.3. Design a two-input multiplexed data latch that does not have the extra propagation delay of the structure of Fig. 2.4.3.

2.4. Sixty-four ICs are to be interconnected to form a circuit that will be tested using scan techniques. The ICs will be packaged on four PC boards, each containing 16 ICs. Each IC has 1024 internal latches connected into a scan path. Assume that the scan data out (SDO) is driven by a tri-state driver which is enabled by the scan clock.

     Consider the three following options for interconnecting the scan path of the individual ICs into the circuit scan path.

1. Connect the 64 ICs serially into a single scan path.
2. Connect the 16 ICs on each PC board into a single scan path and add control logic to select the board to be scanned.
3. Use control logic to select the specific IC to be scanned.

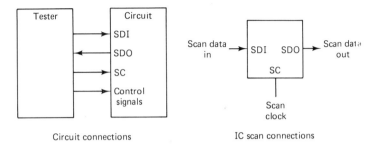

Circuit connections   IC scan connections

Figure P2.4

Do the following:

(a) For each option, draw a block diagram of the circuit showing scan path connections and any control logic. How many control signals are needed? How much control logic must be added?

(b) For each option, compute the number of bits of data that must be scanned in and out to load a test pattern into the entire circuit and scan out the test result.

(c) For each option, compute the average number of bits of data that must be scanned in and out to load a test pattern into a single IC and scan out the test result.

(d) Briefly (one paragraph) describe appropriate criteria for choosing which of these options should be selected.

2.5. Eight identical ICs are connected as shown in Fig. P2.5-1. Each IC has 64 internal latches in the scan path.

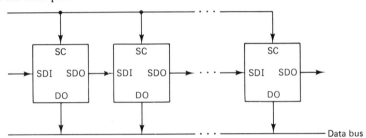

Figure P2.5-1

The output $D0$ is a tri-state output whose enable signal is driven by the first latch in the scan chain and whose data value is driven by the second latch in the scan chain (see Fig. P2.5-2).

To test this circuit of eight ICs, it is desired to scan in the following data string (reading from left to right):

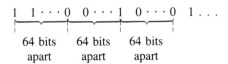

(a) Why is this not a suitable test pattern to scan-in to this circuit?

(b) Describe three methods for solving this problem.

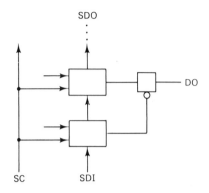

Figure P2.5-2

2.6. Consider the circuit shown below. The flip-flops have two clocked ports and are connected to form a scan path. The combinational logic for this circuit is shown below:

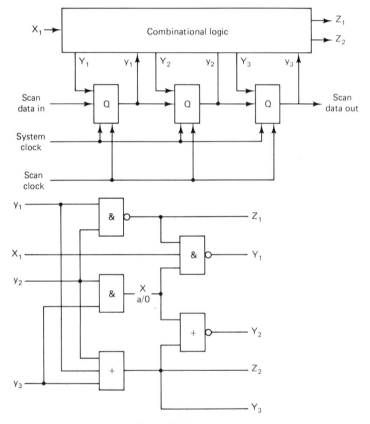

Figure P2.6

It is desired to test for the fault $a/0$ in the combinational logic.

(a) Use path sensitization to find a test for $a/0$. Show the sensitized path on the combinational logic diagram in Fig. P2.6.

(b) In what order are the values for the bits y_1, y_2, and y_3 scanned in and out?

	In	Out
First bit		
Second bit		
Third bit		

(c) Complete the testing sequence information below.

   (1) Scan in the following test vector y values.

$$y_1 =$$

$$y_2 =$$

$$y_3 =$$

   (2) Set the test value on input X_1.

$$X_1 =$$

   (3) After signal propagation is complete, check the circuit outputs.

	Good circuit	Faulty circuit
Z_1		
Z_2		

   (4) Apply one pulse to the system clock.

   (5) Scan out and check the new y values.

	Good circuit	Faulty circuit
y_1		
y_2		
y_3		

2.7. Figure P2.7 shows the structure of an (AND–OR) PLA. A FIT (function independent testing) Hong/Fujiwara design is to be used to realize the functions given by the following maps.

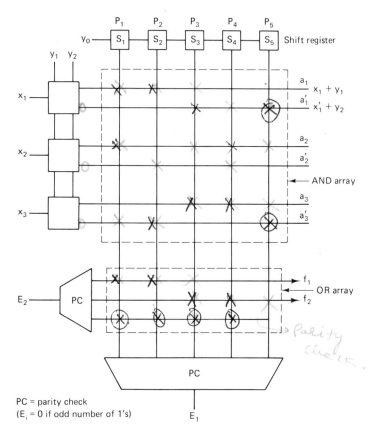

Ⓧ even parity

PC = parity check
(E_i = 0 if odd number of 1's)

Figure P2.7

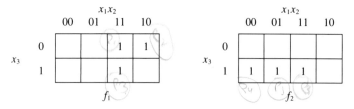

(a) Determine the product terms needed to realize these functions and indicate them on the Karnaugh maps above. Use a minimum number of product lines. On the diagram on the next page, place ×'s at all intersections that should have crosspoints connected.

(b) Write expressions for the product terms realized and label the terms on the Karnaugh maps above:

$P_1 =$; $P_2 =$; $P_3 =$;
$P_4 =$; $P_5 =$;

(c) Fill in the following table with the appropriate set of test patterns (assume that the shift register has been tested):

										Check all tests that detect:	
S_1	S_2	S_3	S_4	S_5	X_1	X_2	X_3	Y_1	Y_2	$a_1/0$	$a_1'/1$
1	0	0			1	1	1		1	X	
1	0	0						1		X	
0	1	0			1	1	1		1	X	
0	1	0						1		X	
0	0	1			1	1	1		1	X	
0	0	1						1		X	
0	0		1		1	1	1		1	X	
0	0		1					1		X	
0	0			1	1	1	1		1	X	
0	0			1				1		X	
0	0	0	0	0	0	1	1	0	1		X
0	0			0	1	0	0	1	0		X
0	0			0	1	0	1	0	1		X
0	0			0	0	1	0	1	0		X
0	0			0	1	1	0	0	1		X
0	0			0	0	0	1	1	0		X

2.8. It is desired to test the multiplexer shown in Fig. P2.8 for stuck-at faults on the inputs and output.

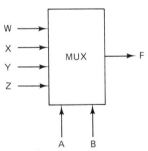

Figure P2.8

(a) How many test patterns are needed for exhaustive testing?

(b) Assume that random test patterns are generated with equal probability of a "1" or a "0" for each bit. For each fault in the table below, list the conditions under which it will be detected (e.g., $X = Y = 0$) and the probability that the pattern conditions will be satisfied by a single random test pattern.

W	X	Y	Z	A	B	F
0	x	x	x	0	0	0
1	x	x	x	0	0	1
x	0	x	x	0	1	0
x	1	x	x	0	1	1
x	x	0	x	1	0	0
x	x	1	x	1	0	1
x	x	x	0	1	1	0
x	x	x	1	1	1	1

Fault	Conditions for detection	Probability
$F/1$		
$X/0$		
$A/0$		
$A/0\ X/0$		

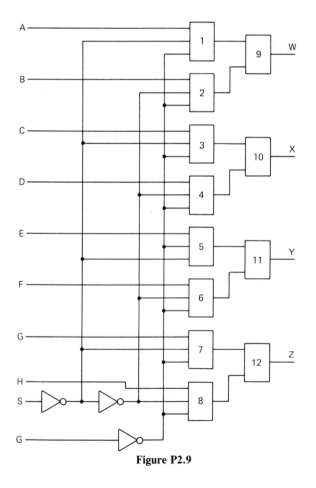

Figure P2.9

2.9. In the circuit shown in Fig. P2.9, generate the dependency list for each output (i.e., the set of inputs each output depends on). From this list determine a suitable partitioning of the gates. The goal is to test each partition independently.

(a) How many input patterns are needed to test the function realized by each output if we were to do these tests in sequence (i.e., test W first, then X, etc.).

(b) Write down 16 input patterns (each pattern is a binary vector of 10 bits) that exhaustively test the function realized by each output line; this time all four output lines are tested in parallel.

2.10. In the parity generator circuit shown in Fig. P2.10, determine how many inputs are needed to test the function generated by each output line. How many tests are needed to test the output line marked EVEN exhaustively? Rather than exhaustively testing the whole circuit, determine a set of partitions that can be exhausted with fewer test patterns than 20 input patterns each (keep the number of partitions under six). Write down the

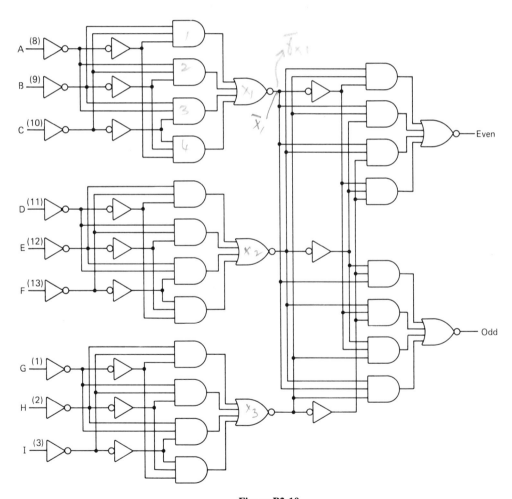

Figure P2.10

necessary number of (9-bit vector) test patterns needed to exhaustively test all your partitions.

2.11. Shown in Fig. P2.11 is the circuit for a dual four-input multiplexer. A pseudo-exhaustive test set is to be developed.

    (a) Write down the dependence matrix and the partitioned dependence matrix for this circuit.

    (b) Write down the RVTS for this circuit.

    (c) List any stuck-at faults that are not detected by the set of part (b).

    (d) List any bridging faults that are not detected by the set of part (b).

    (e) Use partitioning techniques (autonomous test) to obtain a minimum-length pseudo-exhaustive test set. (Show the partitions used.)

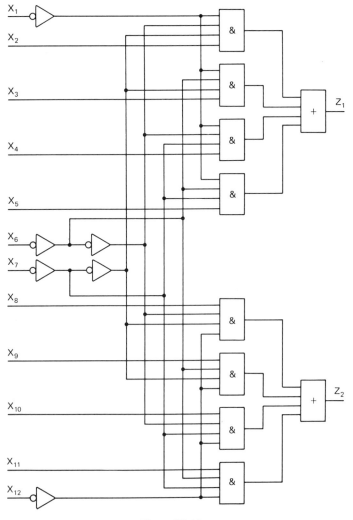

Figure P2.11

    (f) List any stuck-at faults not detected in part (e).

    (g) List any bridging faults not detected in part (e).

    (h) Repeat parts (e), (f), and (g) with the restriction of not more than three partitions for each output.

2.12. The circuit shown in Fig. P2.12 is used to compact a stream of input data to produce a signature; this signature is used to distinguish between error-free patterns (P_c) and erroneous patterns (P_e). Assume that P_c has the following values:

Time	8 7 6 5 4 3 2 1 0
P_c	1 0 1 0 1 1 0 0 1

    (a) Determine which of the following patterns will be indistinguishable from P_c. (*Hint:* You do not have to calculate the actual signature.)

Pattern	P_e values at time: 8 7 6 5 4 3 2 1 0	Distinguished	Not distinguished
a	1 1 0 1 1 1 0 0 1		
b	1 0 0 0 0 0 0 0 1		
c	1 1 1 1 0 1 0 0 1		
d	1 1 0 0 0 1 0 0 1		

    (b) There are only two P_e's with fewer than 3 bits in error that cannot be distinguished from P_c. Write down these two patterns:

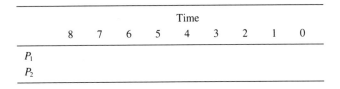

	Time							
	8	7	6	5	4	3	2	1	0
P_1								
P_2								

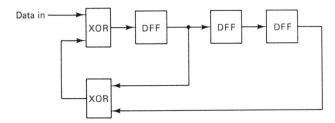

Figure P2.12

Chapter 3

FAULT SIMULATION

Y. Levendel
P. R. Menon

3.1. INTRODUCTION

Logic simulation is an important member of any set of computer-aided design tools for digital systems. This is especially true in the design of large highly reliable systems. In this chapter simulation techniques are discussed with emphasis on fault simulation in the VLSI environment.

3.1.1. Simulation Applications

Figure 3.1.1 shows the role of logic simulation in the hardware design process. Although many of the activities in Fig. 3.1.1 are outside the scope of this chapter, they are shown for completeness.

The two principal applications of logic simulation are design verification and fault analysis. Design verification requires the use of a simulator that predicts the behavior of the normal circuit, based on the analysis of a model of that circuit. This type of simulation, often called *true-value simulation,* is used for determining the output sequence that will be produced by any specified input sequence. It can also be used for producing fairly accurate timing diagrams for the outputs or internal points in the circuit, based on specified rise and fall delays for devices in the circuit. True-value simulation can also identify oscillations and races, if any, for the simulated input sequence. In short, simulation can be used to increase the confidence in the circuit design, prior to its prototyping. Since finding design errors constitutes a major part of the design process, simulation can reduce the time for detection of errors and, therefore, shorten the design interval [MONA82].

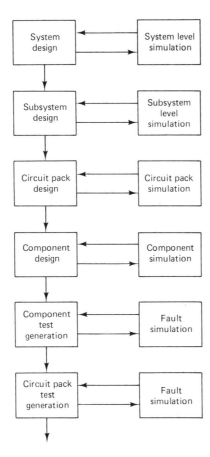

Figure 3.1.1 Simulation in the design process.

Another application of true-value simulation is the production of probe data for factory testing. In this case, simulation is used to produce expected responses of signals at probing points in the circuit. This response is stored in the tester and compared with probe data of the circuit under test in order to identify malfunctions.

Fault simulation determines the behavior of the circuit in the presence of each of the faults from a specified set. Due to the large number of potential faults in any large circuit, and the complexity of the simulation algorithms, it is usually assumed that only a single fault can be present in the circuit at any time. One of the uses of fault simulation is to determine the *fault coverage* of a given test sequence. The fault coverage is normally defined as the ratio of the number of detected faults to the total number of simulated faults. It is a measure of test quality. This information can be used for improving the test sequence, if necessary. Fault simulation is also used for building dictionaries of the *signatures* of the different faults for the purpose of fault location [CHAN66]. These signatures are stored in a data base. Actual failure patterns collected from the circuit under test are compared with fault signatures in the data base to find the closest match and thereby identify the most probable failure.

3.1.2. Levels of Simulation

At the highest level of simulation (i.e., the level with the least amount of detail) is *architectural simulation*, used for evaluating system architectures. Architecture simulators do not simulate logic signal values, but they simulate the data flow in the system in order to identify bottlenecks and determine throughputs [ELLE81]. They are used to study the performance of computers, communication networks, and so on.

Functional simulation, also called *register-transfer-level simulation*, may be viewed as the highest level of logic simulation. Here the circuit to be simulated is modeled as an interconnection of functional blocks, whose behavior is described using a computer hardware description language (CHDL) such as the Digital Design Language (DDL) [DULE67] or the Function Definition Language (FDL) [CHAP77]. The primary purpose of simulation at this level is the verification of the high-level design of a system before the detailed logic design is done. Functional level fault simulation is useful for fault analysis to a limited extent, when a more detailed fault simulation is not feasible or not desired. If the circuit to be simulated is very large, a combination of functional and gate-level fault simulation may be a feasible alternative to a detailed fault simulation of the complete circuit.

Gate-level simulation is by far the most widely used tool for both design verification and fault analysis. At this level of detail, it is possible to simulate not only the logical behavior of a circuit, but also some of its timing characteristics. However, present-day technology is already pushing gate-level simulation on general-purpose computers to its limits. The number of elements to be simulated can be reduced by using more complex elements, such as flip-flops, registers, and memories.

Two additional levels of simulation may be identified below the gate level. These are the *transistor level* [BRYA81, CHAW75, NHAM80, BOSE82] and the *circuit level* [NAGE75]. In both these levels, circuits are modeled as interconnections of transistors, resistors, and capacitors. At the switch-level, simulation is performed by treating the transistors as switches, with delay characteristics determined from the circuit description. In circuit-level simulation, the circuit behavior is determined by solving circuit equations. While transistor-level simulation is feasible for circuits with up to a few thousands gates, circuit-level simulation is usually limited to circuits with a few hundred gates. Thus the latter is useful for obtaining detailed timing diagrams showing the dynamic behavior of cells realizing specific functions, for use within larger circuits.

Due to the inability to simulate large circuits at the desired level of detail, it has become necessary to use a *mixed-mode simulation* strategy. Although it is possible to simulate circuits containing functional, gate-, and circuit-level primitives, the most commonly used combinations are functional and gate level [CHAP76], and gate and circuit level [AGRA80, JOHN80, NEWT79]. The parts of the circuit to be analyzed are modeled at the lowest level, with the higher-level descriptions modeling the environment in which the parts of interest operate. For example, if faults are to be simulated in one part of a large circuit, a gate-level description of that part may be simulated in conjunction with a functional level description of the rest of the circuit.

Functional simulation would then be used to propagate signal values from the primary inputs of the circuit to the gate-level part, and also for determining fault-free and faulty values of the primary outputs of the circuit.

Various fault simulation techniques will be studied in this chapter. The emphasis will be on techniques for functional-level simulation, since it appears to be essential for simulating VLSI circuits. Gate-level simulation has been discussed extensively in the literature [SESH65, CHAP74b, ULRI74] and will be touched on only briefly here. Architectural, transistor, and circuit-level simulation are beyond the scope of this chapter.

3.1.3. Architecture of a Simulator System

Simulators may be classified as *general-purpose simulators* and *specialized simulators*. In a general-purpose simulator (Fig. 3.1.2), the simulator itself is separate from the circuit model. The circuit model is provided by the user as a description in a circuit description language, and a data structure is constructed by a compiler. Similarly, the stimuli to be applied to the circuit are provided by the user and translated into a data structure by a compiler. The simulator is a system of programs that determines signal values and supervises and synchronizes the flow of signal changes in the circuit model.

The most important attribute of the general-purpose simulator is its flexibility. The same simulator may be used over and over again, and only the circuit model will be different. This allows uniformity in the circuit description, and the model prepared for simulation may be used for other purposes (physical design, documentation, etc.). The existence of libraries containing frequently used circuit components facilitates modeling. Also, the user aids that allow users to monitor simulation results may become very powerful and are reusable. Although extremely useful, these user aids will not be included in this chapter.

In a specialized simulator (Fig. 3.1.3), the simulator mechanism is embedded in the circuit model. That is, the circuit description is part of the executable code and not contained in a separate data structure. It is generally programmed using a standard programming language (C, FORTRAN, ALGOL, PASCAL, etc.).

Specialized simulators are tailored for specific applications and must be replaced when the simulation of a new circuit is desired. They are generally cheaper than general-purpose simulators but cannot be used for other design activities. Because of these limitations, specialized simulators will not be discussed here.

3.2. CIRCUIT MODELING

The simulation of the behavior of a circuit requires the construction of a circuit model, called simply a *circuit* whenever there is no ambiguity. This model is an abstraction of the real circuit, which retains as much information as needed to perform logic simulation at the desired level of detail. In addition, the circuit model may be used for

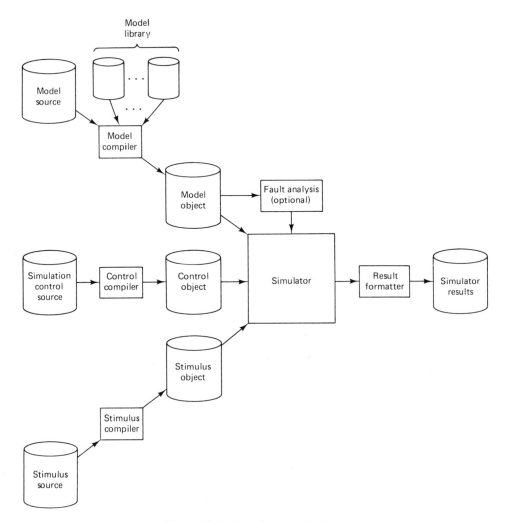

Figure 3.1.2   General-purpose simulator.

various computerized activities other than simulation (routing, placement, documentation, etc.).

A circuit consists of an interconnection of its *access terminals* (inputs and outputs) and *circuit bodies*. Each circuit body is composed of at least one *circuit description*, which is defined as either a *component circuit* or an *elementary circuit*. A component circuit is composed of other circuits *(parts)*. An elementary circuit may be a *primitive circuit*, whose behavior is predefined in the system (gates, flip-flops, memories, etc.) or a *user circuit*, whose behavior is described using tables [CAPA], graphs [AKER78], or a computer hardware description language (CHDL) [CHAP77].

Consider the circuit of Fig. 3.2.1. Circuit *A* is formed by the interconnection of elementary circuits *B* (type T_1), *C* (type T_2), and *D* (type T_3) and a component circuit

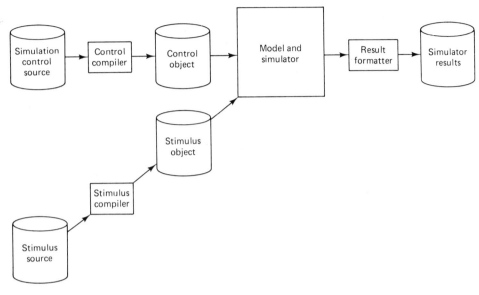

Figure 3.1.3 Specialized simulator.

E (type T_4). *B* and *C* are primitive circuits defined in the system. They are specified in terms of their *access terminals* and *types*. *D* is a user circuit whose behavior is specified in a suitable language. T_4 is a component circuit defined by the user in terms of primitive circuits and their interconnections.

A more formal definition of a circuit is given in Fig. 3.2.2. The double colon (::) denotes a definition. An asterisk (*) is used to repeat an item zero or more times. The repetition applies to the contents of the braces preceding the asterisk. The vertical

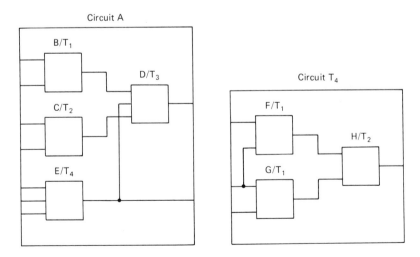

Figure 3.2.1 Circuit.

bar (|) between items means the disjunction (OR) of these items, and a dot (·) indicates the ordered conjunction of items (series). The boldfaced items are elementary items which need no further formal definition.

circuit	:: **type**.{access terminal}*.circuit body
circuit body	:: circuit descr.{circuit descr.}*
circuit descr.	:: component circuit | elementary circuit
elementary circuit	:: **primitive circuit** | user circuit
user circuit	:: user description
component circuit	:: {part}*.{net}*
part	:: **type.part name**.{terminal instance}*
net	:: **connection**.{terminal instance}*
access terminal	:: **input** | **output**

Figure 3.2.2 Circuit syntax.

The syntax of Fig. 3.2.2 (line 2) allows for multiple definition of a circuit (e.g., gate and behavioral descriptions). Although keywords may be necessary in an actual implementation, none has been specified here to simplify the discussion. The inputs and outputs are access terminals of the circuit under consideration. A *connection* is a continuous electrical connection. *Nets* (connections and terminals) are used to connect circuits. *Terminal instances* are "owned" by both the nets and the circuits, in the sense that they are terminals of a net and also access terminals of the parts connected to that net.

It should be noted that the definition is implicitly recursive through the type, which refers to another circuit. The definition of a component circuit is a finite recursion and the circuits used inside the definition may in turn be defined using the same mechanism. This recursive definition may produce many circuits and this continues until an elementary circuit is reached. This is a circuit for which no further recursive definition is needed.

The connectivity of a circuit may be augmented by additional information needed for simulation. For instance, delays may be assigned to gates and circuit terminals in addition to the timing information embedded in the user description (see Section 3.5). Simple examples of a component circuit (Exclusive-OR) and a primitive circuit (NAND) are given in Fig. 3.2.3.

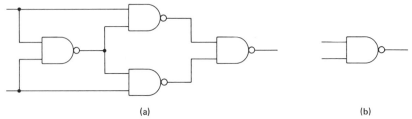

(a)   (b)

Figure 3.2.3 Circuit examples: (a) Component circuit (Exclusive-OR); (b) primitive circuit (NAND).

3.3. LOGIC VALUES

In digital simulation, the actual signals which are propagated through the circuit are modeled using *logic values*. Since digital circuits operate traditionally on an on–off basis, only a few values are needed to represent the signal values.

A minimal set of logic values consists of 0, 1, and x, where x denotes an unknown value [JEPH69]. The unknown value is needed in simulation to represent unknown initial states and signals whose values cannot be determined because of races and oscillations. In some technologies, such as TTL totem pole and MOS, it is necessary to model two additional states: high impedance and bus conflict. Accurate simulation of MOS circuits requires knowledge of signal values and also associated impedances [HAYE82, LEVE81a].

Table 3.3.1 gives a set of logic values that will cover most technologies. In MOS technologies, bus signals which are not actively driven will display "soft" 0 or 1 logic values (values $Z0$ or $Z1$), due to capacitances on the bus. These values may be overriden by regular logic values without damage to the circuits. A similar effect occurs in TTL technology, but the impedances are not high enough to keep the capacitances charged and the voltage level becomes unknown (value Zx).

TABLE 3.3.1
LOGIC VALUES

0	Zero
1	One
x	Unknown
$Z0$	Soft zero
$Z1$	Soft one
Zx	Soft unknown
ax	Analog unknown

The soft values are used to model high impedances in MOS technologies and the analog unknown is used to model a conflict on a bus. Different subsets of this set of values, which are closed under logic operations, may be used for logic simulation of different technologies.

Consider the subsets S_1, S_2, S_3, and S_4 (Table 3.3.2) of the set of logic values given in Table 3.3.1

TABLE 3.3.2 CLOSED
SETS OF LOGIC VALUES

S_1	$\{0, 1\}$
S_2	$\{0, 1, x\}$
S_3	$\{0, 1, x, Zx, ax\}$
S_4	$\{0, 1, x, Z0, Z1, Zx, ax\}$

S_1 and S_2 are the classical sets of logic values for simulation. S_3 and S_4 can accommodate TTL totem-pole and MOS gates [LEVE81a]. In MOS technologies, signals in high-impedance states may "remember" previous signal values. This is why set S_4 includes three soft values $Z0$, $Z1$, and Zx. As can be seen in the definitions of AND, OR, NOT, and BUS (Table 3.3.3), all the sets are closed under logic operations. Therefore, the logic operations may be implemented using S_4 and applied on any of the subsets S_1, S_2, and S_3.

TABLE 3.3.3 OPERATOR DEFINITION

(a) AND

	0	1	x	$Z0$	$Z1$	Zx	ax
0	0	0	0	0	0	0	0
1	0	1	x	0	1	x	x
x	0	x	x	0	x	x	x
$Z0$	0	0	0	0	0	0	0
$Z1$	0	1	x	0	1	x	x
Zx	0	x	x	0	x	x	x
ax	0	x	x	0	x	x	x

(b) OR

	0	1	x	$Z0$	$Z1$	Zx	ax
0	0	1	x	0	1	x	x
1	1	1	1	1	1	1	1
x	x	1	x	x	1	x	x
$Z0$	0	1	x	0	1	x	x
$Z1$	1	1	1	1	1	1	1
Zx	x	1	x	x	1	x	x
ax	x	1	x	x	1	x	x

(c) NOT

	0	1	x	$Z0$	$Z1$	Zx	ax
	1	0	x	1	0	x	x

(d) BUS

	0	1	x	$Z0$	$Z1$	Zx	ax
0	0	ax	x	0	0	0	ax
1	ax	1	x	1	1	1	ax
x	x	x	x	x	x	x	x
$Z0$	0	1	x	$Z0$	Zx	Zx	ax
$Z1$	0	1	x	Zx	$Z1$	Zx	ax
Zx	0	1	x	Zx	Zx	Zx	ax
ax	ax	ax	x	ax	ax	ax	ax

The above is only one aspect of signal modeling, namely the ability of representing various technologies. When hardware designers are interested in other aspects of logic design, a different set of logic values may be needed. For instance, a set of nine logic values has been used for better timing analysis [FANT74]. This set includes values representing rising and falling signals and hazardous transitions. S_2 is a subset of this set, and the other six values correspond to hazard-free transitions and transitions containing dynamic and static hazards [EICH64].

Another method of representing signal values is by means of combinations of values and strengths. Typical values are 0, 1, unknown, and indeterminate; strengths are driving, forcing and high impedance. Each combination of strength and value will correspond to a "logic value" as defined earlier [LEVE81a].

3.4. DELAYS AND TIMING

The simplest form of delay is the *transport delay*. This is the time it takes for an input change to reach the output of a gate, independent of the direction of the change. When the delay depends on the direction of the change, *rise and fall delays* must be used [SZYG72]. At the beginning of simulation, there may be transitions from an unknown state (x) to a known state (0 or 1). The rise (fall) time will be used as the transition delay from x to 1 (0). The concept of rise and fall delays must be extended to model specific technologies. For instance, the modeling of a CMOS tristate driver may require six transition delays, one for each of the following transitions: 0 to 1, 0 to $Z0$, 1 to 0, 1 to $Z1$, $Z0$ or $Z1$ to 0, $Z0$ or $Z1$ to 1.

Ambiguity delays are a refinement of rise and fall delays [CHAP71]. An ambiguity region for the rise (fall) delay is defined as the interval between the minimum and the maximum rise (fall) delays. During that interval, the logic value is undefined (x). The algebra underlying the ambiguity regions is a ternary algebra [YOEL64]. The ambiguity regions tend to accumulate along sensitive paths causing sequential circuits to latch unknown states, thus producing pessimistic results. For this reason, this delay model is not frequently used.

In the ambiguity model, a delay may assume any value between the minimum and the maximum with equal probability. An attempt has been made to model the delay ambiguity using a Gaussian distribution of the signal transition time around a nominal value [MAGN77]. An incoming transition distribution is combined with the intrinsic gate delay distribution to obtain the distribution of the output signal. However, complications occur when the combination of two or more input distributions is required to produce the output transition distribution, because the incoming distributions may not be independent (due to reconvergent fan-outs and feedback lines).

Short pulses may not carry enough energy to reverse the polarity of the device output. It may be desirable to suppress such pulses during simulation if their duration is below a certain threshold, called the *inertial delay*. Pulse suppression has also been called *high-frequency rejection* [CHAP71]. Since this effect is not properly a delay, the name *inertial threshold* may be more appropriate. Also, the inertial threshold may be combined with other delay models. The exact treatment of inertial thresholds may require complicated procedures [BREU76].

3.5. USER DEFINED DESCRIPTION

3.5.1. Behavior Tables

Combinational and sequential circuits may be represented by user-defined tables. These are similar to truth tables, as illustrated by the example of a master-slave JK flip-flop (Fig. 3.5.1). A discrete behavior of the flip-flop is assumed in that events occur at integer time units. The internal state is represented by q_M (master), q_S (slave), and q_{Cl} (clock), and capital letters denote the next values of these variables. J, Cl, and K are inputs and p and q are outputs. It was necessary to create the state q_{Cl} in order to remember the previous value of the clock and allow for a clock change to trigger the flip-flop memory changes.

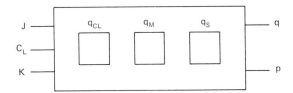

Figure 3.5.1   JK-flip-flop state representation.

The flip-flop behavior is described in Table 3.5.1. The "—" denotes unspecified entries.

TABLE 3.5.1   *JK* FLIP-FLOP BEHAVIOR

q_{Cl}	q_M	q_S	J	Cl	K	Q_{Cl}	Q_M	Q_S	q	p
0	—	—	—	0	—	0	q_M	q_S	q_S	$\overline{q}_S$
—	—	—	0	—	0	Cl	q_M	q_S	q_S	$\overline{q}_S$
—	—	—	0	1	1	1	0	q_S	q_S	$\overline{q}_S$
—	—	—	1	1	1	1	$\overline{q}_M$	q_S	q_S	$\overline{q}_S$
—	—	—	1	1	0	1	1	q_S	q_S	$\overline{q}_S$
1	—	—	—	0	—	0	q_M	q_M	q_M	$\overline{q}_M$

The table contains two parts: the input (left) region, which includes inputs and previous states, and the output (right) region, which includes outputs and next states. Entries in the output region may be Boolean expressions. Timing may be associated with any column or any entry in the right region of the table, by specifying integer-valued delays.

3.5.2. Computer Hardware Description Languages

Many computer hardware description languages (CHDLs) have been designed and used in the past. Initially, CHDLs were used to provide an unambiguous description of computer architectures [CHU72]. Later, the simulation of CHDLs provided an important method of design verification [CHAP77], and fault simulation of CHDLs was used for the evaluation of test quality for large circuits which could not be modeled completely at the gate level [MENO78].

Because of the variety of constructs and dialects [BELL71, CHU72, DIET75, CHAP77], it is impossible to present here a comprehensive study of CHDLs.* Only the basic features of CHDLs as embodied in the *User Function Description Language* (UFDL) will be discussed. UFDL is a fictitious language patterned after FDL [CHAP 77] but broader in its syntactic framework.

Language constructs of UFDL.   Entities, such as inputs, outputs, states, and registers, are represented by variables in UFDL descriptions. Variable types must be declared at the beginning of the user description. Registers are declared using the **REG** declaration. For instance,

$$\mathbf{REG}\ R1[1 \rightarrow 16],\ R2[16];$$

declares two registers $R1$ and $R2$ of 16 bits each. $R2$ starts at bit 0, by default.

Memories can be declared using the **MEM** declaration. The declaration

$$\mathbf{MEM}\ M[1 \rightarrow 256{:}32];$$

defines 256 words of 32 bits each. State variables are defined using the **STATE** declaration.

$$\mathbf{STATE}\ S[0 \rightarrow 27];$$

defines a vector of 28 states of type integer, by default. Any undeclared variable is considered a state. The **LOGIC** declaration defines the set of logic values used. The declaration

$$\mathbf{LOGIC}\ A\{0, 1, x\}$$

associates the values 0, 1, and x with variable A, and the declaration

$$\mathbf{LOGIC}\ \{0, 1, x\}$$

states that all the variables have values from the same set. Registers and memories are naturally of logical type, whereas state variables are of type integer. A departure from this requires an explicit type definition. It should be noted that access terminals as defined in Section 3.2 are *ipso facto* UFDL variables in a user-defined description. Therefore, access terminals may be of any of the types mentioned above.

Following is a list of operators:

1. *Logical operators* (**AND, OR, NOT, NAND, NOT, XOR, EQUIV**): These operators may operate on registers, bit by bit or on all the bits of one register, except the NOT operator, which operates on every bit of one register. The operands of the logical operators may also be scalar variables.

---

* For more information on CHDLs, the reader is referred to the *Proceedings* of the CHDL symposia (1972, 1975, 1979, 1981, 1983).

2. *Comparison operators:* The comparison operators are *greater than* ($>$), *less than* ($<$), *less than or equal to* ($<=$), *greater than or equal to* ($>=$), *equal* ($=$), and *not equal* ($!=$). The operands may be variables or vectors. The result of any comparison operation is a logic value: 1 if it is true and 0 if it is false.

3. *Arithmetic operators:* The arithmetic operators are addition ($+$), subtraction ($-$), multiplication ($*$), and division ($/$). These operators may be applied to integers or vectors of logical type.

4. *Bit reorganization:* These operators are Shift Right (SR), Shift Left (SL), Rotate Right (RR), Rotate Left (RL), and Concatenate (C), which operate on vectors.

5. *Assignment:* The transfer ($\leftarrow$) moves contents of variables and registers and may perform higher bit truncation or zero padding, in case of length mismatch between the operands.

These operators are unary (act on one operand) or binary (act on two operands) and, together with parentheses, they can be used to form expressions.

Unit delays are implicitly associated with assignments. For instance,

$$A \leftarrow B + C;$$

will be executed in one unit of delay. This implicit assumption may be modified in several ways. First, a delay may be assigned to a statement

$$A \leftarrow B + C \quad \textbf{DELAY } 5;$$

A delay may also be assigned to variable A, using the following declaration at the head of the description:

$$\textbf{DELAY } A: 5;$$

This declaration will apply to every occurrence of a transfer to A.

There are two basic decision constructs:

1. *Binary decision construct:* Its syntax is

$$\textbf{IF } C \textbf{ THEN } B_1 \textbf{ ELSE } B_2 \textbf{ IFEND;}$$

where C is a condition (expression) and B_1 and B_2 are blocks, composed of UFDL statements (including decision constructs).

2. *Multiway decision construct:* Its syntax is

$$\textbf{TEST } E_0;$$
$$\textbf{CASE } E_1 : B_1;$$
$$\textbf{CASE } E_2 : B_2;$$

.

.

.

$$\textbf{CASE } E_n : B_n;$$
$$\textbf{DEFAULT}: B_{n+1};$$
$$\textbf{TESTEND};$$

where E_i are expressions and B_i are blocks. The value of the expression E_0 is matched against the value of each E_i, and in case of match the block B_i is executed; if no match occurs, the default block B_{n+1} is chosen. More complex situations are stated in Problem 3.11.

It may be useful to describe the behavior of a circuit in terms of past and present values of some variable. The **HIST** (history) declaration provides this capability. For instance, the declaration

$$\textbf{HIST } A\,(2);$$

defines a variable A with a history of 2 (one present and one past value). A change of that variable may be checked by evaluating the expression

$$(A \textbf{ AND } (\textbf{NOT } A(-1))) \textbf{ OR } ((\textbf{NOT } A) \textbf{ AND } A(-1))$$

The concept of history, explicitly stated here, is implicit in the flip-flop example of Fig. 3.5.1 (state variable q_{Cl}). The **HIST** declaration can be omitted since the history can be determined by lexical analysis of the UFDL description.

Interpretation.   There are two main interpretations of UFDL, *sequential* interpretation and *parallel* interpretation. In order to distinguish between them, the following declarations are used:

$$\textbf{PAR UFDL};$$

or

$$\textbf{SEQ UFDL};$$

The parallel interpretation is assumed by default. Functions using the parallel and sequential interpretations will be called *nonprocedural* and *procedural* functions, respectively.

In the sequential interpretation, the statements are evaluated sequentially in a way similar to programs. Since the statements are executed one after the other, the latest values of variables are used to evaluate the expressions on the right-hand sides of assignments. Classically, each assignment statement is executed instantaneously; namely, the delay is zero. However, it is possible to associate delays with the assignments. For instance,

$$\textbf{DELAY } 1;$$

will associate a unit delay with all the transfers. In the sequential interpretation, the default is zero delay; in this case, the functional block has no delay and this may present difficulties in modeling. Two solutions are available. First, the statement

$$A \leftarrow B + C \ \textbf{DELAY} \ 5;$$

in the middle of a block will suspend the execution for five units of delay, meaning that subsequent UFDL statements do not get executed, even if they have no delay. Second, delays may be assigned to the terminals of the user-defined circuit to compensate for the absence of timing in the transfers.

In procedural functions, the **DELAY** declaration causes the sequential execution to be suspended. This requires external synchronization in the execution mechanism (see Section 3.9.3). For instance, if all the statements have a unit delay, the execution must be suspended after each statement and resumed at the next time frame.

In the parallel interpretation, all the statements are evaluated in parallel and each statement is executed with its specified delay (one unit by default). Delays may be associated with all types of transfers, including transfers to states.

The basic difference between the interpretations is illustrated by the following example:

$$A \leftarrow B \ \textbf{DELAY} \ 1;$$

$$C \leftarrow A \ \textbf{DELAY} \ 1;$$

Initially, let $A = C = 0$ and $B = 1$. Both interpretations are described in Fig. 3.5.2. In the parallel interpretation, C remains 0 because it received the previous value of A. This interpretation corresponds to the Huffman model of a sequential circuit [HUFF54] (Fig. 3.5.3).

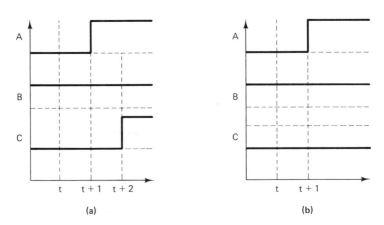

Figure 3.5.2 Timing in (a) sequential and (b) parallel interpretations.

Figure 3.5.3 Huffman model of a sequential circuit.

In the parallel interpretation, two cases may be distinguished: a synchronous model and an asynchronous model. In the asynchronous model, a change in state variables will cause reexecution of the user description, which may in turn cause changes in state variables. In the synchronous model, no reexecution occurs, corresponding to the case where a sequence of state changes is prevented by the clock. By default, state variables are asynchronous and registers and memories are synchronous. By using the **SYNC** declaration, synchronous state variables may be defined. For instance,

$$\textbf{PAR UFDL};$$
$$\textbf{STATE } S[1 \rightarrow 8];$$
$$\textbf{SYNC } S;$$

provides a description, where a change of state variables S will not cause a reexecution of the user description.

The parallel interpretation may be locally overridden using the **IMM** (immediate) declaration. For instance,

$$\textbf{IMM } B,C;$$

will force a sequential evaluation of the following two statements, by making the transfers to B and C immediate:

$$B \leftarrow A;$$

$$C \leftarrow B;$$

The assignment operator in both these statements is called an *immediate* assignment. The *simultaneous* execution of two "immediate" blocks of statements may lead to a critical race. An example of this situation is the case, where a variable, say A, is used on the right side of a transfer in one immediate block and on the left side of a transfer in another immediate block. Depending on the order of appearance of these blocks, the CHDL execution may yield different results. Similarly, if a variable appears on the left side of a transfer in two immediate blocks which are executed simultaneously, this may lead to conflicting assignments of that variable.

The sequential interpretation may be modified to include parallel sections, using the **COBEGIN** statement, which allows the initiation of parallel processes. Here, too, we may encounter critical races. An example of the **COBEGIN** statement is given next.

$$\textbf{COBEGIN}$$
$$\textbf{BLOCK} : B_1;$$
$$\textbf{BLOCK} : B_2;$$
$$.$$
$$.$$
$$.$$
$$\textbf{BLOCK} : B_n;$$
$$\textbf{COEND};$$

where $B_1, \ldots, B_n$ are blocks of UFDL statements to be executed in parallel. The **COBEGIN** declaration locally reverses the sequential nature of the description; however, each block internally remains sequential in nature.

In both interpretations, phase control may be performed by using semaphores to signal between processes and potentially halt the execution of one process until a predefined condition becomes true, using the **WAIT FOR** *condition* statement. Its syntax is

WAIT FOR *C*

where *C* is a condition.

In principle, both the parallel and the sequential interpretations are equivalent, since each one may be modified to include constructs belonging to the other interpretation. However, the UFDL syntax for parallel interpretation does not include a powerful construct analogous to **COBEGIN** to create sequentiality among parallel blocks. The only construct in this spirit is the **IMM** construct, which affects single variables and assignments into them. Therefore, the dominant feature of the parallel interpretation remains the ability of asynchronous modeling and that of the sequential interpretation remains the ability of high-level abstraction. The difference between the two interpretations has strong implications on the evaluation of CHDLs (Section 3.9).

An example of UFDL circuit description.   A limited arithmetic logic unit is given next.

CIRCUIT: *ALU*   *inputs*
    INPUT: $A[8]$, $B[8]$, $C[2]$;   *A/B, C are inputs*
    OUTPUT: $R[17]$;   *2 inputs*
        SEQ UFDL;
            REG $D[4]$;
            $D \leftarrow$ **DECODE**(C);
            TEST T;
                CASE $D[0]$: $R \leftarrow A + B$;
                CASE $D[1]$: $R \leftarrow A - B$;
                CASE $D[2]$: $R \leftarrow A * B$;
                CASE $D[3]$: $R \leftarrow A / B$;
            TESTEND;

The **DECODE** operator decodes the two bits of vector C. **T** stands for true and is tested against the decoder outputs, $D[1]$, $D[2]$, $D[3]$, and $D[4]$. The execution will follow one of the four cases. Note that the function is defined as **SEQ**, so that the result of decoding C is used immediately to select the operation to be performed.

3.6. CIRCUIT CAPTURE AND EXPANSION

The hierarchical structure of a circuit may be captured using graphical input or textual input in an appropriate language at each level of the hierarchy. At any level of the hierarchy, a user may refer to library circuits, instead of defining the component circuits using lower-level parts at that time. The structure of a circuit and its lower-level references define a finite tree structure.

Graphical input and textual input are *compiled* into identical computer models. The circuit description used for simulation is a single-level description but the language syntax is recursive since the definition of a circuit refers to other circuits by using their types (Fig. 3.2.2). The inherent recursion is not instantiated in that every circuit refers only to circuits one level below in the hierarchy. A single-level model can be constructed from a hierarchical description by a compiler using a recursive algorithm. However, the use of different libraries is facilitated by separating the overall process into two processes: *component compilation* and *circuit expansion*. Component compilation uses the description of each component circuit in terms of its next level parts, if any. The expansion process uses the product of compilation and produces a single-level circuit model, appropriately structured for simulation. The single-level circuit model is produced by replacing every component circuit by its more detailed lower-level model until an elementary circuit is encountered.

As an example of the use of separate circuit expansion and component compilation, consider the verification of the design of a circuit consisting of a number of large blocks. The design verification process may consist of simulating the entire circuit with all blocks described in UFDL, followed by several resimulations with different blocks described at the gate level. To accomplish this, the highest-level circuit description and the different blocks are compiled separately, the latter including UFDL models as well as gate-level models. The circuit model for each simulation is constructed using the expansion process with the compiled model of the main circuit and appropriate compiled models of the blocks.

The computer model used in the expansion process is a graph composed of *main vertices* (MV), *secondary vertices* (SV), *main edges* (ME), and *secondary edges* (SE). The main vertices are used to represent elementary circuits. The secondary vertices are used to represent terminals and primary inputs and outputs. The secondary edges describe the relationship between main vertices and secondary vertices. For instance, an edge between a main vertex (elementary circuit) and a secondary vertex (output) means that the elementary circuit owns the output. Secondary edges are directed from input to elementary circuit and from elementary circuit to output. The main edges represent fan-out lines between terminals. An example is given in Fig. 3.6.1. Later, during simulation, this graph model will allow flow of information from primary inputs to primary outputs along directed edges and through terminals and elementary circuits.

The following is a pseudocode version of the expansion algorithm. Several approaches to the expansion algorithm are possible (Problem 3.1), and one of them is given below.

Routine Expansion

    1. Search for circuit in main file
    2. If not found, then search in library files

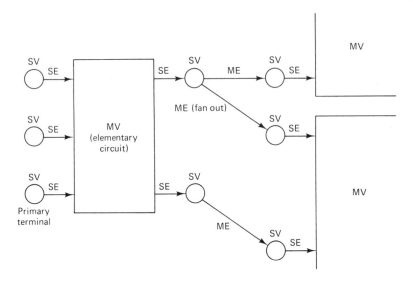

Figure 3.6.1   Graph model of a circuit.

3. If not found, then terminate
4. If circuit is not elementary, then for all parts in circuit
    a. create terminals, which are secondary vertices
    b. call *Expansion*
5. If circuit is elementary, then:
    a. if circuit is primitive, then create main vertex and return
    b. if circuit is UFDL, then compile, create main vertex, and return
6. Connect nets to terminals

End Expansion

This algorithm is a rather crude procedure which needs to be tuned to specific situations, but it accurately reflects the essential steps. It must be followed by a procedure to simplify the net connections. Also, it assumes that all the circuits needed are kept in a compiled form, namely using a graph model. If this is not the case, the algorithm may be modified to call a text compiler. The user-defined circuits are kept in a "source" file before compilation and compiled into an "object" file. Similarly, library circuits in a "source" form are compiled into a library, which is kept in an object form.

Although fully expanded single-level models are usually used in simulation, unexpanded circuit models may be used instead [WILL79]. The circuit definition of Fig. 3.2.2 allows for multiple circuit descriptions. The circuit expansion must be guided by the user for the proper selection of the alternate models. Only fully expanded single-level models will be considered in this chapter.

3.7. SIMULATION MODELS FOR ELEMENTARY CIRCUITS

Several computer models are possible, and only the most commonly used are given here. An elementary circuit (element) model consists of a data area or *state description,* an *evaluation mechanism* and a *symbol table.* The symbol table is necessary for information retrieval by the user during simulation (Fig. 3.7.1).

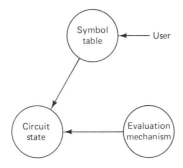

Figure 3.7.1   Elementary circuit model.

The evaluation mechanism may be *built-in, executable code,* or *interpretive.* The built-in mechanism is used for primitive circuits and the interpretive mechanism is generally used for user-defined elementary circuits. Executable code is also used for user-defined elementary circuits, especially when a programming language (e.g., FORTRAN or C) is used for the description.

Independent of the evaluation mechanism used, each instance of the elementary circuit is allocated a state representation in the form of an area of storage with a fixed location for every variable. Any reference to that location is made using a displacement (index) with respect to the beginning of the storage area of the elementary circuit.

A number of computer models are described in the following sections. All of these models are adequate for true-value simulation. However, it will be shown that some fault simulation methods cannot accommodate all the computer models of CHDL elements.

3.7.1. Built-in Representation

An appropriate evaluation routine is called by the simulator, based on the type of element. The routine "knows" the structure of the circuit state and does not require any user information. Commonly used gates and functions (AND, OR, Exclusive-OR, flip-flops, etc.) are treated in this manner.

3.7.2. Table Representation

The table in Fig. 3.7.2, called an *evaluation table,* has two regions. The entries in the state regions are logic values of input signals and state variables. The entries in the output region are pairs composed of a pointer to an expression and a delay.

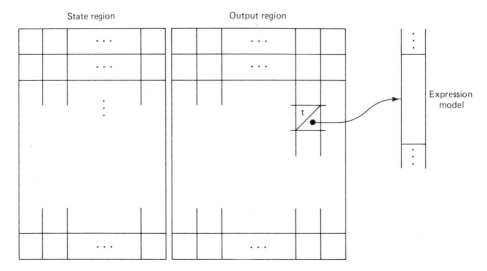

Figure 3.7.2   Table representation.

Each expression in the description provided by the user is compiled into a computer model consisting of a symbol table and an expression model. The reverse Polish notation [KNUT73] is one popular representation of expressions in the evaluation table.

During simulation, this table is accessed by a table evaluation mechanism that is composed of a search algorithm and an expression evaluation procedure. Given an input combination, the search algorithm finds the proper row of the table. The expression evaluation procedure computes the corresponding values of the output signals. More generally, for a sequential circuit, the input region contains input and previous state-variable values, and the output region includes expressions for output and next state values.

3.7.3. CHDL Representation

Expressions and decision constructs are the basic elements of CHDL representations. Expressions are treated as in table representations.

Each CHDL construct can be represented by a directed graph whose vertices correspond to actions (decision or execution). Directed edges labeled "next" indicate the order in which the actions are to be performed. In addition, decision vertices have one outgoing edge corresponding to each test outcome. A graph for an entire CHDL description can be obtained by combining the graphs for simpler constructs.

Consider the following example:

> **TEST** A;
>   **CASE** B: **IF** C **THEN** B_1 **ELSE** B_2 **ENDIF**;
>   **IF** D **THEN** B_3 **ELSE** B_4 **ENDIF**;
>   **CASE** E: **IF** F **THEN** B_5 **ELSE** B_6 **ENDIF**;
>   **DEFAULT**: B_7; B_8;
> **TESTEND**;

where A, B, C, D, E, and F are expressions, and B_1, B_2, ..., B_8 are executable blocks. The graph representation of this example is given in Fig. 3.7.3a.

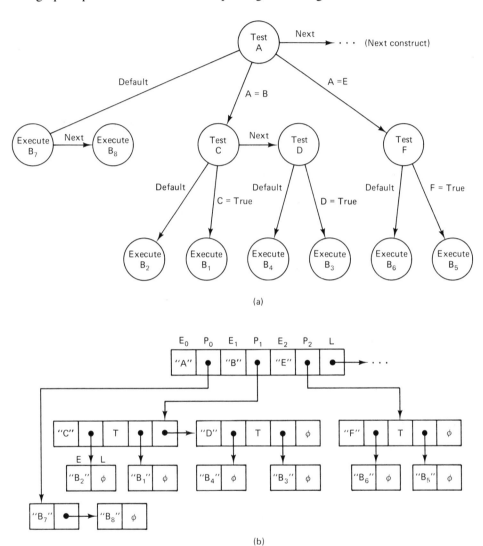

Figure 3.7.3 Graph model for CHDL.

The graph can be represented by a data structure containing nodes and pointers. A decision node is represented as a vector of pairs $\{E_i, P_i\}$ and a lateral pointer L (to the "next" node). E_i is a pointer to an expression and P_i is a pointer to another node. E_0 is the pointer to a *test expression* and P_0 is the pointer to a *default node*. E_1, E_2, ..., E_{n-1} are pointers to the potential *matching expressions* and P_1, P_2, ..., P_{n-1} are the corresponding pointers to other nodes (decision or execution nodes). The lateral pointer is used to point to the next statement contained in the same block. Execution nodes are pairs $\{E, L\}$ where E is the pointer to an expression and L is a lateral pointer.

A data structure representing the graph of Fig. 3.7.3a is shown in Fig. 3.7.3b. In the figure, T is a reserved symbol for the logical constant true, and pointers to expressions are denoted by quoted expressions. Φ denotes an empty pointer.

During the evaluation of a user defined block, E_0 is matched against all E_i and, in case $E_0 = E_j$, the pointer P_j is chosen. If no match is found, the pointer P_0 is chosen. Note that binary and multi-way decision mechanisms are treated in the same way.

The CHDL model evaluation mechanism is composed of a graph-traversal mechanism and an expression evaluation mechanism. The graph-traversal mechanism gets the results from the evaluation of the expressions E_i, compares these results, and chooses the proper path in the graph. This corresponds to the way the decision mechanisms in a programming language are evaluated to choose the proper path and execute the instructions which are on this path. The only difference is that in the present context the decision graph is explicity traversed.

An alternative model for a decision construct is a Boolean representation. For instance,

$$\textbf{IF } C \textbf{ THEN } D \textbf{ ELSE } E \textbf{ ENDIF};$$

may be represented as

$$CD+\overline{C}E; \tag{3.7.1}$$

More generally, the CHDL text modeled in Fig. 3.7.3 may be represented as follows (see Problem 3.10):

$$(A=B)(CB_1+\overline{C}B_2)+(A=B)(DB_3+\overline{D}B_4)+$$
$$(A=E)(FB_5+\overline{F}B_6)+(\overline{A=B})(\overline{A=E})(B_7) \tag{3.7.2}$$

where $A=B$ is the equivalence operation between A and B. Since each B_i represents a block with assignments to a number of variables, Equation 3.7.2 represents a number of equations, one for each variable to which an assignment is made.

As seen in Sections 3.11 and 3.12, the various other models are used (sometimes exclusively) in different fault simulation methods.

3.7.4. Programming Language Model

One method of architectural modeling [ELLE81] consists of a "super C-language" which is aimed at modeling hardware. A preprocessing of the model produces a C-language [KERN78] script, which is in turn compiled by the C-compiler. The compiled code and its data are linked with the simulator program and during evaluation of the user-defined circuit the control is passed to the compiled code. Other programming languages, such as PASCAL, may also be extended to CHDLs [HILL79]. This type of model presents a problem in fault simulation in that fault insertion and propagation in the user-defined model is difficult (Section 3.11).

3.7.5. *Alternate Modeling*

The simulation model of a CHDL construct may or may not have the same structure as the user description. For instance, the model of Fig. 3.7.3 had the same tree structure as the CHDL description. However, this need not be the case and user and computer models may be different. This is the case in the algebraic model of Eq. (3.7.2) equivalent to the graph of Fig. 3.7.2.

Expressions may be modeled as graphs or translated into executable code by compilation. Similarly, decision mechanisms may be modeled as tables or translated into executable code, and tables may be modeled as executable code.

Various combinations of the foregoing models are possible. All models except executable code are independent of the logic values which are coded into the operator evaluation.

3.8. *GENERAL SIMULATION ALGORITHM*

Logic simulation algorithms and data structures have been discussed in detail in several textbooks and papers [FRIE71, BREU76, HARD67, ARMS72, ULRI74]. Only a brief outline of the general simulation algorithm, necessary for understanding fault simulation techniques, will be presented here.

In its simplest form, logic simulation involves computing the next state and outputs of a circuit, given its present state and applied stimuli. This can be accomplished by computing the output and next state of each element (elementary circuit) in the circuit using the connectivity, element type, and delay information contained in the circuit model. This method is rather inefficient, because it computes the next states and outputs of elements even when their inputs and states have not changed.

The most widely used method of simulation is the *event-driven* method (sometimes called *trace directed*), which essentially propagates the effects of signal changes through a circuit [MENO65, ULRI65]. The change of any signal in the circuit is called an *event*. The main operations to be performed in an event-driven simulation algorithm are scheduling of events, processing of events, evaluation, and event list management. These operations are applicable to both gate-level and functional level simulation. True-value simulation and the different methods of fault simulation differ mainly in the definition and processing of events.

3.8.1. *Scheduling*

In true-value simulation, an event represents a signal change and consists of the identity of the changing signal and its new value. Events are generated as a result of primary input changes and the evaluation of elements. All the events for a particular time are kept in a list, called the *event list,* for that time. Insertion of events in the event list for the appropriate tim is called *scheduling*.

For efficient simulation, only signal *changes* should be inserted in the event list. This requires comparing the computed value of each signal with its present value if a change has not already been scheduled. If a change has been scheduled, the newly computed value must be compared with the last scheduled value, before the new value is scheduled. Suppression of pulses of short duration ("high-frequency rejection or spike suppression") can also be performed at this time.

For detecting a spike, the newly computed value of a signal is compared with its last scheduled value. A spike is present if the values are different and the time between the last scheduled change and the new change to be scheduled is smaller than a prespecified value (inertial threshold). The spike is suppressed by deleting the last scheduled event and ignoring the new change.

An alternative method of scheduling, which is useful when spike suppression is not required, consists of scheduling the updating of all computed signal values, and determining whether or not an actual change has occurred at the time of updating. Although this method is simpler than the first method, it may result in some inefficiencies due to unnecessary schedulings.

When different rise and fall delays are simulated, it may be necessary to cancel certain scheduled events in order to obtain correct results. For example, consider the circuit of Fig. 3.8.1, where gate A has a delay of 3, and gate B has rise and fall delays of 10 and 5, respectively. If the input to the circuit changes at time 0, the output will be scheduled to change to 1 at 13, and to 0 at 8. Clearly, the output should not change to 1 at all, and the event scheduled for time 13 must be canceled.

Figure 3.8.1 Difficulty in delay treatment.

The first method of scheduling is more appropriate in this case. The last scheduled time must be retained in addition to the last scheduled value for each gate, in order to determine the events that must be canceled. In some high level functions, different delays may be associated with changes of the same signal, depending on the actual operation being performed by the function. A more complex scheduling method will be necessary to handle this correctly. For the sake of simplicity, the second method of scheduling will be used in the different fault simulation algorithms to be presented.

3.8.2. Processing Scheduled Events

The processing of scheduled events consists of updating signal values and determining the elements to be evaluated as a consequence of the signal change. If all updates are scheduled, whether or not the new value is different from the preceding one (as in the alternative method discussed above), the processing of scheduled events occurs only for true events (i.e., where new and previous values are different).

For every event in the event list at the current simulated time, the signal value is updated to its new value. If the updated signal is the output of an element, its fan-outs are traced and the appropriate input of each fan-out element is updated to the new value. The fan-out element to be evaluated is put on a list, called the *evaluation list*, if it is not already there. If the event involves updating a state variable of an element, the element itself is put on the evaluation list.

After all the updates and fan-out processing for a particular simulated time have been performed, the elements on the evaluation list are evaluated. In this method, sometimes called the "two-pass" method, an element is evaluated only after all the changes to its inputs and state variables for a particular time have been made. An alternative "single-pass" method evaluates an element as soon as any of its input or state variables changes [ULRI68]. This method is efficient when multiple-input changes to elements are infrequent. Multiple-input changes will require deletion of events and reevaluation of elements, making the method inefficient for high-level elements.

3.8.3. Evaluation

Evaluation consists of computing the output(s) and next state (if the element has memory) of elementary circuits (elements) in the circuit model. An element may be a primitive or a user-defined function. Primitives may be gates such as NAND, NOR, AND, OR, and NOT or higher-level primitives such as flip-flops, registers, RAMs, and ROMs, which are predefined in the particular system. The evaluation of primitives is performed by *evaluation routines*. User-defined elements are described in a CHDL. Evaluation of CHDL elements will be discussed in Section 3.9.

3.8.4. Event List Management

A simple method of maintaining event lists during simulation is shown in Fig. 3.8.2. There is a linked list of events for each time, with an event list header with pointers to the first and last events in the list. These pointers simplify retrieving events for a particular time and adding events to the end of an event list. The event list headers are also linked together in the order of increasing time.

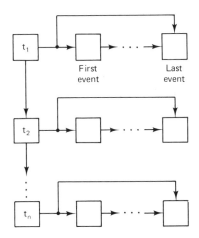

Figure 3.8.2 Simple event lists.

A more efficient mechanism for event list management is the *time wheel* [ULRI68, ULRI76]. The event lists on the time wheel are separated by fixed increments of simulated time (Fig. 3.8.3), allowing faster access to events for a desired time.

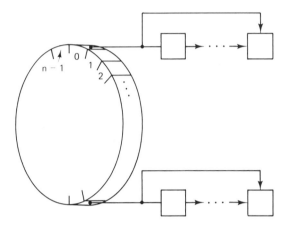

Figure 3.8.3 Simple time wheel.

An embodiment of the time wheel, which is particularly efficient if most of the delays in the circuit are less than some integer N, is obtained by dividing the events into a *near range* and a *remote range* (Fig. 3.8.4). This is a combination of time wheel (near range) and linked list (remote range). Events scheduled for any time less than N from the current time are treated as being in the near range, and all other events in the remote range. The event list header for any time t in the near range can be accessed by using $t \bmod(N)$ as the index. Accessing event list headers in the remote range will require searching the headers for the desired time. Events in the remote lists in the range t to $t + N - 1$ are moved to the near range whenever $t \bmod(N) = 0$. With this scheme, all event retrieval during simulation can be made from the near range using the indexing method mentioned earlier.

An efficient method of list management for unit delay simulation is the *dual list* method, with present and next event lists [CHAP74b]. Due to its limited applicability, this method will not be discussed further.

3.8.5. The Algorithm

The following algorithm assumes that primary input changes, ordered by time, are contained in a file. Simulation control, such as stopping and resuming simulation, are not shown.

Simulation algorithm

Routine simulation

WHILE there are input changes and/or events pending
    1. Advance time to smaller of next input change and scheduled event

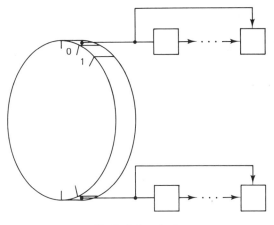

Simple timing wheel

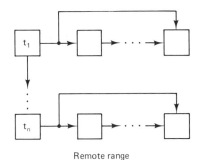

Remote range

Figure 3.8.4   Timing wheel with remote range.

2. Put input changes, if any, on event list for present time.
3. FOR every element in event list for present time
   a. Update signal value.
   b. IF updated signal is a state variable
         THEN put element on evaluation list, if not already there.
         ELSE FOR every fan-out of signal
             a. Update input of fan-out element.
             b. Put fan-out element on evaluation list, if not already there.
4. FOR every entry on evaluation list
   a. Evaluate element.
   b. Schedule generated events.

End simulation

3.9. EVALUATION ALGORITHMS

The evaluation of circuit elements during simulation can be divided into two types: evaluation of primitives and evaluation of user-defined functional elements (user circuits). Methods for the former have been discussed extensively in the literature [BREU76]. They all involve the use of system routines which compute the new values of outputs and state variables using logical operations or table look-up. Truth tables and zoom tables [ULRI72] are widely used with table-look-up methods. The emphasis here will be on user-defined functional elements.

3.9.1. Functional Evaluations

The representation of any user-defined functional element consists of two parts: the behavioral description of the function (Section 3.7.3) and the state description of the function. The behavioral description expresses the output and next state of the element as functions of its inputs and present state. It is static in nature, and a single description is sufficient for each type of functional element, independent of the number of times the element is used in the circuit. On the other hand, the state description, which consists of values of the inputs and state variables of the function, is dynamic. A separate copy of the state description must exist for each instance of a functional element.

If the evaluation of a function requires the detection of edges or pulses, the state description must also contain an appropriate number of previous values of some variables. For example, a rising edge on a signal corresponds to a present value of 1 and a previous value (one unit of time earlier) of 0. Detection of this edge requires knowledge of two consecutive values of the signal at all times. A pulse of width N can be identified by examining the present value and the past N values. In general, any waveform of finite length can be identified by retaining a sufficient number of previous values.

The sequence of present and past values of a variable is called its *history*. The history of variables may be implemented as shift registers. If all the values in the history of a variable are not equal, the history shift register must be "pushed" once per time frame, even if the variable does not change. During pushing, all values are moved by one time unit. The oldest value is discarded and the new value becomes the present value. Pushing a history shift register will result in a change in the waveform of previous values, and the function must be evaluated.

The method of evaluating a functional element depends on how the behavioral description is represented. The behavior of some relatively simple functional elements can be represented by zoom tables, which are similar to truth tables. The evaluation of a function represented by a zoom table involves computing an index for present values of inputs and the present state of the function from its state description. This index is used to look up the next state and the outputs of the function from the zoom table.

Another type of behavioral description, especially useful for high-level functional elements, consists of machine language instructions executable in the host computer. The evaluation of a functional element with such a behavioral description requires only a transfer to the sequence of executable instructions, with a pointer to the appropriate state description to be used as data for the sequence of instructions. This method is used in architectural-level simulators such as AIDE [ELLE81].

As discussed in Section 3.7.3, the behavior of a functional element can be represented by a graph. The graph consists of one or more trees. Each vertex of such a tree represents either a decision or a computation. There is branch from a vertex a to a vertex b if, and only if, the decision or computation represented by vertex b is to be executed as a result of the execution of vertex a. Decisions and computation represented by the vertices of the graph may also involve arithmetic or logical expressions and/or data transfers. Expressions are usually represented in the reverse Polish (postfix) notation.

The evaluation of a function described by a graph is essentially a graph traversal. At each decision vertex, the expressions required for making the decision are evaluated using the information contained in the state description of the function and the appropriate branch emanating from the vertex is traversed. In the case of computation vertices, expressions are evaluated using data contained in the state description. Data transfers required are accomplished by scheduling the update of outputs and/or state variables at times specified in the behavioral description of the function. Evaluation of expressions represented in the reverse Polish notation can be done efficiently using a stack mechanism [KNUT73].

The results of the evaluation of a function depend on the type of interpretation (i.e., parallel or sequential) of the behavioral description. This is the topic of the following two sections.

3.9.2. Nonprocedural Functions (Parallel Interpretation)

As discussed earlier, the evaluation of a nonprocedural function requires the computation of its next state and output, using only the values of the inputs and the state of the function at the beginning of the evaluation. Two different types of nonprocedural functions are possible: synchronous and asynchronous.

In synchronous functions, every state transition is assumed to be caused by some input change (typically, a clock input). Hence a function is evaluated if and only if one or more of its inputs change. If a state variable changes, it is updated at the appropriate time, but the function is not reevaluated as a result of this change. Therefore, it is necessary to distinguish between input variables and state variables in the data structure.

In the case of asynchronous functions, a change in one or more state variables may cause additional state-variable changes. The function may make a sequence of state transitions in response to an input change, until a stable state is reached or another input change occurs. This behavior is simulated by scheduling a function for evaluation, whenever any of its inputs or state variables change.

A function may depend on rising and/or falling edges or pulses of specified widths on some of its inputs. In such cases, a sufficient number of previous values of these inputs are stored in the state description of the function, as the history of the variable. The history shift register must be pushed once per simulated time frame, as long as the shift register does not contain identical values.

3.9.3. Procedural Functions (Serial Interpretation)

The evaluation of these functions is similar to the execution of programs in that operations are performed in the logical sequence in which they are encountered. Since procedural functions usually represent higher levels of abstraction than nonprocedural ones, they are treated as synchronous functions, and no reevaluations are performed as a result of state-variable changes.

When a transfer with **DELAY** is encountered, the evaluation of the function must be suspended and rescheduled for a later time, determined by the **DELAY** and the present time. The point in the behavioral description at which the evaluation is to be resumed must also be saved with each rescheduling. At the specified time, the evaluation of the function must be resumed at the appropriate point.

The **WAIT FOR** *condition* statement will also result in the suspension of the function, and resumption when the condition is satisfied. Since the condition is a function of the inputs and the functional element will be entered for evaluation when any input changes, conditions can be checked to determine whether any suspended evaluations are to be resumed.

DELAY constructs have the potential of introducing races in procedural functions (see Section 3.14.4). The inputs to a function may change exactly when a suspended execution is to be resumed, or the times for the resumption of two suspended executions may coincide. The results of the evaluation may depend on the order of evaluation of the segments of the functional description, making these races critical. Such races can be resolved by performing the evaluations in a fixed order, or changing all affected variables to x. Ideally, functional descriptions should not contain any critical races. Critical races are discussed further in Section 3.14.4.

3.10. FAULT MODELING

3.10.1. Gate-Level Faults

The most widely used fault model in gate-level simulation is the *single stuck fault*. Any single lead in the circuit may be stuck at a constant value, 0 or 1. A test sequence that detects a very large percentage of all single stuck faults in a gate-level circuit is likely to detect a large percentage of actual faults in the circuit, even when the stuck fault model does not represent actual failure mechanisms.

Another type of fault that is simulated at the gate level consists of *short circuits* between leads (CHAP74b). Since the number of all shorts in a circuit may be prohibitively large, only faults between adjacent leads or pins, as determined from the physical layout, are usually simulated. Simulation of shorts is discussed in Section 3.14.5.

Not all physical faults in a circuit can be modeled by the fault types listed above. An example of a fault that cannot be modeled as above is the open junction fault in CMOS circuits. A transistor-level simulator, such as MOTIS [BOSE82], is ideally suited for simulating such faults. Using the stuck fault model for simulating these faults requires modification of the circuit model by adding dummy gates [WADS78]. However, they can be simulated at the gate level without modifying the circuit model by using additional logic values [LEVE81a].

3.10.2. Faults in Functional-Level Circuits

An obvious class of faults that can be simulated at a functional level consists of stuck faults on the inputs and outputs of each functional element (*pin faults*). However, a test sequence that detects all such faults may not even exercise the function completely. To obtain a better estimate of the fault coverage in a circuit described at the functional level, it is necessary to simulate additional types of faults.

Faults that affect the behavior of a functional element will be called *functional faults*. The simplest example of functional faults consists of state-variable stuck faults. For instance, one bit of a register may be stuck at zero.

Control faults, which affect conditional transfers in CHDL descriptions, constitute another type of functional fault. A control fault is defined as a fault that causes a control variable or expression to have an incorrect value. Such faults will result in the traversal of incorrect paths in the graph representation of the functional element. An example of a control fault is a control variable or expression stuck at a constant value. Although the correspondence between control faults and physical faults is not apparent, testing for control faults in addition to the stuck faults is likely to improve the true fault coverage, by exercising parts of the function not exercised otherwise [LEVE82a].

Another class, called *general function faults*, consists of faults whose effects are known but cannot be modeled by the fault types considered so far. Consider a function f containing an expression E such that

$$f = f(\underline{x}, \underline{y}, E(\underline{x}, \underline{y})) \qquad (3.10.1)$$

where $\underline{x}$ and $\underline{y}$ are the input and state variables, respectively, of the function. The general function fault α transforms the expression E to an expression E_α, so that the faulty function becomes f_α, where

$$f_\alpha = f(\underline{x}, \underline{y}, E_\alpha(\underline{x}, \underline{y})) \qquad (3.10.2)$$

Although this type of fault is very general, its usefulness is limited by the need for describing each such fault individually.

General function faults can be specified in the CHDL description of a function using fault variables [MENO78]. For example, a fault α that causes an expression to be complemented can be described by

$$\textbf{IF}(a) \ \textbf{THEN} \ Q = x(y + z)$$
$$\textbf{ELSE} \ Q \ = \bar{x} + \bar{y}\,\bar{z}$$

where a is the fault variable associated with α and $a = 1(0)$ if the fault is present(absent).

3.10.3. Fault Collapsing

The time required for fault simulation can be reduced without any loss of information by identifying equivalent faults and simulating only one fault from each equivalence class. Most of the equivalent faults can be identified by local analysis of the neighborhood of each gate [SCHE72]. Other equivalences are more complicated to identify.

For AND (NAND) gates, all the inputs stuck at 0 and the output stuck at 0(1) form an equivalence class. Similarly, for OR (NOR) gates, the input stuck at 1 faults and the output stuck at 1(0) fault form an equivalence class. Therefore, it is sufficient to simulate only the output stuck faults in these cases.

If a gate has a single fan-out, its output stuck faults are equivalent to the input stuck faults of the fan-out gate, and the latter need not be simulated. In the case of inverters, the input stuck faults are equivalent to the output stuck at the opposite values. In a chain of inverters with no fan-out, it is sufficient to simulate the faults on one of the inverters.

It is also useful to delete faults that can be shown to be undetectable by analyzing the topology of the circuit. Examples of such faults are faults along paths that cannot reach any observable output. These are the result of unused outputs on some devices. Another class of undetectable faults are those on leads set to constant values. For example, the stuck at 0 fault on a lead set to a constant value of 0 (e.g., ground) cannot be detected. However, the faults in the latter category do not cause any slowdown in most methods of fault simulation, since their effects do not propagate.

Another concept that is useful for fault collapsing, but *only in combinational circuits* when no fault location information is required is *fault dominance* [SCHE72]. A fault α is said to *dominate* a fault β if every test that detects β also detects α. The dominating fault α need not be simulated for determining fault coverage in combinational circuits. For example, the output stuck at 0 fault on a NAND gate in a combinational circuit need not be simulated, since it dominates all input stuck at 1 faults on the same gate. The foregoing type of dominance relations are not applicable in sequential circuits. A test sequence that detects a stuck at 1 fault on an input of a NAND gate may not detect the output stuck at 0 fault on the same gate [BREU76]. Therefore, this type of fault dominance cannot be used for fault collapsing, in general.

3.11. FAULT SIMULATION METHODS

In fault simulation, it is necessary to determine the fault-free value of every signal in the circuit, and also the values of these signals in the presence of the faults from a prespecified set. The various methods of fault simulation differ in their complexity, speed, storage requirements, accuracy, and the levels of models that can be simulated efficiently.

Simulating one fault at a time is, perhaps, the simplest method of fault simulation. First, the fault-free circuit is simulated. Each fault is then inserted by suitable modification of the circuit model, and the modified circuit is simulated. Stuck faults are inserted by simply setting the stuck signal to the appropriate constant value. This signal can be prevented from changing by flagging it as constant or by disconnecting it from any device that is driving it. Other types of faults may require more complex circuit modification.

The one-at-a-time method is slower than the other methods that are discussed in the following three sections. However, the storage requirements of this method are less than the other methods. In spite of its inefficiency in speed, this method may be useful when the host computer is small [CAPA].

The following sections present the three widely used methods of fault simulation: parallel simulation, deductive simulation, and concurrent fault simulation. They attempt to speed up simulation by processing a number of faults at the same time, and represent different trade-offs between simulation speed and computer storage requirement.

3.12. PARALLEL FAULT SIMULATION

Parallel simulation takes advantage of the word-oriented nature of operations in the host computer to simulate the effects of a number of faults simultaneously [SESH65]. The number of faults simulated during one pass of the simulator is usually determined by the word length of the host computer. It is also possible to use the same algorithm for simulating larger numbers of faults simultaneously if the host machine has efficient methods of handling long bit strings (as in multiple precision arithmetic). Multiple passes through the simulator are usually necessary when the number of faults is large.

3.12.1. Gate-Level Parallel Simulation

Parallel simulation is simplest at the gate level with two logic values and stuck-type faults. In this case, a word of length n is used to hold the fault-free value and $n - 1$ faulty values of every signal in the circuit.

The logic performed by a gate is simulated by performing the corresponding logical operation(s) on the words representing its input values. A stuck at 1 fault on a lead is injected by ORing a word, called a *fault mask*, containing a 1 in the bit position for the faulty value and 0s elsewhere, to the word representing the signal values on the lead. Similarly, a stuck at 0 fault can be injected by ANDing a word with a 0 in the faulty value position, and 1s elsewhere.

Example 1. Consider the two-input AND gate shown in Fig. 3.12.1a, with inputs a and b, and output c. This gate is part of a larger circuit not shown here. Let w_a, w_b, and w_c be the words representing the signal values, and m_0 and m_1 the masks for injecting c stuck at 0 and c stuck at 1, respectively. The fault-free and faulty values (Fig. 3.12.1b) are computed by

$$w_c = w_a w_b m_0 + m_1 \qquad (3.12.1)$$

In Fig. 3.12.1, the word length is assumed to be 8. The leftmost bit represents the fault-free value. The second and third bits represent the values in the presence of the fault c stuck at 0 and c stuck at 1, respectively. Looking at w_a, one notices that the signal on lead a in the presence of the fault c stuck at 0 is different from the fault-free value. This is possible only if the circuit containing this gate has a feedback loop containing c and a. Although the inputs to the AND gate in the presence of c stuck at 0 are both 1s, the output if forced to 0 by the fault injection process.

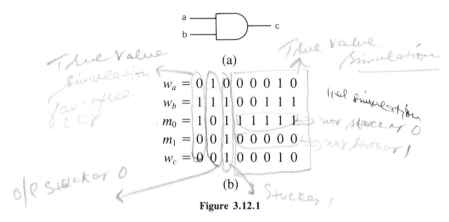

Figure 3.12.1

As pointed out in Section 3.3, two logic values are usually not sufficient for accurate logic simulation. At the very least, a third value, usually represented by x or u, is needed to represent unknown signal values. Coding techniques are required, when more than two logic values are used.

Two bits are necessary for representing each signal value in three-valued logic simulation. Two words will be used for representing a set of fault-free and faulty values: namely, a *1-word* and a *0-word*. A pair of bits, one from the same position in each of the two words will represent each logic value. This coding is similar to that used in test generation [CHAP74a]. Table 3.12.1 shows a code that can be used for representing three values.

TABLE 3.12.1
CODING FOR THREE
LOGIC VALUES

a^0	a^1	a
1	0	0
0	1	1
0	0	x
1	1	Unused

With the code of Table 3.12.1, the operation $c = ab$ is replaced by

$$w_c^0 = w_a^0 + w_b^0 \qquad (3.12.2a)$$

$$w_c^1 = w_a^1 w_b^1 \qquad (3.12.2b)$$

Similarly, $c = a + b$ corresponds to

$$w_c^0 = w_a^0 w_b^0 \qquad (3.12.3a)$$

$$w_c^1 = w_a^1 + w_b^1 \qquad (3.12.3b)$$

Finally, $c = \bar{a}$ is simulated by

$$w_c^0 = w_a^1 \qquad (3.12.4a)$$

$$w_c^1 = w_a^0 \qquad (3.12.4b)$$

For a general switching function $z = f(a, b, c, \ldots)$,

$$w_z = f(w_a, w_b, w_c, \ldots) \qquad (3.12.5)$$

It can be shown (see Problem 3.14) that

$$w_z^1 = f^1(w_a^1, w_b^1, \ldots) \qquad (3.12.6a)$$

$$w_z^0 = (f^1(w_a^1, w_b^1, \ldots))^0 = f^0 \qquad (3.12.6b)$$

where f^1 is obtained from f by attaching the superscript 1 to every uncomplemented expression in f and replacing every complement by the superscript 0. f does not have to be a sum of products, and the AND and OR operators are unchanged. These superscripts act like operators and simplifications are handled by using the following rules:

$$(x^1)^0 = x^0 \qquad (3.12.7)$$
$$(x^1)^1 = x^1 \qquad (3.12.8)$$
$$(x^0)^1 = x^0 \qquad (3.12.9)$$
$$(x^0)^0 = x^1 \qquad (3.12.10)$$

where x is any expression. The 1-operator is a neutral operator and the 0-operator is similar but not identical to the complement. Note that

$$x^1 \neq \overline{(x^0)} \qquad (3.12.11)$$

f^0 can also be obtained from $\bar{z}$ (see Problem 3.15).

Let w_c and w_c' be the words representing the signal values of c before and after injecting the local fault on c, respectively. Equation (3.12.1) can be generalized to

$$w_c' = w_c m_0 + m_1 \qquad (3.12.12)$$

and, using the various rules in the algebra of Problem 3.15, one can show (see Problem 3.16) that

$$w_c'^1 = w_c^1 m_0^1 + m_1^1 \qquad (3.12.13a)$$

$$w_c'^0 = w_c^0 m_1^0 + m_0^0 \qquad (3.12.13b)$$

where $m_0^1 = \overline{(m_0^0)} = m_0$ and $m_1^1 = \overline{(m_1^0)} = m_1$. This is true because there is no possible unknown status for the injection of a local fault.

Example 2. Based on the previous set of equations, the three-input NAND gate of Fig. 3.12.2a can be simulated using the following set of equations:

$$w_d'^1 = (w_a^0 + w_b^0 + w_c^0)\, m_0^1 + m_1^1 \tag{3.12.14a}$$

$$w_d'^0 = w_a^1 w_b^1 w_c^1\, m_1^0 + m_0^0 \tag{3.12.14b}$$

Here m_0^0 and m_0^1 are the masks for d stuck at 0, and m_1^0 *and* m_1^1 for d stuck at 1. The masks shown in Fig. 3.12.2b assume that the second and third bits from the left represent signal values with d stuck at 0 and d stuck at 1, respectively.

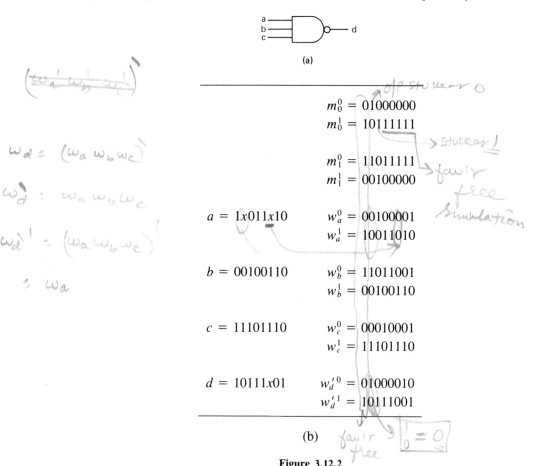

(a)

$$m_0^0 = 01000000$$
$$m_0^1 = 10111111$$

$$m_1^0 = 11011111$$
$$m_1^1 = 00100000$$

$a = 1x011x10$ $w_a^0 = 00100001$
                $w_a^1 = 10011010$

$b = 00100110$ $w_b^0 = 11011001$
                $w_b^1 = 00100110$

$c = 11101110$ $w_c^0 = 00010001$
                $w_c^1 = 11101110$

$d = 10111x01$ $w_d'^0 = 01000010$
                $w_d'^1 = 10111001$

(b)

Figure 3.12.2

The method discussed above for three logic values can be extended to any number of logic values by coding them using a sufficient number of bits [JEA78,

LEVE81a]. For n logic values, $p = \lceil \log_2 n \rceil$ words are needed for each signal x, namely $x^0, x^1, x^2, ..., x^{p-1}$. The logic value of a faulty signal simulated in position i is represented by the ith bits of all the words $x^0, x^1, ..., x^{p-1}$, and this forms the coding of this signal. The propagation function of an element z is mapped into p propagation functions $z^0, z^2, ..., z^{p-1}$ (see Problem 3.17).

3.12.2. Functional-Level Parallel Simulation

Since parallel simulation uses word-oriented logical operations, functional descriptions must be converted into two-valued Boolean expressions before parallel simulation can be used. Note that in the preceding section, multivalued logic was converted to two-valued logic by the use of codes for parallel simulation even at the gate level.

One approach to functional simulation is to automatically generate a gate-level description of each function for simulation [SZYG73]. This needs no modification of the parallel simulation algorithm. It also has the advantage that the simulation of each functional block can be event driven inside the functional boundaries. That is, the evaluation of a functional block will cease as soon as there is no more activity in its gate-level representation.

A disadvantage of the approach outlined above is that the gate-level representation of functional blocks increases the size of the model, defeating a central purpose of functional-level modeling. This disadvantage can be overcome by using Boolean equations to represent CHDL constructs [MENO78]. Operations such as arithmetic operations and shifting must be represented by equivalent Boolean expressions. In three-valued parallel simulation, *a pair of words must be associated with each function input, output, and state variable.*

As will be seen later, transformation of CHDL descriptions into Boolean equations is necessary for deductive simulation also. This transformation requires the following: (1) conversion of control constructs into Boolean equation; (2) representation of arithmetic and other non-Boolean operation in terms of Boolean expressions; and (3) transformation of expressions in multivalued logic into two-valued logic using appropriate coding.

1. *Conversion of control constructs into Boolean equations:* The simplest control construct in a CHDL is the binary decision, which has the general form

   IF y **THEN** $z = A$
   ELSE $z = B$ **ENDIF**;

   where y, A, and B are expressions, and z may be a single binary variable or an array of variables. If y can only have the value of 0 or 1, the above construct can be represented by

$$z = yA + \bar{y}B \tag{3.12.15}$$

   However, if the value of y may also be unknown (i.e., it is a three-valued variable), this equation will produce the value $z = x$ if $y = x$ and $A = B = 1$.

This is clearly incorrect. For three-valued simulation, the decision construct must be replaced by the following equation [WU79]:

$$z = yA + \bar{y}B + AB \qquad (3.12.16)$$

Multiway decisions can be transformed into a set of Boolean expressions in an analogous manner by coding the outcomes of tests with binary variables. For example, consider a four-way branch based on the value of a variable (or expression) y, which can assume the values 0, 1, x, or z.

CASE ($y = 0$): $q = a$;

CASE ($y = 1$): $q = b$;

CASE ($y = z$): $q = c$;

CASE ($y = x$): $q = d$;

a, b, c, and d may be binary variables or expressions. Coding $y = 0$ by $(y_1, y_2) = (0, 1)$, $y = 1$ by $(y_1, y_2) = (1, 0)$, $y = z$ by $(y_1, y_2) = (1, 1)$, and $y = x$ by $(y_1, y_2) = (0, 0)$, we have

$$q = \bar{y}_1 y_2 a + y_1 \bar{y}_2 b + y_1 y_2 c + \bar{y}_1 \bar{y}_2 d \qquad (3.12.17)$$

2. *Conversion of arithmetic and other expressions into Boolean expressions:* Arithmetic expressions can be converted into Boolean expressions using logical expressions for realizing the arithmetic operators. For example, the addition of two integers can be modeled by representing each integer as an array of binary variables and the addition operation by the equations representing a ripple carry adder.

3. *Transformation of multivalued logic expressions into binary logic expressions:* The procedure for performing this is similar to that used in Section 3.12.1 for three logic values.

Example 3.   Consider a tri-state driver, whose behavior is specified by Table 3.12.2. The inputs of the element are a and e, and the output is b.

TABLE 3.12.2 TRI-STATE DRIVER

		0	1	z	x
	0	z	z	z	z
e	1	0	1	x	x
	z	x	x	x	x
	x	x	x	x	x

(column header: a)

This tri-state driver can be represented as follows:

CASE ($e = 0$): $b = z$;

$$\textbf{CASE } (e = 1): \quad \textbf{IF } (a = z) \textbf{ THEN } b = x;$$
$$\textbf{ELSE } b = a;$$

$$\textbf{CASE } (e = z): \quad b = x;$$

$$\textbf{CASE } (e = x): \quad b = x;$$

These statements yield the following four-valued logic equation:

$$b = (e = 0)z + (e = 1)(a = z)x$$
$$+ (e = 1)\ \overline{(a = z)}a$$
$$+ (e = x)x + (e = z)x \qquad (3.12.18)$$

Using the codes 01, 10, 11, and 00 to represent the values 0, 1, z, and x, respectively, we have

$$b_1 = \overline{e}_1 e_2 + e_1 \overline{e}_2 a_1 \overline{a}_2 \qquad (3.12.19)$$
$$b_2 = \overline{e}_1 e_2 + e_1 \overline{e}_2 \overline{a}_1 a_2 \qquad (3.12.20)$$

as an equivalent to the original tristate driver.

The equations representing functional primitives can be represented in reverse Polish form. The operations involved are binary or unary, and a stack mechanism can be used for their evaluation. Fault-free and faulty values are computed using word-oriented operations as discussed earlier.

3.12.3. Parallel Simulation Algorithm

The parallel simulation algorithm is similar to the general algorithm described in Section 3.8.5 with the following differences;

1. The new value in each event is replaced by one or more words representing the fault-free and faulty values of the signal to be updated.
2. Logical equations similar to Eqs. (3.12.13a) and (3.12.13b) are used for element evaluations. These equations include the injection of faults using fault masks. Word-oriented computations are performed so that fault-free and faulty values are computed simultaneously.

When the number of faults to be simulated is large, multiple passes through the simulation algorithm will be used.

3.12.4. Activity in Parallel Simulation

In multiple-pass parallel fault simulation performed on a computer with word size n, the fault-free circuit and $n - 1$ faulty circuits are simulated in each pass. For a three-valued logic system, two computer words are required. An event is defined as a triplet: {signal, word pair, time}. During any pass, simulation activity will continue until no more events are created. Events will be created even if only one faulty circuit is active and all the faults represented in the active signal will be evaluated. However, there is no additional cost incurred by this evaluation, since word-oriented computer operations are used.

As a variation of parallel simulation, it is possible to use p pairs of words for each signal, rather than one pair, so that pn circuits can be simultaneously simulated as a vector. Fault j will always have the same word position k in the p words pairs associated with each signal. Assuming that the faults and the words are numbered in an increasing order starting from 0, the word position of fault j is

$$k = \text{integer}\,((j+1)/n)$$

This method eliminates the recurrent overhead of multiple-pass simulation, such as fan-out search. It should be noted that, usually, only a small fraction of the faulty signals are different from the fault-free signal. Therefore, most of the vector bits are identical to the fault-free signal bits (corresponding faults have no effect on the signal). This results in increased processing during the evaluation phase which may consume all or part of the savings in the fan-out search. It has been experimentally found that when the number of faults in one pass is multiplied by a constant m the activity (number of events) decreases by $m' < m$ [LEVE83b] (i.e., the number of events becomes greater than $1/m$).

This inefficiency can be removed by using the concept of *selective event*, which is a quadruplet: {signal, word position, word pair, time}. The word position allows the selective simulation of active words only. The fan-out search for several selective events on the same signal may be saved by means of *vector events*, defined as the ordered p-tuples composed of p selective events: $se_1, se_2, \ldots, se_p$.

To better evaluate the usefulness of vector events, two cases must be studied:

1. There is no fault-free circuit change. Only the words that include faulty signal changes will participate in the vector event. This situation represents the largest savings.
2. There is a fault-free circuit change. As stated earlier, all the words that include signals identical to the fault-free signal will participate in the vector event. This results in the potentially large overhead.

3.13. DEDUCTIVE FAULT SIMULATION

A relatively large number of faults can be simulated in one pass using the deductive method. Instead of computing signal values for all faults being simulated, this method computes signal values for the fault-free circuit, and deduces the faults that will cause each signal to have a value different from its fault-free value [ARMS72]. This method is ideally suited for two-valued simulation, and has been extended to handle the unknown value. Extensions to multivalued simulation have also been proposed [LEVE81b].

3.13.1. Gate-Level Simulation with Two Logic Values

During simulation, a *true* (fault-free) *value* and a *fault list* are associated with every lead in the circuit. The fault list associated with a lead is the set of faults such that any one of them will cause the signal value on the lead to be opposite to its true value. This implies that any fault absent from the fault list of a lead at any time during simulation has no effect on its signal value at that time.

The deductive simulation method involves determining the output true values and fault lists of elements from their input true values and fault lists. The true value of an element output is computed whenever one or more of its input true values change. The output fault list is computed whenever any of its input true values or fault lists change.

Set algebra is used for fault list computations. The equation used for computing the output fault list of a gate depends not only on the type of the gate but also on its input values.

Example 4.   Consider the three-input AND gate of Fig. 3.13.1, with inputs a, b, and c and output d. Let the fault list associated with each lead be denoted by the corresponding uppercase letter.

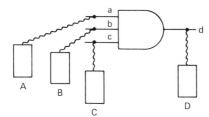

Figure 3.13.1

If $a = 1$, $b = 0$, $c = 1$, then $d = 0$. The output d will become 1 if a fault causes b to become 1, but leaves a and c unchanged. That is, any fault in B but not in A or C must also be in D.

$$D = B - (A \cup C) \tag{3.13.1}$$

Denoting stuck faults by lead names with the stuck value as subscript, let

$$A = \{p_1, q_0, r_1\}$$
$$B = \{q_0, r_0, s_1\}$$
$$C = \{r_1, s_0\}$$

where p, q, r, and s are leads elsewhere in the circuit. Then

$$D = \{r_0, s_1\}$$

The faults r_0 and s_1 may be thought of as having propagated through the AND gate. If the set of faults being simulated consists of stuck at 0 and stuck at 1 on all gate outputs, the fault d_1 must be added to the list to give

$$D' = \{r_0, s_1, d_1\}$$

If all the inputs of the AND gate of Fig. 3.13.1 have true value 1, a fault on any of the gate inputs would propagate to the gate output. Therefore,

$$D' = A \cup B \cup C \cup \{d_0\}$$

is the expression for the output fault list after fault injection.

Fault list equations for different types of gates can be obtained as in the example above. Let I_0 and I_1 represent the sets of gate inputs with values 0 and 1, respectively. Let the inputs of each gate be denoted by $x_1, x_2, \ldots, x_n$. Fault lists associated with these inputs are $X_1, X_2, \ldots, X_n$. Table 3.13.1 shows the equations for computing the output fault list for each type of gate under different input conditions. ϕ denotes the empty set.

TABLE 3.13.1   OUTPUT FAULT LIST COMPUTATION FOR BASIC GATES

Gate type	Input condition	Output fault list
AND, NAND	$I_0 = \phi$	$\bigcup_{x_i \in I_1} X_i$
	$I_0 \neq \phi$	$\bigcap_{x_i \in I_0} X_i - \bigcup_{x_i \in I_1} X_i$
OR, NOR	$I_1 = \phi$	$\bigcup_{x_i \in I_0} X_i$
	$I_1 \neq \phi$	$\bigcap_{x_i \in I_1} X_i - \bigcup_{x_i \in I_0} X_i$
NOT		X_1

In circuits with feedback, the effects of a fault originating from an input or output of a gate may propagate back to the inputs of the same gate through the feedback. Such faults must be deleted from the input fault lists of the gate, and faults associated with the gate reinserted, based on the true values of the gate inputs and output. For example, consider the case $a = 1$, $b = 0$, $c = 1$ in Fig. 3.13.1. If the fault list B contains the fault d_0, it must be deleted from the list. The fault d_1 is then added to the output fault list. Note that if d_0 is not deleted, the output fault list will contain d_0. Since the true value of the output is 0, the presence of d_0 in the output fault list means that d will have the value 1 if d is stuck at 0—obviously incorrect!

3.13.2. Three-Valued Deductive Simulation

The two-valued simulation technique can be extended to handle unknown signal values using the concept of conditionally detectable faults (*star faults*) [ARMS72,

CHAP74b]. If the true value of a signal on a lead is 0 or 1, but the signal value in the presence of a fault α is unknown, the fault α is included in the fault list of the lead as a star fault, denoted by $\alpha*$. The presence of $\alpha*$ in a fault list indicates that it could not be determined whether or not the fault α would result in an incorrect signal on the lead.

If the true value of a signal is unknown (x), it cannot be determined whether any fault α will cause the faulty value to be different from the true value. This fact can be represented by associating a symbolic fault list $U*$ with leads with unknown true value, U being the set of all simulated faults (universe).

Three-valued deductive simulation requires a method of fault list computation in the presence of unknown signal values. A simple example will be used to explain the method.

Example 5.   Consider a three-input AND gate with inputs a, b, c and output d, and let $a = 0$, $b = 1$, $c = x$. The ouput fault list D can be computed for the two cases, $c = 0$ and $c = 1$:

$$\text{for } c = 0, D = (A \cap C) - B$$

$$\text{for } c = 1, D = A - B - C$$

Clearly, $\phi \subseteq D \subseteq A - B$ in both cases. Using the star fault notation,

$$D = (A - B)*$$

(i.e., all faults in the set $A - B$ are star faults).

More generally, consider an arbitrary gate with a number of input values that are unknown. If the gate output is unknown, the output fault list must be $U*$. If the output true value is known, the longest output fault list is obtained when all the unknown inputs assume the nondominant value for this gate type and have null fault lists associated with them. Since the shortest output fault list obtainable is the null list, all the faults in the list obtained by changing x to the nondominant value must be changed to star faults. Assigning the nondominant value and the empty fault list to a gate input is computationally equivalent to ignoring the input.

The general procedure for fault list computation in the presence of unknown signal values is as follows:

1. Compute the true value of the gate output.
2. If the true value is unknown, make the propagated fault list $U*$; end.
3. Otherwise, compute the propagated fault list, ignoring the unknown inputs. Change all faults in the propagated list to star faults. Correct for local faults that may have propagated to the gate inputs via feedback paths; end.

The fault lists $U*$ associated with unknown signal values never participate in fault list computations. Therefore, for all practical purposes, null fault lists are frequently associated with signals that have unknown values.

The discussion above considered only the cases where star faults are generated at gate outputs when one or more gate input true values are unknown. Star faults can also be generated as a result of oscillations and critical races.

If a fault causes the signal value on a particular lead to oscillate (but the fault-free circuit does not oscillate), that fault will continue to appear in and disappear from the fault list of the lead. It is changed to a star fault if the number of changes exceeds a preset threshold.

Critical races are identified by simultaneous changes on specified pairs of leads called *race pairs*. The identification of a fault-induced critical race will require a knowledge of the present and past true values of a race pair and the associated fault lists.

With star faults introduced by any of the mechanisms above, the set operations used in fault list computations must be modified. The additional rules for this purpose follow from the definition of star fault and are given below:

$$\{\alpha\} \cap \{\alpha^*\} = \{\alpha^*\} \qquad \{\alpha\} \cup \{\alpha^*\} = \{\alpha\}$$
$$\{\alpha\} - \{\alpha^*\} = \{\alpha^*\} \qquad \{\alpha^*\} - \{\alpha\} = \{\}$$

The treatment of unknown signal values by using star faults ignores the cases where the fault-free circuit value is unknown but the faulty value is known. This can lead to incorrect results as shown in the following example [LEVE79].

Example 6. Consider the part of the circuit of Fig. 3.13.2 shown in solid lines. The D flip-flops are clocked once after applying each input to a, using clock lines which are not shown. The results of simulating the part of the circuit shown in solid lines for the input sequence 011 and fault b stuck at 0, denoted by α, using the deductive method are shown in Table 3.13.2a. Each entry in the table gives the true

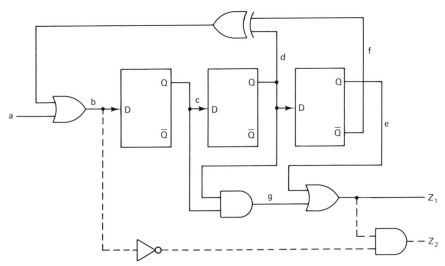

Figure 3.13.2

TABLE 3.13.2
(a) DEDUCTIVE SIMULATION RESULTS

t	a	b	c	d	e	f	g	z_1
0	$x\{\alpha*\}$	$x\{\alpha*\}$	$x\{\alpha*\}$	$x\{\alpha*\}$	$x\{\alpha*\}$	$x\{\alpha*\}$	$x\{\alpha*\}$	$x\{\alpha*\}$
1	$0\{\}$	$x\{\alpha*\}$	$x\{\alpha*\}$	$x\{\alpha*\}$	$x\{\alpha*\}$	$x\{\alpha*\}$	$x\{\alpha*\}$	$x\{\alpha*\}$
2	$1\{\}$	$1\{\alpha\}$	$1\{\alpha\}$	$x\{\alpha*\}$	$x\{\alpha*\}$	$x\{\alpha*\}$	$x\{\alpha*\}$	$x\{\alpha*\}$
3	$1\{\}$	$1\{\alpha\}$	$1\{\alpha\}$	$1\{\alpha\}$	$x\{\alpha*\}$	$x\{\alpha*\}$	$1\{\alpha\}$	$x\{\alpha*\}$

(b) FAULT-FREE/FAULTY VALUES

t	a	b	c	d	e	f	g	z_1
0	x/x	$x/0$	x/x	x/x	x/x	x/x	x/x	x/x
1	$0/0$	$x/0$	$x/0$	x/x	x/x	x/x	$x/0$	x/x
2	$1/1$	$1/0$	$1/0$	$x/0$	x/x	x/x	$x/0$	x/x
3	$1/1$	$1/0$	$1/0$	$1/0$	$x/0$	$x/1$	$1/0$	$1/0$

value and fault list associated with a lead, after the clock has been applied and the circuit has settled. Table 3.13.2b shows the fault-free/faulty values obtainable by simulating the fault-free and faulty circuits separately. From the tables it is seen that although the fault α is detected at output z_1 by the particular input sequence, the results of deductive simulation show it only as a potentially detectable (star) fault.

The errors produced by deductive simulation may not be always pessimistic. It can be verified that the fault α in the complete circuit of Fig. 3.13.2 (including the dashed portion) is not detected at the output z_2 by the input sequence 011. However, it appears as a star fault at z_2, in deductive simulation.

An approximation that is sometimes used in deductive fault simulation with three logic values is to assume that no faults are propagated through a gate if one or more of its inputs have unknown values [CHAP74b]. It may appear that this approximation is conservative in that some faults that reach a circuit output as star faults may not reach the output at all. The following example shows that some star faults may be incorrectly declared as detected by the approximate method.

Example 7 [LEVE79]. Consider the circuit of Fig. 3.13.3, with fault $\alpha = b$ stuck at 1, and inputs $a = x$, $b = 0$. The output fault list obtained by deductive fault simulation is $Z = \{\alpha*\}$. The approximate method yields $Z = \{\alpha\}$, although the fault is clearly not detected, if the unknown signal a has the value 1.

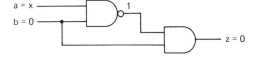

Figure 3.13.3 Incorrect results obtained by approximate method.

The potential inaccuracy in deductive simulation is due to the fact that not all combinations of fault-free and faulty values are represented by a true value and a fault list. Since each signal may have three logic values 0, 1, or x, there are nine combinations of fault-free and faulty values to be represented. The combination of true value and fault list can represent the following six values accurately: $0/0$, $0/1$, $0/x$, $1/0$, $1/1$, $1/x$. The combinations $x/0$, $x/1$, x/x are not distinguishable, since they are all represented by the true value of x and the null fault list (or $U*$).

The potential inaccuracy in deductive simulation can be removed by representing each signal value by two binary variables [LEVE80]. A fault list is associated with each of these variables. Using two variables a_0 and a_1 to represent a variable a, so that $a_0 = 1$, $a_1 = 0$ for $a = 0$, $a_0 = 0$, $a_1 = 1$ for $a = 1$, and $a_0 = a_1 = 0$ for $a = x$, any fault α for which a has a fault-free value of 0 and faulty value of 1 will be represented by $a_0 = 1\{\alpha\}$, $a_1 = 0\{\alpha\}$. If the faulty value is unknown, only the fault list associated with the variable whose true value is 1 will be non-null (i.e., $a_0 = 1\{\alpha\}$; $a_1 = 0\{$ $\}$). The fault-free/faulty value pair $x/0$, which cannot be represented by a single true value and fault list, can be represented by $a_0 = 0\{\alpha\}$; $a_1 = 0\{$ $\}$. All the possible combinations of a fault-free signal a and a faulty signal a_α and their representation using two variables and two fault lists are given in Table 3.13.3. The combinations which are not in the table would create the impossible faulty or fault-free code $(1,1)$. Capital letters denote fault lists.

TABLE 3.13.3 FAULT LISTS AND FAULT-FREE/FAULTY SIGNALS

a_0/A_0	a_1/A_1	a	a_α
0{ }	0{ }	x	x
0{α}	0{ }	x	0
0{ }	0{α}	x	1
0{ }	1{ }	1	1
0{ }	1{α}	1	x
0{α}	0{α}	1	0
1{ }	0{ }	0	0
1{α}	0{ }	0	x
1{α}	0{α}	0	1

When each signal is represented by two binary variables, two Boolean functions are necessary for representing each logical operation or function, as discussed earlier for parallel simulation. These functions are used for computing the values and fault lists associated with the output.

Example 8.   Consider a NOR gate with inputs a, b, c and output d. Using two binary variables denoted by subscript 0 and 1 for representing each signal, the logic function realized by the gate is given by

$$d_0 = a_1 + b_1 + c_1$$

$$d_1 = a_0 b_0 c_0$$

Denoting fault lists by upper case letters, let the input values and fault lists be

$$a_0 = 1 \quad A_0 = \{\alpha, \beta\}$$
$$a_1 = 0 \quad A_1 = \{\alpha, \beta\}$$
$$b_0 = 0 \quad B_0 = \{\alpha, \delta\}$$
$$b_1 = 1 \quad B_1 = \{\alpha, \gamma, \delta\}$$
$$c_0 = 1 \quad C_0 = \{\epsilon\}$$
$$c_1 = 0 \quad C_1 = \{\epsilon\}$$

Note that the fault γ is contained in the list B_1 but not in B_0. Therefore, the presence of fault γ will result in $b_0 = b_1 = 0$ (i.e., $b = x$).

The output true value and fault list (only faults propagating through the gate) are given by

$$d_0 = 1 \quad D_0 = B_1 - A_1 - C_1 = \{\gamma, \delta\}$$
$$d_1 = 0 \quad D_1 = B_0 - A_0 - C_0 = \{\delta\}$$

Using the star fault notation, these values and fault lists correspond to

$$a = 0 \quad A = \{\alpha, \beta\} \qquad b = 1 \quad B = \{\alpha, \gamma^*, \delta\} \qquad c = 0 \quad C = \{\epsilon\}$$

and

$$d = 0 \quad D = B - A - C = \{\gamma^*, \delta\}$$

Now, consider the case

$$a_0 = 1 \quad A_0 = \{\alpha, \beta\}$$
$$a_1 = 0 \quad A_1 = \{\alpha, \beta\}$$
$$b_0 = 0 \quad B_0 = \{\alpha, \gamma\}$$
$$b_1 = 0 \quad B_1 = \{\beta, \delta\}$$
$$c_0 = 1 \quad C_1 = \{\delta, \epsilon\}$$
$$c_1 = 0 \quad C_0 = \{\epsilon\}$$

The true values and fault lists of a and c are

$$a = 0 \quad A = \{\alpha, \beta\}$$
$$c = 0 \quad C = \{\delta^*, \epsilon\}$$

The true value of b is x, but the faults affecting it cannot be represented by a single fault list. The faults α and γ cause b to become 0, while the faults β and δ cause it to become 1. The true value of the output is unknown, since

$$d_0 = a_1 + b_1 + c_1 = 0$$

$$d_1 = a_0 b_0 c_0 = 0$$

The output fault lists are

$$D_0 = A_1 + B_1 + C_1 = \{\alpha, \beta, \delta, \epsilon\}$$

$$D_1 = B_0 - A_0 - C_0 = \{\gamma\}$$

indicating that the fault γ will cause the output to become 1 and any of the faults $\{\alpha, \beta, \delta, \epsilon\}$ will cause the output to become 0. This case cannot be simulated correctly using the concept of star faults.

3.13.3. Higher-Level System Primitives

An efficient method of simulating system primitives like latches and flip-flops is by means of tables containing equations for fault list computation. Since the fault list computations depend on the input and state of the primitive, the table must contain the next state, and output, and the set algebraic equations for computing the associated fault lists for every combination of inputs and state variables. The equations can be derived by analyzing the behavior of the primitive, from a gate-level realization of the primitive [ARMS72, LEVE74], or from its next state and output equations.

Consider a general switching function $z = f(a, b, c, \ldots)$. It is possible to calculate the output fault list Z, using an expression containing the inputs a, b, c, $\ldots$ and the input fault lists A, B, C, $\ldots$ [LEVE74]. Defining the mixed Exclusive-OR $p \oplus P$ of a logic value p and a fault list P by

$$p \oplus P = P \qquad\qquad \text{if } p = 0$$

$$p \oplus P = \bar{P} = U - P \qquad \text{if } p = 1$$

the following equation for the output fault list is obtained:

$$Z = f(a, b, c, \ldots) \oplus F(a \oplus A, b \oplus B, c \oplus C, \ldots) \qquad (3.13.2)$$

where F is obtained from f by replacing AND and OR in f by intersection and union, respectively (see Problem 3.18).

3.13.4. Functional Elements

As in the case of parallel simulation, user-defined functional elements must be represented by Boolean equations for deductive simulation. The transformations to be performed are identical to those described in Section 3.12.2. The equations representing functional elements can be stored in postfix form. A stack mechanism is used for the evaluations, each item on the stack consisting of a true value and a pointer to a fault list. Operations to be performed consist of binary and unary logical operations, and assignments. Each logical operation requires of a true-value computation and a fault list computation, the set of operations used in the latter depending on the true values of the operands. *A fault list must be associated with each function input, output, and state variable*.

Functional faults in user-defined functions can be simulated using fault variables [MENO78]. Associated with each functional fault α is a fault variable a with a constant true value 0 and fault list $\{\alpha\}$. If the fault α causes a function to change from f to f_α, the composite functional behavior can be represented by

$$f' = af_\alpha + \overline{a}f$$

Since a has a true value of 0, the true value of f' will be the value of f. The fault α will cause a to become 1 and the output will change if, and only if, $f \neq f_\alpha$. The output fault list can be computed directly from the equation for f'.

3.13.5. Activity in Deductive Simulation

There are two types of activity in deductive simulation, true-value changes and fault list changes. True-value changes are usually accompanied by fault list changes, but the fault list associated with a signal may change even when its true value does not change [LEVE74].

Consider a signal s and the fault s stuck at 0, denoted by α. In the presence of α, the signal s will remain 0 even if the true value of the signal undergoes the transition 0–1–0–1. As a result of these true-value changes, α must appear, disappear, and reappear in the fault list of s. These events cause fault list recomputations.

A situation where a true value changes but a fault α remains permanently in the fault list happens when the signal value under the fault α is always the complement of the true value. Also, the fault α can remain as a star fault in a fault list if the signal under the fault remains unknown. However, the likelihood of a fault list to remain unchanged when the true-value changes is very low.

Whenever the true value of any input or state variable of an element changes, the element must be evaluated. Since fault propagation through an element depends on the true values and fault lists on its inputs and state variables, fault list computations must also be performed. However, if only the fault lists associated with the inputs and/or state variables change, only the new fault lists need be computed.

An important aspect of activity in deductive simulation is the "coupling" between all the faults contained in a fault list. The algorithm essentially treats each fault list as an entity. Thus, the appearance or disappearance of a single fault in an input fault list of a gate will require the entire output fault list of the gate to be computed.

3.13.6. Deductive Simulation Algorithm

The algorithm is similar to the general simulation algorithm with the following exceptions:

1. Events are now of two types, namely:
   a. True value changes usually accompanied by fault list changes.
   b. Fault list changes with no true value changes.

2. Evaluation is now composed of:
   a. True value evaluation, due to true value change.
   b. Fault list computations, due to true value and/or fault list change.
3. Fault injection and fault deletion must be performed. Fault injection corresponds to local fault effects, and fault deletion is done to correct feedback effects of faults.

3.14. CONCURRENT FAULT SIMULATION

Concurrent fault simulation [ULRI74] has some of the features of one-fault-at-time simulation and also some of those of deductive simulation. The evaluations of fault-free and faulty signal values are done explicitly, one at a time. However, only those elements whose inputs and/or states in the presence of any fault are different from their fault-free values are evaluated. This is accomplished by maintaining *fault state lists*, analogous to the fault lists used in deductive simulation. A fault state list, consisting of *fault states*, is associated with each element of the circuit. Each fault state consists of a fault identifier (fault number) and the state of the element (inputs, outputs, and state variables) in the presence of the particular fault. The *fault-free state* of the element (usually identified by fault number 0) is also contained in the fault state list of that element. The fault state list of an element will contain a particular fault state if and only if the state of the element in the presence of the fault is different from its fault-free state. Note that, unlike fault lists in deductive simulation, fault state lists are associated with elements and not with signals.

As the fault-free and faulty signal values change during simulation, some fault states may become identical to the corresponding fault-free states. This process is called *convergence*, and the fault states involved are deleted from the fault state list. Signal changes may also result in some fault states values that were previously identical to the corresponding fault-free states to become different. This process, called *divergence*, requires the addition of new fault states to fault state lists.

The following example shows the processes of convergence and divergence during concurrent simulation. These processes will be discussed in greater detail in subsequent sections.

Example 9. Figure 3.14.1a shows a part of a circuit, and the effects of faults α, β, and γ, which are assumed to be elsewhere in the circuit. In the figure, fault states of an element are shown as copies of the element labeled with the faulty values and the fault identifier. The fault state of an element p for a fault α is denoted by $p(\alpha)$, and its fault-free state by $p(0)$. The fault α causes the inputs (and the output) of gate g_1 to be different from the corresponding fault-free values. This is represented by the fault state $g_1(\alpha)$. The differences in the signal values at gates g_3 and g_4 in the presence of fault α are similarly represented by $g_3(\alpha)$ and $g_4(\alpha)$.

The element g_2 is an *SR* flip-flop, where Q represents both the state of the flip-flop and its output. The fault state $g_2(\beta)$ represents a difference in an input value,

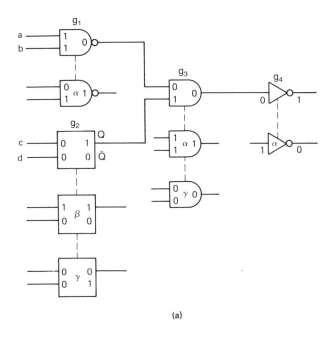

(a)

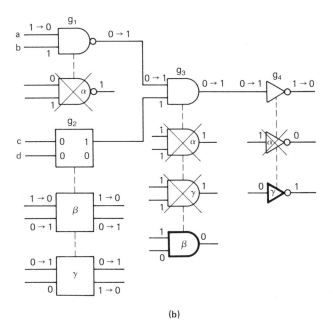

(b)

Figure 3.14.1

but no difference in the state. On the other hand, $g_2(\gamma)$ represents a difference in the state, but not in the inputs. Note that gate g_3 has a fault state $g_3(\gamma)$ in its fault state list but no $g_3(\beta)$, since the input values of gate g_3 in the presence of the fault β are identical to the corresponding fault-free values.

Representing the signal on a lead p in the presence of a fault δ by $p(\delta)$, Fig. 3.14.1b shows the stable state of circuit after the following signal changes have occurred:

$$a(0): \quad 1 \rightarrow 0$$

$$c(\gamma): \quad 0 \rightarrow 1$$

$$c(\beta): \quad 1 \rightarrow 0$$

$$d(\beta): \quad 0 \rightarrow 1$$

The change of the fault-free signal a, i.e., $a(0)$, causes $g_1(\alpha)$ to become identical to g_1. $g_1(\alpha)$ is therefore deleted. Similarly, $g_3(\alpha)$ and $g_4(\alpha)$ are also deleted due to fault-free signal changes.

The change of $c(\gamma)$ causes the outputs $g_2(\gamma)$ to become the same as g_2. However, since the inputs of $g_2(\gamma)$ are different from those of g_2, $g_2(\gamma)$ is not deleted. The inputs of $g_3(\gamma)$ now become identical to those of g_3, and $g_3(\gamma)$ is deleted.

The changes of $c(\beta)$ and $d(\beta)$ cause the fault state of $g_2(\beta)$ to diverge from its fault-free state. Since g_2 drives g_3, the inputs of g_3 in the presence of the fault β will be different from their fault-free values. Hence a fault state $g_3(\beta)$ is created (shown by heavy lines). The divergence of the fault β at the gate g_3 will cause a divergence at gate g_4, as shown in the figure.

Before presenting the concurrent simulation algorithm, some of the data structures used in the algorithm will be discussed.

3.14.1. Data Structures

As mentioned earlier, fault-free and faulty signal values that are different from the fault-free values are represented by fault state lists associated with elements. The values in a fault state are not restricted to binary values. A fault state may represent values of different arbitrary types of variables (such as integers, characters, etc.), allowing considerable flexibility in the description of the element.

The fault state may also contain additional information used during simulation. This includes information regarding whether or not the fault represented by the fault state is local to the element, and whether any value updates or evaluations have been scheduled for the fault state.

It is clear from Example 9 that fault states are deleted from fault state lists and added to these lists during simulation. To facilitate insertion and deletion of fault states, integers are used as fault identifiers, 0 being used as identifier of the fault-free case. The fault states within each list are ordered by fault number.

To keep fault state lists ordered by fault number during simulation and minimize searching, the list of fault states of each element to be evaluated at any simulated time are also kept ordered by fault number. Linked list structures are used for all these lists to facilitate insertion and deletion. The events on the scheduler are also grouped by elements and ordered by fault number.

3.14.2. Fault Insertion

A fault is inserted for simulation by creating a fault state of the element for the particular fault. For a stuck-type fault, the fault state is constructed by copying the fault-free state of the element and setting the faulty variable to the stuck value. The fault state is marked as that of a local fault.

Prior to evaluating an element in the presence of a local fault, the faulty variable must be set to its stuck value, since it may have changed as a result of feedback in the circuit. Recall that in deductive simulation, local faults of an element were deleted from the output fault lists of the element. Local faults that would make each element output different from its fault-free value were determined based on the true values, and inserted in the output fault lists. Setting faulty variables to the stuck values before evaluation performs the same function.

Two methods are available for handling the fault states of local faults. In one method, fault states of local faults are never deleted as a result of convergence. In the second method, local fault states are deleted exactly like other fault states. However, if any fault-free input or state value of an element changes, the local fault states must be created and scheduled for evaluation. The first method leads to a simpler algorithm than the second, but requires more storage. The first method is assumed for the rest of the discussion.

All faults to be simulated are inserted during initialization, at the beginning of simulation. Their effects are propagated so as to obtain a set of consistent fault states throughout the circuit. The concurrent simulation algorithm to be discussed in the following sections can be used for this purpose by ignoring all delays in the circuit.

3.14.3. Convergence

As mentioned earlier, a fault state of an element may become identical to its fault-free state during simulation due to signal changes in either state or both. To determine this convergence, the fault state must be compared with the fault-free state. Since the fault state is to be deleted if it is identical to the fault-free state, the comparison should be made only when no updates into the fault state or evaluations using the particular fault state are scheduled. Therefore, convergence checks will be made immediately after updating state or output variables, provided that no events for the fault state have been scheduled.

The fault states of an element that must be compared to the fault-free state depend on whether or not the latter has changed. Note that if the fault-free state or a fault state changes, the element will be evaluated, and one or more updates scheduled.

If no fault-free state change has occurred, only those fault states that changed (and therefore were evaluated and updated) need be compared with the fault-free state. On the other hand, if the fault-free state changes, all the fault states in the fault state list of the element must be compared with the fault-free state, because a fault state that did not change may have become identical to the new fault-free state.

Example 10.   In Fig. 3.14.2a, only the fault states α and γ have changed. Since the fault-free state has not changed, only these two fault states need be compared with the fault-free state. The fault α which has become identical to the fault-free state is deleted.

In Fig. 3.14.2b and c, the fault-free state has changed. In both cases, all the new fault states must be compared to the new fault-free state. The fault states that have become identical are deleted, as shown.

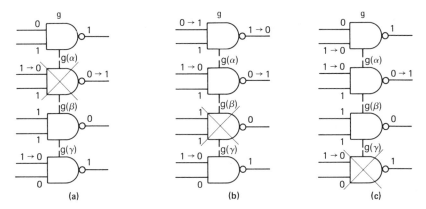

Figure 3.14.2   Convergence.

3.14.4. Divergence

An output value in a fault state may become different from the corresponding fault-free value due to changes in either or both values. When an output value in a fault state becomes different from the fault-free value, it would be necessary to create fault states for the fan-out elements of the output, if such fault states do not already exist.

As in the case of convergence detection, the set of fault state outputs to be compared to the fault-free output depends on whether or not the fault-free output changed. If there has been no change, only the fault state outputs that have changed need be considered. In the case of fault-free output change, all fault states in the fault state list are candidates for divergence check. In both cases, the newly divergent faults must satisfy the following conditions: their previous faulty output values are the same as the previous fault-free output value; and the new faulty output values are different from the new fault-free output value. It is only for a subset of these faults that new fault states have to be created for fan-out elements.

Example 11.   Figure 3.14.3 shows a case where the fault-free output of gate g_1 did not change, but the outputs of $g_1(\alpha)$, $g_1(\beta)$, and $g_1(\delta)$ changed. The only new divergences are faults β and δ. Note that although the output of $g_1(\alpha)$ also changed, the faulty state and the fault-free state were different before and after the change. The fan-out element g_2 already has a fault state for δ, since the other input to the gate has a value different from its fault-free value. Therefore, it is sufficient to create a fault state for β, as shown by heavy lines in the figure.

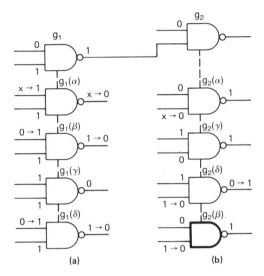

Figure 3.14.3   Divergence.

3.14.5. Fan-out Processing

When an output value of a fault-free state or fault state of an element changes, the changes must be propagated to the appropriate fault-free/fault state of each fan-out element. The divergence processing discussed in the preceding section guarantees that for every fault with output value different from the fault-free value, an appropriate fault state will exist in the fault state list of each fan-out element. However, if a fault state was deleted due to convergence, the fault state list of a fan-out element may or may not contain a fault state for the deleted fault. If a fault state does not exist, no action is necessary. If the fault state exists, the appropriate input value is updated.

If a fault-free output changes, the change must be propagated not only to the fault-free states of the fan-out elements, but potentially to some fault states also, as shown in the following example.

Example 12.   Consider the example of Fig. 3.14.4. A change in the fault-free value of g_1 must be propagated to the appropriate input of $g_3(\beta)$, because the signal from gate g_1 to gate g_3 is not affected by fault β.

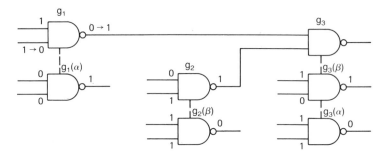

Figure 3.14.4   Fan-out processing.

In general, when an output of an element g_1 is connected to an input of an element g_2, any fault α such that there is a fault state for α in the fault state list of g_2 but not in that of g_1 must receive the fault-free value of the output.

3.14.6. Concurrent Simulation Algorithm

The concurrent simulation algorithm is obtained by incorporating the processes of fault injection, convergence, and fan-out processing discussed in the preceding sections in the general simulation algorithm. The following algorithm assumes that fault state lists, events, and evaluation lists are organized as discussed in Section 3.14.1.

Concurrent simulation algorithm

Routine simulation

Insert faults by creating fault states for local faults.

Evaluate all elements with local faults.

WHILE there are scheduled events pending
  Simulate time frame ($t = 0$) ignoring all delays

WHILE there are input changes and/or scheduled events
  Advance to nearest time for which there are input changes or scheduled events.
  Simulate time frame. Generate outputs.

end simulation

The step "Simulate time frame," which forms the core of the concurrent simulation algorithm, follows:

FOR every fault-free and faulty element for which updates are scheduled
  FOR every state variable update
    Update new value in fault state.
    Schedule evaluation of element if state has changed and element is not yet scheduled.
  Determine convergence of fault state if no fault activity scheduled.
  Delete convergent fault state.

FOR every output variable update
    Update scheduled values in fault states.
    Determine convergence of fault states with no more scheduled activity.
    Delete convergent fault states.
    Put fault identifiers and new values of changed signals in a list,
    called the propagation list.
    Put fault identifiers and new values of signals that did not change
    but became different from fault-free value (due to change of latter)
    in the propagation list.
    FOR every fan-out element and every entry in the propagation list
        IF new value is different from the new fault-free value AND
        the fault state list of fan-out element does not contain
        a fault state for the particular fault
            Create new fault state for the fault.
        Update input value in fault state.
        Schedule evaluation of fan-out element with the fault state.
    IF fault-free value changed
        FOR every fault in the fault state list of the fan-out element, but
        not in that of the source
            Update input value in the fault state to the new fault-free value.
            Schedule fan-out element for evaluation, with the fault state.
  Evaluate all elements scheduled for evaluation.
END

This algorithm requires only one traversal of each fault state list involved.

3.14.7. Activity in Concurrent Simulation

From the algorithm discussed in the preceding section, it is clear that the activities associated with different faults are independent of each other. However, there is some coupling between fault-free activities and fault activities in the process of convergence and divergence. Thus, even if a faulty signal does not change, changes in the corresponding fault-free signal may cause it to become the same as or different from the latter, resulting in the deletion or creation of the corresponding fault state.

3.14.8. Functional-Level Simulation

One of the main advantages of concurrent simulation over the deductive and parallel methods is that arbitrary functions can be evaluated directly. No transformations of CHDL descriptions into Boolean equations or special encodings are necessary. Evaluations can also be faster because only one path through a decision graph need usually be traversed.

    The procedure for functional-level concurrent simulation is essentially the same as that for gate-level simulation, provided that a fault state list is associated with every function. However, the method may be inefficient in storage usage, when functions with very large numbers of internal variables, such as RAMs, are to be simulated. In the fault state of a function with a large memory, only a small number of variables may have values which are different from the good values. A data compaction scheme for reducing the storage requirements in such cases, at the expense of execution speed, is discussed in Section 3.15.

3.15. DATA STRUCTURES AT THE FUNCTIONAL LEVEL

For functional-level fault simulation, information about fault-free and faulty values must be maintained for internal variables in addition to inputs and outputs. Internal variables include state variables, register and memory bits, and previous values of inputs.

In parallel simulation, a word (or a set of words) is used for each input, output, and internal variable. If history registers are used for identifying input edges and pulses, they will also contain a word (or a set of words) for each previous input value stored. A temporary word (or a set of words) is also needed for each temporary variable during the evaluation of procedural functions.

In deductive simulation, a logic value and fault list is associated with each input, output, and state variable. The logic values and fault lists associated with these variables are computed using the Boolean expressions representing the function in a way similar to gates. In procedural functions, true values and fault lists are needed for temporary variables. However, they need not be retained after the evaluation of a function. If history registers are used, *history push* consists of pushing the true value and also the fault list.

In concurrent simulation, a copy of the state description is maintained (in principle) for each fault in the fault state list of a functional element. This will include inputs, outputs, internal variables, and histories. However, maintaining the complete state description is feasible only if the number of variables is relatively small, since the fault state is associated with the functional element rather than the variables of the element.

A summary of the data structure for functional elements is represented in Figs. 3.15.1 to 3.15.3 for the three fault simulation methods.

A data compaction scheme is necessary for large state descriptions in concurrent simulation. One possible scheme is described now. The complete state is stored only for the fault-free case. For each fault state which differs from the fault-free one, a state difference list is maintained, containing the variable and its faulty value, for every variable that has a value different from the fault-free value. When a faulty function is to be evaluated, a temporary fault state is constructed from the fault-free state and the state difference list. When a faulty variable value is to be updated during simulation, the state difference list of the faulty node is searched to determine if it is in the list. If it is, the value is updated in the list and compared with its fault-free value. If they are the same, the faulty value is deleted from the state difference list. If the list does not contain the particular variable and the new faulty value is different from the fault-free value, an entry is created in the state difference list, and the new value is updated. Since updating a faulty value requires searching, inserting into, and deleting from the state difference lists, it would be desirable to maintain these lists as linked lists, ordered by variables. If there are too many differences to be maintained for one faulty state, the overhead for data compression may defeat the purpose of the method. The crossover point is expected to be around 10% difference between the faulty and fault-free states.

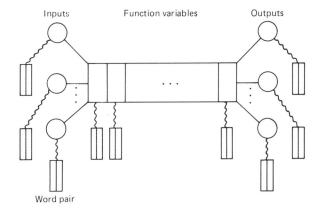

Figure 3.15.1 Functional parallel simulation data structure.

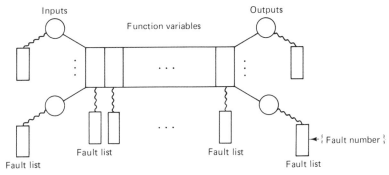

Figure 3.15.2 Functional deductive simulation data structure.

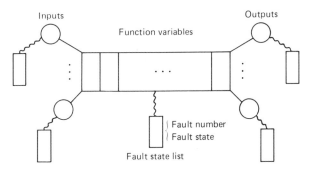

Figure 3.15.3 Functional concurrent simulation data structure.

Executable code produced by a compiler from a programming language description of functional behavior was mentioned in Section 3.7.4 as a possible model for high-level functions. While such models are adequate for true value simulation of functions, they lead to difficulties when used for fault simulation.

1. Deductive and parallel simulation require the executable code to evaluate equations which must be generated from user descriptions.
2. Deductive simulation requires the manipulation of fault lists. The problem of generating executable code to perform this from a programming language user description has not been solved.

Functional behavior described by executable code may be used in concurrent simulation. However, certain restrictions must be placed so that signal value information can be transmitted between the simulator and the function.

3.16. FAULT INJECTION AT THE FUNCTIONAL LEVEL

3.16.1. Parallel Simulation

As in the case of gate-level simulation, fault masks are used for injecting faults in functions. If both stuck at 0 and stuck at 1 faults on function variables are to be injected in two-valued parallel simulation, a pair of fault masks are associated with each variable to be faulted. As discussed earlier, the stuck at 1 mask is ORed to the word containing the values, whereas the stuck at 0 mask is ANDed to the word. General function faults are injected as stuck at 1 faults on the corresponding fault variables. Control faults can be injected by assigning each control expression to a temporary variable, and associating a pair of fault masks with the temporary variable.

In three-valued parallel simulation where two words are used to represent a set of fault-free and faulty values, a pair of masks are necessary for each fault to be injected. One of these is to be ORed to one of the value words and the other is to be ANDed to the other value word as shown earlier. The method can be extended to multivalued simulation (Problem 3.28).

Faults on inputs to functions are injected at the beginning of each evaluation. Faults on outputs and state variables are injected whenever they are scheduled for update. In nonprocedural functions, the value of each output or state variable will be updated only once during each evaluation. However, variables in procedural functions may be updated more than once during each evaluation, and fault injection on the variable to be updated must be done immediately after each update.

3.16.2. Deductive Simulation

In deductive simulation, certain faults on variables which propagate back to the same input variables must be deleted from fault lists of those variables. The stuck fault opposite to the current true value of the variable must then be added to the fault list of each variable. In the case of input variables, these operations must be performed immediately before the evaluation of the function. In the case of state variables and output variables, they must be performed when the true value or fault list of a variable is scheduled for update.

Fault variables used for modeling general function faults do not require this type of processing. They have a constant true value of 0, and a fault list consisting of a single fault, the general function fault represented by the particular fault variable. Since no assignments are made to any fault variable, their true value and fault lists remain constant. Variables used for modeling control faults are temporary variables. They are reevaluated every time, and the appropriate control faults added to their fault lists.

As in the case of parallel simulation, the only difference between nonprocedural and procedural functions is that, in the latter case, multiple updates of the same variable may be required during the same function evaluation. For each of these updates, the operations of deleting and inserting faults discussed above must be performed.

3.16.3. Concurrent Simulation

Fault injection with concurrent simulation is simpler than the other two methods because faults are handled individually during evaluation. To evaluate a function with an input variable stuck, the input is set to the faulty value prior to evaluation. Assuming that faulty internal variables, output variables, and temporary variables for simulating control faults are set to their faulty values during initialization, it is sufficient that the evaluation routine not schedule any updates for these variables. Since fault variables used for simulating general function faults are never assigned values during evaluation, they will remain unchanged once they are set.

3.17. SPECIAL FAULT SIMULATION PROBLEMS

3.17.1. Oscillations and Hyperactivity in Fault Simulation

During simulation, some signal values in the fault-free circuit or one or more faulty circuits may oscillate. Correct identification of an oscillation requires establishing that the circuit (fault-free or faulty) is in the same state at two different times. Since this is impractical, a count of the number of events after the last change in any primary input is often used for detecting oscillations.

The effects of a fault that causes oscillations will appear to be different in the three methods of fault simulation. In parallel simulation, there is no distinction between fault-free and faulty circuit activities. On the other hand, in concurrent fault simulation, fault-free and faulty circuit activities are handled separately. Therefore, if a fault causes oscillations, only one faulty circuit will continue to be active.

In deductive simulation, true values become stable as soon as the fault-free circuit stabilizes. Any fault that causes oscillations will repeatedly appear in and disappear from fault lists, as shown in the following example.

Example 13. The circuit of Fig. 3.17.1 is simulated in Table 3.17.1 when input a is changed from 0 to 1. Fault lists are denoted by capital letters. The faults of interest are signals a, b, c, d, and e stuck at 0 and 1 (a_0, a_1, b_0, b_1, c_0, c_1, d_0, d_1, e_0 and e_1).

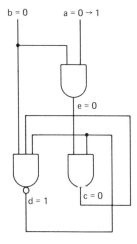

Figure 3.17.1 Oscillatory circuit.

The simulation is started from a stable state for $a = 0$ and $b = 0$ at time $t = 0$. The change of fault-free signal a does not propagate beyond e and further simulation involves only fault list changes. All true values and fault lists are identical at times $t = 3$ and $t = 6$ and the simulation will continue indefinitely if a simulation limit on the number of events or a time limit is not set. From the fault lists C and D, it is clear that the fault b_1 causes the circuit to oscillate.

TABLE 3.17.1   DEDUCTIVE SIMULATION OF OSCILLATIONS

t	a	A	B	C	D	E
0	0	$\{a_1\}$	$\{b_1\}$	$\{c_1, e_1\}$	$\{d_0\}$	$\{e_1\}$
1	1	$\{a_0\}$	$\{b_1\}$	$\{c_1, e_1\}$	$\{d_0\}$	$\{e_1\}$
2	1	$\{a_0\}$	$\{b_1\}$	$\{c_1, e_1\}$	$\{d_0\}$	$\{b_1, e_1\}$
3	1	$\{a_0\}$	$\{b_1\}$	$\{b_1, c_1, e_1\}$	$\{d_0\}$	$\{b_1, e_1\}$
4	1	$\{a_0\}$	$\{b_1\}$	$\{b_1, c_1, e_1\}$	$\{b_1, d_0\}$	$\{b_1, e_1\}$
5	1	$\{a_0\}$	$\{b_1\}$	$\{c_1, e_1\}$	$\{d_0\}$	$\{b_1, e_1\}$
6	1	$\{a_0\}$	$\{b_1\}$	$\{b_1, c_1, e_1\}$	$\{d_0\}$	$\{b_1, e_1\}$

Hyperactivity in deductive simulation has been shown to consume a large amount of computer resources [CHAP74b, LEVE74]. Hyperactive faults [CHAP74b] are faults which cause a large amount of list computations, and their removal will substantially reduce the simulation cost. Oscillatory faults are well understood, but hyperactive faults have not been well characterized; it is possible that hyperactive and oscillatory faults are the same class. It has also been shown [LEVE74] that the existence of oscillatory faults causes the complexity (worst case) of the deductive simulation with n feedback lines to be of the order of 2^{2^n}, compared to a complexity of the order of 2^n in the absence of oscillatory faults. Obviously, this causes a serious cost increase. One method of reducing simulation time is to remove from simulation any fault that is still active after a predetermined amount of computer resources have been used [CHAP74b]. *Early fault termination*, which removes a fault from simulation after a limited number of detections, may be helpful in some cases in limiting the amount of activity allowed to a fault after detection. However, it would apply only to those hyperactive faults which are detected. Another drawback of early termination is the inability to construct dictionaries of failure symptoms spanning the entire simulation interval.

It must be noted that, in deductive simulation, the existence of one active fault will cause the computation of fault lists, even if all the other faults are inactive. This is a disadvantage of deductive fault simulation, which does not exist in the "one-at-a-time" or the concurrent methods, since in both of these the faults may be treated independently. Parallel fault simulation stands somewhat in the middle, in that n faults are packed together and one fault activity results in the activity of other faults in the set. On the other hand, the partition of simulation into several passes insulates the passes from one another.

3.17.2. Initialization

At the beginning of simulation, it may be impossible to determine the value of the signals in the circuit, and the unknown value x is used. In the presence of a fault, some signal values may be known, in spite of the fact that the fault-free signals are unknown (Fig. 3.17.2). Conversely, it is possible that a fault-free signal will become known in the course of simulation, while the same faulty signal remains unknown.

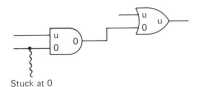

Stuck at 0

Figure 3.17.2   Initialization of faulty circuit $\propto$.

Since, in parallel simulation, all fault-free and faulty signals are represented independently, these differences are preserved during simulation. The initialization phase of parallel simulation includes the following steps:

1. Set all bits to unknown values.
2. Inject local faults and propagate the values until stability is reached.

Figure 3.17.3 shows how the example of Fig. 3.17.2 is handled in concurrent simulation. The initialization phase of concurrent simulation is left as an exercise (see

Problem 3.23). In deductive simulation, all the lists associated with unknown signals are empty, because the combinations of unknown fault-free values and known faulty values cannot be represented (Section 3.13.2).

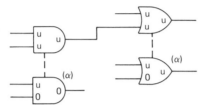

Figure 3.17.3   Concurrent simulaton of fault α.

An important problem in fault simulation initialization is that setting of signals to a set of known values by a user. Since this set of known values for the fault-free circuit must be consistent, a consistency analysis must be performed. Also, the faulty signal values are generally unknown and this fact should be reflected in the way fault simulation is initialized. Some of the faulty values that may be known (e.g., stuck values) and their effect on other signal values must also be represented.

3.17.3. Bidirectional Elements

The discussion so far has been under the assumption that the signal flow in all the elements in the circuit are from a set of input terminals to a disjoint set of output terminals. It may not always be possible to model all elements used in practical circuits in this manner. Some examples are tied ANDs and tied ORs formed by connecting together gate outputs in certain technologies, and also buses.

It has been shown that bidirectional devices can be simulated accurately using a model consisting of switches, connectors, and attenuators [HAYE82]. Due to the large number of components needed in such a model, the method does not appear to be practical for very large circuits.

Figure 3.17.4 shows a modification of the circuit that permits a bidirectional tied AND to be treated as an ordinary AND gate. All the fanouts from gates driving the tied-AND are moved to the output of an AND gate replacing it. Simulation can then be carried out in the usual manner. The method can be generalized to other types of bidirectional devices. A disadvantage of this method is that the outputs of gates driving bidirectionals may be incorrect if examined directly. This problem can be solved by flagging the element as driving a bidirectional, and fetching the value from the output of the ordinary gate representing the bidirectional, when the output of the driver is needed.

An alternative method of simulating bidirectionals without modifying the connectivity of the original circuit requires maintaining two values associated with every element output driving a bidirectional. One value, called the *computed* value, is the value determined from the elements inputs and element type. The signal value on the bidirectional element is then determined from the computed values of its drivers and the type of the bidirectional element. The output values of the elements driving the

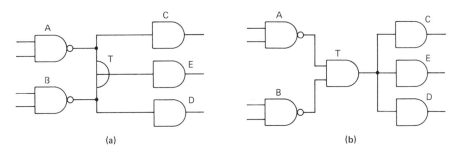

Figure 3.17.4   (a) Original circuit; (b) modified circuit.

bidirectional are then *forced* to the same value as the bidirectional, if they are different.

For example, consider the two NAND gates A and B connected to a tied-AND T as shown in Fig. 3.17.5a. Since the output of both the NAND gates are 1, the tied-AND has a value 1, as shown in the figure. Figure 3.17.5b shows the effect of A changing to 0. The value on the tied-AND becomes 0, and gate B is forced to this value (indicated by *). If the output of gate A returns to 1, the tied-AND and the outputs of both A and B return to 1.

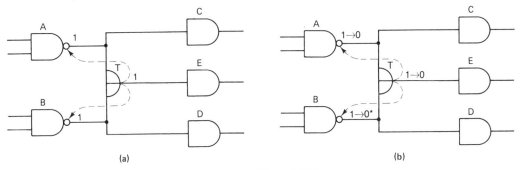

Figure 3.17.5

It is important to note that the computed values of driving gates must be used for computing the value of the bidirectional. However, other gates driven by the drivers, such as gate D in Fig. 3.17.5, receive the forced value. This method is applicable also to other types of bidirectional elements, such as tri-state buses.

The above method is also applicable when a number of bidirectional devices are connected together, if all the bidirectional elements are of the same type. All the bidirectionals are updated to the same value, and their drivers are forced to that value if they differ from it. The details of the implementation are heavily dependent on the data structures used and will not be discussed here.

For fault simulation, all the operations that are performed at the time of a signal update must also be performed when values are forced. Although this method is more complicated than the preceding one, it has the potential of enabling the simulation of faulty open connections between nets.

Bidirectional terminals are often associated with user defined circuits for use as both input and output ports. The simulation of external nets connected to the bidirectional terminals is performed as explained above. However, the simulation of the internal connection to the bidirectional terminal requires the maintenance of calculated and forced logic values, as well as combination rules to calculate the resultant values.

3.17.4. Races

The simultaneous change of a pair of signals is called a *race*. The race is said to be *critical* if the next state or output of the circuit depends on the order in which the signals actually change. For example, consider the pair of cross-connected NAND gates of Fig. 3.17.6, with signal values as shown. If both the inputs change simultaneously to 1, the circuit will oscillate. However, in practice, the circuit will respond to one of the two changes before it responds to the other. It is easily seen that the outputs of the NAND gates will depend on which change occurs first. Hence the race is critical.

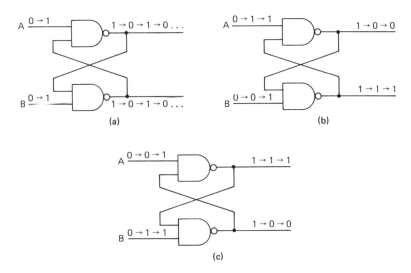

Figure 3.17.6 (a) Simultaneous change; (b) A changes first; (c) B changes first.

In simulation, any pair of signals such that a simultaneous change of signal values on them will result in a critical race is called a *race pair*. Simulating simultaneous changes on race pairs requires a knowledge of the effects of the races on the elements connected to them. A more general but probably more pessimistic method is to set both the racing signals to the unknown value x and propagate the x through the fanouts of the race pair.

Races can occur in the fault-free circuit or in the presence of faults. The faults that cause races are called *race faults*. From the discussion in Section 3.10 it is clear that the case in which there is a race in the fault-free circuit but no race in the presence of a fault cannot be represented in the classical deductive method. When the fault-free signal value is known, race faults will appear as star faults. In the parallel and concurrent methods, no special handling of unknown values resulting from races is necessary.

The effects of critical races can be simulated by using the following method. If leads *a* and *b* form a race pair, an element *R* is introduced as shown in Fig. 3.17.7a. The behavior of *R* can be described functionally by

$$\text{IF } ((a \oplus a(-1)) \ \& \ (b \oplus b(-1)))$$
$$\text{THEN } c = x; \ d = x;$$
$$\text{ELSE } c = a; \ d = b;$$
$$\text{ENDIF};$$

Another method is shown in Fig. 3.17.7b where the connections to *R* are bidirectional. This would require the values computed by *R* to be forced on the leads *a* and *b* as discussed in Section 3.17.3.

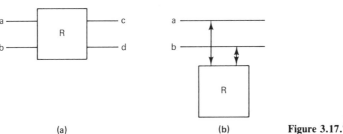

(a)   (b)   **Figure 3.17.7**

Two different types of critical races can occur in user-defined functions. The first type consists of races between inputs. Whether or not such races are critical can be determined by an analysis of the functional description. Once the race pairs have been identified, they can be handled in essentially the same manner as discussed above for gates.

The second type consists of races in procedural functions containing DELAYs and WAITs, as discussed in Section 3.9.3. These races cannot be identified by simultaneous changes of signals on any set of leads. Determining whether or not a race is critical would require the evaluation of different sections of the functional description which have become active at the same time, in all possible orders and comparing the results. Since this may be impractical, the only feasible solution seems to be to assign the unknown value to all affected variables.

3.17.5. Shorted Signals

Shorted signals are common failures during the manufacturing process, and simulation of shorts [CHAP74b] is an important test quality measurement tool. Here a universal model for shorted signal simulation is discussed. The model requires a minor connectivity modification and may be used with any of the simulation methods discussed earlier.

Consider a short between signals a and b. A special element f is inserted on signals a and b; it has two inputs, a and b, and two outputs, c and d (Fig. 3.17.8). Assuming the short to perform an AND function (0-dominance), the faulty and fault-free functions are described in Table 3.17.2. One-dominance can be treated in an analogous manner.

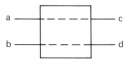

Figure 3.17.8

TABLE 3.17.2

Inputs		Fault-free		Faulty	
a	b	c	d	c	d
0	0	0	0	0	0
0	1	0	1	0	0
1	0	1	0	0	0
1	1	1	1	1	1

In two-valued parallel simulation, computer words will be attached to a, b, c, and d, and the fault propagation is trivial.

$$w_c = w_a \tag{3.17.1}$$

$$w_d = w_b \tag{3.17.2}$$

The fault injection produces the words w_c' and w_d'.

$$w_c' = w_c(\overline{m} + w_d) \tag{3.17.3}$$

$$w_d' = w_d(\overline{m} + w_c) \tag{3.17.4}$$

The word m is a mask that has a 1 in the position devoted to the shorted fault and 0 elsewhere. Problem 3.24 addresses more than two logic values.

In deductive fault simulation, fault lists A, B, C, and D are associated with a, b, c, and d, respectively. Again, the fault propagation equations can be derived from the equations

$$c = \overline{f}a + ab \tag{3.17.5}$$

$$d = \overline{f}b + ab \tag{3.17.6}$$

where f is the fault variable representing the short. With these equations, the fault is automatically injected into C for $a = 1$, $b = 0$ and into D for $a = 0$, $b = 1$. In concurrent fault simulation, the fault state of the short will be in the list of the added element, and output values in the presence of the short will be computed $c = d = ab$.

Instead of Table 3.17.2, a functional description of the short may be used as in the treatment of races. As in the case of race analysis, a special bidirectional element may be used for modeling a short, minimizing the circuit modification required.

3.18. COMPARISON OF FAULT SIMULATION METHODS

3.18.1. Logic Values

In the context of a three-valued system of logic values, it has been shown that deductive simulation is more pessimistic than both parallel and concurrent simulation [LEVE79]. Parallel simulation and concurrent simulation are equivalent in accuracy, since each fault is treated independent of the fault-free circuit in parallel simulation, and the fault information is preserved in concurrent simulation in the form of fault states. However, if a fault-free signal is unknown, no information about faulty values of that signal is maintained in deductive simulation. Hence some loss of information occurs.

In order to accommodate modern technologies, larger sets of logic values must be used [LEVE81a]. Deductive and parallel simulation are well defined only in the context of a switching algebra, since both require the existence of switching expressions for the functional elements being simulated. Although the extension of both methods is simple for three logic values [ARMS72], it is possible but complicated for more than three values [LEVE81b].

Since, in concurrent simulation, all the faults are treated in the same way as the fault-free circuit, this method can accommodate an unrestricted set of logic values [ABRA77, LEVE78, LEVE81b].

3.18.2. Functional Representation

In both deductive and parallel simulation, functional blocks must be modeled using switching functions [MENO78, LEVE81b]. This either restricts element modeling to switching functions or requires a nontrivial mapping of nonswitching functions into a set of switching functions. In concurrent simulation, there is no such restriction on functional modeling, because of the decoupling between faulty and fault-free behaviors.

A tabular comparison of the various modeling techniques with respect to simulation requirements is presented in Table 3.18.1. The entries which are (not) marked mean that the technique described in the corresponding row is (not) applicable for the corresponding simulation method. The table shows that concurrent fault simulation has fewer modeling limitations than the other fault simulation methods.

3.18.3. Timing

In principle, deductive and parallel simulation assume identical timing for the fault-free and faulty circuits, since these are strongly coupled. It has been shown that

TABLE 3.18.1

	True value	Parallel	Deductive	Concurrent
Boolean equation model	×	×	×	×
Non-Boolean equation model	×			×
Graph model	×			×
Table model	×			×
Compiled code	×	×		×

simulation with more detailed timing is possible with these methods, and that different rise and fall times may be associated with individual faults [KJEL77, LEVE81b]. However, this will cause more computations involving faults which are normally inactive, because of the strong coupling between fault-free and faulty signal changes in both methods.

In concurrent simulation, the timing of each fault will be handled independently and, therefore, the additional computation will be minimum. In addition, this simulation method may be used to analyze the tolerance of the design to timing variations. For instance, the impact of the variation of the delay of a gate can be deduced by simulating k different delay values for this gate as k different independent failures originating from the gate. If the k delays are uniformly distributed around the nominal (fault-free) value, the sensitivity of the design to delay variations may be characterized by the number of "faults" (delay variations) that are "detected" (cause a different circuit behavior). If the design is insensitive to all the "faults" (variations in delay), the design is considered to be tolerant of the delay variations. The concurrent simulation mechanism lends itself very well to this kind of simulation, since the activities of the delay "faults" are independent.

3.18.4. Computer Storage Requirements

In parallel simulation, the computer storage requirement is fixed for a given circuit and for the number of faults simulated in one pass. Simulating a larger number of faults will require multiple passes rather than an increase in storage requirements. During deductive and concurrent simulation, the storage requirements will depend on a number of factors, such as circuit activity and circuit sequentiality. Highly sequential circuits require more storage due to longer test sequences and longer fault lists associated with circuit elements.

Concurrent simulation of gates is expected to require more storage than deductive simulation for two reasons. First, each fault is represented by a fault identifier and a fault state, instead of just a fault identifier. Second, there are more entries in the concurrent fault list, as demonstrated next.

Consider a gate g with inputs $x_1, x_2, \ldots, x_n$ and output z. Let G be the set of faults in the concurrent fault state list associated with g, and $X_1, X_2, \ldots, Z$ the deductive fault lists associated with $x_1, x_2, \ldots, x_n, z$, respectively. The following relations hold (ignoring local faults on gate g):

$$G = \bigcup_{i=1}^{n} X_i$$

$$Z \subseteq \bigcup_{i=1}^{n} X_i$$

Therefore, we have

$$|G| \geq |Z|$$

which means that the size of the concurrent fault list associated with a gate is greater than the size of the deductive fault list associated to the output of the gate. Actual measurements indicate that concurrent simulation of gates requires 30 to 40% more storage than deductive simulation.*

In the case of functions, the situation is different. Let $x_i (i = 1$ to $n)$, $z_i (i = 1$ to $k)$ and $y_i (i = 1$ to $m)$ be the inputs, outputs, and state variables, respectively. Deductive fault lists associated with these variables are denoted by uppercase letters. Let F be the set of faults in the concurrent fault state list associated with the function. The deductive and concurrent fault lists associated with inputs and ouputs contain the same faults. However, we have

$$F = \bigcup_{i=1}^{m} Y_i + \bigcup_{i=1}^{n} X_i$$

$$|F| \leq \sum_{i=1}^{m} |Y_i| + \sum_{i=1}^{n} |X_i|$$

In other words, the concurrent fault list has fewer entries than the sum of the entries in the deductive fault lists associated with the input and internal variables of the function. On the other hand, each entry is larger in concurrent simulation, since a state copy is needed. The result of comparing the storage requirements is inconclusive.

The increase in storage requirements implies the need for a multiple-pass concurrent simulation mechanism. The total fault population is partitioned into smaller subsets and the subsets are simulated in independent simulation runs. The partitioning of the fault population may be done as a preprocessing step using predictive techniques (static partitioning) or performed when the need arises (dynamic partitioning). In the dynamic mode, the fault set is partitioned during the course of simulation and a subset of faults is removed from simulation. The good circuit state and the faulty circuit states

---

*Authors' unpublished work.

for these faults are stored. Simulation then continues for the active set. Later during simulation, preferably at a user-defined breakpoint, simulation will be halted again and resumed for the dormant subset at the point where it was previously interrupted. Dynamic fault set partitioning may have to be invoked repeatedly if the storage requirements become excessive.

3.18.5. Execution Speed

In parallel simulation, all the faults are simulated independently of the fact that most of the faults cause only a few signals to be different from the fault-free values. This does not occur in deductive and concurrent simulation, since the fault lists include only faults that cause divergences from the fault-free behavior. An earlier comparison (CHAN74) between parallel and deductive simulation demonstrated that parallel simulation is faster than deductive simulation for highly sequential circuits. A more precise study of execution speeds of all three methods is not yet available.

3.19. OPEN ISSUES AND DIRECTIONS

Several issues, difficulties, and problems in fault simulation have been identified and deserve special attention.

3.19.1. Fault Modeling

The fault model for CHDL functions covers fewer physical faults than the gate-level fault model. By raising the level of representation, the user is losing some confidence in test evaluation through fault simulation. Two questions emerge from this situation: What is the degradation in test evaluation accuracy? Is there a better fault model than the usual models (stuck-type fault models) and the models proposed in Section 3.9?

3.19.2. Alternative Fault Simulation Methods

The analysis of sensitive traces may provide a cheaper fault simulation method [ABRA83, LEVE83a]. This method is a reversal of the critical cube test generation [THOM71, WANG75] and is essentially based on the observation that failures along a sensitive trace are detected at the circuit outputs along the sensitive path. Although faster than traditional fault simulation, it has been shown that the method is pessimistic in that certain faults detected by multiple path sensitization are not identified as detected by the critical trace method [LEVE83a] The method is well understood for gate-level fault simulation. However, more exploration of the method for functional models is needed.

3.19.3. Special-Purpose Hardware

The computer costs associated with fault simulation grow with circuit complexity. Concurrent fault simulation, which has advantages with user-defined models, is wasteful in computer storage and this in turn results in a degradation of performance. It is believed that the solution is not only in finding better algorithms but also, and perhaps mainly, in the implementation of special-purpose computers for simulation (SPCS).

Pioneering work has been done in several places, and implementation has been done or is under way. These methods exploit concurrency in simulation, resulting in a substantial speedup. The methods used belong to two main categories. In the first category, the simulation algorithm is mapped into hardware, step by step; this results in a functional partitioning of the simulation algorithm onto a system of processors. This produces an architecture, where most activities are pipelined, except element evaluation, which can be performed in a loosely connected parallel mode [ABRA82, BART80]. An example of such an architecture is given in Fig. 3.19.1.

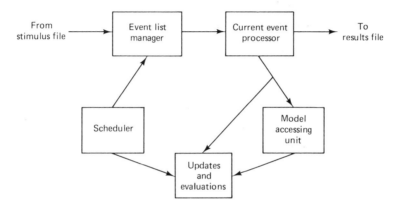

Figure 3.19.1 Mapping of the simulation algorithm into hardware.

Estimates of the time required for the various steps of the algorithm of Section 3.8.3 indicate that all the steps require roughly the same amount of time in gate-level true-value simulation [ABRA82]. The evaluation of functional elements requires much more time, depending on the function size. This observation leads to a pipelined processing of the active events in one time frame. To reduce the bottleneck of functional evaluation, several functional evaluators operate in parallel with one gate-level evaluator [ABRA82]. At every simulated time frame, the pipelined processing is initiated until the pipeline operates at full steady-state capacity. When the last event for the current time frame has been processed, the pipeline becomes empty and the process is restarted for the next time frame. It should be noted that the processing for one time frame cannot start before the processing for the previous time frame has been finished. This architecture can be implemented with custom processors or commercial components (e.g., microprogrammable microprocessors). The latter approach results in performance degradation, but allows easier architecture modification.

The second architecture category takes advantages of the inherent concurrency of signal activity in the simulated circuit. The simulated circuit is partitioned and mapped onto the simulator hardware architecture. This results in an array architecture

[DENN82, LEVE82, KOIK83]. Each processing unit processes the simulation of a set of elements, assigned to it, and all the processing units execute an identical algorithm. An example of this type of architecture is given in Fig. 3.19.2.

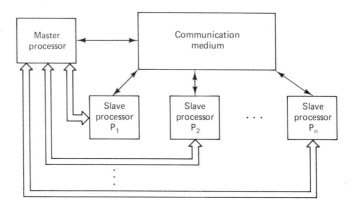

Figure 3.19.2

There are several variations in the second category. Special circuit partitioning techniques may help minimize the total processing time by maximizing the concurrency in event processing [LEVE82]. For best results, the structure used for interprocessor communication should be such that the communication time and processing time for simulating one time frame are approximately equal, to prevent bottlenecks. It has been shown that a time-shared parallel bus is adequate for functional simulation, but a faster crosspoint matrix structure will be optimal for gate-level simulation [LEVE82]. Mixed functional-gate-level simulation requires a mixed architecture with bus and crosspoint matrix.

A compiled simulation algorithm has been used in [DENN82], whereas an event-oriented algorithm is used in [KOIK83, LEVE82]. These architectures differ in terms of the processing allocated to the slave processor, the input/output processor, and the communication medium.

Since fault simulation is considerably costlier than true-value simulation, an important open issue is that of discovering all possible concurrencies in fault simulation and choosing the architecture that takes advantage of them. In principle, there are two types of concurrency during fault simulation. The first one is the same as in true-value simulation and was just discussed. The second type occurs as a result of simulating the effects of a number of faults simultaneously. Signals on the same lead, associated with different faults, may be active at the same time. The parallel simulation algorithm takes advantage of this type of concurrency.

An important feature of the architecture of a special-purpose computer for fault simulation (SPCFS) should be its ability to exploit both types of concurrency. The array architecture discussed above has been extended to fault simulation [LEVE83b]. Further work is needed to determine the best approach for an SPCFS.

SPCSs present several advantages:

1. An SPCS provides a higher computing power for simulation than traditional general-purpose computers. A speedup of 30 times is expected from a low-cost special architecture using microprocessors [ABRA82]. Higher gains are expected with special-purpose circuits [DENN82].
2. The computing cost is very low, because simulation is computation intensive and because of the simplicity of an SPCS installation.
3. The affordability and speed of an SPCS enables the tightening of the interface between simulators and factory testers.This is true for true-value simulation, which is used in the factory for probe guiding and for fault simulation. For this reason, the development of a special-purpose computer for fault simulation is needed.

The first two advantages would contribute to the speedup of the hardware design process.The third advantage allows the creation of an independent self-sufficient factory test workstation, linked to an SPCS or an SPCFS, thus reducing the testing cost and the turnaround time. This test station allows the fast processing of test design changes involving the factory tester.

REFERENCES

[ABRA77] Abramovici, M., M. A. Breuer, and K. Kumar, "Concurrent Fault Simulation and Functional Level Modeling," *Proc. 14th Des. Autom. Conf.*, pp. 128–137, June 1977.

[ABRA82] Abramovici, M., Y. H. Levendel, and P. R. Menon, "A Logic Simulation Machine," *Proc. 19th Des. Autom. Conf.*, pp. 65–73, June 1982.

[ABRA83] Abramovici, M., P. R. Menon, and D. T. Miller, "Critical Path Tracing—An Alternative to Fault Simulation," *Proc. 20th Des. Autom. Conf.*, pp. 214–220, June 1983.

[AKER78] Akers, S. B., "Binary Decision Diagrams," *IEEE Trans. Comput.*, pp. 508–516, June 1978.

[AGRA80] Agrawal, V. D., A. K. Bose, P. Kozak, N. H. Nham, and E. Pacas-Skewes, "A Mixed-Mode Simulator," *Proc. 17th Des. Autom. Conf.*, pp. 618–625, June 1980.

[ARMS72] Armstrong, D. B., "A Deductive Method for Simulating Faults in Logic Circuits," *IEEE Trans. Comput.*, vol. C-21, pp. 464–471, May 1972.

[BART80] Barto, R., and S. A. Szygenda, "A Computer Architecture for Digital Logic Simulation," *Electron. Eng.*, pp. 35–66, Sept. 1980.

[BELL71] Bell, C. G., and A. Newell, *Computer Structures: Readings and Examples*, McGraw-Hill, New York, 1971.

[BOSE82] Bose, A. K., P. Kozak, C. Y. Lo, H. N. Nham, E. Pacas-Skewes, and K. Wu, "A Fault Simulator for MOS LSI Circuits," *Proc. 19th Des. Autom. Conf.*, Las Vegas, pp. 400–409, June 1982.

[BREU76] Breuer, M. A., and A. D. Friedman, *Diagnosis and Reliable Design of Digital Systems*, Computer Science Press, Woodland Hills, Calif., 1976.

[BRYA81] Bryant, R. E., "MOSSIM: A Switch-Level Simulator for MOS LSI," *Proc. 18th Des. Autom. Conf.*, pp. 786–790, June 1981.

[CAPA] *CAPABLE 4000 Logic Simulation System User Manual*, Computer Automation Industrial Products Division, IPM-28932-00.

[CHAN66] Chang, H. Y., and W. Thomis, "Methods of Interpreting Diagnostic Data for Locating Faults in Digital Machines," *Bell Syst. Tech. J.*, vol. 46, no. 2, pp. 289–317, Feb. 1966.

[CHAN74] Chang, H. Y., S. G. Chappell, C. H. Elmendorf, and L. D. Schmidt, "Comparison of Parallel and Deductive Fault Simulation Methods," *IEEE Trans. Comput.*, vol. C-23, no. 11, Nov. 1974.

[CHAP71] Chappell, S. G., and S. S. Yau, "Simulation of Large Asynchronous Logic Circuits Using an Ambiguous Gate Model," *Proc. Joint Comput. Conf.*, AFIPS Fall 1971, pp. 651–661.

[CHAP74a] Chappell, S. G., "Automatic Test Generation for Asynchronous Digital Circuits," *Bell Syst. Tech. J.*, vol. 53, pp. 1477–1503, Oct. 1974.

[CHAP74b] Chappell, S. G., C. H. Elmendorf, and L. D. Schmidt, "LAMP: Logic Circuit Simulators," *Bell Syst. Tech. J.*, vol. 53, pp. 1451–1476, Oct. 1974.

[CHAP76] Chappell, S. G., P. R. Menon, J. F. Pellegrin, and A. M. Schowe, "Functional Simulation in the LAMP System," *Proc. 13th Des. Autom. Conf.*, pp. 42–47, June 1976.

[CHAP77] Chappell, S. G., P. R. Menon, J. F. Pellegrin, and A. M. Schowe, "Functional Simulation in the LAMP System," *J. Des. Autom. Fault Tolerant Comput.*, vol. 1, no. 3, pp. 203–216, May 1977.

[CHAW75] Chawla, B. R., H. K. Gummel, and P. Kozak, "MOTIS—An MOS Timing Simulator," *IEEE Trans. Comput.*, vol. C-22, pp. 901–910, Dec. 1975.

[CHU72] Chu, Y., "Introducing the Computer Design Language," *Proc. IEEE COMPCON 72*, pp. 215–218, Sept. 1972.

[DENN82] Denneau, M. M., "The Yorktown Simulation Engine," *Proc. 19th Des. Autom. Conf.* pp. 55–59, June 1982.

[DIET75] Dietmeyer, D. L., and J. R. Duley, "Register Transfer Languages and Their Translation," *Digital System Design Automation*, M. A. Breuer, Ed., Computer Science Press, Woodland Hills, Calif., pp. 117–218, 1975.

[DULE67] Duley, J. R., "DDL—A Digital System Design Language," Ph.D. dissertation, University of Wisconsin, Madison, 1967.

[EICH64] Eichelberger, E. B., "Hazard Detection in Combinational and Sequential Switching Circuits" *Proc. 5th Ann. Symp. Switching Circuit Theory Logical Des.* pp. 111–120, 1964.

[ELLE81] Ellenberger, D. J., and Y. W. Ng, "AIDE—A Tool for Computer Architecture Design," *Proc. 18th Des. Autom. Conf.*, Nashville, Tenn., pp. 796–803, June 1981.

[FANT74] Fantauzzi, G., "An Algebraic Model for the Analysis of Circuits," *IEEE Trans. Comput.*, vol. C-23, pp. 576–581, June 1974.

[FRIE71] Friedman, A. D., and P. R. Menon, *Fault Detection in Digital Circuits*, Prentice-Hall, Englewood Cliffs, N. J., 1971.

[HARD67] Hardie, F. H., and R. J. Suhocki, "Design and Use of Fault Simulation for Saturn Computer Design," *IEEE Trans. Electron. Comput.*, vol. EC-16, pp. 412–429, Aug. 1967.

[HAYE82] Hayes, J. P., "A Fault Simulation Methodology for VLSI," *Proc. 19th Des. Autom. Conf.*, Las Vegas, Nev. pp. 393–399, June 1982.

[HILL79] Hill, D. D., and W. Van Cleemput, "SABLE: A Tool for Generating Structured Multilevel Simulation," *Proc. 16th Des. Autom. Conf.*, pp. 272–279, June 1979.

[HUFF54] Huffman, D. A., "The Synthesis of Sequential Switching Circuits," *J. Franklin Inst.*, vol. 257, pp. 161–190, Mar. 1954, and pp. 275–303, Apr. 1974.

[JEA78] Jea, Y. H., and S. A. Szygenda, "Boolean Vector Algebraic Structures: Properties and Applications to Digital Logic Simulation," *Comput.-Aided Des.*, vol. 11, no. 6, pp. 315–323, Nov. 1979.

[JEPH69] Jephson, J. S., R. P. McQuarrie, and R. E. Vogelsburg, "A Three-Valued Computer Design System," *IBM Syst. J.*, vol. 8, pp. 178–188, 1969.

[JOHN80] Johnson, W., J. Crowley, M. Steger, and E. Woosley, "Mixed-Level Simulation from a Hierarchical Language," *J. Digit. Syst.*, pp. 305–336, Fall 1980.

[KERN78] Kernighan, B. W., and D. D. Ritchie, *The C Programming Language*, Prentice-Hall, Englewood Cliffs, N. J., 1978.

[KJEL77] Kjelkerud, E., and O. Thessen, "Techniques for Generalized Deductive Fault Simulation," *J. Des. Autom. Fault Tolerant Comput.*, vol. 1, pp. 377–390, October 1977.

[KNUT73] Knuth, D. E., *The Art of Computer Programming: Fundamental Algorithms*, 2nd ed., Addison-Wesley, Reading, Mass., 1973.

[KOIK83] Koike, N., K. Ohmori, H. Kondo, and T. Sasaki, "A High Speed Logic Simulation Machine," *Proc. Spring COMPCON83*, pp. 446–451, Feb.–Mar. 1983.

[LEVE74] Levendel, Y. H., "Some Experiments and Problems in Fault Simulation," *Tech. Rep.*, Math-71, University of the Negev, May 1974.

[LEVE78] Levendel, Y. H., and W. C. Schwartz, "Impact of LSI on Logic Simulation," *Proc. Spring COMPCON78*, San Francisco, Feb. 1978.

[LEVE79] Levendel, Y. H., and P. R. Menon, "Unknown Signal Values in Fault Simulation," *Dig., 9th Annu. Int. Conf. Fault Tolerant Comput.*, Madison, Wis., pp. 125–128, June 20–22, 1979.

[LEVE80] Levendel, Y. H., and P. R. Menon, "Comparison of Fault Simulation Methods—Treatment of Unknown Signal Values," *J. Digit. Syst.*, vol. 4, no. 4, pp. 443–459, Winter 1980.

[LEVE81a] Levendel, Y. H., P. R. Menon, and C. E. Miller, "Accurate Simulation Models for TTL Totempole and MOS Gates and Tristate Devices," *Bell Syst. Tech. J.*, vol. 60, no. 7, pp. 1271–1287, Sept. 1981.

[LEVE81b] Levendel, Y. H., and P. R. Menon, "Fault Simulation Methods—Extensions and Comparison," *Bell Syst. Tech. J.*, vol. 60, no. 9, pp. 2235–2258, Nov. 1981.

[LEVE82] Levendel, Y. H., P. R. Menon, and S. H. Patel, "Special Purpose Computer for Logic Simulation Using Distributed Processing," *Bell Syst. Tech. J.*, vol. 61, no. 10, pp. 2873–2909, Dec. 1982.

[LEVE83a] Levendel, Y., and P. R. Menon, "The *-Algorithm: Critical Traces in Functions and CHDL Constructs," *Dig., 13th Annu. Intl. Symp. Fault Tolerant Comput.*, Milan, Italy, pp. 90–97, June 1983.

[LEVE83b] Levendel, Y., P. R. Menon, and S. Patel, "Parallel Fault Simulation Using Distributed Processing," *Bell Syst. Tech. J.*, vol. 62, no. 10, pp. 3107–3137, Dec. 1983.

[MAGN77] Magnhagen, B., "Practical Experiences from Signal Probability Simulation of Digital Design," *Proc. 14th Des. Autom. Conf.*, New Orleans, pp. 216–219, June 1977.

[MENO65] Menon, P. R., "A Simulation Program for Logic Networks," Bell Laboratories Internal Memorandum, Mar. 1965.

[MENO78] Menon, P. R., and S. G. Chappell, "Deductive Fault Simulation with Functional Blocks," *IEEE Trans. Comput.*, vol. C-27, pp. 687–695, Aug. 1978.

[MONA82] Monachino, M., "Design Verification for Large Scale LSI Designs," *Proc. 19th Des. Autom. Conf.*, pp. 83–90, June 1982.

[NAGE75] Nagel, W., *SPICE2, A Computer Program to Simulate Semiconductor Circuits*, ERL Memo, ERL-M520, University of California, Berkeley, May 1975.

[NEWT79] Newton, A. R. "Techniques for the Simulation of Large Scale Integrated Circuits," *IEEE Trans. Circuits Syst.*, vol. CAS-26, pp. 741–749, Sept. 1979.

[NHAM80] Nham, H. N., and A. K. Bose, "A Multiple Delay Simulator for MOS LSI Circuits," *Proc. 17th Des. Autom. Conf.*, pp. 610–617, June 1980.

[SCHE 72] Schertz, D. R., and G. Metze, "A New Representation for Faults in Combinational Digital Circuits," *IEEE Trans. Comput.*, vol. C-21, pp. 858–866, Aug. 1972.

[SESH 65] Seshu, S., "On an Improved Diagnosis Program," *IEEE Trans. Electron. Comput.*, vol. EC-14, pp. 76–79, 1965.

[SZYG72] Szygenda, S. A., "TEGAS2—Anatomy of a General Purpose Test Generation and Simulation System for Digital Logic," *Proc. 9th Des. Autom. Workshop,* Dallas, pp. 116–127, June 1972.

[SZYG73] Szygenda, S. A., and A. A. Lekkos, "Integrated Techniques for Functional and Gate Level Digital Logic Simulation," *Proc. 10th Des. Autom. Conf.*, pp. 159–172, June 1973.

[THOM 71] Thomas, J. J., "Automatic Diagnostic Test Programs for Digital Networks," *Comput. Des.*, pp. 63–67, August 1971.

[ULRI65] Ulrich, E. G., "Time-Sequenced Logic Simulation Based on Circuit Delay and Selective Tracing of Active Network Paths," *Proc. 20th ACM Natl. Conf.*, pp. 437–448, 1965.

[ULRI68] Ulrich, E. G., "Series/Parallel Event Scheduling for the Simulation of Large Systems," *Proc. 23rd ACM Natl. Conf.*, pp. 279–287, Aug. 1968.

[ULRI72] Ulrich, E. G., Baker, T., and L. R. Williams, "Fault-Test Analysis Techniques Based on Logic Simulation," *Proc. 9th Des. Autom. Workshop*, pp. 111–115, June 1972.

[ULRI74] Ulrich, E. G., and T. Baker, "Concurrent Simulation of Nearly Identical Digital Networks," *Computer*, vol. 7, pp. 39–44, Apr. 1974.

[ULRI76] Ulrich, E. G., "Non-integral Event Timing for Digital Logic Simulation," *Proc. 13th Des. Autom. Conf.*, pp. 61–67, June 1976.

[WADS78] Wadsack, R. L., "Fault Modeling and Logic Simulation of CMOS and MOS Integrated Circuits," *Bell Syst. Tech. J.*, vol. 57, no. 5, pp. 1449–1474, May-June, 1978.

[WANG75] Wang, D. T., "An Algorithm for the Generation of Test Sets for Combinational Logic Networks," *IEEE Trans. Comput.*, vol. C-24, pp. 742–746, July 1975.

[WILL79] Williams, W. J. Y., and R.W. McGuffin, "A High Level Logic Design System," *Proc. 4th Int. Symp. Comput. Hardware Descr. Languages,* Palo Alto, Calif., pp. 40–46, Oct. 1979.

[WU79] Wu, K., "Synthesis of Accurate and Efficient Functional Modeling Techniques for Performing Design Verification of VLSI Digital Circuits," Ph.D. dissertation, University of Texas, Austin, Dec. 1979.

[YOEL64] Yoeli, M., and S. Rinon, "Application of Ternary Algebra to the Study of Static Hazards," *J. ACM*, vol. 11, no. 1, pp. 84–97, Jan. 1964.

PROBLEMS

3.1. Is the expansion algorithm in the text a depth-first algorithm or a breadth-first algorithm?

3.2. Demonstrate how a CHDL description can be transformed into a circuit of NAND gates. Can the two models be made equivalent from the point of view of timing by proper delay insertion?

3.3. Repeat Problem 3.2 for incomplete descriptions.

3.4. Write an evaluation algorithm for a switching expression given in reverse Polish form.

3.5. Using UFDL, construct a model for a 16-bit arithmetic-logic unit which performs the following operations: addition, subtraction, AND, and OR.

3.6. Write an algorithm for CHDL function evaluation, using the data structure described in the text.

3.7. Can internal, input, and output states be identified by scanning a CHDL description? If your answer is yes, give appropriate rules. Can any variable serving as both an input and an output ("I/O port") be characterized?

3.8. How is sequentiality of a circuit reflected in its CHDL decriptions? Can sequentiality be recognized by CHDL scan?

3.9. Can races in CHDL blocks be determined during simulation? How?

3.10. For the CHDL description of Fig. 3.7.3, demonstrate the correctness of Eq. (3.7.2).

3.11. In a n-ary decision mechanism, is it necessary that the conditions be disjoint? What are the implications of nondisjoint conditions on the corresponding expressions in the decision branches and on the evaluation mechanism?

3.12. Write a dynamic fault partitioning algorithm for concurrent simulation and integrate it in the fault simulation algorithm.

3.13. Same as Problem 3.12 for deductive simulation.

3.14. Show the correctness of Eqs. (3.12.6a) and (3.12.6b), and demonstrate how to obtain f^0 from $\bar{z}$.

3.15. Define the algebra of the 1-operator and the 0-operator mentioned in Section 3.12.1. Is it a switching algebra? Do the de Morgan laws exist in this algebra?

3.16. Show the correctness of Eqs. (3.12.13a) and (3.12.13b).

3.17. Consider a system of four logic values, 0, 1, x and z, where x and z are the unknown and the high impedance, respectively. Find a coding for these values and define the propagating functions of the AND, OR, and NOT for parallel simulation.

3.18. Show the correctness of Eq. (3.13.2). Is the formula valid for three logic values? (*Hint:* $x \oplus X$ is the list that causes signal x to be 1.)

3.19. Demonstrate that the code 11 can never occur during logical operations using the coding of Table 3.12.1.

3.20. Is it correct to set the initial deductive fault list to the empty set? Could the empty set be made to mean that no fault is detected? Or that, since the signals are initially unknown, all the faulty signals are also unknown?

3.21. Is it possible that a true-value change causes no fault list change in deductive simulation?

3.22. In deductive simulation, t is the time of a change of true value x or fault list X. $x(+)$ and $X(+)$, $x(-)$, and $X(-)$ are the true value and fault list after and before the change, respectively. What is the meaning of the following sets?

$$X(-)X(+)$$
$$\overline{X(-)}X(+)$$
$$X(-)\overline{X(+)}$$
$$\overline{X(-)}\ \overline{X(+)}$$

Answer the question for all combinations of $x(-)$ and $x(+)$.

3.23. Do you expect the initial fault lists to be empty in concurrent simulation? Will that cause any difference between deductive and concurrent simulation during the initialization phase? Compare with parallel simulation.

3.24. Find the propagation and injection equations for three-valued parallel simulation of shorts.

3.25. What is the mechanism for simulating shorts between three signals? Solve this problem for the three major fault simulation methods.

3.26. Demonstrate the deductive propagation rules when inputs of elements are partially unknown and outputs are known (Section 3.13.2). Can that be extended to functions with state variables?

3.27. How are the faults initialized in parallel, deductive, and concurrent simulation when the user requires a forced initialization to known fault-free signal values? Is the result pessimistic? Why?

3.28. Demonstrate how to perform fault injection in parallel simulation for the stuck values $\{0, 1, x, z\}$.

3.29. Can the problem of Example 9 be solved by considering the fan-in of elements rather than considering the fan-out only? What are the trade-offs?

3.30. Can a fault simulator be used as a true-value simulator? What are the costs and benefits?

Chapter 4

CODING THEORY FOR FAULT-TOLERANT SYSTEMS

B. Bose
J. Metzner

4.1. INTRODUCTION

It is desirable, and in some cases vital, that data in a computer remain correct when written into memory, stored, read from memory, communicated, or manipulated. The complexity of modern computers makes it impractical to depend solely on reliable components and devices for reliable operation. Some redundancy is needed for the detection and/or correction of errors which will invariably occur as information is being stored, transferred, or manipulated.

An extensive theory of error-control coding has been developed [BERL68, LIN70, PETE71]. The primary emphasis of this theory has been the design of reliable communication systems. The problem of reliable computation differs significantly from the problem of reliable communication. For example, communication error-control schemes usually assume perfectly reliable computing and processing at the transmitter and receiver, have less severe restraints on computation time for error correction, and are subject to different statistics of error occurrences than those that occur in computer systems. Nevertheless, the principles that have been discovered by communication coding theorists are so fundamental that they also are basic to the understanding and design of error control for reliable computation.

An important consideration is the relative use of error detection and error correction. Error detection normally results in an interruption in the computation, followed by possibly a retry of some or all of past computations, possibly a switching from use of a presumed faulty part of the computer to a presumed reliable part, or possibly some maintenance procedure. On the other hand, error correction permits the computation process to continue uninterrupted. This would seem to favor error correction over error detection, but there are some mitigating factors. For a given amount of redundancy, if the number of error patterns which the decoder attempts to correct is increased, the probability of an undetected error increases; and the computational decoding complexity increases rapidly as the amount of error-correction capability is increased.

In communication, error detection combined with acknowledgment and retransmission protocols often provides a satisfactory method of obtaining extremely reliable communication in the presence of communication channel symbol errors. However, in computing, if the presence of errors is detected in a word retrieved from memory, there may be no way of determining what the correct word is.

In this chapter the general principles of error-correcting codes and decoding schemes are explained. It is then shown how these coding principles can be applied to fault tolerance in various aspects of the computer system: memory, arithmetic, logic, and communication.

4.2. ERROR MODELS

Most errors in computer systems are caused by faults, which are faulty or failed components of the system. In the absence of faults errors can occur due to random disturbances or noise. Such errors are rare except in communication over a long distance.

The types of error statistics which occur in memory, logic, and arithmetic circuits are many and varied. We can attempt to categorize them by reference to the following qualities depicted on scales with opposing properties on the two ends.

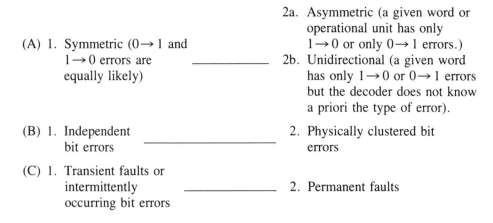

(A) 1. Symmetric ($0 \rightarrow 1$ and $1 \rightarrow 0$ errors are equally likely)

2a. Asymmetric (a given word or operational unit has only $1 \rightarrow 0$ or only $0 \rightarrow 1$ errors.)

2b. Unidirectional (a given word has only $1 \rightarrow 0$ or $0 \rightarrow 1$ errors but the decoder does not know a priori the type of error).

(B) 1. Independent bit errors

2. Physically clustered bit errors

(C) 1. Transient faults or intermittently occurring bit errors

2. Permanent faults

With respect to each quality, statistics could fall in some middle range of the scale rather than the extreme. For example, in (A), the errors could be predominately, but not entirely, $1 \rightarrow 0$; in (B), errors could be only lightly dependent, or perhaps clustered in a byte, while independent between bytes; in (C), some bit faults could be of a semipermanent nature, with errors in that bit occurring more frequently than normal, but at random.

Let us now look into some physical source of errors in computer circuits to see how they relate to these general models.

It is important to observe at the outset that error statistics are strongly influenced by how the data are organized. For example, if the bits of a coded word are stored in physically remote places, their errors are more likely to be independent, whereas if the bits of a word are located physically close, there is a greater chance that errors will be clustered.

In the case of semiconductor random access memories, if the memory is organized as bits per card, any defect in the memory card will affect the corresponding card bit positions. Defects in separate cards tend to be independent, and hence these types of errors could be modeled as independent bit errors.

The advent of very large scale integration (VLSI) technology has pushed the bits per card to a cluster of bits, or a byte, per card memory organization. In this type of byte-per-card memory organization a single card defect may affect many bits in that card. Also, a single fault in one of the data paths is likely to affect many bits within the byte. These types of errors are referred to as *byte errors*. Now, we can assume independent byte errors, but error clusters within a byte.

In the case of magnetic tape units there are several causes of errors. These include oxide particles on the head, oxide particles on the tape, voids in the oxide coating of the tape, dust and foreign particles on the tape, and head and tape damage due to handling. These defects usually affect only one track of the tape, but they result in a (possibly large) cluster of errors on a track.

For the past three decades most of the codes have been developed under the fault assumption of symmetric errors. The errors in magnetic tapes and some of the random access memories can be considered as symmetric errors. On the other hand, the failure in the memory cells of some of the LSI single-transistor-cell memories and metal-nitride-oxide semiconductor (MNOS) memories are most likely caused by the leakage of charge. If we represent the presence of charge in a cell by 1 and the absence of charge by 0, the errors in these types of memories can be modeled as $(1 \rightarrow 0)$-type asymmetric errors. This is because the charge cannot be created except by a rewrite process, and hence $(0 \rightarrow 1)$-type errors in the memory cells are almost impossible.

In considering situations where all errors in a coded block are of one type (all $1 \rightarrow 0$ or all $0 \rightarrow 1$), two different cases are distinguished. The errors are called *asymmetric* if only one of the two types of errors can occur and it is known a priori which type that is. The errors are called *unidirectional* if all the errors in any given code block must be of one type (either all $1 \rightarrow 0$ or all $0 \rightarrow 1$), but it is not known a priori which of the two types has occurred.

Finally, the various faults in many LSI/VLSI devices—the read-only memories—provide a clear illustration of how unidirectional errors are caused in practice. The likely sources of unidirectional errors in some of these devices are [PRAD80b]:

1. *Address decoder:* Single and multiple faults in address decoders result in either no access or multiple access. No access yields an all-0-word readout. Multiple access causes the OR of several words to be read out, resulting in unidirectional errors if the correct word is among those accessed.

2. *Word line:* An open word line may cause all bits in the word beyond the point of failure to be stuck at 0. On the other hand, two word lines shorted together will form an OR function beyond the point where they are shorted. In either case the resulting errors are unidirectional.

3. *Power supply:* A failure in the power supply usually results in a unidirectional error.

Also, in some of the recently developed shift register memories a stuck-at fault in one of the shift registers will result in a constant 0 or 1 from that shift register. These errors can be modeled as unidirectional errors.

In Section 4.5 we will discuss the fundamental theory of asymmetric and unidirectional error correction/detection and develop codes for these types of errors.

4.3. BASIC STRUCTURAL PROPERTIES OF PARITY CHECK CODES

Parity check codes are important because they have a good mathematical structure which simplifies the task of designing error-correcting codes which are simple to implement and effective for the detection and correction of errors. A description of their structure is closely related to the very basic properties of groups, rings, fields, and vector spaces [PETE71, MACL67]. The following section lists these basic properties, which will later be used in describing the characteristics of parity check codes.

4.3.1. Groups, Rings, Fields, and Vector Spaces

Groups. A group G is a set of elements and a defined operation for which certain axioms hold. Let a, b, c, be any elements of G (not necessarily distinct). Let $a \cdot b = c$ denote: a operated with b yields c. The properties that must be satisfied are the following:

1. For any a, b, in G, $a \cdot b$ is in G (closure property).
2. For any a, b, c in G, $(a \cdot b) \cdot c = a \cdot (b \cdot c)$ (associative property).
3. There is an identity e in G such that

$$e \cdot a = a \cdot e = a$$

for all a in G.

4. For each a in G, there is an inverse, a^{-1}, such that

$$a \cdot a^{-1} = a^{-1} \cdot a = e.$$

An Abelian (or commutative) group is defined as a group for which the commutative law also is satisfied:

$$a \cdot b = b \cdot a$$

for all a, b in G. A subset H of elements in a group G is called a *subgroup* of G if H itself is a group.

One example of a group is the group G_1 of integers modulo 5 with the operation addition. The members of G_1 are 0, 1, 2, 3, 4. The identity e is 0. The integers 2 and 3 are inverses of each other, as are 1 and 4. Another example of a group is the group G_2 of nonzero integers modulo 5 with the operation multiplication. The members of G_2 are 1, 2, 3, 4. In G_2, the identity e is 1; 2 and 3 are inverses of each other; and 4 is its own inverse. Both groups G_1 and G_2 are Abelian. G_1 has no subgroup except the single identity element 0. G_2 has a subgroup of two elements: 1 and 4.

Rings, fields, and vector spaces.   A *ring R* is a set of elements with two operations defined. We can call one operation addition and call it $a + b$, and the other multiplication, denoted ab, but the operations need not be ordinary addition and multiplication. A ring must satisfy the following axioms. The elements a, b, c referred to are not necessarily distinct.

1. The set R is an Abelian group under addition.
2. For any a and b in R, ab is in R (closure).
3. For any a, b, and c in R, $a(b + c) = ab + ac$ and $(b + c)a = ba + ca$ (distributive law).

A ring is called *commutative* if for any a, b in R, $ab = ba$. The additive identity is denoted as 0.

As an example of a ring consider the integers modulo 4 with the two operations addition and multiplication. The reader may easily verify that the three axioms are satisfied for the integers modulo 4 (or for integers modulo any other integer for that matter). It is worth noting, however, that elements in a ring do not necessarily have a multiplicative inverse. For example, in the ring of integers modulo 4, there is no element a such that $2a = 1$, so 2 does not have a multiplicative inverse, even though it has an additive inverse ($2 + 2 = 0$). The existence of a multiplicative inverse often is a desirable property, so we consider an important special kind of ring called a *field*.

A *field F* is commutative ring with a multiplicative identity (denoted as 1) in which every nonzero element has a multiplicative inverse. Coding theory is concerned with fields having a finite number of elements. A field of q elements is denoted as GF(q), where GF stands for Galois field. More details of field structure will be discussed when certain specific codes and error control schemes are introduced.

A *vector space V* is a set of elements called vectors over a field F which satisfies the following axioms:

1. The set V is an Abelian group under addition.

2. For any v in V and any field element c in F, a product cv, which is a vector, is defined. (Field elements also are called *scalars*.)

3. (Distributive law). If u and v are in V and c is in F,

$$c(u + v) = cu + cv$$

4. (Distributive law). For v in V and c and d in F,

$$(c + d)v = cv + dv$$

5. (Associative law). If v is in V and c and d are in F,

$$(cd)v = c(dv) \qquad \text{and} \qquad 1v = v$$

A subset of a vector space which is also a vector space is called a *subspace*. It will be assumed the reader is familiar with the concepts of linear independence and dimension of a vector space.

4.3.2. Matrix Description of Parity Check Codes

A general binary parity check (n, k) code is a linear one-to-one mapping of each binary k-tuple, $(d_1, \ldots, d_k)$, which represents the data, into a binary n-tuple, $(x_1, x_2, \ldots, x_n)$, $n > k$, called a code "word." In matrix notation,

$$[x_1 \quad x_2 \quad \cdots \quad x_n] = [d_1 \quad d_2 \quad \cdots \quad d_k] \begin{bmatrix} g_{11} & \cdots & g_{1n} \\ \vdots & & \\ g_{k1} & \cdots & g_{kn} \end{bmatrix} \qquad (4.3.1)$$

The g_{ij} are each 0 or 1, and arithmetic is modulo 2 ($1 + 1 = 0$, $1 \times 1 = 1$, $0 \times 1 = 1 \times 0 = 0 \times 0 = 0$). In abbreviated notation,

$$\bar{x} = \bar{d}G \qquad (4.3.2)$$

In order to have a one-to-one mapping between the set of 2^k data sequences and the corresponding 2^k code words, it is necessary and sufficient that the k rows of G (considered as vectors) be linearly independent. The matrix G is called the *generator matrix*. For example,

$$G = \begin{bmatrix} 1 & 1 & 0 & 0 & 1 & 0 \\ 1 & 0 & 1 & 1 & 1 & 0 \\ 0 & 1 & 1 & 0 & 1 & 1 \end{bmatrix} \qquad (4.3.3)$$

is the generator matrix of a $(6, 3)$ parity check code. The eight data sequences map into eight code words as follows:

Data	Code word
000	000000
001	011011 ← row 3 of G
010	101110 ← row 2 of G

011	110101	← row 2 + row 3 (modulo 2)
100	110010	← row 1 of G
101	101001	
110	011100	
111	000111	

Parity check codes are also called *linear codes,* due to the linearity of relation (4.3.1). More general nonbinary linear codes are sometimes considered, where the g_{ij}, d_i, and x_j are field elements from GF(q). In the general case there are q^k code words with matrix relations (4.3.1).

Systematic parity check codes.   For a systematic parity check code, the first k columns of $[G]$ form a $k \times k$ identity matrix:

$$\bar{x} = \bar{d} \begin{bmatrix} 1 & & 0 & \vdots & \\ & 1 & & \vdots & P \\ 0 & & 1 & \vdots & \end{bmatrix} \qquad (4.3.4)$$

so we can write $G = [I_k \ \vdots \ P]$, which indicates that G is partitioned into a $k \times k$ identity submatrix for the first k columns, and a submatrix $[P]$ for the last $n - k$ columns. For a systematic parity check code, the first k code bits are identical to the k data digits, and the last $n - k$ code bits are called the *parity check digits.* The systematic form is usually preferred for practical purposes, since the data can be extracted directly from the code word after checking has been completed.

Interchanging rows of the generator matrix and adding rows to other rows by vector modulo 2 addition does not change the set of code words but does change which data sequences are associated with which code word. By such operations it is always possible to convert a nonsystematic (n, k) code into a systematic (n, k) code having the same set of code words except for a possible rearrangement of the order of the digits.

For the systematic code

$$\bar{x} = (d_1, d_2, \ldots, d_k, p_1, p_2, \ldots, p_{n-k})$$

where $p_1, \ldots, p_{n-k}$ are called the *parity check digits.* Given

$$P = \begin{bmatrix} \alpha_{11} & \cdots & \alpha_{1,n-k} \\ \vdots & & \vdots \\ \alpha_{k1} & & \alpha_{k,n-k} \end{bmatrix} \qquad (4.3.5)$$

The parity digits can be related to the data digits by the equations

$$p_j = \sum_{i=1}^{k} \alpha_{ij} d_i \qquad 1 \le j \le n - k \qquad (4.3.6)$$

We can rewrite Eq. (4.3.6) as

$$\sum_{i=1}^{k} \alpha_{ij} d_i \oplus p_j = 0 \qquad j = 1, 2, \ldots, n - k \qquad (4.3.7)$$

Equation (4.3.7) illustrates why the p_j are called parity check digits. In matrix form Eq. (4.3.7) becomes

$$[d_1 \quad d_2 \quad \cdots \quad d_k \quad p_1 \quad p_2 \quad \cdots \quad p_{n-k}]\begin{bmatrix} \alpha_{1,1} & \alpha_{1,2} & \cdots & \alpha_{1,n-k} \\ \vdots & \vdots & & \vdots \\ \alpha_{k1} & \alpha_{k2} & & \alpha_{k,n-k} \\ 1 & 0 & & 0 \\ 0 & 1 & & 0 \\ 0 & 0 & & 0 \\ \vdots & \vdots & \ddots & \vdots \\ 0 & 0 & & 1 \end{bmatrix} = \bar{0} \qquad (4.3.8)$$

or, in abbreviated form,

$$\bar{x}\begin{bmatrix} P \\ I_{n-k} \end{bmatrix} = \bar{0} \qquad \text{where } I_{n-k} \text{ is an } (n-k) \times (n-k) \text{ identity matrix}$$

An alternative form of (4.3.7) is

$$[P^T \; \vdots \; I_{n-k}]\bar{x}^T = \bar{0}^T \qquad (4.3.9)$$

where T stands for transpose. ($\bar{x}^T$ is a column vector and $\bar{0}^x$ is a column of zeros.)

4.3.3. Vector-Space Properties of Parity Check Codes

The binary digits 0 and 1 with modulo 2 addition and ordinary multiplication form a field of two elements. The set of binary n-tuples with bit-by-bit modulo 2 addition is a vector space over the binary field. The set of 2^k code words of an (n, k) code is a subspace of the space of binary n-tuples. The subspace is of dimension k. Relating to the G matrix, this subspace consists of all the linear combinations of the k linearly independent rows of G. Similar statements can be made for the nonbinary case where the symbols are from GF(q).

The subspace of code words can also be defined as the set of all vectors $\bar{x}$ in the space of "binary" n-tuples such that

$$\bar{x}H^T = \bar{0} \qquad \text{or} \qquad H\bar{x}^T = \bar{0}^T \qquad (4.3.10)$$

where H is a $(n-k) \times n$ matrix whose $n-k$ rows are linearly independent. Comparing with Eq. (4.3.8), it is seen that for systematic codes H can be derived from G as

$$H_{\text{systematic}} = [P^T \; \vdots \; I_{n-k}] \qquad (4.3.11)$$

Two vectors $\bar{a}$ and $\bar{b}$ are orthogonal if $\bar{a}\,\bar{b}^T = 0$. Note from Eq. (4.3.9) that $\bar{x}$ is orthogonal to every row of H, and thus is orthogonal to every vector in the $(n-k)$-dimensional space spanned by the rows of H. Such a vector is said to be in the null space of the row space of H, and this null space of dimension k is the set of code words. Note that H is not unique for a given code as any basis of the row space could serve as the rows of H.

To illustrate the principle above and others to follow, consider a $(7, 4)$ systematic code for which

$$
G = \begin{bmatrix} 1 & 0 & 0 & 0 & 1 & 1 & 0 \\ 0 & 1 & 0 & 0 & 1 & 1 & 1 \\ 0 & 0 & 1 & 0 & 1 & 0 & 1 \\ 0 & 0 & 0 & 1 & 0 & 1 & 1 \end{bmatrix} \tag{4.3.12}
$$

Thus

$$
P = \begin{bmatrix} 1 & 1 & 0 \\ 1 & 1 & 1 \\ 1 & 0 & 1 \\ 0 & 1 & 1 \end{bmatrix} \tag{4.3.13}
$$

and

$$
H = \begin{bmatrix} 1 & 1 & 1 & 0 & 1 & 0 & 0 \\ 1 & 1 & 0 & 1 & 0 & 1 & 0 \\ 0 & 1 & 1 & 1 & 0 & 0 & 1 \end{bmatrix} \tag{4.3.14}
$$

The reader may verify that each row of G is orthogonal to each row of H. If we added row 2 of H to row 3, we would obtain

$$
H' = \begin{bmatrix} 1 & 1 & 1 & 0 & 1 & 0 & 0 \\ 1 & 1 & 0 & 1 & 0 & 1 & 0 \\ 1 & 0 & 1 & 0 & 0 & 1 & 1 \end{bmatrix} \tag{4.3.15}
$$

The set of sequences orthogonal to all rows of H' remains the same 16 code words which are generated by G.

4.3.4. Error Checking and the Syndrome

The presence of errors in a binary n-tuple can be represented as an error vector $\bar{e}$ which has ones in just the positions which are in error. Thus, if $\bar{x}$ is the correct n-tuple and $\bar{y}$ is the erroneous n-tuple,

$$
\bar{y} = \bar{x} \oplus \bar{e} \tag{4.3.16}
$$

where the operation $\oplus$ represents vector addition with binary components added modulo 2 (i.e., $011010 \oplus 101001 = 110011$).

The presence of errors can be tested for by computing the quantity

$$
\bar{s}^T = H\bar{y}^T \tag{4.3.17}
$$

If there are no errors, $\bar{s}$ will be zero. If $\bar{s}$ is not zero, there must be one or more bit errors. Substituting Eq. (4.3.11) in Eq. (4.3.12) we see that

$$\bar{s}^T = H(\bar{x}^T + \bar{e}^T) = H\bar{x}^T + H\bar{e}^T = H\bar{e}^T \qquad (4.3.18)$$

Thus $\bar{s}$ depends only on the error pattern and not on the code word. For this reason it is called a *syndrome*, or symptom of the error. If $\bar{s}$ is zero, it is not necessarily true that there are no errors, since any error pattern that matches exactly one of the 2^k code words will produce a zero syndrome. However, this is 2^k out of 2^n possible patterns, and if n is significantly greater than k, such error patterns will be rare.

For the code represented by Eqs. (4.3.12) to (4.3.14), suppose that

$$\bar{x} = (1 \quad 0 \quad 1 \quad 0 \quad 0 \quad 1 \quad 1)$$

$$\bar{e} = (0 \quad 0 \quad 0 \quad 0 \quad 0 \quad 1 \quad 0)$$

so that

$$\bar{y} = (1 \quad 0 \quad 1 \quad 0 \quad 0 \quad 0 \quad 1)$$

Then

$$\bar{s}^T = \begin{bmatrix} 1 & 1 & 1 & 0 & 1 & 0 & 0 \\ 1 & 1 & 0 & 1 & 0 & 1 & 0 \\ 0 & 1 & 1 & 1 & 0 & 0 & 1 \end{bmatrix} \begin{bmatrix} 1 \\ 0 \\ 1 \\ 0 \\ 0 \\ 0 \\ 1 \end{bmatrix} = \begin{bmatrix} 0 \\ 1 \\ 0 \end{bmatrix} \qquad (4.3.19)$$

Note that $\bar{s}$ is identical to column six of H as it should be, since the error is in position six. Note that no other column of this H has the same pattern. Thus this is the only *single* bit error pattern which could have caused the observed syndrome. There are, however, 15 other error patterns (e added to each of the 15 nonzero code words) which could have caused this syndrome, but all the other error patterns have more than one bit error.

4.3.5. Group Properties of Parity Check Codes

The set of code word vectors $\bar{x}_i$, $i = 1, 2, \ldots, 2^k$, form an Abelian group under vector modulo 2 addition. Also, they are a subgroup of the Abelian group of 2^n binary n-tuples under vector modulo 2 addition.

Starting with a subgroup H of l elements, the $n = lm$ elements of the whole group G can be displayed in an array of m disjoint sets, called *cosets*, one of which is the subgroup H. To form the array, let $h_1, h_2, \ldots, h_l$, the members of H, be the first row, with $h_1 = e$, the identity. Then take some element g_2, $g_2 \in G$, $g_2 \notin H$ and make a second row of l distinct elements, where $g_2 h_i$ is the ith element. It can be proven that the $g_2 h_i$, $i = 1, 2, \ldots, l$, are distinct from each other and from members of H. This second row is called the left coset $g_2 H$. The leftmost element g_2 is called the *coset leader*. One then selects an element $g_3, g_3 \in G$, $g_3 \notin H$, $g_3 \notin g_2 H$, and forms another coset for the third row. Continuing, we get m rows of elements which are all the lm elements of G appearing once each.

For the case of binary parity check (n, k) codes, the tabulation appears as follows:

TABLE 4.3.1   Group of 2^n n-tuples subdivided into cosets of the code word subgroup

	$\bar{x}_1 = \bar{0}$	x_2	$x_3 \cdots$	$x_2 k$	$\leftarrow$ Code word subgroup
2^{n-k} cosets	$\bar{g}_2,$	$\bar{g}_2 \oplus \bar{x}_2$		$\bar{g}_2 \oplus \bar{x}_2 k$	
	$\vdots$				
	$\bar{g}_{2^{n-k}.}$	$\cdots\cdots\cdots\cdots\cdots$		$\bar{g}_{2^{n-k}} \oplus \bar{x}_2 k$	

Table 4.3.1 also provides a valuable insight into the relation between error patterns and syndromes. Each of the 2^n possible errors patterns is identical to one member of the Table 4.3.1 array. All members of the same coset have the same syndrome, as

$$H(\bar{g}_i^T + \bar{x}_j^T) = H\bar{g}_i^T \qquad (4.3.20)$$

Also, two members of two different cosets have different syndromes, and there is a one-to-one relation between the 2^{n-k} cosets and the 2^{n-k} syndromes. In the nonbinary case, there is a similar array of q^n elements relating to the subgroup of q^k code words.

For the $(7, 4)$ code of (3.12), the subgroup of 16 code words subdivides the group of 128 7-tuples into eight cosets which correspond to the eight different syndromes.

4.3.6. Distance Properties of Parity Check Codes

Define the weight of an n-tuple as the number of nonzero terms in it. Define the Hamming distance d between two code words as the number of positions in which the two words differ. The following properties can be deduced for parity check codes.

1. The number of words of Hamming distance d from any given word is the same as the number of words of weight d, for all $0 < d < n$. As a corollary, the minimum distance $d_{\min}$ between two different code words is the weight of the lowest nonzero weight code word.

2. To correct all error patterns of weight e or less, we must have $d_{\min} > 2e$.

3. The set of correctible error patterns must be such that no two are in the same coset.

For the code of Eq. (4.3.3) it is seen that the minimum weight of any code word is 3, so the minimum distance between any two code words is 3.

For the code of Eq. (4.3.12) each of the seven single error patterns has a different syndrome because each column of H is different, and thus each is in a different coset. The eighth coset consists of the code word subgroup which is associated with the zero syndrome. Thus property 3 is satisfied for the set of all single error patterns. Then by property 2 it follows that d_{min} is at least 3 for this code. The reader may verify that d_{min} is exactly 3.

4.3.7. Polynomial Algebra and Cyclic Codes

A cyclic code is a parity check code which has the additional property that every cyclic shift of a code word is a code word. For example, if $(c_{N-1}, c_{N-2}, \ldots, c_0)$ is a code word, so is $(c_{N-2}, c_{N-3}, \ldots, c_0, c_{N-1})$.

Cyclic codes are most conveniently described as polynomials, and some knowledge of polynomial algebra and finite field theory is essential for a full understanding of literature dealing with cyclic codes. The n-tuple or vector $(c_{n-1}, c_{n-2}, \ldots, c_0)$ can be written instead as a polynomial

$$c(X) = c_{n-1}X^{n-1} + c_{n-1}X^{n-2} + \cdots + c_1X + c_0 \qquad (4.3.21)$$

This polynomial is called a polynomial over a field $GF(q)$ when the coefficients are elements of $GF(q)$. Usually, $q = 2$ and the coefficients are binary. A key concept is that of "modulo a polynomial" and the related Euclid division algorithm. Let $f(X)$ and $p(X)$ be any two polynomials over a finite field and let the degree of $p(X)$ be at least 1. Then the Euclid division algorithm states that there are unique polynomials $q(X)$ and $r(X)$, called the *quotient* and *remainder*, respectively, such that

$$f(X) = q(X)p(X) + r(X) \qquad (4.3.22)$$

where the degree of $r(X)$ is less than the degree of $p(X)$. We then say that $r(X)$ is congruent to $f(X)$ modulo $p(X)$:

$$r(X) = f(X) \quad [\text{mod } p(X)] \qquad (4.3.23)$$

The most important modulo base polynomial for cyclic codes is $X^n - 1$. In particular,

$$1 = X^n \quad [\text{mod } X^n - 1] \qquad (4.3.24)$$

As a consequence, $Xc(X) \quad [\text{mod } X^n - 1]$ is a one-step left cyclic shift of $c(X)$. From Eq. (4.3.21)

$$Xc(X) = c_{N-1}X^n + c_{N-2}X^{n-1} + \cdots + c_1X^2 + c_0X$$

Reducing modulo $X^n - 1$, X^n *is replaced by 1*, so that

$$Xc(X) \quad [\text{mod } X^n - 1] = c_{N-2}X^{n-1} + c_{N-3}X^{n-2} + \cdots + c_1X^2 + c_0X + c_{N-1}$$
$$(4.3.25)$$

Thus, in modulo $X^n - 1$ polynomial arithmetic, if $c(X)$ is a code word, so is $X^ic(X)$ and, since in a parity check code any sum of code words is a code word,

$$\sum_i \alpha_i X^i c(X) = f(X)c(X) \quad [\text{mod } X^n - 1] \qquad (4.3.26)$$

is a code word, where $f(X)$ is any polynomial with binary coefficients [or, in general, with GF(q) field element coefficients].

We have seen that a general parity check code can be specified by its generator *matrix G*. It turns out that the set of code words for an (n, k) cyclic code is uniquely specified by a generator *polynomial* $g(X)$. The following properties show how $g(X)$ determines the cyclic code.

1. $g(X)$ is the unique lowest-degree nonzero code polynomial having unity coefficient in its highest-degree term. If there were two such code polynomials, then by the additive group property their difference would be a code polynomial, but the difference would be of lower degree because the leading terms cancel.
2. The degree of $g(X)$ is $n - k$. This will follow from properties 3 and 4 below.
3. Each of the 2^k code words of a binary cyclic code can be expressed as a multiple of $g(X)$ in the form

$$\sum_{i=0}^{k-1} \alpha_i X^i g(X)$$

where each α_i is 0 or 1. (Or similarly, for the nonbinary case of q^k code words with $\alpha_i \varepsilon$ GF(q).) It is easily seen that these 2^k combinations are all different and (based on Eq. (4.3.26)) all code words. That any code word must be of this form can be proven by assuming the contrary: Some $m(X)$ is not a multiple of $g(X)$. Then, by the Euclid division algorithm,

$$m(X) = q(X)g(X) + r(X)$$

or

$$m(X) - q(X)g(X) = r(X) \qquad (4.3.27)$$

By Eq. (3.26), $q(X)g(X)$ is a code word. By the additive group property, $m(X) - q(X)g(X)$ is a code word. Then, by Eq. (4.3.27), $r(X)$ is a code word of degree less than $g(X)$, which is a contradiction unless $r(X) = 0$, which contradicts $m(X)$ not being a multiple of $g(X)$.
4. The set of code polynomials $g(X), Xg(X), \ldots, X^{k-1}g(X)$ is a linearly independent set. All 2^k code words can be generated by linear combinations of these k code words.
5. $g(X)$ must be a factor of $X^n - 1$. To prove this, assume the contrary:

$$X^n - 1 = q(X)g(X) + r(X), \qquad r(X) \neq 0, \text{ degree } r(X) < \text{ degree } g(X)$$

Modulo $X^n - 1$,

$$0 = [q(X)g(X) + r(X)]_{\text{MOD}_{X^n - 1}}$$

or

$$-[q(X)g(X)]_{\text{MOD } X^n - 1} = r(x) \qquad (4.3.28)$$

The left side of Eq. (4.3.28) is a code word; thus $r(X)$ is a code word; since degree $r(X) <$ degree $g(X)$, $r(X) = 0$.

As an illustration consider a length 7 binary cyclic code whose generator matrix is

$$g(X) = X^3 + X + 1 \qquad (4.3.29)$$

Property 5 is verified by factoring $X^7 - 1$ (same as $X^7 + 1$ for binary digits) as

$$X^7 + 1 = (X + 1)(X^3 + X + 1)(X^3 + X^2 + 1) \qquad (4.3.30)$$

The code has three check digits by property (2). The four linearly independent code words specified in property 4 are:

As polynomials	As 7-tuples
$X^3 + X + 1$	0001011
$X^4 + X^2 + X$	0010110
$X^5 + X^3 + X^2$	0101100
$X^6 + X^4 + X^3$	1011000

The 16 code words are the linear combinations of these four words.

Encoding a cyclic code.   Define a data polynomial as

$$d(X) = d_{k-1}X^{k-1} + d_{k-2}X^{k-2} + \cdots + d_1X + d_0 \qquad (4.3.31)$$

where $d_{k-1}, d_{k-2}, \ldots, d_0$ are the data digits. One way of encoding a cyclic code is to perform the multiplication.

$$c(X) = d(X)g(X) \qquad (4.3.32)$$

by means of a shift register circuit as shown in Fig. 4.3.1.

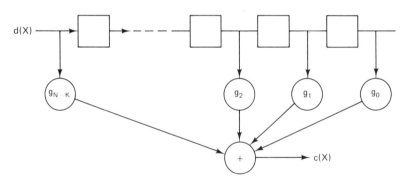

Figure 4.3.1 Nonsystematic cyclic encoding with a shift register.

The digit d_{k-1} goes into the register first, followed by d_{k-2}, then d_{k-3}, and so on. The circled (g_i) represent multiplication by g_i (0 or 1), and the symbol $\oplus$ indicates a modulo 2 adder [in the general case a GF(q) adder]. The code digits come out in the order $c_{n-1}, c_{n-2}, \ldots, c_1, c_0$.

The procedure above yields a nonsystematic encoding of the cyclic code, as the data do not appear explicitly as a subsequence of the output code digits. The encoding can be made systematic with the aid of the technique described below.

Consider

$$X^{n-k}d(X) = d_{k-1}X^{n-1} + \cdots + d_0 X^{n-k} \tag{4.3.33}$$

By the Euclid division algorithm,

$$d_{k-1}X^{n-1} + \cdots + d_0 X^{n-k} = q(X)g(X) + r(X) \tag{4.3.34}$$

where if $g(X)$ is the degree $n - k$ generator polynomial, $r(X)$ is the unique remainder of degree less than $n - k$. Adding $r(X)$ to both sides (binary coefficients) yields

$$d_{k-1}X^{n-1} + \cdots + d_0 X^{n-k} + r(X) = q(X)g(X) \tag{4.3.35}$$

The left side of Eq. (4.3.35) is seen to be a multiple of $g(X)$; thus it is a code polynomial. If

$$r(X) = p_{n-k-1}X^{n-k-1} + \cdots + p_1 X + p_0, \tag{4.3.36}$$

then the coefficient sequence for the code polynomial is

$$d_{k-1}, d_{k-2}, \ldots, d_0, p_{n-k-1}, \ldots, p_0$$

which is seen to be systematic.

It is easy to design a feedback shift register circuit to divide $d(X)$ by $g(X)$ in order to find the remainder $r(X)$. The circuit for this is shown in Fig. 4.3.2. In this case d_{k-1} is fed in first, followed by $d_{k-2}, d_{k-3}, \ldots$ until d_{k-1} reaches the rightmost position. Then k shift rights are performed, after which the digits of $r(X)$ appear in the register with p_{n-k-1} at the extreme right.

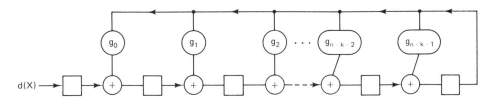

Figure 4.3.2   Feedback shift register for systematic cyclic encoding.

The same feedback shift register used for encoding can also be used for error detection. Similar to what was done with vectors, we can define an observed polynomial $y(X)$ and an error polynomial $e(X)$ by

$$y(X) = c(X) + e(X) \tag{4.3.37}$$

We can divide $y(X)$ by $g(X)$. If $y(X)$ is not a code word, there will be a remainder. We can call this remainder the syndrome polynomial $s(X)$.

$$s(X) = \text{remainder } \frac{y(X)}{g(X)} \tag{4.3.38}$$

This remainder can be found by the same feedback shift register circuit illustrated in Fig. 4.3.2. However, instead of feeding in data, we feed in the observed sequence represented by $y(X)$, starting with y_{n-1}. After y_{n-1} reaches the rightmost position, we shift k times, after which $s(X)$ appears in the register.

The syndrome polynomial also can be valuable for error correction as well as error detection. Some error-correction schemes will be described in the next section.

4.4. CLASSES OF PARITY CHECK CODES AND GENERAL DECODING SCHEMES

For any parity check code, error detection can be accomplished by the operation (4.3.17) on the observed sequence $\bar{y}$; or if the code is cyclic, it can be accomplished even more simply by computing the syndrome polynomial as in Eq. (4.3.38). The general error-correction problem when errors are detected is not so straightforward, however. Over the years, coding schemes have evolved which have gradually increased the amount of error correction which can be performed with a constrained number of computational steps. Concurrently, the time and hardware cost to perform a given number of computational steps has greatly decreased. The combination of these two trends is leading to broader application for error-correcting techniques.

4.4.1. Hamming Single-Error-Correcting Codes

Although single error correction is almost trivial compared to the general error-correction problem, the Hamming single-error-correcting codes [HAMM50] are very important for practical purposes and as a key to the understanding of more complex error-correcting schemes.

It was seen from the discussion about Table 4.3.1 that it is possible to correct all single errors if and only if each single error pattern is in a different coset of the standard array, which is equivalent to stating that each single error pattern has a different syndrome. Also by observation of Eq. (4.3.17), if each column of matrix H is different and nonzero, in the binary case each single error pattern will yield a different syndrome. If the code has $m = n - k$ check digits, there are $2^m - 1$ nonzero syndromes and H can have as many as $2^m - 1$ columns. Thus the longest single-error-correcting code having m check digits is of length $2^m - 1$. The resulting $(2^m - 1, 2^m - 1 - m)$ code is called a Hamming single-error-correcting code.

The code with H given by (4.3.14) is a (7, 4) Hamming single-error-correcting code. The ordering of columns can always be chosen so that the Hamming single-error-correcting code is systematic. Sometimes it may be convenient to arrange the columns so that column i is the binary representation of the number i; then the syndrome is the binary representation of the single error location. However, for $m > 4$ this is not compatible with the systematic code requirement. In any case, single-error correction can readily be accomplished by a combinational circuit having the syndrome as input and n outputs, such that each of the n different single-error syndromes produces a 1 at just the output position that corresponds to the single error position.

Hamming single-error-correcting codes have the advantage that they require the fewest possible check digits for their code lengths. However, they have the disadvantage that no room is left for detection of any events of greater than one error in a code block. Any such event is interpreted wrongly as a single error because each nonzero syndrome is matched with one of the single-error events. The addition of a single additional parity digit which is the modulo 2 sum of all the other digits can improve this situation somewhat by detecting all double error patterns in addition to correcting all single-error patterns. For example, if we convert the (7, 4) single-error-correcting code of Eqs. (4.3.12) to (4.3.14) into an (8, 4) single-error-correcting double-error-detecting code, the parity check matrix becomes

$$H = \begin{bmatrix} 1 & 1 & 1 & 0 & 1 & 0 & 0 & 0 \\ 1 & 1 & 0 & 1 & 0 & 1 & 0 & 0 \\ 0 & 1 & 1 & 1 & 0 & 0 & 1 & 0 \\ 1 & 1 & 1 & 1 & 1 & 1 & 1 & 1 \end{bmatrix} \qquad (4.4.1)$$

We see that the eight columns of H are still all different (different nonzero syndrome for each single-error pattern) and all end in a 1. Any double-error pattern yields a nonzero pattern (vector sum of two columns) which ends in a zero. These patterns are detected as errors which are not single-bit errors.

Altogether there are $2^8 - 1$ possible bit-error patterns. Table 4.4.1 explains the disposition of each possible error pattern.

TABLE 4.4.1   ENUMERATION OF ERROR EVENT DISPOSITION FOR THE (8, 4) CODE ILLUSTRATION.

Syndrome	Result
0000	15 patterns that imitate code words are not detected. (These all have at least four errors.)
XXX1	8 single-error patterns are corrected. 8×15 other patterns with these syndromes are erroneously interpreted as a wrong single-error pattern. (These all have at least three errors in the pattern.)
YYY0	The 7×16 patterns with these syndromes [including all $\binom{8}{2} = 28$ double error patterns] are detected but not corrected.

4.4.2. BCH Cyclic Codes

Cyclic codes are an important class of parity check codes which have a structure which makes them easier to implement than general parity check codes. The most important subclass of cyclic codes is the BCH class [BOSE 60, CHIE 64]. The BCH codes include Hamming single-error-correcting codes as a special case, and include design rules for codes that correct up to any specified maximum number of correctible errors.

Finite field properties.   To help explain their capabilities and properties we must extend the discussion of finite fields with polynomial elements begun in Section 4.3.7. The elements of a field form an Abelian group under addition, so the additive properties are as discussed in Eq. (4.3.2). We now state without proof the multiplicative and other important properties for a field of q elements [GF(q)].

1. The $q - 1$ nonzero elements form an Abelian group under multiplication. Define β^i as the multiplication of a string of i β's, $\beta \ldots \beta$, and define β^{-i} as the multiplicative inverse. The smallest positive r such that $\beta^r = 1$ is called the *order* of the element β.

2. Every field contains at least one element α whose order is $q - 1$, such that α, $\alpha^2, \ldots, \alpha^{q-1}$ are all the $q - 1$ distinct nonzero elements. Such an element is called a *primitive element*.

3. The order of a field must be a power of a prime (i.e., $q = p^m$, where p is a prime).

4. Any GF(p), where p is prime, is isomorphic to the field of integers modulo p.

5. Any GF(p^m), p a prime, is isomorphic to the field of polynomials over GF (p) modulo an irreducible polynomial of degree m. [An irreducible polynomial over GF(p) is a polynomial which cannot be factored into polynomials with coefficients in GF(p).]

6. The $q - 1$ nonzero elements of the field are all the $q - 1$ roots of $X^{q-1} - 1$.

7. Let α be a primitive element of GF(p^m), where p is a prime, and let i_j be an element of GF(p). Then any $\beta \in$ GF(p^m) can be written as

$$\beta = i_{m-1}\alpha^{m-1} + i_{m-2}\alpha^{m-2} + \cdots + i_1\alpha + i_0 \qquad (4.4.2)$$

As an illustration, consider GF(2^3). By property 5, it has the structure of the field of polynomials over a binary field modulo a degree 3 irreducible polynomial. Because we will often be considering field elements as roots of a polynomial in X, if we wish to express the field elements themselves as polynomials we must use a different variable name, say t, for the polynomials representing the field elements. Thus let $t^3 + t + 1$ be the degree three irreducible polynomial for this GF(2^3) example.

Suppose that we take the field element $\alpha = t$ and take its successive powers to see if it is primitive.

$$\alpha = \underline{t}$$

$$\alpha^2 = \underline{t^2}$$

$$\alpha^3 = t^3 \equiv \underline{t + 1}$$

$$\alpha^4 = \underline{t^2 + t} \qquad\qquad (4.4.3)$$

$$\alpha^5 = t^3 + t^2 \equiv \underline{t^2 + t + 1}$$

$$\alpha^6 = t^3 + t^2 + t \equiv t + 1 + t^2 + t \equiv \underline{t^2 + 1}$$

$$\alpha^7 = t^3 + t \equiv \underline{1}$$

Thus it is seen that $\alpha = t$ is primitive and the seven underlined expressions in Eq. (4.4.3) are the seven nonzero field elements expressed as polynomials over GF(2).

Multiplication by t modulo an irreducible polynomial is readily accomplished with a feedback shift register.

Figure 4.4.1 is a shift register that multiplies by $\alpha = t$ modulo $t^3 + t + 1$. The shift register contents from left to right are the coefficients (a_0, a_1, a_2) of a field element expressed as a polynomial $a_2 t^2 + a_1 t + a_0$. Multiplication by t is a shift to the right, but if there is a t^2 term, instead of shifting it out to a box representing t^3, the feedback connections effectively replace what would be t^3 by $t + 1$. This is exactly what is required according to the modulo $t^3 + t + 1$ rules of operation. If one starts with $\alpha = t$, (010) in the feedback register, successive shifts produce all seven nonzero field elements in succession in the same order as in (4.3); further shifts would repeat the pattern.

Coefficients of:

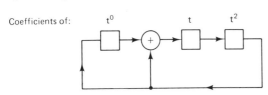

Figure 4.4.1   Multiplication by t modulo $t^3 + t + 1$.

From the discussion above it can be observed that there are three different ways by which it may be convenient to represent a nonzero field element of GF(q^m):

1. As a power of a primitive element
2. As a polynomial over GF(q): $a_{m-1}t^{m-1} + a_{m-2}t^{m-2} + \cdots + a_0$
3. As a vector of m components: $(a_{m-1}, a_{m-2}, \ldots, a_0)$

BCH cyclic codes [BOSE 60].   In this important class of cyclic codes the code is specified in terms of field elements which must be roots of the generator polynomial. Before considering the general case, we will show that the set of code words (written as polynomials) of a Hamming single-error-correcting code of length $2^m - 1$ consists of those polynomials which have a primitive element $\alpha \in$ GF(2^m) as a root. Let $n = 2^m - 1$ and

$$c(X) = c_{n-1}X^{n-1} + \cdots + c_1 X + c_0$$

Then if α is a root of $c(X)$, we have the equation, in matrix form,

$$[\alpha^{n-1}\alpha^{n-2} \cdots \alpha^1 \alpha^0] \begin{bmatrix} c_{n-1} \\ c_{n-2} \\ \vdots \\ c_0 \end{bmatrix} = 0 \qquad (4.4.4)$$

Equation (4.4.4) resembles the parity check matrix equation (4.3.10). In fact, if each power of α is replaced by a column vector corresponding to the vector representation of the field element, then

$$[\alpha^{m-1} \quad \alpha^{m-2} \quad \cdots \quad \alpha^1 \quad \alpha^0]$$

becomes

$$\begin{bmatrix} a_{m-1,m-1} & \cdots & a_{m-1,1} & a_{m-1,0} \\ a_{m-2,m-1} & & \vdots & \vdots \\ a_{0,m-1} & & a_{0,1} & a_{0,0} \end{bmatrix}$$

which is just like the H matrix. For GF(2^3),

$$[\alpha^6 \quad \alpha^5 \quad \alpha^4 \quad \alpha^3 \quad \alpha^2 \quad \alpha \quad 1]$$

becomes

$$\begin{bmatrix} 1 & 1 & 1 & 0 & 1 & 0 & 0 \\ 0 & 1 & 1 & 1 & 0 & 1 & 0 \\ 1 & 1 & 0 & 1 & 0 & 0 & 1 \end{bmatrix}$$

which is seen to be identical to the condition on H to have a single-error-correcting $(7,4)$, Hamming code [in the general case, a $(2^m - 1, 2^m - 1 - m)$ single-error-correcting Hamming code].

The cyclic structure of this code permits use of a sequential circuit for single-error correction, which is simpler than the general single-error-correction combinational circuit referred to at the beginning of this section. Figure 4.4.2 shows the basic elements of this circuit. After the seven received code digits are shifted simultaneously into the buffer and feedback shift register (FSR) the FSR will contain the syndrome [equivalent to the remainder after division by $g(x) = 1 + x + x^3$]. If there is a single error in the first received digit (x^6 coefficient), the resulting syndrome will be α^6 or equivalently $t^2 + 1$ or

$$\begin{bmatrix} 1 \\ 0 \\ 1 \end{bmatrix}$$

This pattern will produce a 1 output of the AND gate, which will add modulo 2 to the

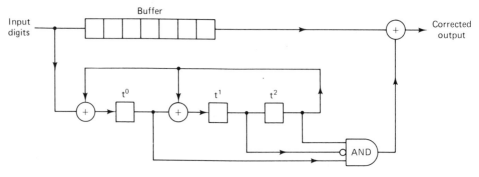

Figure 4.4.2

first digit coming out of the buffer and change (correct) its value. The next six successive shifts of the FSR will produce each of the other nonzero patterns, but none of these will produce a 1 at the AND-gate output; thus the other digits will not be changed. If the single error is in the $(1 + i)$th digit, $6 > i > 1$, the syndrome will be α^{6-i}, and after i shifts α^6 will appear in the FSR and a 1 will appear at the AND-gate output. This will occur just when digit $i + 1$ is coming out of the buffer. Thus any single error gets corrected as it comes out of the buffer.

A general BCH code is specified by the parameters q, m, α, r, and d. An element α is in the field $GF(q^m)$, and the code consists of all polynomials over $GF(q)$ of degree $n - 1$ or less which have as roots all of the following elements:

$$\alpha^r, \quad \alpha^{r+1}, \quad \ldots, \quad \alpha^{r+d-2}$$

The code length n is the order of α. Usually, α is primitive and $n = q^m - 1$.

The code specification can be shown in matrix form as follows:

$$\begin{bmatrix} \alpha^{(n-1)(r+d-2)} & \cdots & \alpha^{r+d-2} & \alpha^0 \\ \alpha^{(n-1)(r+d-3)} & \cdots & \alpha^{r+d-3} & \alpha^0 \\ \vdots & & & \\ \alpha^{(n-1)(r+1)} & & \alpha^{r+1} & \\ \alpha^{(n-1)r} & & \alpha^r & \alpha^0 \end{bmatrix} \begin{bmatrix} C_{n-1} \\ C_{n-2} \\ \vdots \\ C_1 \\ C_0 \end{bmatrix} = [0]^T \qquad (4.4.5)$$

If the root matrix in Eq. (4.4.5) is converted to the binary entry ($q = 2$) form of H, there would be $m(d - 1)$ rows. However, some of these rows are dependent, and it can be shown that the number of check symbols [also the degree of the generator polynomial $g(X)$] is less than or equal to $m(d - 1)/2$. Also, it can be shown that the minimum distance between any two code words is at least d. Thus the code could correct all patterns of errors containing a number of errors less than $d/2$.

The explanation of the procedure for correcting multiple errors is too lengthy and complex to be described here. The reader may refer to [BERL68] or [LIN83] for more information. Hardware requirements are roughly proportional to md, and decoding time is roughly proportional to mn. The multiple error-correction techniques have practical application for efficient communication over noisy channels, but normally would not be cost-effective in computer systems.

4.4.3. Reed–Solomon Code, Concatenated Codes, and Product Codes

Reed–Solomon codes [REED54, REED60] are a class of BCH codes where $m = 1$ and $q = p^l$, where p is a prime (in most cases $p = 2$). Then, since $m = 1$, the field of coefficients is the same as the field of roots. To specify a code with minimum Hamming distance of d, we have

$$g(X) = \prod_{i=r}^{r+d-2} (X - \alpha^i) \qquad (4.4.6)$$

The code length is $q - 1$ and the number of check digits is $d - 1$. The minimum

Hamming distance d is the greatest possible for any code having $d - 1$ check digits (the digits here are q-ary, not binary).

As an illustration, suppose that $q = 8$, $d = 4$, $r = 1$. Let the GF(2^3) be as described previously: polynomials modulo $t^3 + t + 1$ over GF(2), with $\alpha = t$. The code length is seven octal digits, with three octal check digits. It can correct all single errors and detect all double errors. We require that $g(x)$ have the roots $\alpha = t$, $\alpha^2 = t^2$, $\alpha^3 = t + 1$.

$$g(X) = (X - t)(X - t^2)(X - t - 1) = X^3 + (t^2 + 1)X^2 + tX + t^2 + 1 \quad (4.4.7)$$

Each octal digit can be written as a length 3 binary sequence, so the code is a (21, 12) binary code which can correct all binary error patterns which are confined to a single block of three binary digits corresponding to an octal digit. Examples of code words written as binary sequences are

$$g(X): \quad 000\ 000\ 000\ 001\ 101\ 010\ 101$$

$$X^3 g(X): \quad 001\ 101\ 010\ 101\ 000\ 000\ 000$$

$$tX g(X): \quad 000\ 000\ 010\ 001\ 100\ 001\ 000$$

Another possibility is that the 2^l field elements in the Reed–Solomon code can be the 2^l code words of an (n_1, l) binary code instead of the 2^l binary sequences of length l. This gives the code what is called a *concatenated code structure* [FORN66]. The (n_1, l) code for the field elements is called the *inner code*. The outer code is a $(q - 1, q - d)$ Reed Solomon code with q-ary digits. Looking at both outer and inner code as a single binary block code, this composite code is of length $n = n_1(q - 1)$ and has $l(q - d)$ binary data digits. If the inner code has minimum distance d_1 between code words, the composite code has minimum distance $d_1 d$.

Decoding can be accomplished by cooperation between an inner decoder for the (n_1, l) binary inner code and an outer decoder for the overall code. The most direct procedure is for the inner code to be used first to correct whatever errors it can. Then the (possibly) corrected l-bit bytes are supplied to the Reed–Solomon outer decoder for correction and/or detection of any remaining errors. An alternative or supplemental procedure is that the inner decoder could in some cases detect but not correct errors in its byte, and supply an "erasure" symbol to the outer decoder in such a case. The outer decoder would have to have the capability of discovering the erased byte contents (see Section 4.6.1).

Iterated codes [ELIA54, PETE71]   Consider the two-dimensional array of digits shown in Fig. 4.4.3. Suppose that each row is a code word of an (n_1, l_1) parity check code, and each column is a code word of an (n_2, l_2) code. The iterated two-dimensional code (also called a *product code*) is then a $(n_1 n_2, l_1 l_2)$ code. If the (n_1, l^1) code has minimum distance d_1 and the (n_2, l_2) code has minimum distance d_2, the product code has minimum distance $d_1 d_2$.

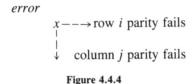

Figure 4.4.3

The iterated code structure is a very convenient one for simplifying the error correction/detection process. As one application, errors can be corrected even if the row and column codes are used only for error detection, as exemplified below.

Example 1.   Suppose that each row and column contains but a single parity bit for error detection. A single error in row i, column j of the array could be corrected by observing that only the parity of row i and column j would fail to check, as illustrated in Fig. 4.4.4.

error

$x---\rightarrow$ row i parity fails

$\downarrow$ column j parity fails

Figure 4.4.4

Example 2.   Suppose that each row is a more powerful error-detecting code employing a substantial number of parity bits, but each column has a single parity bit. Suppose say, that five errors occur, but all in row i. Most likely parity would fail in row i, and the five columns where parity fails would locate the five errors (see Fig. 4.4.5).

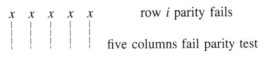

Figure 4.4.5

Another decoding rule could be first to use the horizontal code to correct errors, thereby hopefully reducing the total number of errors, and then use the vertical codes to reduce the errors remaining. This simple scheme does not correct all patterns of errors that the two-dimensional code is capable of correcting, but more elaborate correcting schemes designed to increase the set of corrected error patterns might not be worth the added computational effort.

4.4.4. Modified Codes [BERL68]

Code classes such as BCH and Reed–Solomon codes have restrictions on code lengths and code rates. In order to expand the freedom of choice of lengths and rates, codes sometimes are modified by deleting or adding digits. An important example of this is the shortened cyclic codes, which are formed by omitting some of the message digits. (Or one could pretend that these omitted message digits were always set to zero.) By choosing a $g(X)$ of moderate degree from an extremely long code, the number of message digits in a block can be varied over a wide range while employing a fixed number of check digits. Other variations include punctured codes, where certain check digits are deleted, and extended codes, where check digits are added to the code.

4.4.5. Erasures and Erasure Decoding

Sometimes a certain location in memory involving one or many bits is known to be faulty. In this case the bit or set of bits known to be unreliable can be represented as an erasure symbol, indicating that it is unknown. A similar effect occurs in concatenated codes where, as mentioned in Section 4.3, the inner decoder detects the presence of errors in some subblock and the outer decoder interprets this subblock as being "erased."

The ability to decode erased bits conveniently is very much dependent on how the code is organized relative to the physical location of data bits. If each code block is such that bits within a block come from physically relatively independent locations, a large cluster of erased bits may involve only one or a few bits in each code block. An example of a good structure for this purpose is the two-dimensional iterated code described in Fig. 4.4.5. Referring to Fig. 4.4.5, suppose that the rows represent bits which are physically interrelated, whereas bits in a column are in physically independent locations. Then a physical fault may result in erasure of a single row, but this only affects one bit in each column.

The capability of a block parity check code to correct erasures is easily stated. A parity check code with Hamming distance of d symbols has the capability of discovering the value of all cases of up to $d - 1$ erased symbols, assuming that none of the unerased symbols are in error. The general decoding procedure involves the simultaneous solution of a set of linear equations with the erased symbols as the unknowns [EPST58]. This general procedure would be too complex for most applications. Two-dimensional iterated codes or a concatenated code provide more convenient decoding at some cost in number of discoverable erasures. Cyclic codes have convenient properties for decoding erasures that occur in bursts or clusters (see Section 4.4.6). Also, a block code with internal convolutional structure [METZ82] has been suggested for convenient decoding of large numbers of erasures.

Burst error or erasure correction. The correction of errors or erasures in bursts is much simpler in general than the correction of errors occurring in random positions. It is easy to accomplish burst error correction with cyclic codes [PETE71]. The main component of the decoder is the feedback shift register with connections determined by $g(X)$ as illustrated in Fig. 4.3.2. The received sequence $y(X)$ is fed into the register, which produces a result which is a syndrome:

$$s(X) = \text{remainder } \frac{y(X)}{g(X)} \tag{4.4.8}$$

Also, let β be the set of all error bursts of length B or less. The length of an error burst is defined as the total number of symbols from the first error in the code block through the last error, inclusive. The interior symbols may or may not be in error, in any pattern. Let

$$y(X) = c(X) + e_\beta(X), \tag{4.4.9}$$

where $e_\beta(X)$ is the error polynomial, and assume that $e_\beta(X) \in \beta$. Let us suppose that the code has the capability of correcting all bursts of length B or less, which means no two such bursts are in the same coset or have the same syndrome.

Suppose, for example, that the degree of $e_\beta(X)$ is less than $n - k$. This means the burst lies entirely within the last $n - k$ positions.

$$s(X) = \text{Rem} \frac{y(X)}{g(X)} = \text{Rem} \frac{e_\beta(X)}{g(X)} = e_\beta(X), \tag{4.4.10}$$

since degree $[g(X)]$ is $n - k$ and degree $[e_\beta(x)] < n - k$. Thus the error burst is revealed. Suppose instead that degree $[e(x)] \geq n - k$. Then, on dividing $y(X)$ by $g(X)$, the remainder will not be $e_\beta(X)$. However, the remainder will not be any other member of β, since only one member of β can have a given syndrome.

It can be shown that $B < n - k$. Thus, if we try cyclically shifting the input and dividing for each cyclic shift, we must find some case where the cyclic shift of $e_\beta(X)$ will be of degree $< n - k$. Thus we try

$$\text{Rem} \frac{[X^i y(X)]_{\text{mod} X^n - 1}}{g(X)} = \text{Rem} \frac{[X^i e_\beta(X)_{\text{mod} X^n - 1}}{g(X)} \tag{4.4.11}$$

until some i is found where

$$\text{degree } [X^i e_\beta(X)]_{\text{mod} X^n - 1} < n - k$$

We then discover the burst and move it back i positions cyclically to where it really occurred. If all attempts fail, the error pattern must be something other than a burst in β.

The cyclic code structure is also convenient for decoding any cluster of erasures which is confined to any span of $n - k$ consecutive positions. Cyclically shift the n bits of a code word until the K highest-degree terms contain no erased bits. Call this known part of the code block

$$w(X) = a_{n-1}X^{n-1} + \cdots + a_{n-k}X^{n-k} \tag{4.4.12}$$

Divide $w(X)$ by $g(X)$ and obtain the remainder $r(X)$. If there are no errors in the positions corresponding to $w(X)$, then $r(X) + w(X)$, cyclically shifted back to the original position, will be the correct code word and the erasure values will be revealed. If there are errors as well as erasures, the parts of $r(X)$ corresponding to unerased digits usually will contain disagreements with the observed bits. Correction of both errors and erasures in the same block usually is a complex task.

4.4.6. Importance and Availability of Error Detection

Specialized parity check codes have been developed primarily because their structure has certain regularities which simplify the task of correcting errors. Error correction succeeds only if the error pattern is one of the set of correctible errors. For example, in the ordinary Hamming single-error-correcting code, the presence of two errors will not be detected and will result in a third bit error.

The number of correctible error patterns for an (n, k) block code is at most 2^{n-k}, which can be a *tiny fraction* of the total of 2^n possible error patterns. This proportionally small set of correctible error patterns may be adequate to correct all but a minute fraction of occurring errors, *provided* that error statistics obey perfectly known statistical laws—this is a consequence of the statistical regularities involving a large number of independent or near independent trials. However, in a large complex system there are many possible physical sources of errors whose statistics are imperfectly known both as to relative frequency of occurrence of the underlying phenomenon and number and relative location of affected bits. Thus, for highly fault-tolerant system design, it may not be safe to rely on the error pattern being in a relatively small correctible set. To provide this necessary extra safety we must have the capability for error detection. This could be accomplished by backing off somewhat from using the full error-correcting capability of the code. It is a fortunate consequence of laws of large numbers that at a small cost in error-correcting capability we can greatly increase the protection against undetected errors in case an unusual error pattern occurs. This will be demonstrated below.

Consider a binary (n, k_0) parity check code. Suppose that the decoding scheme for this code allows correction of any of Q different error patterns for each code word,* as shown in Fig. 4.4.6. Suppose that we denote by f the ratio of number of corrected sequences to total possible number of sequences.

$$f = \frac{Q \cdot 2^{k_0}}{2^n} \tag{4.4.13}$$

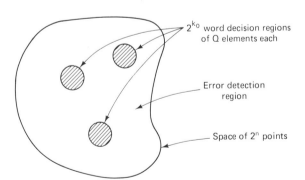

2^{k_0} word decision regions of Q elements each

Error detection region

Space of 2^n points

Figure 4.4.6 Decision space of 2^n binary n-tuples.

*For cases such as stuck-at fault where the likelihood of an error pattern is dependent on the code word pattern, the size of each error pattern set might not be the same. However, the general principles being discussed would remain the same.

If we tried to use the fullest error-correcting capability we would choose $Q = 2^{n-k_0}$ and would have $f = 1$; but then any uncorrectible error pattern would be undetected. Suppose that we replace c of the k_0 data bits by check bits, keeping the same size Q. Then

$$f = 2^{-c}$$

It is this exponential dependence of f on c which makes it easy to obtain great safety at little cost in efficiency.

As a numerical example, suppose that $n = 300$, $k_0 = 270$, $c = 30$. Then

$$f = 2^{-30} = 10^{-9}$$

Thus, at a cost of reduction of data efficiency from 90% $[(270/300) \times 100]$ to 80%, the chance of an unusual error pattern causing an undetected error has been reduced from near unity to 1 in a billion. For larger n, even less efficiency reduction would be needed for a given amount of protection.

An alternative method is to permit full error correction for each code block, but add check bits for error detection which check over several code blocks. This is a good way to keep a small ratio of number of check bits for error detection to number of information bits. A disadvantage is that if the check fails, all blocks in the checking set must be considered unreliable, instead of just one block.

It might seem at first that error detection violates the primary goal of a fault-tolerant system, which is to continue computing successfully despite any errors that may occur in the course of computation. However, error detection often is just one step in the overall error correction and resultant correct operation of the system. For example, in communication error detection leads to retransmission and eventual correct reception; in computation or memory retrieval it may lead to a retry, which could lead to a correct result if the errors are due to a transient rather than permanent fault; or the computation could be backed up and retried with different or repaired facilities; or the computation might have been done in duplicate facilities, such that error detection in one facility results in taking the output from the other facility; or bits detected in error by one code may also be part of another error correcting code, as with iterated or concatenated codes.

4.5. UNIDIRECTIONAL AND ASYMMETRIC CODES

4.5.1. Unidirectional Error Correcting/Detecting Capabilities of Binary Block Codes

The error statistics are said to be *unidirectional* if, for any code word, either (1) all the errors in the word are 0 to 1 or, (2) all the errors in the word are 1 to 0. However, the decoder does not know a priori whether event type (1) or (2) has occurred.

Let e_i be 0 or 1 according to whether bit i is correct or not. Then, in the case of unidirectional errors, if $(a_n, a_{n-1}, \ldots, a_1)$ is the correct word, $a_i \in [0, 1]$, a word with errors is represented either by $(a_n + e_n, a_{n-1} + e_{n-1}, \ldots, a_1 + e_1)$ if all the errors are 0 to 1, or by $(a_n - e_n, a_{n-1} - e_{n-1}, \ldots, a_1 - e_1)$ if all the errors are 1 to 0. If $e_1 + e_2 + \cdots + e_n = t$, we say that t errors have occurred in the received word. In order to study the unidirectional error-correcting/detecting capabilities of binary codes, the following parameter is useful.

Let X and Y be any two n-tuples over GF(2). Let $N(X, Y)$ denote the number of $1 \rightarrow 0$ crossovers from X to Y.

For example, if $X = 1011$ and $Y = 0101$, then $N(X, Y) = 2$ and $N(Y, X) = 1$. In general $N(X, Y) \neq N(Y, X)$. Also note that we can express the Hamming distance $D(X, Y)$ as

$$D(X, Y) = N(X, Y) + N(Y, X) \tag{4.5.1}$$

The following two theorems give the unidirectional error correcting/detecting properties of binary block codes.

Theorem 1. A code C is capable of detecting all unidirectional errors iff it satisfies the following condition:

$$\text{for all } X, Y \in C, \quad N(X, Y) \geq 1 \tag{4.5.2}$$

Theorem 2. A code C is capable of correcting t-(symmetric) errors and detecting multiple (all) unidirectional errors iff it satisfies the following condition:

$$\text{for all } X, Y \in C, \quad N(X, Y) \geq t + 1 \tag{4.5.3}$$

4.5.2. Unidirectional Error-Detecting codes

There are two known unidirectional error-detecting codes: m-out-of-n codes and the Berger codes.

m-out-of-n codes. In the m-out-of-n code each code word has weight m and the length of the code words is n. If there are unidirectional errors in a code word, the corrupted word will have weight more than m in the case of $0 \rightarrow 1$ errors, and less than m in the case of $1 \rightarrow 0$ errors. In both cases the unidirectional errors can be detected. These codes are nonsystematic in the sense that the information bits cannot be separately identified from the check bits. Among all unidirectional error detecting codes the $\lfloor n/2 \rfloor$-out-of-n code or $\lceil n/2 \rceil$-out-of-n code has the highest information rate [FRIE 62].

Berger codes. These are systematic unidirectional error detecting codes. Let $(a_k a_{k-1} \cdots a_1)$ be a given information symbol, where $a_i \in$ GF(2) for $i = 1, 2, \cdots, k$. Count the number of 0s in the information symbol and append this in binary form as the check symbol. For example, if 1010100 is the given information symbol, then the check symbol is 100 because there are four zeros in the information symbol. Now we will discuss why this code detects all unidirectional errors.

1. If there are unidirectional errors in the information part, the number of zeros in the information symbol of the corrupted word will be greater than the check value in the case of $1 \rightarrow 0$ errors and less than the check value in the case of $0 \rightarrow 1$ errors.

2. If there are unidirectional errors in the check part, the number of zeros in the information symbol of the corrupted word will be less than the check value in the case of $0 \rightarrow 1$ errors and greater than the check value in the case of $1 \rightarrow 0$ errors.

3. Finally, if there are unidirectional errors in both information and check symbols, the number of zeros in the information part of the corrupted word will increase in the case of $1 \rightarrow 0$ errors and decrease in the case of $0 \rightarrow 1$ errors. On the other hand, the check value of the corrupted word will decrease in the case of $1 \rightarrow 0$ errors and increase in the case of $0 \rightarrow 1$ errors. So in both cases the number of zeros in the information part cannot be the same as the value of check part in the corrupted word. In all cases we can detect multiple unidirectional errors.

Note that the number of check bits for the Berger code is $\lfloor \log_2(k + 1) \rfloor$, where k is the number of information bits. The following theorem gives the optimality property of Berger codes.

Theorem 3.   The Berger codes are optimal systematic unidirectional error-detecting codes.

Proof: Let the number of information bits of the code be k. Now consider the following $k + 1$ information symbols.

$$000 \cdots 000$$
$$000 \cdots 001$$
$$000 \cdots 011$$
$$000 \cdots 111$$
$$\vdots \qquad \vdots$$
$$111 \cdots 111$$

For a code to be capable of detecting all unidirectional errors, the check symbols for the above $k + 1$ information symbols must all be distinct [i.e., the code must use at least $\lceil \log_2(k + 1) \rceil$ check bits]. Since the Berger code uses exactly this number of check bits, the Berger codes are optimal systematic unidirectional error detecting codes.

4.5.3. Unidirectional Error-Correcting/Detecting Codes

In this section we describe systematic single-error-correcting and multiple (all) unidirectional error-detecting codes. By putting $t = 1$ in Theorem 2 we have the following lemma.

Lemma.   A code C is capable of correcting single errors and detecting multiple unidirectional errors iff it satisfies the following condition:

$$\text{for all } X, Y \in C, \qquad N(X, Y) \geq 2 \qquad (4.5.4)$$

Note that if a code satisfies the property above, the Hamming distance of the code is at least 4, so the code is also capable of detecting double (symmetric) errors. Codes satisfying the condition (4.5.4) are referred to as *single-error-correcting and multiple-unidirectional-error-detecting* (SEC-MUED) codes.

Code construction.   First we give k distinct weights to the k information bits where the weights are the k least positive integers which are not powers of 2 (i.e., the integers are 3, 5, 6, 7, 9, 10, etc.). Two types of checks are appended to the information symbols given. The sum of the weights of the information bits of value 0 is calculated and appended to the information symbol in binary form. More formally, if $(a_k a_{k-1} \cdots a_1)$ is the given information symbol, where $a_i \in 0, 1$, and $w_k, w_{k-1}, \cdots,$ w_1 are the least k positive integers not powers of 2, the value of type 1 check B is

$$B = \sum_{i=1}^{k} \bar{a}_i w_i \qquad (4.5.5)$$

For example, let $X = (1010\ 1101)$ be the given information symbol. Then the weights of these bit positions are 3, 5, 6, 7, 9, 10, 11 and 12. The value of type-1 check symbol will be $0 \times 3 + 1 \times 5 + 0 \times 6 + 0 \times 7 + 1 \times 9 + 0 \times 10 + 1 \times 11 + 0 \times 12 = 25$. Hence the partial code word after appending the first check symbol will be

$$\begin{array}{cc}
1010\ 1101 & 011001 \\
\text{Information} & \text{Type 1} \\
\text{bits} & \text{check}
\end{array}$$

Now the weights of type 1 check bits are the positive integers which are powers of 2.

The number of 0s in the information and in type 1 check symbols is counted and it is appended in binary form as the type 2 check. For the given example the code word after appending the type 2 check symbol is as follows:

$$\begin{array}{cccc}
12,11,10,9\ \ 7,6,5,3 & 32,16,8,4,2,1 & \\
1\ 0\ \ 1\ 0\ \ 1\ 1\ 0\ 1 & 0\ \ 1\ 1\ 0\ 0\ 1 & 0110 \\
\text{Information bits} & \text{Type 1 check} & \text{Type 2 check}
\end{array}$$

So the given example is a $(18, 8)$ systematic code.

It can be proved that the code constructed by the method described above satisfies the condition given in the lemma above. Now we discuss the error-correction and error-detection procedure [BOSE82b].

Decoding algorithm.   Let $(a_k a_{k-1} \cdots a_1 b_r b_{r-1} \cdots b_0 d_s d_{s-1} \cdots d_0)$ be the received word where $(a_k a_{k-1} \cdots a_1)$ is the information part, $(b_r b_{r-1} \cdots b_0)$ is the type 1 check and $(d_s d_{s-1} \cdots d_0)$ is the type 2 check. Let $B = \sum_{i=0}^{r} b_i 2^i$ be the value of type 1 check and $D = \sum_{i=0}^{s} d_i 2^i$ be the value of type 2 check.

Step 1:   (No error) From the information part of the received word find the value of check 1 value B' (i.e., $B' = \sum_{i=1}^{k} c_i w_i$). If $|B' - B| = 0$ there is no error in the information or type 1 check part. (Correct type 2 check part can be obtained easily.)

Step 2:   (Single error) If $|B' - B| = w_i$, complement the bit with weight w_i. Now find the number of 0s in the information and check 1 type. Let it be D'. If $|D' - D| = 0$, a single error has been corrected.

Step 3:   (Multiple unidirectional errors) If w_i does not belong to the weight set or $|D' - D| \neq 0$, this implies multiple unidirectional errors in the received word.

The following example illustrates the decoding procedure. The erroneous bits of the received word are marked.

Example 3.   Let the number of information bits be 8 and the received word be 1010 1101 011001 0110. Then $B = 25$ and $D = 6$. Also, by calculating the type 1 check from the received word, we get $B' = 25$. Since $|B' - B| = 0$, there is no error in the information or in the type 1 check bits. Also since $|D' - D| = 6 - 6 = 0$ there is no error in the type 2 check bits.

Suppose that the received word is 10$\underline{00}$ 1101 011001 0110. Then $B' = 35$ and hence $|B' - B| = |35 - 25| = 10$. After complementing the bit with weight 10 we get the word 1010 1101 011001 0110. Now $D' = 5$ and $|D' - D| = 0$. So single error has been corrected.

Suppose that the received word is 1010 1101 011$\underline{1}$01 0110. Then $B' = 25$ and $B = 29$, so $|B' - B| = 4$. After complementing the bit with weight 4 the word will be 1010 1101 011001 0110. Now $D = 6$ and $D' = 6$, so $|D - D'| = 0$. Again a single error has been corrected.

Finally, in order to illustrate multiple unidirectional error detection, let the received word be 1010 $\underline{0}$100 $\underline{0}$11000 0110. Now $B = 24$ and $B' = 35$, so $|B' - B| = 11$. After complementing the bit with weight 11, we get the word as 1110 0100 011000 0110. But now $D = 6$ and $D' = 8$ and hence $|D' - D| = 2 \neq 0$. So we can detect multiple unidirectional errors.

The code above requires approximately $3 \log_2 k$ check bits, where k is the number of information bits. The following theorem gives a lower bound for the number of check bits.

Theorem 4 [BOSE81].   Any systematic single-error-correcting and multiple-unidirectional-error-detecting code requires at least $\lceil 2 \log_2 k \rceil$ check bits.

4.5.4. Asymmetric Error-Correcting Codes

In the case of asymmetric errors it is known that only one type of error can occur in the received word. If we assume that the error can be of $1 \rightarrow 0$ type, there will not be any $0 \rightarrow 1$-type errors in the received words. The asymmetric distance defined below is useful in studying the asymmetric error-correcting capabilities of binary block codes.

The *asymmetric distance* $D_a(X, Y)$ between two n-tuples X and Y over GF(2) is defined as

$$D_a(X, Y) = \max[N(X, Y), N(Y, X)] \tag{4.5.6}$$

For example, if $X = 1011$ and $Y = 0110$, then $N(X, Y) = 2, N(Y, X) = 1$, and hence $D_a(X, Y) = 2$.

The significance of the asymmetric distance is given in the following theorem.

Theorem 5 [CONS79].   A code C is capable of correcting t-asymmetric errors iff the minimum asymmetric distance of the code is at least $t + 1$.

Note that if the minimum Hamming distance of a code is d, the minimum asymmetric distance of the code is at least $\lfloor (d + 1)/2 \rfloor$. So if a code is capable of correcting t-symmetric errors, it is also capable of correcting t-asymmetric errors. Since the conditions required for asymmetric error correction are less restrictive than that of symmetric error correction, one can expect to construct better information rate codes for asymmetric errors. In the following section we briefly explain single-asymmetric-error-correcting codes devised by Constantine and Rao [CONS79]. Although these are nonsystematic codes, the information rates of these are better than that of Hamming codes.

4.5.5. Single-Asymmetric-Error-Correcting Code

For a code to be capable of correcting single asymmetric errors the minimum asymmetric distance must be at least 2. This can be seen from Theorem 5 by putting $t = 1$. We now describe the group-theoretic codes.

Let G be an Abelian group of order $n + 1$ with elements $a_0 a_1 \cdots a_n$. Let GF(2^n) be the set of all binary n-tuples. Now define a function T from GF(2^n) to F as follows:

$$T: \text{GF}(2^n) \rightarrow G \tag{4.5.7}$$

such that

$$T((c_n c_{n-1} \cdots c_1)) = \sum_{i=1}^{n} c_i a_i$$

where

$$c_i a_i = \begin{cases} a_i & \text{for } c_i = 1 \\ a_0 & \text{for } c_i = 0 \end{cases}$$

The summation defined above is the group operation. Note that the function T partitions the set of n-tuples into $n + 1$ equivalence classes, say $c_0 c_1 c_2 \cdots c_n$, based on where the given n-tuple maps. The following example illustrates the above concepts.

Example 4.   Consider the set of all 4-tuples and take the group as z_5. Now T is a function from $GF(2^4)$ to z_5. If $(a_4 a_3 a_2 a_1)$ is a 4-tuple over $GF(2)$, then

$$T((a_4 a_3 a_2 a_1)) = (4 \times a_4 + 3 \times a_3 + 2 \times a_2 + 1 \times a_1) \mod 5.$$

Then

$$C_0 = 0000,\ 0110,\ 1001,\ 1111$$
$$C_1 = 0001,\ 0111,\ 1010$$
$$C_2 = 0010,\ 1011,\ 1100$$
$$C_3 = 0011,\ 0100,\ 1101$$
$$C_4 = 0101,\ 1000,\ 1110$$

We now show that each of the C_i's forms a single-asymmetric-error-correcting code.

Theorem 6 [CONS79].   The minimum asymmetric distance of any C_i for $i = 0, 1, 2, \ldots, m$ is at least 2.

Before going to the error-correcting procedure, note that $C_0 + C_1 + C_2 + \cdots + C_n = 2^n$ and hence there exists a C_i such that $C_i \geq 2^n/(n + 1)$. It can be proved that the set C_0 contains the maximum number of code words. The bound above is interesting because the maximum number of single (symmetric)-error-correcting code words with length n is $\leq 2^n/(n + 1)$. To find the actual number of code words in C_0 and which group gives the maximum number of code words require a sound background in group theory and these problems are discussed in [CONS79].

Now we will discuss how the error-correction procedure can be carried out. We will assume that C_0 is the set of code words and only $(1 \rightarrow 0)$ type of asymmetric errors can occur in the code words.

Let $X = (C_n C_{n-1} \cdots C_1)$ be the received word. Let $T(X) = b$. If $b = a_0$ there is no error in the received word. If there is a $1 \rightarrow 0$ error at location j, we must have $T(X) + a_j = a_0$ (i.e., $b + a_j = a_0$). Therefore, $a_j = a_0 - b$, from which we can find out the position in error.

Example 5.   Let C_0 given in Example 4 be the set of code words. Here the Abelian group is Z_5. Let 1111 be the correct code word and 1011 be the erroneous message. Since $1 \times 4 + 0 \times 3 + 1 \times 2 + 1 \times 1 = 2 \not\equiv 0$ mod 5 we know that there exists an error in the message. The error position is given by $0 - 2 = 3$ mod 5 and hence we can complement the third bit to get the correct word 1111.

4.6. CODES FOR COMPUTER MEMORIES

4.6.1. Codes for Byte-per-Card Memory Organization

Section 4.2 has discussed how error statistics are influenced by how data are organized in memory. A common arrangement is the byte-per-card organization depicted in Fig. 4.6.1. With this organization the most frequent error events are: (1) a single byte error, with several bit errors within that byte, or (2) a single bit error.

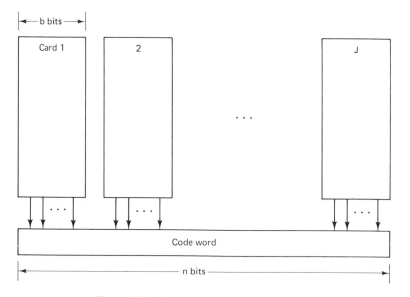

Figure 4.6.1 Byte-per-card memory organization.

Single-error-correcting and byte-error-detecting codes. This is a class of codes which has the following properties if the errors are confined to a byte of b bits:

1. If the byte in error contains only a single bit error, the error is corrected.
2. If the byte in error contains more than one error, the presence of errors always is detected, but error correction is not attempted.

   Theorem 7. A binary linear code with parity check matrix H is single-error correcting and byte-error detecting if and only if:

1. The column vectors of H are distinct and nonzero.

2. A sum of two or more column vectors in a byte of H is neither zero nor a column vector of H.

Condition 1 ensures that a single bit error can be corrected. Condition 2 ensures that a byte in error containing more than one bit error will be detected and will not look like a single bit error.

Code construction.   The following code was developed by Bossen et al. [BOSS78].

Let b be the bits per byte and r be the number of check bits, where $r > b$. Then the binary linear code described by a parity check matrix H shown below is capable of correcting single errors and simultaneously detecting byte errors.

$$H = \begin{bmatrix} M_1 & M_2 & M_3 & \cdots & M_J \\ Q & Q & Q & \cdots & Q \end{bmatrix} \tag{4.6.1}$$

where

$$Q = \begin{bmatrix} 0 \\ 0 \\ \vdots \\ \vdots \\ 0 \end{bmatrix} I_{b-1} \tag{4.6.2}$$

$$J = 2^{r-b+1} - 1 \tag{4.6.3}$$

and M_i contains b identical columns, each equal to the binary representation of integer i. Here H is an $r \times Jb$ matrix, Q is a $(b - 1) \times b$ matrix, and M_i is an $(r - b + 1) \times b$ matrix. For example, if $r = 6$ and $b = 4$, we will have a $(28, 22)$ code with parity check matrix

$$H = \begin{bmatrix} 0000 & 0000 & 0000 & 1111 & 1111 & 1111 & 1111 \\ 0000 & 1111 & 1111 & 0000 & 0000 & 1111 & 1111 \\ 1111 & 0000 & 1111 & 0000 & 1111 & 0000 & 1111 \\ \cdots & \cdots & \cdots & \cdots & \cdots & \cdots & \cdots \\ 0100 & 0100 & 0100 & 0100 & 0100 & 0100 & 0100 \\ 0010 & 0010 & 0010 & 0010 & 0010 & 0010 & 0010 \\ 0001 & 0001 & 0001 & 0001 & 0001 & 0001 & 0001 \end{bmatrix}$$

It is obvious that the code of Eq. (4.6.1) satisfies condition 1 of Theorem 7. As to condition 2, if byte i has an even number of errors, the first $r - b + 1$ components of the syndrome (which come from M_i) will be zero, which is not the case for a single error; if byte i has an odd number (>1) of errors, the last $b - 1$ components of the syndrome (which come from Q) will have two or more nonzero terms, whereas a single bit error would result in zero or one nonzero term in this group.

Decoding.   The decoders for the proposed codes will be essentially those for shortened Hamming codes. The only additional circuitry needed is to detect the presence of byte errors. This can be easily done by monitoring the syndrome. The decoder for $b = 4$ and $r = 6$ is given in Fig. 4.6.2. The single-bit-error-correcting circuit is enabled ($A = 0$) only if the syndrome is single-bit error and an error is detected ($A = 1$) if the syndrome is nonzero and the single-bit-error-correcting circuit is not enabled.

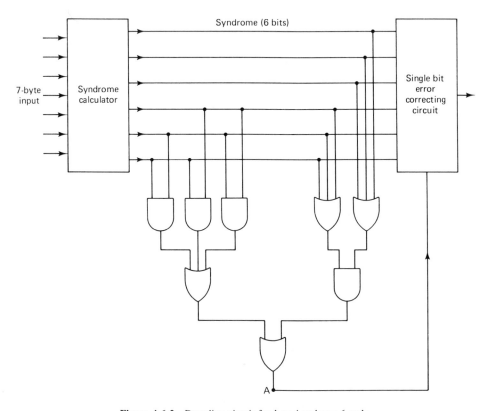

Figure 4.6.2   Decoding circuit for $b = 4$ and $r = 6$ code.

When $b \geq 5$, by using the same number of check bits, Reddy [REDD78] has proposed codes which are capable of correcting single errors and detecting byte and double random errors. These double errors can be in different bytes. If we want to detect double and byte errors and correct single errors, the column of the H matrix must satisfy the following third condition together with the two conditions given in Theorem 7.

3. A sum of two column vectors of H is neither zero nor a column vector of H.

Code construction.   The binary linear code described by the following H matrix is capable of correcting single errors and detecting double and byte errors.

$$H = \begin{bmatrix} M_1 & M_2 & \cdots & M_j \\ Q & Q & \cdots & Q \end{bmatrix} \qquad (4.6.4)$$

where

$$Q = Q_E = \begin{bmatrix} & 0 \\ & 1 \\ I_{B-1} & 1 \\ & \vdots \\ & 1 \end{bmatrix} \quad \text{for } b = \text{even}$$

$$\qquad (4.6.5)$$

$$Q = Q_0 = \begin{bmatrix} & 1 \\ & 1 \\ I_{b-1} & 1 \\ & \vdots \\ & 1 \end{bmatrix} \quad \text{for } b = \text{odd}$$

$$J = 2^{r-b+1} - 1$$

Here M_i is as in Eq. (4.6.1), that is, M_i is an $r - b + 1 \times b$ matrix whose columns are b copies of the binary representation of integer i. Q is a $(b - 1) \times b$ matrix consisting of the identity matrix of dimension $(b - 1)$ followed by an all-1 column in the case of b an odd integer or followed by column with first bit 0 and all other bits 1 in the case of b an even integer. J is the maximum number of cards and hence the length of the code word is $n = Jb$, with r check bits. The reader may refer to [REDD78] for proof that this construction has the stated property.

Byte-error-correcting codes. By taking the b bits of a card as a symbol from $GF(2^b)$, the codes discussed in Section 4.4 (with $q = 2^b$) can be used to correct byte errors. Note that in this case each check symbol must also be of length b bits. To correct single byte (symbol) errors we must choose a H matrix with symbols from $GF(2^b)$ such that the columns of H are all distinct and the linear combination of any two columns must not be equal to zero. We have seen that for the binary Hamming single-error-correcting code we obtained minimum distance 3 by taking the columns of the H matrix to be the $2^r - 1$ distinct binary r-tuples. However, if we take the symbols to be b bit bytes ($b > 1$) and form H as an $r \times (2^{br} - 1)$ matrix of byte symbols in which the columns are all possible distinct nonzero r-tuples, we do not get a single byte-error-correcting distance 3 code. The reason is that some nontrivial linear combination of two columns may be zero. To overcome this, out of each class of column vectors that are scalar multiples of each other only one is chosen, say the one having a 1 as its first nonzero component. For $r = 2$ and $b = 2$ we can have the following check matrix:

$$H = \begin{bmatrix} 0 & 1 & 1 & 1 & 1 \\ 1 & 0 & 1 & \alpha & \alpha^2 \end{bmatrix} \qquad (4.6.6)$$

In this case no two columns are linearly dependent and hence the distance of the code is 3.

If there is a single error, the syndrome will be merely the transpose of the erroneous symbol column multiplied by some scalar β. Then the syndrome will have β as its leading nonzero symbol. By dividing the syndrome by its leading nonzero symbol β, we get a column vector of H corresponding to the position of the error. Now correction can be accomplished by subtracting β from this symbol of the erroneous message.

The code above is sometimes referred to as a generalized Hamming code. Bossen has discussed a fast decoding algorithm for this code in [BOSS70].

As mentioned earlier, if we devise the error-correcting code by taking each of the b bits as a symbol from $GF(2^b)$, the check symbols are also of length b bits. By taking a byte as a convenient cluster of b individual bits instead of a symbol from $GF(2^b)$, Hong and Patel have developed single-byte-error-correcting code [HONG72], which we will discuss shortly. Here the check bits may or may not be clustered as bytes and the number of check bits need not be a multiple of b when the number of check bits r is not an exact multiple of b with $r > 2b$. The information rate of these codes is better than that of a generalized Hamming code.

This code is best described by using the parity matrix H. Let the number of check bits be r and $r \geq 2b$. Since r need not be a multiple of b we can put $r = q_1 b + q_2$ where $0 \leq q_2 < b$. The leftover q_2 check bits, if any, may form a special check byte. Another way is to form $(q_1 - 1)$ regular size check bytes and allow a special check byte of length $b + q_2$. Let α be a primitive element in $GF(2^{r-b})$. Then the code described by the following parity matrix is capable of correcting single byte errors.

$$H = [H_{r,b} \; \vdots \; I_r] \qquad (4.6.7)$$

where

$$H_{r,b} = \begin{bmatrix} I_b & I_b & & I_b & & I_b \\ A_1 & A_2 & \cdots & A_i & \cdots & A_{2^{r-b}-1} \end{bmatrix} \qquad (4.6.8)$$

$$A_i = [\alpha^i \alpha^{i+1} \quad \cdots \quad \alpha^{i+b-1}] \qquad (4.6.9)$$

and I_r is an $r \times r$ identity matrix. Note A_i is an $(r - b) \times b$ matrix whose columns are nonzero $GF(2^{r-b})$ elements written as vectors (see Section 4.4). Now the first $2^{r-b} - 1$ symbols, say $B_1 B_2 \cdots B_{2^{r-b}-1}$, form the information part and the last q_1 symbols, say $C_1 C_2 \cdots C_{q_1}$, form the check part. Here each symbol is of length b bits except the special symbol C_{q_1} which is of length $b + q_2$. We will now see why the code is capable of correcting a single byte error. Let the message be $C = B_1 B_2 \cdots B_{2^{r-b}-1} \ C_1 C_2 \cdots C_{q_1}$. Then the syndrome is given by

$$CH^T = [B_1 \cdots B_{2^{r-b}-1} \quad C_1 \cdots C_{q_1}] \begin{bmatrix} I_b & A_1^T \\ I_b & A_2^T \\ \vdots & \vdots \\ I_b & A_{2^{r-b}-1}^T \\ \hline & I_r \end{bmatrix} \qquad (4.6.10a)$$

$$CH^T = [S_1 S_2 \cdots S_{q_1}] \qquad (4.6.10b)$$

where S_i is b bits long for $i = 1, 2, \dots, q_1 - 1$, and S_{q_1} is $b + q_2$ bits long. If there is a byte error in one of the check bytes, only one of the corresponding syndromes, say S_i, will not be equal to zero. On the other hand, if there is a byte error in one of the information symbols, S_1 will not be equal to zero. Moreover, the following reasoning shows that at least one of the other syndrome symbols must be nonzero.

Suppose that the ith information symbol is the corrupted symbol. Let

$$S_1 = [a_0 a_1 \cdots a_{b-1}] \qquad \text{where } a_i \in \text{GF}(2) \qquad (4.6.11)$$

Note that S_1 will correspond to the actual error pattern within the erroneous byte. Then, comparing Eq. (4.6.11) with Eqs. (4.6.9) and (4.6.10), we see that

$$[S_2 \cdots S_{q_1}]^T = a_0 \alpha^i + a_1 \alpha^{i+1} + \cdots + a_{b-1} \alpha^{i+b-1}$$
$$= \alpha^i (a_0 + a_1 \alpha + \cdots + a_{b-1} \alpha^{b-1}) \qquad (4.6.12)$$

Now $\alpha, \alpha^2, \dots, \alpha^{b-1}$ are linearly independent because $r - b \geq b$. Therefore, $a_0 + a_1 \alpha + \cdots + a_{b-1} \alpha^{b-1} \neq 0$ when one of the a_i's is not zero. Therefore,

$$[S_2 \cdots S_q]^T = \alpha^s \qquad (4.6.13)$$

for some s. Hence, if there is an error in one of the information symbols, then $S_1 \neq 0$ and also at least one of the other S_i will not be equal to zero. Thus errors in a check symbol can be distinguished from errors in an information symbol.

Also, note that the errors in distinct check symbols give distinct syndromes. Now we will show that the errors in distinct information symbols also give distinct syndromes. As mentioned before, the syndrome S_1 indicates the erroneous bits within the corrupted information symbol. If the same bits of any two information symbols, say i and j, where $i \neq j$ are in error, even though the syndromes corresponding to S_1 will be the same, the syndromes corresponding to $S_2 S_3 \cdots S_{q_1}$ will be distinct. If we get the same syndromes, then, with the S_1 of Eq. (4.6.11),

$$\alpha^i (a_0 + a_1 \alpha + \cdots + a_{b-1} \alpha^{b-1}) = \alpha^j (a_0 + a_1 \alpha + \cdots + a_{b-1} \alpha^{b-1}) \qquad (4.6.14)$$

Since at least one of a_i's is not zero, we get $\alpha^i = \alpha^j$ and hence $i = j$. This is a contradiction because we assumed that $i \neq j$. Thus errors in distinct information symbols yield distinct syndromes.

Let us see now how decoding can be accomplished. If there is an error in the check symbol, say C_j, then only S_j will not be zero where $1 \le j \le q_1$ and all other syndromes will be zero. The nonzero bits of S_j correspond to the error bits within C_j; so these errors can be corrected by complementing the corresponding bits. On the other hand, if one of the information symbols is in error, say B_i, where $1 \le i \le 2^{r-b} - 1$, the error bits within B_i are given by the syndrome S_1.

Now we need to find the erroneous byte. The syndrome $[S_2 S_3 \cdots S_{q_1}] = [\alpha^s]$ is useful in finding the byte in error. As we have seen from (4.6.12) and (4.6.13) we can put

$$\alpha^s = \alpha^i(a_0 + a_1\alpha + \cdots + a_{b-1}\alpha^{b-1}) \tag{4.6.15}$$

Since α is a primitive element in $GF(2^{r-b})$ we can put $a_0 + a_1\alpha + \cdots + a_{b-1}\alpha^{b-1} = \alpha^t$.

We can design the decoding circuit as follows. The syndrome S_1 (which is α^t) can be stored in register ER1, and $[S_2 \cdots S_{q_1}]$ (which is α^s) in register ER2. Let ER1 have feedback connections corresponding to the primitive polynomial with root α in $GF(2^{r-b})$. Then shifting ER1 will be like multiplying by α (see Section 4.2 and Fig. 4.4.1). Shift the contents of ER1 until the contents of ER1 equals that of ER2. This will occur after i shifts, since $\alpha^i\alpha^t = \alpha^s$. Thus the position number i of the erroneous symbol is found. Once we know the erroneous symbol, error correction can be accomplished by using S_1.

When $r \ge 3b$ we can get still better information rate single-byte-error-correcting codes. By a method of iterative concatenation, see [HONG72], the codes can be extended to obtain "perfect" codes. The code is called *perfect* if all the 2^r syndromes are used to correct the 2^r distinct error patterns, including all the single-byte-error patterns and the error-free pattern. Perfect codes have no error detection beyond the error-correction capability, however, so if it is desired to have error detection as well as error correction, perfect codes have no special value.

4.6.2. Codes for Mass Storage Systems

An important goal in mass storage systems is to obtain a high density of bit storage. However, as bit density is increased, the frequency of random errors increases, and the number of bits covered by a defect of given size increases. Error-corrrecting codes provide the prospect of increasing bit density while maintaining overall reliability. There is some loss in effective bit density due to the redundancy required for error correction, but there can be a significant net gain in achievable bit density for a given reliability as a result of employing sophisticated error-correction techniques which are tailored to the physical structure and error characteristics of the storage medium.

The sources of noise and errors in mass storage systems are many and varied. Berlekamp [BERL80] has attempted to categorize the noise as an additive contribution of (1) media noise, (2) writing noise, and (3) reading noise. When data are read, errors caused by writing and some media failures will be persistently wrong for any reading, whereas reading noise and some media defects will produce different error patterns for different readings. More sophisticated error-correcting and error-detecting codes can tolerate a greater number of either persistent or intermittent errors. Rereading is used when uncorrectable errors are detected and is a way of eventually obtaining correct data when there are reading noise or intermittent media-caused errors. However, if the reading or intermittent noise is above some level, an excessive number of rereadings would be required on the average. A more effective strategy suggested in [BERL80] for this situation is to save successive rereadings and use a majority rule decision for each bit prior to applying the overall error correcting and detecting code.

The general ideas discussed above are applicable to disk, magnetic tape, and probably most other forms of mass storage as well, although the exact choice of codes and decoding method would be somewhat different for different systems and media types. The following section serves as an illustration for the case of magnetic tape storage systems.

Codes for magnetic tapes.   In most magnetic tapes data storage is organized with multiple tracks. However, there is an important recently developed mass storage tape system in which data are organized in single-track format [PATE80]. In this section we first will discuss codes for the multitrack format, and then will describe a code which has been developed for a single-track format.

A common situation in the multitrack system is for the errors in a section of the tape to be in a (possible large) cluster, but usually confined to a single track. Often, the erroneous track or tracks can be identified prior to employing the error-correcting capabilities of the overall code.

Following is a discussion of codes useful for correcting single track errors in magnetic tapes. If the erroneous tracks are known, these codes can be used to correct two track errors. By taking the b bits of a track as a byte, the byte-error-correcting codes discussed in Section 4.6.1 are used here to correct track errors.

The codes discussed here are used in IBM magnetic tape units and the error-correcting properties of these codes are discussed in [BROW70], [PATE74], and [SLOA76]. Even though the codes can be developed for any arbitrary number of tracks, for our discussion we will assume that the number of tracks is equal to 9. The code gives the highest information rate when the number of bits in a track byte is $n - 1$, where n is the number of tracks. So in our case we assume that the number of bits in a track byte is 8.

The code used is called a *cyclic redundancy check* (CRC) code. It has the data format shown in Fig. 4.6.3.

B_1 through B_7 denote the 7 bytes of information in standard 8-bit bytes. B_0 denotes the check byte computed from the information bytes. The ninth track is simply an overall vertical parity check (VPC) on the other eight tracks. The number of bits in a code word is 72 and the number of check bits is equal to 16.

For a natural description of the code the track vectors of the code word will be used as track bytes, denoted by Z_i's in Fig. 4.6.4. Now our task is to correct errors in Z_i's.

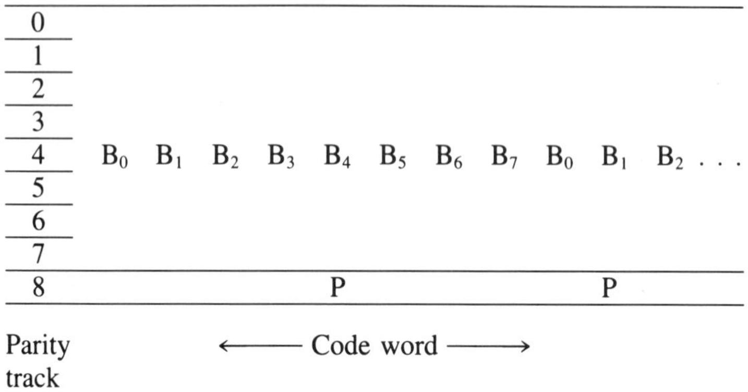

0	
1	
2	
3	
4	B_0 B_1 B_2 B_3 B_4 B_5 B_6 B_7 B_0 B_1 B_2 . . .
5	
6	
7	
8	P P

Parity $\longleftarrow$ Code word $\longrightarrow$
track

Figure 4.6.3 Code word divided into eight columns.

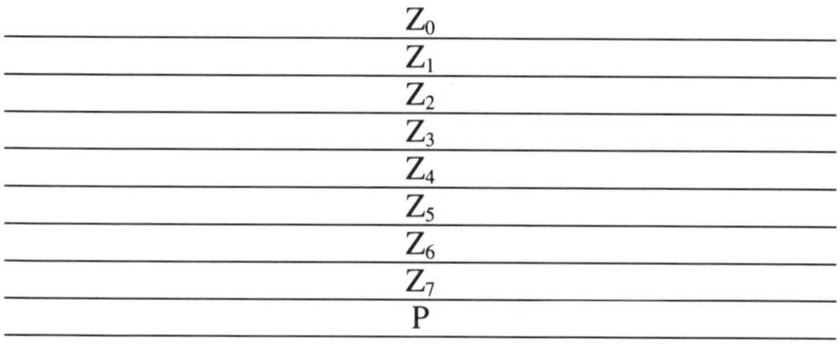

Z_0
Z_1
Z_2
Z_3
Z_4
Z_5
Z_6
Z_7
P

Figure 4.6.4 Horizontal track bytes. These bytes are subject to errors and correction.

If we represent Z_i and B_j as

$$Z_i = (Z_{i0}, Z_{i1}, \ldots, Z_{i7}) \qquad B_j = \begin{bmatrix} B_{oj} \\ B_{1j} \\ \vdots \\ B_{7j} \end{bmatrix} \qquad (4.6.16)$$

then $Z_{ij} = B_{ij}$ (i.e., Z_{ij} and B_{ij} represent the same ith track and jth column bit). Also, the vertical parity check (VPC) P is given by the vector module 2 sum

$$P = Z_0 + Z_1 + \cdots + Z_7 \qquad (4.6.17)$$

Now visualize the 72 bits of the code word written serially in the order

$$(Z_0 : Z_1 : \cdots : Z_7 : P)$$

The parity matrix for the code can then be written as

$$H = \begin{bmatrix} I_8 & \vdots & I_8 & \vdots & I_8 & \vdots & I_8 \\ \alpha^0 \ \alpha^1 \ \cdots \ \alpha^7 & \vdots & \alpha^1 \ \alpha^2 \ \cdots \ \alpha^8 & \vdots \cdots & \alpha^7 \ \alpha^8 \ \cdots \ \alpha^{14} & \vdots & 0 \end{bmatrix} \quad (4.6.18)$$

where α is a primitive element of GF(2^8) written as an 8-bit column vector.

Let u be the correct code word and let $v = u + e$ be an erroneous code word. Then the syndrome is given by

$$S = vH^T = (u + e)H^T = eH^T = [S_1 \ \vdots \ S_2] \quad (4.6.19)$$

where S_1 and S_2 are 8-bit row vectors. If there is no error, obviously S will be zero. If the errors are confined to the parity track, it is easily seen that S_2 will be zero and S_1 will be nonzero. If the errors are in exactly one of the information tracks, S_1 will have the same pattern as the errors in the track, and S_2 will contain information to locate which track is in error.

To see how the erroneous track is located, let $S_1 = (a_0 a_1 a_2 a_3 a_4 a_5 a_6 a_7)$, where $a_i \in$ GF(2) and not all $a_i = 0$. Then if the errors are in track i,

$$S_2^T = a_0\alpha^i + a_1\alpha^{i+1} + \cdots + a_7\alpha^{i+7}$$
$$= \alpha^i(a_0 + a_1\alpha + a_2\alpha^2 + \cdots + a_7\alpha^7) \quad (4.6.20)$$

Since $1, \alpha, \alpha^2, \ldots, \alpha^7$ are linearly independent $a_0 + a_1\alpha + \cdots + a_7\alpha^7 \neq 0$ and also $\alpha^i \neq 0$. Therefore, $S_2 \neq 0$.

Suppose that we define

$$\beta = (a_0 + a_1\alpha + a_2\alpha^2 + \cdots + a_7\alpha^7) \quad (4.6.21)$$

Note that β can be computed directly from S_1. Then

$$\alpha^i = S_2\beta^{-1} \quad (4.6.22)$$

Since $\alpha^i \neq \alpha^j$ if $i \neq j$ in the range $0 \leq i, j \leq 7$, computation of α^i uniquely discovers track i as the location of the errors, while S_1 specifies the error pattern. Alternatively, the decoding could be done by successively multiplying S_1 by powers of α and comparing with S_2, as described in the discussion following Eq. (4.6.15).

The code described by the parity check matrix (4.6.18) is also capable of correcting two erasure errors (i.e., if the tracks in error are known, the code can correct two track errors). This can be seen from the following argument.

Let the tracks in error be i and j where $0 \leq i \leq 8$ and $0 \leq j \leq 8$. Let $i < j$ and the error patterns in i and j be, respectively,

$$E_i = (a_{i0} a_{i1} a_{i2} \cdots a_{i7}) \quad \text{and} \quad E_j = (a_{j0} a_{j1} a_{j2} \cdots a_{j7})$$

where $a_{pq} \in$ GF(2). The syndromes S_1 and S_2 are given by

$$S_1 = E_i + E_j = (a_{i0} + a_{j0}, a_{i1} + a_{j1} \cdots a_{i7} + a_{j7}) \qquad (4.6.23)$$

$$S_2 = \alpha^i \beta_1 + \alpha^j \beta_2 \qquad j \neq 8 \qquad (4.6.24)$$

or

$$S_2 = \alpha^i \beta_1 \qquad j = 8$$

where

$$\beta_1 = (a_{i0} + a_{i1}\alpha + \cdots + a_{i7}\alpha^7)$$

$$\beta_2 = (a_{j0} + a_{j1}\alpha + \cdots + a_j\alpha^7) \qquad (4.6.25)$$

Define $V = S_{10} + S_{11}\alpha + \cdots + S_{17}\alpha^7$, where $S_1 = (S_{10}S_{11} \cdots S_{17})$. Then

$$\beta_1 + \beta_2 = V \qquad \text{or} \qquad \beta_1 = \beta_2 + V \qquad (4.6.26)$$

Since V, S_2, i, and j are known, we can solve Eqs. (4.6.24) and (4.6.26) to get

$$\beta_2 = \begin{cases} (\alpha^{-1}S_2 + V)(1 + \alpha^{j-1})^{-1} & \text{if } j \neq 8 \\ \alpha^{-i}S_2 + V & \text{if } j = 8 \end{cases} \qquad (4.6.27)$$

From the discussions above we can see that the code can be used to correct single track errors if the track in error is unknown or two track errors if the tracks in error are known.

For convenient implementation of encoding and decoding the parity check matrix of the code can be represented in a slightly different way. By grouping the B characters together we can rearrange the H matrix of (6.18) as follows:

$$H_1 = \begin{bmatrix} B_0 & B_1 & B_7 & \vdots & P \\ \hline 11111111 & O & & \vdots & \\ & 11111111 & O & \vdots & \\ & & \cdots & \vdots & I_b \\ O & O & 11111111 & \vdots & \\ \hline \alpha^0\alpha^1 \cdots \alpha^7 & \alpha^1\alpha^2 \cdots \alpha^8 & \cdots & \alpha^7\alpha^8 \cdots \alpha^{14} & \vdots & 0 \end{bmatrix} \qquad (4.6.28)$$

The H_1 matrix defines the code words in terms of the column bytes ($B_0B_1 \cdots B_7$). This leads to a faster implementation of the encoding–decoding process, as described below.

Implementation. The code can be generated by using an irreducible polynomial $g(x)$ of degree 8. The polynomial chosen in [PATE74] is $g(x) = 1 + x^3 + x^4 + x^5 + x^8$. The check byte B_0 can be generated such that B_0 satisfies the equation

$$B_0 = B_1\alpha + B_2\alpha^2 + \cdots + B_7\alpha^7 \qquad (4.6.29)$$

where $\alpha = x$. (We can use a shift register (SR) with feedback connections correspond to $g(x)$.) The connections are shown in Fig. 4.6.5. Initially, SR contains zeros. The information bytes B_7, B_6, . . . , B_1 are successively exored with the contents of the SR and shifted in the SR. After shifting B_1, the register SR will contain the character B_0 which can be written on the tape as the check character. As each character is read in, the vertical parity bits can also be generated and written on the vertical parity track.

Input: $B_0 B_1 B_2 B_3 B_4 B_5 B_6 B_7$

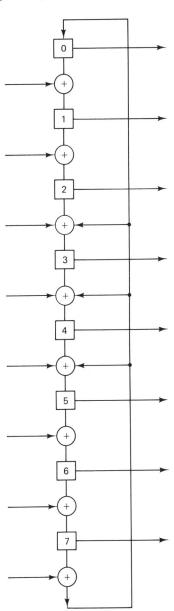

Figure 4.6.5   Feedback shift register corresponding to $g(x) = x^8 + x^5 + x^4 + x^3 + 1$.

To correct single track errors we can use two shift registers, EPR (error pattern register) and SR. The feedback connections for both EPR and SR correspond to $g(x)$. As each character is read in, the error pattern can be found from VPC and this can be stored in EPR. The characters $B_7, B_6, \ldots, B_0$ are shifted into SR in that order. At the end of this process if both EPR and SR are zero, this implies that there is no error. If EPR is not zero and SR is zero, the vertical parity track is in error and this can be corrected by Exclusive ORing the EPR bits with that of vertical parity tracks. If both SR and EPR are not zero, shift the EPR such that the contents of EPR is the same as that of SR. The number of shifts gives the track in error. By EXORing the initial contents of EPR to the bits of this erroneous track we can get the correct message.

By using Eq. (4.6.24) we can also correct double track errors and this is discussed in [PATE74]. In the case of the double-track-error-correction scheme the number of error patterns corrected by the code is $2^8 \times 2^8 = 2^{16}$. This is because there are 2^8 error patterns possible for one track. On the other hand, there are exactly $2^8 \times 2^8 = 2^{16}$ distinct syndromes. Therefore, this code is optimal.

4.6.3. The IBM Mass Storage System

In this tape storage system [PATE80] data are organized in single "stripes" which run diagonally across the tape rather than in multiple tracks. Each stripe contains 4096 bytes of information. This is then expanded to a data stream of 4160 bytes with the addition of two bytes of cyclic redundancy check and additional startup and filler bits. This data stream is then organized into sections and segments of the stripe with additional redundancy added, in the format shown in Fig. 4.6.6.

Each of the 20 segments of the stripe is independently encoded. Each segment consists of 13 data sections followed by two check sections. Each section is 129 bits long, consisting of 16 bytes of binary information with an overall odd-parity bit. This sequence of 129 bits is encoded into a 258-digit sequence by what is called a "zero modulation" technique [PATE75], followed by a known synchronization signal (see Appendix 1 of [PATE80]). The large extra redundancy of the zero modulation technique provides detection of most error patterns that might occur within a section. The detection of errors in a section is reported to the decoder of the error-correction code for error recovery.

An error-correcting code word consists of one byte from each section of a segment; 13 of these are data bytes and two are check bytes (see Fig. 4.6.6). There are 16 such code words in a segment. The interleaving of code words among the sections permits correction of error patterns extending over hundreds of bits, such as may occur due to dust particles or other magnetic tape problems.

The structure of the 16-byte code word is somewhat similar to the byte-error-correcting codes described in the beginning of this section. The parity check matrix, written with bytes represented as abstract elements in $GF(2^8)$, is

$$H = \begin{bmatrix} 1 & 1 & 1 & 2 & \cdots & 1 \\ 1 & \alpha & \alpha^2 & \alpha^3 & \cdots & \alpha^{14} \end{bmatrix} \qquad (4.6.30)$$

where α is an element of order 15 in $GF(2^8)$. If the bytes are elements in $GF(2^8)$, the check equations are

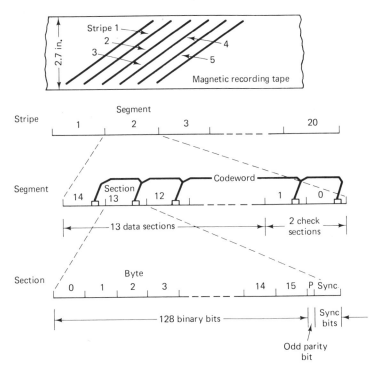

Figure 4.6.6   Stripe data format. (Copyright 1980 by International Business Machines Corporation; reprinted with permission from *IBM Journal of Research and Development*, vol. 24, no. 1, p. 33, January 1980.)

$$\beta_0 + \beta_1 + \beta_2 + \cdots + \beta_{14} = 0$$
$$\beta_0 + \alpha\beta_1 + \alpha^2\beta_2 + \cdots + \alpha^{14}\beta_{14} = 0 \qquad (4.6.31)$$

If detection of errors in a section has been reported, the byte from that section is treated as an erasure. If there are two erasures but no other errors, Eq. (4.6.27) always provides two independent equations in two unknowns, which permits the decoder to fill in both erasures. Alternatively, if there are no erasures the code can correct any single-byte error, or it can detect any double-bit error.

The H matrix also could be expressed in binary form much as was done in Eqs. (4.6.8) and (4.6.18). The field elements then are represented as 8×8 matrices in H. The representation of the field elements as matrices is convenient for describing the decoder implementation. This approach is used in [PATE80], and the reader may refer to that reference for a description of practical decoding circuits.

The IBM 3850 mass storage system is a good example of application of fault tolerance at several stages. First, there is error-detection capability within each section; then there are the code words across sections which allow correction of detected errors and/or possible further error detection. Finally, the entire data stream of the stripe contains two check bytes which could be used after the two processes above and in most cases would detect any faults left by the first two processes.

4.7. ARITHMETIC CODES

Coding requirements for checking arithmetic operations are somewhat different than requirements for correcting and detecting errors in memory. This section discusses codes designed for checking arithmetic errors. Although designed primarily for arithmetic, these codes have possible application in data transmission and memory protection as well.

Any integer N can be expressed relative to a radix r as

$$N = a_{n-1}r^{n-1} + a_{n-2}r^{n-2} + \cdots + a_0 \qquad (4.7.1)$$

where $0 \le a_i < r$ for $i = 0, 1, \cdots, n - 1$. The number is written $(a_{n-1}a_{n-2} \cdots a_0)$. For example, 14 in binary form is

$$(1110) = 1 \cdot 2^3 + 1 \cdot 2^2 + 1 \cdot 2^1 + 0 \cdot 2^0$$

The arithmetic weight of N, denoted by $W(N)$, is the minimum number of nonzero terms when expressed in the form

$$N = b_{n-1}r^{n-1} + b_{n-2}r^{n-2} + \cdots + b_0 \qquad (4.7.2)$$

where $b_i \in \{0, \pm 1, \pm 2, \ldots, 1 \pm (r - 1)\}$. It is easy to see that $W(N) = W(-N)$. For binary arithmetic, $r = 2$, and the b_i are in the set $0, 1, \bar{1}$, where $\bar{1}$ stands for -1.

The arithmetic weight of 14 in binary is 2, because 14 can be expressed as (10010) (i.e., $14 = 1 \cdot 2^4 + 0 \cdot 2^3 + 0 \cdot 2^2 - 1 \cdot 2^1 + 0 \cdot 2^0$).

The arithmetic distance between two numbers N_1 and N_2 is defined as the arithmetic weight of $N_1 - N_2$. For example, when $r = 2$, the distance between 31 and 39 is 1 because $31 - 39 = -8 = -2^3$.

The definition of arithmetic distance above matches very closely to the types of errors that can occur in an arithmetic operation. For instance, consider the addition of two numbers 31 and 2 in binary (i.e., $011111 + 000010 = 100001$). Suppose that there is a carry failure at the second digit. Then the result will be $011101 = 29$. This carry failure changes four digit positions of the result. However, the failure is counted as a single error because the arithmetic weight of $2^2 = 4 = 33 - 29$ is defined to be 1.

Let C be an arithmetic code. Then it can be shown that:

1. The code C is capable of detecting d or fewer errors iff the arithmetic distance of C is at least $d + 1$.

2. The code C is capable of correcting t or fewer errors iff the arithmetic distance of C is at least $2t + 1$.

3. The code C is capable of correcting t or fewer errors and detecting up to d $(d \ge t)$ errors iff the arithmetic distance of C is at least $t + d + 1$.

4.7.1. AN Code and Single-Error Detection

In an *AN* code a given integer N is represented by the product AN for some suitable constant A. A is called the *check base*.

Now consider the addition of two numbers N_1 and N_2. The sum of the numbers in code form is $AN_1 + AN_2 = A(N_1 + N_2)$, which is equal to the coded form of their sum. Therefore, the coded numbers can be added in an ordinary adder.

There is a cost in number of radix r digits to represent a set of numbers. If N_M is the largest actual number to be represented, the number of digits to be provided must exceed $\log_r AN_M = \log_r A + \log_r N_M$ instead of $\log_r N_M$.

The ability to check for errors is based on the fact that a coded number must be a multiple of A. Suppose that an error E occurs in the sum. Then the result R will be

$$R = A(N_1 + N_2) + E = AN_3 + E \tag{4.7.3}$$

To check for errors, divide R by A and find the remainder. If $E = 0$, there will be no remainder. The remainder in general can be represented as R modulo A, denoted by $|R|_A$. Now

$$|R|_A = |AN_3 + E|_A = |E|_A \tag{4.7.4}$$

Analogous to Eq. (4.3.13), $|E|_A$ is called the *syndrome*. A nonzero syndrome indicates that an error or errors have occurred.

In the radix-r representation the syndromes corresponding to single errors are of the type $|ar^i|_A$, where $1 \le a < r$. In order to detect all single errors, the syndromes corresponding to single-error patterns must all be nonzero. If the check base A is chosen such that A and r are relatively prime with $A > r$, then $|ar^i|_A \ne 0$. In particular, note that r and $r + 1$ are relatively prime for $r \ge 2$ and hence if the check base A is equal to $r + 1$, the *AN* code will be capable of detecting any single error. The number of extra radix r digits needed to provide this error detection is no more than 2, since $2 > \log_r(r + 1)$, $r \ge 2$. This is true no matter how many digits are used for representing the actual numbers.

The class of codes with $A = r^c - 1$ for some positive constant c has certain advantages because the residue modulo A can be obtained without division. Let $X = (a_{n-1}a_{n-2} \cdots a_0)$ be a code word of such an *AN* code in the radix r representation. Let this sequence be partitioned into l bytes of c digits each as follows:

$$(a_{n-1} \quad \cdots \quad a_{(l-1)c} \quad \cdots \quad a_{2c-1} \quad \cdots \quad a_c \quad a_{c-1} \quad \cdots \quad a_0)$$
$$\underleftrightarrow{\quad B_{l-1} \quad} \qquad \underleftrightarrow{\quad B_1 \quad} \; \underleftrightarrow{\quad B_0 \quad}$$

If we define

$$B_i = a_{ic} + a_{ic+1}r + \cdots + a_{ic + c-1}r^{c-1} \tag{4.7.5}$$

then

$$x = B_{l-1}r^{(l-1)c} + B_{l-2}r^{(l-2)c} + \cdots + B_1r^c + B_0 \tag{4.7.6}$$

Now

$$|r^{jc}|_{r^c-1} = 1 \qquad \text{for all } j \geq 0$$

hence

$$|x|_{r^c-1} = |B_{l-1} + B_{l-2} + \cdots + B_0|_{r^c-1} \qquad (4.7.7)$$

From Eq. (4.7.7) it is seen that the residue can be obtained by adding the bytes modulo $r^c - 1$ instead of by dividing.

In the binary case A can be 3, 7, 15, 31, and so on. As an example, let $A = 7$ and $N = (100\ 011\ 110)$. Adding the partitions:

$$
\begin{array}{r}
110 \\
011 \\
100 \\
\hline
1101
\end{array}
$$

Reducing modulo 7:

$$1101 \rightarrow 101 + \underbrace{001}_{} = 110 \quad \text{(remainder)}$$

Since N is 286 in decimal, it is easily verified that Rem $(286/7) = 6$, which is the decimal equivalent of 110.

4.7.2. Single-Error-Correcting AN Codes

In order to correct all of some set of error patterns, the syndromes corresponding to each pair of error patterns in the set must be different and nonzero. The syndromes corresponding to single errors are of type $|\pm ar^j|_A$ for $0 \leq j \leq n - 1$ and $1 \leq a < r$, where n is the length of the code and r is the radix. In particular for binary numbers the syndromes are of type $|\pm 2^j|_A$ for $0 \leq j \leq n - 1$, so an appropriate check base A must be elected to get distinct nonzero syndromes.

Suppose that A is a prime. Then the integers modulo A are a field (see Section 4.3). Suppose that 2 is a primitive element (see Section 4.4) of the field. Then its order is $A - 1$, and $2^0, 2^1, 2^2, \ldots, 2^{(A-1)/2} = -1, -2, \ldots, 2^{A-2} = -2^{(A-3)/2}$ are all distinct. For example, 2 is primitive element (order 10) of GF(11): $2^0 = 1, 2^1, 2^2 = 4$, $2^3 = 8$, $2^4 = 5$, $2^5 = 10 = -1$, $2^6 = 9 = -2$, $2^7 = 7 = -2^2$, $2^8 = 3 = -2^3$, $2^9 = 6 = -2^4$.

If the range of integers is restricted so that $AN < 2^{(A-1)/2}$, the syndromes corresponding to single errors are all distinct. Therefore, an AN code with A a prime, 2 a primitive element of GF(A), and the maximum integer range less than $2^{(A-1)/2}$ is capable of correcting all single errors. For example, the range of BCD numbers is from 0 to 9. 19 is a prime with 2 as a primitive root and $9 \cdot 19 < 2^{(19-1)/2} = 512$. Thus a $19N$ code of BCD numbers is capable of correcting all single errors.

Let -2 but not $+2$ be a primitive element of GF(A). Let the maximum value of N be less than $2^{(A-3)/2}/A$. Then it can be proved that this code is also capable of correcting all single errors. Moreover, it can be proved that the two codes described above are perfect single-error-correcting codes.

The discussion above is for binary numbers. Higher-order radix *AN* codes are discussed in [RAO74].

4.7.3. Separate Codes

A separate code is one in which the information and the check are processed separately. The advantage of a separate code is that the arithmetic and checking operations can be done in parallel. Therefore, the speed of the system is not deteriorated by the addition of redundant bits to the check part.

Consider the use of a separate code to check the operation addition. Let the check corresponding to the information symbol N be denoted by $C(N)$, so a code word is of the form $[N, C(N)]$.

A system as shown in Fig. 4.7.1 can be used to check the operation. There are two operations involved in the addition of the code words. The operation $+$ is ordinary addition done on the information part and the operation $*$ is done on the check part. If $C(N_1) * C(N_2) = C(N_1 + N_2)$, the output of the checker will be consistent with the output of the adder (i.e., the sum of the two code words yields another code word, which implies the code is closed under addition). If the code satisfies the closure condition above, it restricts the code to a very special type given by the following theorem [PETE71].

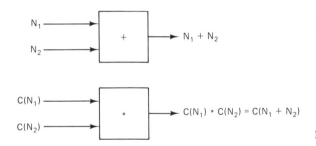

Figure 4.7.1   Separate adder and checker.

Theorem 8.   If there are fewer check symbols than integers in the permissible range of integers and if the check symbols $C(N)$ satisfy the equation $C(N_1) * C(N_2) = C(N_1 + N_2)$, $C(N)$ must be the residue of N modulo b in coded form, where b is the number of distinct check symbols and $*$ is addition modulo b.

By virtue of the result above any separate code which is closed under addition must be of the form $[N, N_b]$.

AN codes described in the preceding section are nonseparate. However, to every *AN* code there corresponds a mod A separate code with the same distance and essentially the same redundancy, as shown below.

Let $s = \lceil \log_r A \rceil$. Then every integer less than A can be represented as a s-digit number in radix-r form. Consider the code in which the check symbol $C(N)$ for N is the residue modulo $-r^s N \bmod A$. Then

$$-r^s N = Aq + C(N)$$

or

$$r^s N + C(N) = -Aq$$

Since $r^s N + C(N)$ is a multiple of A this is a code word in the AN code. But if $r^s N + C(N)$ is represented in radix-r representation, the low s digits correspond to the check $C(N)$ and the higher-order digits correspond to information N. So this is a separate code. Moreover, the minimum distance of this separate code will be at least the minimum distance of the AN code.

4.7.4. Separate Codes in a Finite Ring Arithmetic

Since the size of a computer word is finite, any arithmetic operation on the numbers N_1 and N_2 will give a finite value. Let Z_m denote the finite ring of integers modulo m, namely $0, 1, 2, \ldots, m - 1$. The additive inverse of N in Z_m is given by $\overline{N} = m - N = -N \bmod m$. The additive inverse of a number N is often called the complement of N.

The arithmetic weight defined earlier satisfies the condition $\omega(N) = \omega(-N)$. However, in the finite ring A_m, $\omega(N)$ may not be equal to $\omega(-N)$. For example, in Z_{31}, $\omega(16) = 1$ but $\omega(-16) = \omega(15) = 2$. This is an undesirable feature because a carry propagation error at the ith bit of an adder may result in an error syndrome of $|+2^i|_m$ or $|-2^i|_m$. But these two error syndromes have different arithmetic weights. To alleviate this problem the modular arithmetic weight is defined below as first introduced by Rao and Garcia [RAO71].

The modular arithmetic weight of an integer n in Z_m, denoted by $\omega_m(N)$, is given by

$$\omega_m(N) = \min[\omega(N), \omega(\overline{N})]$$

For example, in binary representation the modular arithmetic weight of 15 in Z_{31} is 1 because $\omega(15) = 2$ and $\omega(\overline{15}) = \omega(16) = 1$.

The modular arithmetic distance between two numbers N_1 and N_2 in Z_m, denoted by $D_m(N_1, N_2)$, is the modular weight of $N_1 - N_2$ that is,

$$D_m(N_1, N_2) = \omega_m(N_1 - N_2) = \omega_m(N_2 - N_1)$$

The modular distance defined above is, in general, not a metric. However, if the number system is in radix complement, in which case $m = r^k$ or in diminished radix complement, in which case $m = r^k - 1$ for some k, the modular system defined above is a metric.

If the modular distance is a metric, it can be shown that:

1. A code C in Z_m is capable of detecting d or fewer errors iff the minimum modular arithmetic distance is at least d.

2. A code C in Z_m is capable of correcting t or fewer errors iff the minimum modular arithmetic distance is at least $2t + 1$.

3. A code C in Z_m is capable of correcting t or fewer errors and detecting up to d $(d \geq t)$ errors iff the minimum modular arithmetic distance is at least $t + d + 1$.

It is shown in Theorem 8 that any separate code must be a residue code. There is no restriction placed on N_1 and N_2 and their sum. However, in a computer N_1 and N_2 will be represented by k-bit numbers, so the numbers can be treated as the elements in Z_m and their sum as $N_1 + N_2$ mod m. A generalization of Theorem 8 is given by Rao [RAO74] in the case of a finite ring. In the following theorem the symbol $\oplus$ indicates the mod m operator.

Theorem 9.   Let N_1 and N_2 be elements in Z_m. Let $C(N)$ denote the check symbol for the number $N \in Z_m$. Let $C(N)$ need no more digits than $N \in Z_m$. Then $C(N_1 + N_2) = C(N_1) * C(N_2)$ holds iff for some A:

1. $C(N) = |N|_A$,
2. $*$ denotes addition modulo A, and
3. A divides m.

Condition 3 is an extra restriction for a separate code to be closed under addition in a finite ring of integers.

Suppose that a system which uses two's-complement arithmetic has 8 data bits. The number representation can be considered as elements in Z_{256} (i.e., $m = 2^8 = 256$). If one wants to design a separate single-error-detecting code, by Theorem 9, the check base A must divide 2^8. Therefore, the check base A must be of the form 2^i. The error values corresponding to single errors are of the type $|\pm 2^j|_{256}$ for $j = 0, 1, 2, \ldots, 7$. However, if $A = 2^i$ and $i < 8$, the code cannot detect all single errors. This is because for single errors of the type $+2^j$ with $j \geq i$, $|+2^j|_A = 0$. So the only possibility is that $A = 2^8$, which results in duplication of the information symbol.

For a one's-complement system m will be equal to 255, so the check base can be any one of 3, 5, 15, 17, 51, 85, 255. The error values corresponding to single errors are in the set $\{1, 2, 4, 8, 16, 32, 64, 127, 128, 191, 223, 239, 247, 251, 253, 254\}$. Since none of the possible check bases divide any of the error vectors, any divisor of 255 can be taken as a check base. Note that when $A = 255$ the resultant code is a duplication that is not efficient.

4.7.5.   Biresidue Binary Codes for Single-Error Correction

A code word in this code is of the form $(N, |N|_{A1}, |N|_{A2})$, where $N \in Z_m$. This is a separate code closed under modulo m addition so that both A_1 and A_2 must divide m.

If the system uses the radix complement number system, in particular 2's complement, this code will result in triplication of the information range. This is because both A_1 and A_2 must divide $m = 2^k$. Moreover, the syndrome corresponding to each single error must be distinct and nonzero. These conditions force $A_1 = 2^k$ and $A_2 = 2^k$. Hence the code is not very efficient; so it is considered that the system uses a one's-complement number system.

It has been mentioned before that if the check base is of the form $2^c - 1$, it is very easy to generate the residues. Hence in the biresidue codes the check bases are assumed to be of the form $A_1 = 2^a - 1$ and $A_2 = 2^b - 1$.

Let the numbers a and b be relatively prime and let $k = a \cdot b$. Then $2^k \equiv 1 \bmod(2^a - 1)$ because $2^k \equiv (2^a)^b \equiv (1)^b \equiv 1 \bmod(2^a - 1)$. Therefore, $2^a - 1$ divides $2^k - 1$. Similarly, it can be proved that $2^b - 1$ divides $2^k - 1$ so that the biresidue code with $A_1 = 2^a - 1$, $A_2 = 2^b - 1$, and $m = 2^k - 1$ is closed.

Let $x = (N, |N|_{A1}, |N|_{A2})$ be a biresidue code word with check bases A_1 and A_2 as defined above. Define a syndrome corresponding to a code word x as a pair (s_1, s_2), where $s_1 = (|N - |N|_{A1}|_{A1})$ and $s_2 = (|N - |N|_{A2}|_{A2})$. If there is no error in the code word, $s_1 = 0$ and $s_2 = 0$. Any single error in the information will be of the form $|\pm 2^i|_m$ for $i = 0, 1, 2, \ldots, k - 1$. Therefore, a single error in the information part will result in a syndrome $s_1 = \pm 2^i \bmod 2^a - 1$ and $s_2 = \pm 2^i \bmod 2^b - 1$. It is shown below that the syndromes corresponding to these single errors are all distinct.

If both a and b are greater than 1, $2^i \neq 0 \bmod 2^a - 1$ and $2^i \neq 0 \bmod 2^b - 1$ for $0 \leq i < k$.

Suppose that $2^i = 2^j \bmod 2^a - 1$, then $2^{i-j} = 1 \bmod 2^a - 1$. Therefore, $2^a - 1$ divides $2^{i-j} - 1$ and hence a divides $i - j$. Similarly, if $2^i = 2^j \bmod 2^b - 1$, then b must divide $i - j$. Since $\gcd(a, b) = 1$, ab must divide $i - j$ but $i - j < k$. Therefore, the only possibility is that $i - j = 0$.

Moreover, if $-2^i = 2^j \bmod 2^a - 1$, then $2^{i-j} = -1 \bmod 2^a - 1$. Then $2^a - 1$ divides $2^{i-j} + 1$. This is possible only if $a = 2$. Similarly, if $-2^i = 2^j \bmod 2^b - 1$, then b must be equal to 2. Therefore, if a and b are distinct, then for each single error in the information part there corresponds a distinct nonzero pair of syndromes s_1 and s_2.

If there is a single error in the check part, then $s_1 = \pm 2^i \, 0 \bmod 2^a - 1$ and $s_2 = 0$, or vice versa. Thus any single error in the code word gives a distinct syndrome and hence all the single errors can be corrected. An example is given below to illustrate these concepts.

Example 6. Let $A_1 = 7 = 2^3 - 1$, $A_2 = 15 = 2^4 - 1$, and $k = 4.3 = 12$. Therefore, $m = 2^{12} - 1$. The syndromes corresponding to each of the single errors are given in Table 4.7.1. Moreover, note that any single error in the first check part results in $s_1 \neq 0$ and $s_2 = 0$ and that in the second check part result in $s_1 = 0$ and $s_2 \neq 0$. Therefore, these errors can also be corrected.

TABLE 4.7.1   ERROR SYNDROMES FOR SINGLE ERRORS IN A
BIRESIDUE CODE WITH $a = 3$, $b = 4$, and m

i	Syndrome of $+2^i$ $(s_1 = 2^i_7 \quad s_2 = 2^i_{15})$	Syndrome of -2^i $(s_1 = -2^i_7 \quad s_2 = -2^i_{15})$
0	(1, 1)	(6, 14)
1	(2, 2)	(5, 13)
2	(4, 4)	(3, 11)
3	(1, 8)	(6, 7)
4	(2, 1)	(5, 14)
5	(4, 2)	(3, 13)
6	(1, 4)	(6, 11)
7	(2, 8)	(5, 7)
8	(4, 1)	(3, 14)
9	(1, 2)	(6, 13)
10	(2, 4)	(5, 11)
11	(4, 8)	(3, 7)

4.8. ON CHECKING ERRORS IN LOGICAL OPERATIONS

There are a total of 16 different logical functions of two variables x and y. The six functions 0, 1, x, y, $\bar{x}$, and $\bar{y}$ are trivial because they depend upon only one or neither of the arguments. The other 10 nontrivial functions are $x \oplus y$, $x \odot y$, $x \cdot y$, $x \cdot \bar{y}$, $\bar{x} \cdot y$, $\bar{x} \cdot \bar{y}$, $x + y$, $x + \bar{y}$, $\bar{x} + y$, and $\bar{x} + \bar{y}$. This section discusses error correcting and detecting codes for these nontrivial operations.

As seen in the preceding sections, errors in memory, data transmission, or in an arithmetic operation can be checked by using a few check bits. However, to check errors in any nontrivial logical operations except EXOR and EQUIVALENCE, it has been shown [PETE59] that no less than duplication is possible. Errors in the EXOR and EQUIVALENCE operations can be checked by using linear codes.

Let the processor configuration be as shown in Fig. 4.8.1. A more general model will be described later. Here x and y are two k-bit binary vectors, and the logical processing device performs the logical operation on corresponding x and y bits in parallel, which yields the k-bit output vector z. Check symbols $a(x)$ and $b(y)$ are derived from x and y, respectively, and are processed by an independent checking

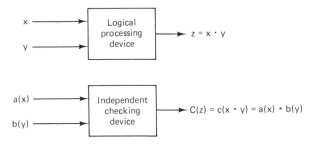

Figure 4.8.1   Separate processor and checker.

device to yield an output $a(x) * b(y)$. Check symbol $c(z)$ is derived from output z, and this should match the checking device output. That is,

$$c(z) = a(x) * b(y) \qquad (4.8.1)$$

The procedure above has been stated in very general terms, without assuming what kind of operation is performed by the independent checking device. Nevertheless, it is shown below that at least 2^k distinct check symbols are required to detect single errors in any nontrivial logical operation except EXOR and EQUIVALENCE.

Suppose that the processor performs the logical AND operation. Detection of single errors requires that whenever only one of the bits in the output vector is incorrect, the error can be detected. So if z and z' are two output vectors which differ exactly in one position, we require that $c(z) \neq c(z')$. Let x and x' be two different vectors. Let position i be one of the positions where they differ, and let D_i be the vector with one at the ith position and zero at all other positions. Then $x \cdot D_i$ and $x' \cdot D_i$ differ in exactly one position. Therefore, $c(x, D_i) \neq c(x'D_i)$ so $a(x) * b(D_i) \neq a(x') * b(D_i)$. Clearly, then $a(x) \neq a(x')$. This implies for every possible input vector the corresponding check symbol must be distinct. As a consequence no simpler method than duplication is possible for detecting single errors in a logical AND operation.

A similar argument can be given for detecting single errors in any nontrivial logical operation except EXOR and its complement EQUIVALENCE, for which distance two linear codes can be used to detect single errors.

Before describing the conditions for error correction, a general model of the processor configuration is shown in Fig. 4.8.2. The separate processor and checker configuration is a special case of this configuration. The k-bit vectors x and y are encoded into the n-bit vectors $u(x)$ and $v(y)$, respectively. $w(z)$ is the encoded version of the k-bit vector z, where $z = x * y$. In this configuration of the processor, the encoders and the decoders are assumed to be completely reliable. It is also assumed that the digits are processed digit by digit and thus one error in processing can effect only one digit.

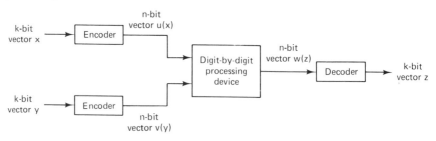

Figure 4.8.2   Block diagram of a digit-by-digit processor.

In the absence of errors in $w(z)$, let $w(z)$ be a single-valued function of z. Under this condition Peterson and Rabin [PETE59] have shown that if $*$ is any nontrivial Boolean operation other than EXOR or EQUIVALENCE, the length n of $w(z)$ has to be at least $d \cdot k$ for the system to be capable of correcting $\lfloor (d-1)/2 \rfloor$ errors at the output. This is equivalent to replicating the input vectors d times.

However, by relaxing the condition that $w(z)$ is not a single-valued function of z, an efficient error control technique for logical processors is given by Pradhan and Reddy [PRAD72]. The technique is described below.

Any logical function involving two input vectors x and y can be expressed in Reed-Muller canonical form as

$$x * y = c_0 I \oplus c_1 x \oplus c_2 y \oplus c_3 x \cdot y \qquad (4.8.2)$$

where $c_i \in \{0, 1\}$ and I is an all-1 vector. For example, $x \cdot y$ can be obtained by taking $c_0 = 0$, $c_1 = 0$, $c_2 = 0$, and $c_3 = 1$. Similarly, $x + y$ can be obtained by taking $c_0 = 0$, $c_1 = 1$, $c_2 = 1$, and $c_3 = 1$. Now consider the Reed-Muller code (RMC) with length $n = 2^m$. If x and y belong to the ith order RMC, $i \le [m/2]$, then $x * y$ must be the code word in the $2i$th-order RMC. This is because $x \cdot y$ is a code word in the $2i$th-order RMC. Moreover, since I, x, and y are in the ith-order RMC they must also be in the $2i$th-order RMC. Thus any linear combination of I, x, y, and $x \cdot y$ must be in the $2i$th-order RMC.

In the processor configuration, let the encoders be the encoders of a systematic ith-order RMC, $i \le [m/2]$, and let the decoder be the decoder for a $2i$th-order RMC. Therefore, $u(x)$ and $v(y)$ are code words in the ith-order RMC and $w(z)$ is a code word in the $2i$th-order RMC. Since the minimum distance of a $2i$th-order code is 2^{m-2i}, the scheme is capable of correcting up to $(2^{m-2i} - 1)/2$ errors and detecting 2^{m-2i-1} errors.

It can be proved that the maximum efficiency, k/n, is less than or equal to $1/2$ for any error control scheme for the logical processor of the type shown in Fig. 4.8.2. For the proposed scheme let $n = 2^m = 2^{2l}$. For minimum distance to be 4, a $[2(l-1)]$-order RMC can be taken at the output. In that case the efficiency k/n is given by

$$\frac{k}{n} = \frac{2^{m-1} - \binom{m}{m/2} \Big/ 2}{2^m} \qquad (4.8.3)$$

$$\approx \frac{1}{2} \qquad \text{as } m \to \infty$$

Thus the error-control scheme described is almost optimum for single-error correction. Further, it can be proved that this scheme is asymptotically optimum, even for d error correction.

4.9. COMMUNICATION CODING

With the trend toward greater emphasis on distributed computing, communication over a significant distance often is a necessary part of computer system operation. A fault-tolerant computer system may require that communication be carried out virtually error-free. This is despite the fact that the communication medium often is subject to significantly greater frequency of errors and much greater variability of conditions than the ordinary computing environment. Nevertheless, if variable time delay can be tolerated, virtually error-free communication can be assured using rather straightforward procedures. Schemes employing error detection and retransmission strategies (denoted ARQ systems [MOOR60] are relatively simple to implement and can assure that a message is virtually certain to get through correctly [METZ60], but with variable delay depending on the number of retransmissions required. More sophisticated error-correcting codes combined with error detection-retransmission can allow achievement of high data rate efficiency and usually less delay.

Although fault-tolerant computer systems usually can tolerate some variability in the time taken to perform a given task, there usually is a limit to how long a particular task or subtask is permitted to take for completion. Unfortunately, a wide variation in delay often is invariable in communication because (1) communication channels often are shared with others and the amount of user demand is highly variable, (2) underlying noise conditions vary unpredictably in many communication channels, and (3) techniques that ensure virtually error-free communication of a certain block of data inherently introduce variable delay (i.e., variable number of retransmissions). Thus variable delay inherent to communication must be considered in the fault-tolerant system design.

4.9.1. Error-Free Communication Over a Noisy Data Link

Computer communication normally is carried out in a network shared by a number of users. This section is restricted to the study of how reliable communication can be accomplished over a single noisy data link between a single pair of terminals. Later we will see how the basic principles explained here fit into the problem of communication in an extensive computer communication network.

Use of block codes with sufficient error detection to make the fraction f defined by Eq. (4.4.13) very small is one part of the solution to achieving virtually error-proof data communication. A second part involves treatment of the acknowledgment or retransmission request via a return signal. An acknowledgment misinterpreted as a repeat request results simply in a word unnecessarily repeated, whereas a retransmission request misinterpreted as an acknowledgment results in failure to receive that word. By using an asymmetric decision rule at the return channel receiver which highly favors the repeat request interpretation, the probability of misinterpreting a repeat request as an acknowledgment can be made negligible. A third part of the problem is to provide means whereby the forward channel receiver can ascertain whether a decoded word is new information or an unrequested repeat. This is accomplished by including a label (also called a *sequence number*) in the data part of each code word. The interaction of these mechanisms is explained below.

The communication can be either "stop-and-wait" or continuous [BENI64]. Some communication paths can support communication in only one of the two directions at a given time—this is referred to as a *half-duplex channel*. If communication can be carried out simultaneously in both directions, the channel is called a *full-duplex channel*. For a half-duplex channel the sender must stop after sending a message block or blocks, and wait for the return acknowledgment(s) before sending new information or retransmission. For a full-duplex channel the sender has the option of sending message blocks continuously and simultaneously receiving return acknowledgments of past transmitted blocks.

4.9.2. Stop-and-Wait ARQ Protocols

Figure 4.9.1 illustrates stop-and-wait transmission where a stream of code words are sent from A to B, while acknowledgments are sent from B to A. In the figure, time advances horizontally and position varies vertically. A indicates that a word (or acknowledgment) cannot be decoded reliably due to excessive noise or errors. Each code word carries a 1-bit label digit (also called *sequence number*) which alternates between 0 and 1 for successive new words. The words to be sent are denoted x, y, z, . . . and the subscripts denote the attached label bit. Station B sends back the label bit of the last new word decoded (or in some schemes the next new word expected). If the return label cannot be decoded at A, or if it is the label of the word prior to the word last sent, then A retransmits the word last sent; if the return label is decoded as the label of the word last sent, this is treated as an acknowledgment and A sends the next new message block. At the receiving end, identical labels (as when y_1 was received twice in Fig. 4.9.1) indicate to B that the second y_1 is an unrequested retransmission, and it can be discarded. (Note that it might be unwise to rely on identical data content of successive words to identify an unrequested repeat, since sometimes it may actually be desired to send the same data block twice in succession.) We see that failure to decode a return label does not result in any final error; only a possible unnecessary retransmission of a word. On the other hand, reception of the wrong label on the return channel must be avoided, since it could result in A believing that B had successfully received a message when in fact B had not. Application of a decoding rule with a very large error-detection region (Section 4.7) on the return channel can ensure that this type of error almost never happens.

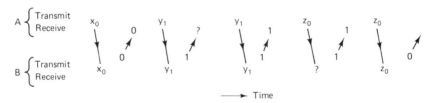

Figure 4.9.1

In some cases data are being sent in both directions. Often this occurs on a one-to-one basis, with one word sent from A to B followed by a word from B to A, then a word from A to B, and so on. Then an acknowledgment label digit from B to A can be embedded as part of the data in a word going from B to A, and a similar procedure can be used from A to B. Due to the large error-detection region, either a word is decoded correctly with near certainty, in which case the embedded label digit also is correct, or it cannot be decoded, in which case the label digit is not decoded either. (If one station has no data to send at any particular time, a dummy word containing no data but only the acknowledgment label can be sent.)

In the two-way data flow case, greatest flexibility is obtained by providing two labels or sequence numbers in each code word: one to identify the forward-going code word, and one to carry the return acknowledgment sequence number. It is also possible to use a protocol with only one sequence number using the rule: send a new word when and only when a new word is received from the other station [METZ65]. However, the two-sequence number approach provides better flexibility [GRAY72] by not forcing the acknowledgment rates in the two directions to be synchronized. Also, with the two-sequence number approach the return sequence number could be encoded separately, or the encoding could be constructed in such a way that the return sequence number could be decoded in many cases where the word as a whole could not be decoded [METZ74].

4.9.3. Continuous Transmission ARQ Protocols

In many situations it is inefficient for a transmitting station to defer sending new data while awaiting acknowledgment. Protocols are available which permit continuous transmission of new data. These can be categorized as either *go-back* [REIF61, BENI64, MORR78] or *selective repeat* [METZ60, METZ65, GATF74, EAST80, MILL80] protocols. Before explaining the difference between these categories, some characteristics common to these two types of continuous transmission schemes will be described.

Assume at this point that each word sent out is indiviually acknowledged or not acknowledged (later we will see that this one-to-one correspondence is not essential). Let J be the number of consecutive words sent out before the sender is able to ascertain from the return signal whether the first of these J has been acknowledged. In the continuous transmission case more than one bit is required for sequence numbering. The minimum requirement is $\log_2 J$ bits. In the illustrations to follow, suppose that $J = 4$ and the sequence number is three bits, representing the decimal numbers 0 through 7. Let A be sending to B the message blocks a_0, b_1, c_2, d_3, e_4, f_5, g_6, h_7, i_0, j_0, k_2, . . . , where the subscripts indicate the accompanying sequence number. As acknowledgment, B returns to A the sequence number of the last new word block decoded successfully, Fig. 4.9.2 illustrates the procedure when all decodings are successful. Note that b_1, c_2, and d_3 are sent out before the return acknowledgment of a_0 is decoded by A, but that before it is decided whether to transmit e_4, station A has time to learn if a_0 was acknowledged.

Go-back protocols.   In this procedure, if a word is not acknowledged, the sender goes back and retransmits the unacknowledged word and the $J-1$ words after it which were sent during the waiting interval. Figure 4.9.3 illustrates how the protocol

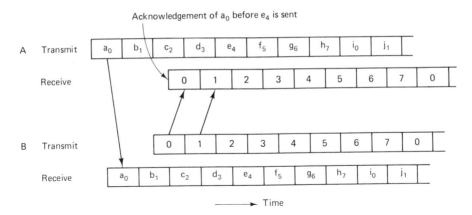

Figure 4.9.2 Continuous transmission with no failures.

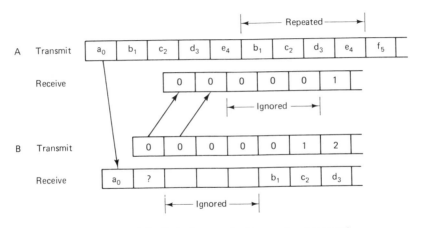

Figure 4.9.3 Go-back protocol with an undecodable word.

works if a forward word is not decoded (indicated by a). At the expense of greater complexity, the received words at B indicated as ignored could be decoded, which would improve efficiency in case one of the retransmissions c_2, d_3, and c_4 later turned out to be nondecodable. Figure 4.9.4 shows the go-back-J protocol in operation when a return sequence number is not decoded. Note that station B can recognize the unrequested A repeats by their sequence number and discard them.

Selective repeat protocols. The go-back-J procedure is inefficient if decoding failures are frequent or if propagation time is very long, resulting in a very large J. In such cases it may be more desirable to selectively repeat only those words for which a decoding failure actually occurred. Two methods of accomplishing this are shown below.

One of the procedures, which we will call the *circulating memory procedure* [METZ60, METZ65], can be described in terms of a clockwise circulating ring

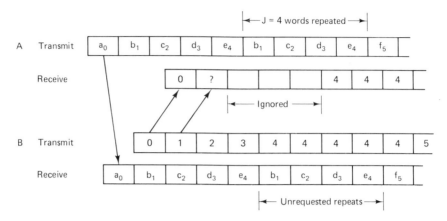

Figure 4.9.4   Go-back protocol with a return signal undecodable.

memory by J storage elements which is located at the transmitter. This is shown in Fig. 4.9.5. When a new word is to be transmitted, the switch is placed in position P and the new word enters position one of the storage ring at the same time it is transmitted and other words in the ring move one step clockwise, with the word in J discarded. By the time a word in memory comes around to position J it is known whether it has been acknowledged. If not, no new word is entered, the switch is placed in position Q, and the word that was in location J is retransmitted and returned to position 1 as the ring shifts. If it has been acknowledged and no other word in the ring is too far back (to be explained later) the switch moves to position P for new word transmission.

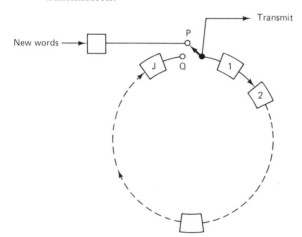

Figure 4.9.5   Circulating memory transmission control.

The sequence number normally is prescribed by an l-digit binary number and thus has 2^l different values which advance cyclically. The sequence number is used at the receiver to reassemble the message in proper order (since the selective repeat policy sometimes results in words received out of order) and to distinguish new words from unrequested repeats. Ambiguity is prevented if the transmitter obeys the rule: don't transmit and enter a new word into the ring if the new sequence number would be advanced by $2^l - J$ or more, cyclically, from the oldest word still in the ring memory [METZ65]. Then the receiver is certain that the most advanced accepted word could not have been sent if there was an unacknowledged word prior to the window, so every decoded sequence number unambiguously locates the word within the given window.

Another possible selective repeat protocol is an *interlacing* procedure [METZ60, METZ65]. In this procedure, J separate stop-and-wait chains are simply interleaved in time, sort of as a J-slot time multiplexing. If there are about J different users sharing the channel, this is a simple and natural procedure. If a single user's data are interlaced there may be substantial buffering requirements for message reassembly, as the J separate chains will not necessarily each have the same number of decoding failures in a given time period.

4.9.4. Standard Data Link Control Procedures

The desire for greater compatibility for interaction of differing systems has led to the development of certain standard data link control procedures and formats [DAVI79, CARL80]. The trend is toward bit-oriented rather than character-oriented protocols due to the greater flexibility and efficiency of the former. Principal standards are a national standard (ADCCP) and an international standard (HDLC); these two standards are similar in most respects. The standards permit continuous transmission in both directions. Data are transmitted in basic transmission unit blocks or frames. The frame format is shown in Fig. 4.9.6. The flag sequences, which denote the start and end of the frame, each consist of the bit pattern 01111110. The data link control mechanism ensures that this flag pattern does not appear elsewhere by having the transmitting end insert a 0 whenever five consecutive ones are observed and having the receiving end delete such zeros. The address field consists of one or more octets (8-bit groups) identifying the station that is to receive or is sending that frame.

Flag	Address Field	Control Field	Information Field	Frame Check Sequence	Flag

Figure 4.9.6 Basic frame format.

The control field normally consists of 8 bits, but can be extended to 16 bits by a mode command. There are three different control field formats: information transfer, supervisory, and unnumbered. The information transfer format is identified by a 0 in the first bit of the field. The remainder of the field contains a 3-bit send sequence number, a 3-bit receive sequence number, and a poll/final; alternatively, in the extended form the send and receive sequence numbers are alloted 7 bits each. Supervisory frames begin with 10 as the first 2 bits of the control field. There are four such types of frames which are used to control data flow or error recovery; these are called receive ready, receive not ready, reject, and selective reject. The field also contains a sequence number identifying an expected next frame number. Unnumbered frames begin with 11 in the first 2 bits of the control field. The remaining bits of this field provide for up to 32 different kinds of control frames for setting various modes and other commands. The reader may refer to Chapter 6 of [DAVI79] for a more complete description.

The information field is of unspecified length. It is followed by a 16-bit frame check sequence field prior to the closing flag sequence. This is computed based on a cyclic code with generator polynomial $x^{16} + x^{12} + x^5 + 1$. The 16 check bits are computed from the bits in the address, control, and information fields by the technique described in Section 4.3 of finding the remainder on dividing the information sequence (as a polynomial) by the generator polynomial. It does not matter that the number of bits in the information polynomial is variable. The receiver uses division by the same polynomial to detect errors. If errors are detected, the frame is discarded and ignored.

ARQ protocols are based primarily on the send and receive sequence numbers. A return sequence number identifies the next information frame expected and, in the normal mode, automatically acknowledges reception of all frames with sequence numbers preceding it. The sender waits a certain specified time for an acknowledgment. If it does not come back, the sender retransmits (go-back strategy) that frame and any others sent after it. Unlike in the systems described previously, it is not necessary that the receiver acknowledge every frame, as long as the frame acknowledgment can be returned within the specified time period. Note that the variable frame size necessitates use of such a procedure rather than the ones previously where the frame sizes were fixed.

The supervisory frames *reject* (REJ) and *selective reject* (SREJ) are provided as means of improving efficiency in some cases. REJ is a negative acknowledge which the receiver can return immediately on a frame check sequence failure, thereby usually reducing the number of unnecessary retransmissions. The SREJ frame allows the receiver to reject one specific frame (identified by a receive sequence number sent with the frame), while acknowledging all prior frames. This procedure is limited to allowing only one outstanding selective reject at a time, whereas the circulating memory procedure described previously was not so restricted.

Efficient operation on noisier channels.   The standard data link control procedure is designed for channels where the bit error rate is low—an average of much less than one bit error per frame. Higher error rates would result in excessive retransmissions. Also, false flag patterns would occur fairly frequently with higher error rate, resulting in the receiver wrongly judging the beginning or end of a frame. This would almost always result in a frame check failure, but in about 1 out of 2^{16} of these cases the erroneous length frame would check.

Noisier channels could be operated efficiently if error correction were used in addition to error detection [LEUN81]. Error-correction schemes would be difficult to employ unless a fixed frame size were used. A fixed frame size could permit use of a simple frame synchronization signal which would eliminate the need for a flag sequence and virtually eliminate misplacements of the beginning and end of the frame.

Where channel capacity is at a premium, there is justification for operating the channel in a noisier mode. This is because if a channel is virtually error-free at the current mode of usage, a higher rate can be achieved by sending, say, multilevel signals instead of binary, or at a higher signaling rate (if bandwidth permits). This would result in a higher effective bit rate, but a noiser channel. A quantitative discussion of the trade-offs involved is beyond the scope of this book. The reader may refer to a text in communication theory, such as [WOZE65]. Also, certain memory ARQ techniques [METZ63, SIND77, METZ79, LIN79] which save the information in the first frame transmission and combine it with its retransmission could be used to improve efficiency further in the fixed-frame-size mode.

4.9.5. Data Networks

It was shown that reliable communication can be attained by adhering to the following three principles:

1. Provide for sufficient error checking to make negligible the probability of undetected error.
2. Provide for retransmission of any data that are not positively acknowledged; retransmission is made unless the sender is virtually certain that the message has been correctly received.
3. Provide sequence number identification for each message unit to permit recognition of unrequested retransmissions and unambiguous reassembly of messages received out of order.

Thus far we have considered only the case of a single data link between two stations and a uniform flow of data between stations. However, computer communication more frequently is carried out over a network shared by a number of users, and the data communication needs of the users usually are highly variable with time. The problem of reliable and efficient communication in a data network is considerably more complex than in the single-link uniform data flow case; nevertheless, the three basic principles listed above remain the key to reliable communication.

The process of two users communicating through a computer communication network is being standardized through a "layering" model. An example of this is the seven-layer ISO reference model [ZIMM80] illustrated in Fig. 4.9.7.

Protocols are designed to govern the rules for communication between "peers" at the same level. These protocols at a given level ideally are independent of what protocols or procedures are used at lower levels.

Error-correcting and error-detecting codes primarily have application at the data link level and at the transport level. There are two principal ways that high reliability can be assured for information transmission from user A to user B.

1. User A can supply its information to the network level and rely on the network or networks to convey the information reliably to user B. As the message

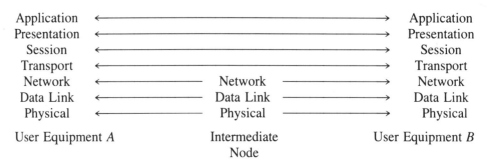

Figure 4.9.7   Seven-layer ISO reference model.

traverses each link of the network, check bits are appended and data link control procedures are employed to ensure reliable transmission over that link.

2. User A can request an acknowledgment return message from user B at the transport level. The unit of acknowledgment is not necessarily the same as the frame unit in the individual link control procedure; it normally would be a larger "message unit." As part of this procedure user A could add check bits to its message unit. These check bits would be carried along just like other data through the network to user B. User B can then perform error detection at its transport layer and send an acknowledgment message back through the network to user A. This method, which can be referred to as an *end-to-end protocol*, is recommended when the reliability of the network is not sufficient for the needs of user A.

Networks usually can be classified as circuit switched or packet switched. *Circuit-switched networks* set up a specific route for all data flowing between users A and B during a particular session. This could either be a fixed-capacity connection (as a solid connection of wires dedicated to that circuit or a fixed number of time slots in time-division multiplexing dedicated to the circuit) or a dynamically allocated capacity connection (called a *virtual circuit*), where the fixed route is maintained but the amount of capacity allocated (or number of time slots provided) varies dynamically according to user needs. In a circuit-switched network error control is normally on an end-to-end basis according to a format determined by the communicating users. It is theoretically possible for the nodes on the path to assist in error control in a manner that is transparent to the users, but in practice this assistance has been limited to making binary decisions for each digit.

In a *packet-switched network* all network information is transferred in fixed-size packets, and the network takes on the responsibility of delivering the packets reliably in order to the destination address. There is a standard protocol (X25) by which the user interfaces with the network. Through this interface the user can obtain one of three different types of facilities: *datagram*, where an individual packet is sent to any specific destination by whatever path the network chooses at the time; *permanent virtual circuit*, whereby a specific path has been reserved between user A and user B, and all packets exchanged between them will follow that path; and *virtual call*, where a particular path is set up from user *A* to user *B* only for the duration of a "call," during which a number of packets (which can be numbered consecutively and are delivered in order) are sent over the path. For further details of the X25 procedure, see [DAVI79, Chap. 6].

REFERENCES AND BIBLIOGRAPHY

[BENI64] Benice, R. J., and A. H. Frey, Jr., "An Analysis of Retransmission Systems," *IEEE Trans. Commun. Technol.* vol. 12, no. 4, pp. 135–145, Dec. 1964.

[BERG61] Berger, J. M., "A Note on Error Detecting Codes for Asymmetric Channels," *Inf. Control*, vol. 4, pp. 68–73, Mar. 1961.

[BERL68] Berlekamp, E. R., *Algebraic Coding Theory*, McGraw-Hill, New York, 1968.

[BERL80] Berlekamp, E. R., "The Technology of Error-Control Codes," *Proc. IEEE,* vol. 68, no. 5, pp. 564–593, May 1980.

[BOSE60] Bose, R. C., and D. K. Ray-Chandhuri, "On a Class of Error Correction Binary Group Codes," *Inf. Control*, vol. 3, pp. 68–79, 1960.

[BOSE80a] Bose, B., "The Theory and Design of Unidirectional Error Codes," Ph.D. thesis, *Dept. of Computer Science and Engineering, Southern Methodist University,* Dallas, May 1980.

[BOSE80b] Bose, B., and T. R. N. Rao, "Unidirectional Error Codes for Shift Register Memories," *Dig., 10th Annu. Int. Symp. Fault-Tolerant Comput.*, Kyoto, Japan, pp. 26–28, Oct. 1–3, 1980.

[BOSE81] Bose, B., "On Systematic SEC-MUED Codes," *Dig., 11th Annu. Int. Symp. Fault-Tolerant Comput.*, Portland, Me., pp. 265–267, June 24–26, 1981.

[BOSE82a] Bose, B., and T. R. N. Rao, "Theory of Unidirectional Error Correcting/Detecting Codes," *IEEE Trans. Comput.*, vol. C-31, no. 6, pp. 520–530, June 1982.

[BOSE82b] Bose, B., and D. K. Pradhan, "Optimal Unidirectional Error Detecting/Correcting Codes, *IEEE Trans. Comput.*, vol. C-31, no. 6, pp. 564–568, June 1982.

[BOSS70] Bossen, D. C., "*b*-Adjacent Error Correction," *IBM J. Res. Dev.*, vol. 14, pp. 402–408, July 1970.

[BOSS78] Bossen, D. C., L. C. Chang, and C. L. Chen, "Measurement and Generation of Error Correcting Codes for Package Failures," *IEEE Trans. Comput.*, vol. C-27, no. 3, pp. 201–204, Mar. 1978.

[BROW70] Brown, D. T., and F. F. Sellers, "Error-Correction for IBM 800-Bit-Per-Inch Magnetic Tape," *IBM J. Res. Dev.*, vol. 14, pp. 384–389, July 1970.

[CARL80] Carlson, D. E., "Bit-Oriented Data Link Control Procedures," *IEEE Trans. Commun.*, vol. COM.-28, no. 4, pp. 465–467, Apr. 1980.

[CART76] Carter, W. C., and C. E. McCarthy, "Implementation of an Experimental Fault-Tolerant Memory System," *IEEE Trans. Comput.*, vol. C-25, no. 6, pp. 557–568, June 1976.

[CHIE64] Chien, R. T., "Cycle Decoding Procedures for the Bose–Chandhuri–Hocquenghem Codes," *IEEE Trans. Inf. Theory*, vol. IT-10, pp. 357–363, 1964.

[CHIE73] Chien, R. T., "Memory Control beyond Parity." *IEEE Spectrum*, pp. 18–23, July 1973.

[CONS79] Constantin, S. D., and T. R. N. Rao, "Group Theoretic Codes for Binary Asymmetric Channel," *Inf. Control.* vol, 40, no. 1, pp. 20–26, Jan. 1979.

[COOK73] Cook, R. W., W. H. Sisson, T. F. Storey, and W. N. Toy, "Design of a Self-Checking Microprogram Control," *IEEE Trans. Comput.*, vol. C-22, pp. 255–262, Mar. 1973.

[DAVI79] Davies, D. W., D. L. Barber, W. L. Price, and C. M. Solomonides, *Computer Networks and Their Protocols,* Wiley, New York, 1979.

[EAST80] Easton, M. C., "Batch Throughput Efficiency of ADCCP/HDLC/SDLC Selective-Reject Protocols," *IEEE Trans. Commun.*, vol. COM.-28, no. 2, pp. 187–195, Feb. 1980.

[ELIA54] Elias, P., "Error Free Coding," *IRE Trans. Inf. Theory,* vol. IT-4, pp. 29–37, 1954.

[EPST58] Epstein, M. A., "Algebraic Decoding for a Binary Erasure Channel," *IRE Natl. Conv. Rec.*, vol. 6, pt. 4, pp. 56–69, 1958.

[FORN66] Forney, G. D., *Concatenated Codes*, MIT Press, Cambridge, Mass., 1966.

[FRIE62] Frieman, C. V., "Optimal Error Detection Codes for Completely Asymmetric Binary Channel," *Inf. Control*, vol. 5, pp. 64–71, Mar. 1962.

[GATF74] Gatfield, A. G., "ARQ Error Control on the Satellite Channel," *Int. Conf. Commun. Conf. Rec.*, pp. 22 B.1–22 B.5, 1974.

[GRAY72] Gray, J. P., "Line Control Procedures," *Proc. IEEE*, vol. 60, pp. 1301–1312, Nov. 1972.

[GRAY77] Gray, J. P., "Network Services in Systems Network Architecture," *IEEE Trans. Commun.*, vol. COM.-25, no. 1, pp. 104–115, Jan. 1977.

[HAMM50] Hamming, P. W., "Error Detecting and Correcting Codes," *Bell Syst. Tech. J.*, vol. 29, pp. 147–160, 1950.

[HONG72] Hong, S. J., and A. M. Patel, "A General Class of Maximal Codes for Computer Applications," *IEEE Trans. Comput.*, vol. C-21, pp. 1322–1331, Dec. 1972.

[HSIA70] Hsiao, M. Y., "Optimum Odd-Weight Column Codes," *IBM J. Res. Dev.*, vol. 14, no. 4, pp. 395–401, July 1970.

[ISO76] Data Communication-High Level Data Link Control *Procedures—Int. Standard 150/DIS 4335,* International Organization for Standardization, Geneva, 1976.

[KIM59] Kim, W. H., and C. V. Frieman, "Single Error Correcting Codes for Asymmetric Channel," *IRE Trans. Inf. Theory,* pp. 62–66, June 1959.

[LEUN81] Leung, C. S. K., and A. Lam, "Forward Error Correction for an ARQ Scheme," *IEEE Trans. Commun.*, vol. COM-29, pp. 1514–1519, Oct. 1981.

[LIN70] Lin, S., *An Introduction to Error-Correcting Codes*, Prentice-Hall, Englewood Cliffs, N. J., 1970.

[LIN79] Lin, S., and J. S. Ma, "A Hybrid ARQ System with Parity Retransmission of Error Correction," IBM Res. Rep. 7478 (32232), Jan. 11, 1979.

[LIN83] Lin, S., and D. J. Costello, Jr., *Error Control Coding*, Prentice-Hall, Englewood Cliffs, N. J., 1983.

[LOCK75] Lockitt, J. A., A. G. Gatfield, and R. R. Dobyns, "A Selective-Repeat ARQ System," *Proc. 3rd Int. Conf. Digit. Satellite Commun.*, Kyoto, Japan, Nov. 1975.

[MACL67] Maclane, S., and G. Birkhoff, *Algebra*, Macmillan, New York, 1967.

[METZ60] Metzner, J. J., and K. C. Morgan, "Reliable Fail-Safe Binary Communication," *IRE Wescon Conv. Rec.*, vol. 4, pt. 5, pp. 192–206, 1960.

[METZ63] Metzner, J. J., and K. C. Morgan, "Cumulative Decision Techniques for Error-Free Communication Systems," *New York Univ., College of Engineering, Fourteenth Scientific Report*, Air Force Contract AF 19(604)–6168, July 1963.

[METZ65] Metzner, J. J., and K. C. Morgan, "Word-Selection Procedures for Error-Free Communication Systems," New York Univ., Second Sci. Rep., Contract A. F. 19(628)-4321, June 1965.

[METZ74] Metzner, J. J., "A Technique for Separation of Data and Acknowledgment Signals in Two-Way Feedback Communication," *IEEE Trans. Commun.*, vol. COM-22, pp. 881–883, June 1974.

[METZ79] Metzner, J. J., "Improvements in Block-Retransmission Schemes," *IEEE Trans. Commun.*, vol. COM.-27, no. 2, pp. 525–532, Feb. 1979.

[METZ82] Metzner, J. J., "Convolutionally Encoded Memory Protection," *IEEE Trans. Comput.*, vol. 6, pp. 547–551, June 1982.

[MILL80] Miller, M. J., and S. Lin, "The Analysis of Some Selective-Repeat ARQ Schemes with Finite Receiver Buffer," *NTC '80 Conf. Proc.*, Houston, Tex., Nov. 30–Dec. 3, 1980.

[MOOR60] Moore, J. B., "Constant Ratio Code and Automatic-RQ on Transoceanic H F Services," *IRE Trans. Commun. Syst.*, vol. CS-8, no. 1, pp. 72–75, Mar. 1960.

[MORR78] Morris, J. M., "On Another Go-Back-N ARQ Technique for High Error Rate Conditions," *IEEE Trans. Commun.*, vol. COM.-26, pp. 187–189, Jan. 1978.

[PARH78] Parhami, B., and A. Avizienis, "Detection of Storage Errors in Mass Memories Using Low-Cost Arithmetic Error Codes," *IEEE Trans. Comput.*, vol. C-27, no. 4, pp. 302–308, Apr. 1978.

[PATE74] Patel, A. M., and S. J. Hong, "Optimal Rectangular Code for High Density Magnetic Tapes," *IBM J. Res. Dev.*, vol. 18, pp. 579–588, Nov. 1974.

[PATE75] Patel, A. M., "Zero Modulation Encoding in Magnetic Recording," *IBM J. Res. Dev.*, vol. 19, pp. 366–378, 1975.

[PATE80] Patel, A. M., "Error Recovery Scheme for the IBM 3850 Mass Storage System," *IBM J. Res. Dev.*, vol. 24, no. 1, pp. 32–42, Jan. 1980.

[PETE59] Peterson, W. W., and M. O. Rabin, "On Codes for Checking Logical Operations," *IBM J. Research Develop.*, vol. 3, pp. 163–168, 1959.

[PETE71] Peterson, W. W., and E. J. Weldon, *Error-Correcting Codes*, MIT Press, Cambridge, Mass., 1971.

[PRAD72] Pradhan, D. K., and S. M. Reddy, "Error Control Techniques for Logic Processors," *IEEE Trans. Comput.*, vol. C-21, no. 7, pp. 1331–1337, Dec. 1972.

[PRAD77] Pradhan, D. K., and S. M. Reddy, "Fault-Tolerant Fail-Safe Logic Network," *Proc. COMPCON*, pp. 361–363, Mar. 1977.

[PRAD80a] Pradhan, D. K., "A New Class of Error Correcting–Detecting Codes for Fault-Tolerant Computer Applications," *IEEE Trans. Comput.*, vol. C-29, no. 6, pp. 471–481, June 1980.

[PRAD80b] Pradhan, D. K., and J. J. Stiffler, "Error Correcting Codes and Self-Checking Circuits," *Computer*, vol. 13, no. 3, pp. 27–37, Mar. 1980.

[RAO71] Rao, T. R. N. and O. N. Garcia, "Cyclic and Multiresidue Codes for Arithmetic Operations," *IEEE Trans. Inf. Theory*, vol. IT-17, pp. 85–91, Jan. 1971.

[RAO74] Rao, T. R. N., *Error Coding for Arithmetic Processors*, Academic Press, New York, 1974.

[REDD78] Reddy, S. M., "A Class of Linear Codes for Error Control in Byte-per-Card Organized Digital Systems," *IEEE Trans. Comput.*, vol. C-27, no. 5, pp. 455–459, May 1978.

[REED54] Reed, I. S., "A Class of Multiple-Error Correcting Codes and the Decoding Scheme," *IRE Trans. Inf. Theory*, vol. PGIT-4, pp. 38–49, 1954.

[REED60] Reed, I. S., and G. Solomon, "Polynomial Codes over Certain Finite Fields," *J. Ind. Appl. Math.*, vol. 8, pp. 300–304, 1960.

[REIF61] Reiffin, B., N. G. Schmidt, and H. L. Yudkin, "The Design of an Error-Free Data Transmission System for Telephone Circuits," *AIEE Trans. Commun. Electron.*, vol. 80, pp. 224–231, July 1961.

[SIND77] Sindhu, P. S., "Retransmission Error Control with Memory," *IEEE Trans. Commun.*, pp. 473–479, May 1977.

[SLOA76] Sloane, N. J. A., "A Simple Description of an Error-Correcting Code for High-Density Magnetic Tape," *Bell Syst. Tech. J.*, vol. 55, no. 2, pp. 157–165, Feb. 1976.

[STIF78] Stiffler, J. J., "Coding for Random Access Memories," *IEEE Trans. Comput.*, vol. C-27, no. 6, pp. 526–531, June 1978.

[VARS73] Varshamov, R. R., "A Class of Codes for Asymmetric Channel and a Problem from Additive Theory of Numbers," *IEEE Trans. Inf. Theory*, vol. IT-19, no. 1, pp. 92–95, Jan. 1973.

[WAKE78a] Wakerly, J. F., "Detection of Unidirectional Multiple Errors Using Low-Cost Arithmetic Codes," *IEEE Trans. Comput.*, vol. C-27, no. 4, pp. 302–308, Apr. 1978.

[WAKE78b] Wakerly, J. F., *Error Detecting Codes, Self-Checking Circuits and Applications*, Elsevier North-Holland, New York, 1978.

[WOZE65] Wozencraft, J. M., and I. M. Jacobs, *Principles of Communication Engineering*, Wiley, New York, 1965.

[ZIMM80] Zimmerman, H., "OSI Reference Model—the ISO Model of Architecture for Open System Interconnection," *IEEE Trans. Commun.*, vol. COM-28, pp. 425–432, Apr. 1980.

PROBLEMS

4.1. In the code example of Eq. (4.3.12) to (4.3.14), demonstrate that each row of G is orthogonal to each row of H.

4.2. For the (8, 4) code with the H matrix given by Eq. (4.4.1):

(a) If $S^T = \begin{bmatrix} 1 \\ 0 \\ 1 \\ 1 \end{bmatrix}$, what can be concluded?

(b) If $S^T = \begin{bmatrix} 1 \\ 1 \\ 1 \\ 1 \\ 1 \end{bmatrix}$, what possible double errors could have occurred?

4.3. A binary parity check code has the following generator matrix:

$$G = \begin{bmatrix} 1 & 1 & 1 & 1 & 0 & 0 & 1 \\ 1 & 0 & 1 & 1 & 1 & 1 & 1 \\ 0 & 1 & 1 & 0 & 1 & 0 & 1 \end{bmatrix}$$

(a) List the set of code words.
(b) What is the error-correcting capability of this code?
(c) Find the generator matrix for a systematic code having the same set of code words.
(d) Find an H matrix for this code based on Eq. (4.3.11).

4.4. A (12, 4) code is used for correction of all possible single errors and detection of some other error patterns.
(a) How many different error patterns have the same syndrome as a single error in position six?
(b) What fraction of all possible error patterns will fool the decoder into attempting to correct a single error when in fact there is more than one error?
(c) What fraction of the 2^{12} possible error patterns are detected as errors but are recognized as not being single errors?

4.5. List the members of GF(2^4) as polynomials modulo $X^4 + X + 1$. Find a primitive element α and express all nonzero polynomial members of GF(2^4) as powers of α. Draw a feedback shift register for multiplying by X modulo $X^4 + X + 1$.

4.6. Prove that the $q - 1$ nonzero elements of GF(q) form an Abelian group under multiplication.

4.7. Prove that the $q - 1$ nonzero elements of GF(q) are all roots of $X^{q-1} - 1$.

4.8. Investigate the error-correcting properties of the length 15 cyclic code whose generator polynomial over GF(2) is the irreducible polynomial $g(X) = X^4 + X + 1$.

4.9. A (10, 4) cyclic code has generator polynomial $g(X)$. Let

$$c(X) = c_9 X^9 + c_8 X^8 + c_7 X^7 + c_6 X^6 + c_5 X^5 + c_4 X^4 + c_3 X^3 + c_2 X^2 + c_1 X + c_0$$

be a code word. Suppose that all the digits except c_9, c_2, c_1, and c_0 get erased. Show how c_8, c_7, . . . , c_3 can be derived from the known values by means of polynomial operations. Also show the equivalent shift register operations.

4.10. Prove that among all unidirectional error-detecting codes the $\lfloor n/2 \rfloor$-out-of-n code or the $\lceil n/2 \rceil$-out-of-n code has the highest information rate.

Chapter 5

Coding Techniques in Fault-Tolerant, Self-Checking, and Fail-Safe Circuits

Yoshihiro Tohma

5.1. INTRODUCTION

This chapter reviews coding techniques that enhance circuit capability for fault tolerance and reliable operation. Implementation of circuits with self-checking and fail-safe properties is also discussed. The application of error-correcting codes to memories is not included here; these codes are presented in Chapter 4.

First, a variety of error-detecting codes and techniques for the parity prediction are reviewed in Section 5.2. Section 5.3 covers the synthesis of self-checking circuits, emphasizing self-checking checkers, a subject about which many papers continue to appear.

Section 5.4 deals with techniques for fault tolerance in combinational circuits. The application of error-correcting codes to adders and a fault-masking technique by retry are described. Fault-tolerant sequential circuits are discussed in Section 5.5, which includes not only the general principles used to make sequential circuits fault tolerant, but also some special design practices.

The operation of an asynchronous sequential circuit is often unreliable, since it may suffer from some ambiguity due to the lack of a control signal for definite timing. Special care must be taken in asynchronous sequential circuit design, particularly when assigning states. In this context, design methods of fault-tolerant asynchronous sequential circuits will be discussed in Section 5.6.

Although fail-safe sequential circuits are not strictly fault tolerant, their synthesis will be described in Section 5.7, since the concept of fail-safe circuits is close to that of self-checking circuits.

5.2. ERROR-DETECTING CODES AND THEIR APPLICATIONS

5.2.1. Review of Error-Detecting Codes

Mechanisms for error detection are widely employed, since all countermeasures for fault tolerance can be initiated only after the detection of the occurrence of fault. Among those mechanisms is the utilization of error-detecting codes, including the simple scheme of duplication comparison of circuit operation.

The essential feature of error-detecting codes is to preserve a characteristic property common to each code word. When an error occurs in a code word, this common property will be violated, and thus its occurrence will be detected. Furthermore, the selection of this common property affects the complexity of real implementation.

Since many error-detecting codes have proved to be of practical significance, some of them will be briefly reviewed below. We restrict our discussion to codes of binary tuples, of which each component takes a value 1 or 0. In some cases, a binary tuple will be viewed as a tuple of bytes of b-bit width each.

Let us begin with definitions of errors in a code word.

Definition 1.   An error that affects only a single component value is called a *single error*, while an error affecting multiple component values is referred to as a *multiple error*. The component value affected by an error may change from 0 to 1, or vice versa.

Definition 2.   An error that affects only component values within a byte of b-bit width is classified as a *single b-adjacent error*. An error affecting component values over multiple bytes is referred to as a *multiple b-adjacent error*.

Definition 3.   When all components affected by a multiple error change their values in one direction from, say, 0 to 1, or vice versa, this multiple error is called a *unidirectional error*.

Throughout this chapter, the summation in modulo 2 will be denoted by Σ for notational convenience.

Parity check code.   Let a binary tuple $\mathbf{a} = (a_{n-1} a_{n-2} \ldots a_0 a_c)$ be an arbitrary code word of the *parity check code*, where $a_{n-1}, a_{n-2}, \ldots, a_0$ represent information bits and a_c is a check bit. a_c is given by

$$a_c = \sum_{i=0}^{n-1} a_i \qquad (5.2.1)$$

This definition of the parity check code means that the total number of 1s in every code word is kept even. Therefore, a multiple error at the odd number of bit positions is detected.

There is an alternative scheme, in which a_c is determined by

$$a_c = \left(\sum_{i=0}^{n-1} a_i \right) \oplus 1 \qquad (5.2.2)$$

Here the total number of 1s in every code word is kept odd.

The former and the latter schemes will be referred to as the even and odd parity schemes, respectively. In the even parity scheme, $(00 \cdot \cdot \cdot 0)$ is regarded as a code word, but may result from a stuck-at-0 fault at the output of a circuit. Therefore, the odd parity scheme may be preferred in some applications.

The application of the parity check code to information transmission paths, such as a data bus or a memory, is straightforward. However, the implementation of the parity check in logic circuits is somewhat complicated.

The simple extension to the parity check code is the two-dimensional parity check (the product code). See Problem 5.1.

Checksum code.   A code word of the *checksum code* is an n-tuple of information bytes $\mathbf{X}_{n-1}, \mathbf{X}_{n-2}, \ldots, \mathbf{X}_0$ with an attached check byte $\mathbf{X}_c$ of b-bit width each:

$$(\mathbf{X}_{n-1}\mathbf{X}_{n-2} \ldots \mathbf{X}_0\mathbf{X}_c) \qquad (5.2.3)$$

where $\mathbf{X}_c$ is given by

$$\mathbf{X}_c = \left(\sum_{i=0}^{n-1} \mathbf{X}_i \right) \bmod 2^b \qquad (5.2.4)$$

The summation of all information bytes in modulo 2^b will be called the *checksum*.

Any single b-adjacent error violates the equality (5.2.4), and therefore its occurrence can always be detected. As discussed in Section 5.2.2, however, some double and triple errors may not be detected. When $b = 1$, the checksum code reduces to the parity check code.

Berger code.   The *Berger code* [BERG61] can be viewed as another extension to the parity check code. In the even parity check code scheme, the number of information bits of value 1 is counted in modulo 2, and only one check bit representing this count is attached. On the other hand, the Berger code employs enough check bits to represent the net count of information bits of value 0, instead of 1, in a binary form. When a code word includes k information bits, the count may take at most the value k. Therefore, the required number r of check bits is

$$r = \lceil \log_2(k + 1) \rceil \qquad (5.2.5)$$

where $\lceil x \rceil$ is the minimum integer not less than x.

It is readily understood that a single error will violate the equality between the count of information bits of value 0 and the binary representation of check bits.

The Berger code is of particular interest, because it detects the occurrence of any multiple unidirectional error.

Residue/inverse residue code.   Let N be a positive integer represented in binary form. The residue R of N for divisor A is denoted by

$$R = N \bmod A \tag{5.2.6}$$

The concatenation of N and R, (NR), is called a code word of the *residue code* with check base A, while $(N(A - R))$ is referred to as a code word of the *inverse residue code*.

The residue code has its advantage in arithmetic operations. Consider two positive integers N_1 and N_2 together with their respective residues R_1 and R_2. Then

$$(N_1 \pm N_2) \bmod A = (R_1 \pm R_2) \bmod A \tag{5.2.7}$$

$$(N_1 N_2) \bmod A = (R_1 R_2) \bmod A \tag{5.2.8}$$

Therefore, the arithmetic operation above can be checked by comparing the residue of the result of the operation on N_1 and N_2 with the result of the operation in modulo A on R_1 and R_2 (see Fig. 5.2.1).

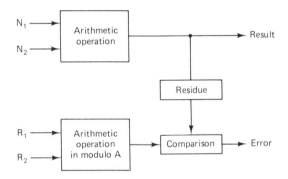

Figure 5.2.1   Checking by residues.

Unfortunately, residues do not preserve the similar property in the division. Instead, we rely on the following equation:

$$N_2 - S = QN_1 \tag{5.2.9}$$

where Q and S are the quotient and the remainder, respectively, in dividing N_2 by N_1. Again, let R_Q and R_S be residues of Q and S for divisor A, respectively. Then

$$(R_2 - R_S) \bmod A = (R_Q R_1) \bmod A \tag{5.2.10}$$

An integer is represented in practice by a register with a fixed number of bits. Since there is a fixed number of bits, a sum can possibly overflow.

Assume that the sum of two integers N_1 and N_2 exceeds the maximum integer M, which the register can represent. Then $N_1 + N_2 - M$, instead of $N_1 + N_2$ itself, will be placed in the register and the residue will be calculated from this content. The residue thus calculated is, of course, not necessarily equal to $(R_1 + R_2) \bmod A$. The following theorem gives us the condition that guarantees the equality.

Theorem 1.   If and only if M is a multiple of A,

$$(N_1 + N_2 - M) \bmod A = (R_1 + R_2) \bmod A \qquad (5.2.11)$$

If a byte-sliced operation is employed, a circuit may be used repeatedly for a particular bit position of each byte. When this circuit becomes faulty, those bit positions of each byte will be affected. For example, consider residue code word 0010001101011010, of which the first 12 bits are information bits and the last four bits represent the residue for $A = 15$. Assume the code word is sliced into bytes of 4-bit width each and the output of a circuit used repeatedly for the last bit position of each byte is now stuck at 1. Then, the code word turns out to be

$$0011^*, \ 0011, \ 0101, \ 1011^*$$

where asterisks indicate errors introduced by the fault. This erroneous tuple is again a code word of the residue code and, therefore, the occurrence of the fault is not detected. The inverse residue code can avoid this sort of misdetection.

Low-cost code.   The complexity in real implementation of residue codes is greatly influenced by the choice of check base A. Consider an integer X of a form

$$X = (X_{n-1} X_{n-2} \cdots X_0) \qquad (5.2.12)$$

where X_i for $i = 0, 1, \ldots, n - 1$ is a byte of b-bit width. When the check base, A, is equal to $2^b - 1$, where b is an integer greater than 1, the residue calculation is simplified. This is because

$$X_c = X \bmod (2^b - 1) = \left(\sum_{i=0}^{n-1} X_i \right) \bmod (2^b - 1) \qquad (5.2.13)$$

The addition in modulo $2^b - 1$ can be performed well by a b-bit binary adder with the end-around carry. For example, consider the residue of $X = 101111001$ ($= 377D$) for $A = 111$ ($= 2^3 - 1 = 7D$). Since $b = 3$, X is partitioned into bytes of 3-bit width each, 101, 111, and 001. These are then added to each other with the end-around carry. (see Fig. 5.2.2). The residue code with check base $A = 2^b - 1$ is called the *low-cost code* [AVIZ71a]. It is practiced not only in specially designed fault-tolerant computer systems [AVIZ71b] but also in many commercial ones [AMDA].

Here, we see the resemblance between the 1's complement and the low-cost code. Consider, as an example, $X = 100010001$ and $A = 111$. By the definition itself, the residue of X for A is 0, while the 3-bit binary adder with the end-around carry will give 111 as its residue. Thus the residue 111 should be regarded equivalent to 0. A way to avoid this ambiguity is studied by Wakerly [WAKE76].

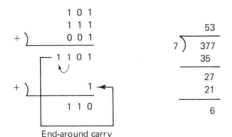

Figure 5.2.2   Calculation of the residue.

By a single error at the jth ($j = 0, 1, \ldots, b - 1$) bit position of a byte $\mathbf{X}_i$ ($i = 0, 1, \ldots, n - 1$), X changes to such $\hat{X}$ as

$$\hat{X} = X \pm 2^j 2^{ib} \tag{5.2.14}$$

Therefore,

$$\hat{\mathbf{X}}_c \equiv \hat{X} \bmod (2^b - 1) \neq \mathbf{X}_c$$

Further, when a single error occurs at a bit position of $\mathbf{X}_c$, the erroneous residue $\hat{\mathbf{X}}_c$ obviously differs from $X \bmod 2^b - 1$.

Hence any single error is detectable. The undetectability of double and triple errors is discussed in Section 5.2.2.

A single b-adjacent error at byte $\mathbf{X}_i$ ($i = 0, 1, \ldots, n - 1$) or $\mathbf{X}_c$ of a code word will change those bytes to $\hat{\mathbf{X}}_i$ or $\hat{\mathbf{X}}_c$, respectively, where

$$\hat{\mathbf{X}}_i = \mathbf{X}_i + \mathbf{e} \qquad \text{or} \qquad \hat{\mathbf{X}}_c = \mathbf{X}_c + \mathbf{e} \tag{5.2.15}$$

and

$$0 < |\mathbf{e}| \leq 2^b - 1 \tag{5.2.16}$$

When $\mathbf{X}_i$ or $\mathbf{X}_c$ changes from $(00 \cdots 0)$ to $(11 \cdots 1)$, or vice versa, *error magnitude* $|\mathbf{e}| = 2^b - 1$. Except in these cases, $\mathbf{e} \bmod 2^b - 1 \neq 0$. Therefore, the low-cost code with check base $2^b - 1$ can detect a single b-adjacent error, other than one which changes a byte from $(00 \cdots 0)$ to $(11 \cdots 1)$, or vice versa.

AN code.   Let N be an integer to be encoded in the *AN* code. Then the code word of N is the product of N and check base A of an integer. Thus the identification of information bits and check bits in a code word is impossible—that is, the *AN* code is not a systematic code in general. However, we can easily construct a systematic code from *AN* code. In fact, the inverse residue code is nothing but an *AN* code (see Chapter 4).

The code word of the addition of two integers N_1 and N_2 is $A(N_1 + N_2)$ by the definition itself. However, integers to be encoded are generally limited by the maximum value M. In this case, the code word of $N_1 + N_2$ is

$$A(N_1 + N_2) \bmod (AM)$$

The residue of any code word for check base A is, of course, 0. Therefore, any error yielding nonzero residue is detectable.

As we have seen, a single error at the ith bit position of a code word has an error magnitude of $\pm\, 2^i$. If A is not a power of 2,

$$\pm\, 2^i \bmod A \neq 0$$

and this error is detected accordingly. On the other hand, assume A to be 2^j. The undetectable error with magnitude $\pm\, 2^j$ can exist, provided that N is not identically equal to 0—a trivial case. Hence the necessary and sufficient condition for any single error being detectable in the nontrivial AN code is that the check base is not equal to a power of 2.

A more detailed discussion on the AN code is given in [RAO74].

Constant-weight code. The total number of 1s in a code word is defined as the *weight* of the code word. In the *constant-weight code*, every code word preserves its weight as a predetermined constant. If a code word consists of n bits with its weight k, this code is alternatively referred to as the k-out-of-n code or $\binom{n}{k}$ code.

Since $\binom{5}{2} = 10$, the $\binom{5}{2}$ code was used to represent decimal digits in early computers. Many self-checking and fail-safe circuits use the constant-weight code. The $\binom{n}{1}$ code, called the one-hot code, is used for address decoders. It may also be used for the state assignment of asynchronous sequential circuits.

Obviously, any unidirectional error causes the weight of a code word to differ from the predetermined constant.

5.2.2. Comparative Evaluation of the Undetectability of Double and Triple Errors in Checksum and Residue Codes

In this section the undetectability of double errors in the checksum code is considered first. This is readily extended to the case of the low-cost code. The undetectability of triple errors in both codes will be evaluated later.

Definition 4. By the undetectability of double (triple) errors, we mean the fraction of the number of undetectable double (triple) errors to the total number of all possible double (triple) errors.

Since a double error in a single byte of the checksum code is always detected, it suffices to consider such a double error that affects two bits in different bytes. Assume that the ith ($i = 0, 1, \ldots, b - 1$) bit and the jth ($j = 0, 1, \ldots, b - 1$) bit in two different information bytes are erroneous. The checksum reduces to

$$\hat{\mathbf{X}}_c = \{\mathbf{X}_c \pm (2^i \pm 2^j)\} \bmod 2^b \qquad (5.2.17)$$

For example, if the ith bit changes its value from 0 to 1 and the jth one from 1 to 0, $\hat{\mathbf{X}}_c$ will be

$$\hat{\mathbf{X}}_c = (\mathbf{X}_c + 2^i - 2^j) \bmod 2^b$$

Thus a double error affecting two bits in different information bytes is not detected, provided that

$$\pm (2^i \pm 2^j) \bmod 2^b = 0 \tag{5.2.18}$$

Even in the case where a double error affects two bits, one in an information byte and one in the check byte, the condition for this error being undetected is the same as Eq. (5.2.18). Thus Eq. (5.2.18) can be regarded as the general expression of the condition in which a double error is not detected.

By enumerating the number of cases that follow Eq. (5.2.18) as well as that of all possible double errors, the undetectability of double errors can be evaluated as follows:

Theorem 2 [USAS78].   The undetectability of double errors in the checksum code for $n \geq 2$ is given by

$$\mathbf{F}_2 = \frac{1}{2}\left(1 + \frac{1}{b}\right)\frac{n}{b(n + 1) - 1} \tag{5.2.19}$$

In the low-cost code, however, the two cases of $b = 2$ and $b > 2$ must be considered separately [WAKE78]. For $b > 2$ it suffices to consider such double errors that affect two different bytes, as in the case of the checksum code. Thus the condition in which double errors are undetectable is quite similar to Eq. (5.2.18) and is expressed as

$$\pm (2^i \pm 2^j) \bmod (2^b - 1) = 0 \tag{5.2.20}$$

For $b = 2$, in contrast, the cases of $\pm (2^i + 2^{i-1})$ for $i = 1$ and $\pm(2^i - 2^i)$ for $i = 0$ and 1 satisfy Eq. (5.2.20). Note here that some of the double errors in a single byte may fall in the first category. Taking this into account, we can enumerate the number of undetectable double errors.

Theorem 3 [WAKE78].   The undetectability of double-errors in the low-cost code for $n \geq 2$ is

$$\mathbf{F}_2 = \begin{cases} \dfrac{1}{2}\dfrac{n}{b(n + 1) - 1} & \text{when } b > 2 \tag{5.2.21} \\[3ex] \dfrac{1}{2} & \text{when } b = 2 \tag{5.2.22} \end{cases}$$

Similarly, we obtain the following theorems:

Theorem 4 [USAS78].   The undetectability of triple errors in the checksum code for $n \geq 2$ is evaluated by

$$F_3 = \frac{3}{4} \frac{(n + 1)n}{\{b(n + 1) - 1\}\{b(n + 1) - 2\}} \qquad \text{when } b > 1 \qquad (5.2.23)$$

Theorem 5.   The undetectability of triple errors in the low-cost code for $n \geq 2$ is evaluated by

$$F_3 = \frac{3}{4} \frac{(n + 1)n}{\{b(n + 1) - 1\}\{b(n + 1) - 2\}} \qquad \text{when } b > 3 \qquad (5.2.24)$$

$$= \frac{1}{4} \frac{(n + 1)(5n + 2)}{(3n + 2)(3n + 1)} \qquad \text{when } b = 3 \qquad (5.2.25)$$

$$= \frac{1}{4} \qquad \text{when } b = 2 \qquad (5.2.26)$$

Note that X_c of magnitude $2^b - 1$ is assumed to appear in the evaluation of Theorems 3 and 5.

5.2.3. Parity Prediction

Since the parity check is incorporated into many applications, various tricks for parity prediction will be described in detail. Use of parity prediction requires an alternative way to compute the output check bit of the logic circuit.

In a parity-checked logic circuit, the input and the output are generally encoded in a parity check code. The predicted value of the output check bit is computed from the values of input check bits, given the nature of logic/arithmetic operation performed by the circuit. The circuit operation is then checked by comparing this predicted value of the check bit with the one obtained from the output itself. The parity prediction in such simple arithmetic circuits as adders, multipliers, dividers, and counters will be discussed first. Next, a way to determine the value of output check bits in general logic circuits will be shown.

In the following discussion, the even parity scheme is assumed.

Parity prediction in arithmetic circuits

Binary adder

Let $\mathbf{a} = (a_{n-1} \cdots a_0 \, a_c)$ and $\mathbf{b} = (b_{n-1} \cdots b_0 \, b_c)$ be two inputs to a binary adder. $(a_{n-1} \cdots a_0)$ and $(b_{n-1} \cdots b_0)$ are two operands to be added, while a_c and b_c are check bits of $\mathbf{a}$ and $\mathbf{b}$, respectively. The encoded output of the adder will be $\mathbf{s} = (s_{n-1} \cdots s_0 \, s_c)$, where $(s_{n-1} \cdots s_0)$ are determined by the ordinary binary addition of $(a_{n-1} \cdots a_0)$ to $(b_{n-1} \cdots b_0)$, and s_c is the check bit for $(s_{n-1} \cdots s_0)$. Then

$$s_c = \sum_{i=0}^{n-1} s_i$$

$$= \sum_{i=0}^{n-1} a_i \oplus \sum_{i=0}^{n-1} b_i \oplus \sum_{i=0}^{n-1} c_i$$

where c_i $(i = 1, \ldots, n - 1)$ is the carry from the $(i - 1)$th bit position and c_0, being 0 in many cases, represents the carry from the outside of the adder.

Since $\sum_{i=0}^{n-1} a_i$ and $\sum_{i=0}^{n-1} b_i$ are equal to a_c and b_c, respectively, the equation above reduces to

$$s_c = a_c \oplus b_c \oplus \sum_{i=0}^{n-1} c_i \qquad (5.2.27)$$

The value of s_c thus predicted will be compared with the one defined by $\sum_{i=0}^{n-1} s_i$, as shown in Fig. 5.2.3.

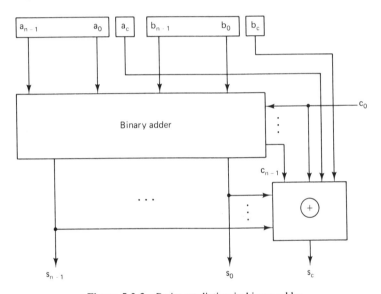

Figure 5.2.3 Parity prediction in binary adder.

In practice, special care must be taken, because an error at a carry may propagate through the circuit. For example, an error that changes c_i to $\hat{c}_i$ may also change some s_j and c_j $(j \geq i)$ to $\hat{s}_j$ and $\hat{c}_j$, respectively, so that the resulting equality

$$\hat{s}_{n-1} \oplus \cdots \oplus \hat{s}_i \oplus s_{i-1} \oplus \cdots \oplus s_0$$
$$= a_c \oplus b_c \oplus (\hat{c}_{n-1} \oplus \cdots \oplus \hat{c}_i \oplus c_{i-1} \oplus \cdots \oplus c_0)$$

would fail to indicate the occurrence of that error. In Fig. 5.2.4a, carry circuits are duplicated to avoid this failure and one of them is used for the adder, while the another is connected to the circuit for the parity prediction.

Instead of the basic ripple-carry adder above, many applications employ carry

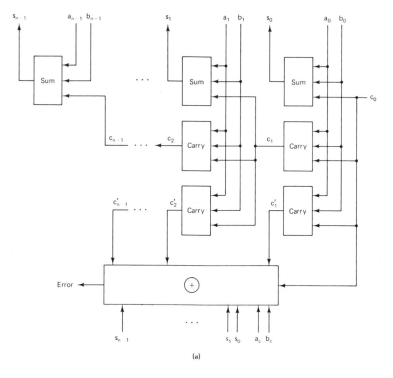

(a)

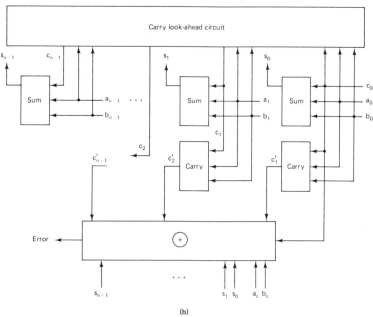

(b)

Figure 5.2.4   Parity-checked binary adder.

look-ahead adders, in which a similar parity prediction technique can be incorporated, as shown in Fig. 5.2.4b.

Addition based on the binary-coded-decimal code is usually carried out in two stages. In the first stage, two operands are added by a 4-bit binary adder, while the second stage modifies the result of the first stage to a form of the binary-coded-decimal code. The check bit is predicted at each stage, and therefore, the circuit configuration for the parity-checked decimal adder is as shown in Fig. 5.2.5.

Binary multiplier. The multiplication of $(a_3 a_2 a_1 a_0)$ and $(b_3 b_2 b_1 b_0)$ can be performed by an array of full/half adders, as shown in Fig. 5.2.6. This approach obviously requires a lot of hardware, but is feasible today with the growing demand for faster multipliers and decreasing LSI hardware cost. In Fig. 5.2.6,

$$p_0 = a_0 b_0$$

$$p_1 = a_0 b_1 \oplus a_1 b_0$$

$$p_2 = a_0 b_2 \oplus a_1 b_1 \oplus a_2 b_0 \oplus c_{1,1}$$

$$p_3 = a_0 b_3 \oplus a_1 b_2 \oplus a_2 b_1 \oplus a_3 b_0 \oplus c_{2,1} \oplus c_{1,2}$$

$$p_4 = a_1 b_3 \oplus a_2 b_2 \oplus a_3 b_1 \oplus c_{3,1} \oplus c_{2,2} \oplus c_{1,3}$$

$$p_5 = a_2 b_3 \oplus a_3 b_2 \oplus c_{3,2} \oplus c_{2,3} \oplus c_{1,4}$$

$$p_6 = a_3 b_3 \oplus c_{3,3} \oplus c_{2,4}$$

$$p_7 = c_{3,4}$$

Therefore, denoting the check bit for $(p_7 \cdots p_0)$ by p_c,

$$p_c = \sum_{i=0}^{7} p_i$$

$$= \left(\sum_{i=0}^{3} a_i \right) \left(\sum_{i=0}^{3} b_i \right) \oplus \sum_{i=1}^{3} \sum_{j=1}^{4} c_{i,j} \qquad (5.2.28)$$

$$= a_c b_c \oplus \sum_{i=1}^{3} \sum_{j=1}^{4} c_{i,j}$$

This appears to be an immediate extension to Eq. (5.2.27). Based on the Eq. (5.2.28), the parity-checked multiplier is constructed as shown in Fig. 5.2.7. Note that carry circuits are again duplicated. One of the duplicated carries is used to compute the product, while the other is connected to the EX-OR gate circuit, which predicts the value of p_c.

Binary divider. Figure 5.2.8a shows a cellular realization of dividers of the nonrestoring type, where $\mathbf{X} = (x_8 x_7 x_6 x_5 x_4 x_3 x_2 x_1 x_0)$ and $\mathbf{d} = (d_4 d_3 d_2 d_1 d_0)$ represent a dividend and a divisor, respectively. The sign bit of the dividend is represented by x_8,

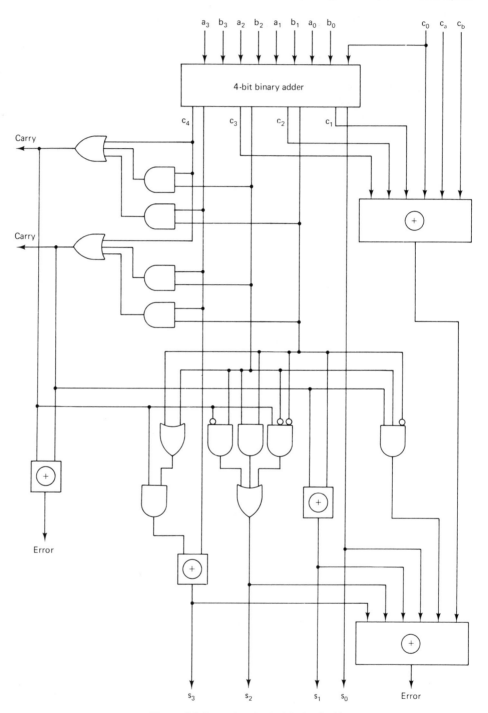

Figure 5.2.5   Parity-checked decimal adder.

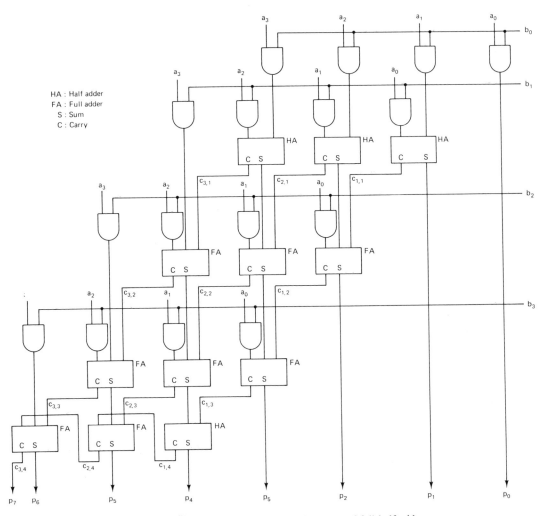

Figure 5.2.6 Multiplier using array of full-half adders.

while d_4 denotes the divisor's sign. When both the dividend and the divisor are positive, the sign bits are 0.

Each cell, denoted by $CAS(i,j)$, i, $j = 0$, 1, . . . , 4, is a controlled adder/subtractor, with detailed structure as illustrated in Fig. 5.2.8b. Then

$$a_{i,j} = q_{i+1} \oplus d_j \tag{5.2.29}$$

$$r_{i,j} = r_{i+1,j-1} \oplus c_{i,j} \oplus a_{i,j} \tag{5.2.30}$$

$$c_{i,j+1} = r_{i+1,j-1} \, c_{i,j} \vee c_{i,j} \, a_{i,j} \vee a_{i,j} \, r_{i+1,j-1} \tag{5.2.31}$$

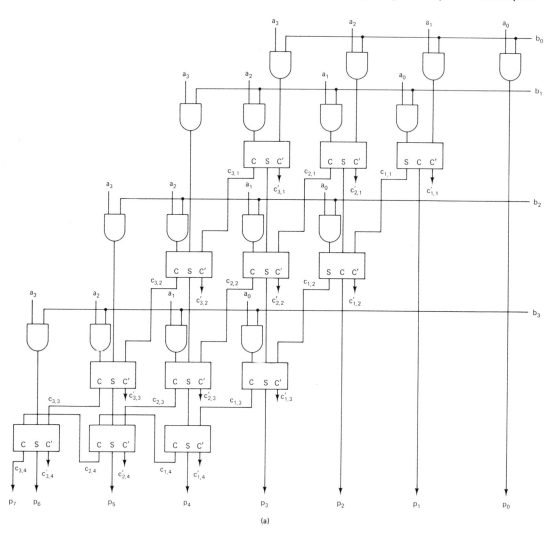

Figure 5.2.7 Parity-checked multiplier.

The row of $r_{i,j}$'s, $j = 0, 1, \ldots, 4$, constitutes a partial remainder $\mathbf{r}_i$, of which the leftmost bit is the sign bit of $\mathbf{r}_i$ and satisfies the following relation:

$$\bar{r}_{i,4} = q_i \qquad\qquad (5.2.32)$$

for $i = 0, 1, \ldots, 4$.

The value of q_{i+1} determines whether subtraction or addition should be performed to obtain $r_{i,j}$. When $q_{i+1} = 1$, subtraction is carried out by adding the one's complement of d_j together with carry $c_{i,j}$ from the lower-significant-bit position. Since the initial subtraction must always be carried out, $q_5 = 1$.

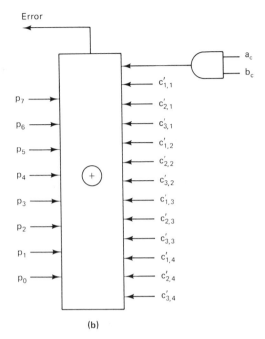

(b)

Figure 5.2.7 (cont.)

In Fig. 5.2.8a, some bits are given specific names as shown below. For $i, j = 0,$
$1, \ldots, 4,$

$$r_{0,j} = r_j \qquad r_{i,4} = r_{i+4}$$

$$r_{i+1,-1} = x_i \qquad r_{5,j-1} = x_{j+4} \qquad (5.2.33)$$

$$c_{i,5} = q_i$$

Noting these designations, we see

$$r_k = x_k \oplus \sum_{i+j=k} c_{i,j} \oplus \sum_{i+j=k} a_{i,j} \qquad (5.2.34)$$

for $k = 0, 1, \ldots, 8$. Therefore,

$$\sum_{k=0}^{8} r_k = \sum_{k=0}^{8} x_k \oplus \sum_{i=0}^{4} \sum_{j=0}^{4} c_{i,j} \oplus \sum_{i=0}^{4} \sum_{j=0}^{4} a_{i,j} \qquad (5.2.35)$$

However,

$$x_c = \sum_{i=0}^{8} x_k$$

$$d_c = \sum_{k=0}^{4} d_k$$

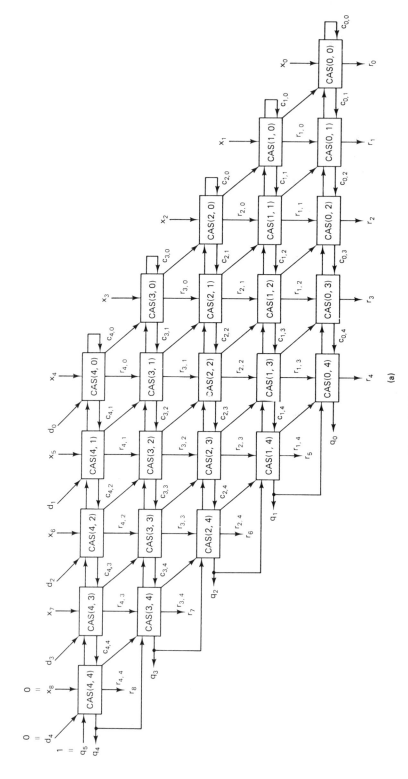

Figure 5.2.8 Cellular divider.

(a)

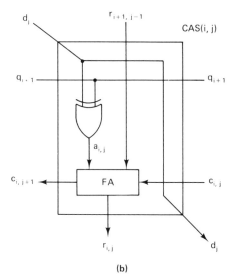

(b)   **Figure 5.2.8** (cont.)

$$\sum_{i=0}^{4} \sum_{j=0}^{4} c_{i,j} = \sum_{i=0}^{4} \sum_{j=1}^{4} c_{i,j} \oplus \sum_{i=0}^{4} q_{i+1}$$

$$\sum_{i=0}^{4} \sum_{j=0}^{4} a_{i,j} = \sum_{i=0}^{4} \sum_{j=0}^{4} (q_{i+1} \oplus d_j) = \sum_{i=0}^{4} q_{i+1} \oplus \sum_{j=0}^{4} d_j$$

Substituting these relations into Eq. (5.2.35), we obtain

$$\sum_{k=0}^{8} r_k = x_c \oplus d_c \oplus \sum_{i=0}^{4} \sum_{j=1}^{4} c_{i,j}$$

Hence

$$r_c \equiv \sum_{k=0}^{3} r_k = x_c \oplus d_c \oplus \sum_{i=0}^{4} \sum_{j=1}^{4} c_{i,j} \oplus \sum_{k=4}^{8} r_k \qquad (5.2.36)$$

In the implementation of the parity prediction above, the carry generation at each CAS (i,j) is again duplicated as shown in Fig. 5.2.9a. One of the duplicated carries is used for predicting the check bit of the final remainder. One can also predict q_c by using duplicated quotient bits.

In this example, the number of information bits of **d** is even. When it is odd (and accordingly **x** has two times as many information bits as **d**), Eq. (5.2.35) will vary slightly. In such cases, we need some means for detecting errors in **d**.

The parity prediction for dividers of the restoring type is a little more complicated. For those, and for dividers with the carry look-ahead and/or carry save mechanisms as well, refer to [FURU83].

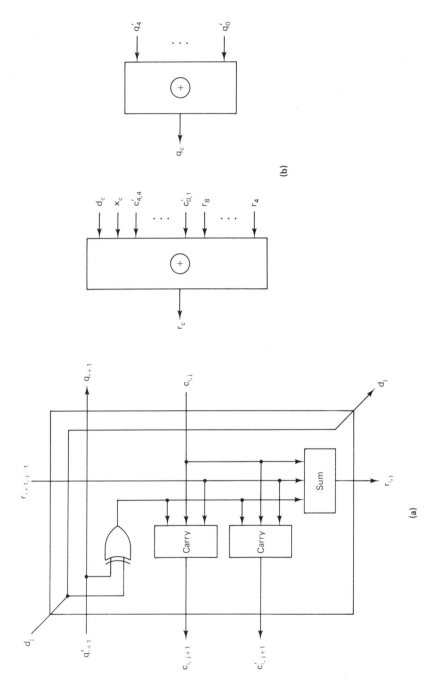

Figure 5.2.9 Modification of CAS (i, j) and parity prediction.

Binary counter.   A binary counter may be regarded as an adder, of which one input is the content of the counter itself and another input is the primary input x. Since x consists of only one bit and takes either value 1 or 0, its check bit, denoted by x_c, is always equal to x.

The counter changes its state upon receipt of $x = 1$, and therefore, we shall consider only that case.

Let p_n and p_{n+1} be check bits of the present and the next contents of the counter, respectively. Then, as in the case of adders,

$$p_{n+1} = p_n \oplus x_c \oplus p_c = p_n \oplus p_c \oplus 1 \qquad (5.2.37)$$

where p_c is the summation of carries in modulo 2. When the number of carries of value 1 is even, $p_c = 0$ and hence

$$p_{n+1} = p_n \oplus 1 = \overline{p_n} \qquad (5.2.38)$$

That is, the check bit of the counter must be complemented to indicate its new value. In the case where the number of carries of value 1 is odd, the check bit remains unchanged.

Figure 5.2.10 shows the structure of a parity-checked counter. Note that inputs t_2 and t_3 represent the carries, so their duplicated signals are counted by an EX-OR circuit. The check bit is realized by a toggle flip-flop, and its input is energized to change the state of the flip-flop, whenever Eq. (5.2.38) is satisfied.

Parity prediction in logic circuits

Complementation.   For convenience, let us denote the 1's (2's) complement of a tuple $(a_{n-1} \cdots a_0)$ by $(a_{n-1} \cdots a_0)^{c(1)} [(a_{n-1} \cdots a_0)^{c(2)}]$. Since $(a_{n-1} \cdots a_0)^{c(1)}$ is the one obtained simply by complementing each component, it is readily understood that the check bit of $(a_{n-1} \cdots a_0)^{c(1)}$ is either the same as or the complement of the check bit of the original form $(a_{n-1} \cdots a_0)$, depending on whether n is even or odd. However, the determination of the check bit of $(a_{n-1} \cdots a_0)^{c(2)}$ is a little more complicated, because 1 must be added to $(a_{n-1} \cdots a_0)^{c(1)}$ to obtain $(a_{n-1} \cdots a_0)^{c(2)}$, and the number of carries of value 1 generated in this addition must also be taken into account.

Several cases for the two's complement and the one's complement are summarized in Table 5.2.1.

Shift.   The cyclic rotation of information bits in any direction obviously does not affect the check bit. In shifting, there are two kinds: the arithmetic shift and the logical one. In the arithmetic left shift, value 0 will be put into the rightmost vacant bit position. In the arithmetic right shift, the original value at the leftmost bit position will remain the same. That is, the value of the sign bit of the shifted word is the same as that of the old one. The logical shift inserts the new value 0 in the vacant bit position at the leftmost or rightmost end of the word, regardless of the direction of the shift.

The value of the check bit will change, according to values of the shifted out bit and the inserted one. For example, suppose that a word $(a_{n-1} a_{n-2} \cdots a_1 a_0)$ is

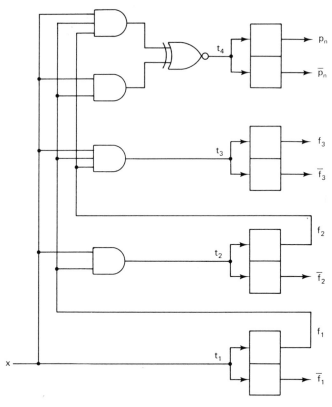

Figure 5.2.10 Parity-checked counter.

TABLE 5.2.1

(a)

Number of information bits	Check bit of the original form	
	0	1
Even	0	1
Odd	1	0

1's complement

(b)

Number of information bits	Check bit of the original form			
	0		1	
	Even-number carries	Odd-number carries	Even-number carries	Odd-number carries
Even	1	0	0	1
Odd	0	1	1	0

2's complement

changed to $(a_{n-1}\,a_{n-1}\,a_{n-2} \cdots a_1)$ by the arithmetic right shift. If $a_{n-1} = a_0$, the new check bit $a_c^{(1)}$ is the same as the old one, a_c. However, $a_c^{(1)}$ will be the complement of a_c when $a_{n-1} \neq a_0$. Thus $a_c^{(1)}$ can be expressed as follows.

$$a_c^{(1)} = a_c \oplus (a_{n-1} \oplus a_0)$$

Table 5.2.2 summarizes the change of the check bit in the arithmetic and the logical shifts.

TABLE 5.2.2

Rotate / shift	New check bit
Rotate	$a_c^{(1)} = a_c$
Arithmetic	
Left	$a_c^{(1)} = a_c \oplus a_{n-1}$
Right	$a_c^{(1)} = a_c \oplus a_{n-1} \oplus a_0$
Logical	
Left	$a_c^{(1)} = a_c \oplus a_{n-1}$
Right	$a_c^{(1)} = a_c \oplus a_0$

OR/AND operation.   Given binary tuples $\mathbf{z} = (z_{n-1} \cdots z_0)$, $\mathbf{y} = (y_{n-1} \cdots y_0)$ and $\mathbf{x} = (x_{n-1} \cdots x_0)$, assume that for $i = 0, 1, \ldots, n - 1$,

$$z_i = x_i \vee y_i \tag{5.2.39}$$

and

$$z_c = \sum_{i=0}^{n-1} z_i \tag{5.2.40}$$

$$y_c = \sum_{i=0}^{n-1} y_i \tag{5.2.41}$$

$$x_c = \sum_{i=0}^{n-1} x_i \tag{5.2.42}$$

Then

$$z_c = \sum_{i=0}^{n-1} (x_i \vee y_i) = \sum_{i=0}^{n-1} (x_i \oplus y_i \oplus x_i y_i)$$

$$= x_c \oplus y_c \oplus \sum_{i=0}^{n-1} (x_i y_i) \tag{5.2.43}$$

This means that a (bit-by-bit) OR operation can be checked by the circuit as shown in Fig. 5.2.11. $\mathbf{z}'$ is a vector obtained by a (bit-by-bit) AND operation.

This configuration looks almost the same as the straightforward duplication-comparison scheme, but differs from it with respect to the error-detecting capability

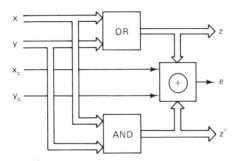

Figure 5.2.11   Parity-checked OR circuit.

at the input. In the simple duplication-comparison scheme, even a single error at an input line cannot be detected. Assume, however, that $(\hat{\mathbf{x}}\,\hat{x}_c)$ is not a code word of the parity check code. That is,

$$\hat{x}_c = \left(\sum_{i=0}^{n-1} \hat{x}_i \right) \oplus 1$$

Then

$$\sum_{i=0}^{n-1} \hat{z}_i = \hat{x}_c \oplus y_c \oplus \sum_{i=0}^{n-1} (\hat{x}_i y_i) \oplus 1 \qquad (5.2.44)$$

and therefore the occurrence of the error is always indicated by $e = 1$ in the circuit of Fig. 5.2.11. Because of the configurational symmetry, the circuit of Fig. 5.2.11 may be regarded as a parity-checked AND circuit.

The Reed-Muller code can be used for providing parity prediction in AND/OR operation [PRAD72b].

General logic.   Consider, as a general case, that output $\mathbf{z}$ of a circuit is determined by a function $\mathbf{F}$ of $\mathbf{x}^0, \mathbf{x}^1, \ldots, \mathbf{x}^{m-1}$ as shown in Fig. 5.2.12a. $\mathbf{F}$ is $(F_{n-1}, F_{n-2}, \ldots, F_0)$, where for $\mathbf{x}^i = (x_{n-1}^i \; x_{n-2}^i \cdots x_0^i)$, $i = 0, 1, \ldots, m-1$, and $\mathbf{z} = (z_{n-1} \cdots z_0)$,

$$z_j = F_j(x_j^{m-1}, x_j^{m-2}, \cdots, x_j^0) \qquad j = 0, 1, \ldots, n-1 \qquad (5.2.45)$$

It is always possible to decompose F_j in such a way [KHOD79] that

$$F_j(x_j^{m-1}, x_j^{m-2}, \ldots, x_j^0)$$

$$= x_j^{m-1} \oplus x_j^{m-2} \oplus \cdots \oplus x_j^0 \oplus R_j(x_j^{m-1}, x_j^{m-2}, \ldots, x_j^0) \qquad (5.2.46)$$

since $R_j(x_j^{m-1}, \ldots, x_j^0)$ can be defined by

$$R_j(x_j^{m-1}, x_j^{m-2}, \ldots, x_j^0)$$

$$= F_j(x_j^{m-1}, x_j^{m-2}, \ldots, x_j^0) \oplus x_j^{m-1} \oplus \cdots \oplus x_j^0 \qquad (5.2.47)$$

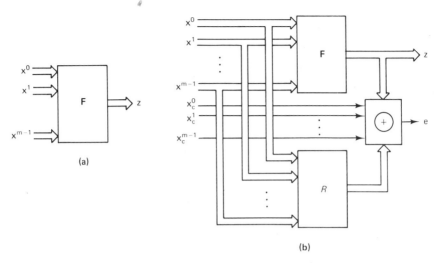

Figure 5.2.12   Parity check for a general logic circuit.

Therefore, the output check bit, z_c, is predicted by

$$z_c = \sum_{j=0}^{n-1} z_j = \sum_{j=0}^{n-1} \{x_j^{m-1} \oplus \cdots \oplus x_j^0 \oplus R_j(x_j^{m-1}, \ldots, x_j^0)\}$$

$$= \sum_{k=0}^{m-1} x_c^k \oplus \sum_{j=0}^{n-1} R_j(x_j^{m-1}, \ldots, x_j^0) \tag{5.2.48}$$

where x_c^k is the check bit for $\mathbf{x}^k$. Thus output $\mathbf{z}$ is checked by the circuit of Fig. 5.2.12b. For details of other error-detecting circuits, refer to [SELL68].

5.3. SELF-CHECKING CIRCUITS

5.3.1. Incentive and Definitions

Incentive.   As shown in the preceding sections, encoding the output of a circuit is certainly effective for the detection of errors if they manifest themselves in the output. However, the utilization of error-detecting codes does not necessarily guarantee the detection of a fault developed in the circuit.

Here the error and the fault must be carefully distinguished from each other. The error is an incorrect outcome due to a fault, while the fault is a change of behavioral nature of the circuit under consideration. Although a circuit can tolerate the development of faults for a while, subsequent occurrence of more faults may have an adverse effect on circuit operation.

In the circuit of Fig. 5.3.1, it is assumed that the primary input $\mathbf{x}$ to a functional unit and its output $\mathbf{y}$ are encoded in an error detecting code—say, the parity check

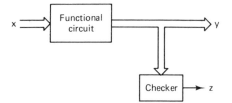

Figure 5.3.1 Output checker.

code. The existence of an error in **y** is accordingly indicated by z of value 1. Because of this encoding, however, the range of **y** is indeed limited to a subset of the set of all possible l-tuples, $\{0, 1\}^l$, where l is the number of variables employed to represent **y**. This limitation of the output range (input domain to the checker) can compromise the detection of a fault.

Consider, for example, the parity checker with three inputs a, b, and c as shown in Fig. 5.3.2. Inputs a and b represent information bits, while input c is the check bit under the even parity scheme. Therefore, the normal input combinations of a, b, and c cover only those tuples as shown in Fig. 5.3.3. By normal inputs, we mean inputs applied during the normal operation. For any of these input combinations, output z must, of course, be 0. Therefore, outputs of G_4, G_5, and G_6 should always take value 1 in the fault-free operation of the checker. This implies, however, that stuck-at-1 faults at any output of these gates would be overlooked during normal input excitation.

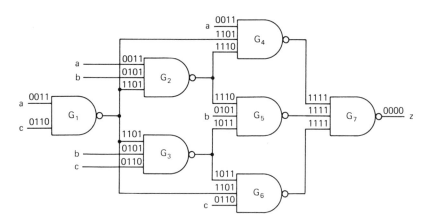

Figure 5.3.2 Three bit parity checker.

a	b	c	z
0	0	0	0
0	1	1	0
1	0	1	0
1	1	0	0

Figure 5.3.3 Input domain.

These stuck-at-1 faults give no adverse effect to the normal circuit operation, in the sense that the checker responds correctly to the normal input. However, they make the checker function incomplete. For example, consider that $(abc) = (010)$ is applied erroneously to the checker. Because of the stuck-at-1 fault at the output of G_5, output z is not 1, but 0.

Therefore, it is desirable for checkers to have the capability to test for the occurrence of a fault within the checker by a normal input, as well as to detect an error at the input itself. This is the motivation for investigating the synthesis of self-checking checkers.

Further, by the use of self-checking techniques, transient and permanent faults are detected during normal operation, and software diagnostic programs will be simplified or eliminated.

The original idea of self-checking circuits can be traced back to the paper by Carter and Schneider [CART68]. The concept was formulated later by Anderson and Metze [ANDE73] and defined in more detail by Wakerly as the totally/partially self-checking circuits [WAKE74], [WAKE78]. In this chapter we simply refer to them as self-checking circuits, since the partially self-checking circuits are not considered here.

Definitions.   Let us call the input domain and the output range in normal operation the input code space and the output code space, respectively. The input code space will be designated by X, while Z represents the output code space. The output of a circuit under consideration is defined by a logic function $z(\mathbf{x})$ of input $\mathbf{x}$ in the fault-free operation. $z(\mathbf{x})$ will change to $\hat{z}_f(\mathbf{x})$ if the fault f develops in the circuit. We assume a prescribed set, F, of faults which may develop in the circuit.

Definition 5.   A circuit is called *fault-secure* with respect to F if and only if

$$\hat{z}_f(\mathbf{x}) \notin Z \qquad \text{or} \qquad z_f(\mathbf{x}) = z(\mathbf{x}) \tag{5.3.1}$$

for any $\mathbf{x} \in X$ and $f \in F$.

This definition implies that $\hat{z}_f(\mathbf{x})$ never takes an incorrect output value in Z. Inversely, when $\hat{z}_f(\mathbf{x})$ belongs to the output code space, it necessarily takes a correct value.

Definition 6.   A circuit is called *self-testing* with respect to F if and only if

$$\forall f \in F, \quad \exists \mathbf{x} \in X, \quad \hat{z}_f(\mathbf{x}) \notin Z \tag{5.3.2}$$

By observing an output that does not belong to the output code space, we know that a fault has occurred in the circuit. Therefore, Eq. (5.3.2) means that whether the circuit contains a fault of F or not can always be tested by at least one normal input.

Based on the two definitions above, the self-checking circuit is defined as follows.

Definition 7.   A circuit is *self-checking* with respect to F if and only if it is fault-secure and self-testing.

The following definitions concern self-checking checkers:

Definition 8.   A circuit is called *code-disjoint* if and only if

$$\forall \mathbf{x} \notin X, \qquad z(\mathbf{x}) \notin Z \qquad\qquad (5.3.3)$$

The code disjointness can be viewed as a formalization of the capability to detect input errors.

Definition 9.   A circuit is the *self-checking checker* if and only if it is self-checking and code-disjoint.

There is a class of circuits called fail-safe circuits in close connection with the self-checking circuit. In the context of fail-safe circuits, a set of the so-called safe outputs is defined. This set, designated by Z_s, may or may not be a subset of Z. Then the definition of fail-safe circuits is as follows:

Definition 10.   A circuit is called *fail-safe* with respect to F if and only if

$$\forall f \in F, \quad \forall \mathbf{x} \in X, \qquad \hat{z}_f(\mathbf{x}) = z(\mathbf{x}) \quad \text{or} \quad \hat{z}_f(\mathbf{x}) \in Z_s \qquad (5.3.4)$$

When $Z_s \cap Z = \emptyset$, the condition above is the same as that of the fault-secureness. The clear difference between the self-checking circuit and the fail-safe circuit is that the existence of the test by at least one normal input is required in the former, but not in the latter. The realization of fail-safe sequential circuits will be discussed in Section 5.7.

5.3.2. Fault Models and Basic Structure

Fault models.   The synthesis of self-checking circuits is obviously closely connected with the type of faults involved. Based on physical conditions, faults are modeled as stuck-type faults, short/open-circuited faults, bridging faults, intermittent/ stationary faults, and so on. Among those, the most popular model is the stuck type of fault. That is, a faulty signal line is assumed to be stuck at a constant value e, say, 1 or 0. The stuck-at-e fault at a line l will be denoted by l/e. Throughout this section we assume the occurrence of a single stuck-type fault.

The implication of l/e differs slightly, depending on whether l is the input or the output line of a gate. When faulty line l_1 is the output line of a gate, as shown in Fig. 5.3.4a, all fan-out lines connected to l_1 are assumed to be stuck simultaneously at the same value. In contrast, let input line l_{11} of gate G_2 be stuck at e, as shown in Fig. 5.3.4b. Input line l_{12} of G_3 is assumed to carry the correct signal, even if it is connected to l_{11} at the output of G_1.

This might look strange. However, the input-line fault in this context does not model the actual stuck line, but represents the manifestation of the internal defect of a gate at its input terminal. For example, suppose that an input line of a TTL NAND gate is disconnected within the chip. This fault then gives the same effect as the stuck-at-1 fault at that input line only. The treatment of a stuck-type fault at the input

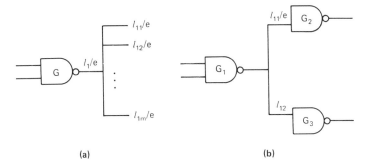

Figure 5.3.4   Output-line/input-line faults.

line of a gate is generally more complicated than that of a stuck-type fault at the output line, because the number of cases to be examined for the former fault is generally greater than that for the latter.

Basic structure.   The following requirements on the basic structure of self-checking circuits is the immediate consequence of Definition 7.

Theorem 6 [CART68].   A self-checking circuit needs to have at least two output lines, each of which must take values 1 and 0 during normal operation.

Proof: Assume the circuit to have only one output line. If this line takes only one value, say, 1 during normal operation, the stuck-at-1 fault at this line cannot be detected by any normal input. Therefore, the output line must take values 1 and 0 according to the normal excitation of the input. This means, however, that the output noncode space is null, and therefore, the condition for self-testing is by no means satisfied. Q.E.D.

5.3.3. Self-Checking Checkers

Parity checker [CART68].   As an example, suppose that $(x_8 x_7 \cdots x_0)$ represents a code word of the odd parity scheme. Divide the set of variables into two groups, say, $\{x_8, x_6, x_4, x_2, x_0\}$ and $\{x_7, x_5, x_3, x_1\}$, and connect variables of each group to the inputs of the tree of EX-OR gates as shown in Fig. 5.3.5.

In the normal operation, the number of 1's in the former group is odd and that in the latter is even, or vice versa. Therefore, the pair of two outputs, $(z_2 z_1)$, will take (10) or (01), but never (00) and (11). That is, $Z = \{(01), (10)\}$.

If a gate, say G_2, generates incorrect output, this erroneous signal always propagates to z_2 to change its value. Therefore, $(z_2 z_1)$ will take (00) or (11) in this case, which does not belong to Z. Thus this circuit evidently satisfies the condition of the fault-secureness.

Note that an arbitrary combination of input values at any gate can be applied by

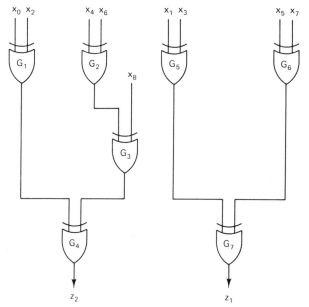

Figure 5.3.5 Self-checking parity checker.

a normal excitation at the primary input. Therefore, when a fault occurs at a gate, there exists at least one normal primary input to manifest an error at one of the two outputs. Therefore, this circuit is self-testing.

Obviously, this circuit is code-disjoint.

Constant-weight code checkers

$\binom{2k}{k}$ *code checker.* Among constant-weight codes, a code where k is equal or nearly equal to half n is the most interesting, because it has the greatest number of code words for a given n. Therefore, the self-checking checkers for $\binom{2k}{k}$ code will be described first.

Figure 5.3.6 shows the circuit configuration of the checker [ANDE73]. In this circuit, $2k$ input variables are divided into two groups as $\{a_k, a_{k-1}, \ldots, a_1\}$ and $\{b_k, b_{k-1}, \ldots, b_1\}$. Two output functions z_2 and z_1 are defined as follows:

$$z_2 = \bigvee_{i=0}^{k} T(k_a \geq i)\,T(k_b \geq k - i) \qquad \text{for odd } i \qquad (5.3.5)$$

$$z_1 = \bigvee_{i=0}^{k} T(k_a \geq i)\,T(k_b \geq k - i) \qquad \text{for even } i \qquad (5.3.6)$$

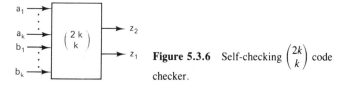

Figure 5.3.6 Self-checking $\binom{2k}{k}$ code checker.

where the operator $\bigvee$ performs ORing on product terms $T(k_a \geq i)T(k_b \geq k - i)$ over the indicated i's. $T(k_a \geq i)$ is a threshold function. That is, it takes value 1 if and only if weight k_a of tuple $(a_k a_{k-1} \cdots a_1)$ is equal to or greater than i. $T(k_b \geq k - i)$ is the similar function.

In the case of $k = 3$,

$$z_2 = T(k_a \geq 1)T(k_b \geq 2) \bigvee T(k_a \geq 3)T(k_b \geq 0)$$

$$= (a_3 \bigvee a_2 \bigvee a_1)(b_3 b_2 \bigvee b_2 b_1 \bigvee b_1 b_3) \bigvee a_3 a_2 a_1 \qquad (5.3.7)$$

$$z_1 = T(k_a \geq 0)T(k_b \geq 3) \bigvee T(k_a \geq 2)T(k_b \geq 1)$$

$$= b_3 b_2 b_1 \bigvee (a_3 a_2 \bigvee a_2 a_1 \bigvee a_1 a_3)(b_3 \bigvee b_2 \bigvee b_1) \qquad (5.3.8)$$

Therefore, the circuit is as shown in Fig. 5.3.7a.

Equations (5.3.7) and (5.3.8) can also be decomposed, as shown below.

$$z_2 = T(k_a \geq 1)\{T(k_b \geq 2) \bigvee T(k_a \geq 3)\}$$

$$z_1 = T(k_b \geq 1)\{T(k_a \geq 2) \bigvee T(k_b \geq 3)\}$$

Based on these equations, we obtain the circuit of Fig. 5.3.7b.

In the normal operation of the circuit, k_a and k_b vary from 0 to k, respectively, keeping the following relationship:

$$k_a + k_b = k \qquad (5.3.9)$$

First, assume that k_a is equal to an odd integer i, and accordingly $k_b = k-i$. $T(k_a \geq i) = 1$ and $T(k_b \geq k-i) = 1$, implying that $z_2 = 1$. On the other hand, for an even integer $j > i = k_a$, $k - j < k - i = k_b$, implying $T(k_a \geq j) = 0$. Further, if $j < i$, $k - j > k - i$ and $T(k_b \geq k - j) = 0$. Thus $z_1 = 0$. It can similarly be proved that $z_2 = 0$ and $z_1 = 1$, when k_a is equal to an even integer. Hence the output code space is $\{(01), (10)\}$.

If an output, say z_2, takes erroneous value, $(z_2 z_1)$ will change to (00) or (11), which is obviously out of the code space (fault-secure).

It is rather complicated to verify the self-testing property of the circuit. For this purpose, the circuit configuration of z_2 is redrawn as shown in Fig. 5.3.8., where each threshold function of $T(k_a \geq i)$ and $T(k_b \geq k - i)$ is assumed to be realized by a two-level AND-OR network. Input variables to an AND gate in $T(k_a \geq i)$ are i variables taken out of a_k, a_{k-1}, . . . , and a_1, while $k - i$ variables out of b_k, b_{k-1}, . . . , and b_1 are connected to an AND gate of $T(k_b \geq k - i)$. Thus $\binom{k}{i}$ AND gates are used in $T(k_a \geq i)$, while $T(k_b \geq k - i)$ has $\binom{k}{k-i}$ ANDs.

Since z_2 takes both values of 1 and 0 during normal input excitations, any stuck-at-1 or stuck-at-0 fault at the output line of OR gate G_0 can be tested by a normal input. The stuck-at-1 fault at the output line of an AND gate, say, G_A, is equivalent to that of G_0, and hence we examine the stuck-at-0 fault at the output line of G_A. There exists, however, such a normal input that only the output line of G_A takes value 1 and others take value 0. Thus it tests this fault as well as the stuck-at-0 fault at an input line of G_A.

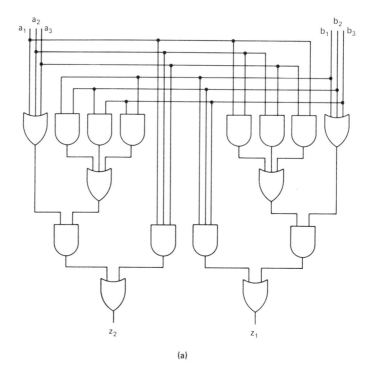

(a)

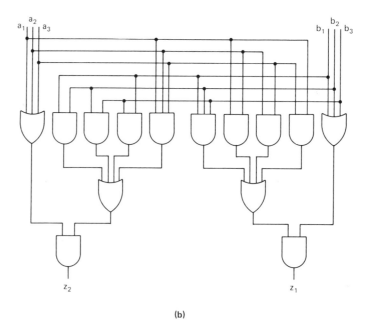

(b)

Figure 5.3.7 Self-checking $\binom{6}{3}$ code checker.

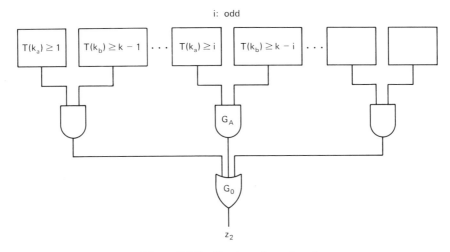

Figure 5.3.8 Circuit configuration of z_2.

Note that the pair of two input lines of any AND gate takes (01) or (10), but never (00), when z_2 is 0. This means that the stuck-at-1 fault at the input line of an AND gate can be tested as well.

The remaining faults to be examined in $T(k_a \geq i)$ are stuck-at-0 faults at output lines and stuck-at-1 faults at input lines of AND gates in Fig. 5.3.9, because other faults are equivalent to those already examined.

It is possible to have only the output of an AND gate, with its input variables, $a_{\mu 1}, a_{\mu 2}, \ldots,$ and $a_{\mu i}$, taking value 1 and all other AND gates taking outputs of value 0. This primary input tests $l_2/0$.

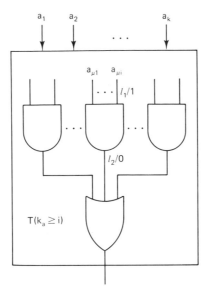

Figure 5.3.9 Faults in $T(k_a \geq i)$.

In order to test $l_1/1$, it suffices to apply such input combination with $k_a < i$ that

$$a_{\mu 1} = a_{\mu 2} = \cdots = a_{\mu(i-1)} = 1$$

$$a_{\mu i} = 0$$

The total number of tests for detecting all of these faults accounts for 2^k.

The proof of the code-disjointness is left to the reader as an exercise.

It might look possible to construct self-checking checkers for general $\binom{n}{k}$ codes, following equations similar to Eqs. (5.3.5) and (5.3.6). However, n must be equal to $2k$, if the circuit follows the same configuration as shown in Figs. 5.3.8 and 5.3.9 [ANDE73]. A method to bypass this limitation will be shown later.

$\binom{n}{1}$ **code checker.**   It has been shown that a $\binom{n}{1}$ code checker with a self-checking property can be constructed by using a code converter from the $\binom{n}{1}$ code to the $\binom{2k}{k}$ code and by connecting this converter to the self-checking $\binom{2k}{k}$ code checker [ANDE73]. This realization, however, requires many gates and multiple logic levels.

Izawa showed a different construction technique. The basic idea was to convert the $\binom{n}{1}$ code to the $\binom{n}{n-1}$ code and then lead it to the output of the $\binom{2}{1}$ code [IZAW81]. His realization requires only three logic levels with at most $n + 2 + \lfloor n/2 \rfloor(1 + n - 2\lfloor n/2 \rfloor)$ gates in total. Here $\lfloor x \rfloor$ is the maximum integer not greater than x.

An example of Izawa's method is illustrated in Fig. 5.3.10, which shows the detailed structure of the $\binom{8}{1}$ code checker. Note that eight input variables are divided into two groups $\{x_3, x_2, x_1, x_0\}$ and $\{x_7, x_6, x_5, x_4\}$, of which each variable is connected to an input of the corresponding OR gate. Further, two variables from each group are paired with each other. For example, x_0 makes a pair with x_4, x_1 with x_5, x_2 with x_6, and x_3 with x_7. One of the inputs, say of G_0, which is associated with x_0, is connected to G_4. This G_4 is associated with x_4, the counterpart of x_0. These two inputs are commonly driven by G_{04}. Input variables of G_{04} are all of those except x_0 and x_4. We call such gates as G_{04} the shared gates in the subsequent reference. For other gates, inputs are connected similarly.

Numbers attached to each line represent their signal values under the condition of $x_0 = 1$ and $x_1 = x_2 = \cdots = x_7 = 0$. Observe that outputs of G_0 through G_7 make a code word of $\binom{8}{7}$ code. AND gates G_8 and G_9 convert this code word into $(z_2\, z_1) = (01)$.

Clearly, each fault at input or output lines of G_0 through G_9 can be tested by some of normal input excitations. Further, the stuck-at-1 fault at the output line of G_{04} and, accordingly, at an input line of this gate will change the output of G_4 from 0 to 1, and

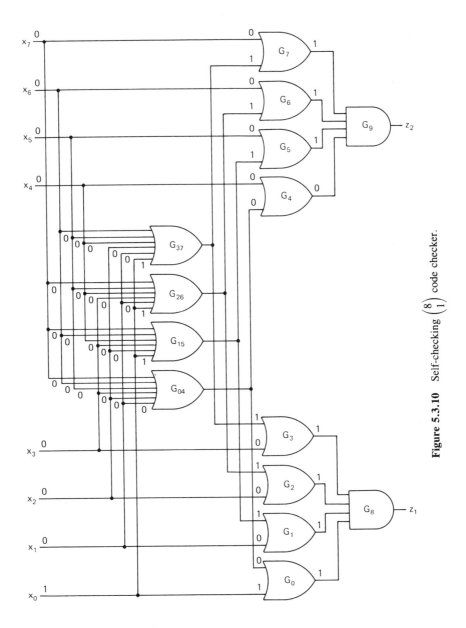

Figure 5.3.10 Self-checking $\binom{8}{1}$ code checker.

$(z_2\, z_1)$ from (01) to (11) as well. On the other hand, the stuck-at-0 fault at the output line of G_{15} and, accordingly, at the input line of this gate will change the output of G_1, resulting in $(z_2\, z_1) = (00)$. Because of the symmetry of the circuit structure, we conclude that other faults at input or output lines of any shared gates can be tested by other normal inputs.

When n is an odd integer greater than 3, the circuit has a different structure. An example of $n = 7$ is shown in Fig. 5.3.11. In this figure, the output of G_i for $i = 0$, 1, . . . , 6 represents an OR expression with all variables except x_i, as in the case of an even n. Namely,

$$
\begin{array}{ll}
G_{\bar{0}}: & x_1 \vee x_2 \vee x_3 \vee x_4 \vee x_5 \vee x_6 \\[4pt]
G_{\bar{1}}: & x_0 \qquad\ \ \vee x_2 \vee x_3 \vee x_4 \vee x_5 \vee x_6 \\[4pt]
G_{\bar{2}}: & x_0 \vee x_1 \qquad\ \ \vee x_3 \vee x_4 \vee x_5 \vee x_6 \\[4pt]
G_{\bar{3}}: & x_0 \vee x_1 \vee x_2 \qquad\ \ \vee x_4 \vee x_5 \vee x_6 \\[4pt]
G_{\bar{4}}: & x_0 \vee x_1 \vee x_2 \vee x_3 \qquad\ \ \vee x_5 \vee x_6 \\[4pt]
G_{\bar{5}}: & x_0 \vee x_1 \vee x_2 \vee x_3 \vee x_4 \qquad\ \ \vee x_6 \\[4pt]
G_{\bar{6}}: & x_0 \vee x_1 \vee x_2 \vee x_3 \vee x_4 \vee x_5
\end{array}
$$

To factor these expressions, shared gates G_{04} through G_{36} are used. They are made of pairs of variables as shown in Fig. 5.3.12. The factorization is as follows: $G_{\bar{i}}$ for $i = 0$, 1, and 2 is factored by outputs of G_{04}, G_{15}, and G_{26}, except $G_{i(i+4)}$. In place of $G_{i(i+4)}$, the output of $G_{3(i+4)}$ is added.

On the other hand, $G_{\bar{3}}$ is factored by all outputs of G_{04}, G_{15}, and G_{26}.

For $G_{\bar{i}}$, $i = 4, 5$, and 6, $G_{3(i+1)}$ (when $i + 1$ equals 7, however, G_{34} must be used instead of G_{37}), G_{04}, G_{15}, and G_{26}, except $G_{(i-4)i}$ are used. Further, in place of $G_{(i-4)i}$, only x_{i-4} is added.

Thus, the above expressions turn out to be

$$
\begin{array}{ll}
G_{\bar{0}}: & (x_3 \vee x_4) \vee (x_1 \vee x_5) \vee (x_2 \vee x_6) \\[4pt]
G_{\bar{1}}: & (x_0 \vee x_4) \vee (x_3 \vee x_5) \vee (x_2 \vee x_6) \\[4pt]
G_{\bar{2}}: & (x_0 \vee x_4) \vee (x_1 \vee x_5) \vee (x_3 \vee x_6) \\[4pt]
G_{\bar{3}}: & (x_0 \vee x_4) \vee (x_1 \vee x_5) \vee (x_2 \vee x_6) \\[4pt]
G_{\bar{4}}: & (x_3 \vee x_5) \vee x_0 \vee (x_1 \vee x_5) \vee (x_2 \vee x_6) \\[4pt]
G_{\bar{5}}: & (x_3 \vee x_6) \vee (x_0 \vee x_4) \vee x_1 \vee (x_2 \vee x_6) \\[4pt]
G_{\bar{6}}: & (x_3 \vee x_4) \vee (x_0 \vee x_4) \vee (x_1 \vee x_5) \vee x_2
\end{array}
$$

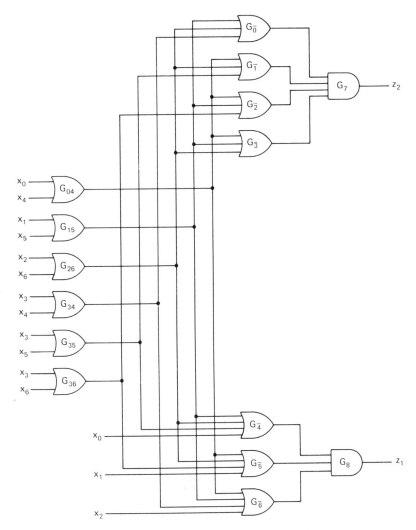

Figure 5.3.11   Self-checking 1-out-of-7 code checker.

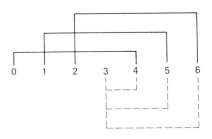

Figure 5.3.12   Factorization.

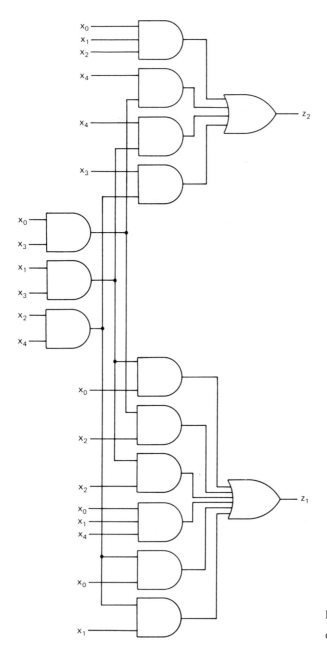

Figure 5.3.13   Self-checking $\binom{5}{3}$ code checker.

$\binom{n}{k}$ *code checker.*   Izawa's approach can be extended to the more general case of $\binom{n}{k}$ codes. An example of the construction of the self-checking $\binom{5}{3}$ code checker is illustrated in Fig. 5.3.13. For details of the factorization of input variables for obtaining shared gates and the verification of the self-checking property, refer to [NANY83].

Another design technique is to convert the $\binom{n}{k}$ code to the $\binom{n'}{1}$ code, where n' is equal to $\binom{n}{k}$. This code is then checked by the self-checking $\binom{n'}{1}$ code checker, as shown in Fig. 5.3.14. The conversion of the $\binom{n}{k}$ code to the $\binom{n'}{1}$ code can be accomplished simply by a row of k-input AND gates, of which the total number is obviously $\binom{n}{k}$.

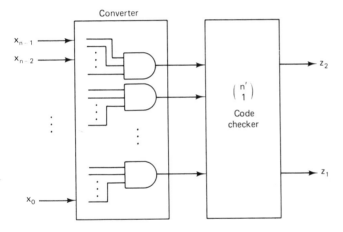

Figure 5.3.14   Self-checking realization of $\binom{n}{k}$ code checker.

Marouf and Friedman argued the case where n' less than $\binom{n}{k}$ could be chosen [MARO78b]. Self-checking checkers for the specific classes of k-out-of-$(2k + 1)$, $(k + 1)$-out-of-$(2k + 1)$, and k-out-of-$(pk + l)$ codes have been investigated by Reddy [REDD74] and Wang and Avizienis [WANG79].

Berger code checker.   The basic idea of self-checking checkers for the Berger code is to generate the replicated check bits of values complementary to the original ones and to compare them by a two-rail comparator. The circuit configuration is illustrated in Fig. 5.3.15, where X_I and X_c represent information and check bits, respectively. The check bits generator can be any type of irredundant combinational circuit.

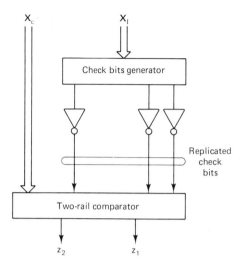

Figure 5.3.15 Self-checking Berger code checker.

Let $|\mathbf{X}_I|$ and $|\mathbf{X}_c|$ be numbers of information and check bits, respectively. Then, any fault adversely affecting the functional behavior of the check bits generator is detected by at least one normal input excitation, since $\mathbf{X}_I$ normally ranges over all $2^{|\mathbf{X}_I|}$ input combinations. However, Ashjaee and Reddy pointed out that special care must be paid to the test for a fault in the two-rail comparator, when $|\mathbf{X}_I| \neq 2^{|\mathbf{X}_c|} - 1$ [ASHJ77]. If this is the case, $\mathbf{X}_c$ (and its complemented counterpart $\overline{\mathbf{X}}_c$) may not exhaust all combinations, and therefore, the self-testing property may not be assured.

For example, the Berger code for $|\mathbf{x}_I| = |\mathbf{x}_C| = 2$ is $\{00\underline{10}, 01\underline{01}, 10\underline{01}, 11\underline{00}\}$, where underlines indicate check bits. The signal values at the lines of the two-rail comparator for these check bits are shown in Fig. 5.3.16. Input signals not underlined are the replicated check bits. Note that G_3 takes only the value 0, and therefore, the stuck-at-0 fault at the output line of this gate cannot be tested by any of the normal input excitations. Ashjaee and Reddy showed a way to detour this difficulty, introducing a code "equivalent" to the Berger code.

Marouf and Friedman [MARO78a] revealed the detailed structure of the check bits generator even for the case of $|\mathbf{x}_I| \neq 2^{|\mathbf{x}_c|} - 1$, giving a way of testing the generator and the comparator itself. Their method of constructing the generator is based on the interconnection of half/full adders. When $|\mathbf{x}_I| = 2^{|\mathbf{x}_c|-1}$, they use a special comparator with four output lines, claiming that no self-checking two-output-line comparator has been discovered.

Two-rail code checker. In the two-rail scheme, a signal is represented by a pair of two variables $(x_i\, x_i')$, of which each component is complementary to the other. Therefore, $(x_i\, x_i')$ takes only such tuples as (01) and (10) in normal operation. This concept is readily extended to the case of a tuple of signals. That is, an n-tuple of signals $(x_{n-1} \cdots x_0)$ is represented by $((x_{n-1}\, x_{n-1}')(x_{n-2}\, x_{n-2}') \cdots (x_0\, x_0'))$, where the equalities $x_{n-1} = \bar{x}_{n-1}'$, $x_{n-2} = \bar{x}_{n-2}'$, . . . , $x_0 = \bar{x}_0'$ must hold. The two-rail code checker is to check these conditions.

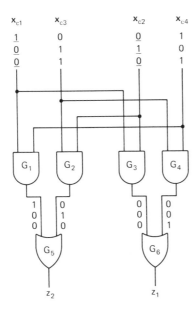

Figure 5.3.16   Undetectable stuck-at-0 fault in two-rail comparator.

The two-rail code checker for $n = 2$ is shown in Fig. 5.3.16. When $x_{C1} = \bar{x}_{C3}$ and $x_{c2} = \bar{x}_{C4}$, (z_2, z_1) is (01) or (10), but never (00) or (11). If any of the conditions above fails or a fault occurs at any line of the checker, $(z_2 \, z_1)$ will be (00) or (11), instead of (01) or (10). The self-testing property of this circuit can be verified easily.

It is straightforward to obtain the two-rail code checker for an arbitrary n simply by interconnecting the circuits above in a tree structure.

5.3.4. Self-Checking Functional Circuits.

An example of a self-checking binary adder is shown in Fig. 5.3.17, where the two-rail scheme is employed [SELL68]. The construction of general circuits with the self-checking property is discussed in [SMIT77]. Several designs of self-checking microprocessors/computers are described in [RENN78, SEDM78, WAKE78, CROU79, CROU80, CHAV82, TSAO82, CART77, and TOY78].

5.4. FAULT TOLERANCE IN COMBINATIONAL CIRCUITS

The idea of introducing redundancy to improve the reliability of combinational circuits originates from papers published in the 1950s. Since then, redundancy has been recognized as a realistic means for constructing reliable systems. Redundancy can be applied at the component part, functional unit, and module levels, although the emphasis is shifting these days from the first two levels to the last one.

Moore and Shannon [MOOR56a, MOOR56b] first showed that the reliability of a relay could be improved to any desired extent by replicating it in the form of a

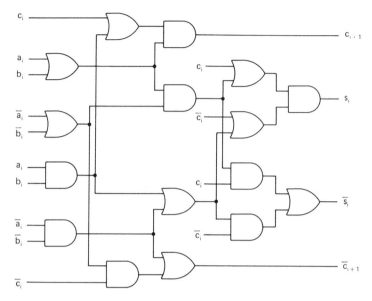

Figure 5.3.17   Self-checking binary adder.

series/parallel connection. In contrast, von Neumann [NEUM56] proposed a scheme where a signal was represented simultaneously on multiple signal lines with voters. Some errors on signal lines are corrected by taking a majority vote on all signal lines. A tier of two levels of AND-OR gates has been shown to have the correcting capability as well [PIER65]. Quadded logic [TYRO62] can be viewed as replication. Triple modular redundancy (TMR) [BROW61] may be one of the most successful applied techniques. However, we will only consider here some other topics which look interesting from the coding point of view.

5.4.1. Adders with Parity Check Matrix

The incorporation of error-correcting codes into logic circuits was investigated earlier by Armstrong [ARMS61] and Chaudhuri [RAYC61]. Their methods, however, were infeasible, because determining the output check bits was prohibitively complicated. All schemes utilizing error-correcting codes have to assume the perfect operation of error-correcting circuits. If the circuits are complex, the possibility of the occurrence of a fault in those circuits is not negligible and therefore, may prevent these schemes from practical applications. Thus the following technique may not be practical, but it will be explained for theoretical interest.

Fujiwara and Haruta [FUJI81] extended the idea of Section 5.2.3 to incorporate the parity check matrix into adders. For clarity, let us rewrite Eq. (5.2.48) for the case of the addition of two operands, $\mathbf{a} = (a_{k-1} \cdots a_0)$ and $\mathbf{b} = (b_{k-1} \cdots b_0)$. The sum will be denoted by $\mathbf{s} = (s_{k-1} \cdots s_0)$. Then

$$s_c = \sum_{j=0}^{k-1} s_j$$

$$= \sum_{j=0}^{k-1} (a_j \oplus b_j \oplus R_j(a_j, \ldots, a_0, b_j, \ldots, b_0)) \qquad (5.4.1)$$

Note that F_j, which expresses s_j, is not a function of only a_j and b_j, in contrast to that of Eq. (5.2.45). Accordingly, $a_{j-1}, \ldots, a_0, b_{j-1}, \ldots, b_0$, as well as a_j and b_j, are included in $R_j(a_j, \ldots a_0, b_j, \ldots, b_0)$. $R_j(a_j, \ldots, a_0, b_j, \ldots, b_0)$ is another expression of the carry from the lower-significant-bit position. For convenience, $R_j(a_j, \ldots, a_0, b_j, \ldots, b_0)$ will be expressed simply by $R_j(\mathbf{a}, \mathbf{b})$.

Suppose that $\mathbf{a}$, $\mathbf{b}$, and $\mathbf{s}$ are encoded in an error-correcting code by a parity check matrix H, such as

$$H = [P \mid I] \qquad (5.4.2)$$

where P is a matrix of r rows and k columns, while I is a $r \times r$ identity matrix. Then r check bits for $\mathbf{s}$ are calculated by

$$\mathbf{c_s} \equiv (c_{s,r-1} \, c_{s,r-2} \cdots c_{s,0})$$
$$= \mathbf{s}P^T = \mathbf{a}P^T \oplus \mathbf{b}P^T \oplus \mathbf{R}P^T \qquad (5.4.3)$$

where $\mathbf{R} = (R_{k-1}(\mathbf{a}, \mathbf{b})R_{k-2}(\mathbf{a}, \mathbf{b}) \cdots R_0(\mathbf{a}, \mathbf{b}))$.

$\mathbf{a}P^T$ and $\mathbf{b}P^T$ are check bits for $\mathbf{a}$ and $\mathbf{b}$, respectively. Denoting these by $\mathbf{c_a}$ and $\mathbf{c_b}$,

$$\mathbf{c_s} = \mathbf{c_a} \oplus \mathbf{C_b} \oplus \mathbf{R}P^T \qquad (5.4.4)$$

Thus

$$\mathbf{d} = \mathbf{s}P^T \oplus \mathbf{c_a} \oplus \mathbf{c_b} \oplus \mathbf{R}P^T \qquad (5.4.5)$$

gives the syndrome, indicating an error pattern that may appear in $\mathbf{s}$.

The circuit configuration of this scheme is illustrated in Fig. 5.4.1. Note that errors in $\mathbf{c_a}$ or $\mathbf{c_b}$, as well as in $\mathbf{s}$, can be corrected. However, as described previously, the circuit enclosed by the dashed line must operate correctly in order to correct the error successfully. Unfortunately, it might require more hardware for this circuit than for the adder itself.

5.4.2. Fault Masking by Retry

Suppose that the output g of a gate in the circuit of Fig. 5.4.2 is stuck at e, $e = 1$ or 0. The primary output y of the circuit will be given by an erroneous function $F^f(\mathbf{x})$, instead of the true $F(\mathbf{x})$, where $\mathbf{x}$ is the primary input to the circuit. In general, $F^f(\mathbf{x})$ may be such that $F^f(\mathbf{x}) \geq F(\mathbf{x})$ holds at one input, while $F^f(\mathbf{x}) \leq F(\mathbf{x})$ may hold at another input. Since this ambiguity is not desirable, we focus our attention on such circuits as defined below.

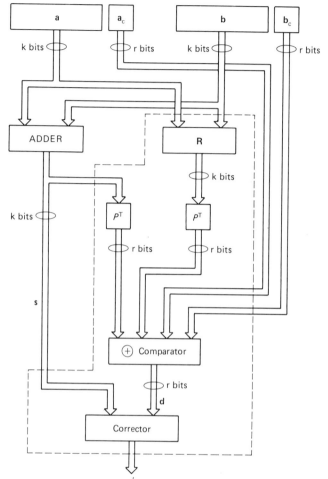

Figure 5.4.1 Implementation of parity check matrix.

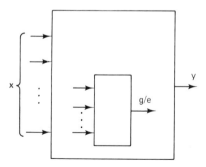

Figure 5.4.2 Logic circuit.

Definition 11.   A circuit is called *f-monotonic* (with respect to the prescribed set of faults) if and only if either $F^f(\mathbf{x}) \geq F(\mathbf{x})$ or $F^f(\mathbf{x}) \leq F(\mathbf{x})$ holds over the entire domain of $\mathbf{x}$.

Here the occurrence of a single fault of the stuck type at the output of a gate is assumed. Then, tree circuits of NOT, AND, and OR gates are *f*-monotonic. Moreover, circuits of NOT, AND, and OR gates, in which all paths between a fan-out gate and a reconvergent gate include either an even or an odd number of NOT gates, also meet the *f*-monotonicity. Thus the *f*-monotonicity is not a very restrictive condition for the construction of circuits.

Now assume that $F^f(\mathbf{x}) \geq F(\mathbf{x})$ at any input. Such a situation as $F^f(\mathbf{a}) = 1 > 0 = F(\mathbf{a})$ may happen at some input $\mathbf{a}$. However, if $F(\mathbf{x})$ takes value 1 at the complemented input $\overline{\mathbf{a}}$, $F^f(\overline{\mathbf{a}}) = F(\overline{\mathbf{a}}) = 1$. That is, the fault is masked by the complementation of the input. Note that the output is always guaranteed to get complemented by the input complementation if the circuit is self-dual. Thus, we reach the following conclusion.

Theorem 7 [SHED78].   If a circuit is composed of *f*-monotonic and self-dual modules, a fault in any module can be masked by the complementation of the primary input.

In order to apply this basic idea to real circuits, the primary input and the primary output each must be attached by an additional bit, called the *mode bit*, to indicate whether the original version of information bits or the complement is used. When $x_m = 0$, the information bits of the primary input are assumed to represent the original version. On the other hand, $x_m = 1$ means that the current information bits are complemented. Similarly, y_m is the mode bit for the primary output.

Next the primary output of the circuit should be represented by some error-detecting code, because retry with the complemented input can be initiated only by the detection of an error at the output.

Let $\mathbf{y}$ be an output code word. Its complement, $\overline{\mathbf{y}}$, will appear by complementating the input. Therefore, $\overline{\mathbf{y}}$ must also be a code word. This imposes some restrictions on the error-detecting codes available.

Finally, a building module of the circuit may not be self-dual. However, such a module can always be made self-dual by incorporating its dual together with the mode bit m, as shown in Fig. 5.4.3. C and C_D are the original and its dual modules, respectively. Outputs from these modules are switched by the multiplexer under the control of m.

Figure 5.4.4a shows an example of the application of the scheme above to a multiplier. Note that the sum output as well as the carry output of a full adder is self-dual. They can easily be constructed to have the *f*-monotonicity property. However, AND gates which perform the multiplication between the multiplicand and a bit of the multiplier must be modified, as shown in Fig. 5.4.4b. a_m and b_m are the mode bits of two operands, respectively. p_m connected to a_m in this case is also the mode bit of the product. Half adders in Fig. 5.2.7a are replaced by full adders, to which b_m is applied.

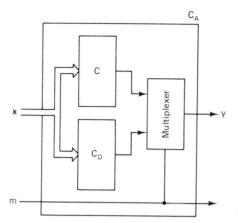

Figure 5.4.3   Modification of module.

The parity check codes are used for the two operands and the product. The mode bit is taken into consideration in determining the check bit. For example, the check bit of the multiplicand is given by

$$a_c = \left(\sum_{i=0}^{3} a_i \right) \oplus a_m$$

Then, in order to make the complement of any code word a code word again, the number of information bits must be even.

For other arithmetic circuits, refer to [TAKE80] and [FURU83].

5.4.3. Further Topics

Pradhan and Reddy have proposed applying the Reed–Muller code to logic circuits, noting the Reed–Muller expansion of logical functions [PRAD72a, PRAD72b, PRAD74b]. The application of the *AN* code has been studied thoroughly by Rao[RAO74]. It is known that the biresidue code corrects a single error in arithmetic circuits [RAO70, RAO74]. To make implementation easy, the combination of the parity check on each byte with the residue code on the whole code word has been proposed [RAO77]. Neumann and Rao argued a byte-error-correcting code [NEUM75]. Pradhan recently developed a new class of codes which are capable of both correcting *t* random errors and detecting any number of unidirectional errors [PRAD80].

A fault-tolerant capability in a two-level AND-OR network has been investigated by Pradhan and Reddy [PRAD74a]. From the testability point of view, the capability of masking faults in combinational circuits has also been revealed by Gray and Meyer [GRAY76]. Yamamoto et al. [YAMA70] and Reynolds and Metze [REYN78] have discussed fault detection in a manner similar to the fault masking by retry technique.

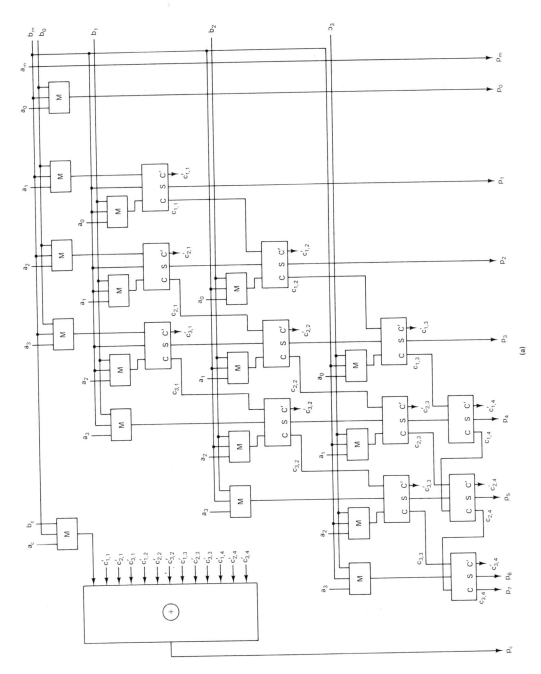

Figure 5.4.4 Multiplier capable of fault-masking.

(a)

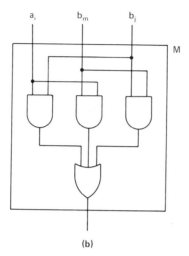

(b)   **Figure 5.4.4** (cont.)

5.5. FAULT-TOLERANT SEQUENTIAL CIRCUITS

For realizing sequential machines, state must be encoded by the state variables. In addition to the minimum number of state variables required for the state assignment, redundant variables should be provided to improve fault tolerance and reliable operation.

Here we restrict our attention to the problem concerned with malfunctions at state variables. This means that input and output variables of the circuit are assumed to be fault-free at any time. The extension to more general cases is a simple matter. Only stuck-type faults will be considered throughout this section.

5.5.1. General Approach

A *sequential machine* $M(X, Q, Z, \delta, \omega)$ is defined by the following 5-tuple:

$$\left.\begin{array}{l} X\text{: set of input symbols} \\[4pt] Q\text{: set of states} \\[4pt] Z\text{: set of output symbols} \\[4pt] \delta\text{: state transition function, } \delta\colon X \times Q \to Q \\[4pt] \omega\text{: output function, } \omega\colon X \times Q \to Z \end{array}\right\} \qquad (5.5.1)$$

Further,

$$\mathbf{q}^{(1)} = \delta(\mathbf{x}, \mathbf{q}) \qquad \mathbf{x} \in X, \quad \mathbf{q} \in Q \qquad (5.5.2)$$

will be called the *next state* of the present state $\mathbf{q}$ for input $\mathbf{x}$.

In the description above, we assumed tacitly the concept of discrete time.

Specifically in this section, all actions of the sequential machine are interpreted to take place at the instant of the clock signal. This type of sequential machine is called *synchronous*. Thus the terms *present* and *next* mean the present instant and the next instant of the clock signal, respectively. Various considerations of asynchronous sequential circuits appear in Section 5.6.

In the same context, the machine produces the present output $\mathbf{z}$, such as

$$\mathbf{z} = \omega(\mathbf{x}, \mathbf{q}) \qquad \mathbf{x} \in X, \quad \mathbf{q} \in Q \tag{5.5.3}$$

when input $\mathbf{x}$ is applied to the machine at state $\mathbf{q}$.

Each state of Q is assigned a unique binary n-tuple, by a state assignment function. An n-tuple of $\{0, 1\}$ is represented by $(y_n y_{n-1} \cdots y_1)$ in general, where y_i's $(i = 1, 2, \ldots, n)$ are called *state variables*. Hereafter, $\mathbf{q}$ and an n-tuple of values of state variables will be used interchangeably to represent a state of Q. y_i at $\mathbf{q}$ is denoted by $(\mathbf{q})_i$.

Then, the state transition function δ defines the state variable functions as follows: For $i = 1, 2, \ldots, n$,

$$y_i^{(1)} = F_i(\mathbf{x}, y_n, \ldots, y_1)$$
$$= (\delta(\mathbf{x}, (y_n \cdots y_1)))_i \tag{5.5.4}$$

That is, $F_i(\mathbf{x}, y_n, \ldots, y_1)$ gives the value of y_i at the next state of $\mathbf{q} = (y_n \cdots y_1)$ for input $\mathbf{x}$.

The state-variable functions may be incomplete, because they are defined only on Q. In order to realize M which is tolerant of t faults, we augment Q to include some faulty n-tuples defined below and provide means to limit values of state variables in a prescribed range even under the existence of faults.

Now, let Q be a set of binary n-tuples in which each n-tuple is separated from any other element of Q by a Hamming distance not less than $2t + 1$. Since such a Q is obviously a t-error-correcting code, well-established coding theory helps us find the desired sets. Then define a set of faulty n-tuples for $(y_n \cdots y_1) \in Q$ to be

$$R(y_n \cdots y_1) = \{(\hat{y}_n \cdots \hat{y}_1) \mid \hat{d}_H((\hat{y}_n \cdots \hat{y}_1), (y_n \cdots y_1)) \le t\} \tag{5.5.5}$$

where $\hat{d}_H$ represents the Hamming distance between two n-tuples. Thus Q is augmented to such Q_{aug} as

$$Q_{\text{aug}} = Q \cup \{R(y_n \cdots y_1) \mid (y_n \cdots y_1) \in Q\} \tag{5.5.6}$$

and the state-variable functions are redefined on this augmented Q_{aug}. For any $(y_n \cdots y_1) \in Q$, $F_i(\mathbf{x}, y_n, \ldots, y_1)$ is completely the same as that of Eq. (5.5.4). In addition, for $\forall (\hat{y}_n \cdots \hat{y}_1) \in R(y_n \cdots y_1)$ and $\forall \mathbf{x} \in X$,

$$F_i(\mathbf{x}, \hat{y}_n, \ldots, \hat{y}_1) = F_i(\mathbf{x}, y_n, \ldots, y_1) \qquad i = 1, 2, \ldots, n \tag{5.5.7}$$

$(\hat{y}_n \cdots \hat{y}_1) \in R(y_n \cdots y_1)$ can be viewed as a faulty state $\hat{\mathbf{q}}$ in a sphere with its center $\mathbf{q} = (y_n \cdots y_1)$ and the radius t. The state transition defined by Eq. (5.5.7) is depicted schematically in Fig. 5.5.1. It is assured by this design and by the independent construction of excitation circuits for state variables that under the existence of

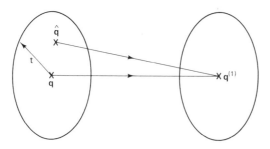

Figure 5.5.1   State transition from a faulty state.

at most t faults, M will travel through (faulty) states which are separated by Hamming distance t or less from the centers of their respective spheres [MEYE71, SAGA69].

The output function of M must also be defined in terms of state variables. With the influence of faults in mind, we specifiy the function Ω on Q_{aug} to be

$$\forall\ (y_n \cdots y_1) \in Q \qquad \forall\ \mathbf{x} \in X$$

$$\mathbf{z} = \Omega(\mathbf{x}, (y_n \cdots y_1)) = \omega(\mathbf{x}, (y_n \cdots y_1)) \qquad (5.5.8)$$

Further,

$$\forall\ (\hat{y}_n \cdots \hat{y}_1) \in R(y_n \cdots y_1) \qquad \forall\ \mathbf{x} \in X$$

$$\mathbf{z} = \Omega(\mathbf{x}, (\hat{y}_n \cdots \hat{y}_1)) = \Omega(\mathbf{x}, (y_n \cdots y_1)) \qquad (5.5.9)$$

Such a definition as Eq. (5.5.9) is always possible, because each center of spheres is separated from others by at least Hamming distance $2t + 1$, and all spheres are mutually disjoint.

Equations (5.5.8) and (5.5.9) mean that M will produce an identical output, no matter which state M takes in a sphere. Thus M appears in effect fault-free of its input–output behavior, even if it has at most t faults.

5.5.2. Majority Decoding

When Q is a linear code, the utilization of a characteristic property of the code may give us a simpler realization than that obtained by the direct application of the general approach above. We see one such example in the application of the majority-decodable codes [RUDO67].

Consider the parity check matrix shown below [REED70].

$$\mathbf{H} = \begin{bmatrix} 110 & 100 \\ 011 & 010 \\ 101 & 001 \end{bmatrix} \qquad (5.5.10)$$

. Let $(y_3\ y_2\ y_1\ c_3\ c_2\ c_1)$ be a code word. An example of assigning code words to states of a modulo-8 counter is shown in Fig. 5.5.2. Equation (5.5.10) implies

y_3	y_2	y_1	c_3	c_2	c_1	Q	δ x \ 0	1
0	0	0	0	0	0	q_0	q_0	q_1
0	0	1	0	1	1	q_1	q_1	q_2
0	1	0	1	1	0	q_2	q_2	q_3
0	1	1	1	0	1	q_3	q_3	q_4
1	0	0	1	0	1	q_4	q_4	q_5
1	0	1	1	1	0	q_5	q_5	q_6
1	1	0	0	1	1	q_6	q_6	q_7
1	1	1	0	0	0	q_7	q_7	q_0

Figure 5.5.2   State assignment to a modulo-8 counter.

$$c_3 = y_3 \oplus y_2$$
$$c_2 = y_2 \oplus y_1$$
$$c_1 = y_3 \oplus y_1$$

giving the following equalities:

$$\left.\begin{aligned}
y_3 &= y_2 \oplus c_3 = y_1 \oplus c_1 \\
y_2 &= y_1 \oplus c_2 = y_3 \oplus c_3 \\
y_1 &= y_3 \oplus c_1 = y_2 \oplus c_2
\end{aligned}\right\} \tag{5.5.11}$$

Note that each y_i ($i = 1, 2,$ and 3) has three alternative representations: y_i itself and two more expressions. Further, any single erroneous variables among y_3 through c_1 can affect only one of the three representations. For example, suppose that y_2 is erroneous. Then only $y_2 \oplus c_3$ out of the three representations for y_3 is erroneous. In the representations for y_2, y_2 itself is erroneous, while $y_1 \oplus c_2$ and $y_3 \oplus c_3$ are correct. Similarly, y_1 and $y_3 \oplus c_1$ are correct in contrast to erroneous $y_2 \oplus c_2$ in the representations for y_1.

Therefore, the correct value of y_i, denoted by y_{ci}, is determined by the following majority vote:

$$\left.\begin{aligned}
y_{c3} &= Maj\{y_3, y_2 \oplus c_3, y_1 \oplus c_1\} \\
y_{c2} &= Maj\{y_2, y_1 \oplus c_2, y_3 \oplus c_3\} \\
y_{c1} &= Maj\{y_1, y_3 \oplus c_1, y_2 \oplus c_2\}
\end{aligned}\right\} \tag{5.5.12}$$

and

$$\left.\begin{aligned}
\bar{y}_{c3} &= Maj\{\bar{y}_3, \bar{y}_2 \oplus c_3, \bar{y}_1 \oplus c_1\} \\
\bar{y}_{c2} &= Maj\{\bar{y}_2, \bar{y}_1 \oplus c_2, \bar{y}_3 \oplus c_3\} \\
\bar{y}_{c1} &= Maj\{\bar{y}_1, \bar{y}_3 \oplus c_1, \bar{y}_2 \oplus c_2\}
\end{aligned}\right\} \tag{5.5.13}$$

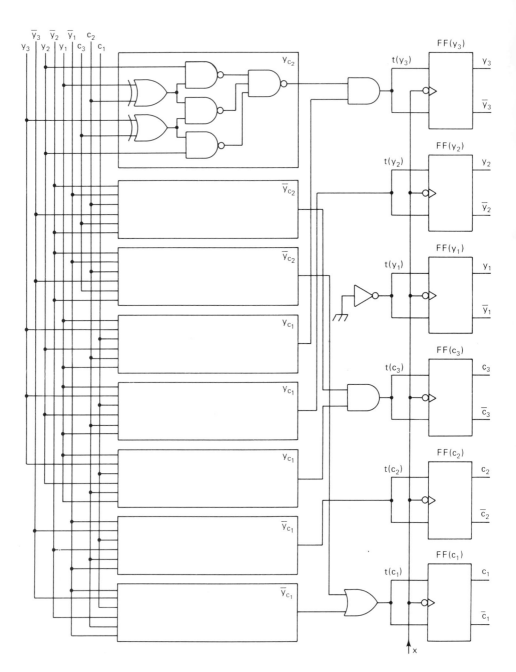

Figure 5.5.3   Fault-tolerant modulo-8 counter.

where

$$Maj\{a, b, c\} = ab \vee bc \vee ca \qquad (5.5.14)$$

Assume here that state variables y_i ($i = 1$, 2, and 3) and c_j ($j = 1$, 2, and 3) are realized by toggle flip-flops $FF(y_i)$ and $FF(c_j)$, respectively. Then, excitations $t(y_i)$ to $FF(y_i)$ and $t(c_j)$ to $FF(c_j)$ can be defined only in terms of y_i's, because c_j's depend on y_i's by **H**. [Alternatively, we may view a cube ($y_3\ y_2\ y_1 - - -$) as a set of states similar to the sphere described in Section 5.5.1 and use them to simplify the excitation functions.] Thus

$$\left.\begin{aligned}
t(y_3) &= xy_2y_1 & t(c_3) &= x\bar{y}_2\,y_1 \\
t(y_2) &= xy_1 & t(c_2) &= x\bar{y}_1 \\
t(y_1) &= x & t(c_1) &= x(\bar{y}_2 \vee \bar{y}_1)
\end{aligned}\right\} \qquad (5.5.15)$$

For fault tolerance, the $y_i/\bar{y}_i$'s in the equations above are substituted for the $y_{ci}/\bar{y}_{ci}$'s of Eq. (5.5.12) or (5.5.13). However, care must be taken to prevent the malfunction of a majority voter from affecting multiple flip-flops. For example, y_1 is included three times in the above equations, and, accordingly, three circuits constructed independently for y_{ci} must be used to drive $t(y_3)$, $t(y_2)$, and $t(c_3)$. Hence the circuit configuration is as shown in Fig. 5.5.3.

5.5.3. Excitations of JK Flip-Flops

Russo [RUSS65] showed another shortcut for determining excitations to *JK* flip-flops in a counter. Here, states of the counter are assigned code words of a code with the minimum Hamming distance three. Before presenting the details of the procedure, some definitions and terminologies should be described.

For a given flip-flop, a state where the J/K-input must be driven to the value 1 in normal operation is called the *valid y-state* of the J/K-input. Contrarily, if the excitation to the J/K-input must be 0 at a state in normal operation, this state is referred to as the *valid n-state* of the J/K-input. The valid y-state and the valid n-state of the J/K-input will be denoted by $y(J/K)$ and $n(J/K)$, respectively. However, there may be several valid y/n-states of the J/K-input of a flip-flop. In such a case, they will be attached with appropriate subscripts as $y_i/n_i(J_j/K_j)$. Sometimes, they are simply called valid y/n-states. Examples of valid y-states and valid n-states together with the state assignment of a modulo-6 counter are shown in Fig. 5.5.4.

We denote the minterm associated with a valid y-state or valid n-state by $m\{y(J/K)\}$ or $m\{n(J/K)\}$, respectively. Let P be a product term of some state variables (which are represented by the outputs of flip-flops). Then P is said to cover a valid y-state or valid n-state, respectively, provided that

$$m\{y(J/K)\} \leq P \qquad \text{or} \qquad m\{n(J/K)\} \leq P \qquad (5.5.16)$$

Now, we are ready to give the following definition.

	Flip-flops						Valid y/n-states											
Q	1	2	3	4	5	6	J_1	K_1	J_2	K_2	J_3	K_3	J_4	K_4	J_5	K_5	J_6	K_6
q_0	1	1	1	1	1	1		$y(K_1)$		$y_1(K_2)$	$y_1(J_3)$	$y_1(K_3)$	$n(J_4)$	$y_1(K_4)$	$y_1(J_5)$	$y_1(K_5)$	$y_1(J_6)$	$y_1(K_6)$
q_1	0	0	0	0	0	0	$n_1(J_1)$		$n(J_2)$									
q_2	0	0	1	0	1	1	$n_2(J_1)$		$y_1(J_2)$		$n(J_3)$	$y_2(K_3)$	$y_1(J_4)$	$n(K_4)$	$y_2(J_5)$	$y_2(K_5)$		$n(K_6)$
q_3	0	1	0	1	0	1	$y(J_1)$		$y_2(J_2)$	$y_2(K_2)$	$y_2(J_3)$			$y_2(K_4)$				$y_2(K_6)$
q_4	1	0	0	1	1	0		$n_1(K_1)$					$y_2(J_4)$		$y_3(J_5)$	$y_3(K_5)$	$n(J_6)$	$y_2(K_6)$
q_5	1	1	1	0	0	0		$n_2(K_1)$		$n(K_2)$		$n(K_3)$					$y_2(J_6)$	

Figure 5.5.4 Valid y/n-states.

388

Definition 12.   If d variables of P must be complemented in order to cover a valid y/n-state, the extended Hamming distance between P and this valid y/n-state is defined to be d.

Suppose that the excitation to the J/K-input of the ith flip-flop is represented by

$$J_i/K_i = P_{i1} \bigvee P_{i2} \bigvee \cdots \bigvee P_{ik} \qquad (5.5.17)$$

where $\{P_{ij}\}$, $(j = 1, 2, \ldots, k)$ is a set of such product terms of state variables that each P_{ij} covers a valid y-state of the J_i/K_i-input. Then $\{P_{ij}\}$ can be chosen so as to satisfy the following two conditions.

1. For any valid y-state of the J_i/K_i-input, elements of $\{P_{ij}\}$ can be collected into a subset $\{P_{iu}\}$ such that each element of $\{P_{iu}\}$ covers this valid y-state and there is no variable commonly included in all elements of $\{P_{iu}\}$.
2. Each element of $\{P_{ij}\}$ is separated from any valid n-states of the J_i/K_i-input by an extended Hamming distance of 2 or more.

Consider, for example, the excitation to J_1-input. Since $\mathbf{q}_3$ is the only valid y-state, P_{ij} will be a product term of the appropriate variables taken from $\{\bar{f}_1, f_2, \bar{f}_3, f_4, \bar{f}_5, f_6\}$. In order to follow condition 2, we first look at variables which take different values in the valid y-state and the valid n-state of the J_1-input. The values of variables 2, 4, and 6 (outputs of flip-flops 2, 4, and 6) in the valid y-state differ from those in the valid n_1-state. This is expressed by

$$y\text{—}n_1: (2, 4, 6) \qquad (5.5.18)$$

Similarly,

$$y\text{—}n_2: (2, 3, 4, 5) \qquad (5.5.19)$$

From these two expressions we see that the product term of variables 2 and 4 meets condition 2. However, it does not suffice to take only one product term, since alone it does not satisfy condition 1. Therefore, we look for other product terms of three variables. Obviously, the product terms of variables $(2, 3, 6)$, $(2, 5, 6)$, $(3, 4, 6)$, and $(4, 5, 6)$ are possible candidates. From these terms, we finally choose the product terms of variables $(2, 4)$, $(2, 3, 6)$, and $(3, 4, 6)$, which give the following excitation:

$$J_1 = f_2 f_4 \bigvee f_2 \bar{f}_3 f_6 \bigvee \bar{f}_3 f_4 f_6 \qquad (5.5.20)$$

What is assured by determining excitations in this way? When a flip-flop malfunctions, the counter may move to a state apart from a valid y-state by Hamming distance 1. Even in such a case, the J-inputs and K-input of all flip-flops except the erroneous one never miss the required excitation of value 1, because in the excitations to those flip-flops, there is at least one product term, which is free of the malfunction of the erroneous flip-flop. (Note that there is no variable common to all product terms in an excitation.) On the other hand, inputs of flip-flops except the erroneous one cannot be excited incorrectly by the value 1, because of condition 2 for choosing product terms.

5.6. FAULT-TOLERANT ASYNCHRONOUS SEQUENTIAL CIRCUITS

5.6.1. State Assignment

The operation of asynchronous circuits is expected to be faster than that of synchronous circuits, since it depends only on the delay of signals propagating through the circuit.

However, the lack of a definite clocking system gives rise to an uncertainty in the circuit operation, and undesirable results may occur. One well-known problem is the race between state variables in sequential circuits. When two or more state variables are changing their values, they compete with each other, and the destination state may be different from that of the design specification, depending on which variable takes its new value first.

To avoid the race between state variables, two approaches are possible. One is to use a state assignment in which the transition takes place only between states, which are represented by two n-tuples separated from each other by Hamming distance one. In this case the race never occurs, because only one state variable will change its value in any state transition.

If the destination state in a transition were determined uniquely even under the presence of the race, nothing would be adversely affected. This kind of race is called *noncritical*. A second approach is to make all races noncritical. In this approach, there exists at least one state variable, called the *controlling variable*, that does not change its value during the transition and determines the final values of the changing variables. Thus the changing variables may vary in any order and the race is obviously noncritical.

Although many aspects of the first approach are known [UNGE69], only techniques of the second approach are described here in connection with the fault-tolerant design of asynchronous sequential circuits.

Separation by controlling variables. Assume that input x_1 is applied to the circuit of Fig. 5.6.1, where transition $q_b \rightarrow q_c$, $q_e \rightarrow q_c$ or $q_d \rightarrow q_a$ may occur. Among these, transition $q_b \rightarrow q_c$ causes a race between y_3 and y_2. However, y_1 remains at the value 1 during the transition to the destination state q_c. On the other hand, y_1 remains constant at value 0 during transition $q_d \rightarrow q_a$. Therefore, transitions $q_b \rightarrow q_c$ and $q_e \rightarrow q_c$ are never confused with transition $q_d \rightarrow q_a$. That is, the circuit is prevented from going to an intermediate state in $q_d \rightarrow q_a$ during transition $q_b \rightarrow q_c$ or $q_e \rightarrow q_c$. In this context, $q_b \rightarrow q_c$ (and $q_e \rightarrow q_c$) is said to be separated from $q_d \rightarrow q_a$ by the value of y_1. y_1 is referred to as the controlling variable with respect to x_1.

We find similar situations for other inputs. At input x_2, for example, $y_3 = 1$ distinguishes $q_c \rightarrow q_d$ from $q_e \rightarrow q_b(y_3 = 0)$, and $y_3 = 1$ also separates it from the stable state $q_a(y_3 = 0)$. (This stable state can be viewed as transition $q_a \rightarrow q_a$.) Further, $q_e \rightarrow q_b$ and q_a are separated by the value y_1. Thus y_3 and y_1 are the controlling variables with respect to x_2. With more detailed inspection, the reader will realize that

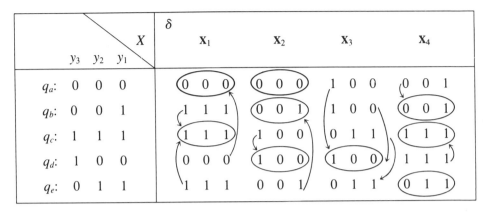

Figure 5.6.1 Separation by controlling variables.

any pair of transitions which may occur at an input and have different destination states is separated by a controlling variable or a combination of controlling variables.

A question may arise: By what means can we find such a state assignment that guarantees the separation described above? A systematic procedure was first shown by Liu [LIU63] and refined later by Tracey [TRAC66]. The basic idea of their approach is to find a collection of K-set dichotomies (K-set is a set of a stable state and unstable states which lead to this stable state at an input, and K-sets with respect to the same input are paired to make K-set dichotomies) and controlling variables such that each controlling variable separates as many K-set dichotomies as possible. The procedure gives the state assignment in a custom-tailored fashion. The complexity of the procedure depends heavily on the nature of the flow table and is almost prohibitive in many real applications.

The universal separating system, discussed next, gives us a set of n-tuples that can be arbitrarily assigned to states without regard to the structure of the flow table.

Universal separating system.   First, formal definitions for the (2, 2) separating system are given.

Definition 13.   A pair of two blocks is called the *n-tuple* (state) *dichotomy* if each block is made of n-tuples (states).

Sometimes, we simply call it the dichotomy.

Definition 14.   The (2, 2) separating system is a set of n-tuples such that for an arbitrary dichotomy of which each block consists of two n-tuples of the set, there exists at least one component variable which takes value 1 at every n-tuple in a block of the dichotomy, but value 0 at every n-tuple in another block.

The (1, 1) separating system and the (2, 1) separating system can be defined similarly. The (i, j) separating system will be represented in the form of a matrix, of which each row is an n-tuple of the set.

The concept of the (2, 2) separating system originates from Liu [LIU63]. He showed that the equidistant code [BERL68] could be used as the (2, 2) separating system. It is presented in a more precise form below.

Theorem 8. Let n and d be the length of code words and the Hamming distance between code words of an equidistant code, respectively. An equidistant code satisfying

$$n = 2d - 1 \qquad (5.6.1)$$

is the (2, 2) separating system.

An example of such equidistant codes is shown in Eq. (5.6.2).

$$
C = \begin{bmatrix}
y_7 & y_6 & y_5 & y_4 & y_3 & y_2 & y_1 \\
0 & 0 & 0 & 0 & 0 & 0 & 0 \\
1 & 0 & 1 & 1 & 1 & 0 & 0 \\
0 & 1 & 0 & 1 & 1 & 1 & 0 \\
0 & 0 & 1 & 0 & 1 & 1 & 1 \\
1 & 0 & 0 & 1 & 0 & 1 & 1 \\
1 & 1 & 0 & 0 & 1 & 0 & 1 \\
1 & 1 & 1 & 0 & 0 & 1 & 0 \\
0 & 1 & 1 & 1 & 0 & 0 & 1
\end{bmatrix} \qquad (5.6.2)
$$

The maximum-length sequence code as well as the orthogonal code [BERL68] without the first bit of each code word are other examples.

According to the Plotkin bound, the number of code words, N, of the equidistant code that meets Eq. (5.6.1) must obey

$$n \geq N - 1 \qquad (5.6.3)$$

Therefore, the number of variables required for encoding 2^m states by the equidistant code is optimally

$$n = 2^m - 1 \qquad (5.6.4)$$

Note that all equidistant codes are not necessarily the (2, 2) separating systems [NANY80], as is demonstrated by a $\binom{n}{1}$ code.

The equidistant code may or may not be linear. Pradhan and Reddy first investigated the relation between the (2, 1) separating system and the linear code [PRAD76]. Their interesting results can be immediately extended to the case of (2, 2) separating systems [NAKA78]. Let d_{max} and d_{min} be the maximum and the minimum Hamming distances among code words, respectively.

Theorem 9. A linear code that satisfies the following condition is the (2, 2) separating system.

$$4d_{min} > 3d_{max} \qquad (5.6.5)$$

The next theorem gives us the direct form of a generator matrix for the (2, 2) separating system.

Theorem 10 [NANY77].   A linear code with its generator matrix as

$$\mathbf{C}_T = [\mathbf{I}_m \mid {}_m\mathbf{C}_2 \mid {}_m\mathbf{C}_3] \qquad (5.6.6)$$

is the (2, 2) separating system, where

$\mathbf{I}_m$: $m \times m$ identity matrix

${}_m\mathbf{C}_2$: matrix of all m-bit column vectors of weight 2

${}_m\mathbf{C}_3$: matrix of all m-bit column vectors of weight 3

The number of code words generated by Eq. (5.6.6) is obviously 2^m, while the length of code words is

$$
\begin{aligned}
n &= m + \binom{m}{2} + \binom{m}{3} \\
&= \frac{m^3 + 5m}{6}
\end{aligned}
\qquad (5.6.7)
$$

Further, ways to synthesize larger separating systems by the composition of smaller ones were investigated by Friedman et al. [FRIE69] and Nanya and Tohma [NANY78]. Friedman et al. [FRIE69], Kuhl and Reddy [KUHL78], and Nanya and Tohma [NANY79] presented (2, 2) separating systems, in which each state was assigned multiple n-tuples.

5.6.2. Fault-Tolerant Design

In Fig. 5.6.2, consider the state transition $\mathbf{q}_c \rightarrow \mathbf{q}_d$ at input $\mathbf{x}_2$. State variables $(y_3 y_2)$ will change their values from (11) to (00), while y_1 keeps its value constant at 1. Since y_3 changes asynchronously with respect to y_2, $(y_3 y_2 y_1)$ may intermittently take any one of the four tuples (111), (101), (011), and (001) during the state transition. The set of these four tuples is called the *transition cube* spanned by (111) and (001), and is denoted by $V(--1)$. Sometimes the transition cube is represented simply by V. Note that the transition cube is identified by the value(s) of component variable(s) which remain(s) unchanged during the transition.

Another transition may occur from $\mathbf{q}_e$ to $\mathbf{q}_a$ at input $\mathbf{x}_2$. In this case, the transition cube is $V(--0) = \{(000), (010), (100), (110)\}$. Obviously, $V(--1)$ and $V(--0)$ are mutually disjoint, because they are separated by the value of y_1, the controlling variable.

Now, let us consider the effect of a fault in an exciting circuit for a state variable, which is constructed independent of other exciting circuits. When a changing variable, say y_3, takes an erroneous value 1 in the transition from $\mathbf{q}_c$ to $\mathbf{q}_d$, the circuit may stop

X \ y_3 y_2 y_1	δ X_1	X_2	X_3	X_4
q_a: 0 0 0	0 0 0	0 0 0	0 0 1	1 0 0
q_b: 1 0 0	1 1 1	0 0 0	0 0 1	1 0 0
q_c: 1 1 1	1 1 1	0 0 1	1 1 0	1 1 1
q_d: 0 0 1	0 0 0	0 0 1	0 0 1	1 1 1
q_e: 1 1 0	1 1 1	0 0 0	1 1 0	1 1 0

Figure 5.6.2 State transition.

at a state where $(y_3\, y_2\, y_1)$ still belongs to $V(--\,1)$. This malfunction does not matter in the sense that the erroneous state is still separated from other transition cubes and the true destination state is easily distinguished from those in other transitions.

If the controlling variable y_1 makes an error, however, the circuit may transfer to a state in which $(y_3 y_2 y_1)$ belongs to $V(--\,0)$. Thus the information about the true destination is lost, and recovery from this malfunction is impossible.

The concept of the distance between two transition cubes helps us cope with this difficulty.

Definition 15. The minimum Hamming distance between a member of a transition cube V_1 and that of another transition cube V_2 is defined to be the distance between V_1 and V_2.

The distance between $V(--\,0)$ and $V(--\,1)$ described above is 1, because they are separated by only one variable. In the context of the distance between transition cubes, we say that an improper transition from $V(--\,1)$ to $V(--\,0)$ or vice versa such as that described previously is attributable to distance one between these two transition cubes.

In the analogy to error-correcting codes, we see that if any two transition cubes of different destination states at an arbitrary input are separated by distance $2t + 1$ or more, the confusion between these two transition cubes is avoided even upon the occurrence of errors on at most t state variables, and, accordingly, these errors are tolerated [PRAD73].

The remark is in order that multiple faults within an exciting circuit for a state variable can cause a single error on that state variable alone, because the exciting circuit shares no gates with other exciting circuits. Consider, as an example, the circuit of Fig. 5.6.3 [PRAD73]. At $x = 0$, there are two transition cubes, $V(---\,101)$ and $V(---\,010)$. Since they are separated by distance three (i.e., three controlling variables y_3, y_2, and y_1), each destination state can be identified even when an error is present at any one of these controlling or changing variables.

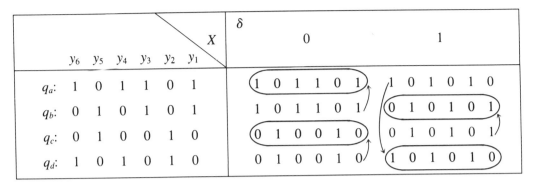

Figure 5.6.3 Design example.

When $(y_6 y_5 y_4 y_3 y_2 y_1)$ lies in $V(---101)$, their final values at the destination state are

$$y_6^{(1)} = 1 \qquad y_5^{(1)} = 0 \qquad y_4^{(1)} = 1$$
$$y_3^{(1)} = 1 \qquad y_2^{(1)} = 0 \qquad y_1^{(1)} = 1$$

while they are

$$y_6^{(1)} = 0 \qquad y_5^{(1)} = 1 \qquad y_4^{(1)} = 0$$
$$y_3^{(1)} = 0 \qquad y_2^{(1)} = 1 \qquad y_1^{(1)} = 0$$

when $(y_6 y_5 y_4 y_3 y_2 y_1)$ is traveling in $V(---010)$. Thus we know that $y_6^{(1)}$, $y_4^{(1)}$, $y_3^{(1)}$, and $y_1^{(1)}$ must be one only when $(y_6 y_5 y_4 y_3 y_2 y_1)$ is in $V(---101)$.

As described previously, the characteristic of $V(---101)$ is $y_3 = 1$, $y_2 = 0$, and $y_1 = 1$. In order to tolerate a single error at any one of these controlling variables, we use the majority function $Maj(y_3, \bar{y}_2, y_1)$, which is still sufficient for discriminating $V(---101)$ from $V(---010)$. Thus

$$y_6^{(1)} = \bar{x}\, Maj(y_3, \bar{y}_2, y_1) \lor \cdots$$
$$= \bar{x}(y_3 \bar{y}_2 \lor \bar{y}_2 y_1 \lor y_1 y_3) \lor \cdots$$

$y_4^{(1)}$, $y_3^{(1)}$, and $y_1^{(1)}$ can be expressed similarly.

On the other hand, $y_5^{(1)}$ and $y_2^{(1)}$ take value 1 only when $(y_6 y_5 y_4 y_3 y_2 y_1)$ belongs to $V(---010)$. Therefore,

$$y_5 = \bar{x}\, Maj(\bar{y}_3, y_2, \bar{y}_1) \lor \cdots$$
$$= \bar{x}(\bar{y}_3 y_2 \lor y_2 \bar{y}_1 \lor \bar{y}_1 \bar{y}_3) \lor \cdots$$

and the expression for $y_2^{(1)}$ is similar.

Observing transition cubes at $x = 1$ in the same way, we obtain expressions of $y_i^{(1)}$, $i = 1, 2, \ldots, 6$, for $x = 1$. Thus

$$y_6^{(1)} = \bar{x}\, Maj(y_3, \bar{y}_2, y_1) \vee x\, Maj(y_6, \bar{y}_5, y_4) = y_4^{(1)}$$

$$y_5^{(1)} = \bar{x}\, Maj(\bar{y}_3, y_2, \bar{y}_1) \vee x\, Maj(\bar{y}_6, y_5, \bar{y}_4)$$

$$y_3^{(1)} = \bar{x}\, Maj(y_3, \bar{y}_2, y_1) \vee x\, Maj(\bar{y}_6, y_5, \bar{y}_4) = y_1^{(1)}$$

$$y_2^{(1)} = \bar{x}\, Maj(\bar{y}_3, y_2, \bar{y}_1) \vee x\, Maj(y_6, \bar{y}_5, y_4)$$

For example, suppose that the circuit concerned with y_1 is faulty. Then, during the transition from $\mathbf{q}_b$ to $\mathbf{q}_a$ at $x = 0$, y_1 may take an erroneous value. Regardless of whether y_1 is 1 or 0, however, $y_6^{(1)}$, $y_4^{(1)}$, and $y_3^{(1)}$ will be excited properly, because y_3 and y_2 take on correct values of 1 and 0, respectively, and therefore, $Maj(y_3, \bar{y}_2, y_1)$ correctly takes value 1. Further, $y_5^{(1)}$ and $y_2^{(1)}$ will be excited correctly by the value 0, since $Maj(\bar{y}_3, y_2, \bar{y}_1) = 0$ independent of the value of y_1. Thus $(y_6 y_5 y_4 y_3 y_2 y_1)$ will finally be $(10110-)$, which, under the assumption of a single error on a state variable, cannot be regarded as any destination state other than $\mathbf{q}_a$.

Then, consider that input x changes its value to 1. Since $(y_6 y_5 y_4 y_3 y_2 y_1) = (10110-)$ belongs to $V(101---)$ and the controlling variables just take their correct values, all state variables except y_1 will be excited correctly, resulting in

$$(y_6 y_5 y_4 y_3 y_2 y_1) = (10101-)$$

Of course, this tuple is uniquely associated with the true destination state, (101010).

The output circuit can also be made tolerant of errors on state variables by incorporating voters on controlling variables. The circuit of this configuration, however, is vulnerable to a fault at a voter as well as a gate in the output circuit. In order to tolerate these faults, the output of the circuit should be encoded by an error-correcting code.

The essential key to this design process is to separate transition dichotomies by multiple controlling variables. Pradhan and Reddy have investigated the number of controlling variables in equidistant linear codes [PRAD73].

Theorem 11 [PRAD73].   The equidistant linear code of 2^m code words, where $n = 2^m - 1$, $m \geq 3$, and $d = 2^{m-1}$, has at least 2^{m-3} controlling variables for any dichotomy.

They also argued the way of constructing $(2, 2)$ separating systems, in which each dichotomy is separated by d_t variables [PRAD73].

Emphasizing the importance of error detection, Maki and Sawin [MAKI74] point out that by a fault-tolerant design, the circuit would be made immune to the occurrence of a fault, and no maintenance action would be taken for this masked fault. Thus a second fault which develops later might not be tolerated.

In their design, each K-set is assigned a state variable. Therefore, any K-set dichotomy is separated by at least two controlling variables and the circuit is capable of detecting an error on a state variable. Further, the duplicate of a given asynchronous sequential circuit is provided with a mechanism to switch the circuit operation from one circuit to its duplicate. This switching mechanism and a part of the error-detecting circuit must work correctly as a hard core.

In a similar context, Pradhan also proposes the synthesis of fault-secure asynchronous sequential circuits [PRAD78], which is based on the complete separating system. The concept of the complete separating system is a restriction to the separating system as defined below.

Definition 16.   The (i, j) complete separating system is a set of n-tuples such that for any ordered dichotomy of i n-tuples and j n-tuples, there exists at least one component variable taking value 1 in i n-tuples, but value 0 in j n-tuples.

For details of the nature and the synthesis of complete separating systems, refer to [MAGO73].

5.7. FAIL-SAFE SEQUENTIAL CIRCUITS

Fail-safeness may be considered to be one of the important attributes of reliable operation, because it guarantees (with respect to a prescribed set of faults) the production of a correct or safe-side output of the circuit even with the malfunction of circuit operation.

A typical environment in which the fail-safe approach has realistic significance is the area of railway traffic control. The red signal gives a warning of something dangerous and makes every observer careful, while the green signal indicates that everything is normal. If the green signal is lit erroneously by some malfunction, it may cause a catastrophe. Therefore, the equipment to control the traffic is said to be safer if it incorrectly turns on the red signal or no signal, but not the green signal under the existence of a fault.

There are two categories of fail-safe circuits: the combinational and the sequential. In this chapter, we focus our attention on fail-safe sequential circuits. Here sequential circuits are again assumed to be synchronous.

A fault within the circuit may affect the state transition function as well as the output function. However, assuming the occurrence of a single fault, either the state transition function or the output function will become faulty ones which we denote by $\hat{\delta}$ and $\hat{\omega}$, respectively. The problem of making the circuit fail-safe against $\hat{\omega}$ can be reduced to the construction of fail-safe combinational circuits, and therefore, we will consider the effect of $\hat{\delta}$ only. We regard a fault to occur and accordingly δ to change when the first error manifests itself. The primary input is always assumed to be correct.

The set of all sequences of input symbols of X will be denoted by $\bar{X}$. $\delta(\bar{\mathbf{x}}, \mathbf{q})$, $\bar{\mathbf{x}} \in \bar{X}$ represents the final state, to which the circuit at initial state $\mathbf{q}$ will move by the application of an input sequence $\bar{\mathbf{x}}$. When the null input sequence λ is applied, $\delta(\lambda, \mathbf{q})$ is defined to be $\mathbf{q}$ itself.

In order for the concept of fail-safe circuits to be meaningful, the safe-side output must be defined a priori. Let Z and Z_s be the output code space in normal operation and the set of safe-side outputs, respectively. Then the formal definition of fail-safe sequential circuits is as follows:

Definition 17. Let $\bar{\mathbf{x}} = \bar{\mathbf{x}}'\mathbf{x}$ be an arbitrary input sequence applied to the circuit at initial state $\mathbf{q}$. The circuit is said to be fail-safe if and only if

$$\hat{\mathbf{z}} \equiv \omega(\mathbf{x}, \hat{\delta}(\bar{\mathbf{x}}', \mathbf{q})) \in Z_s$$

or

$$\hat{\mathbf{z}} = \mathbf{z} \equiv \omega(\mathbf{x}, \delta(\bar{\mathbf{x}}', \mathbf{q})) \tag{5.7.1}$$

for any $\mathbf{q} \in Q$.

However, most investigations so far have not followed this definition directly but have considered more limited cases for analytical convenience.

Let $\hat{Q}$ be a set of such states as

$$\hat{Q} = \{\hat{\mathbf{q}} \mid \exists \, \bar{\mathbf{x}} \in \bar{X}, \, \exists \, \mathbf{q} \in Q, \, \hat{\mathbf{q}} = \hat{\delta}(\bar{\mathbf{x}}, \mathbf{q})\} \tag{5.7.2}$$

A convenient way to realize fail-safe sequential circuits is to make sure that

$$Q \cap \hat{Q} = \phi \tag{5.7.3}$$

This means that under the existence of a fault, the circuit will never move to a state of Q but will remain in $\hat{Q}$ after the transition from a state of Q to that of $\hat{Q}$. Thus it follows that the circuit will produce the safe-side output if we assign an appropriate output of Z_s to each state of $\hat{Q}$.

Next we consider the realization of fail-safe sequential circuits, using two structural models, the delay model and the flip-flop model. The first model is illustrated in Fig. 5.7.1a, and the second model is shown in Fig. 5.7.1b.

$D_n, D_{n-1}, \ldots, D_1$ in the first model are delay elements which propagate their input signals to their output terminals one clock period later. $F_n, F_{n-1}, \ldots, F_1$ are combinational circuits determining the next values of $y_n, y_{n-1}, \ldots, y_1$, respectively. ω is the output circuit of the sequential circuit.

In the second model, however, state variables are represented by outputs of flip-flops, $FF_n, FF_{n-1}, \ldots, FF_1$. J-K flip-flops are assumed throughout this section. $\theta_n, \theta_{n-1}, \ldots, \theta_1$ are combinational circuits exciting $J_n, J_{n-1}, \ldots, J_1$, respectively, while $\psi_n, \psi_{n-1}, \ldots, \psi_1$ are those for exciting $K_n, K_{n-1}, \ldots, K_1$.

5.7.1. Delay Model

Rather than present the design procedure in general terms, we prefer to explain it by using the example in Fig. 5.7.2a. To ensure Eq. (5.7.3), a $\binom{n}{k}$ code is employed for the state assignment, as shown in Fig. 5.7.2b, where $n = 4$ and $k = 2$. Further, an arbitrary code word, (1100) in this case, is excluded.

State variable functions are expressed in two forms, the on-set realization and the off-set realization. In relation to the excluded code word (1100), the off-set realizations are used for $y_4^{(1)}$ and $y_3^{(1)}$, while the on-set realizations are applied to $y_2^{(1)}$ and $y_1^{(1)}$. In the on-set realization, we look at binary value 1 at every code word assigned to each state of Q. For $y_1^{(1)}$, as an example, it takes value 1 in (0101), (1001),

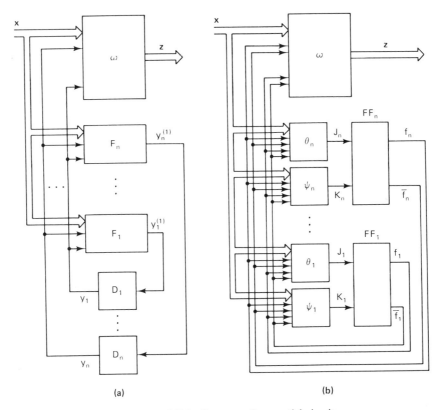

Figure 5.7.1   Structure of sequential circuits.

	δ	
X	0	1
Q		
q_a	q_a	q_b
q_b	q_b	q_c
q_c	q_d	q_e
q_d	q_c	q_e
q_e	q_e	q_e

(a)

				δ								
			X	0				1				
y_4	y_3	y_2	y_1									
0	1	0	1	0	1	0	1	1	0	0	1	
1	0	0	1	1	0	0	1	0	1	1	0	
0	1	1	0	0	0	1	1	1	0	1	0	
0	0	1	1	0	1	1	0	1	0	1	0	
1	0	1	0	0	1	0	1	1	0	1	0	

(b)

Figure 5.7.2   Sequential circuit.

(0110), and (1010) at $x = 0$, while in (0101) at $x = 1$. Regarding any 4-tuple with its weight different from 2 as a don't-care term, $y_1^{(1)}$ can be expressed as

$$y_1^{(1)} \equiv F_1(x, y_4, y_3, y_2, y_1)$$

$$= \bar{x}(y_3 y_1 \vee y_4 y_1 \vee y_3 y_2 \vee y_4 y_2) \vee x y_3 y_1 \tag{5.7.4}$$

Similarly,

$$y_2^{(1)} \equiv F_2(x, y_4, y_3, y_2, y_1)$$

$$= \bar{x}(y_3 y_2 \vee y_2 y_1) \vee x(y_4 y_1 \vee y_3 y_2 \vee y_2 y_1 \vee y_4 y_2) \qquad (5.7.5)$$

These two expressions are called the *on-set realizations*.

Similarly, we note where the binary value 0 occurs at every assigned code word. For example, $y_3^{(1)}$ takes value 0 in (1001) and (0110) at $x = 0$, and in (0101), (0110), (0011), and (1010) at $x = 1$. Considering don't-care terms in the same way, we can express $y_3^{(1)}$ as

$$\bar{y}_3^{(1)} = \bar{x}(\bar{y}_3 \bar{y}_2 \vee \bar{y}_4 \bar{y}_1) \vee x(\bar{y}_4 \bar{y}_2 \vee \bar{y}_4 \bar{y}_1 \vee \bar{y}_4 \bar{y}_3 \vee \bar{y}_3 \bar{y}_1)$$

Complementing both sides of the equation above gives

$$y_3^{(1)} \equiv F_3(x, y_4, y_3, y_2, y_1)$$

$$= \{x \vee (y_3 \vee y_2)(y_4 \vee y_1)\}\{\bar{x} \vee (y_4 \vee y_2)(y_4 \vee y_1)(y_4 \vee y_3)(y_3 \vee y_1)\} \qquad (5.7.6)$$

Similarly,

$$y_4^{(1)} \equiv F_4(x, y_4, y_3, y_2, y_1)$$

$$= \{x \vee (y_4 \vee y_2)(y_4 \vee y_1)(y_4 \vee y_3)(y_3 \vee y_1)\}\{\bar{x} \vee (y_3 \vee y_2)\} \qquad (5.7.7)$$

These two expressions are the *off-set realizations*.

Note that all state variable functions are positive [FRIE75] in any state variable, regardless of whether they are expressed in the on-set realization or in the off-set realization. Following these realizations, we can construct combinational circuits for determining $y_i^{(1)}$, $i = 1, 2, 3$, and 4, without NOT gates except those for primary input variables. This is illustrated in Fig. 5.7.3.

Figure 5.7.4 shows the state transition based on the normal state variable functions. Suppose that, say, $F_3(x, y_4, y_3, y_2, y_1)$ has become an erroneous function $\hat{F}_3(x, y_4, y_3, y_2, y_1)$ by developing a stuck-at-1 fault at the output of a gate in the combinational circuit for $y_3^{(1)}$. Since this circuit has no internal NOT gates,

$$\hat{F}_3(x, y_4, y_3, y_2, y_1) \geq F_3(x, y_4, y_3, y_2, y_1) \qquad (5.7.8)$$

Further, an error manifests itself at a transition from a state $(\alpha_4 \alpha_3 \alpha_2 \alpha_1)$ to the next state $(\alpha_4^{(1)} \alpha_3^{(1)} \alpha_2^{(1)} \alpha_1^{(1)})$, where an erroneous destination state $(\hat{\alpha}_4^{(1)} \hat{\alpha}_3^{(1)} \hat{\alpha}_2^{(1)} \hat{\alpha}_1^{(1)})$ actually occurs, instead of the correct $(\alpha_4^{(1)} \alpha_3^{(1)} \alpha_2^{(1)} \alpha_1^{(1)})$. Because of the inclusion relation (5.7.8), the weight of $(\hat{\alpha}_4^{(1)} \hat{\alpha}_3^{(1)} \hat{\alpha}_2^{(1)} \hat{\alpha}_1^{(1)})$, denoted by $|(\hat{\alpha}_4^{(1)} \hat{\alpha}_3^{(1)} \hat{\alpha}_2^{(1)} \hat{\alpha}_1^{(1)})|$, is not equal to, but greater than 2. More precisely,

$$\hat{\alpha}_i^{(1)} \geq \alpha_i^{(1)} \qquad (5.7.9)$$

for $i = 1, 2, 3$, and 4. In our example of Fig. 5.7.5, let us assume that $(\alpha_4 \alpha_3 \alpha_2 \alpha_1) = (0110)$, $(\alpha_4^{(1)} \alpha_3^{(1)} \alpha_2^{(1)} \alpha_1^{(1)}) = (1010)$, and $(\hat{\alpha}_4^{(1)} \hat{\alpha}_3^{(1)} \hat{\alpha}_2^{(1)} \hat{\alpha}_1^{(1)}) = (1110)$.

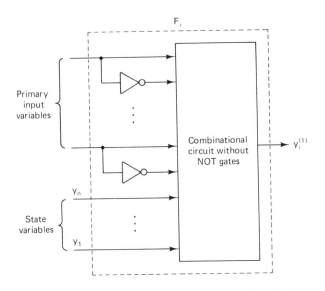

Figure 5.7.3 Exciting circuit for $y_i^{(1)}$.

Now consider the next state $(\hat{\alpha}_4^{(2)}\,\hat{\alpha}_3^{(2)}\,\hat{\alpha}_2^{(2)}\,\hat{\alpha}_1^{(2)})$ of this erroneous (1110) at $x = 1$ in comparison with the correct next state of correct (1010).

By substituting $\hat{\alpha}_4^{(1)} = 1$, $\hat{\alpha}_3^{(1)} = 1$, $\hat{\alpha}_2^{(1)} = 1$, $\hat{\alpha}_1^{(1)} = 0$ into y_4, y_3, y_2, y_1 of $F_i(x, y_4, y_3, y_2, y_1)$ for $i = 1, 2, 3$, and 4, respectively, we get values of state variables given by the normal state variable functions. Since the number of state variables with value 0 is less than 2 in (1110),

$$F_4(x, 1, 1, 1, 0) = F_3(x, 1, 1, 1, 0) = 1 \tag{5.7.10}$$

independent of the value of x. Further, if we note both the inclusion relation (5.7.9) and the monotonicity in $F_2(x, y_4, y_3, y_2, y_1)$ and $F_1(x, y_4, y_3, y_2, y_1)$, we see that

$$\left.\begin{aligned} F_2(x, 1, 1, 1, 0) &\geq F_2(x, 1, 0, 1, 0) \\ F_1(x, 1, 1, 1, 0) &\geq F_1(x, 1, 0, 1, 0) \end{aligned}\right\} \tag{5.7.11}$$

$F_2(x, 1, 0, 1, 0)$ and $F_1(x, 1, 0, 1, 0)$ represent values of y_2 and y_1 at the correct next state of correct (1010). However, recall that no normal state is assigned (1100). Therefore, at least one of $F_2(x, 1, 0, 1, 0)$ and $F_1(x, 1, 0, 1, 0)$ (the former in this example) takes value 1. Under the existence of the fault, the next state of (1110) must be determined by the faulty $\hat{F}_3(x, y_4, y_3, y_2, y_1)$ together with other normal state variable functions. However, the inclusion relation (5.7.8), in addition to Eqs. (5.7.10) and (5.7.11), implies that $\left|(\hat{\alpha}_4^{(2)}\,\hat{\alpha}_3^{(2)}\,\hat{\alpha}_2^{(2)}\,\hat{\alpha}_1^{(2)})\right| > 2$. That is, the erroneous next state of erroneous (1110) does not belong to Q.

Here, let us clarify a set of faults covered. In reference to Fig. 5.7.3, a stuck-at-1 or 0 fault is assumed to develop at the output of a NOT gate for a primary input variable, or at the output of a gate in the box designated as combinational, or even at the output of the delay element for a state variable. Then we summarize the property above as the concluding theorem [TOHM71].

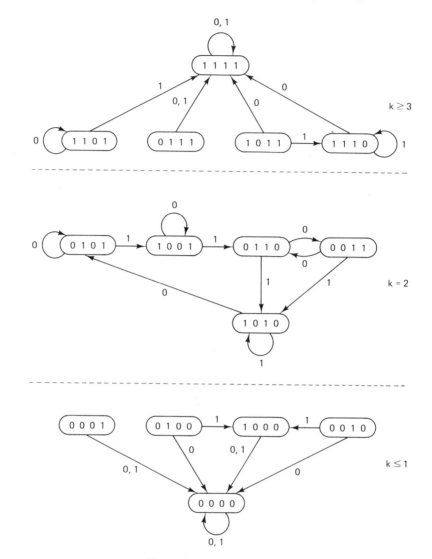

Figure 5.7.4 State transition.

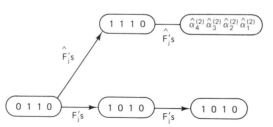

Figure 5.7.5 Erroneous state transition.

Theorem 12.   By the combined use of the on-set realization and the off-set realization under the state assignment of a $\binom{n}{k}$ code, we can construct a sequential circuit that will never go out of $\hat{Q}$ once the circuit transfers to a state of $\hat{Q}$ from a state of Q upon the occurrence of a fault of the prescribed set.

The condition of excluding a code word from the state assignment can be relaxed with an additional care [TOHM71]. Furuya [FURU72], Diaz et al. [DIAZ74a], Wang and Chuang [WANG75], and Sawin [SAWI74b] investigated the conditions for constructing fail-safe sequential circuits using only the on-set realization. Das and Chuang considered the use of the Berger code instead of the constant-weight code [DAS74].

Takaoka and Ibaraki approached the problem from a different point of view, following the direct definition of Eq. (5.7.1) [TAKA73]. In their method, a state variable function may not be positive in all state variables. For details, refer to the literature.

5.7.2. Flip-Flop Model

When the flip-flop model is used, a different approach should be considered. Here each state of Q will be encoded in the parity check code. Suppose that the even parity scheme is incorporated.

Consider a case where the circuit is to move from state $\mathbf{q} \in Q$ to its destination $\mathbf{q}^{(1)}$ by the application of an input $\mathbf{x}$. Instead, the circuit will transfer to an erroneous state $\hat{\mathbf{q}}^{(1)}$ upon the occurrence of a fault. Let $\hat{\mathbf{q}}^{(1)}$ and $\mathbf{q}^{(1)}$ be represented by $(\hat{y}_n^{(1)} \cdots \hat{y}_1^{(1)})$ and $(y_n^{(1)} \cdots y_1^{(1)})$, respectively. Since a single variable is in error at $\hat{\mathbf{q}}^{(1)}$,

$$d_H((\hat{y}_n^{(1)} \cdots \hat{y}_1^{(1)}), (y_n^{(1)} \cdots y_1^{(1)})) = 1 \tag{5.7.12}$$

Then define set $\hat{Q}$ to be

$$\hat{Q} = \{(\hat{y}_n \cdots \hat{y}_1) \,|\, \exists\, (y_n \cdots y_1) \in Q,$$
$$d_H((\hat{y}_n \cdots \hat{y}_1), (y_n \cdots y_1)) = 1\} \tag{5.7.13}$$

Since $(\hat{y}_n \cdots \hat{y}_1)$ has odd parity,

$$Q \cap \hat{Q} = \phi \tag{5.7.14}$$

As far as normal operation is concerned, state variable functions have not yet been specified on $\hat{Q}$. To realize the fail-safe property, however, let us design state variable functions on $\hat{Q}$ as shown below. For $i = 1, 2, \ldots, n$,

$$\forall \mathbf{x} \in X \quad \forall \ (\hat{y}_n \cdots \hat{y}_1) \in \hat{Q}$$

$$F_i(\mathbf{x}, \hat{y}_n, \cdots, \hat{y}_i, \cdots \hat{y}_1) = \hat{y}_i \tag{5.7.15}$$

In terms of the state transitions, this design implies that the circuit at state $(\hat{y}_n \cdots \hat{y}_1) \in \hat{Q}$ will stay at the same state, independent of the input applied. In this context, this design is called the *state trapping technique*.

Q together with $\hat{Q}$ may not exhaust $\{0, 1\}^n$. Any n-tuple of $\{0, 1\}^n - \{Q \cup \hat{Q}\}$ can obviously be treated as a don't-care term.

Figure 5.7.6 shows a design example. In normal operation, this circuit acts like a counter with three states. The code words assigned to these normal states are (000), (011), and (110). The set of n-tuples separated from these normal states by Hamming distance 1 is $\{(001), (010), (100), (111)\} = \hat{Q}$. Observe that the next state of a state of $\hat{Q}$ is specified to be the same as itself, regardless of the value of x. State (101) remains unspecified as the don't-care term.

f_3 f_2 f_1	δ 0	1
Q 0 0 0 0 1 1 1 1 0	0 0 0 0 1 1 1 1 0	0 1 1 1 1 0 0 0 0
$\hat{Q}$ 0 0 1 0 1 0 1 0 0 1 1 1	0 0 1 0 1 0 1 0 0 1 1 1	0 0 1 0 1 0 1 0 0 1 1 1
1 0 1	*	*

Figure 5.7.6 Design example.

In order to achieve the state transition as specified, the J-input and the K-input of each flip-flop must be excited properly. How to construct these excitation circuits is well described in textbooks on the theory of sequential circuits. For the circuit of Fig. 5.7.6, excitation functions of the J_i-input and the K_i-input for $i = 1, 2$, and 3 are

$$J_3(x, f_3, f_2, f_1) = x f_2 f_1$$

$$K_3(x, f_3, f_2, f_1) = x f_2 \bar{f_1}$$

$$J_2(x, f_3, f_2, f_1) = x \bar{f_3} \bar{f_1}$$

$$K_2(x, f_3, f_2, f_1) = x f_3 \bar{f_1}$$

$$J_1(x, f_3, f_2, f_1) = x \bar{f_3} \bar{f_2}$$

$$K_1(x, f_3, f_2, f_1) = x \bar{f_3} f_2$$

The circuit configuration is illustrated in Fig. 5.7.7.

Note that the θ_i and ψ_i circuits can each be constructed with NOT gates only; otherwise they can be constructed for complementing some of primary input variables without internal NOT gates. Complemented state variables are supplied by flip-flops themselves.

In this realization we take into consideration a fault at the output of a gate in the

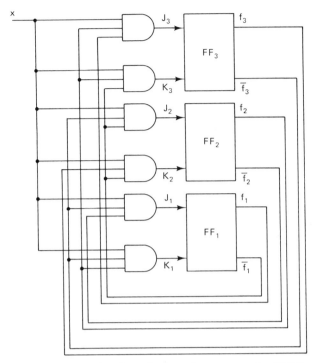

Figure 5.7.7 Scale-3 counter.

θ_i or ψ_i circuit, a fault at the output of a NOT gate for a primary input variable, and a fault at the output of a flip-flop. Further, we assume that the complemented output $\bar{f}_i$ of a flip-flop will also be stuck at $\bar{e}\,(e = 1$ or $0)$, whenever its counterpart f_i is held at e by a fault, or vice versa.

We divide the faults above into two classes:

Class 1
  (i) Stuck-at-1 faults at gates in θ_i circuits.
  (ii) Stuck-at-0 faults at gates in ψ_i circuits.
  (iii) Stuck-at-1 faults at f_i's.

Class 2
  (iv) Stuck-at-0 faults at gates in θ_i circuits.
  (v) Stuck-at-1 faults at gates in ψ_i circuits.
  (vi) Stuck-at-0 faults at f_i's.

The first fault of Class 1 affects circuit operation, incorrectly exciting the J-input of a flip-flop. A flip-flop reset is possibly missed by the second fault, because the K-input of the flip-flop may not be excited when it is to be excited. The third fault may directly cause the circuit to have a false value of a state variable. The immediate consequence of all these adverse effects is a transition to an erroneous state $\hat{\mathbf{q}}^{(1)} \in \hat{Q}$, in which a state variable takes a false value of 1, instead of a true value of 0.

In contrast, a fault of class 2 could transfer the circuit to a state of $\hat{Q}$, where a state variable improperly takes the value 0.

What will happen at the next transition from $\hat{\mathbf{q}}^{(1)}$? Let us consider each case of faults above.

Assume that $J_i(\mathbf{x}, f_n, \ldots, f_1)$ has become faulty $\hat{J}_i(\mathbf{x}, f_n, \ldots, f_1)$ due to a stuck-at-1 fault in θ_i circuit. As described above, $\hat{f}_i^{(1)}$ takes value 1 improperly in $\hat{\mathbf{q}}^{(1)}$. The circuit is designed to again have $\hat{f}_i^{(2)}$ of value 1 at a state $\hat{\mathbf{q}}^{(2)}$ next to $\hat{\mathbf{q}}^{(1)}$. Note that $K_i(\mathbf{x}, \hat{f}_n^{(1)}, \ldots, \hat{f}_1^{(1)}) = 0$ is essential, and the value of $J_i(\mathbf{x}, \hat{f}_n^{(1)}, \ldots, \hat{f}_1^{(1)})$ is of no matter at this state transition from $\hat{\mathbf{q}}^{(1)}$ to $\hat{\mathbf{q}}^{(2)}$. This means that faulty $\hat{J}_i(\mathbf{x}, \hat{f}_n^{(1)}, \ldots, \hat{f}_1^{(1)})$ has no adverse effects and, therefore, the transition $\hat{\mathbf{q}}^{(1)} \rightarrow \hat{\mathbf{q}}^{(2)}$ will be performed as specified in the design. That is, the circuit is trapped at $\hat{\mathbf{q}}^{(1)}$.

For example, suppose that J_3 is stuck at 1. At state (000), J_3 takes erroneous value 1 for $x = 1$. The state of the circuit will change improperly to (111), while the true transition is $(000) \rightarrow (011)$. At (111), however, the value of J_3 can be arbitrary, K_3 being specified definitely as 0. Therefore, by the application of x of any value, f_3 is held at 1 even under the presence of the fault at J_3. Since other state variables are excited as specified, the circuit will be trapped at (111).

We can verify in a similar way that the circuit will be trapped at a state of $\hat{Q}$ after the circuit moves to an erroneous state upon the occurrence of another fault in class 1 or in class 2.

We summarize the observation above as a theorem, which follows. We express the state transition function on the extended domain $Q \cup \hat{Q}$ by Δ, which is specified as

$$\left. \begin{array}{l} \forall \mathbf{x} \in X, \quad \forall \mathbf{q} \in Q, \quad \Delta(\mathbf{x}, \mathbf{q}) = \delta(\mathbf{x}, \mathbf{q}) \\ \forall \mathbf{x} \in X, \quad \forall \hat{\mathbf{q}} \in \hat{Q}, \quad \Delta(\mathbf{x}, \hat{\mathbf{q}}) = \hat{\mathbf{q}} \end{array} \right\} \qquad (5.7.17)$$

Theorem 13. [TOHM74].   Let $\hat{\Delta}$ be the modification of Δ by a fault of the prescribed set. Then

$$\forall \mathbf{x} \in X, \quad \forall \hat{\mathbf{q}} \in \hat{Q}, \quad \hat{\Delta}(\mathbf{x}, \hat{\mathbf{q}}) = \hat{\mathbf{q}} \qquad (5.7.18)$$

5.7.3. Further Topics

The problem of realizing unate state variable functions is discussed more extensively by Mago [MAGO73]. Diaz argues the realization of self-checking and fail-safe sequential circuits [DIAZ74b]. Fail-safe asynchronous sequential circuits and the related topics have been investigated by Sawin and Maki [SAWI74a, SAWI75], Patterson and Metze [PATT74], Mukai and Tohma [MUKA74, MUKA76], Chuang [CHUA75], Pradhan [PRAD78], and Masuyama and Yoshida [MASU75].

REFERENCES

[AMDA] Amdahl 470V/6-II Machine Reference Manual.

[ANDE73] Anderson, D. A., and G. Metze, "Design of Totally Self-Checking Check Circuits for m-Out-Of-n Codes," *IEEE Trans. Comput.*, vol. C-22, no. 3, pp. 263–269, Mar. 1973.

[ARMS61] Armstrong, D. B., "A General Method of Applying Error Correction to Asynchronous Digital Systems," *Bell Syst. Tech. J.,* vol. 40, pp. 577–593, Mar. 1961.

[ASHJ77] Ashjaee, M. J., and S. M. Reddy, "On Totally Self-Checking Checkers for Separable Codes," *IEEE Trans. Comput.,* vol. C-26, no. 8, pp. 737–744, Aug. 1977.

[AVIZ71a] Avizienis, A., "Arithmetic Error Codes: Cost and Effectiveness Studies for Application in Digital System Design," *IEEE Trans. Comput.,* vol. C-20, no. 11, pp. 1322–1331, Nov. 1971.

[AVIZ71b] Avizienis, A., G. C. Gilley, F. P. Mathur, D. A. Rennels, J. A. Rohr, and D. K. Rubin, "The STAR (Self-Testing and Repairing) Computer: An Investigation of the Theory and Practice of Fault-Tolerant Computer Design," *IEEE Trans. Comput.,* vol. C-20, no. 11, pp. 1312–1321, Nov. 1971.

[BERG61] Berger, J. M., "A Note on an Error Detection Code for Asymmetric Channels," *Inf. Control,* vol. 4, no. 1, pp. 68–73, Mar. 1961.

[BERL68] Berlekamp, E. R., *Algebraic Coding Theory,* McGraw-Hill, New York, 1968, pp. 315–318.

[BROW61] Brown, W. G., T. Tierney, and R. Wasserman, "Improvement of Computer Reliability through the Use of Redundancy," *IRE Trans. Electron. Comput.,* vol. EC-10, no. 3, pp. 407–416, Sept. 1961.

[CART68] Carter, W. C., and P. R. Schneider, "Design of Dynamically Checked Computers," *Proc. IFIP-68,* pp. 878–883, Aug. 1968.

[CART77] Carter, W. C., G. R. Putzolu, A. B. Wadia, W. G. Bouricius, D. C. Jessep, E. P. Hsieh, and C. J. Tan, "Cost Effectiveness of Self Checking Computer Design," *Dig., 7th Annu. Int. Symp. Fault-Tolerant Comput.,* Los Angeles, pp. 117–123, June 28–30, 1977.

[CHAV82] Chavade, J., and Y. Crouzet, "The P.A.D.: A Self-Checking LSI Circuit for Fault-Detection in Microcomputers," *Dig., 12th Annu. Int. Symp. Fault-Tolerant Comput.,* Santa Monica, Calif., pp. 55–62, June 22–24, 1982.

[CHUA75] Chuang, H. Y. H., "Fail-Safe Asynchronous Machines with Multiple Input Changes," *Dig., 5th Annu. Int. Symp. Fault-Tolerant Comput.,* Paris, pp. 124–129, June 18–20, 1975.

[CROU79] Crouzet, Y., and C. Landrault, "Design of Self-Checking MOS-LSI Circuits, Application to a Four-Bit Microprocessor," *Dig., 9th Annu. Int. Symp. Fault-tolerant Comput.,* Madison, Wis., pp. 189–192, June 20–22, 1979.

[CROU80] Crouzet, Y., and C. Landrault, "Design Specification of a Self-Checking Detection Processor," *Dig., 10th Annu. Int. Symp. Fault-Tolerant Comput.,* Kyoto, Japan, pp. 275–277, Oct. 1–3, 1980.

[DAS74] Das, S., and H. Y. H. Chuang, "A Unified Approach to the Realization of Fail-Safe Sequential Machines," *Dig., 4th Annu. Int. Symp. Fault-Tolerant Comput.,* pp. 3-2 to 3-6, June 1974.

[DIAZ74a] Diaz, M., J. C. Geffroy, and M. Courvoisier, "On-Set Realization of Fail-Safe Sequential Machines," *IEEE Trans. Comput.,* vol. C-23, no. 2, pp. 133–138, Feb. 1974.

[DIAZ74b] Diaz, M., "Design of Totally Self-Checking and Fail-Safe Sequential Machines," *Dig., 4th Annu. Int. Symp. Fault-Tolerant Comput.,* pp. 3-19 to 3-24, June 1974.

[FRIE69] Friedman, A., R. L. Graham, and J. D. Ullman, "Universal Single Transition Time Asynchronous State Assignments," *IEEE Trans. Comput.,* vol. C-18, no. 6, pp. 541–547, June 1969.

[FRIE75] Friedman, A. D., and P. R. Menon, *Theory and Design of Switching Circuits,* Computer Science Press, Woodland Hills, Calif., 1975, pp. 101–103.

[FUJI81] Fujiwara, E., and K. Haruta, "Fault-Tolerant Arithmetic Logic Unit Using Parity-Based Codes," *Trans. Inst. Electron. Commun. Eng. Jap.,* vol. E64, no. 10, pp. 653–660, Oct. 1981.

[FURU72] Furuya, K., "A Study on Fail-Safe Systems," Graduation dissertation, Tokyo Institute of Technology, Mar. 1972 (in Japanese).

[FURU83] Furuya, K., Y. Akita, and Y. Tohma, "Logic Design of Fault-Tolerant Dividers Based on Data Complementation Strategy," *Dig., 13th Annu. Int. Symp. Fault-Tolerant Comput.,* Milan, Italy, pp. 306–313, June 1983.

[GRAY76] Gray, F. G., and J. F. Meyer, "Algebraic Properties of Functions Affecting Optimum Fault Tolerant Realizations," *IEEE Trans. Comput.,* vol. C-25, no. 11, pp. 1078–1088, Nov. 1976.

[IZAW81] IZAWA, N., "3-Level Realization of Self-Checking 1-Out-Of-n Code Checkers," *1981 IECE Nat. Conv. Inf. Syst., Inst. Electron. Commun. Eng. Jap.,* no. 504, Oct. 1981 (in Japanese).

[KHOD79] Khodadad-Mostershiry, B., "Parity Prediction in Combinational Circuit," *Dig., 9th Annu. Int. Symp. Fault-Tolerant Comput.,* Madison, Wis., pp. 185–188, June 20–22, 1979.

[KUHL78] Kuhl, J. G., and S. M. Reddy, "Multicode Single Transition Time State Assignment for Asynchronous Sequential Machines," *IEEE Trans. Comput.,* vol. C-27, no. 10, pp. 927–934, Oct. 1978.

[LIU63] Liu, C. N., "A State Variable Assignment Method for Asynchronous Sequential Switching Circuits," *J. ACM,* vol. 10, pp. 209–216, Apr. 1963.

[MAGO73] Mago, S., "Monotone Functions in Sequential Circuits," *IEEE Trans. Comput.,* vol. C-22, no. 10, pp. 928–933, Oct. 1973.

[MAKI74] Maki, G., and D. H. Sawin III, "Fault-Tolerant Asynchronous Sequential Machines," *IEEE Trans. Comput.,* vol. C-23, no. 7, pp. 651–657, July 1974.

[MARO78a] Marouf, M. A., and D. A. Friedman, "Design of Self-Checking Checkers for Berger Codes," *Dig., 8th Annu. Int. Symp. Fault-Tolerant Comput.,* Toulouse, France, pp. 179–184, June 21–23, 1978.

[MARO78b] Marouf, M. A., and A. D. Friedman, "Efficient Design of Self-Checking Checkers for m-Out-Of-n Codes," *IEEE Trans. Comput.,* vol. C-27, no. 6, pp. 482–490, June 1978.

[MASU75] Masuyama, H., and N. Yoshida, "Fail-Safe Asynchronous Sequential Circuits," Tech. Rep. EC-75-13, Inst. of Electron. Commun. Eng. Jap., June 1975 (in Japanese).

[MEYE71] Meyer, J., "Fault Tolerant Sequential Machines," *IEEE Trans. Comput.,* vol. C-20, no. 10, pp. 1167–1177, Oct. 1971.

[MOOR56a] Moore, E. F., and C. E. Shannon, "Reliable Circuits Using Less Reliable Relays, Part I," *J. Franklin Inst.,* vol. 262, pp. 191–208, Sept. 1956.

[MOOR56b] Moore, E. F., and C. E. Shannon, "Reliable Circuits Using Less Reliable Relays, Part II," *J. Franklin Inst.,* vol. 262, pp. 281–297, Oct. 1956.

[MUKA74] Mukai, Y., and Y. Tohma, "A Method for the Realization of Fail-Safe Asynchronous Sequential Circuits," *IEEE Trans. Comput.*, vol. C-23, no. 7, pp. 736–739, July 1974.

[MUKA76] Mukai, Y., and Y. Tohma, "A Masked-Fault Free Realization of Fail-Safe Asynchronous Sequential Circuits," *Dig., 6th Annu. Int. Symp. Fault-Tolerant Comput.*, Pittsburgh, Pa., pp. 69–74, June 21–23, 1976.

[NAKA78] Nakajima, T., and Y. Tohma, "A Way of Construction of Universal STT Assignment for Asynchronous Sequential Circuits—(2, 2) Separating Systems and Their Relations to Linear Codes," Tech. Rep. EC-78-30, Inst. Electron. Commun. Eng. Jap., Sept. 1978 (in Japanese).

[NANY77] Nanya, T., "Universal STT State Assignments for Asynchronous Sequential Circuits," *Trans. Inst. Electron. Commun. Eng. Jap.*, vol. J60-D, no. 10, pp. 846–853, Oct. 1977 (in Japanese).

[NANY78] Nanya, T., and Y. Tohma, "On Universal Single Transition Time Asynchronous State Assignments," *IEEE Trans. Comput.*, vol. C-27, no. 8, pp. 781–782, Aug. 1978.

[NANY79] Nanya, T., and Y. Tohma, "Universal Multicode STT State Assignments for Asynchronous Sequential Machines," *IEEE Trans. Comput.*, vol. C-28, no. 11, pp. 811–818, Nov. 1979.

[NANY80] Nanya, T., "Asynchronous Switching Circuits," *J. Inst. Electron. Commun. Eng. Jap.*, vol. 63, no. 7, pp. 752–759, July 1980 (in Japanese).

[NANY83] Nanya, T., and Y. Tohma, "A 3-Level Realization of Totally Self-Checking Checkers for m-Out-Of-n Codes," *Dig., 13th Annu. Int. Symp. Fault-Tolerant Comput.*, Milan, Italy, pp. 173–176, June 1983.

[NEUM56] von Neumann, J., "Probabilistic Logic and the Synthesis of Reliable Organisms," in *Automata Studies*, C. E. Shannon and J. McCarthy, Eds., Princeton University Press, Princeton, N.J., 1956, pp. 43–98.

[NEUM75] Neumann, P. G., and T. R. N. Rao, "Error Correcting Codes for Byte-Organized Arithmetic Processors," *IEEE Trans. Comput.*, vol. C-24, no. 3, pp. 226–232, Mar. 1975.

[PATT74] Patterson, E. E., and G. Metze, "A Fail-Safe Asynchronous Sequential Machine," *IEEE Trans. Comput.*, vol. C-23, no. 4, pp. 369–374, Apr. 1974.

[PIER65] Pierce, W. H., *Failure Tolerant Computer Design*, Academic Press, New York, 1965.

[PRAD72a] Pradhan, D. K., and S. M. Reddy, "A Design Technique for Synthesis of Fault-Tolerant Adders," *Dig., 2nd Annu. Int. Symp. Fault-Tolerant Comput.*, Newton, Mass., pp. 20–24, June 19–21, 1972.

[PRAD72b] Pradhan, D. K., and S. M. Reddy, "Error-Control Techniques for Logic Processors," *IEEE Trans. Comput.*, vol. C-21, no. 12, pp. 1331–1336, Dec. 1972.

[PRAD73] Pradhan, D. K., and S. M. Reddy, "Fault-Tolerant Asynchronous Networks," *IEEE Trans. Comput.*, vol. C-22, no. 7, pp. 662–669, July 1973.

[PRAD74a] Pradhan, D. K., and S. M. Reddy, "Design of Two-Level Fault-Tolerant Networks," *IEEE Trans. Comput.*, vol. C-23, no. 1, pp. 41–48, Jan. 1974.

[PRAD74b] Pradhan, D. K., "Fault-Tolerant Carry-Save Adders," *IEEE Trans. Comput.*, vol. C-23, no. 12, pp. 1320–1322, Dec. 1974.

[PRAD76] Pradhan, D. K., and S. M. Reddy, "Techniques to Construct (2, 1) Separating Systems from Linear Error-Correcting Codes," *IEEE Trans. Comput.*, vol. C-25, no. 9, pp. 945–949, Sept. 1976.

[PRAD78] Pradhan, D. K., "Asynchronous State Assignments with Unateness Properties and Fault-Secure Design," *IEEE Trans. Comput.*, vol. C-27, no. 5, pp. 396–404, Mar. 1978.

[PRAD80] Pradhan, D. K., "A New Class of Error-Correcting/Detecting Codes for Fault-Tolerant Computer Applications," *IEEE Trans. Comput.*, vol. C-29, no. 6, pp. 471–481, June 1980.

[RAO70] Rao, T. R. N., "Biresidue Error-Correcting Codes for Computer Arithmetic," *IEEE Trans. Comput.*, vol. C-19, no. 5, pp. 398–402, May 1970.

[RAO74] Rao, T. R. N., *Error Coding for Arithmetic Processors*, Academic Press, New York, 1974.

[RAO77] Rao, T. R. N., and H. J. Reinheimer, "Fault-Tolerant Modularized Arithmetic Logic Units," *Proc. 1977 NCC*, pp. 703–710, June 1977.

[RAYC61] Ray-Chaudhuri, D. K., "On the Construction of Minimally Redundant Reliable System Designs," *Bell Syst. Tech. J.*, vol. 40, pp. 595–611, Mar. 1961.

[REDD74] Reddy, S. M., "A Note on Self-Checking Checkers," *IEEE Trans. Comput.*, vol. C-23, no. 10, pp. 1100–1102, Oct. 1974.

[REED70] Reed, I. S., and A. C. L. Chiang, "Coding Techniques for Failure Tolerant Counters," *IEEE Trans. Comput.*, vol. C-19, no. 11, pp. 1035–1038, Nov. 1970.

[RENN78] Rennels, D. A., A. Avizienis, and M. Ercegovac, "A Study of Standard Building Blocks for the Design of Fault-Tolerant Distributed Computer Systems," *Dig., 8th Annu. Int. Symp. Fault-Tolerant Comput.*, Toulouse, France, pp. 144–149, June 21–23, 1978.

[REYN78] Reynolds, D. A. and G. Metze, "Fault Detection Capabilities of Alternating Logic," *IEEE Trans. Comput.*, vol. C-27, no. 12, pp. 1093–1098, Dec. 1978.

[RUDO67] Rudolph, L. D., "A Class of Majority Logic Decodable Codes," *IEEE Trans. Inf. Theory*, vol. IT-13, no. 4, pp. 305–307, Apr. 1967.

[RUSS65] Russo, L. R., "Synthesis of Error Tolerant Counters Using Minimum Distance Three State Assignments," *IEEE Trans. Electron. Comput.*, vol. EC-14, no. 6, pp. 359–366, June 1965.

[SAGA69] Sagalovich, Y. L., "Complexity of the Combinational Unit under Noise Immune Coding of the States of an Automaton," *Probl. Peredachi Inf.*, vol. 5, no. 3, pp. 37–45, 1969.

[SAWI74a] Sawin, D. H., III, and G. Maki, "Asynchronous Sequential Machines Designed for Fault Detection," *IEEE Trans. Comput.*, vol. C-23, no. 3, pp. 239–248, Mar. 1974.

[SAWI74b] Sawin, D. H., III, "Fail-Safe Synchronous Sequential Machines Using Modified On-Set Realizations," *Dig., 4th Annu. Int. Symp. Fault-Tolerant Comput.*, pp. 3–7 to 3–12, June 1974.

[SAWI75] Sawin, D. H., III, and G. Maki, "Fail-Safe Asynchronous Sequential Machines," *IEEE Trans. Comput.*, vol. C-24, no. 6, pp. 675–677, June 1975.

[SEDM78] Sedmak, R. S., and K. L. Liebergot, "Fault Tolerance of a General Purpose Computer Implemented by Very Large Scale Integration," *Dig. 8th Annu. Int. Symp. Fault-Tolerant Comput.*, Toulouse, France, pp. 137–143, June 21–23, 1978.

[SELL68] Sellers, F. F., M. Y. Hsiao, and L. W. Bearnson, *Error Detecting Logic for Digital Computers*, McGraw-Hill, New York, 1968.

[SHED78] Shedletsky, J. J., "Error Correction by Alternate Data Retry," *IEEE Trans. Comput.,* vol. C-25, no. 2, pp. 106–117, Feb. 1978.

[SMIT77] Smith, J. E., and G. Metze, "The Design of Totally Self-Checking Combinational Circuits," *Dig., 7th Annu. Int. Symp. Fault-Tolerant Comput.,* Los Angeles, pp. 130–134, June 28–30, 1977.

[TAKA73] Takaoka, T., and T. Ibaraki, "Fail-Safe Realization of Sequential Machines," *Inf. Control,* vol. 22, pp. 31–55, 1973.

[TAKE80] Takeda, K., and Y. Tohma, "Logic Design of Fault-Tolerant Arithmetic Units Based on the Data Complementation Strategy," *Dig., 10th Annu. Int. Symp. Fault-Tolerant Comput.,* Kyoto, Japan, pp. 348–350, Oct. 1–3, 1980.

[TOHM71] Tohma, Y., R. Sakai, and R. Ohyama, "Realization of Fail-Safe Sequential Machines by Using k-Out-Of-n Code," *IEEE Trans. Comput.,* vol. C-20, no. 11, pp. 1270–1275, Nov. 1971.

[TOHM74] Tohma, Y., "Design Technique of Fail-Safe Sequential Circuits Using Flip-Flops for Internal Memory," *IEEE Trans. Comput.,* vol. C-23, no. 11, pp. 1149–1154, Nov. 1974.

[TOY78] Toy, W. N., "Fault-Tolerant Design of Local ESS Processors," *Proc. IEEE,* vol. 66, no. 10, pp. 1126–1145, Oct. 1978.

[TRAC66] Tracey, J. H., "Internal State Assignments for Asynchronous Sequential Machines," *IEEE Trans. Electron. Comput.,* vol. EC-15, no. 4, pp. 551–560, Aug. 1966.

[TSAO82] Tsao, M. M., A. W. Wilson, R. C. McGarity, C. J. Tseng, and D. P. Siewiorek, "The Design of C Fast: A Single Chip Fault Tolerant Microprocessor," *Dig., 12th Annu. Int. Symp. Fault-Tolerant Comput.,* Santa Monica, Calif., pp. 63–69, June 22–24, 1982.

[TYRO62] Tyron, J. G., "Quadded Logic," in *Redundancy Techniques for Computing Systems,* R. H. Wilcox and W. C. Mann, Eds., Spartan Books, Bensalem, Pa., 1962, pp. 205–228.

[UNGE69] Unger, S. H., *Asynchronous Sequential Switching Circuits,* Wiley, New York, 1969.

[USAS78] Usas, A., "Checksum vs. Residue Codes for Multiple Error Detection," *Dig., 8th Annu. Int. Symp. Fault-Tolerant Comput.,* Toulouse, France, p. 224, June 21–23, 1978.

[WAKE74] Wakerly, J. F., "Partially Self-Checking Circuits and Their Use in Performing Logical Operations," *IEEE Trans. Comput.,* vol. C-23, no. 7, pp. 658–667, July 1974.

[WAKE76] Wakerly, J. F., "One's Complement Adder Eliminates Unwanted Zero," *Electronics,* vol. 49, no. 3, pp. 103–105, Feb. 5, 1976.

[WAKE78] Wakerly, J. F., *Error Detecting Codes, Self-Checking Circuits and Applications,* Elsevier North-Holland, New York, 1978.

[WANG75] Wang, L. L., and H. Y. H. Chuang, "On the Improvement of Fail-Safe Synchronous Machine Design Using On-Set Realization," *Dig., 5th Annu. Int. Symp. Fault-Tolerant Comput.,* Paris, p. 255, June 18–20, 1975.

[WANG79] Wang, S. L., and A. Avizienis, "The Design of Totally Self-Checking Circuits Using Programmable Logic Arrays," *Dig., 9th Annu. Int. Symp. Fault-Tolerant Comput.,* Madison, Wis., pp. 173–180, June 20–22, 1979.

[YAMA70] Yamamoto, H., T. Watanabe, and Y. Urano, "Alternating Logic and Its Application to Fault Detection," *Proc. IEEE Int. Comput. Group Conf.,* pp. 220–228, June 1970.

PROBLEMS

5.1. Consider a two-dimensional parity check. That is, information bits are arranged in an array form as shown in Fig. P5.1 and check bits are added to each row and column of this array. There are four options in applying the even or odd parity scheme to each row and to each column. However, the element at $\times$ may encounter such a contradiction that it cannot follow both schemes for the row and for the column of check bits. Show an example of this sort of contradiction. Verify that no contradiction may arise if the even parity scheme is employed both in rows and in columns of the array.

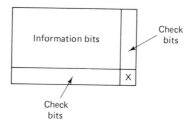

Figure P5.1

5.2. Concerning Eq. (5.2.18), enumerate the number of cases where random double errors are not detected in the checksum code. By a random double error we mean that values of two arbitrary bits are erroneous.

5.3. Verify that n, the length of code words including a check bit of the parity check code, must be even if the bit-by-bit complement of any code word is also a code word.

5.4. Suppose that two input operands **x** and **y** and output **z** of the circuit of Fig. P5.4 are 5-tuples as $(x_3 x_2 x_1 x_0 x_c)$, $(y_3 y_2 y_1 y_0 y_c)$, and $(z_3 z_2 z_1 z_0 z_c)$, respectively, where

$$x_c = \sum_{i=0}^{3} x_i$$

$$y_c = \sum_{i=0}^{3} y_i$$

$$z_c = \sum_{i=0}^{3} z_i$$

and for $i = 0, 1, 2,$ and 3

$$z_i = 1 \qquad \text{if and only if } x_i \leq y_i$$

Determine the formula to predict the value of z_c.

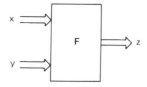

Figure P5.4

5.5. Construct a self-checking checker for $\binom{6}{1}$ code by using Izawa's method.

5.6. Construct a self-checking checker for $\binom{8}{4}$ code by using Anderson and Metze's method.

5.7. Demonstrate that the circuit of Fig. 5.3.11 is self-testing.

5.8. In the network of EX-OR gates of Fig. P5.8, $(x_3 x_2 x_1 x_0)$ is a binary representation of an integer N such that $0 \le N \le 9$, while x_c is the check bit of the odd parity scheme. Is this circuit self-testing? Assume that a fault may develop at the input as well as the output line of an EX-OR gate. If it is not self-testing, permute labels of primary input lines so as to make the circuit self-testing.

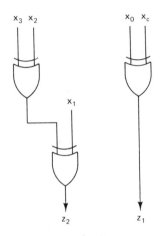

Figure P5.8

5.9. Verify the code disjointness of a $\binom{2k}{k}$ code checker which is based on Eqs. (5.3.5) and (5.3.6).

5.10. Suppose that two binary operands, $(x_4 x_3 x_2 x_1)$ and $(y_4 y_3 y_2 y_1)$, are encoded into $(x_4 x_3 x_2 x_1 c_3 c_2 c_1)$ and $(y_4 y_3 y_2 y_1 d_3 d_2 d_1)$ by the parity check matrix

$$\mathbf{H} = \begin{bmatrix} 1 & 1 & 0 & 1 & 1 & 0 & 0 \\ 1 & 0 & 1 & 1 & 0 & 1 & 0 \\ 0 & 1 & 1 & 1 & 0 & 0 & 1 \end{bmatrix}$$

Design the circuit enclosed by the dashed line in Fig. 5.4.1 and demonstrate that a single error at an output line of the 4-bit binary adder can be corrected.

5.11. Let $(\mathbf{a}, \mathbf{r})$ be a code word of the low-cost code with check base $A = 2^b - 1$, where $\mathbf{a}$ is the n-bit binary representation of a nonnegative integer. $\mathbf{r}$ represents the residue of $\mathbf{a}$ for divisor A in a b-bit binary form. Verify that the bit-by-bit complementation of $(\mathbf{a}, \mathbf{r})$ is also a code word of the same code if b divides n.

5.12. Let $X = (\mathbf{x}_{n-1} \cdots \mathbf{x}_0 \mathbf{x}_c)$ be a code word of the check-sum code, where $\mathbf{x}_i$, $i = 0, 1, \ldots, n - 1$, is a byte of b information bits and $\mathbf{x}_c$ is given by

$$\mathbf{x}_c = \left(\sum_{i=0}^{n-1} \mathbf{x}_i \right) \bmod 2^b$$

Verify that the necessary and sufficient condition of n, the number of information bytes, for the bit-by-bit complementation of any code word of the check-sum code being again a code word of the same code is

$$n = K2^b + 1$$

where K is a nonnegative integer.

5.13. Following the general approach described in Section 5.5.1, encode each state of a mod-8 counter into the Hamming single-error-correcting code and design the counter so as to tolerate a single fault.

5.14. Using Russo's method, determine the excitations to J-K flip-flops which realize the state transition, as shown in Fig. P5.14.

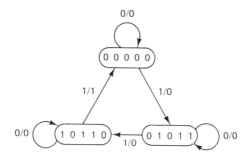

Figure P5.14

5.15. Design a fault-tolerant asynchronous sequential circuit of Fig. P5.15 by Pradhan's method.

$y_6 y_5 y_4 y_3 y_2 y_1$ \ X	δ x_1	x_2	x_3
1 0 1 0 1 1	0 1 0 0 1 1	1 0 1 1 0 0	(1 0 1 0 1 1)
0 1 0 1 0 0	0 1 0 0 1 1	(0 1 0 1 0 0)	(0 1 0 1 0 0)
0 1 0 0 1 1	(0 1 0 0 1 1)	0 1 0 1 0 0	1 0 1 0 1 1
1 0 1 1 0 0	(1 0 1 1 0 0)	(1 0 1 1 0 0)	0 1 0 1 0 0

Figure P5.15

5.16. Using the method of Section 5.7.1 together with a $\binom{5}{3}$ code, design a fail-safe sequential circuit of Fig. P5.16.

5.17. Figure P5.17b is the realization of the sequential machine of Fig. P5.17a. Draw the state transition among all possible $(f_3 f_2 f_1)$'s (we have eight such tuples) with the assumption that the output line of gate 4 (AND gate) is stuck at 1. Is the state trapping practiced?

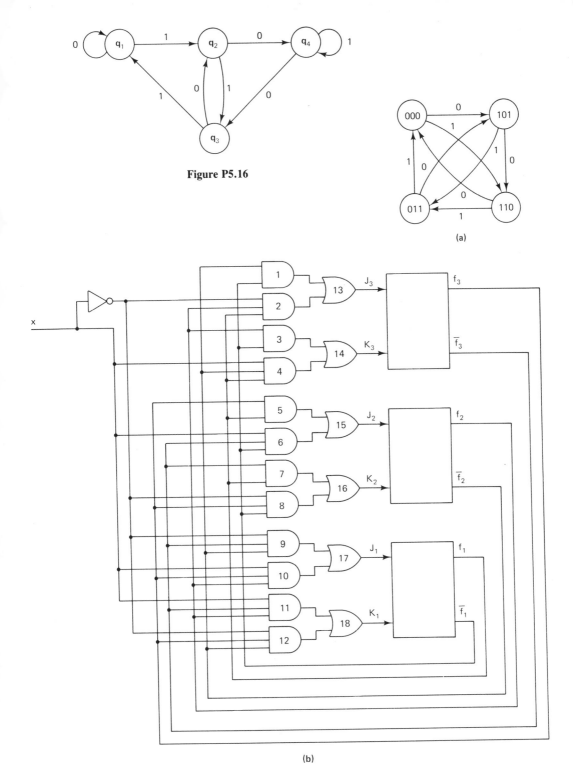

Figure P5.16

(a)

(b)

Figure P5.17

Index